MONTANA

A State Guide Book

MONTANA

A STATE GUIDE BOOK

✸

*Compiled and Written by the Federal Writers' Project
of the Work Projects Administration
for the State of Montana*

AMERICAN GUIDE SERIES

ILLUSTRATED

*Sponsored by Department of Agriculture, Labor
and Industry, State of Montana*

THE VIKING PRESS · NEW YORK

MCMXXXIX

Republished 1978
SCHOLARLY PRESS, INC.
19722 E. Nine Mile Rd., St. Clair Shores, Michigan 48080

JUN 15 1979

F
731
F44

Federal Works Agency

WORK PROJECTS ADMINISTRATION

F. C. HARRINGTON, *Commissioner*

FLORENCE KERR, *Assistant Commissioner*

HENRY G. ALSBERG, *Director of the Federal Writers' Project*

Library of Congress Cataloging in Publication Data

Federal Writers' Project. Montana.
    Montana; a state guide book.

    Original ed. issued in series: American guide series.
    Bibliography: p.
    1. Montana. 2. Montana--Description and travel--
Guide-books. 3. Automobiles--Road guides--Montana.
I. Series: American guide series.
F731.F44 1973   917.86'04'3   73-4364
ISBN 0-403-02176-6

FIRST PUBLISHED IN SEPTEMBER 1939

COPYRIGHT 1939 BY DEPARTMENT OF AGRICULTURE, LABOR AND
INDUSTRY, STATE OF MONTANA

PRINTED IN U.S.A. BY AMERICAN BOOK—STRATFORD PRESS

55

Preface

THE first Montana guidebook, published in 1865, described only one route—the Mullan Military Wagon Road, completed in 1862—but took in a lot of territory nevertheless. Its formidable title was *Miners and Travelers' Guide to Oregon, Washington, Idaho, Montana, Wyoming, and Colorado,* and its author, Captain John Mullan, was the builder of the road. The captain started his single "tour" at Walla Walla, Washington, and carried it across mountains of Idaho and Montana, and through the Clark Fork, Little Blackfoot, Prickly Pear, and Sun River Valleys to Fort Benton, allowing 47 days for the 624-mile trip. He described Indians and road conditions likely to be encountered; gave detailed advice on equipment, supplies, and care of horses and wagons; and declined responsibility for the welfare of travelers who took unauthorized short cuts:

"42nd day—Move to Bird Tail Rock, 15 miles; road excellent; water and grass at camp; willows for fuel but scant; it would be wise to pack wood from the Dearborn or Sun Rivers, according to which way you are traveling. . . .

"47th day—Move to Fort Benton, 27 miles if you camp at the springs, or 11 miles if you camp at Big Coulee. The latter never was a portion of my road, but was worked out by Major Delancey Floyd Jones, and I am not responsible either for its location or the character of the work performed."

Today Mullan's road is obliterated from the landscape and from the memories of all but the oldest pioneers; a network of modern highways spans the "northwestern territories" he wrote about. The *Miners and Travelers' Guide* still exists to tell in what manner travelers once made their difficult and devious way across the plains and "shining mountains," but its life as a guidebook ended in the 1880's. Now, after a hiatus of two or three generations this volume presents the Montana of 1939 with the background of a relatively short but fascinating past, against which are set the immediate daily experiences and concerns of the people, and the patterns of contemporary economic, social, and cultural life. It attempts to convey an impression of the beautiful and varied natural setting in Montana's recreational areas.

The Writers' Project is deeply indebted to many governmental agencies, local, State, and Federal, to commercial associations and travel agencies, to historical societies and to many public and private libraries for information and assistance. Various faculty members of Montana State University and Montana State College acted as consultants in their respective professional fields. Major Evan W. Kelley, Regional Forester, U. S. Forest Service, placed the informational resources of the regional offices at the disposal of the project. Mr. George C. Ruhle, Associate Park Naturalist, and Mr. Channing Howell, Park Ranger, were consultants for the Glacier National Park chapter. Mr. James Willard Schultz and the late Mr. Frank B. Linderman contributed authentic material concerning several Indian tribes and reservations.

Miss Esther Leiser, Reference Librarian, Missoula Public Library, Miss M. Catherine White, Reference Librarian, Montana State University, and Mrs. Anne McDonnell, Assistant Librarian, Montana State Historical Library, rendered valuable research assistance. Finally, thanks are due to Dr. Paul C. Phillips, State Director of the Historical Records Survey of the Works Progress Administration, and to Dr. H. G. Merriam, Professor of English, Montana State University, who critically read the final copy.

BYRON CRANE, *State Director*
JOHN A. STAHLBERG, *Editor*

Contents

CONTENTS

CONTENTS

CONTENTS

IV. Appendices

Illustrations

LIST OF ILLUSTRATIONS

LIST OF ILLUSTRATIONS

LIST OF ILLUSTRATIONS

Maps

General Information

(For highways and other transport routes, see State and special maps in pocket of back cover.)

Railroads: Chicago, Milwaukee, St. Paul and Pacific (the Milwaukee); Northern Pacific (NP); Great Northern; Chicago, Burlington & Quincy (the Burlington); Union Pacific (UP); Minneapolis, St. Paul & Sault Ste. Marie (the Soo); Butte, Anaconda & Pacific (BAP); Gilmore & Pittsburgh; Montana Western; White Sulphur Springs & Yellowstone Park; Montana, Wyoming & Southern. Direct service to Glacier and Yellowstone National Parks in season (June 15–Sept. 15). *(See TRANSPORTATION.)*

Bus Lines: Northland Greyhound (Chicago to Seattle); Washington Motor Coach (intrastate and interstate; connections with Northland Greyhound); Burlington Transportation (Billings to Denver); Intermountain Transportation (Great Falls to Salt Lake City); Meisinger's Stages (Missoula to Salmon, Idaho); Butte-Deer Lodge Transport; Interstate Transit (Williston, N. D.—Eastern Montana); Motor Transit. Feeder lines to main bus and rail routes.

Air Lines: Northwest Airlines (Chicago to Seattle) lands at Glendive, Miles City, Billings, Butte, Helena, and Missoula; Wyoming Air Service (Billings to Pueblo, Colo.); Western Air Express (Great Falls to Salt Lake City) stops at Helena and Butte, and in season at West Yellowstone, western gateway to Yellowstone National Park. *(See TRANSPORTATION MAP.)*

Highways: Nine US, transcontinental or with transcontinental or international connections. Two E.-W. main routes (US 2 and 10), 4 N.-S. (US 87, 89, 91, and 93). Arterials mostly oiled; laterals graded and graveled. Winter travelers should ascertain road conditions. Especially spectacular highways are Going-to-the-Sun (Glacier National Park) and Red Lodge-Cooke City (Absaroka National Forest and Beartooth Mts.), open during summer tourist season. State highway commission maintains nine "ports of entry" which provide maps, pamphlets, and information concerning parks, Indian reservations, fishing streams, dude ranches, hotels and resorts. Roadside epigraphs mark historic points. Inspection at Canadian border. Gas tax, 6¢.

Mountain and Forest Trails for hiking and riding number hundreds. Maps are available at U. S. Forest Service offices in Livingston (Absaroka National Forest), Billings (Custer), Dillon (Beaverhead), Hamilton (Bitterroot), Thompson Falls (Cabinet), Kalispell (Flathead), Butte (Deer Lodge), Bozeman (Gallatin), Helena (Helena), Great Falls (Lewis and Clark), Libby (Kootenai), Missoula (Lolo).

Motor Vehicle Laws are enforced by State Highway Patrol. Speed limit on marked curves, 40 m.; in towns on Federal highways, 25 m. Hand signals. Vehicles entering main highways stop, yielding right-of-way to vehicles already on highways. Vehicles broken down must be marked at night by front and rear flares or lanterns, and be removed from roadway as soon as possible. School zone and other markers must be observed; cattle crossings are marked at 600 ft. *Prohibited* are reckless driving at any speed, passing on hills or where view is obstructed, and parking on highways. (For local regulations, see *CITIES.*)

Accommodations: All types in larger cities; comfortable in most villages. Modern tourist camps (many municipal) and camping or picnic sites on all highways. Widely varying dude ranch accommodations, from $25 wk. Cabins and hotels at mountain and hot springs resorts; the latter usually have warm and cold plunges as well as natural hot baths. No scarcity of accommodations except in cities when annual or special events draw large crowds. Many dude ranches, hot springs resorts, and mountain lodges offer reduced winter rates.

Climate and Equipment: Summer travelers should be prepared for warm days and cool nights. Medium-weight clothing and coat or sweater for evening wear are sufficient in general, but vacations at high altitudes require a supply of warm clothing. In regions infested by wood ticks, clothing should be selected that will prevent the ticks from reaching the skin. For outings, old clothes and light but strong shoes with flexible cord or rubber composition soles are best; hobnails are seldom an advantage. Suitable equipment is sold in all Montana trading centers. Guides (licensed by the State fish and game commission) and horses may be obtained through chambers of commerce or game wardens. For winter vacations, heavy outdoor clothing is needed.

(*Recreational Areas:* See *Recreation, Forests, Glacier National Park, Tours,* State map.)

Fishing: Season, May 21 to March 14 of following year. Licenses: resident, $2 (includes upland and migratory bird hunting license); non-resident, $3.50; special 10-day tourist, $1.50; alien, $10; issued by game wardens, sporting goods dealers, highway "ports of entry." All except special tourist licenses expire April 30 succeeding date of issue. Licenses not required of children under 15, or of visitors in Glacier National Park. Daily limit, 25 game fishes or 20 lbs. and 1 fish; 5 fishes less than 7 in. long, except sunfish, yellow perch, ringed perch. In Glacier Park the limit (variable) is 10 fishes per day per person in most waters. Game fish may be taken only by hook and line, with rod in hand. Defined as game fish are trout (mountain, rainbow, cutthroat or native, eastern brook, Dolly Varden, Loch Leven, Steelhead, Mackinaw); salmon (chinook, silver, sockeye); grayling; Rocky Mountain whitefish; perch (yellow, ringed); black bass (large-mouth, small-mouth); sunfish; northern pickerel; pike (wall-eyed, yellow, great northern).

Game Birds: Upland game-bird hunting season, variable. Licenses: resident, $2 (see *Fishing*); non-resident, $10; alien, $50 (includes fish and big game licenses). Limit, 3 male birds a day. Defined as upland game birds are grouse (sharp-tailed, blue, sage, ruffed); prairie chicken; fool hen; quail; ptarmigan; wild turkey; Hungarian partridge; Chinese (ring-necked) pheasant. Hunting of migratory waterfowl (wild duck, wild goose, brant) is subject to Federal regulations under the Migratory Bird Act. *(See FAUNA.)*

Big Game: Regulations vary from region to region. General deer and elk hunting season, Oct. 15–Nov. 15; bear, Oct. 15–May 14 of following year. Antelope, moose, caribou, and buffalo may not be taken, nor may cub bears or female bears with cubs. State fish and game commission may open any region to hunting of Rocky Mountain sheep and goats for limited periods. Deer and elk hunting restricted to definite areas. Limit, 1 male deer with horns 4 in. or longer; 1 bull elk (in some sections, 1 elk of either sex). Licenses: resident, $3; non-resident, $30; alien, $50 (resident and alien licenses cover all hunting and fishing). Predatory animals may be hunted and trapped without license. Prohibited: hunting in Glacier National Park; hunting game birds or animals from automobile, airplane, powerboat, sailboat, or any power-towed device. Hunters should obtain additional information when purchasing license.

Camping Restrictions: When fire hazard is great, travelers may have to obtain permits (issued at points of entry; no red tape) before entering national forests. Ax, shovel, and water bucket must be carried. All travelers must obey the following *Forest Fire Prevention Rules:* In making camp, scrape away all inflammable material from a spot 5 ft. in diameter. Dig hole in center and keep your fire in the hole. Keep it small. Do not build fire near trees, logs, or brush. Be sure matches, pipe ashes, cigarette and cigar stubs are dead before throwing away; even then, don't toss into brush, leaves, or needles; step on them, break matches in two. In breaking camp, stir coals while soaking with water. Turn small sticks, and drench both sides. Wet ground around fire. If without water, stir in earth and tread down until packed tightly over and around fire. Be sure the last spark is dead.

Liquor Regulations: Intoxicating liquors are dispensed by Montana State Liquor Stores and licensed dealers in all cities and county seats and many villages. State Stores generally open daily from 12 m. to 8 p.m., except Sundays and holidays, but local regulations vary. Saloons open 8 a.m. to 2 a.m.; Sundays and holidays 1 p.m. to 2 a.m. Purchasers' permit 50¢ a year; non-residents' permit (good for 30 days) 50¢. Liquor may not be consumed on store premises or purchased by minors (under 21). Beer (4%) is sold at bars, taverns, gardens, restaurants, and hotels.

Precautions: Sunburn should be guarded against at high elevations. Carry cold cream on hikes. On glacier and mountain trips, *protect the eyes* with amber goggles. Use extreme care in the matter of *drinking water.* Spring water at its source is safe, as is mountain water at high altitudes (usually) and water at designated public campgrounds. Water from rivers or abandoned wells is unsafe.

Snakes: Rattlesnakes occur in the western valleys and south of the Missouri River on the plains; abundant in some areas. High-top shoes and stout leggings protect the legs; use hands sparingly in climbing over rocky places. In treatment of rattlesnake bite, a ligature, preferably rubber, should be bound above the wound, which should be opened by an incision not deeper than ¼ in. Suck the wound, if necessary, to induce bleeding; but lips and mouth should be free from sores. Do not cauterize. Do not take whisky. Get a doctor.

Mosquitoes, while not a disease-carrying species, are a nuisance in some areas. A low smudge is of aid in driving them away. So is a vessel of oil of citronella mixed with an equal amount of spirits of camphor and half as much oil of cedar. Soap rubbed on bites eases discomfort. Ammonia and alcohol in equal parts also help.

Wood Ticks: Rocky Mountain spotted fever is a very serious disease carried to man exclusively by wood ticks. To infect, a tick must penetrate the skin enough to feed, remaining for 2 hrs. or longer. Hikers and campers in tick-infested country should not wear shorts or other clothing that does not protect the skin. They should examine the body and clothing frequently, and take advantage of the vaccination offered by the United States Public Health Service. In removing a tick from the body, a firm straight pull is best. Treat bite immediately with silver-nitrate or other cauterants. Tick season: early spring until about mid-July, depending upon conditions of moisture and heat. *(See FAUNA.)*

Black Widow Spiders are few in number. They are small, shiny black, and marked with a red hourglass on lower surface of abdomen. Treatment for bite: put patient to bed; apply iodine to wound, and give large quantities of non-alcoholic fluids to drink. Get a doctor.

Public Information Service: Montanans, Inc., Gold Block, Helena; Montana Highway Commission, Helena; Highway Commission ports of entry at Columbia Falls, Monida, West Yellowstone, Gardiner, Rockvale, Wyola, Miles City, Culbertson, and junction of US 10 and 93 NW. of Missoula; Highway Patrol officers; regional headquarters of the U. S. Forest Service, Missoula; forest supervisors' headquarters at Livingston, Dillon, Hamilton, Thompson Falls, Billings, Butte, Bozeman, Kalispell, Helena, Libby, Great Falls, and Missoula; all ranger stations; chambers of commerce in the larger cities; Montana Automobile Association offices at chambers of commerce or largest hotels in Missoula, Kalispell, Butte, Great Falls, Helena, Billings, Havre, Glendive, Glasgow, Hamilton, Lewistown, Miles City, Livingston, and Wolf Point.

Calendar of Events

("nfd" means no fixed date)

Jan.	1st week	Anaconda	Winter Sports Carnival (4 days)
Jan.	nfd	Arlee	Blue Jay Dance at Flathead Reservation
Feb.	pre-Lenten	Butte, Anaconda, Great Falls	Mesopust Croatian Celebration
May	1st week	Havre	Music Festival
May	1st week	Camas Prairie	Bitterroot Feast of Flathead Indians
May	17	Sheridan County	Norwegian Independence Day
May	nfd	Missoula	Interscholastic and Intercollegiate Meets
June	13	Butte	Miners' Union Day
June	24	Frenchtown	St. John's Day
June	1st week	Hardin	Rodeo
June	4th week	Rocky Boy Reservation	Rocky Boy Indian Ceremonial Dances
June	nfd	State-wide	Sheep Shearing
July	3-5	Red Lodge, Butte, Kalispell, Lewistown, and other places	Independence Day Celebrations and Rodeos
July	4	Whitefish	Regatta
July	1st week	Browning	Blackfeet Medicine Lodge Ceremonial and Sun Dance
July	1st week	Fort Peck Reservation	Assiniboine and Sioux Ceremonial and Sun Dance
July	1st week	Belknap Agency	Assiniboine and Gros Ventre Ceremonial and Sun Dance
July	2nd week	Butte, Wolf Point, Livingston	Rodeos
July	2nd week	Blackfeet Reservation	Blood Indian Medicine Lodge Ceremonial and Sun Dance
July	3rd week	Blackfeet Reservation	Piegan Medicine Lodge Ceremonial and Sun Dance
July	3rd week	Thompson Falls	Regatta
July	3rd week	Cut Bank	Horse Races
July	4th week	Crow Agency	Crow Ceremonial and Sun Dance
July	nfd	Deer Lodge	Tri-State Semi-Pro Baseball Tournament
July	nfd	Arlee	Flathead War Dances
Aug.	2	Butte	Miners' Field Day
Aug.	1st week	Polson	Cherry Regatta
Aug.	1st week	Cooke	Rodeo
Aug.	2nd week	Great Falls	North Montana Fair

CALENDAR OF EVENTS

Aug. 3rd week	Billings	Midland Empire Fair and Rodeo
Aug. 3rd week	Missoula	Western Montana Fair
Aug. 3rd week	Crow Agency	Crow Indian Fair
Aug. nfd	Hamilton	Harvest Festival
Aug. nfd	Georgetown Lake	Montana Championship Regatta
Sept. 1st week	Miles City	Eastern Montana Fair
Sept. 15-16	Billings	Mexican Fiesta
Sept. 30	Chinook	Pageant: Battle of Bear's Paw
Oct. nfd	Butte	State University-State College Football Game

PART I

Montana: The General Background

Contemporary Montana

MONTANA is too large and diverse for definition or characterization in general terms. Children in its schools are taught that the name Montana means "mountains," but many of them see only prairies rolling to the horizon. They are told that Montana is still a great ranching State, where cattle graze and cowboys ride, but some of them, as in Butte, see only ore dumps, great dark sheds, and barren buttes.

To the dry-land farmer in the eastern part of the State, Montana is a vast agricultural plain checkered with brownish fallow land and fields of green wheat that ripen to a dusty gray-gold in August; or it is a drab waste seen through a haze of wind-blown soil. For him the mountains of the western part exist chiefly as the goal for some long-deferred vacation.

To the resident of the mountain region, Montana is a land of rich valleys, small thriving cities, and uncounted mineral treasures. He hesitates to admit that anything important or interesting can exist in the immensities of dead brown grass and gray stubble that make up the eastern two-thirds of his State. At best, he believes, tank towns are there, and cattle and wheat. Less than best means badlands, coyotes, tumbleweeds, and dust.

These attitudes of high valley dweller and plainsman derive, on the one hand, from knowledge of the importance of the western region, the greater economic security of its rural population, and its relative wealth in people and in cultural opportunity; on the other, from knowledge of the sheer immensity of the plains and from the comfortable thought that the crops and livestock they produce are worth more to the State, in prosperous times, than are the minerals dug in the mountainous area.

The people vary less than might be expected, considering that they live far apart and in widely contrasting environments. They number only 3.7 per square mile, compared with 41.3 for the Nation, and are thus as scattered as the residents of Baltimore would be if distributed over Maryland, Delaware, New Jersey, New York, and New England. But they make frequent long trips, and think of a hundred-mile drive to a Saturday night dance as part of the regular order of living. Modern highways, built mostly since 1925, have emphasized this trait by making communication easier. A "neighborhood" on the plains, or the "environs" of a city, may include points separated by distances that would seem absurd to a stranger.

Where physical vastness in land and resources is an accepted fact, people are likely to be prodigal in measuring the size of their enterprises. The copper industry is most conspicuous for its leviathan structure. But every cowpuncher scales his ambition to the proportions of the great old-time cattle outfits. Every farmer wants to own or rent more land, buy more and bigger farming machines, and then acquire still more land to keep his machines profitably employed. Little avarice or scheming is involved in this continued reaching out; there is plenty of land for everyone. Montanans are merely so accustomed to vastness that anything less than huge seems trivial to them.

The compulsion to be big is solidly rooted in the State's history, with its traditions of big fur companies, big cattle and sheep outfits, and big mining operations. During Montana's period of greatest growth (1880–1920), size became an end in itself. Population increased 1,400 percent, and still more manpower was needed. Many argued that the area and resources of this "Treasure State" warranted a population of millions. Here day-laborers could become owners, and owners could become wealthy. To gain wealth in the new empire (Montanans liked the word) became the hope of everyone. The prime requirement was to "get in on the ground floor."

Even when expansion itself faltered, with the post-War failure of prices and credit, the habit of thinking in terms of expansion continued. Farmers, however, remembered that Montana is semiarid, and began to use moisture-conserving tillage methods. The mining industry had serious troubles: profits on Butte copper dwindled in competition with open-cut operations elsewhere; silver was not in demand; coal had two rivals, oil and gas, growing steadily in importance. In business, sales were slow, collections difficult. The trend of population was away from the State.

After 1922, crops and prices improved, and the market quickened for lumber and minerals. Agricultural expansion gained momentum until 1930, with emphasis on mechanization and larger farm units. Even when mines, smelters, and sawmills ceased operations, and grain prices fell to staggering lows, it did not stop at once. "We can't quit now," said the farmers. "We're in too deep. The only way out is to till more land and cut per-acre production costs." But drought and dust made even large-scale cultivation useless; when crop control was introduced most Montana farmers were glad to adopt it.

A FARMER—STOCKMAN

In the dry-land areas striking changes are taking place. Between 1920 and 1930 farmers believed that, by the use of summer fallow, they had solved the problem of growing crops without irrigation. But in the 1929 drought they had the appalling experience of seeing the loosened soil blown away, and with it their laboriously evolved technique. Some left defeated. Those who remained are trying to devise new techniques. Throughout the middle 1930's, two movements of population were in progress—one from the dry-land areas to the irrigated or irrigable valleys, another from outlying villages and hamlets to county seats and larger centers. The latter movement seems the result of better highways through these centers and of increased chances for employment in them. The migration has produced a new phenomenon—that of ghost towns on the prairie.

The farmer of western Montana has in large part escaped the problems of the eastern section, and has developed a happier, more confident agriculture. Spared the one-crop limitation, he has developed less of the gambling spirit that distinguishes the dry-lander; instead, he shows a tendency to work according to plan, for there is far greater likelihood that his plans will be realized. Between the two stand the cattle and sheep growers, somewhat less secure than the western farmer, but less affected by weather hazards than the dry-lander.

In Montana's "wide, open spaces" the cowpuncher no longer rides hour after hour, unimpeded by fences. He wears few fancy togs and carries no gun; he is a workingman who does his job well and cares nothing about the traditions of the motion-picture West. But he does ride. In at least the southeast quarter of the State, the resident, male or female, who cannot sit a horse well is a rarity.

Increasing tourist trade and a growing dude ranch industry have made Montanans think of themselves as hosts, and has added a certain smoothness to the simple good-fellowship and bluff hospitality of older times; but, among themselves, they remain informal and respect few artificial conventions. Hospitality, as proud a tradition West as South, has come down from the days when a rancher's home was everyone's castle and a good citizen never locked his door, knowing that a cold, tired, and hungry rider might need to enter and cook a meal.

Montana's is a labor population, and support for labor's aspirations has grown swiftly since 1930. Butte and Great Falls, always potential union towns, are well organized.

The most cynical Montanan is the citizen of Helena, whose days are spent in an atmosphere of politics. Yet his interests are broad, for his live-

BUTTE MINERS

lihood may depend on events in distant parts of the State or Nation. He understands and heartily distrusts politicians. Legislative scandals are his favorite gossip; his jokes are bitter meaningful allusions to such things as the Goddess of Liberty atop the capitol's copper dome (loosened by earthquake and swung about by a big wind, the Goddess turned her back on Helena). He is usually alert for a "spot to land in" in times of political change.

The Butte citizen's blood pressure rises and falls with the price of copper. He opposes war "and yet, when you come to think of it, war would probably raise the price of copper and increase work and wages . . ." Sometimes he is half-convinced that Butte is the real capital of the United States and copper instead of gold the proper standard of values. If he is a miner, or has friends or near relatives in the mines, he is often grim and worried. Butte's streets are crowded nightly with persons intent upon a round of pleasure in bars and gambling places, some seeking to forget the fears of daily existence.

Missoula, Great Falls, and Billings are agricultural centers rather than industrial or political ones; but Missoula has the State University and takes a solemn pride in its cultural position. In Great Falls, copper refining and power production have brought a considerable degree of adjustment to industrial conditions. Great Falls and Billings have retained in large measure the independence and pride in their own way of life that Charlie Russell epitomized during his career as an artist in the State.

The tradition of the self-reliant West exerts a steadily growing influence. *Frontier and Midland,* the magazine published at the State University, labors for a wider understanding of the value of Indians, cowpunchers, farmers, miners, and lumber-jacks as literary source material. Montanans are becoming aware that Montana's cultural possibilities are as vast and relatively unexplored as her material resources.

Natural Setting and Conservation

Physical Characteristics

THE name Montana is derived from the Spanish *montaña,* meaning mountain. The State, third largest in the Union, is bounded on the north by Saskatchewan, Alberta, and British Columbia; on the east by the Dakotas; on the south by Wyoming and Idaho; and on the west by Idaho. Its area is 146,997 square miles, of which 866 square miles is water surface.

Two-thirds of the surface of the State is a plain broken by a network of valleys, many of the smaller ones carrying no water except during rare floods, and by isolated groups of low mountains. The western mountainous section, roughly 200 miles wide, is composed of generally parallel ranges on a northwest-southeast axis, but the Continental Divide follows a meandering course north and south. In the north *(see GLACIER NATIONAL PARK)* the main range of the Rockies fronts the eastern plain, but farther south an increasing spread of ranges lies east of the Divide, comprising the sources of the Missouri River and its tributaries.

The highest peaks are east of the Divide rather than along its crest. Granite Peak (12,990 alt.), near the southern boundary, is the highest point in the State. Fairview (1,902 alt.), on the Dakota boundary, and Troy (1,892 alt.), in the northwest corner, have the lowest altitudes. Montana is generally lower than other Rocky Mountain States. In eastern Montana, along the Yellowstone River and other streams where erosion has been too rapid to allow vegetation to gain foothold, grotesque badlands formations in vivid colors extend for many miles.

Montana's most important eastern rivers are the Missouri and Yellowstone. As evidenced by its broad alluvial plain, the Yellowstone is the older; it also has the most direct course. Its valley, one of the most productive agricultural districts in the State, has terraced landscapes shaped by long processes of land elevation and erosion. The Missouri is the larger river, formed by the junction of the Madison, Jefferson, and Gallatin at Three Forks; it describes a huge, irregular northerly arc on its course eastward. Its valley bottom is narrower, the sides generally lower and smoother than those of the Yellowstone, but more rugged than those of the Milk, an important northern tributary. Between the Missouri and the Yellowstone lies the vast expanse of prairie, cut by tributary streams into grassy uplands and rocky hills.

Clark Fork of the Columbia is the master river of western Montana. Coursing westward from its source near Butte, it is joined by the Blackfoot, the Bitterroot, and the Flathead. Generally slow-running, it becomes turbulent in places. The Kootenai River, which joins it in British Columbia, makes only a brief dip into the northwestern corner of the State. In volume of water, the Kootenai compares with the Missouri.

The Continental Divide separates Montana into distinct climatic divisions, partially protecting the area to the west from severe southwardsweeping cold waves and forcing condensation of much of the moisture carried by westerly winds. Winters west of the Rockies are therefore more moderate, summers cooler, and rainfall more plentiful than in subarid eastern Montana. The State's climate as a whole shows great changeability. In January and February, fierce unpredictable storms may be followed suddenly by warm chinook winds and sunshine. Late freezes and snowfalls may delay spring locally until June, and are not unknown even in July. In any of the mountain areas excessive daytime heat is sure to be relieved by cool nights. Westerly winds prevail.

The mean annual temperature is 42.6°. The warmest areas are in the south-central section traversed by the upper Yellowstone Valley, while the coldest habitable areas are in the northern prairie counties. The highest mean temperature (46.3°) in the State is recorded in the Billings region; Bowen, Beaverhead County, because of its elevation, has the lowest mean, 32.3°. The highest recorded temperature, 117°, occurred on July 20, 1893, at Glendive, Dawson County; the lowest, —65°, at Fort Keogh, Custer County, on January 15, 1888. Usually July is the warmest month and January the coldest. In the eastern section hot winds sometimes cause rapid deterioration of grain crops and range grasses, but in late summer and early autumn the winds become beneficial, curing the grasses to provide excellent fodder. Autumn, dry and temperate, usually lasts until December.

The average annual precipitation is 15.48 inches. In the west, rainfall is distributed through the year, but in the east it is heaviest in late spring and early summer. Mineral County and Bull River Valley in Sanders

THREE FORKS OF THE MISSOURI

County have the heaviest precipitation, 30 to 34 inches. Regions of lightest precipitation are Dell, Beaverhead County, with 8.7 inches, and (curiously, because of its nearness to the place of heaviest precipitation) Lonepine, Sanders County, with 10.3. In 1909 Snowshoe, in Lincoln County, established an all-time record with 79.75 inches; and in 1894 Fort Shaw, Cascade County, parched with 4.24 inches. Averages in eastern Montana range from 12 to 16 inches, but the peculiar topography causes wide variations within small areas. June is usually the wettest month, February the driest.

Snowfall is heaviest in the mountains. Saltese, Mineral County, averages 160 inches; Fallon, Prairie County, 13. Snow on the lower levels has less water content, and diminishes rapidly by melting and evaporation. Strong winds sweep it into drifts, leaving ranges uncovered for grazing. Fall-planted grains, lacking cover, often winter-kill.

The frost-free growing season is longest in low altitudes. The southeast has 125 frostless days yearly, the northeast 123, the southwest 105. In high mountain districts freezing occurs every month. Average number of clear days is 161; partly cloudy, 107; cloudy, 97. The long daylight hours of this latitude stimulate crops.

All geologic periods have left traces in Montana. During the Archaean, the entire region was the bottom of an arm of the Pacific Ocean. It shared the heavy vegetation of the later Paleozoic, and was the swampy residence of Mesozoic reptile terrors. During the mountain building at the close of Cretaceous time, the predecessors of the Rocky Mountains were formed and Montana assumed something like its present surface pattern. Volcanic action upthrust lava in the form of conical hills ranging to several thousand feet in height.

During the Pleistocene epoch four great ice sheets plowed down from the northern part of the continent. Each erased most of the effects of its predecessor; thus the fourth, or Wisconsin, sheet had the most easily traceable influence. Its vast bulk (of an estimated 10,000-foot thickness in places) smoothed out the plains, filled in valleys, and created new stream courses and lakes. It deposited silt in piles hundreds of feet thick and many miles long. But it came only as far as the Missouri River and only east of the Rockies. Similar effects in western Montana were due to the action of piedmont glaciers independent of the Wisconsin sheet.

Great dams or moraines heaped up by the mountain glaciers created hundreds of lakes, two of the largest being the long-dry Missoula Lake, formed by the blocking of Clark Fork of the Columbia, and Flathead Lake, now one of the largest fresh-water bodies in the United States. Other remaining glacial lakes dot the Glacier Park region.

Passing, the glaciers left the surface substantially as it is today. Their less spectacular effects appear in the composition of the State's soils.

An outstanding geologic phenomenon is the Boulder batholith, an intrusive mass of igneous rock, 40 miles in mean width, extending southwest from near Helena to the Big Hole River. Formed at the beginning of the Rocky Mountain building period, it apparently occupies a huge basin whose dissected sides contain remnants of the entire series of sedimentary rocks from pre-Cambrian shales to late Cretaceous sandstones. Its principal rock is a dark coarse granite.

Seventy percent of Montana's exploited mineral wealth is concentrated in Silver Bow County, a division of this region. Gold and silver first brought Butte to the Nation's attention, but copper, zinc, and lead are now of first importance.

Ancient forms of life have left their signatures abundantly in Montana's rocks. The first were one-celled algae, followed several million years later by metazoa, tiny worms. Their marks are found in the Algonkian strata of the Proterozoic era, in the Little Belt Mountains, and in several ranges of the Rockies. Fossil mollusks, snails, corals, and trilobites of Paleozoic age are found throughout Montana. Extensive coal deposits, remains of the luxuriant forests of the Cretaceous and Tertiary periods, are, broadly speaking, the State's most valuable fossils.

Several important discoveries have been made near Harlowton, Wheatland County, including some Paleocene mammals, especially seven species of the condylarth, and the oldest primate remains known to science. An expedition of the American Museum of Natural History under Dr. George Simpson, discoverer of the primate remains, now spends four months each summer in the area. Since 1927, When Dr. Barnum Brown of the Museum uncovered rich fossil deposits in the foothills of the Beartooth Mountains, all southern Montana east of Bozeman has been of interest to paleontologists. Princeton University has a permanent base of operations on Rock Creek, four miles south of Red Lodge, and in 1931 Dr. W. J. Thom of that institution discovered fragments of dinosaur eggs, previously found only in the Gobi Desert. This region extends into Wyoming, where Beartooth Butte is in effect a fascinating open book of geologic history *(see Tour 13A)*.

Several dinosaur skeletons, usually the most publicized of fossils, have been unearthed in Montana. Dr. Barnum Brown discovered an almost complete skeleton of *Tyrannosaurus,* largest and fiercest carnivorous dinosaur, on Hell Creek north of Jordan, Garfield County. In Wheatland County he found one of the smallest dinosaurs known to science. Triceratops, an armored brute larger than a modern rhinoceros, was first found 14 miles south of Glendive, Dawson County. This grotesque animal had a 3-foot horn projecting over each eye; another jutted from its snout; and a collar of bone enveloped its neck like an Elizabethan ruff. A second skeleton, almost complete, was found in Treasure County.

Remains of *Stegosaurus,* weirdest of all armored dinosaurs, were found in 1924 at Sheep Creek, 25 miles north of Great Falls. Besides having hindlegs that boosted its rear skyward while its head was within two feet of the ground, the stegosaur had thick armor plates that stood erect in a staggered row along its back from head to tip of tail.

Partial skeletons of *Ichthyosaurus* and *Plesiosaurus,* seafaring reptiles of the Jurassic, have been found in Cascade and Wibaux Counties. A trachodon jaw is in the Larimer collection at Glendive, together with such oddities as gizzard stones—rocks worn smooth in saurian digestive processes.

Hoplitosaurus, a 15-foot horned toad found 32 miles south of Billings, had been broken into 20,000 pieces by earth movement and exposure. Many other reptile fossils have been taken from the Yellowstone Valley, including two camptosaurs, two nodosaurs, and a tenantosaur, unusual species provisionally named by Henry Fairfield Osborn. The Lewis overthrust, where the Rockies meet the northern plains, is rich in similar remains.

Flora

Montana's more than two thousand species of flowers and many non-flowering plants may be divided into three somewhat overlapping groups —subalpine, montane, and plains.

The subalpine group, characterized by plants that appeared after the recession of the glaciers, or moved in along the mountains from the Arctic, has made the higher altitudes in the northern Rockies famous for their profusion of color in the short midsummer season. When the snowbanks melt and all the flowers bloom at once, the earth is brilliant with glacier lilies, alpine poppies, columbines, white dryads, globeflowers, Indian paint-brushes, asters, and arnicas. The summits are, on the whole, too rigorous for any marked growth of shrubbery, but white and purple heathers, Rocky Mountain laurel, and Labrador teas are present.

The montane group includes most of the coniferous forests, and ranges from the lower border of the subalpine to the valley grasslands. Its most characteristic species is the spire-crowned alpine fir, sometimes associated with Engelmann spruce and white-barked and limber pine (also known as limber-twig pine). There are many shrubs: huckleberries, Menziesia, mountain ash, and scrubby birches and alders. Blue phacelia and, in damp places, red monkey flower and fringed parnassia are conspicuous. In the moister parts of the lower montane forest are Moneses and prince's pine, lowland and Douglas fir, and western larch; but in dry places, lodgepole and western yellow pine, and mountain balsam are more common. Bear grass lifts its beautiful domed column of white blossoms among Mariposa lilies, dogtooth violets, and windflowers. There are many shrubs, such as kinnikinnick, which are not found in the upper montane.

The plains group varies, being characterized on the eastern prairie by grasses such as buffalo and blue grama; in the west, by bunch grasses and by flowers such as the yellow bell, shooting star, bluebell, blanketflower or gaillardia, golden aster, and daisy. On the eastern grasslands are found sand and gumbo lilies, prairie evening primrose, and a little shrubby scarlet mallow with conspicuous waxy petals; clumps of small cacti bear red and yellow blossoms of a delicacy hard to reconcile with the aspect of the plants themselves. Wherever overgrazing, fire, or erosion has destroyed

BEAR GRASS

the soil's water-holding capacity, desert shrubs from the south have crept in; the familiar sagebrush is found with greasewood, sea blite, ranger brush, and mountain mahogany. Moist areas are often called camas prairies because of the blue camas, an onionlike May-blooming plant used by the Indians in making pemmican. Death camas, a plant similar to blue camas, but highly toxic, has caused heavy losses among sheep; even men, mistaking it for blue camas, have been poisoned. It bears a star-shaped flower, usually white; its grasslike leaves are most often folded. Common on the plains are yucca or Spanish bayonet, many species of Pentstemon, and sego lily, which blossoms in nearly every color.

Subsurface moisture encourages stream bank forests composed largely of cottonwood and aspen, but often containing alders, river birches, willow, and the like. In swampy areas, cattail, bulrush, and water plantain flourish beside water buttercups and various mints. Coulees and other favored grassland spots support serviceberry, currant, gooseberry, hawthorn, fragrant mock orange, and wild rose.

The State flower is the bitterroot. Flathead Indians who used its root for food gave it the name later applied to the valley, river, and mountains of the region where it was found most abundantly. It is small, with a rosette of 12 to 18 leaves; its low-set pink blossoms turn white after a few days in the sun. White men called it Lewisia in honor of Captain Meriwether Lewis, and rediviva (Lat., *lives again*) in recognition of its vitality. The gumbo lily, most abundant in Carbon County, is like the bitterroot, and even more beautiful. It is not so commonly found, however.

Montana's four species of cactus are much smaller than southwestern ones. Most common is prickly pear, valued in the East as a houseplant because of the indescribably tender tints of its blossoms. In Montana its beds of sharp spines would make it a pest—if anything so beautiful could be a pest. Cacti are very easily transplanted; a stem set in the ground will take root.

Wild roses are common along mountain trails as well as in coulees on the plains. A low-growing variety sometimes becomes a nuisance in fields.

Sagebrush, common on open plain and hillside, is an erect shrub, one to six feet high, with many branches, silver-gray leaves, and small, clustered yellow flowers.

The Oregon grape of the lower montane forests has bright yellow flowers and glossy green leaves. The stem is thick, the root a yellowish hardwood used by Indians in concocting stomach medicine and spring tonics. In autumn the fruit, a small, blue, rather bitter grape, is used in making jelly. The plant grows in shaded places, often near large rocks. It is conspicuous in autumn, when, after other growth is gone, a single leaf may present an array of orange, brown, and red.

Kinnikinnick, with its small red berries, also provides much autumn color. It grows in great vinelike masses over large rocks; its sturdy root often spreads several feet; its small dark green leaves provide food for deer and other animals. The Indians used its bark for smoking.

Mountain mahogany grows in the hills, and the pussy willow thrives along the banks of streams in all parts of Montana. Foothills and valley are well stocked with edible berries: huckleberries, currants, gooseberries, chokecherries, serviceberries, and buffalo or bull berries. A few wild cherries grow near Martinsdale, in Meagher County. Wild strawberries and raspberries are found in many wooded sections.

WILD ROSES

Montana has many varieties of forage grass. Some of the most important are June, wheat, and pine grasses, bluejoint, and bluestem. Besides the grasses, edible ferns and mosses flourish in the forests. When forage grasses are overgrazed, an almost worthless "cheat grass" sometimes takes their place. Nourishing enough early in the spring, it is spoiled by summer weather.

Foxtail is a detriment to some pastures. At the top of an 8-inch stem it bears a spiculate tassel resembling the tail of a fox. Animals seldom attempt to eat it, but if they do the bristles may stick in their throats. Feather grass and needle grass, both species of Stipa, are other nuisance grasses. When ripe, their twisted awns catch in the wool of sheep, work into the skin and eyes, and cause infections and blindness.

Among Montana's worst weeds are Russian thistle and "Jim Hill" mustard, both tumbleweeds. Easily uprooted or broken off at the base, they roll before the wind, scattering seeds, and then pile up along fences. High winds strike these walls of piled weeds with such force that miles of fence are sometimes torn up and dragged out into the fields.

The lupine, which bears racemes of bright blue flowers followed by seed pods, is often poisonous to animals, particularly sheep. Several varieties of locoweed exist; they resemble lupine, and all have a narcotic effect when eaten.

Quee or *racine de tabac,* used as tobacco by the Indians, grows abundantly in Madison County. The Tobacco Root Mountains were named after it.

Fauna

Montana still is home to an abundance of wild life. The proudly tossed antlers of an elk or buck deer outlined against the sky, a bear shuffling through the underbrush, the flash of a pheasant rocketing from a hidden nest, the gleam of trout rising to a fly through the transparent waters of a mountain stream: these are familiar pictures to frequenters of Montana's forests.

The State has more than 180,000 game and fur-bearing animals in its 12 national forests, uncounted numbers in other wooded regions, and more than 300 species of birds. In the spring of 1936 the Forest Service estimated 65,000 deer, 18,000 elk, 1,600 moose, 1,200 mountain sheep, 4,000 mountain goats, 850 antelope, 5,000 black bears, 470 grizzly bears, and 8 caribou; 16,000 beaver, 1,700 foxes, 8,800 marten, 7,000 mink, 160 otter, and 2,000 miscellaneous fur bearers. In addition, there were approximately 20,000 predatory animals, including 17,000 coyotes, 2,500 wildcats or lynxes, 250 mountain lions, and a few wolves and outlaw bears. Deer and elk are slowly increasing, the 1931 estimate having given their numbers as only 52,000 and 15,000 respectively. Moose, mountain goats, and antelope are nearly at a standstill; mountain sheep are growing fewer. There is a surplus of elk in the Flathead, Lewis and Clark, Gallatin, and Absaroka Forests, where the range is over-grazed to the point of extermination for the most valuable forage plants, and in some places to total denudation. Attempts at control by extension of the hunting season have proven unsatisfactory.

The commonest game birds include Chinese, or ring-necked, pheasant; Hungarian partridge; blue, ruffed, and Franklin (fool hen) grouse; mallard; teal; canvasback and gadwall ducks; and Canadian geese. Montana's State game farm, at Warm Springs, Deer Lodge County, liberated 9,600 Chinese pheasants and hundreds of birds of other species in 1935.

Fourteen fish hatcheries established by the Montana Fish and Game Commission liberate more than 30,000,000 game fish each year. The hatcheries are at Big Timber, Sweet Grass County; Hamilton, Ravalli

WHITE-TAILED DEER "SPARRING"

County; Emigrant, Park County; Libby, Lincoln County; Lewistown, Fergus County; Ovando, Powell County; Polson, Lake County; Red Lodge, Carbon County; Somers, Flathead County; Havre, Hill County; Wolf Creek, Lewis and Clark County; Anaconda; Great Falls; and Miles City.

Spawning stations are at Flint Creek and Steward Mill on Georgetown Lake, Deer Lodge County; Ashley and Rodgers Lake, Flathead County; Hebgen Lake, Gallatin County; Lake Ronan, Lake County; and Lake Francis, Pondera County. A pond cultural station is maintained at Miles City.

From 1911 to 1935 the Somers hatchery liberated more than 150 million fish. Its capacity would permit an annual production of 8,000,000 to 10,000,000 fry and 200,000 fingerlings. It is perhaps the only one in the country that produces grayling, a fish unusually hard to raise because the food of the fry is microscopic, and cannot be prepared in the hatchery.

The Somers grayling are returned soon after hatching to the waters where they were spawned, the Rodgers Lake spawning station, which produced 12,000,000 grayling eggs in 1935. Later they are distributed to lakes and streams, usually in Flathead County.

For several years, land-locked sockeye salmon have been increasing in Flathead Lake; thousands spawn along the east and west shores, and many run up the Swan and Flathead Rivers.

High, almost inaccessible slopes in Glacier National Park, the Mission Range, and the rugged Cabinet Mountains are the stronghold of the mountain goat, an obscure member of the antelope tribe—to which the American "antelope" does not belong. It lives usually above timber line, amid snowbanks, glaciers, and precipices, and feeds chiefly on the short moss that grows on rocks and in crevices. It climbs the sharpest slant easily, and can be approached only from above, being apparently unable to understand that anything can descend upon it.

Buffalo have been wholly restricted to game preserves since the first protective legislation in 1894. On the National Bison Range at Dixon, more than 400 of them graze on the foothills of the Cabinet Mountains in a fenced area of 18,521 acres, and 1,100 have been removed as surplus (see Tour 12).

Bears weighing from 300 to 800 pounds prowl the highlands. Usually they do little damage, eating meat only when driven by hunger. Black bears range all the mountain region, while the rugged Mission Range is the chief habitation of grizzlies. More are seen there than in any other part of the United States.

Among predatory animals, cougar and wolf are most dangerous to young livestock. The weasel and coyote are the worst chicken thieves. Damage to field crops by gophers and jack rabbits yearly reaches a high figure. A prime nuisance is the pack rat, which carries off anything that takes its fancy.

The pelican, with its large ugly fish-pouch jaw, is a bird rare in Montana; but a flock of nearly 1,000 was once seen on Lake Bowdoin, 7 miles east of Malta, Phillips County (see Tour 2). The great blue heron summers along marshy streams. Wild canaries, juncoes, meadow-larks, blackbirds, bobolinks, chickadees, and scores of other bird species are common. A showy but unpopular one is the ubiquitous magpie, a long-tailed, noisy, black and white scavenger that frequents highways in search of gophers and rabbits killed by cars. Peculiarly hateful is its practice of harassing livestock by picking at little wounds and scratches.

Of all the fauna in the State, the greatest menace to life and health is the tick. One species, *Dermacentor andersoni*, of the class popularly known as wood tick, carries tularemia and Rocky Mountain spotted fever to human beings and tick-paralysis to humans and animals. It also causes serious local lesions. The wood tick feeds on many animals; in immature stages it usually fastens upon small rodents, such as mice or squirrels. Like its relative, the dog tick, this species is marked with reddish-brown splotches on the back.

In early spring the ticks emerge from the ground and the bark of stumps. Unable to endure hot dry weather, they disappear from the lower elevations during June and July and from the higher ones in later summer. In order to combat Rocky Mountain spotted fever, the U. S. Public Health Service maintains an experimental laboratory at Hamilton *(see Tour 7)*.

Control efforts have been directed against the small wild animals on which the ticks live, and special attention has been given to systematic dipping of livestock. Attempts were made to destroy the ticks by propagating and liberating minute insects supposedly hostile to them, but the experiment gave no results. *(For first aid in tick bite, see General Information.)*

Several orders of insects seriously threaten the State's forests and farms. The western pine beetle—small, brownish, and cylindrical—bores irregular galleries 9 to 36 inches long under the outer bark of trees. In these it lays 60 to 80 eggs. The developing larvae bore feeding tunnels, from 1 to 3 inches long, ending in small cells where they pass the pupal stage. The adults then bore outward from the cell and migrate to other trees, where the process is repeated. In some areas there are two annual generations of the pine beetles. Fortunately predacious insects and other natural agents destroy most of the eggs and larvae of each brood. Birds destroy many migrating adults. Even so they would increase up to 300 percent yearly but for Forest Service control measures. Another species of beetle confines its attack almost exclusively to Douglas fir.

The pine butterfly, which defoliates yellow and white pine, is black above and white beneath, with white wings netted with black. A few hours after mating, it lays eggs along the needles of the treetops. The eggs remain over the winter and hatch in June; the larvae eat the needles, and in late July, lowering themselves as much as 75 feet by silken threads, pupate in shrubs, grass, fences, and stumps.

Many kinds of grasshoppers and cutworms, army worms, and Mormon crickets, have caused serious damage to Montana agriculture. In contrast, the bee is highly profitable. Annual production per colony averages 100 pounds of high quality white honey; the State total is about 120 carloads. The abundant alfalfa and sweet clover of the irrigated valleys form the major sources of supply. In the fruit-growing counties bees have great value in cross-pollination.

A rare animal in Montana is the axolotl (Mex.: *plays in the water*), a larval salamander found in the pools and mountain lakes of Madison County. Mexicans regard it as edible. It is six to ten inches long, and identical with young *amblystoma tigrinum*, terrestrial salamanders of the warmer parts of the United States and Mexico. The axolotl retains its external gills and breeds in the larval stages. But, should its native pool dry up, it is capable of becoming an adult salamander, adapted to land life.

Rattlesnakes, the only poisonous reptiles in Montana, occur in twenty-three central, southern, and western counties. They average four feet in length, and are yellow to brown with a symmetrical row of darker rounded and separated blotches on the back, narrowly bordered with yellow or white. A distinct V of light color is on the shield above each eye. Natural enemies of destructive rodents, rattlesnakes are also dangerous to man. Occasional organized hunts keep them well under control.

Forests

Forest covers about one-fifth of the State, or a total of 20 million acres, 18 million of which are in national forests. Timber of commercial size and quality occupies nearly half of this acreage, but only 4,636,000 acres can be reached profitably. Even so, the State's merchantable timber totals about 50 billion board feet. Three-fourths of this is west of the Continental Divide; the forests on the eastern slopes and in the southeast corner of the State are chiefly of local value.

The first national forest, then called the Yellowstone Park Timberland Reserve, and today known as Yellowstone National Park, was set aside in 1891. As the idea developed and others were created, they were grouped into districts, or regions, now 10 in number, each supervised by a regional forester and a staff of assistants. Headquarters for Region One, embracing northwestern South Dakota, Montana, northern Idaho, and eastern Washington, is in Missoula. Montana's 12 national forests are the Absaroka, Beaverhead, Bitterroot, Cabinet, Custer, Deer Lodge, Flathead, Gallatin, Helena, Kootenai, Lewis and Clark, and Lolo.

Ponderosa (western yellow) pine makes up about one-fifth of Montana's forests. Commercial stands of it extend along the Kootenai River and Clark Fork of the Columbia; extensive pure stands, resistant to fire, occur on Thompson River and in the Bitterroot and lower Flathead Valleys, and also to some extent on the hills and broken table-lands of Custer National Forest. It serves a variety of purposes in building houses and ships and in the manufacture of furniture, cars, mine timbers, and railroad ties.

Western larch (tamarack) is one of the largest native trees and reaches its best development west of the Continental Divide from Canada to Missoula, where, though it may grow in pure stands, it is usually associated with Douglas fir, the two together constituting 40 percent of Montana's salable timber. Douglas fir is found in all the national forests except Custer. Its eastern limits are the Big Horn, Big Snowy, and Little Rocky Mountains, where it is associated with lodgepole pine. It is more susceptible to fire injury than western larch or yellow pine, but less so than other species.

Lodgepole pine forms extensive forests in the mountains of central Montana, along the main range of the Rockies, and on the upper Missouri drainage; and in many other places it comes in as a temporary forest cover after fires. The best stands are usually 6,000 to 8,000 feet above sea level. It is not favored for lumber, but is used for fuel, mine timbers, poles, and posts. The railroads have used it for cross ties since the first transcontinental road crossed the Rocky Mountains.

The greatest development of western white pine is in the more humid valleys near the Idaho boundary, at 1,500 to 6,500 feet. It is a somewhat temporary species, and may be forced out by cedar and hemlock, which require similar moisture conditions but endure more shade. The wood resembles eastern white pine, for which it is often substituted.

Minor species are Engelmann spruce, lowland white fir, western red cedar and western hemlock. Juniper, ash, and cottonwood grow in limited numbers along streams on the plains, but are suitable only for poles, fence posts, and fuel. Virtually all Montana woods are soft.

Forests, by increasing the absorptive power of the soil, retard the runoff of moisture when snow is melting in the spring, prevent erosion, and decrease the amount of silt carried into streams and reservoirs. The shade prevents rapid evaporation in summer, allowing rain to soak into the ground and augment the supply of ground water, a very real factor in maintaining the flow of streams and springs. One-fourth of Montana's forests are valuable chiefly for watershed protection.

The Civilian Conservation Corps, under the provisions of the Federal Highway Act, builds forest highways for public travel, and forest development roads for use in the care of national forest property. In addition to 1,187 miles of the former and 5,978 miles of the latter, Montana has 22,065 miles of foot and bridle trails. Construction and improvement are constantly in progress.

In 1935, not an unusual year for the destruction of forests, 931 fires burned 18,827 acres of Montana forest. The loss was estimated at $50,679. Lightning caused 503 fires; the others were due to human agencies. The cost of suppressing them was $136,450.

The Forest Service operates about 400 lookout stations, trains observers and firemen, maintains trails, telephone lines, and other equipment, and builds new lookout houses and towers.

The lookout station is a glass-walled, square building perched on a peak observation point. Many stations have radio equipment as well as telephone. With field glasses, a lookout can spot smoke anywhere within the field of vision; then by comparing observations with another lookout at another angle he can exactly locate and quickly direct fire fighters to it. Fire-fighting crews keep in touch with headquarters and with sources of supply by telephone or radio.

Region One has a fire control plan which gives protection on each of its ten worst fire areas at minimum cost. The size of the needed organization is determined beforehand by factors of season, visibility, dryness, winds, and occurrence of fires, all reduced to a single figure accurately expressing the degree or class of danger. Camping restrictions are imposed according to current fire hazard; when danger is extreme forests may be closed entirely (see GENERAL INFORMATION).

Insects yearly destroy millions of feet of timber, and the Forest Service, with the Bureau of Entomology and Plant Quarantine, constantly struggles to control them. Worst is the mountain pine beetle which from 1926 to 1936 destroyed about 5 billion board feet of lodgepole and western white pine in Region One.

A beetle infestation may be controlled if attacked in its early stages. Crews systematically cover the areas to be treated and mark all infected trees, which are recognized by fading foliage or the presence of boring dust. Control is obtained by burning the trunks of the standing trees with an oil spray, or by felling and burning or peeling the logs.

Other pests are the Douglas fir beetle, the ponderosa pine butterfly, the lodgepole needle tyer, and the larch and lodgepole sawflies. The Forest Service Insect Laboratory at Coeur d'Alene, Idaho, carries on a continual search for inexpensive means of eradication.

The Montana Legislature and the Fish and Game Commission have established 22 game preserves. Besides the 1,388,431 acres of refuges in the national forests, there are 1,458,328 acres on which the Forest Service limits grazing of domestic stock to provide forage for game. Nevertheless more than 500,000 acres of privately owned range are needed to supplement Federal range in winter. The sanctuaries are largely in high country, and deep snows often force 70 percent of the animals out of the safety zones, where an abundance of summer feed has built up herds beyond the winter carrying capacity. The results are heavy kills near refuge boundaries when early snows force migration during hunting season; death or lowered vitality from starvation; overgrazing of private ranges; and damage by herd migration to fences, haystacks, pastures, and fields.

The Northern Rocky Mountain Forest and Range Experiment Station in Missoula is one of twelve operated by the Forest Service to develop and test better methods of forest and range management, and to reduce costs. Its studies include tree culture, protection, forest products, and forest and range resources.

At Haugan (See Tour 1, Sec. d), the Forest Service maintains the Savenac Forest Nursery, which supplies 6 million trees annually for planting in Region One. Plantings in Montana run from 800 to 1,000 acres yearly, with a total of 21,623 acres planted up to the end of 1935.

Nearly 7 million acres of national forest land provide excellent grazing in summer, when the lower ranges are dry. Under Forest Service supervision particular ranges are available only to the kind of stock suited to them, and numbers are limited according to the actual feed supply. In 1935 there were 124,000 cattle and 533,000 sheep under permit.

The principal grazing areas lie east of the Rocky Mountains, where forests are mixed grassland and timber, and the elevation favors a good forage crop each season. Cattle are usually allotted the lower grass ranges, while sheep, because of their ability to get over the ground, get the higher, rougher, weedy ones. The open, grassy ridges are best for horses.

The relatively small ranges on the heavily timbered slopes of western Montana support many sheep, and burnt-over forest land affords excellent sheep forage until new growth crowds it out. A few cattle are pastured in the foothills.

This use of national forest land permits the production of thousands of head of additional livestock. As with other national forest receipts, 25 percent of the revenue derived from grazing reverts to the counties in which the forests lie. The rest goes to the national treasury.

Resources and Their Conservation

Of Montana's 94 million acres almost half are more than 5,000 feet in altitude with a restricted growing season, but none the less valuable for grazing and timber. Formerly it was thought the land could be divided into three classes almost equal in extent: farm, grazing, and forested and waste. Through the recent dry years the trend has been to turn back to grazing more and more marginal land, making the estimated present classification: grazing land, about 50 million acres; farm lands, 10 to 12 million. An immediate need is a detailed survey of soils to establish their logical use. Before 1936 only 14 of the 56 counties had such surveys.

Montana soils are fairly well supplied with the basic elements of fertility and they have not been greatly depleted by long-continued cropping. Throughout the State, additions of phosphate greatly increase plant growth. Nearly all the mature soils show the effect of alkali in producing a compact subsoil, in places a dense claypan. White alkali (sodium sulphate), which consists of mineral salts of marine origin, is widely distributed in or just below the top soils. In moderate amounts it is beneficial to plant growth, and often remains unnoticed until excessive irrigation flushes it to the surface, where it becomes a poison to plant life. Except for the expense of tiling, sub-drainage is a perfect solution of this problem.

To know Montana soils one must understand their origin as clayey sediments and marine shales at the bottom of a great inland sea, or as later products of erosion.

The glacial drift that covers the northern plains is from 25 to 50 feet deep, and may exceed 100 feet where ancient depressions were filled. It varies in character, but has in all cases been modified by weathering and vegetation. At present, therefore, the northern top soils range from silty clay, through a series of productive loams, usually clayey rather than sandy, to a stony leached drift. Alluvial deposits border most of the streams; along the Milk River they are wide enough for important agricultural development. The loams and silt loams, well drained and supplied with organic matter, produce bountiful crops of wheat when rainfall is adequate.

In the central and southern plains, which were unaffected by glaciation, the soils are more mature, their nature modified by erosion and by addition of wind-blown volcanic ash from the immense igneous intrusions of the Rocky Mountain building period. The bench lands are characterized by very productive dark brown loams over clay subsoils. They lie too high above the rivers to be irrigable on an important scale. Although they have been widely cultivated, their better use would probably be as grazing land. Along the river bottoms, which are broader than in the north, the alluvial deposits differ in composition according to the character of the formations from which they were eroded, and occupy positions ranging from low flood plains to high, well drained terraces. Readily irrigable, they support large crops of alfalfa, small grains, sugar beets, peas, and other crops.

Along the foot slopes of the Rockies and smaller mountain groups are extensive alluvial fans containing coarse gravel with a thin soil covering. Where soft sandstone, shale, and clay have permitted rapid erosion, the true soil has been stripped off and badlands areas are the result.

The soils of the western valleys are the result of erosion by piedmont glaciers, and of comparatively unimportant alluvial deposits since the glaciers receded. Much of this land has for centuries supported heavy forests. Soil developed under such cover is characterized by a veneer of organic matter over heavy textured, not very friable clayey subsoil. Most cutover land is suited only to grazing.

The parent material of nearly all the agricultural soils was transported. In general, those that have developed as grassland are the better soils, but the character of the subsoil (which must permit drainage) and the surface relief is usually the final determinant of their adaptability to profitable cultivation. As would be expected from their origin, soils throughout the State are characterized by gumbo rather than by sand. In the western valleys there are sandy areas of local extent.

In a region of somewhat deficient rainfall, gumbo has the advantage of retaining moisture as it also retains tenaciously its mineral salts. The disadvantage of gumbo under irrigation is the possible dissolution of these salts and their concentration as alkali at the surface. For that reason not all this land is suited to irrigation.

The unwise expansion of cultivation in dry regions, where soil was formerly held in place by tough-rooted, luxuriant buffalo grass, has exposed much land to soil blowing and the threat of permanent denudation. Present recognition of the danger would allow this land to be returned to permanent grass cover before the damage becomes irreparable.

The annual flow of Montana's rivers, with their sources in the great national forests, is sufficient to cover the whole State with six inches of water—more than enough to irrigate ten million acres. It does not drain off in great floods—for snow at the higher altitudes melts slowly—but assures a flow throughout the summer. Nevertheless, only about two-thirds of the State's two million acres of irrigated land has adequate water in dry years.

Most of Montana's irrigation is in the southern and southwestern counties. Immense central, northern, and eastern areas have no irrigation except of the "flood" or "spot" type; either no water is available, or the lands are not suitable. Tributaries of the Missouri River are used in irrigation, but the river itself contributes very little.

Spot irrigation is gaining in favor in drought areas, and has received some Government support through Works Progress Administration projects. Small dams are built in coulees to capture flood water for use on gardens and patches of fodder. Such small projects are expensive, but their influence for better homes makes them a social investment.

The average farm on large irrigation projects must contain more than 100 acres, because 90 percent of the land is devoted to the raising of hay and grains. Beans and sugar beets each account for only 3 percent and other products make up the difference. More intensive use of irrigated land is not feasible because of climate and distance from consuming centers. The cost of construction on large projects has usually made them uneconomic for the tenant or proprietor, since Montana has no law providing for "conservancy districts" under which the whole community would pay.

The history of irrigation records many difficulties in financing and in meeting charges on the poorer lands. Present indebtedness is a serious obstacle, especially for several projects undertaken about 1919–20, a period of high costs. In contrast, a few of the older projects have retired their bonds and are forging ahead. The benefits of irrigation have been well worth their cost when measured by the public welfare.

Montana's rivers make an average descent of 3,000 feet from source to State line, and could produce 2,500,000 horsepower of electric energy, more than five times their actual production. In annual per capita consumption (2,061 kilowatt hours), Montana ranks first and in present production of electricity, sixth. The State's most extensive project for the utilization of water power, Fort Peck Dam in Valley County (see Tour 10A), is also the country's largest mud dam. Fort Peck will generate 12,000 kilowatts of continuous power.

Many mining regions in the Rocky Mountains started as gold camps. It is a lucky accident for prospectors that gold ore weathers more slowly than other metals and is often discovered in concentrated form where the others have been recombined or diffused. In Montana the six principal metals, copper, silver, lead, zinc, manganese, and gold are usually found mixed, but all six seldom exist in commercial quantities in a single ore. The deposits are found throughout the mountain areas. Sometimes, as at Butte, they are almost inexhaustible.

At Butte the metals occur in a zonal arrangement, one or two predominating in each zone. The central zone is copper; the intermediate, zinc; the outer, manganese. The copper ores (chiefly chalcocite, bornite, and enargite) contain 80 to 240 pounds of copper, 2 ounces of silver, and 1 ounce of gold per ton; zinc ores contain 240 to 280 pounds of zinc, 40 pounds of lead, 5 to 6 ounces of silver, and .008 ounce of gold per ton; manganese ores contain 600 to 760 pounds of manganese.

Cascade, Meagher, Judith Basin, and Glacier Counties have deposits of iron ore. Chromite, a rare mineral in the United States, is found in Carbon, Stillwater, and Park Counties.

Fifty of Montana's fifty-six counties have coal, mostly lignite. Their 38,000 square miles of workable coal fields contain more than 400 billion tons of fuel, of which perhaps 30 billion tons are bituminous or high-grade sub-bituminous. The extensive Fort Union formation underlies most of the eastern end of the State. The best beds are at Colstrip, Rosebud County; Roundup, Musselshell County; Bear Creek, Carbon County; and Griffin, near Sand Coulee. Most of the seams are from 3 to 15 feet thick; some exceed 30 feet. A small amount of anthracite exists in Park County, and deposits of lower Cretaceous coal of coking quality are found at Sand Coulee, Cascade County, and at Lewistown, Fergus County. Lake-bed coal occurs at many places in the mountain region.

In the 1930's the Government spent thousands of dollars to extinguish fires in coal veins, some of which had burned for years. The method in most cases was to dig through the seam and pack dirt between the fire and the unconsumed coal.

The Sweetgrass Arch, a huge upward fold of the earth's crust paralleling the Rockies and extending nearly 200 miles from the Belt Mountains, south of Great Falls, to Lethbridge, Canada, is one of the most important geological formations in Montana. It is 60 miles wide, and embraces five natural gas and petroleum fields. Near Shelby in the center of the arch, a pronounced sag has caused a doming of the strata. This dome contains the oil-bearing sands.

The most productive gas field (also yielding petroleum) is the Cut Back strip, 4 miles wide and 25 miles long, in Toole and Glacier Counties. The gas deposit of the Cedar Creek anticline in Fallon and Dawson Counties is one of the largest in the Northwest. One gas field is near Havre, Hill County, another near Malta, Phillips County.

Major oil fields lie in Petroleum, Pondera, Toole, Carbon, and Glacier Counties; several produce gas as well as oil. Most of Montana's crude oil is of high gravity and readily refined. Formations strongly indicating oil are plentiful on the plains.

Granite, quartzite, marble, limestone, sandstone, and various clays are found in commercial quantities.

Before the White Man

MONTANA is roughly divided by the main range of the Rockies into two archeological provinces. Early Indians spread over both areas, Eastern Plains and Western Plateau, but apparently there was little cultural unity between the two groups before the advent of the horse in the eighteenth century. The eastern portion contains evidence of typical Plains archeology. Recent explorations in the western counties indicate a prehistoric people whose traits of culture were similar to those of the early Puget Sound tribes. In this early period the foods, manner of life, and occupations differed widely; the Plateau Indians probably had migrated eastward from the Pacific Coast, while the Plains Indians had come westward from the Mississippi Valley and beyond.

Evidences of prehistoric man in eastern Montana appear in the form of buffalo cliffs, teepee rings, and peculiar arrangements of stones which suggest various ceremonial uses. A few graves have also been uncovered. Crude pottery was made by the very early inhabitants, but not by the historic tribes.

Before horses were introduced, the Plains Indians obtained meat by still hunts; firing the prairie and then surrounding their quarry; or by drives. The drive was a common method of buffalo hunting. One or more series of stones were arranged in V-shape on a plateau of good grazing ground, with the apex at the edge of a cliff. Large rocks were piled on the floor of the canyon below. With the scene thus prepared, the hunting party stampeded a herd of buffalo toward the V, a number of the Indians hiding along the rock walls of the drive and waving robes to confuse the herd. The frightened beasts plunged over the cliff and perished either as a result of the fall or from the hundreds of arrows that followed.

At the foot of each of the 400 *piskuns* (buffalo cliffs) discovered in Montana, have been found arrowheads, fragmentary buffalo skeletons, and teeth. The ground at the base of the *piskun* on Two Medicine Creek about two miles from US 89 *(see Tour 4, Sec. a)* is white with the tooth enamel of buffalo whose bones have crumbled *(see Tour 11)*.

Teepee rings are circles of stone where lodges once stood. A teepee was a conical tent of animal skins wrapped around three or more poles, with a ventilation hole in the top. The skins were weighted down with stones to retain heat and to prevent their flapping in the wind. Where villages stood, hundreds of these circles remain, sometimes on the surface, sometimes half-buried. In some sections on the plains farmers dug and hauled away innumerable tons of them in preparing the land for cultivation *(see Tour 4)*.

A short distance west of Armstead, near US 91 south of Dillon, is a curious wheel-shaped pattern of stones thought to have had ceremonial uses *(see Tour 6, Sec. c)*. In Inscription Cave on US 87, eight miles east of Billings, are picture writings of unknown age *(see Tour 3, Sec. b)*.

Indian artifacts found in Montana include spearheads, arrowheads, and knives; stone pestles, hammers, and mauls; and red and black soapstone pipes for smoking wild tobacco. Pipes were treasured possessions. "Smoke the peace pipe" is a term universally known, but smoking sometimes signified warlike intent. It also propitiated the spirits of animals killed for food, confirmed friendships, pacified the elements, conveyed thanks for a good harvest, and sealed decisions. Like the coup stick (the Indian's Victoria Cross), the pipe was decorated with eagle feathers to record brave deeds.

Clothing, bags, and mats were made of animal skins, fringed, punctured, dyed, painted, or decorated with porcupine quills. A man wore a hip-length shirt, long leggings, belt, breechclout, moccasins; and cap, headband, fur hat, or feathered bonnet. A woman wore a dress reaching nearly to the ankles, short leggings, moccasins, belt, and headband. Shell earrings and necklaces were often worn, and face and body painting was general. Symbolical tattooing, chiefly of the wrists and forearms, was probably practiced only rarely by either sex.

To the Plains people the great provider of food, shelter, and tools was the buffalo. Bitter intertribal wars were fought over his ranges; his favor was wooed in many ways. If Indians found a peculiar red "buffalo stone," they did a buffalo dance forthwith. If more women than men danced, more cows than bulls would be taken. Some villages had a saying: "Do not steal. A buffalo will search you out and expose you."

The buffalo robe was the Indian's bed; dressed skins covered his lodges; braided strands of rawhide and twisted hair served him as ropes; and the green hide provided him a vessel in which to boil meat, or, when stretched over a frame of boughs, one in which to cross a river. Though deer and elk skins were preferred for other clothing, moccasins and leggings were often of buffalo hide.

From the tough, thick hide of the bull's neck, shrunk hard, the Indians made a shield that would turn a lance or arrow. From dried and hairless rawhide (parfleche), they made carrying cases. They made cannon bones and ribs into tools for dressing hides; shoulder blades lashed to sticks into hoes and axes; hoofs into glue for fastening feathers and heads on arrows. Bowstrings and thread were made of back sinews; spoons, ladles, and ornaments, of the horns; buckets, of the lining of the paunch. The dried skin of the tail, fastened on a stick, was used for a fly brush.

Some time in the eighteenth century, the horse was introduced to Montana Indians, possibly by the Shoshones. After that, modes of living on the two sides of the Rockies grew more similar. As buffalo hunters, the Plains Indians became the best horsemen; the Crow name for a horse was *espheta* (something to hunt with). Other Indian terms for "horse" indicated it as only a bigger and better dog: "medicine-dog," "elk-dog," and the like.

Plains Indians did little trapping, and did not molest "the underwater people"; but the Plateau tribes were eager fishermen and trappers. The women of both regions dug roots for food: chiefly wild turnip on the Plains, and camas, bitterroot, parasitic pine moss, wild carrot, and onion in the mountains. Mixing berries in pemmican (dried and pounded meat) was a Plains practice.

Surviving among Plains Indians are certain early secret societies, such as the Blackfeet Ikunikahntsiks (All Friends). This society is made up of Tsistsiks (Little Birds), youths under 20 years; Kuh-kwo-iks (Pigeons), young warriors; Suyis-Kaisiks (Mosquitos), mature warriors; Mut-siks (Braves), warriors of long experience; and Ikunuts-Omitaiks (All Crazy Dogs), warriors of 40 to 50 years. Other bands of the society, each with its own costume and way of dancing, are extinct.

Crow societies often originated in war parties which, after a successful campaign, met and swore their members to supreme mutual loyalty. The leading ones were the Foxes, War Clubs, Big Dogs, Crazy Dogs, Muddy Hands, and Fighting Bulls. Meetings were held at night, with fires blazing and drums beating as each member recited his deeds of valor. Members were elected upon petition, any warrior who had "counted coup" being eligible. When a member died, his brother could demand his place. The only society limited to one class of members was the Fighting Bulls, made up of aged warriors.

An important duty, especially of Foxes and War Clubs, the most respected societies, was to police the villages and prevent young warriors from venturing out on expeditions alone.

Each society had two tribal coup sticks carried by volunteer bearers from appointment until "snow fell upon their heads" (usually about a year). In the ceremony of appointment, the society chief asked who would next carry the sticks, then passed the pipe. To take the pipe and smoke it signified acceptance of the charge.

One stick was straight, with an eagle feather on the small end. When, in battle, the bearer thrust this stick into the ground, it represented his country, and he must remain and defend it until he died or until a society brother rode between him and the enemy; then it might be removed with honor. The other, the two-feathered "crooked stick," might be moved to a better position at discretion, but must not be lost to an enemy except by the bearer's death.

"Coup" consisted in striking an armed enemy with coup stick, quirt, or bow before otherwise harming him; striking the first enemy in battle; striking the enemy's fortification under fire; stealing a horse tied to a lodge in an enemy camp; or disarming a living enemy. Striking coup with the tribal sticks counted double, for a man was in greater danger while carrying them. In the ceremony of "counting coup," the braves sat around the campfire and listened to the hero's account of his exploit. A warrior wore an eagle feather in his hair to show that he had "counted coup." If he had been wounded, the feather was painted red; but it was more praiseworthy to have "struck coup" without being wounded. To carry an eagle's wing signified that one had accomplished a feat of unusual valor.

The sun dance of the Plains tribes may be regarded as a summer solstice ceremony, an offering to the sky gods. The early fur traders named it the Medicine Lodge, which seems a better term than sun dance, at least in the case of the Blackfeet, with whom dancing is not the important part of the ceremony. The Blackfeet themselves call it O-Kan (Vision). They believe that dreams are actual experiences of the shadow (soul) while the body is inert, and their great annual rite doubtless originated in the visions of some ancient sleeper. A tribal legend tells that once when meat was scarce an old woman, in a vision, learned the use of the "piskun" from one of her animal friends.

The vow to the Sun of which the sun dance is the fulfillment was made among the Crow, Sioux, Cheyenne, and Arapaho by a man, but among the Blackfeet by a woman. In Blackfeet legend it was Tailfeathers Woman who, first of mankind, visited Sun and received his request that sacred lodges be built in his honor. *(For description of Blackfeet sun dance, see Tour 2, Sec. b.)*

The predominant Plains tribes were the Crow and the Blackfeet. Others

were the Assiniboine in the northeast; the Sioux, or Dakota; the Minnetaree (Gros Ventres of the River); the Shoshone (nicknamed "Snakes,"
perhaps because of the tribal symbol in the sign language), widely scattered, living also west of the mountains; the Cheyenne in the southeast;
the Arapaho (White Claymen or Gros Ventres of the Prairie). Not all
Gros Ventres (Big Bellies) were of one stock. The Arapaho and Minnetaree spoke different languages and were bitter enemies. A third tribe
called Gros Ventres of the Mountains (Atsina) spoke the Arapaho
dialect.

The Blackfeet were a loose confederacy of Pikunis (Piegans), Bloods,
and Blackfeet proper, all of Algonquian stock. They camped and hunted
from the North Saskatchewan River to the headwaters of the Missouri.
They were cleanly, warlike people, and famous as horsemen. In their
campaigns they crossed the Rockies and ranged west and south as far as
Great Salt Lake.

The Crow (Absarokee) were a branch of the Hidatsa from the lower
reaches of the Missouri. Legend tells that two women's quarrel over a
buffalo paunch split the Hidatsa into Minnetaree and Crow factions. The
Crow went west to the "land of the lone mountains," settling along the
Yellowstone, Big Horn, Powder, and Wind Rivers, where they became
the most powerful tribe.

The Cheyenne, who probably preceded the Sioux in the upper Mississippi region, were Algonquian. According to their traditions, they were
the first eastern Montana Indians to use horses. The Shoshone roamed and
hunted from the Big Horn Mountains to the Coastal Range. Arapaho
(Algonquian) ranged over a wide territory around the headwaters of the
Missouri and Yellowstone Rivers and were allied at various times with
both Blackfeet and Cheyenne.

Little is known of the earliest inhabitants of western Montana. Skeletal
remains show that they were short and stocky, like modern Coast tribes,
and practiced flexed burial in pits. Charcoal remains suggest cremation,
which was not a custom of the historic Flathead. Trinkets and adorn-
ments, beads of abalone shell and salt-water mollusks, indicate coastal
origin. Legends describe them as courageous, but stupid and cruel. They
lived in pit dwellings little better than holes in the ground.

Despite their name, the Flathead (Salish) Indians never flattened the
heads of infants, as did Coast tribes. The name may have been given them
by their neighbors on the west, whose heads were pointed. They originally
lived in the double lean-to, later adopting a teepee-style dwelling of poles
chinked with grass and earth and covered with hides. Their ceremonial

FLATHEAD INDIAN

dances differed from the sun dance of the Plains, and they had no secret societies. They were, in addition, fish eaters. Otherwise they were so much like Plains Indians that anthropologists account for this only by their yearly migrations to the Plains after they acquired horses.

They dwelt along the shores of Flathead Lake and in the Bitterroot Valley, often crossing the Divide to hunt along the Judith and Mussel-shell Rivers. They recognized kinship with the Kalispel, Coeur d'Alene, Colville, and Spokan, and intermarried with the Nez Percé. The Kalispel are closely related to, and sometimes identified with, the Pend d'Oreille or Hanging Ears, who, like the Flathead and Kootenai, have given their name to a river and a lake.

The Kootenai, who extend from northwestern Montana into northern Idaho and southeastern British Columbia, are usually accounted a distinct stock (Kitunahan), but their speech has similarities to Algonquian which may indicate relationship. It is believed that they lived east of the Rockies, and were driven west by the Blackfeet. They were more warlike than their western neighbors, and were the greatest of deer hunters and tanners of buckskin. They were noted for their birchbark canoes with undershot ends, resembling those used on the Amur River in Siberia. They hunted and traded peaceably with the Flatheads, but were constantly at war with the Blackfeet.

The Indians who came into Montana in the 1880's as the Rocky Boy group were Chippewa from Minnesota and Canadian Cree (see Tour 14). The Bannack, a Shoshonean tribe, ranged over part of southwestern Montana, but lived in Idaho.

History

MONTANA'S history is alive with action and color, a drama in which the characters range from Indians and buckskin-clad trappers to copper kings and skilful modern politicians. The scenes shift from lonely trading posts or settlers' cabins to roaring gold camps; conflict sweeps from Indian battles and the "war of the copper kings" to the dryland farmer's grim struggle against the elements.

An eighteenth century French trader, Pierre Gaultier, Sieur de Varennes de la Verendrye, heard Indian tales of a river that flowed into a western sea. In 1738, after obtaining a grant of the fur trade monopoly from the French Government, he made his way to the Mandan villages in what is now North Dakota, then returned to Montreal by way of Fort La Reine, near the site of Winnipeg.

In 1742 he sent two of his sons, Pierre and François, on another expedition. After long dreary marches across the Dakota plains, they first saw, early in January 1743, the "shining mountains" generally believed to have been the Big Horns of Wyoming and southern Montana. Here the threat of Indian war, and perhaps discouraging reports of what lay ahead, made them return to Montreal.

The elder Verendrye died in 1749, the sons were deprived of their grants, and the French and Indian Wars stopped all expeditions of discovery. In 1763 New France (Canada) passed into British hands, and Louisiana came under the control of Spain. No other white men were to see Montana's "shining mountains" for more than sixty years.

The Lewis and Clark expedition outfitted for its epic adventure at Wood River, Illinois, opposite St. Louis. On May 14, 1804, with a large keelboat, two smaller boats, and a party of thirty-two men, they started, traveling 1,609 miles against Missouri currents before ice on the river compelled them to go into winter quarters in a friendly Mandan village.

The next spring they sent the keelboat back and, using the lighter craft, reached the mouth of the Yellowstone on April 26, 1805. Only Sacajawea, a Shoshone Indian woman, and her French-Canadian husband, Charbonneau, who had joined the party at the Mandan villages as interpreter, had ever been west of that point. A little farther on, the expedition had its first sight of grizzly bears. Lewis later wrote that he would rather meet two Indians than one grizzly.

They reached the mouth of the Marias River June 2, and saw the spray of the Great Falls on June 14. The 18-mile portage around the falls and rapids was enlivened by the first Fourth of July celebration west of the Mississippi. Lewis wrote: "I gave the men a drink of spirits which was the last of our stock. Fiddle was produced and a dance begun which lasted until 9 o'clock, when it was interrupted by rain."

Launching their boats on the upper Missouri July 15, they began the journey through the mountains. On July 19, about 14 miles northeast of the present site of Helena, they poled through a steep-walled canyon which they named the Gates of the Mountains. Six days later they camped at the three forks of the Missouri, naming each stream for a leading statesman: Jefferson, Madison, Gallatin. Sacajawea said it was here, five years earlier, that she had been captured by a band of Minnetaree Indians of the Dakota Nation.

Pushing up the Jefferson River July 30, they were delayed by beaver dams, shallow water, and thick alder and willow growth. Game was much less abundant and supplies were low; it was imperative that they meet with Indians and obtain horses for the journey across the mountains. Up to this point the expedition had not encountered a single Indian.

From the headwaters of the Beaverhead River, Lewis' advance party crossed the Divide through Lemhi Pass, and camped August 12 at the source of a stream flowing west. They were 3,000 miles from the mouth of the Missouri, and on short rations. Next morning they came upon a Shoshone camp. The chief, Cameahwait, was propitiated with presents and persuaded, with a few others, to return with Lewis to the Beaverhead. There, when Clark came up on August 17, it was learned that Cameahwait was Sacajawea's brother. This happy storybook circumstance assured the party of a cordial welcome.

They spent two weeks with the Shoshone, caching their canoes, bringing up their equipment, and trading for horses. Clark explored the Salmon River for some distance, but found it impassable. On August 30 the expedition started north down the Bitterroot Valley with a few unshod horses and an Indian guide, stopping at a spot on Lolo Creek which they named Traveler's Rest. On September 11 they pushed on over Lolo Pass and out of Montana.

At the Mandan villages, in the winter of 1804–05, a party of French-Canadian fur hunters led by François Antoine Larocque of the North-

West Company, offered to accompany the expedition, but Lewis declined the offer. In the spring of 1805 Larocque's party explored the Yellowstone region, buying beaverskins from the Crow.

On June 30, 1806, having returned from the Pacific, the Lewis and Clark expedition divided at Traveler's Rest. Captain Lewis, with nine men, went northward over the present site of Missoula and up the Blackfoot River, crossing the Continental Divide at its headwaters. While exploring the Marias River to learn whether it afforded a trade route to the Saskatchewan, his party skirmished with Gros Ventre Indians, killing two. Of the entire trip, this was the only hostile encounter that ended in fatality.

Clark, with the remainder of the party, crossed through Gibbon's Pass to the Big Hole River, then went down the Beaverhead and Jefferson Rivers to the Missouri. A detail was sent to meet Lewis at the mouth of the Marias, while Clark went overland to the Yellowstone. Near the mouth of that river, on August 12, the expedition was reunited.

Lewis and Clark had found St. Louis eager for news of their discoveries. None was more interested than Manuel Lisa, a New Orleanian of Spanish descent, who had traded with the Osages to the south. Outfitting an expedition of 42 men, he took them up the Yellowstone to the mouth of the Big Horn, where, in 1807, he built Montana's first trading post. Lisa named it Fort Ramon, for his son, but his trappers knew it as Lisa's Fort or Fort Manuel. Within two years he had 350 men working for him, and his organization continued to spread out until his death.

In 1807 he had sent John Colter and Sergeant Potts, veterans of the Lewis and Clark expedition, to the forks of the Missouri to trade with the Indians. Potts was slain by Indians, and Colter narrowly escaped. He made his way back to Lisa's Fort by way of what is now Yellowstone National Park. His account of the region caused fur traders to call it Colter's Hell.

Under the Hudson's Bay Company the British were operating westward to the Rockies and far to the north. Alexander Mackenzie and Simon Fraser, factors, had even penetrated to the Pacific. Although they had missed the Columbia River, their explorations led to the forming of the North-West Company, in whose employ the great David Thompson, with few instruments, explored and mapped the Columbia Basin. Even today his maps are found to be amazingly accurate.

Thompson came to Canada as a Hudson's Bay Company apprentice. He did not like the duties of a factor, and joined the North-West Company as an explorer at a time when the British were being spurred by the prospect of American competition in the Oregon country. In the spring of 1806 he crossed the Rockies and a year later was on the Kootenai River with a group of traders, the first white men to visit many of the tribes west of the Rockies. He built Kootenai House that year, and in November 1809, the Salish House near Thompson Falls. In the spring of 1810 he made several expeditions into the Flathead region. He returned to Canada in 1812 and never again came west; but in his five years of careful work on the Pacific slope he had explored and charted a great and previously unknown region.

In the spring of 1810 Pierre Menard and Andrew Henry built a trading post near Three Forks. The Blackfeet began a series of attacks, and twenty men were killed, among them George Drouillard, the second Lewis and Clark veteran to be killed near this place. Henry crossed the mountains to the headwaters of the Snake and established a post there; Menard and the main party returned to St. Louis.

In 1811 an overland party sent out by John Jacob Astor crossed the southeast corner of Montana. At about the same time a party sent to Astoria by sea landed at the mouth of the Columbia River. Among these were Alexander Ross, a Scot. When Astor's Pacific Fur Company failed because of the War of 1812, Ross joined the North-West Company, and led a motley band of Canadians, half-breeds, Iroquois—even Hawaiians— through the Columbia Basin. In the spring of 1824 he passed through Hell Gate Canyon to the source of Clark Fork of the Columbia, and across the Rockies to the headwaters of the Missouri. After retiring from the fur trade, he became one of the first and most prominent citizens of Winnipeg.

On March 20, 1822, William H. Ashley advertised for 100 "enterprising young men" to engage in the Missouri River fur trade, and the activities of the Rocky Mountain Fur Company then began. Among those who responded were Jim Bridger, Mike Fink, "king of the keelboatmen," and Hugh Glass. Ashley, a Virginian and a brigadier general in the War of 1812, had served as general of the Missouri Militia, and as Lieutenant Governor. Major Andrew Henry, of the ill-fated Three Forks trading post, was his associate.

The first expedition set out from St. Louis on April 15, 1822. At the Arikara villages it encountered hostile Indians and lost a boat and valuable equipment. Ashley returned to St. Louis, but the remainder of the party proceeded upstream and weeks later built Fort Henry at the mouth of the Yellowstone. Ashley's defeat might have been averted, had he taken the warnings of his guide and interpreter, Edward Rose. Of mixed Negro,

Indian, and white blood, Rose bore an unjustified reputation for disloyalty to the soldiers and trappers, probably strengthened by his notoriously sullen nature and mutilated face.

In 1823 Henry pushed up the Missouri as far as Great Falls, but was put to flight by the Blackfeet. He then built a post on the Yellowstone at the mouth of the Big Horn, but again had trouble with Indians, who killed several trappers.

The achievements of the Rocky Mountain Fur Company men, like those of David Thompson, were more important geographically than financially. Hiram Martin Chittenden, the historian, estimated, however, that in the twelve years of its career the company shipped $500,000 worth of beaver to St. Louis; at the same time goods, furs, and horses to the value of $100,000 were stolen. A hundred human lives were lost during the twelve years of exploring and trading.

As trapper, guide, and scout Jim Bridger became the most famous of the mountain men. For about fifty years he traveled over the Rockies, exploring and discovering, his exploits being a frontier byword. Shot by an Indian, he carried an arrow-head in his back for three years, and, when asked by Father de Smet if the wound had not become infected, smilingly replied, "In the mountains, meat never spoils."

The American Fur Company was founded in 1808, with John Jacob Astor for years the only stockholder. In 1822 a St. Louis branch was formed, with Pierre Chouteau, Bernard Pratte, and others as partners. Kenneth McKenzie, one of several former agents of Canadian companies who were enlisted into the service, came in 1827 and was given charge of the company's interests on the upper Missouri. In 1828 he built a large post near the mouth of the Yellowstone not far from the site of the one Henry had abandoned in 1823. McKenzie called it Fort Floyd, but soon afterward it became known as Fort Union.

McKenzie is said to have been the company's ablest trader. He made Fort Union the greatest concentration point of the western fur trade; he obtained the trade of the Blackfeet; he built Forts Piegan, McKenzie, Chardon, Lewis, Benton (on or near Marias River), Cass (Big Horn), and Van Buren (Tongue). Pierre Chouteau, Jr., who was the first to bring a steamboat up to Fort Union (1832), Alexander Culbertson, who succeeded McKenzie as factor, and Malcolm Clark, who helped settle the Prickly Pear Valley near Helena and was killed there by Piegan Indians, all received their training at Fort Union.

Famous visitors to Montana while the fur trade was at its height were George Catlin (1832), American painter of early-day Indian life; Prince

Maximilian of Wied-Neuwied (1833), whose travel journals are among the most valuable records of the period; and John James Audubon (1843), the naturalist.

Fort Lewis, most famous offshoot of Fort Union, was established in 1846. In 1850 it was rebuilt by Major Alexander Culbertson and christened Fort Benton in honor of Senator Thomas Benton of Missouri. This fort is conspicuous in Montana history mainly because of its site at the head of navigation on the Missouri River. Its importance as a fur trading post was secondary, for by 1850, beavers were almost extinct and other kinds of fur were hard to get. Nearly all profit had vanished for independent traders, although at Fort Owen, near Stevensville, the trade carried on into the gold rush period. The first steamer to arrive at Fort Benton was the *Chippewa*, in 1859. In 1862, year of the discovery of gold at Bannack, four boats landed cargoes; five years later there were thirty-nine boats. Then the traffic decreased again, and the last freight arrived in 1888.

An episode of 1854, notable for sheer dash and display, was perhaps the last wild explosion of color in Montana's hunting and trapping era. A wealthy Irish sportsman, Sir St. George Gore, came in with some companions, 40 servants, 112 horses, 12 yoke of oxen, 14 hunting dogs, enough arms and ammunition for a small arsenal, and 6 wagons and 21 carts laden with every luxury of the times. Engaging Jim Bridger as guide, he hunted in the Powder River region and slaughtered so much game that the Indians became resentful. In 1856 Gore drifted down to Fort Union, where he burned his equipment rather than pay the price Major Culbertson asked for transporting it to St. Louis. He spent the winter at Fort Berthold, and returned to St. Louis in the spring of 1857.

The first attempt to find a route for a railroad from St. Paul to the Pacific was made by one of five parties of the Pacific Railway expedition sent out by Secretary of War Jefferson Davis. The expedition, in charge of Governor Isaac I. Stevens of Washington Territory, reached Fort Union on August 1, 1853. Only part of the way surveyed was ever used in railroad building, but a member of the party, Lieutenant John Mullan, later (1858–1862) built the first wagon road over the northern Rockies, from Fort Benton to Walla Walla.

While explorers and trappers were breaking trails in this western country, missionaries also began to come in. Hearing of Christianity from Iroquois employees of the North-West Company, the Flathead and Nez Percé sent four delegates to St. Louis in 1831 asking for missionaries to teach them how to worship the Great Spirit in the white man's way. Two of the envoys died in St. Louis and were buried in the cathedral. Nothing came of the mission at that time, and in 1835, and again in 1839, other envoys repeated the request.

Fired by the story of distant Indians waiting to be converted, Father Pierre Jean de Smet, Belgian Jesuit, traveled to the Rocky Mountains in 1840 by way of the Platte River. He received a delegation of the Flathead on Green River, Wyoming, baptized them, and on July 5 celebrated mass. Then he accompanied the Flathead to the Gallatin Valley, where he left them on August 27 and returned to St. Louis. The following spring, with two priests and four lay brothers, he came back and founded St. Mary's Mission in the Bitterroot Valley.

Late the next winter he obtained a supply of seed at Fort Colville, Washington, and in the spring, at St. Mary's Mission, he planted oats, wheat, and potatoes—Montana's first crop. In 1845 Father Anthony Ravalli, Italian Jesuit, joined him, and the two pioneering priests built the first gristmill in Montana at St. Mary's Mission.

In 1854 the Idaho mission of St. Ignatius was moved by Father Adrian Hoecken to the Mission Valley. Here, twenty years later, a press was installed and a dictionary printed of the Kalispel language. Another mission was established near the site of Choteau, in the heart of the Blackfeet country, but because of the hostility of the Indians, it was moved to the Missouri River and then to Skull Butte above Cascade, becoming known as St. Peter's-by-the-Rock. While St. Ignatius still serves the Flathead, the other missions are now only historic points of interest.

In 1856 a party en route from the Bitterroot Valley to Salt Lake, obtained a small quantity of gold from François Finlay, a quarter-breed Indian known as Benetsee, who had prospected on Gold Creek. Evidently they thought little of their find for they gave it to Richard Grant, who lived in the Deer Lodge Valley near by. In the spring of 1858 John Silverthorne, a packer at Fort Owen, gave Major Culbertson at Fort Benton a small amount of what appeared to be gold dust in exchange for goods. Culbertson sent it to St. Louis; and there it was pronounced gold. Silverthorne had procured the dust from Benetsee.

James and Granville Stuart, returning from California, found gold values as high as ten cents a pan near Benetsee's discovery, but, as they had neither sufficient provisions nor proper tools and were menaced by the Blackfeet, they went on to Fort Bridger on the Oregon Trail. In the summer of 1860 Henry Thomas, known as "Gold Tom," sank a 30-foot shaft in the glacial drift. He made only $1.50 a day, and so he moved on.

The Stuarts returned and, on May 8, 1862, set up the first sluices in

FATHER DeSMET

Montana near the head of Gold Creek. A letter written to their brother Thomas in Colorado, advising him to join them, started a small rush to Montana. Among the prospectors were John M. Bozeman, Samuel T. Hauser, and W. B. Dance.

While the Gold Creek diggings were becoming active, large parties of Colorado miners, bound for Idaho, turned toward the Deer Lodge Valley when they learned that the Idaho gold camps were overrun with men from the coast. On Willard's (Grasshopper) Creek, a tributary of the Beaverhead, John White and William Eads made the first big strike in Montana, July 28, 1862. Bannack, named for an Indian tribe, sprang up overnight.

Many of the gold seekers had left the East to escape the war raging there, but its echoes followed them. Confederate sympathizers named a gulch "Jeff Davis"; Bannack's residential district became "Yankee Flat."

In 1863 the Edgar-Fairweather party from Cottonwood (Deer Lodge) missed a rendezvous with a party from Bannack for a prospecting trip to the Yellowstone Valley and the Black Hills. Turned back by Indians, they made one of the greatest of all gold discoveries in Alder Gulch on May 26. The first year's yield from this gulch was estimated at $10,000,000 or more. At once towns sprang up; in two years Virginia City had 10,000 inhabitants.

Drawn to the new El Dorado, in addition to honest prospectors, were fugitives from older camps, among them Henry Plummer, who became sheriff at Bannack. With him as chief, a gang of highwaymen began operations in 1863 along the wild 90-mile stretch between Alder Gulch and Bannack. Corresponding in cipher, they marked men and coaches for plunder, used stage stops as hang-outs, and killed at least 102 persons.

A group of determined men decided to act. Arresting one George Ives after a particularly brutal murder, they tried him before a miners' court, and, defying the threats of the organized criminals, convicted and hanged him December 21, 1863. Then a secret group calling themselves Vigilantes took up the task of swift and wholesale justice. They hanged Erastus (Red) Yeager and George W. Brown at Laurin on January 4, 1864. Plummer and his chief deputies, Stinson and Ray, were hanged at Bannack on January 10. Altogether, twenty-four "bad men" paid their score between December 20, 1863, and February 5, 1864, and organized robbery and murder on the road ceased.

On July 14, 1864, John Cowen, John Crabb, Robert Stanley, and Gabe Johnson found traces of color in Last Chance Gulch. After prospecting northward in the hope of a richer find, they returned to this "last chance"

—and made a big strike. Other rich gulches were soon found in the same region. Some of the values in Confederate Gulch, thirty miles east of Helena, were sensational, Montana Bar yielding as high as $1,000 per pan and one clean-up of seven days amounting to $114,800.

In May 1864 G. O. Humphreys and William Allison had found placer gold in Silver Bow Creek. The camp boomed for a few seasons, but a dry year (1869) reduced the clean-ups and by 1870 it was almost deserted. In 1875 William Farlin opened rich silver veins in the Travonia mine, and started a boom that made Butte "the silver city" for twenty years. The Travonia was taken over by W. A. Clark, who built a mill to handle the ore.

Montana had been a component successively of Oregon, Washington, Nebraska, Dakota, and Idaho Territories, always with the seat of government far away. Miners' courts had been organized but were largely ineffective; knowledge of law was not a necessary qualification of judges. As people poured in, some local government became a necessity. The organic act of May 26, 1864, created Montana Territory, and Sidney Edgerton became Governor. Three justices were provided. The first Territorial legislature met at Bannack and enacted provisions that form the basis of the present codes.

In 1865 the legislature changed the capital to Virginia City, established the original nine counties, and then adjourned without providing for future meetings. As a result the court refused to recognize the legislative acts, thus creating grave antagonism between bar and people. Congress somewhat eased matters by passing an enabling act for the Legislature of 1867. The new government followed Idaho statutes in legislative and judicial procedure, but among its problems were water rights and mine law, both new branches.

A movement toward statehood in 1865 resulted in Acting Governor Meagher's calling a constitutional convention. Eight of the delegates did not bother to attend. The constitution was sent to St. Louis for printing and was lost somewhere on the way.

At first Montana Indians were not invariably hostile—as shown by the Laramie treaty (1851) and the Isaac I. Stevens treaties (1855)—but government on both sides was inadequate to compel observance of agreements, and frequent clashes resulted.

The Indians soon made it clear that they did not like being confined to reservations, especially when the buffalo sought other pastures. Chiefs and medicine men, who had predicted distress and doom if the whites continued to come in, found many followers. The Government's failure during the Civil War to forward the goods and money promised in treaties made the Indians openly hostile. The Sioux, who were crowded westward, harassed routes of travel and took heavy toll of emigrant trains.

In 1863 John M. Bozeman blazed a road from the Oregon Trail to the Montana gold camps; in 1864 he escorted a large wagon train over it. The Sioux and Cheyenne at once began attacks on the road, and the Blackfeet followed their example in the north. In April 1867 Bozeman was slain by Piegans on Mission Creek, east of Livingston.

To guard the trail Fort C. F. Smith, Montana's first army post, was established on the upper Big Horn in 1866. It irritated the Indians so much that in 1868, a year after the notable Hayfield and Wagon Box fights in which a handful of United States soldiers repulsed hundreds of Indian horsemen, the Government withdrew the troops, declared the region a reservation, and forbade settlers to enter it. For nine years the Bozeman Trail was unused; emigrants came by the Mullan Road from Walla Walla, the water route to Fort Benton, and a road northward from Utah.

In 1876 the War Department launched a campaign against the Sioux and Cheyenne. On June 17 the Sioux, under Crazy Horse, outfought General Crook on the Rosebud. Meanwhile General George A. Custer, with 600 officers and men of the Seventh Cavalry, rode toward the Little Horn. When his scouts brought word that he was approaching a large Indian village, Custer divided his command, sending Major Marcus A. Reno with three troops to the river, and Captain Frederick Benteen with three more to keep to Reno's left and to attack any Indians before him.

Taking somewhere between 208 and 277 (historians differ) men and officers, Custer swung right and soon engaged an overwhelming force on the hills just east of the river. When the firing ceased and the Indians left the field, the only living thing remaining was Comanche, Captain Myles Keogh's wounded horse. Four miles to the south Reno was too busily engaged to know either the whereabouts or the tragic fate of Custer. Although his losses were heavy, Reno saved his command when Benteen came up and, with him, took a defensible position on the bluffs above the river.

The tragedy led to the establishment, later in the year, of Fort Keogh (the beginning of Miles City) at the mouth of the Tongue River. Next year Fort Custer, another cavalry post, was built at the junction of the Big Horn and Little Horn.

The last major Indian battles in the United States were fought with the Nez Percé, who, rather than be confined to their north Idaho reservation,

VIRGINIA CITY

attempted a flight to Canada. Led by their chief, Joseph, they eluded 90 cavalrymen from Fort Lapwai (Idaho) and 300 soldiers under General Howard, and entered Montana over the tortuous Lolo Trail. Captain C. C. Rawn, in command of Fort Missoula (just established), fortified Lolo Pass with 50 regulars and 100 volunteers. Joseph demanded free passage up the Bitterroot Valley, and the citizens, realizing they would not be molested, withdrew their support from Rawn, compelling him to return to Fort Missoula. Meanwhile General John Gibbon had left Helena with 197 officers and men; on August 8, 1877, he found the Nez Percé in Big Hole Basin at the junction of Ruby and Trail Creeks. The battle started at daylight August 9; on the night of August 10 Joseph withdrew, leaving the wounded Gibbon with 69 casualties.

Chief Joseph moved southeast into the Yellowstone Park region, then turned north through Cooke City. Across Montana he retreated, skirmishing with his pursuers but eluding them. The telegraph was his undoing; General Nelson A. Miles of Fort Keogh, being forewarned, headed him off in the Bear Paw Mountains. After a masterly 1,600-mile retreat, encumbered by women, children, and a large band of horses, Joseph engaged in a four-day battle and, on October 8, finally surrendered.

With the way cleared for settlement, the grassy plains and valleys were found to be as ideal for cattle as they had been for buffalo. In 1853 John Grant started a beef herd in Deer Lodge Valley, driving the cattle from the Oregon Trail. He sold out in 1865 to Conrad Kohrs, who also ran a large herd in the Sun River Valley. The first Texas drive was made in 1866 by Nelson Story of Bozeman; the last, about 1888. In the years between, large outfits financed by outside capital occupied most of the Territory. The great difficulty was the long drive to market. In 1874 James Forbes drove a herd to Ogden, Utah, and from there sent it east by rail, the first Montana cattle so shipped. Building of the Northern Pacific and Great Northern brought into being a string of "cowtowns" of which Billings, Miles City, Culbertson, and Havre were typical. The Montana Stock Growers' Association was organized July 28, 1884, with Theodore Roosevelt, then ranching in western Dakota, a charter member. Brand books had been published in 1872, with the Masonic square of Poindexter and Orr, of Beaverhead, the first brand entered. Sheep had first been brought to the Bitterroot Valley in 1857, and, despite heavy depredations by coyotes, they increased steadily until damage to ranges by their close cropping of grass forced reductions.

Statehood and the railroad building era—roughly 1880–1910—ended the days of the open range. Settlers flooded in; sod was broken and fences built; immense counties were split up; cowtowns became small cities; the people of the State set about building a new way of life.

The Territorial government having become thoroughly unsatisfactory, a convention held in Helena on January 14, 1884, drafted a constitution which the people ratified. Five years later Congress passed an enabling act providing for the forming of constitutions and State governments in several western Territories. The delegates, well practiced by then, met once more and drew up a constitution prefaced by the Magna Carta, the Declaration of Independence, the Articles of Confederation, the United States Constitution, and organic and enabling acts. It was ratified at a special election, and the State was admitted to the Union on November 8, 1889.

The new State's resources seemed limitless. Every type of endeavor offered bonanza returns. Silver and gold mines were in flush production; the great copper boom was getting into full swing; immense coal deposits had been discovered; timber products were in demand; a new agriculture was beginning. The people were lusty, adventurous, seeking opportunity.

Nowhere was the struggle for power and wealth more intense than in Butte, which city had come into prominence mainly through the work of William A. Clark and Marcus Daly, lifelong rivals. Clark developed diverse interests, but Daly, having discovered in 1881, by depth explorations in his silver mine, the fabulous richness of the Butte copper deposits, concentrated on the development of his great mining company.

In 1889 F. Augustus Heinze, a young engineer from the Columbia School of Mines, came to Butte. Two years later he inherited $50,000, went to Germany for a few months of study, and returned to found the Montana Ore Purchasing Company. With New York capital he built a smelter to treat ore from small mines, thus gaining a foothold in the industry. Soon he was buying and leasing claims all over the district.

In 1895 he was ready for bigger game. His plans were based on the "law of the apex," under which, within certain limits, an owner could follow any vein that apexed (came to the surface) on his property. In the Butte district, with its faulted and offset geologic structure, it was anybody's guess where a vein apexed. Before a friendly court a good lawyer and "experts," suitably rewarded, could make a convincing case of any claim. On this basis Heinze brought suit against the Anaconda, St. Lawrence, and Neversweat mines—the best of the Butte properties. District Judge Clancy issued an injunction stopping production and throwing thousands out of work. When the angry miners threatened to hang him, he dissolved the injunction; but for eight years thereafter the courts were cluttered with suits and countersuits.

When the Minnie Healy, a claim adjoining the rich Leonard mine, unexpectedly became a heavy producer, Heinze claimed apex rights to the Leonard ore bodies, though his title to the Minnie Healy itself was questionable. The case of the Michael Davitt was even more bitter, developing into an underground battle in which two miners were killed and others barely escaped, while Heinze mined $1,000,000 worth of ore.

After several years of strife the Amalgamated Company, rather than continue a fight costing $1,000,000 a year, bought out Heinze for $14,-000,000 and an interest in a company formed to work his holdings. Heinze went to New York, where, it is said, powerful interests broke him when he attempted to juggle prices on the New York Stock Exchange. His failure is held by some to have been a cause of the 1907 panic.

Other stories from Montana mining history are nearly as exciting although the characters and events do not loom so large. In the Granite Mountain silver mine at Philipsburg, the owner's last shot of powder had been set and the men were putting on their coats to leave, when the blast piled bonanza at their feet.

Before he died in 1900, Marcus Daly had created a great industrial organization, built much of Butte, and founded Anaconda. Meanwhile, with scores of metal mines in the mountains, it was natural that a wider smelting industry should develop. Great Falls, with unlimited water power and extensive coal deposits near by, was an ideal site. The first hydroelectric plant and smelter was established in 1890; within ten years the city became second in the State. A third important smelter was built at East Helena. In Territorial days only a few towns had had more than 2,000 inhabitants; Helena led for many years with about 10,000. The coming of railroads and the admission of Montana to the Union spurred growth, especially in the case of Billings, Havre, Kalispell, Missoula, Miles City, and the mining and smelting towns. Those fortunately placed as distributing centers grew most rapidly. In Bozeman, Missoula, and Dillon, the establishment of units of the University of Montana in 1893, 1895, and 1897, respectively, helped greatly in laying the foundation for later development, both economic and cultural.

Republicans and Democrats had about equal strength in the young State, and politics was lively from the start. It was said at the time that electioneering practices were open to question; this led to many charges of corruption. William A. Clark, a Democrat, was a leading candidate for Senator; Marcus Daly, also a Democrat, was determined to prevent his election. Daly wished to make Anaconda the State capital, while Clark favored Helena. Election to the United States Senate (by the State legislature) hinged on the disputed election of five representatives from Butte. Each party claimed the election of its own delegates, thus deadlocking the legislature. The Republicans sent Wilbur F. Sanders and T. C. Power to the Senate; the Democrats sent W. A. Clark and Martin Maginnis. The Senate seated Republican Sanders and Power. In the capital contest Helena won after two elections (1894) by a small majority.

Clark still aspired to the Senate, but his party did not gain control of the legislature until 1899. Then he was elected; but twenty-seven legislators sent a memorial to Congress charging that he had bought votes. Before the Senate investigating committee could report, Clark resigned. In the absence of Governor Smith from the State, Lieutenant Governor Spriggs appointed Clark to the vacancy. Smith, returning, declared the appointment invalid and appointed Martin Maginnis, whom the Senate refused to seat. The office remained vacant until Clark was elected again in 1901.

The passage of the Reclamation Act of 1902 made farming under large-scale irrigation possible for the first time. In Montana the Huntley project in Yellowstone County (completed 1907) was the first of the large projects and one of the outstandingly successful ones. It was soon followed by others. In the same period (1902–1910) there were large increases in the number of homestead entries in the dry-land areas. The last section settled was the northeastern one, which was still being homesteaded during the early years of the World War. Division of the large older counties into smaller and usually more convenient units continued into the 1920's, in most cases under the guidance of one Dan McKay, a shrewd manipulator who became known to the State as County Splitter McKay.

Meanwhile industry in the State reached something like the limit of logical development under prevailing conditions. In Anaconda the Washoe Smelter, replacing the older, smaller smelter in 1902, gave Montana one of the greatest copper reduction plants in the world. In Great Falls, during the wartime stimulation of markets (1918), a wire, rod, and cable factory was built to make the copper refined in the electrolytic plant into finished products. Oil and lumber production boomed and declined. Sugar refining, flour milling, canning, and meat packing grew slowly. Hydroelectric power production expanded steadily. As in other parts of the United States, the emphasis in transportation development swung to highways; except for a few short branch lines built for special purposes, railroad expansion ended by 1920.

The greatest growth of population after the end of the gold rush period came in the decade between 1880 and 1890, when the number of people increased 365 per cent. This record was never approached again. Later census reports—up to 1930—show that, although the State's growth was still rapid, it became steadily less so; from 1890 to 1900 the increase was 70 per cent; from 1900 to 1910, nearly 55 per cent; from 1910 to 1920, about 46 per cent. Then as drought and price inequalities struck hard at the farmers, and activity in the State's chief industries slumped, the movement of population changed its direction; from 1920 to 1930 there was a decline of slightly more than 2 per cent.

Politically Montana has been somewhat unpredictable during its entire period of statehood. Since 1900 it has invariably cast its electoral votes for the winning Presidential candidate; but, while all but two of its Governors have been Democrats, a majority of the other elective State offices —up to 1933—was held by Republicans.

Socially significant laws include those on compulsory school attendance

(1887) and child labor (1907); the initiative and referendum (1907) and the direct primary (1912); and special laws which protect the health of women at work, and provide for an eight-hour day (1917), and equal wages to men and women for identical work. Under the Workmen's Compensation Act (1915) graduated compensation is paid to those injured in industry, and employers are required to contribute to an insurance fund. An inheritance tax law imposing graduated assessments was passed in 1923, the moneys received to go into educational, conservational, and general funds. A year later the people initiated and passed a law imposing a tax of one-fourth to one per cent on the gross production of metal mines. Laws on grain grading and marketing (1915), livestock and fruit inspection, hail insurance (1917), and education through extension service have aided agriculture. Traffic laws were first passed in 1905, and the State' highway commission was created in 1913. A gasoline tax of five cents (1931) pays for construction of hard-surfaced roads. A planning board, created in 1934, is studying means of bringing resources of the State into more extended use. A highway patrol system was inaugurated in 1935. Montana has two executive bodies not common to all States: a special livestock commission of six members appointed to protect the livestock interests of the State, and a water conservation board whose special interest is irrigation.

In 1916 Jeannette Rankin of Missoula was elected to Congress as the Representative of the western district. She took her seat as the Nation's first Congresswoman the following spring, in the special session which met to declare war on Germany. At first—according to Walter Millis' Road to War (1935)—she did not vote. Then "Uncle Joe" Cannon urged her, "You cannot afford not to vote. You represent the womanhood of the country in the American Congress." "At last," says Millis, "she rose . . . looking straight ahead. 'I want,' she said . . . 'to stand by my country, but I cannot vote for war . . . I vote No.' " Then she "fell back into her seat, pressed her forehead, and began to cry." Her action was widely denounced as discreditable to women and to women's participation in politics, and, from an opposite point of view, it was as widely acclaimed.

Montanans have a fairly warlike tradition. Many of the pioneers were veterans of the Civil War, or had fought Indians. The First Regiment of Montana Infantry won high praise in the Philippines, and their flag in 1905 became the official State flag. The Second Montana Infantry served four and one-half months on the Mexican border in 1916, and in 1917 sailed for France as part of the 163rd Regiment. Montana troops fought at Cantigny, Chateau Thierry, and the Argonne, winning 53 Distin-

JIM BRIDGER

guished Service crosses. In the Argonne, the war cry of the Ninety-first became famous, "(We're from) Powder River; let 'er buck!"

In the early 1920's, while oil and gas fields were being discovered in Montana, oil was indirectly responsible for bringing into Nation-wide prominence two Montana Senators, Thomas J. Walsh and Burton K. Wheeler. Walsh, who led the investigation that unearthed the illegal Tea-pot Dome lease and other irregular leases of naval oil lands, had been Senator from Montana for years; after this episode he became known as.

the inquisitorial genius of the United States Senate and one of the best legal minds in the Nation. In 1933 he was chosen for the post of Attorney-General in the Cabinet of Franklin D. Roosevelt, but died suddenly before taking office. Senator Wheeler became the Vice-Presidential candidate of the Progressive ticket headed by Robert M. La Follette in 1924. When this ticket was defeated he continued as Senator from Montana. In 1937 he acted as spokesman for the group in Congress that opposed the President's court reform plan.

Montana recovered slowly from the depression of the early 1930's; adverse factors included a drought of unprecedented length. Great aids to the State, however, were Federal projects such as Fort Peck Dam and lesser undertakings, and large Federally sponsored programs of soil conservation, irrigation, rural electrification, insect control, and construction of roads, parks, and recreational facilities, under such agencies as the Public Works Administration and Works Progress Administration. In 1935 Helena suffered disastrous earthquakes. Several lives were lost and property damage ran to $4,000,000. Business revival and great activity in mining and oil districts were observed in 1936 and 1937; mines and ore-reduction plants operated at capacity. Eastern Montana, at the same time, was subjected to extreme drought. In the autumn of 1937 some of the Butte mines suspended operations; others followed until, early in the summer of 1938, only one or two remained in operation. In contrast to the gloom in industrial Butte, there was joy in the State's agricultural districts as a rainy summer had brought to maturity the best crops in ten years.

Ethnic Groups

MANY of the early trappers engaged in the Montana fur trade were French-Indian; the managers of the companies were usually English or Scottish, and several of them, who married Indian women, left descendants of mixed blood. Most of the people who poured in when gold was found were native whites from the Midwest and East; those who rushed to the Butte silver and copper ledges were largely German and Irish. Between 1880 and 1900 many immigrants helped build railroads, then turned to farming and lumbering. Thousands of Germans and Scandinavians settled in the dry-land sections after 1900.

Persons of foreign birth or of foreign or mixed parentage made up 45.2 per cent of the population in 1930, according to the U. S. Bureau of Census. Since Canadians, who numbered 31,585, represent no single parent stock, the 30,377 persons of German extraction formed the largest group. They were closely followed by the Norwegians (29,386). Swedes numbering 16,226 and Danes numbering 8,109 brought the figure for persons claiming Scandinavian birth or parentage to 53,721. The British Isles were represented by five groups totaling 52,819 (England, 19,815; Irish Free State, 17,940; Scotland, 8,174; North Ireland, 4,628; Wales, 2,262). Other nationalities represented by more than 5,000 persons were: Russian, 13,761; Jugoslav, 9,278; Italian, 6,325; Finnish, 6,051; and Czechoslovak, 5,078. After 1920, about 2,500 Mexicans came to work in the sugar beet areas (see BILLINGS).

Comparison of the 1930 census figures with those of 1920 show that the number of Indians in Montana is increasing (from 10,956 in 1920 to 14,798 in 1930), while those of Orientals (1,631) and of Negroes (1,256) are declining. A small number of Negroes had drifted as far west as Montana during the brief excitement of Negro migration from the South after the Civil War. There were only 346 in the State in 1880, but by 1890 there were 1,490. Most of them went to such towns as Butte and Helena, and found employment in the mines, hotels, saloons, and gambling rooms; in 1903 a Negro owned and operated a hotel on Main Street in Helena, at which white and Negro guests were served. Circulars had been distributed telling of the Government and railroad lands that could be obtained cheaply, and a few settled on such land and engaged in agriculture. Unlike States to the east, Montana was not affected by the Negro migration during the World War. The peak was reached in 1910, when there were 1,834 Negroes in the State. By 1920 the number had decreased to 1,658. Most Montana Negroes live in Cascade, Silver Bow, Yellowstone, and Lewis and Clark Counties, where several operate retail businesses and a few engage in the professions. They have their own churches, chiefly of the African Methodist Episcopal denomination.

The foreign-born and foreign-parentage elements are found chiefly in local groups. The industrial cities have large numbers of Irish, English, Germans, Jugoslavs, Finns, and Italians; the northeastern farming region has a preponderance of Norwegians and Danes. The northwestern region has a sprinkling of French Canadians. Some of the groups in part retain their native languages or dialects and a few old-country customs.

Among Scandinavian residents no Christmas dinner is complete without *lutfisk* (Sw.)—a dried cod reduced to extreme tenderness in a brine of wood ashes or lye, then cooked and served hot. A vast thin griddlecake called *lefse* (Nor.), made of flour and mashed potatoes, is baked on a floured stove top, and served folded and buttered. Two delightful old customs are slowly passing: *julotta* (Sw.)—a simple service held in the churches before dawn of Christmas Day; and the antics of *julebokker* (Nor.) or "Christmas fools," who go about the countryside in fantastic disguises, invading houses and entertaining their occupants.

Among the Jugoslavs of Butte, Great Falls, and Anaconda, celebration of Christmas begins on the evening of January 6 (Julian calendar) with the preparation of the *badnyak,* a fire of three logs. A family's first visitor after midnight mass is known as the *Polaznik.* He sprinkles a gloveful of wheat on its members, saying "Christ is born"; they reply, "Truly He is born," and sprinkle him with wheat. He kisses one of the logs in the fireplace and is given a present. If he is a close friend he spends the day with the family.

In eastern Montana May 17 is celebrated as Norwegian Independence Day. Swedish, Danish, and Norwegian inhabitants also observe Midsummer Day and Martinmas, usually with small picnics and the serving of special foods in their homes.

A three-day Balkan pre-Lenten celebration, the Mesopust (leave out meat), ends with public exercises on Shrove Tuesday. In symbolic expression of the people's desire to enter Lent spiritually pure, *Slarko Veljacic,* an effigy of their sins and misfortunes, is tried, condemned, dragged through the streets, hanged and burned.

Frenchtown, a small scattered settlement composed of about 140 people of French-Canadian descent, is 15 miles northwest of Missoula. It is of interest for its traces of colonial French culture and patois, though its origin is fairly recent (1864). Many of these people are descended from the Brunswick French of eastern Canada, some of whom have intermarried with the Indians, and others are of the Quebec French. A few of the older people cannot speak or understand English, and many of them speak it brokenly. Few old customs have survived. New Year's Day, however, is the "open house" holiday of the year and on St. John's Day (June 24) a festival is sponsored by the St. Jean Baptiste Society, named for the patron saint of the parish.

In Scottish settlements Burns' birthday is celebrated with bagpipe music, dances, and the rendition of his songs and poems.

Billings beet workers celebrate Mexican independence with a fiesta, September 15-16, at which scenes of the Revolution of 1810 are reenacted in pantomime.

Agriculture

MONTANA, traditionally a mining and stock raising State, is also a great farming region. In a few exceptional years its wheat crop alone has exceeded the entire mineral output in value. Unusual hardships and constant change have beset the development of agriculture, and production was markedly curtailed in the 1930's both by natural conditions and organized crop control programs, yet the average wheat crop continued to exceed 35,000,000 bushels yearly.

The first small crop of grain and vegetables was grown in the Bitterroot Valley in 1842, but Montana had no extensive agriculture until the early 1860's, when successive gold rushes began to populate the western valleys. At first the incomes of those who broke the soil fluctuated with the fortunes of those who followed the mining camps. Then many disappointed prospectors found that they could acquire more gold by raising and selling foodstuffs for miners. In 1865 the land claimed for agricultural uses totaled 80,000 acres.

Meanwhile cattle raising, introduced about 1832, increased more slowly, but was less affected by changes in other fields. In 1856 there were nearly 2,000 beef and milch cattle in the region, and more than 4,000 oxen. Between 1860 and 1880 cattle were trailed to market at Salt Lake City and other distant places; at the same time ranchers drove large herds from Texas to the Montana ranges, where both horses and cattle grew fat and sleek on buffalo grass and other rich forage.

The 1880's and early 1890's were the heyday of the stockman and cowboy, who shared with the miner the task of founding and governing the new State. In 1886–7 the industry met and survived a major disaster, a hard winter when thousands of cattle died.

After 1900 a flood of homesteaders poured into the State. Protesting stockmen were forced out of localities where they had been supreme; grain raising assumed prime importance. For some years the ranchers affected to despise the "honyak," and resisted his advance by cutting fences and pasturing cattle in his fields; but this attitude gave way to a realization that the new settlements offered a rapidly growing market for horses.

CATTLE

From 1900 to 1916 large crops were harvested. Then in the northeast the wheat was damaged by rust; and in 1917 came a drought that was to last three years throughout the State and five years in the eastern part. These misfortunes were aggravated by an economic depression and harsh winters. Farmers, at the mercy of chance, had to depend on Federal loans for seed and feed. Adversity made them cautious; they began summer-fallowing to conserve moisture. Crops improved and power machinery cut labor and production costs. A new period of prosperity culminated in the late 1920's, and was again succeeded by disaster—worse this time, because farmers had invested so heavily in new machines.

Agriculture, especially dry farming, has subsequently undergone readjustment. Strip farming is to some extent replacing summer fallow, which loosens the soil and promotes erosion. Land is cultivated with the one-way disk, which leaves stubble at the surface to hold soil in summer and snow in winter, or with the duck-foot cultivator, which turns up large clods.

Rapidly expanding irrigation tends to reduce the speculative fever for extensive dry-land farming. Individual planning, assisted by Federal and State conservation programs, takes much poor land out of cultivation. But it will take time for native grasses to regain foothold on such land.

From 1919 to 1923, the average annual value of farm products was roughly $90,000,000. This value was taken from 35,000,000 acres, divided into farms of a little more than 600 acres each. In 1927 farm products reached a high of $161,700,000, but in 1935 they dropped back to $100,411,000. The number of farms decreased from 57,677 in 1920 to 47,495 in 1930; at the same time the average size of the remaining farms rose to 955 acres, and the average income rose from $1,560 to $2,030.

The effects of depression years upon the security and welfare of farmers in Montana is traceable in the statistics of the National Resources Committee on tenancy, published in 1935. The report lists 13,985 tenant farmers, or 27.7 per cent of the total. It ranks Montana twenty-seventh in the Nation and third among the western States in the proportion of farmers without equity in the land they occupy.

Montana has great variety in soils, but in general the dark and very dark grayish brown loams of the central, eastern, and northeastern sections are best for farming, being rich in organic material and in many other elements of fertility. They are especially adapted to the production of hard spring wheat, which in many places has been grown exclusively, despite a tendency toward drought-resistant crops such as corn. Because of the severe climate Montana's hardiest crops have always been her best. In the southern counties, where the growing season is longer but rainfall even scantier, more land is reserved for grazing. On the milder and moister western slopes much fruit is grown. The rich dark loams of the Gallatin and other sheltered valleys east of the Divide produce the State's finest and most varied crops of grain, fruit, and vegetables.

Crops: Oats and hay, in great demand for stage lines and military posts, were for a time the leading crops. Wheat, which had originally occupied first rank, became first again in 1914. Although it declined briefly about 1930, because of low grain prices, and hay far exceeded wheat in value for that particular period, the acreage planted to wheat continued the largest and increased in importance in the northeastern counties and the Judith Basin. Montana wheat ranges up to 16 percent in protein content and is harder, heavier, and of finer milling quality than any other American wheat. The chief variety is marquis, although durum also yields well. High prices during the World War brought huge expansion in acreage, but drought prevented an increase in actual production. Hence the farmers

YOUNG FARMER

had to bear higher costs without a corresponding rise in income. In 1936 the yield from 2,239,000 acres was 13,626,000 bushels.

Next in importance are corn and hay. Corn is grown chiefly for feed in the eastern half of the State. Every county produces hay: alfalfa, grain, hay, clover, timothy, and various grasses; it is the leading crop in the upper Yellowstone Valley. Native bluejoint is harvested in several counties. Alfalfa and clover seed are valuable incidental crops. Tame hay in 1936 yielded 1,302,000 short tons on 1,329,000 harvested acres; wild hay yielded 302,000 short tons on 464,000 acres.

All except the highly mechanized farms raise oats and barley for feed. Flax is popular in the eastern and northern counties as a cash crop; Glacier County claims the greatest per acre production in the world. All grain crops are relatively free of weed seeds, and dockage is low; but weeds such as the Russian thistle have complicated cultivation on the plains.

The quality of Montana grains has received wide commercial recognition. Wheat, in particular, often sells at a premium that in large part compensates for the high costs of shipping to distant markets. Wheat, barley,

WHEAT, GRASS VALLEY

oats, flax, rye, timothy seed, and alfalfa seed all have won prizes at important expositions.

Excellent potatoes are grown everywhere in the State. The Yellowstone Valley, especially the irrigated area around Billings, produces Great Northern beans. Canners contract in advance for green peas and garden produce, and seed peas from the irrigated valleys are in great demand in other States. Sugar beets are increasingly grown wherever there is watered land within reach of refineries; they have attained real importance around Missoula, Billings, Sidney, and Chinook. All beets are grown on contract with the refiners, with the price and acreage fixed in advance. Byproduct beet pulp and molasses make rich stock feed; winter fattening of cattle, sheep, and hogs has become a subsidiary industry.

In the milder valleys west of the Continental Divide certain fruits do well. Sweet cherries have been grown in the Flathead Lake region for many years, and sour varieties in the Bitterroot Valley, but extreme bad weather in 1935–36 killed 75 percent of the trees and retarded the development of cherry growing. Apples produced abundantly in the western and south central valleys are popular in eastern markets. Strawberries, raspberries, gooseberries, and huckleberries are increasingly grown.

SHEEP GRAZING ON NATIONAL FOREST LAND

Irrigation: In 1890 farming without irrigation, or dry farming, was thought impossible in Montana. Settlers established themselves along streams and worked out limited but inexpensive diversion systems. Although dry farming later succeeded during the periods of adequate rainfall, the irrigated valleys remained the only areas wholly free from the danger of crop failure. Greatly extended since 1920, irrigation tends to stabilize agriculture even on farms that merely border on watered lands.

Small systems range from wind-driven pumps that water gardens to fair-sized coulee reservoirs capable of serving whole neighborhoods. The largest system is at Valier in Pondera County, with three-fourths of its 80,000 irrigable acres developed. Several others eventually will be larger; altogether perhaps 2,500,000 acres will be irrigated when existing projects are completed.

The Huntley project in Yellowstone County, the first part of which was completed in 1907 under the Reclamation Act of 1902, has in large measure proved the value of big-scale irrigation. It is useful for 24,000 acres, lifting the water from the Yellowstone River by power generated in its own plant.

Livestock: Livestock raising remains a major industry, especially in the southeast and on the mountain slopes. The Blackfeet Indian Reservation is excellent horse country; Gallatin, Fergus, Richland, and Sheridan Counties lead in raising purebred stock. Principal markets within the State are at Billings, Great Falls, and Butte, but much livestock is sold outside the State.

The number of cattle increased until 1919, when there were 1,610,000 head. Reductions were gradual and interspersed with slight increases until 1934, when extreme drought caused heavy sales both in the regular markets and through the Federal Surplus Relief Corporation. Complete failure of feed crops in many sections during 1936-7 caused further decreases; at the beginning of 1937 only a little more than 1,000,000 head remained. Most of the cattle, principally Hereford or Shorthorn, are owned by farmers who cultivate forage crops. Few of the old, vast ranches with famous brands remain.

Dairying is increasing, and butter production exceeds 15,000,000 pounds yearly.

In the early days sheepmen came into conflict with cattle growers, but sheep raising nevertheless expanded rapidly until, in 1901, there were 6,000,000 sheep in the State. The inability of sheep raising to adapt itself to a limited range brought a decline when homesteading began, but the abandonment of many farms during the drought of the 1930's again made room for sheep. In 1936 there were 3,405,000 head, and Montana ranked second to Texas in wool production, with a crop of 30,343,000 pounds. Large bands (10,000 to 40,000) are kept near Billings, Dillon, and Deer Lodge, smaller ones in nearly every county. In all, 3,000 herders are employed. Of the wool markets in the State, Dillon is the largest concentration point.

In the 1890's and early 1900's important horse ranches were operated in the Gallatin and Beaverhead Valleys and in the breaks of Phillips and Valley Counties. Marcus Daly's ranch in the Bitterroot drew national attention as a producer of blooded horses and fine livestock. Montana now has only half as many horses as in 1919, but many dry-land farmers, disappointed with the results of power farming, are turning back to them, and prices show an upward trend. In 1936 horses and mules together totaled 316,000.

Most farms have at least a small flock of poultry. Emphasis is on egg production in the western counties and on market poultry in the plains area. In 1934 egg production exceeded 12,000,000 dozen. Turkeys have become popular in the northeastern counties, where they add considerably to the autumn and winter income on farms. The growers ship cooperatively through turkey marketing associations, thereby effecting large savings in transportation. In 1935 these shipping pools sold about 1,200,000 pounds, or half the State's turkey crop.

Reports for the 1935–6 marketing season showed 161 farmers' selling, buying, and service associations. Their membership was estimated at 28,-980, and their volume of business at $17,740,000.

Labor

BEFORE metal mining became a large scale enterprise in Montana, the miner was his own boss. He staked his claim, bought or built his equipment, panned his pay dirt, and put the product of his labor into his own poke. But when the excitement of rich placer discoveries began to fade—when silver, and then copper, engaged the attention of capital— the position of the individual worker changed. He lacked capital and equipment to compete with promoters. The primitive tools that had served well enough for recovering gold were not adequate for separating copper and silver from the earth. While men of greater means built or financed the machinery of production, and thus controlled this vast natural store of wealth, the worker took wages instead of metal for his labors.

From its small beginnings in the late sixties, silver mining grew to large proportions after 1875, employing mill and furnace workers as well as miners. By the time copper production on a modest scale began, Montana labor had become conscious of its organized strength and its part in the life of the commonwealth. The Knights of Labor were represented in the Territory before 1878 by a few scattered assemblies. An organization in modern trade union form began its existence on June 13, 1878, when less than a hundred miners, many of whom had followed Marcus Daly to Butte from the silver mines of Nevada, joined forces to prevent a threatened wage reduction. In 1881 the organization became known as the Butte Miners' Union. Though born during the silver era, it grew up with the copper industry, and soon became the largest and strongest association of metal miners in the West, with a membership that exceeded 8,000 in its best years (1900–06). A base wage of $3.50 a day for all underground mine workers became the union's unyielding minimum standard. In 1895 the Butte Trades and Labor Council was formed.

The foothold gained by Montana miners encouraged other western labor groups. In Idaho's Coeur d'Alene district in 1892 a bitter strike had been suppressed by the State militia, and its leaders thrown into bull pens. Twelve of them, while serving additional jail sentences, planned a new organization. Forty delegates from the metal mining regions of Colorado,

South Dakota, Idaho, and Montana, including some of the Idaho strike leaders, met in Butte to organize mill and smelter workers and engineers. On May 15, 1893, they founded the Western Federation of Miners. A month later the Federation issued its first charter to the Butte Miners' Union. Federation objectives were establishment of a scale of wages in just proportion to the risks of mine employment, passage of safety laws, prohibition of child labor, and removal of private guards from the mines. Arbitration and conciliation rather than strikes were emphasized in Federation tactics. One of the first important victories gained by the Federation was in support of the eight-hour day. In 1897 a bill embodying the idea was urged in the legislature and in 1901, with the backing of the Western Federation of Miners, the United Mine Workers, and other labor organizations, it became law.

After 1894 the Western Federation grew steadily in membership and influence. It affiliated in 1896 with the American Federation of Labor, but withdrew the following year, disappointed by the A. F. of L.'s failure to send material support to a Leadville, Colorado, mine strike, and by its seeming indifference to the problems of labor in the mountain States. Ed Boyce, president of the Western Federation, was determined to organize the large numbers of unskilled and ill-paid workers in the whole region lying west of the Mississippi, and to that end he launched the Western Labor Union in 1898, known shortly thereafter as the American Labor Union.

Meanwhile, in Butte, the Miners' Union took advantage of a divided enemy. Employers, badly in need of labor's help in their wars with one another, encouraged the unions and openly courted union leaders. When the union asked W. A. Clark, one of the three copper magnates who dominated Butte, to accept the eight-hour day, with no reduction of wages, Clark at first protested that he could not operate his mines on such a schedule. He changed his mind when Dan McDonald of the union convinced him that this was his chance to become the most popular man in Butte, and that, if he failed to grasp it, his rival F. Augustus Heinze, would take the advantage. Clark and Heinze not only yielded to the demand, but hastened to compliment the miners upon their progressive spirit, thus stealing a march on Marcus Daly, who shared the third controlling interest with the Standard Oil Company.

In his *Comical History of Montana* (1912), Jerre C. Murphy, editor of the Butte *Inter-Mountain*, declared that Butte was for a time "the strongest union town on earth," a place in which no employment was possible for a man who did not belong to one or another of the recognized workers' groups. Everything was organized; there was even a chimney sweeps' union composed of two chimney sweeps. Unclassified wage earners made up the membership of a general "Workingman's Union," which once considered the advisability of declaring a boycott against the cemetery because the gravedigger was unable to obtain certain concessions. Union terminology became the common language. When a visiting salesman contradicted some statement made by a local political spellbinder, the speaker demanded, "Who's paying you for talking?" "Nobody," said the salesman, highly offended. "Then you're scabbing the job!" cried the speaker.

At the 1904 convention of the Western Federation of Miners, the delegates, believing in unity for militant industrial organizations, proposed a merger of the American Labor Union and the American Federation of Labor, but neither side responded favorably. The following year the Western Federation of Miners met in Chicago with several independent groups and individuals, including the Socialist Trade and Labor Alliance, and formed the Industrial Workers of the World. The I. W. W. immediately declared itself the implacable enemy of the entire capitalistic system, and at the same time came out strongly for the industrial idea in union organization, as opposed to the craft-union structure of the A. F. of L. Although the Western Federation of Miners endorsed this industrial policy, it soon became dissatisfied with the I. W. W. The published aims of the I. W: W., its program of direct action, and its determination to make converts of all other labor organizations precipitated many conflicts. In 1907 the kidnapping and trial of Charles H. Moyer, Bill Haywood, and George Pettibone, Federation officers, on charges of murdering ex-Governor Steunenberg, of Idaho, widened the breach between the Federation and I. W. W. Although the men were acquitted, partly through the strong defense efforts of the latter, the Federation nevertheless resented its association in the public mind with the left-wing group.

In 1906 F. A. Heinze sold out his Butte interests to the Amalgamated Copper Company, and the Amalgamated alone assumed command of employer strategy in the copper city. Under a 5-year contract signed with the Butte Miners' Union, wages were at that time computed according to the price of copper for the calendar month. When the price exceeded 18 cents, the pay of underground men was $4 a day; at less than 18 cents, it dropped to $3.50. The 8-hour day remained effective. Although the Western Federation of Miners opposed time contracts, and declared this one void, the Butte local held fast. The employers disregarded the contract. Thousands of men were thrown out of work when the late 1907 slump hit the copper industry. When activity was resumed, the wage rate per day was not reduced, but the plan of part-time work adopted by the copper interests lowered monthly income as much as 40 percent in some cases. At the time union officials charged that low-price, unskilled labor was brought in to take the places of experienced miners.

In industries other than metal mining and smelting 1907 was a year of widespread strikes. Telephone, telegraph, and street railway employees, janitors, meat cutters, teamsters, waiters, drug clerks, and machinists went out early in the year, and a strike of Butte and Anaconda printers, pressmen, and stereotypers left both cities without newspapers for six weeks. The chief demand of the strikers was for higher wages.

Recognizing that a profound change had come about in the labor situation in Butte, the more radical elements in the Miners' Union expressed their dissatisfaction in the union elections of 1907 and 1909, and new officials were put in charge of the organization. A brother union, Local 83, made up of mining engineers, then tried to withdraw from the W. F. of M. To prevent their desertion, the Miners' Union instructed the engineers to present paid-up membership cards in Local 83 when they came to work in the Butte mines. Enforcement of this rule by the Miners' Union stopped mining operations for three days.

In the winter of 1909–10, switchmen on the Great Northern Railway went out on strike, and it became impossible to move supplies in the Great Falls area. The railroad and copper interests, acting together, attempted to have miners and smeltermen act as switchmen, but the Butte Miners' Union, after consideration, adopted resolutions of sympathy with the strikers. Thereupon John D. Ryan, acting for the employers, threatened a shut-down in Butte, to begin January 1 and continue for six months, unless the miners consented to aid the railroad. The angry miners met, 5,000 strong, and voted to stand firm. The shut-down order was rescinded.

In 1911 the Western Federation of Miners reaffiliated with the American Federation of Labor. The following year, the Miners' Union, once more under conservative leadership, signed a new contract with the copper company. Wages again were fixed by the price of copper, being $4.25 a day when the price reached 18 cents and $3.50 when it fell below 15 cents. The mines adopted the "rustling card" system under which company-owned employment offices issued cards granting permission to "rustle" (ask for work) at the mines. Before a card could be issued, the applicant was required to give his personal history. Upon taking a job he had to surrender his card.

In the union elections of 1912, a Central Committee for Industrial

Union Organization nominated a ticket in opposition to the conservative leaders headed by Charles H. Moyer, president, and charged the conservatives with election frauds; willingness to make a deal on company terms; official inaction when several hundred Socialist miners were discharged; and refusal to fight the "rustling card" system after the miners had condemned it. The charges were voiced by Thomas Campbell at the 1912 convention, but the convention rejected them and expelled Campbell from the Federation.

Bitterness intensified in 1914, to some extent because of the unsatisfactory ending of the Calumet strike in Michigan the year before. It found expression in a referendum vote of Butte miners that overwhelmingly repudiated the Moyer group and its policies. The majority withdrew from the Butte Miners' Union and formed an independent organization of 4,000 members called the Butte Mine Workers' Union. Hostilities with the older union culminated in rioting, gunfire, and death. The acting mayor and several policemen were injured. Moyer appealed to the Governor for protection from violence, and his appeal, taken by the opposition as a call for troops, enraged them more. Governor Stewart offered to mediate between the two factions, but the new union refused.

A demand that all miners carry its membership cards was the first step of the new union to gain control of employment in the Butte district. Unknown persons dynamited Union Hall on June 23, and Moyer and other officials of the old union fled from Butte. A miners' court met on the flat at the southern limits of Butte, tried several prominent figures of the Western Federation of Miners on the charge of having acted as employers' agents and warned them to leave town. During this time, a mine employment office was blown up. Following this incident, the mine operators asked for martial law. They closed the mines for two days, stopped all negotiations with organized labor, and under the protection of martial law established the open shop. Mucky McDonald and Joe Bradley, the president and vice president of the Mine Workers' Union, were sentenced to prison for 3 to 5 years. On charges preferred by members of the older union, the mayor and sheriff were removed from office for allegedly failing to perform their duties. An effort to amalgamate the unions came to nothing, and the open shop prevailed in Butte copper mines and plants from 1914 to 1934.

Some years before the beginning of the 1912–14 troubles in Butte the I. W. W. had turned to organizing miners and migratory workers in lumber and construction camps and in the agricultural regions. Their plan called for unions of unskilled and skilled workers of every category. The local unions were to be united in national industrial unions, controlled by

"RUSTLERS"

annual conventions and an executive board. As the I. W. W. grew, it became the outstanding expression of labor's dissatisfaction with a leadership that seemed to many workers as unintelligent and untrustworthy—the most formidable rank-and-file revolt of the prewar and World War periods. It demanded immediate working-class victories, and its tactics included the deliberate slowing down of production and the quick or surprise strike—methods that terrified employers, politicians, and conservative union leaders alike.

In June 1917 fire broke out on the 2,400 foot level of the Speculator Mine in Butte and killed 164 men by suffocation. The electricians employed in the mines immediately struck, and when the work of the electricians was undertaken by others, the metal trades workers also went out. A joint strike committee was formed, which demanded the dismissal of the State mine inspector, observance of the mining laws, abolition of "rustling cards," and the increase of wages from $4.75 to $6 a day. Prominent in the councils of the strikers were members of the I. W. W. and former members of the defunct Western Federation of Miners, whose remnants were held together in the International Union of Mine, Mill, and Smelter Workers.

Again Butte was placed under martial law, and Federal troops patrolled the streets leading to the mines. Vigilante organizations attacked the miners and their allies; newspapers whipped public excitement into hysteria; W. A. Clark declared that he would rather flood his mines than recognize the union. The war with Germany was in progress, and there was wild talk of anarchists and pro-Germans. A mass meeting of strikers petitioned the Government to take over the mines, "so that the miners may give prompt and practical evidence of their patriotism," and Congresswoman Jeannette Rankin, in a speech to the strikers, said that if the owners could not operate the mines the Government could.

In the early morning of August 1, 1917, a crowd of gunmen broke into the room of Frank Little, bedridden I. W. W. organizer, who had denounced the troops in Butte as "scabs in uniform." They forced him to the street, fastened him with rope behind an automobile, and dragged him through the city. His body was left hanging from a railroad trestle. Pinned to his clothing was a card bearing the vigilante sign "3-7-77" (the dimensions of a burial pit) and the initials "LDSM."

On July 25 the operators had announced a new sliding scale of wages which would have raised miners' pay on that date to $5.25; but they refused to give up "rustling cards," and the settlement was rejected. On August 24 the smeltermen at Anaconda struck, and an almost complete shut-down of Butte mines and of the Great Falls reduction works followed immediately. Two weeks later the smeltermen and about half the Butte miners accepted a 50-cent wage increase and some concessions on working conditions, and returned to work. The strike ended officially in December 1917. Martial law, however, remained in force for more than a year longer.

The first revolt of lumber workers organized by the I. W. W. took place in 1917 at Eureka, in northwestern Montana. The men demanded wages of $60 per month, an 8-hour day, Sunday and holiday freedom, sanitary kitchens and sleeping quarters, and other concessions. Some of these concessions, including the 8-hour day, later became law. During the same period and for several years to follow, the "wobblies" were prominent among migratory agricultural workers in the central and eastern parts of the State, where, during the rush season of harvesting and threshing, a working day of 15 hours or more had not been unusual. Partly as a result of their activities the 10-hour day became standard in most Montana farm areas, while wages were considerably increased. In Butte, however, the influence of the I. W. W. declined with the failure of a strike in February 1919, which was broken by troops and special deputies after only 11 days. The strike had been called to protest a wage reduction of $1 a day in the Anaconda and Great Falls reduction plants following the postwar collapse of the copper market. Another strike followed in 1920, and on August 21 of that year two men were killed and nineteen wounded when gunmen fired into a picket line on the Anaconda road near the Butte city limits.

The suppressive measures taken by authorities in Butte were similar to those used against the I. W. W. elsewhere in the United States. Wartime prosecutors accused the I. W. W. of taking pay and instructions from German agents, and of disrupting necessary industrial operations. I. W. W. records were confiscated and destroyed, and members were jailed, threatened with lynching, and driven into hiding. In Forsyth, Judge Crum of the District Court was impeached by the State senate, partly for insisting on fair and humane treatment for members of the I. W. W. jailed in his district. The 1918 laws against criminal syndicalism helped to complete the overthrow of the organization. After 1924, little more than the name and a hangover of public alarm remained.

During the 20-year period that ended in 1934, all the crafts in Butte maintained their organizations, but the miners' union was denied recognition. To its record of working-class defeats, this open-shop period added a long death toll from accidents and industrial diseases. The maintenance of safety and health had always presented grave problems in Butte. William D. (Big Bill) Haywood, the militant I. W. W. leader, wrote of Butte as it was about 1900: "There was no verdure of any kind; it had all been killed by the fumes and smoke of the burning ore. The noxious gases came from the sulphur that was allowed to burn out of the ore before it was sent to the smelter. It was so poisonous that it not only killed trees, shrubs, grass, and flowers, but cats and dogs could not live in the city of Butte. Housewives complained that the fumes settling on the clothes rotted the fiber . . . The city of the dead, mostly young miners, was almost as large as the living population . . ."

Figures on mortality in the copper district led the Bureau of Mines and the Public Health Service, both Federal agencies, to begin an investigation in 1916 of working conditions there. The findings, published in 1921, represented four years of study on the relation of underground employment to pneumonia, tuberculosis, and silicosis (also called *miners' consumption*), and pointed out certain hazards to which miners were exposed. Shortly after the Bureau of Mines report was issued, the mining companies announced an expenditure of several million dollars for the installation of protective devices. A later report, submitted by other investigators and published by the Bureau in 1925, stated:

"Although . . . much . . . remains to be done . . . attention is again called to the advances already made—good systems of mechanical ventilation, wet drilling, fireproofing at shafts and stations and around underground electrical installations, training of many men in first aid and use of oxygen breathing apparatus, and the building of an organization to see that improvements are properly maintained."

As a result of legislative action in 1937, a commission was established to study occupational disease in Montana. In a report transmitted to Governor Ayers in January 1939, the commission stated that, due to the many improvements resulting from the recommendations of the Bureau of Mines and the willingness of industrialists to install the recommended improvements, much of the danger of occupational disease had been eliminated; and that there was no pressing need at this time to enact further workers' compensation laws. The commission recommended the establishment of an industrial hygiene division within the State department of health. Such a division was created by a bill passed by the 1939 legislature and enacted into law by the approval of Governor Ayers.

Many improvements followed the establishment of the National Recovery Administration in 1933. As in the rest of the Nation, there were wage increases, shortened hours, fuller observance of safety and sanitary regulations, and a new freedom for workers to organize without fear of discrimination or discharge. Leaders and members of Montana unions immediately strengthened their organizations and prepared to turn these favorable conditions to good account.

In May 1934 the reorganized International Union of Mine, Mill and Smelter Workers in Butte, Anaconda, and Great Falls struck and restored the closed shop in the Butte mines. The strike, which lasted until September, involved all the crafts. For the first time in Butte's history the engineers and pump men, almost indispensable because of the constant influx of water in the mines (see BUTTE), were called out. In addition to the closed shop, the miners won a basic wage of $4.75 a day, with a sliding scale of increases based on the copper price. The work week was fixed at 40 hours, and weekly paydays were adopted. Later in the year the printers at Helena won wage increases after striking for wages equal to those paid by the Great Falls papers.

During the mine strike an attempt was made to split the craft unions away from the industrial unions such as the International Union of Mine,

Mill and Smelter Workers. In a New York conference with representatives of the copper interests, John P. Frey, president of the Metal Trades
Department of the A. F. of L., signed an agreement for some of the
unions without consulting the membership. The agreement was rejected;
the discussions that followed were national in scope, and played a large
part in laying the foundation of the Committee for Industrial Organization.

The victory of the miners at Butte and of the printers at Helena stimulated organization throughout the State. As in the early days, Butte was
again a union stronghold, almost 100 percent organized, and unions in
Great Falls, Anaconda, Missoula, Helena, and Kalispell also attained a
greater effectiveness. In the grazing regions, the International Sheep
Shearers' Union strengthened its position. The passage of the National
Labor Relations Act in 1935 and the establishment under it of the National Labor Relations Board stiffened Government support of organized
labor and brought legal dignity and a measure of justice to the settlement
of labor-employer differences. With the rapid growth to power of the
Committee for Industrial Organization in 1937, the Mine, Mill and Smelter Workers, one of the ten original member unions, took steps to establish a State C. I. O. council. The organization was set up at East Helena
on August 22, 1937, with Archie McLeod of the Great Falls smeltermen
as president and Sylvester Graham of the Butte Miners' Union as secretary.
The change from A. F. of L. to C. I. O. affiliation among the industrially
minded Montana unions came without the bitterness that attended such
changes in the eastern States. C. I. O. and A. F. of L. unions today cooperate in matters affecting the general welfare of Montana labor.

Unions affiliated with the American Federation of Labor are strong
throughout Montana in the service crafts, including in their membership
barbers, retail clerks, and restaurant workers. Other affiliates represent the
railway shopmen, building trades workers, sheep shearers, and, among
the white-collar workers, school teachers.

Organization in all unions has, of course, been carried farthest in
Butte, Great Falls, and western Montana generally. In the eastern part of
the State there has been little organizing except in the building trades
and among the sheep shearers. The United Cannery, Agricultural, Packing,
and Allied Workers (C. I. O.) were able in 1937 to organize the field
workers. The sugar refinery workers, organized in the A. F. of L., signed
an agreement in 1938 with the Great Western Sugar Company.

In many small towns where the number of workers is limited a general
union, somewhat like the old "Workingman's Union" of Butte, includes

all the trades. In Basin, for example, clerks, waiters, and even teachers are organized in the International Union of Mine, Mill and Smelter Workers. Beneath this phenomenon, and woven into the intellectual fabric of the whole State, is a consciousness of the community of interests of all types of workers.

Industry and Commerce

RADITION says that Lewis and Clark found gold in the Bitterroot River in 1805; that some unnamed person found traces of it in Mill Creek near Corvallis in 1852, the year of the real discovery by François Finlay; that priests, including Father De Smet, knew of the existence of the metal but were silent, fearing the effects of a gold rush upon their charges, the Indians. In any case, nothing was done about it.

From the time of Lewis and Clark to that of François Finlay, commercial enterprise in Montana was limited to the fur trade, which enriched the traders, helped pave the way for settlement, and provided much of the color of early Montana history, but also robbed the future State of much of its wealth of wildlife. By 1852 when Finlay, himself a trapper, discovered gold on Gold Creek, west of Garrison, the fur trade was nearly finished. When Finlay's discovery was confirmed by James and Granville Stuart in 1859 and followed by more important discoveries at Bannack (1862), Virginia City (1863), and Last Chance (1864), furs were forgotten in the tumult of a hundred new activities, of which mining at once became the chief. Trade in tools and supplies became highly profitable and encouraged trail and river transportation. Manufacturing began as crude gristmills and ore reduction plants were devised. One of the earliest factories was the *arrastra,* or primitive gold concentrator of the Spanish, a pit in which dragging boulders ground small quantities of ore to a slime that was later treated with quicksilver.

Placer mining was soon succeeded by lode mining. Famous locations of the early period are scattered throughout the central and southern mountains *(see Tours 1, 1A, 6, 8, 15, 16, and 18).* After 1919 gold production fell to about 70,000 ounces a year, but the later rise in the price of gold revived prospecting. Many old mines were reopened, and the operations of regular producers were enlarged. Among the latter are the Spring Hill mine in Grizzly Gulch near Helena, the Golden Messenger at York, and the Ruby Gulch and Little Ben mines near Zortman, where a 300-ton cyanide mill is operated. Small lode mines were developed in Madison and Beaverhead Counties. During the middle 1930's dredging yielded good returns on several old creek bottoms, including Last Chance Gulch, where a machine capable of handling 5,000 cubic yards of gravel a day was put into operation. Montana's 1936 gold production was $6,265,000. Total production between 1862 and 1938 was something like $350,000,000.

The first important silver mine was discovered at Butte in 1865 by William Farlin *(see BUTTE)*. After 1875, when William A. Clark built a ten-stamp mill and a furnace at Butte, silver was the leading Montana metal for about ten years. The Butte district remained the largest producer, but rich deposits were also found at Philipsburg, and in Powell, Cascade, Jefferson, Flathead, Madison, and Beaverhead Counties. Silver mining was revived by high prices after 1933; even old tailings were worked over profitably by modern methods. The 1936 production was $8,650,950; altogether Montana has produced about half a billion dollars' worth of silver.

In 1880 Marcus Daly began mining copper at Butte, and the boss industry of Montana was founded. Copper was at first a bitter disappointment to the miners, yet in less than five years it became the Territory's most important product, and made Butte the center around which its industrial life revolved. At first the ore was shipped to Swansea, Wales, for smelting, and high transportation costs forbade handling of any but the richest ores. In 1884 a plant was built in Butte that converted 500 tons a day into a rich copper concentrate called matte. This made it possible to recover lower grade ores profitably, but the matte was still shipped to Wales for further refining. The first fully equipped reduction plant was built at Anaconda in 1892, to be succeeded ten years later by the great Washoe Smelter *(see Tour 18)*; at the same time (1892) an electrolytic copper refinery was built at Great Falls. None but refined copper has since been shipped out of the State.

With the building of the wire and cable mill at Great Falls in 1918 *(see Tour 14)* the Montana copper industry was rounded out; its operations thereafter included every step from the extraction of ore to the sale of finished products.

In the deep Butte mines air-driven drills stutter like machine guns as they bore into the rock half a mile or more below surface. The men who operate the drills, set the explosive charges, and muck (shovel) the ore into chutes, work strenuously and often under trying conditions. Engineering specifications provide for a system of compressors that force fresh air through pipe lines into the mines, and of exhaust fans that remove foul air. Because of oxidation in the ore, and because of the heat of the

OLD-FASHIONED PLACER MINING

water that seeps into the mines, temperatures sometimes reach 125° F. Large sums of money are spent by employers and union authorities in helping the men learn safe working methods and to acquaint them with first aid practices. Much progress has been made in improving working conditions. Many methods and devices for the protection of life and health among the 7,000 miners have been introduced. Improvements in practice include wet drilling, wetting of "muck piles" before shoveling, and underground spraying. Masks have also been tried. Blasting fills the workings with fumes that remain for hours; therefore, most of the blasting is done between shifts. Electric signal systems are used in all the deep mines.

Butte ore is delivered to the Washoe Smelter at the rate of 1,000 tons an hour. Here 3,500 men guide it on its progress through great ranks of machines and furnaces that extract the metals from the rock with scientific thoroughness and economy. Sent on to Great Falls, it is electrically purified *(see Tour 14)*. Much of it is then passed through dies and stranding machines, to emerge as wire and cable ready for the market. The Great Falls plants employ 2,000 men.

Between 1880 and 1938 fully eleven billion pounds of Montana copper were produced. Most of it came from an area of about six square miles within a larger area which also produces zinc, silver, manganese, lead, and gold; but there are recoverable quantities in twenty-one counties. In all, Silver Bow County, in which are the Butte mines, has produced metals valued at more than $2,000,000,000. The 1936 copper production was $20,112,850.

Zinc, like copper, comes mostly from the Butte district. Until 1916, zinc in combination with other metals was a nuisance. Smelters penalized such ores heavily; when the quantity of zinc was more than 6 percent of metallic content, the penalties became so high as to prohibit refining. It was impossible to separate cleanly either lead and zinc or zinc and copper in commercial volume, as their specific gravities are nearly the same. Zinc in lead ore tended to "freeze" lead furnaces and cause large quantities of both metals to be lost as slag; lead in zinc had the same effect on zinc furnaces. Discovery of the flotation process for separately concentrating these refractory ores, and development of the electrolytic method of refining, revolutionized the industry by making it profitable to mine zinc ores formerly thought worthless. Annual production now exceeds a hundred million pounds.

The lead concentrate obtained in zinc reduction is sent to the smelter at East Helena. The zinc is roasted at the Anaconda or Great Falls zinc plant, then dissolved in dilute sulphuric acid. After treatment with zinc dust, to precipitate its copper and cadmium, the solution is sent to electrolytic cells, and the zinc plated out, 99.9 percent pure.

About a billion pounds of lead have been mined in Montana. Cascade County has produced up to three million pounds in a single year (1928), Broadwater half as much. Mines in several other counties yield heavily. The 1936 production was 37,332,000 pounds.

The smelter at East Helena refines lead, gold, and silver ores and concentrates and zinc plant residues. The material received is given blast furnace treatment; the lead is sent to Omaha for removal of its silver and gold, the zinc to Great Falls for electrolysis. In the East Helena plant smoke is passed through 3,000 woolen bags, which filter out and recover the lead fumes. A slag-fuming plant near the smelter produces from zinc-bearing slag an impure zinc oxide for electrolytic treatment at Great Falls.

There are several byproducts of smelting. Arsenic is recovered by passing furnace gases through electric dust precipitators and settling chambers

ORE FROM BUTTE MINES

on their way to the smokestack. Another product of dust treatment is wood preservative. Sulphuric acid is made by treating sulphur dust from roasted copper concentrates with nitric acid and then spraying it with water. Phosphate rock treated with sulphuric acid produces liquid phosphoric acid which, mixed with more phosphate rock, becomes excellent fertilizer.

A foundry at Anaconda makes 18,000,000 pounds of iron castings and 200,000 pounds of brass castings yearly. Brick factories are operated at Anaconda and Great Falls.

Montana mines produce 43 percent of the Nation's manganese, most of it from high-grade ores at Butte and Philipsburg. Since manganese is used chiefly in the making of steel alloys, most of the ore (25,000 tons annually) is shipped to markets outside the State, and does not exert much influence on local manufactures; a separation mill is, however, operated intermittently at Philipsburg. Considerable quantities of the pure Philipsburg metal are used in making batteries.

Nonmetals: Factories at Hanover in Fergus County and Trident in Gallatin County make 500,000 barrels of cement and plaster yearly from outcrops of Carboniferous and Devonian limestone and shale. Gypsum, used in making cement, is produced in several central counties; lime at Elliston, Red Lodge, and other places; phosphate near Garrison. The annual output of sand and gravel used in construction is valued at something like $2,500,000.

Granite is quarried in Lewis and Clark, Silver Bow, Ravalli, and other mountain counties; sandstone, at Dillon, Columbus, and Billings. A black dolomite marked with golden brown, found at Townsend, is sold as "black-and-gold marble." Travertine, a limy hot springs deposit at Gardiner and elsewhere, was placed on the market in 1932. Madison County produces a banded siliceous rock used in interior decoration.

Vermiculite, mined at Libby, is a silicate similar to black mica which, when heated, expands tenfold and looks worm-eaten (hence the name). It is sold as "zonolite," an insulating material. Calcite, graphite, asbestos, and bentonite are produced in a small way.

Gems: Montana produces more gem sapphires than any other State. The important deposits are in Rock Creek, Granite County; Yogo Gulch, Judith Basin County; and Cottonwood Creek, Powell County. The blue sapphires from Yogo Gulch are often large and of great brilliance and depth of color. A few green, yellow, red, and aquamarine stones have been found. Of 88,000 ounces annually recovered, about 86,000 are used in watch and meter bearings and for other mechanical purposes.

Rubies occur rarely in Cottonwood and upper Rock Creeks. Garnets are recovered from placer gravels in the Tobacco Root and Ruby Mountains. A semi-precious gem, the moss agate, is made handsome by dendritic growths of manganese and iron oxide that form effects resembling wooded landscapes within the translucent rock. Found in the gravels of Yellowstone River from Livingston to Glendive, it is cut and polished at Billings and Miles City.

Mineral Fuels: The vast reserves of coal in the plains region have hardly been touched, though 2,500,000 tons or more are mined every year. Most of the mines are small developments for family or community use; they often consist of only one narrow tunnel with shallow work chambers on both sides, and are quite commonly abandoned for newer workings as soon as caving begins. Larger mines range from relatively lasting shaft and tunnel developments to such spectacular operations as those at Colstrip *(see Tour 1, Sec. a)*. At Roundup and Red Lodge bituminous and sub-bituminous coal is taken from workings that tap 4 and 11 seams respectively. Coal of greater hardness is mined at Red Lodge, Bozeman, and Great Falls. Comparatively little Montana coal is used for industrial purposes, partly because of its low heating power and high ash content and partly because gas is more convenient.

Natural gas was discovered south of Glendive in 1913, and oil at Elk Basin, near Red Lodge, two years later. Since then 15 fields have been found. The first gas field remains the most important, producing 600,-000,000 cubic feet daily, but the first oil field has long been surpassed in production. The best fields are in the Sweetgrass Arch.

The Cut Bank field, the largest producer, runs about 250,000 barrels a month. When new, the Kevin-Sunburst field produced more than 560,000 barrels in one month, but its wells declined four-fifths within a year. Acid-treatment later increased the yield of some wells and caused several dry holes to produce.

In the Cut Bank field wells are comparatively deep, averaging 2,900 feet as against the 1,500 feet of Kevin-Sunburst wells. The oil, easily and cheaply refined, yields 36 percent or more of gasoline. Both fields produce a nearly pure methane gas.

The Elk Basin and Dry Creek fields in Carbon County, from wells more than 5,000 feet deep, produce oil of such quality (60° A.P.I.) that it can be used in internal combustion engines without refining. The Cat Creek field in Petroleum County produces from relatively shallow wells (1,200 feet), but here, too, the oil is of high quality (50° A.P.I.). The initial production of the best wells was more than 3,000 barrels a day.

The chief oil refineries are the skimming and topping plants at or near producing fields; the absorption plant, for converting casing-head gas, at Cut Bank; and the cracking plants at Kevin, Sunburst, and Great Falls. In the first the gasoline and kerosene are simply run off; what remains is fuel oil. More gasoline is recovered by the cracking plants, which break down the molecules of oil by distillation under heat and pressure. No lubricating oil is refined in Montana.   .

Farm Product Processing and Storing: Sugar refining, the largest manufacturing process consequent on agriculture, is carried on at Sidney, Billings, Missoula, and Chinook. The large Billings factory produces nearly 100 million pounds of sugar a year, from 320,000 tons of beets *(see BILLINGS).*

A cannery at Billings packs garden vegetables and pork and beans; others in the agricultural valleys specialize in peas, but handle minor quantities of other vegetables and fruits. About half a million cases are packed yearly.

Of the many creameries and flour mills the largest are at Great Falls, Billings, and Missoula. The products of flour milling, which is perhaps the State's oldest manufacturing enterprise, are worth about $17,000,000 annually. Factories that make cheese, ice cream, and beverages are well distributed. There are several meat-packing plants; the one at Great Falls is rated the largest between Minneapolis and Spokane.

Every village in the wheat-growing areas has grain elevators. Numerous warehouses store beans, peas, potatoes, garden vegetables, and wool.

Lumber and Power: As an employer, the lumber industry is important, providing 6,000 jobs in normal times. Its annual output varies greatly; before the depression of the 1930's the average was about 342,000,000 board feet of lumber and 138,000,000 feet of mine timbers, ties, poles, posts, and fuel valued at more than $10,000,000 altogether. In 1933 the lumber cut had dropped to 125,000,000 feet. Two-fifths of the State's lumber comes from Flathead County, which also has the basis of a large pulpwood industry. The largest sawmills are at Bonner and Libby *(see Tours 2 and 8)*. The Bonner mill's annual capacity is 150,000,000 board feet. In some of the larger cities are factories that make furniture and other finished products.

Power plants on Montana's rivers generate half a million horsepower of electric energy, less than one-fifth of the potential horsepower. The largest development is on the Missouri, especially at Great Falls *(see Tour 14)* and at Helena, where dams have formed three artificial lakes; but there are also plants on the Yellowstone, Clark Fork of the Columbia, and other streams. About half the power generated is used by the metal industry at Butte, Anaconda, Great Falls, and East Helena. Much is used by coal mines and railroads.

Altogether, Montana manufacturers in 1935 employed 9,539 wage earners, and paid them $11,742,178. The total value of the products made was $124,778,215. Much of this total was contributed by enterprises of modest size and merely local importance; most of them were concerned with processing of farm or forest products. Minor manufactured products ranged from saddles and cigars to livestock feed and lamp posts.

Fur farms in western and southern Montana specialize in foxes, muskrats, and Chinchilla rabbits. A farm near Kalispell, besides raising its own silver foxes, "finishes off" pups for Alaskan fox breeders. All native fur bearers are bred to some extent; more than 100,000 pelts are marketed

BONNER SAWMILL

each year. Montana fur farms, it is believed, eventually will supply one-tenth of the Nation's demand.

There are nurseries and greenhouses in all the important centers. In Lincoln County about 400,000 young Douglas firs are cut annually for Christmas trees.

Transportation

DURING the half century between the Lewis and Clark expedition and the first large immigration, Montana was an almost endless wilderness inhabited by Indians and a few trappers and voyageurs, who traveled or transported in canoes, bullboats, and keelboats, or with horses. The Indians were accustomed to the horse- or dog-drawn travois, two trailing poles bearing a sort of platform of hide or basketwork for goods. White men also used it occasionally.

Steamboats appeared on the Missouri as early as 1832, but not until 1859 were they built with sufficiently shallow draft to reach Fort Benton. Navigation was very difficult on the Missouri: the tortuous channel was full of snags and sand bars; and the waterstage, influenced by storms far up in the mountains, changed rapidly. A steamboat tied up for the night in plenty of water might bump bottom by morning. With navigation established and immigration made possible, Fort Benton became the hub from which spread stage lines, freight roads, and pack trails, but the coming of the railroads effaced Fort Benton from the picture.

Freight also entered the Territory from Corinne, Utah, by bull team, a team usually consisting of five yokes. The rate was 8 cents a pound, the speed of travel with well-shod oxen 12 to 15 miles a day. Delays were frequent, for bulls dropped shoes, and the stopping of one team halted the train. Many a stop became an occasion for sampling the shipment of whiskey, invariably a part of the load. The usual method was to start a hoop and bore a hole, draw the sample and replace it with water, then plug the hole and drive back the hoop to conceal the evidence.

The tradition of the "Great American Desert" was slow to die. It was gravely suggested that camel caravan routes into Idaho and Montana be established; in 1856 Congress actually appropriated $30,000 for the purchase of camels for military use in the West. Some of them were brought into Montana from Nevada, where they had been used on the California trail. But pack train men objected that a camel's back was no place for a diamond hitch and Montana trails no place for a camel's feet. One camel was mistaken for a deformed moose by a white hunter; others were killed by Indians. Those remaining stampeded a train of mules loaded with whiskey for the gold camps of Last Chance Gulch, and the whiskey was spilled. Such an accident was more than enough to discredit camels in the Montana of that day.

For a time the stagecoach was the frontier's best answer to the problem of swifter travel. The first coaches were small and uncomfortable four-horse affairs that carried mail, express, and usually a bandit-bait "treasure box" to which only station-masters had a key. The driver's duty was to the goods he carried, and the human freight could take care of itself. Trails were hazardous. At fords the water often rose so high in an hour as to make passage impossible. Concord coaches replaced the early vehicles, to be replaced in turn by the "jerky," an unpleasant contrivance without springs or thoroughbraces.

The idea of a trancontinental railroad had received considerable attention since the Oregon migration, the Mormon exodus, and the California gold rush, but not until 1853 was a survey made of a northern route to the coast. From Fort Union to Helena this route partly coincides with that of the Great Northern Railway; from Helena to the Idaho boundary it becomes almost exactly the road of the Northern Pacific.

Aided by large land grants, which gave to the company twenty alternate sections per mile of non-mineral public land on each side of the right-of-way through the Territories, the Northern Pacific Railway started in 1870 to build east from Puget Sound and west from Duluth. Before construction reached Montana, the panic of 1873 bankrupted the company. The Territorial legislature attempted to pass a bill authorizing counties along the route to borrow construction funds for the Northern Pacific. It was argued that Montana was already paying at least $1,500,000 a year for freighting by wagon and steamboat, and that a railroad would save half. Submitted to the people, the proposal was defeated by 248 votes.

Overland travel from the Union Pacific in Utah had already reduced the long Montana trail when, in 1877, the Utah & Northern Railroad Company was organized. The Utah & Northern began work on a narrow gauge line from Ogden. Again bills were introduced to provide financial aid and were defeated, but the work went on. In a race with the reorganized Northern Pacific, the Utah & Northern won, reaching the site of Dillon in 1880 and Silver Bow in 1881. Rebuilt as a standard gauge line, it later became the Oregon Short Line, now a part of the Union Pacific system.

The Northern Pacific track-laying gangs crossed the eastern boundary and reached Glendive July 5, 1881. Winter halted construction at Miles City, but the following summer it proceeded rapidly up the Yellowstone

STAGECOACH

Valley to meet the crews working eastward. The last 300-mile section lay in the mountains, and the work included construction of tunnels under the long Bozeman Pass (3,654 feet) and Mullan Pass (3,875 feet), at an elevation exceeding 5,500 feet. In a faulted section of the Mullan tunnel extraordinary pressure necessitated constant attention to timbering; experienced mining men from Butte had to finish the job. At Weeksville, northwest of Missoula, a shoulder of the Cabinet Mountains jutted across the way and was removed only by extensive blasting, at a cost of life to many Chinese coolies on the job. A tent city near the scene of operations passed into the control of toughs who terrorized the place until three of their leaders (Dick the Diver, Ohio Dan, and the Barber) were hanged. The Barber, a cripple, was buried where he died; his crutches, like crosses, were set up to mark his grave.

The last spike was driven by Henry Villard, Northern Pacific president, September 8, 1883, near Gold Creek, seven miles west of Garrison. Distinguished visitors were present, and the hammer strokes were recorded by telegraph in New York.

An exciting chapter in railroad history is the story of the Great Northern, formed of the combined railroad properties acquired by James J. Hill and his associates, with additional public timber and mineral domains in Idaho, Montana, and Washington, obtained through an Act of Congress in 1891. Hill bought the bankrupt St. Paul & Pacific Railroad in 1872 and reorganized it as the St. Paul, Minneapolis & Manitoba. In 1886 he began building roadbed and bridges from Minot, Dakota Territory, to Helena. Missouri River steamboats brought up the equipment.

Then he met legal obstacles. He could not build through the great Indian reservations without permission from Congress; and the Northern Pacific fought bitterly the granting of such permission. Like other promoters of his time, Hill took a practical view of political matters. By spring of 1887 he had completed one of the numerous campaigns that made him "the Jay Gould of the Northwest." Meanwhile he had stored great quantities of material at Minot and was ready to proceed. His track layers entered Montana on June 13 and raced up the Missouri and Milk River Valleys, laying a record four miles of track a day. Reaching Havre on September 6, they turned toward Great Falls and Helena over grades prepared by the Montana Central Railroad, also controlled by Hill. At Helena a forcible attempt was made to prevent their building across the Northern Pacific right of way, but a court order blocked it.

The Montana Central was extended to Butte in 1889, and merged with the St. Paul, Minneapolis & Manitoba to form the Great Northern. Since the long swing southward was not suitable for a transcontinental line, John F. Stevens, chief engineer, undertook to find a more direct way. In December 1889 he found Marias Pass, the lowest (5,213 feet) of the passes across the Continental Divide. The result was a main route almost unequalled in scenic interest, surmounting the Divide along the south edge of what became Glacier National Park and winding west through some of the greatest mountains and forests in the country.

The Chicago, Milwaukee, St. Paul & Pacific Railroad began construction in 1906, entering Montana near Baker. It followed a route through the Musselshell Valley, reaching Harlowton in 1908. From Harlowton to Lombard and to Lewistown it used the tracks of the old Central Montana Railroad, known as the "Jawbone Line."

The history of this now important part of the system is diverting. Not only was it promoted by the generous use of "jawbone" (promises or talk), but its builders seemed to have little basis for their hopes, and the public enthusiasm that greeted railroads elsewhere was lacking. Soon after its completion, the Northern Pacific requested a timetable of the new road

FIRST TRAIN AND LAST SPIKE

to incorporate in its own. "There were no towns on the line," said Richard Harlow, president of the Jawbone, "nor . . . any provocation for towns, but . . . I drew up a schedule and located . . . plenty of them. Two young ladies [Fan and Lulu] were visiting at my house. On the timetable you will find . . . Fanalulu just below . . . Ringling."

The Milwaukee crossed the Continental Divide through a 2,290-foot tunnel under Pipestone Pass, and the Bitterroot Range into Idaho through St. Paul Pass Tunnel, 8,771 feet long. At the Montana end of the tunnel, construction gangs built Taft camp, which became, like Weeksville on the Northern Pacific, a wild and lawless place; a thaw once' disclosed fifteen corpses scattered along the trail to the tunnel's mouth. A fire in the winter of 1909–10 reduced the camp to only three small frame structures.

The Milwaukee, built across Montana by a difficult route, was the first great railroad to use electric power extensively. Its entire 438-mile Rocky Mountain section (Harlowton to Avery, Idaho) is electrically operated.

In 1894 the Chicago, Burlington & Quincy Railroad, also reaching toward the Pacific, built a line from the Wyoming boundary to Huntley, east of Billings. But in 1901 the Northern Pacific and Great Northern jointly bought control of it, to prevent construction of a fourth line

EAST SIDE TUNNEL, GOING-TO-THE-SUN

through the State. A branch from Frannie, Wyoming, to Fromberg, built
in 1911, links both railroads with the Burlington's Denver line. In 1935
Montana had 5,194 miles of railroad, a mileage greater than that of any
other Rocky Mountain State.

Because its topography is difficult, its distances vast, and its population
small, Montana was slow to build a modern highway system. Up to 1919,
before the first grant of Federal aid, Montana roads were crude trails,
amazingly smooth when well-worn, but winding and unsuited to speed
and heavy hauling. The first highway (1923) consisted of 26 miles of
concrete pavement between Butte and Anaconda.

The State today is crisscrossed with a network of roads reaching every
habitable place. Eleven highways (5,012 miles) are included in the Federal trunk road system. Most are surfaced with oil, the remainder with
crushed rock or gravel. Thousands of miles of State highways supplement
these. Extraordinary scenic beauty distinguishes Montana 32 (Red Lodge-
Cooke) and the spectacular Going-to-the-Sun Highway across Glacier
National Park. The former rises to about 11,000 feet, the latter to 6,700;
and when it is remembered that road construction anywhere in Montana
entails heroic labor, the building of these two seems almost miraculous.
Both were planned to take full advantage of sightseeing opportunities.

Of the many thousand miles of unmarked roads and trails, 6,500 miles in recent years have been built, improved, or surfaced by the Works Progress Administration, and 2,600 by the Civil Works and the Federal Emergency Relief Administrations. The young men of the Civilian Conservation Corps have built many fire trails in national forests.

Growth of motor freight and passenger bus lines has accompanied highway development. Such lines now have a large part in local and interstate passenger business, and handle the bulk of local small freight. Lower fares and frequent service have greatly increased passenger traffic. Two of the railroads have replaced short branch lines with bus lines of their own.

The first mail, passenger, and express air line in Montana was that of National Parks Airways, which began operations August 1, 1928, between Great Falls and Salt Lake City. In 1937 three air lines served the State, each having connections with transcontinental lines.

One line serves Great Falls, Helena, Butte, and, in summer, Yellowstone National Park; another crosses the State from Glendive to Missoula on the Chicago-Seattle flight; the third connects Billings with Denver and Pueblo.

Education, Religion, and Social Welfare

WHEN two messengers of the Flathead Indians returned to their people in 1840, bringing Father Pierre Jean de Smet from St. Louis, they introduced the learning and faith of an accomplished Jesuit missionary. Father de Smet called two priests into service with him. In 1841 they founded St. Mary's Mission in the Bitterroot Valley, one of the first efforts of the "Black Robes" toward establishing an instructed and pious society in Montana.

Education

Schools were started at Bannack and Nevada City in 1863; it is uncertain which was first. Lucia Darling, a niece of Sidney Edgerton, first Governor of the Territory, taught at Bannack and Kate Dunlap at Nevada City.

"Bannack," wrote Miss Darling, "was tumultuous and rough, the headquarters of . . . highwaymen, and lawlessness and misrule seemed the prevailing spirit . . . But . . . many worthy people . . . were anxious to have their children in school. I was requested to take charge. . . ."

Miss Darling opened the school in October in a room of her own home, the pupils using any books they owned or could borrow from neighbors. Twenty children attended until late fall, when sessions were suspended because of cold. They were resumed in the spring, and the following summer Bannack built a log schoolhouse, which still stands.

Thomas J. Dimsdale, an Oxford graduate who had come to the mountains seeking a cure for consumption, taught school at Virginia City in the winter of 1863–4. Dimsdale, author of *The Vigilantes of Montana*, was a scholar and his school a good one, according to the diary of Granville Stuart. All the town children attended, paying tuition of $2 a week.

An Indian boarding school, the first of its kind in the Northwest, opened in 1864 at St. Ignatius, where a Jesuit mission had been organized ten years earlier. Sisters of Providence from Montreal traveled by way of New York, the Isthmus of Panama, San Francisco, and Vancouver to become its teachers, crossing from Walla Walla to St. Ignatius on horseback. Between 1865 and 1875, numerous Catholic and other private elementary schools were opened for both white and Indian children. Subscription wholly or partly supported many early schools, including those at Helena (January 1865) and at Bozeman (1865–66). The Bozeman school was housed in the back room of a log cabin; the earth made a convenient floor for the half-dozen marble-playing pupils, who could scratch rings in it with a stick.

By an act of the First Legislative Assembly, in 1865, a school system was established for the Territory. Virginia City, the first community to organize a school district under the law, opened a public school in March 1866 in the Union Church, a log building. Other towns followed its example. The first formal report of the Territorial school commissioner (1868) showed 2,000 pupils, 25 organized districts, and 15 schoolhouses.

Judge Cornelius Hedges, a lawyer who came to Montana from Massachusetts in 1864, is credited with organizing the Territorial school system. For five years after his appointment as Superintendent of Public Instruction in 1873, he traveled by stagecoach and horseback over an area eighteen times as large as his native State, visiting and establishing elementary schools of high standard.

In 1893 the State legislature created a State board of education. The State College at Bozeman began its work in the same year, and the State University at Missoula opened two years later. These two, together with the State Normal College at Dillon (1897) and the Montana School of Mines at Butte (1900) were combined to form the University of Montana in 1916. The Eastern State Normal School at Billings and the Northern Montana College at Havre later opened as units of the university.

Free county high schools, which were not provided for in the original school system, were established in 1897 in response to public demand for adequate and widespread educational facilities.

Numerous secondary and college institutions were privately sponsored, particularly before the full development of the public school system. Montana Collegiate Institute at Deer Lodge, which offered a course of study extending from primary grades through college, was founded by subscription in 1878. Four years later it was taken over by the Presbyterian Church. The Methodist Episcopal Church established Montana Wesleyan at Helena in 1888. In 1923 the two institutions merged to form

Intermountain Union College. The Billings Polytechnic Institute, emphasizing practical vocational training, was founded by Lewis T. Eaton and his brother Dr. Ernest T. Eaton in 1907. The institute is supported by an endowment fund, and employment of students in the school shops and on the school farm is part of its program *(see BILLINGS)*. Intermountain Union College moved to the Billings Institute campus when the earthquake of 1935 damaged its buildings so seriously that they had to be abandoned. The two institutions, however, maintain their separate identities.

Carroll College at Helena was established as Mount St. Charles College by the Catholic Church in 1909, and renamed in 1931 in honor of the late Bishop John P. Carroll. A college for women, St. Mary's Institute at Great Falls, and parochial grade and high schools in the principal cities are also maintained by the Catholic Church.

Professional enthusiasm among teachers was evident as early as 1882 when the Territorial Teachers' Association was organized at Helena. This organization was the forerunner of the Montana Education Association which today brings school problems before the public and takes an active part in shaping educational policy.

A war orphans' educational fund was established by law in 1937, to provide educational opportunities for children of sailors, soldiers, and marines who were killed in the World War or who died from other causes between April 1917 and July 1921.

According to data issued by the U. S. Office of Education, Montana has 3,250 public elementary schools and 215 public high schools (1933–34). Approximately 2,000 of its schools are the one-room rural type, but there is a gradual trend toward consolidated schools and transportation of pupils at public expense. Attendance figures show 76,500 public school pupils; 8,000 private and parochial school pupils.

Adult education is gaining momentum and several high schools have night school terms of six weeks during the winter months. Courses in practical and cultural subjects are given; Diesel engineering is particularly popular, as are also courses in business, home economics, and home nursing. The rehabilitation division of the State department of public instruction is in charge of work in adult education, special schools, and agricultural and vocational education. In 1938 the adult education program of the Works Progress Administration got under way in Montana, with classes in Butte, Missoula, and other cities.

Religion

For years the only ministers in Montana were the dozen or so Jesuit priests connected with the missions at St. Mary's and St. Ignatius among the Flathead, and at St. Peter's among the Blackfeet. Protestant missionaries, lacking the black robes and other habiliments that impressed the Indians, were rejected, and went on to Washington and Oregon.

But with the gold seekers, Protestant "sky pilots" came to stay. Methodist, Baptist, and Presbyterian ministers established churches at Bannack and Virginia City in 1864. This followed a period of preaching in saloons, dance halls, and gambling houses, where roulette wheels, card tables, and other paraphernalia were pushed aside to let the "brimstone busters" hold forth. Bishop Daniel S. Tuttle, Episcopalian, was eminent among the clergy of this period. He worked from 1867 to 1880 in the rapidly spreading mining camps, and displayed great organizing ability.

At the same time the Catholic fathers set up white missions at the mining camps, expanding their districts as the need arose. The group of Catholic missionaries of this period included Father Mengarini, who mastered the difficult Flathead language and compiled an Indian-English dictionary; Father Point, co-founder of St. Mary's, who pleased the Indians by painting their portraits; Father Giorda, superior of the Montana missions during the difficult gold rush days; Father Kuppens, who founded the church at Helena; Father Palladino, historian of the Church in Montana; Father Ravalli, and Father de Smet, the most distinguished of them all. The first secular priest was Father de Ryckere, who founded a mission at Deer Lodge and traveled on horseback from mining camp to mining camp over a large district.

In all the early chronicles respectful mention is made of the physical vigor of the pastors. Many eastern candidates for missionary service preferred East Africa or China to frontier Montana, which may explain why the pioneers admired the few who chose to live with them. These clergymen were always ready to ride a hundred miles in any weather to help those in distress, and equally ready to bury an executed desperado. They married and buried, built log churches with their own hands, and assumed full responsibility for the relief of suffering. Frontiersmen who professed no creed responded willingly when such men asked for money or other aid. Many early accounts of the deaths of ministers say merely, "he sickened and died," and make but scant mention of the hardships that contributed to their sickening.

Churches spread with the spreading white population. More than a dozen denominations sent in valiant workers. The Reverend W. W. Van Orsdel in 1872 debarked at Fort Benton in a rainstorm, preached his first sermon in an adobe house with muddy water trickling on him through the roof, and overcame scores of such hardships in his notable career. In addition to being a brilliant preacher, he helped found several schools and hospitals.

Religious activities of some kind entered into the early life of almost every community and served to offset the influence of saloons and brothels. These activities—suppers, bazaars, lectures, and amateur theatricals—often provided the principal, and sometimes the only available, opportunities for a wholesome social life.

The Roman Catholics, the Methodists, and the Lutherans are now the leading denominations, the first equaling all others in number. Total church membership in 1930 was 152,000, or a little more than one in five of the State's population. The Roman Catholics number approximately 74,000, and the Methodists and Lutherans 15,000 each. These are followed in the order named by the Episcopalians, Presbyterians, Congregationalists, Baptists, Disciples of Christ, Latter-Day Saints, and smaller groups.

Social Welfare

Montana has played a pioneer role in social legislation. It was one of the first States to experiment with workmen's compensation, and (simultaneously with Nevada) the first to make provisions for old age pensions (1923). The compensation act of 1910 for the maintenance of a State cooperative insurance fund for miners and laborers in and about mines was declared unconstitutional, but the first compulsory compensation act was passed in 1915. Twice revised in the face of violent opposition, the law sets up a graduated scale of compensation benefits. It provides a maximum allowance of $21 per week for 500 weeks of total disability, and maximum compensations of $8,400 for a widow and $10,500 for a totally and permanently disabled workman. Protective legislation for women and children has also been progressive.

This background enabled the State to function under the Federal Social Security Act with speed and efficiency. With the enactment of social security legislation and its approval by the Federal board, public agencies for social welfare were set up or enlarged to take care of increased activity.

The Montana State Planning Board, created in 1935, in its staff report for the year ending December 1936, estimates that there are 7,000 families who cannot be self-supporting under present conditions, and that from 5,000 to 12,000 farm families have needed some relief from Federal, State, or private agencies during the past twenty years.

It is these families that have been the concern of private agencies—women's clubs, church and fraternal organizations, and family welfare services in the larger cities. No State-wide or uniform plan of social welfare existed up to a few years ago, nor was it needed in normal times. Local assistance—impulsive yet matter-of-fact, and given in the spirit of pioneer mutual help—had been enough. But it proved far from equal to the task of meeting widespread distress; such popular slogans as "Butte will take care of its own" have become more well-meaning than true.

The picture today is one of steady development and growing coordination. Old age assistance, aid for the blind and for dependent children, and unemployment compensation are administered under the Federal Social Security Act by the State department of public welfare, organized in 1937, and by the State board of health. Special institutions care for the insane and feebleminded, the delinquent, the deaf, the blind, and the tubercular. The State board of health, in addition to administering social security services, carries on the usual activities in sanitation, communicable disease, food and drugs, and vital statistics. Serum developed by the U. S. Public Health Service is administered free each spring to combat spotted fever in the western part of the State. The major cities have general hospitals, and there are a few specialized institutions, such as the orthopedic St. Vincent Hospital-School (see BILLINGS).

The State planning board is carrying on surveys and studies to determine State policies for public school education and social welfare. Its welfare section has undertaken a social study of four Montana counties that will include data on causes of unemployment, agencies caring for needy families, physical and mental ill-health and disabilities, housing, and children's problems.

The Arts

Literature

MONTANA, like most communities close to pioneer conditions, has produced only a small body of literature expressive of its life and spirit. Many of its writers have gone outside the State for their material. Of those who have delved fairly deeply into local lore and history, several have limited themselves to some particular phase, such as Indian life. The literature that has developed, while somewhat narrow in scope, is comparatively free both from false sophistication and from cow-country extravagances. When the *Frontier* (later *Frontier and Midland*), originally a student publication, began in the 1920's to take a more prominent place in Northwest literature, there was a notable trend toward careful evaluation and utilization of regional material.

The first inhabitants have received much attention from Montana authors; but the old Indian life is rapidly disappearing, and its interpreters have to depend increasingly on secondary material. Of the literature dealing with the life of the region since white settlement began, the first example is a contemporary account of the activities of road agents and vigilantes, written by Thomas Dimsdale, a Virginia City schoolmaster. *Vigilantes of Montana, or Popular Justice in the Rocky Mountains* was first published as a serial in the *Montana Post* beginning August 26, 1865, and later appeared in book form. A framed poster bearing the original announcement hangs in the lobby of Hotel Leggat in Butte. From this book and from Judge Lew Callaway, an authority on early days in Montana, Hoffman Birney obtained the material for *Vigilantes,* which ran serially in the *Saturday Evening Post* in February and March 1929.

A Trip to the States, by John Allen Hosmer (1850–1907), was printed in Virginia City in 1867, when the author, the son of Montana's first chief justice, was sixteen years old. This, the second book published in Montana, describes an adventurous trip by stage, pirogue, and river steamer from Virginia City to the railroad at Boonesboro, Iowa. The young author not only wrote an entertaining account, but printed it himself on a hand press. "My readers will notice," he apologizes, "that in a great many places where there ought to be full stops, nothing appears but commas, my reason for that is, I had but one small font of type, and scarcely any capitals. One large 'W' was all of that letter I had."

Much of the best writing done later in Montana is historical: accounts of exploration, including the journals of the Canadian David Thompson (1770–1857) and of Henry Edgar (1836–1910), one of the party that discovered Alder Gulch; *Vigilante Days and Ways* (1893), by Nathaniel P. Langford (1832–1911); *Then and Now, or Thirty-six Years in the Rockies* (1900), by Robert Vaughn (1836–1918); *Forty Years on the Frontier* (1925), by Granville Stuart (1834–1918). State histories have been written by Tom Stout, Helen F. Sanders, and Robert G. Raymer.

The journals of David Thompson, the great geographer, have been freely used in subsequent accounts of Northwest exploration, but it was not until the twentieth century that his work gained full recognition. E. C. Coues drew upon the journals in preparing his three-volume work, *New Light on the Early History of the Greater Northwest* (1897). J. B. Tyrrell in 1916 edited Thompson's *Narratives,* which are accounts, taken from the journals, of the latter's explorations. Many other writers have depended on Thompson's maps and descriptions for information about the Northwest region. A biography of Thompson by C. N. Cochrane was published in 1924.

Reputedly the earliest fiction produced in Montana is the novel, *Claire Lincoln,* by Decius M. Wade (1835–1905). It was published in 1875. Writers from various parts of America have frequently used the Northwestern country for background, notably Owen Wister in *The Virginian;* but Montana writers did not claim popular attention until after 1900.

In 1902 *The Story of Mary MacLane,* a forerunner of the modern autobiographical novel, created a sensation. Discussion of its frank revelations swept from end to end of the country and made Mary MacLane (1881–1929) famous. H. L. Mencken devoted a chapter in *Prejudices: First Series* to this "Butte Bashkirtseff," in which he expressed the opinion that Butte was a Puritan town—a suggestion no doubt startling to the citizens.

Among contemporary writers Frank Bird Linderman (1868–1938), Will James, Myron Brinig, and Grace Stone Coates are nationally recognized. Linderman was an adopted member of the Chippewa and Cree tribes and devoted his talents to portraying Indian life and character. As trapper, guide, and prospector he had known the Indians in their own free environment, and his books are inspired by friendly understanding and sympathy. His most significant volume is *American: Life Story of a Great Indian* (1930), the biography of Chief Plenty Coups of the Crow. A novel, *Morning Light* (1930), is a stirring tale of white contact with Indians. *Indian Why Stories* (1915), *How It Came About Stories* (1921), and various other collections contain fine interpretations of Indian myth and folklore. Mr. Linderman served his State in public office as well as in his work as a writer.

Since the appearance of *Cowboys North and South* (1924), Will James has enjoyed wide popularity, particularly among juvenile readers. The books that have been most favorably received are *Smoky* (1926), the story of a cow pony, and the autobiographical *Lone Cowboy* (1930). A protege of the cowboy artist Charlie Russell, James illustrates his own books with line drawings. He lives and works at his 4,000-acre ranch on the Crow Reservation south of Billings.

Myron Brinig, who was born in Minneapolis, Minnesota, may be claimed as one of Montana's most distinguished novelists, not primarily because he spent much of his early life in that State, but because he was a pioneer in the use of the life in Butte and other mining towns as material for realistic fiction. His *Singermann* (1929), *Wide Open Town* (1931), *Sons of Singermann* (1934), and several other novels present an uncompromisingly honest picture, in colorful vibrant prose, of an era of quick fortunes, lusty adventure, and lawlessness. Brinig in his later work introduces western scenes but covers a wider field, as in *The Sisters* (1937), with Saratoga of the nineties as a high point, and in his latest book *May Flavin* (1938). The Montana stories, however, are generally considered his real contribution to literature.

Grace Stone Coates is an active force among present-day Montana writers, both as novelist and poet and in her association with *Frontier and Midland*. Her novel *Black Cherries* (1931) is an extremely delicate and beautiful recollection of childhood on a Kansas farm. (Mrs. Coates was born in Kansas.) The father "who launched yachts on the Mediterranean in the face of blistering prairie winds, and hail, and mortgages"; the mother, a second wife, who liked the black cherry tree and all trees, and the discouragement and sorrow of both parents, are revealed through the daily reactions of a hypersensitive child. Two volumes of verse—*Mead and Mangel-wurzel* (1932), and *Portulacas in the Wheat* (1933)—show the same fine choice of image and detail as the novel, but on the whole lack its power. Mrs. Coates has published many short stories (included in several anthologies) and, with Patrick T. Tucker, the narrative *Riding the High Country* (1933).

One of the best known writers working with Indian material is James Willard Schultz, author of *Blackfeet Tales of Glacier National Park*

(1916), *My Life as an Indian* (1933), and with Jessie Donaldson as co-author, *Sun God's Children* (1930). Schultz married a Blackfoot woman, and has lived with the tribe most of his life. Harriet Laverne Fitzgerald of Great Falls, author of *Black Feather* (1933), and Glendolin Damon Wagner of Billings, co-author with Dr. W. A. Allen of *Blankets and Moccasins* (1933), have used Indian material. In his novel, *The Surrounded* (1936), D'Arcy McNickle has told the grim story of the Salish in their unequal struggle against the whites. McNickle was born and grew up on the Flathead Reservation. *Crow Indians* (1933), by Robert H. Lowie, is an authoritative account of Absaroka tribal life. *Memoirs of a White Crow* (1928) and *A Warrior Who Fought with Custer* (1931), by Dr. Thomas B. Marquis (1869–1935), also deal with the Absaroka people.

Butte, one of the world's most colorful mining camps, has fascinated a number of writers. Much of its literary material, like its ore, has still to be mined, although Myron Brinig has accomplished much in this direction. In *The War of the Copper Kings* (1935), C. B. Glasscock presented Butte's turbulent political and mining history, and Gertrude Atherton, in *Perch of the Devil* (1914), wrote of the same events with more asperity than understanding. *The Sheriff of Silver Bow* (1921), by Berton Braley, shows some comprehension of the city's spirit, but the tone of the book is that of the popular "western."

Life in the smaller towns and on the wheat ranches and beet farms has provided material for several novels. Dale Eunson, who lived at Lewistown, presented realistic rural scenes in *Homestead* (1935); Agnes Getty of Whitefish used the experiences of a village school teacher in the romantic novel *Blue Gold* (1934); *Small Town Stuff* (1932), by Albert Blumenthal, is an uncompromising study of life in Philipsburg, the author's former home.

Taylor Gordon, a Negro singer born in White Sulphur Springs, published his autobiography in 1929. The work, entitled *Born to Be,* deals with his boyhood in Montana. Max Miller, author of *I Cover the Waterfront* (1932) and *Mexico Around Me* (1937), spent his childhood on a homestead near Conrad, and he also tells of his early years in *The Beginning of a Mortal* (1932). B. M. Bower (Bertha Muzzy Sinclair), formerly of Big Sandy, has written several novels dealing with the ranch country of north-central Montana. Her first one, *Chip of the Flying U,* is typical of her work. *The Yankee Bodleys* (1936) is an unusually successful first novel by Naomi Lane Babson of Bozeman. Mildred Walker (Mrs. F. R. Schemm) of Great Falls wrote *Fireweed* (1934), and *Light from Arcturus* (1935), neither of which deals with Montana life.

An old-timer's biography, *Yellowstone Kelly* (1926), contains the memoirs and colorful anecdotes of Luther S. Kelly's scouting days. *Riding the High Country* (1933), by Patrick T. Tucker and Grace Stone Coates, tells of Tucker's adventures in company with the artist Charlie Russell. *Ubet* (1934), by John Barrows, is a well-written account of life in the early 1880's at a stagecoach station in the Judith Gap country.

Contemporary Montana poets include, besides Mrs. Coates, Jason Bolles, Mary Brennan Clapp, Grace Baldwin, Gwendolen Haste, Elliott C. Lincoln, and Norman MacLeod. *Northwest Verse* (1931), compiled by H. G. Merriam, Chairman of the Department of English at Montana State University, and *Western Prose and Poetry* (1932), edited by Rufus A. Coleman, contain poems of both regional and universal significance.

Missoula is the home of *Frontier and Midland,* a nationally circulated quarterly edited and published by H. G. Merriam. It began in 1919 as the *Montanan,* a student publication which soon became the *Frontier.* In 1927 it was taken out of the hands of the students and widened in scope, becoming a regional magazine of the Northwest. *The Midland,* literary magazine of the Middle West, was merged with it in 1933. Emphasizing regional material, the *Frontier and Midland* publishes fiction and poetry of high quality, often presenting writers who, because of the experimental nature of their work, could not get space in popular magazines. Outstanding stories have been republished in the leading annual anthologies.

Handicrafts

Montana Indians knew many handicrafts. The things they made were not merely material necessities; often they represented the tribesman's expression of his love of form and color, and of the sentiments which civilized man voices in more sophisticated art forms. Symbolic designs and traditional patterns possessed a religious and tribal significance.

Earth—yellow, red, green, blue, and black—provided the basis of the paints and dyes with which they decorated their lodges and their persons. They created also colorful designs in feathers and quills. All tribes made clothing of decorated skins, and tools of wood, bone, or stone. They did little carving, but some of their stonework shows amazing skill. They made pipes of clay, baskets of skin, bark, or woven willow *(see Tours 1, 2, 3, 7, 14).*

White men brought handicrafts of their own. Among the most necessary and characteristic were gunsmithing and saddle-making, and such domestic crafts as spinning, knitting, and weaving. With the advance of

YELLOWSTONE KELLY

civilization most of these fell into disuse, but saddle-making has survived and even grown into a minor industry. There are saddlers in Miles City, Butte, Livingston, and Billings who, besides making saddles of outstanding workmanship—some inlaid with gold and silver—produce belts, purses, holsters, traveling bags, and other leather products.

Mary Atwater of Basin started a revival of the ancient handicraft of weaving, which in this region had been practiced chiefly by Swedes trained in their native land. Many Montanans now produce linens, tweeds, and dress fabrics of good quality.

Fine hooked rugs are made in Bole; baskets woven from native reeds in Josephine; sculptured jewelry and carved wood in Billings. The frequently exhibited wood carvings of John Clarke, a full-blooded Blackfoot Indian of Glacier National Park, have gained wide recognition.

Painting

Father Ravalli was Montana's first white artist. Pictures and wooden figures executed by him almost a hundred years ago are preserved at St. Mary's Mission, Stevensville, and at the State historical museum, at Helena. Since his time, Montana has produced a number of artists who left to make their careers elsewhere, and several who remained in the State and devoted their talents to the portrayal of its colorful life and history.

The greatest of them, a noteworthy painter and sculptor, was Charles M. Russell (1864–1926), the "cowboy artist" of Great Falls, whose log cabin studio, purchased at his death by his native city, is the State's only important art museum. Opened to the public in 1930 as the Charles M. Russell Memorial Museum, it contains 320 catalogued items, covering every period of his career. Many of the pictures and relics remain as he left them, and in his studio is perpetuated something of the spirit of his life, of his long years as a cowboy, his great and enduring friendship with the Indians, and his unique and dramatic interpretation of the making of the West.

Russell came west from St. Louis as a boy, in the days of the great cattle ranches. His first sketches were made for the entertainment of fellow workers in the cow camps. His work first aroused attention outside the State for its treatment of a subject suggested by the terrible winter of 1886–87, during which a neighboring cattle outfit lost almost its entire herd. The artist's report of this event to the owner was the expressive *Last of Five Thousand,* which depicts a starving cow standing in the snow while a coyote waits hungrily near by. After 1914, when an exhibition of his work was held in the Doré Galleries in London, Russell's paintings brought rapidly increasing prices; his last work, unfinished, sold for $30,000.

An extensive collection of his work is on exhibit in the Mint at Great Falls, and a few examples are in the State capitol at Helena. A few of his earlier sketches, oils, and water colors, portraying the Indian in native surroundings and depicting cowboy life in the days when buffalo and longhorn cattle shared the range, are held privately. Hundreds of letters, illustrated with sketches, are treasured by his friends.

Critics agree that Russell was a skilful draftsman and colorist, and that his faithful portrayal of life in the Montana of his time is a significant contribution to American art. He was the author of *Trails Plowed Under* (1923) and *Good Medicine* (1929), containing his illustrations.

Edgar S. Paxson (1852–1919), while not Russell's equal in artistic talent, did much to memorialize the West he knew as soldier and frontiersman. Like Russell he lived and painted in several Montana cities, finally building a rustic studio in Missoula. Examples of his work are found in the State capitol, the Billings Public Library, and the Missoula County Courthouse (murals). In the Natural Science Building of the University of Montana is *Custer's Last Stand,* the large canvas Paxson regarded as his masterpiece. He worked on it intermittently for 21 years, putting into it the figures of more than 200 soldiers and Indians, some of whom he had known in life.

Ralph De Camp (1858–1936), the third of Montana's noted frontier painters, is remembered for his landscapes. Born in New York, he studied in Milwaukee, Duluth, and Philadelphia. Working on a Red River boat, he attracted the attention of Charles Fee of the Northern Pacific Railway, who brought him to Yellowstone Park. From 1896 to 1924 he lived in Helena, and several of his paintings hang in the State capitol there. The best known is a representation of the Gates of the Mountains *(see Tour 6),* but his own favorite is one that depicts the grief of his son Renan at having killed a bird with his air gun.

Photographs of artistic and historic value were made by Richard Throssel and L. A. Huffman, mostly in the period between 1870 and 1900. Throssel, who was part Crow, made some outstanding prints of Indian life: *Game of Arrows, Salute to the Sun God,* and others.

Leader of Montana's contemporary artists is Will James, cowboy author-illustrator of Pryor. Born in 1892 in a covered wagon amid rough surroundings, he wrangled horses at an age when most boys are in school, riding the range from Canada to Mexico. His refreshing and original pen drawings, packed with the action of everyday life on the range, are among the most authentic interpretations of cowboy life today. Many of his oils of Montana subjects are widely popular.

Good work has been done by Hart Merriam Schultz (Lone Wolf), a son of James Willard Schultz; Branson Stevenson, a Great Falls etcher; Irvin Shope, Missoula mural painter employed by the State highway commission; and Weinold Reiss, a German-born painter who spends part of each year among the Blackfeet, and directs a summer art school in Glacier Park. His style is of more recent derivation than that of the native Montanans, most of whom have followed in the path of Russell. *The Blackfeet Indians* (1935) contains some of his portraits. Many younger artists are emerging, some of them with the aid of the Federal Art Projects of the Works Progress Administration.

On April 7, 1938, the Butte Art Center was opened to the public with a circulating exhibition supplied by the Federal Art Project and many works by Montana artists. Sponsored by the project and by the Butte Art Association, the center has been planned to provide wide opportunity to study, appreciate, and enjoy the visual arts. Its program includes exhibitions, free art instruction, an extension program of educational services, and a library, research, and reproductions division.

Music

Musical activities in Montana are confined largely to schools and colleges, although several cities and towns have creditable bands, and the Servian Orthodox Church in Butte has an outstanding choral group. The highly regarded bands of Montana State College and the University of Montana make annual tours of the State, giving concerts in the principal cities. The Butte Mines Band, under the leadership of Samuel Treloar, who founded it in 1887, has won national competitions at Salt Lake City, Denver, and Los Angeles, and has played for five Presidents. Its excellence may or may not, as one writer suggested, be due to the fact that "their occupation is such as to develop their lung capacities and thereby give greater zest and tone," but it is certainly notable among bands whose members earn a livelihood in occupations other than music.

Butte and Great Falls have amateur symphony orchestras. In Butte, Irish orchestras specialize in jigs and reels; Jugoslavs dance to the traditional music of the *Kolo;* and a German *Lieder* club regularly rehearses the airs of the fatherland. All national groups in the industrial centers have transplanted in some measure their native folk music. Cowboy songs are popular everywhere in the State.

Two singers have achieved prominence. Marie Montana (Ruth Waite) of Helena, operatic and concert soprano, has appeared in both Europe and America. Taylor Gordon of White Sulphur Springs has made concert tours in America and has achieved notable success in London and Paris as a singer of Negro spirituals.

Musical composition in Montana never developed beyond a modest beginning, although at least one composer, Lowndes Maury, Jr., has attempted symphonic music besides writing for the piano, string quartet, and various solo instruments.

The Theater

In the great days of the road Montana saw the best shows. Katie Putnam, Nellie Boyd, Emma Juch, Ferris Hartman, and the Tivoli Opera Company came in their own stagecoaches, and were followed by Lotta Crabtree, Bernhardt, Modjeska, Clara Morris, Fanny Davenport, Agnes Huntington, Stuart Robson, the Barrymores, Robert B. Mantell, Blanche Bates, Minnie Maddern Fiske, Henrietta Grossman, Mrs. Leslie Carter, Mrs. Pat Campbell, Lillian Russell, Grace George, William Faversham.

Today moving pictures, occasionally supplemented with vaudeville of the touring type, supply Montana's dramatic entertainment. Though its residents supposedly see cowboy life at first hand, the State prefers "western" films, especially in the smaller cities.

The drama is kept alive by scattered groups of amateur players, among whom the Montana Masquers, a university group, has taken the lead. Experiments in writing and presenting original plays are carried on at the State college, the university, and Billings Polytechnic Institute. Little theaters have been organized, but with slight success. In Billings a civic group under the sponsorship of service clubs, organized in 1936, has had a good start.

Architecture

When white men came, Montana Indians were living in lodges made of skins, sticks, and mud, usually in the conical tepee form. The first buildings of the invaders were crude log cabins, chinked with clay. Most of these have fallen into decay, but a few examples dating from the 1860's are well preserved. On the plains the only building material available to the pioneers was the turf that stretched from horizon to horizon. Furrows were carefully plowed to obtain sodblocks of uniform size. These were laid in tiers to form the four walls. A pole framework covered with sod formed the roof. The door and its frame were of wood; holes left for windows were sometimes curtained with burlap or canvas, but often left uncovered. A sod house was rarely larger than ten feet square, and two or three days' labor completed it. It was excellent for shutting out the harsh prairie winters, but dusty and rude. A few examples still stand in the northeast *(see Tour 2)*, the section last settled. With the coming of sawmills and railroads, homes became plain box-type buildings of clapboards or red brick, purely utilitarian; the false-front (a façade that extended some distance above the actual building, to suggest an additional story) for business houses became standard.

Building boomed in the 1880's and 1890's. Copper kings and gold barons vied with one another in building ornate, costly residences. It was the period of "gingerbread" decoration and architectural absurdities; but here and there appeared simple and handsome houses. Remaining examples include the Worden house (1875) in Missoula, a frame dwelling built in the style of early New England farm houses; the Morgan Evans house (1883) on Warm Springs Creek *(see Tour 18)*, a brick building of modified Colonial design; and the Marcus Daly house (1885) in Anaconda, another adaptation of Colonial style.

Buildings of the past century, such as the red-brick box dwelling introduced from the Mormon communities of Utah, predominate on many streets in the older cities, but on the whole the cities show a diversity of treatment in the modern manner. The most common residential style is the Georgian Colonial; architects estimate that half of the new homes follow this tradition, having white columns, shuttered windows, hipped roofs, and slightly projecting cornices. Somewhat less common are the English and Mediterranean types, of which the latter is certainly incongruous in Montana.

Most business buildings are conservative in treatment, with little ornamentation. Schools have improved vastly; many excellent ones have been built with PWA funds. The Great Falls high school and the groups at the State college and the university are designed in a somewhat modified Renaissance idiom that suits the Montana landscape, a style introduced by George H. Carsley, Helena architect, and Cass Gilbert, designer of the Woolworth Building in New York. The older public buildings tend toward the neoclassic design, best exemplified in the State capitol at Helena. The newer ones are almost invariably in modern style.

Church buildings are usually unpretentious and utilitarian, sturdy in

ST. HELENA CATHEDRAL

PROSPECTOR'S HOME

construction rather than distinctive in style. However, St. Helena Cathedral in Helena and the Presbyterian Church in Great Falls are good examples of Gothic design. The design of the cathedral is based upon that of the Cathedral of Cologne in Germany, the only decided change being the trefoil or cloverleaf window over the arch of the middle front doorway. Von Herbulis, European architect who helped design the Votive Church in Vienna, drew the plans.

Ranch buildings and summer homes in the mountains are usually of logs hewed, in most instances, on the interior surface only. The logs extend beyond the corners, where they are notched together, and are either sawed off uniformly or, if the ends are chopped, allowed to protrude at random. Outside chinking is usually of cl. y and gypsum; inside, of cedar strips. Old-style roofs are of cedar shakes nailed to poles placed lengthwise, but in recent construction rafters, board ceilings, and composition shingles are favored. There are examples of fine log work near Red Lodge, at Swan and Flathead Lakes, and around Lake McDonald (see Glacier National Park). The slightly modified Swiss chalets of Glacier Park have a rightness in relation to their setting that nothing in the State, unless it be the old-fashioned prairie sod house, has ever equaled.

The Press

THE first news sheet published in Montana (name unknown) was printed in Virginia City in January 1864, on a small press brought by ox team from Denver. Wilbur F. Sanders was the editor; John A. Creighton, who later founded Creighton University at Omaha, was printer's devil.

The *News Letter,* a small paper printed by Francis M. Thompson, appeared in Bannack two or three months later. The press was hand-operated and used mostly for business purposes; no copy of the short-lived *News Letter* is extant.

The first newspaper of consequence was the *Montana Post,* published by John Buchanan and M. M. Manner. Arriving in Virginia City in 1864 —after an adventurous trip on the steamer *Yellowstone* from St. Louis to Fort Benton—they set up their equipment in a cabin cellar. The events of the trip were the chief matter of the first two issues, but the publishers planned wide news service. An introductory editorial said: "We have correspondents in the various mining camps, who will keep our readers well posted on what is going on in . . . our young and rapidly growing territory." The first issue appeared August 27, 1864; the 960 copies sold quickly at 50¢ each, usually in gold dust. Before the third issue, Buchanan and Manner sold out for $3,000.

The Republican *Montana Post* was followed in 1865 by another Virginia City weekly, the *Montana Democrat.* The publisher freighted all his supplies from Salt Lake City.

The *Lewiston Radiator* (1865) was Helena's first newspaper. Press and supplies were brought across the snowy passes by mule train from Idaho's Snake River country. At first independent, it became a Republican organ, the Helena *Herald.*

Other gold camp weeklies were the *Rocky Mountain Gazette* (Helena, 1866), the *Independent* (Deer Lodge, 1867), the *New Northwest* (Deer Lodge, 1868), and the Missoula and Cedar Creek *Pioneer* (Missoula, 1870), which later became the *Daily Missoulian.* The *Independent* became one of the strongest advocates of Helena in the impending capital location fight.

These early newspapers, filled with zestful matter pertaining to gold strikes, Indian raids, hold-ups, and range affairs, held up a faithful mirror to frontier life, but they softened the reflection a little in dealing with politics. They were eagerly received, for printed matter was scarce. News from the East came most quickly through Salt Lake City, whose newspapers, brought in by stage, were much clipped by Montana editors.

Railroad building brought a boom in newspaper publication, as towns sprang up along the routes; but it did not last long, and several papers reversed the usual order of newspaper evolution by becoming weeklies after having been dailies. The Livingston *Enterprise* started as a daily when the construction crews approached in 1883, became a weekly when the boom collapsed the following year, and did not return to daily publication until 1912.

In the turbulent 1890's, W. A. Clark and Marcus Daly fought for control of public opinion, and acquired ownership or control of most of the influential publications. Copper-knuckled editorials followed. In Billings, whose first newspaper had adopted the hard-boiled slogan, "We did not come to Montana for our health," Shelby E. Dillard was editor of the *Vociferator* and a sharp critic of public affairs.

Animosities among the powerful papers subsided as their economic interests began to grow identical. Lesser journals continued in the pugnacious tradition of the earlier press, but their alignment changed from one of owning faction against owning faction to one of public interest against corporate interests. After 1917 Bill Dunne issued more or less regularly the small and sometimes violent but always vital Butte *Daily Bulletin*.

"It is doubtful," wrote Oswald Garrison Villard in the *Nation,* July 9, 1930, "if in any other State the press is . . . so deeply involved in the great economic struggle . . . at the bottom of our political life." He declared that the same corporation "generously runs both Republican and Democratic dailies," and that in Missoula a single versatile editor wrote at one time the arguments for both sides. In 1928 W. A. Clark, Jr., launched the *Montana Free Press,* at first a very promising effort to achieve journalistic independence on an effective scale; but the expenses of the paper were ruinous, and he gave it up within a year.

Butte has a morning paper, and an evening paper without Sunday edition. This pattern is repeated in Great Falls, Missoula, and Helena. Of 120 newspapers published, 20 are dailies.

Recreation

HISTORICALLY, and by popular preference, recreation in Montana is associated with camping, hunting, and fishing. The favorite recreation (except "going to town") of the old-time cowboy was to throw a diamond hitch around a pack of grub and bedding, and start for the mountains to bring in a lion, bighorn sheep, grizzly bear, mountain goat, deer, antelope, or elk. The pattern was fixed before white men came, having been the Indian way of life for uncounted generations. Since the time of Sir St. George Gore, the first "dude," the State has attracted famous sportsmen, some of whom have come with elaborate equipment to hunt big game and try the mountain streams for trout.

Present emphasis is on fishing rather than hunting, but either is readily available; even the larger cities are near forest reserves and primitive areas. Many tourists find the opportunity for camping out under ideal conditions the State's greatest attraction.

Few regions offer finer inducements to the tourist with a camera. Roads twisting along water courses through hills and mountains reveal striking views at almost every turn, often with a lone horseman, a herd of sheep or cattle, or an abandoned cabin adding a human touch to nature's display. Because much of the scenery is above any plane of vision possible through a window, a good horse or an open car with the top down is the best conveyance. A lens filter is essential; besides capturing the spectacular cloud effects common over the mountains, it guards against overexposure in the clear air.

Camping: In organizing an outing, dude ranches are undoubtedly the best resource for the uninitiated. They arrange for "roughing it" near the main lodge or for extensive pack trips, according to the taste and aptitude of the guest. They are not summer resorts in the usual sense; their hospitality is more personal. Under the supervision of a dude wrangler, guests participate in riding the range, roping, branding, and other ranch and roundup activities; in shooting, fishing, canoeing, swimming, campfire entertainments, pack trips, mountain climbing—even placer mining.

Most people, however, bring their own outfits in trailer or car, pick a spot that affords opportunity for their favorite sport, and pitch camp. Wood is free, fish and berries help out the larder; the expense is often less than that of staying at home. Secluded campgrounds within a few miles of stores and gas stations are often equipped with fireplaces and tables, piped water, and other conveniences. Many people lease summer home sites near forest lakes or running streams.

Except during periods of extreme fire hazard, the forests are open for all forms of recreation not detrimental to them. Prospecting and mining are permitted as on other public lands, and not a few people spend their vacations with pick, shovel, and sluice box, obtaining gold dust in the manner of earlier days.

The camper who enjoys solitude will of course find it most readily in the less advertised localities. Ten great primitive areas, uncommercialized and without roads or habitations other than an occasional ranger station or lookout tower, are available to those who really wish to rough it. The areas are:

Absaroka, in the Absaroka Forest near Yellowstone Park, a 64,000-acre tract of high wooded mountains. It has a large count of deer, elk, and bear, and good trout fishing.

Beartooth, in the Custer Forest, 230,000 acres of bare, lofty peaks (including Granite), glaciers (including Grasshopper), and lakes *(see Tour 13A).* It offers superb scenery and opportunities for climbing.

Mission Mountains, 67,000 acres of spectacular scenery in the Flathead Forest on the east slope of the Mission Range. Grizzly bear and mountain goat abound. Among its peaks and precipices are glaciers, lakes, and a profusion of alpine flowers.

South Fork of the Flathead, Sun River, and *Pentagon* are contiguous primitive areas, South Fork and Pentagon in the Flathead, Sun River in the Lewis and Clark Forest. The 625,000-acre South Fork area, accessible by pack horse from dude ranches in the Swan River and Blackfoot country, is wild and rugged but with excellent camp sites. It is richly stocked with fish and game. The Pentagon, 95,000 acres, is one of the wildest of all primitive areas; few white men have passed through it. Three-fourths of the Sun River area, 240,000 acres, is a game preserve, used by part of the Nation's second largest herd of elk. Its stupendous limestone peaks compare with those of Glacier Park. Indians still hunt there.

Spanish Peaks, 50,000 acres of rugged crests and cliffs rising from the valleys of the Gallatin Forest; it contains 20 alpine lakes.

Cabinet, 90,000 acres in the Cabinet Forest, a region of heavy snows among high summits rising between deep river valleys.

TROUT STREAM

Selway-Bitterroot, 1,870,000 acres mostly in Idaho but partly in the Bitterroot and Lolo Forests, Montana. The scenery is imposing and the hunting excellent on both sides of the State line.

Anaconda-Pintlar, 145,000 acres in the Deer Lodge, Beaverhead, and Bitterroot Forests. It lies on the high summits of the Continental Divide, with heavy forest sloping away on either hand. There are moose, elk, deer, and bear.

The best season for a camping trip is after June 15. Before that, snow is excessive at the higher altitudes, the ground muddy, mosquitoes and ticks are active, and the streams too full for fishing. Floral displays on the mountain meadows are best in early July.

Fishing: In the mountain lakes and streams, bass, grayling, whitefish, most varieties of trout, and other game fish may be taken even by the tyro. The Madison River and its tributaries are renowned for large, fighting rainbow. Native blackspot trout ("flats") and Dolly Varden ("bulls") abound in the northwestern lakes and larger streams. Both are taken by trolling or casting (fly or spinner according to season). Almost every mountain stream teems with 6- to 10-inch trout which rise readily to the fly and are perhaps the best of all fish to "smell up a pan." There is excellent fishing in superb surroundings in the Kootenai River region near Libby; on the North and South Forks of the Flathead River; on the headwaters of the Swan and Clearwater Rivers and in the Clearwater Lakes east of the Mission Range; in the tributaries of Clark Fork of the Columbia west of Thompson Falls; in Rock Creek east of Missoula, and Hebgen and Red Rock Lakes west of Yellowstone Park; in Big Hole, Beaverhead, Madison, Boulder, Stillwater, and Gallatin Rivers; in Clark Fork of the Yellowstone; in the Beartooth Lakes; and in many other localities.

Best fishing in the lakes is between June 15 and July 15; in the streams, after July 15. During the hot, lazy days of September there is usually a lull, although the expert fly-fisher on good waters will catch a few. Large land-locked salmon are taken from Flathead Lake by trolling or snagging in late September and October.

Hunting: Elk, deer, and bear are the most numerous big game. Rocky Mountain goats are hunted only in limited areas. Nearly all counties east of the Rockies are closed to elk hunting, many to deer hunting. Closed areas in any part of the State are changed from year to year, however; it is best, before planning a hunt, to get latest information from the Fish and Game Commission, Helena.

Chinese pheasant, Hungarian partridge, and various kinds of grouse are plentiful in all parts of the State. The many lakes out of Kalispell and Missoula, the Missouri River and the artificial lakes along it, and the lakes, reservoirs, and sloughs in northern and eastern Montana are very good places for duck hunting. *(For fish and game laws, see General Information.)*

Mountain Climbing: The State has 25 peaks 12,000 feet or more in height, any of which challenges the skill of an expert climber. Innumerable summits—only slightly lower—present equal difficulties. The best climbing is in the Beartooth and Absaroka Mountains and Glacier Park (guides available); here the typical ascent begins over forest trails that extend to the timber line, then up loose talus slopes to precipitous cliffs; beyond these are difficult rock seams and buttresses, leading to easier inclines near the summit. In August and later, snow can be avoided on most mountains, and only a few retain patches of ice that the climber must cross. Although many mountains can be climbed by experienced mountaineers without special equipment, it is wise to carry at least a rope

and ax, for there is usually some ticklish bit that should be attempted only with an anchor to windward. Most climbs require only one day for the trip to the summit and back, provided there is a trail to timber line. Without a trail to follow, the dense forest, full of windfalls, is likely to be tedious.

Riding: Nearly all dude ranches furnish horses without extra cost, riding being as much a part of the fare as the food. At low-priced lodges, hot springs resorts, and national parks, there is an extra charge. Small outfitters in mountain towns specialize in saddle trips into the back country. The rate for guides, horses, equipment, and food averages about $8 a day per person in parties of three or more. Large parties usually get a lower rate; persons traveling alone must pay slightly more.

Good horsemen willing to look after their riding stock and to do without guides can usually rent ranch horses inexpensively and conveniently. An experienced camper provided with proper maps has no real need for a guide. The main difficulty in looking after rented horses is to keep them near. Horses sometimes take a notion to travel homeward over-night, and even when hobbled can cover several miles in a few hours. As they seldom separate, it is usually best to picket one or two securely on the best grass and hobble the others near by.

Hiking: Glacier National Park offers the best hiking, with 900 miles of safe, well-kept trails through some of the most beautiful scenery in the Rockies. In less developed areas an extensive hike entails carrying a bed roll and food, as supply points are infrequent. The best plan is to select a supply base and make several 1- or 2-day excursions from it, then catch a ride to another base.

Hikers in the Rockies should carry a topographic map of the chosen area. Although most of the main trails are marked at intersections, some are not; and a wrong choice of trail late in the day may be a serious inconvenience. To hike alone except on familiar trails is unwise; an injured hiker might wait a long time for help. To hike without any trail at all is dangerous even for groups. Any safe route would likely have at least a game trail, since animals have been making such trails for thousands of years. Game trails, however, may not lead anywhere in particular. Both the Park Service and the Forest Service urge hikers to discuss their plans with a ranger before setting out into new country.

Swimming: A swim in a clear mountain lake or river rewards the hiker or horseman at the end of many Montana trails. In some places the water is not long on its way from a melting glacier, but after the first gasp it not only isn't bad, it's perfect. The swimmer unaccustomed to such water should not stay in too long or swim too far unaccompanied by a boat, for it is colder than he may realize.

Most of the cities have public pools with tempered water, and a score of hot springs resorts offer water as hot as can be borne comfortably. Besides plunges, the resorts usually have saddle horses, tennis courts, and other accommodations. Many tourists prefer hot springs to tourist camps, for the sake of a warm plunge at the end of the day.

Fossil Hunting: All Montana is a promising field for fossil hunters, but the best areas are south of the Missouri, where the stream courses are deeply eroded. Caves, rock shelters, and gravel slides in the breaks along the major rivers are good places to search. If a fossil or artifact is discovered, it is important to dig around it only enough to establish that it is a real find, and then report it to the School of Mines at Butte. A geologist will be sent to identify the stratum in which it is imbedded and to authenticate the discovery.

Prospecting: Not all the pay dirt in Montana has yet been found;

there remain many gulches that have been but lightly prospected. Most prospectors get only 50¢ to $2 out of a day's work, but the possibility that the gold panner who finds a little in a creek may find more in a lode nearby is alluring.

Prospecting requires only a long-handled shovel and a pan. For actual placer mining a ditch is dug, and a few boards and nails made into a sluice box about 6 feet long, a foot wide, and a few inches deep. A strip of carpet is laid on the bottom; over it are placed several pieces of wire screen for riffles. The box is set at a slight angle to allow coarse material to run out; water from the stream is led into it. The gold caught in the riffles settles in the carpet, which is washed at the end of the day to recover the embedded metal. The foot of gravel next to bedrock is richest.

Rodeos: The modern outgrowth of the old-time roundup is a more popular spectacle at Montana fairs than horse racing, though races are used as part of the rodeo. Rodeo events also include bronco riding, bulldogging *(see Glossary)*, calf roping, steer riding (without saddle), and milking of wild cows.

Some of the riders are young fellows in from the range, eager to display their ability and perhaps win a purse. Others, including a few women, are professionals traveling from rodeo to rodeo, usually "grubstaked" by the people who organize the show, furnish the buckers and other stock, and manage the brisk run-off of events. The most spirited buckers, often as famous as their riders, learn to make the 10 seconds allowed for a ride all too long for any but the most expert "busters." *(For principal rodeos, see CALENDAR OF EVENTS.)*

Winter Sports: Montana has every advantage for winter sports—plenty of snow and clear, cold weather; an open, hilly terrain; and people with a tradition for skiing and kindred activities. Organization was begun in 1934 when Casper Oimoen, captain of America's 1932 and 1936 Olympic ski teams, came to Anaconda to supervise construction of a ski jump. It turned out to be one of the fastest jumps in the country; tournaments held there attracted the foremost performers and helped popularize all winter sports. The annual winter carnival now features ski jumping, cross country ski running, hockey, dog sledding, speed and figure skating, and bobsledding.

Following the example of Anaconda, other cities are organizing their winter sports activities, collaborating with the recreational program of the Works Progress Administration.

Motorboat Racing: Although the sport is in its infancy in Montana, some exciting races have been held on Flathead Lake and at Anaconda and Thompson Falls. Most of the motors used are of the outboard type. Regattas are held at Whitefish and at Hauser Lake, 12 miles north of Helena. The lake created by Fort Peck Dam will provide further opportunities for speedboat enthusiasts.

Golf: Not many years ago the rough was so well named and so extensive that a few players invented "Montana golf," using no ball between greens, but simply basing the result of a stroke on the perfection of form in making it. The game had a certain Scotch merit. There are now some good well-kept golf courses. A few boast grass greens, but others use only an oily composition based on granulated smelter slag, which makes the greens black. Fairways have scant grass; the lie of the ball is likely to satisfy anyone's craving for variety. The average greens fee is 50 cents. Most clubs, while private, welcome visitors belonging to other clubs. A few dude ranches have small courses.

Other Sports: Tennis courts are available at most towns and dude ranches. A State league plays amateur and professional baseball, with clubs in the larger cities. Football is played in schools and colleges, with outstanding teams at the university and the State college. Basketball is perhaps the most popular competitive sport. Nearly every fair-sized school and town has a team, and local rivalries are often both spirited and bitter. Bowling is a winter sport in several cities. Montana likes rough and hearty sports, and has produced some prize fighters who have graduated into the big arenas. Its most celebrated ring battle was the Dempsey-Gibbons fight at the little oil town of Shelby, July 4, 1923. Significantly, Montanans never forget to mention that Shelby was just a "little oil town" at the time.

PART II
Cities and Towns

‹‹‹‹‹‹‹‹‹‹‹‹‹‹‹‹‹‹‹❖›››››››››››››››››››››

Billings

Railroad Station: Union Station, Montana Ave. between 22nd and 24th Sts. for Great Northern Ry., Northern Pacific Ry., and Chicago, Burlington & Quincy R.R.
Bus Stations: Union Terminal, 108 N. 26th St., for Greyhound, Burlington Trailways, Washington Motor Coach, Motor Transit Co. 512 N. 27th St. also for Motor Transit. 2302 1st Ave. N. for Northern Pacific Transport. Chapple's Drug Store, Montana Ave. and Broadway, for Billings Interurban.
Airport: On Rimrock, 2.2 m. NW. by Lindbergh Blvd., for Northwest Airlines and Wyoming Air Service. Taxi 50¢.
City Busses: Fare 10¢.
Taxis: 1st zone, 1 passenger, 25¢; 2nd zone, 1 or 2, 50¢; 3rd zone, 1 to 3, 75¢.
Traffic Regulations: Speed limit 15 m.p.h. downtown, 25 in residential sections, 12 within 100 yards of school in session. Parking downtown 1hr., at post office 10 min.; free near courthouse, 200-300 N. 27th St., and on 3rd Ave. N. at Broadway.
Street Numbering: Avenues numbered from N. P. Ry. both ways, streets numbered NE. to SW. to Division St., thence E. to W.

Accommodations: Eleven hotels, many tourist camps; during large gatherings newspapers list homes with spare rooms.

Information Service: Commercial Club, N. 27th St. at 3rd Ave. N.; Rod and Gun Club, Boothill Mound at E. edge of city off Rimrock Dr.
Radio Station: KGHL (950 kc.).
Motion Picture Houses: Four.
Swimming. Athletic Park, 901 N. 27th St.; South Park, 600 S. Broadway; free.
Golf: Hilands Club, 1.5 m. N. over Polytechnic Dr.; Billings Country Club, 2 m. N. on Lindbergh Blvd.; Hiltop Club, 1.5 m. E. on US 10 and L. on Lake Elmo Rd. (greens fees 25¢ and 35¢).
Tennis: Billings Polytechnic Institute, 3 m. NW. on Polytechnic Dr.; Eastern Montana Normal School, 1500 N. 30th St.; Pioneer Park, between Grand Ave. and Ave. G.
Ice Skating: Athletic Park, 901 N. 27th St.; South Park, 600 S. Broadway; Terry Ave. & 5th St. W.
Shooting: Billings Rod & Gun Club, Boothill Mound off Rimrock Dr.; Yellowstone Rifle Club, 2915 1st Ave. N.
Bowling: Basement of Babcock Theater, Broadway and 3rd Ave. N.

Annual Events: Motor caravans to Custer Battlefield, May 30. Motorcycle climb, Polytechnic pageant, pioneer banquet, shooting, golf, and tennis tournaments, early summer. Swimming tournament, July 4. Midland Empire Fair, August. Mexican fiesta, September 15-16. Turkey shoot, late November.

BILLINGS (3,117 alt., 16,380 pop.), seat of Yellowstone County and third largest city of Montana, lies on the west bank of the Yellowstone River. On the east beyond the river, and on the north, buff sandstone cliffs known as the Rimrock rise 400 feet above the valley floor. On the south, the high hills flatten down to a plain that slopes westward toward Clark Fork of the Yellowstone. From the streets of the city the valley seems an irregular bowl, rather than the great trough it is in reality, and mountains loom up at its southwestern rim. Though the snow-covered Beartooths are

60 miles away, the clearness of the air sometimes makes the city seem to lie almost at their feet.

Except at the west end of town there are no diagonal streets. The gridiron pattern is laid on a northeast-southwest axis, following the railroad, which cuts the town completely in two. Only a few widely separated crossings connect the halves.

On the north side are the main business section, most of the public buildings, and the better residential districts. Most of the buildings are clean and fresh. Increasing use of electricity and gas protects them from much of the smoke and dust of the average city. At night the business section is neon-lighted in all the colors of the rainbow.

The south side is the older part of Billings. At its southern limit is the sugar refinery, the city's biggest industrial plant. Along the railroad are flour mills, lumberyards, and the warehouses of some of the leading distributing plants in Montana. In between, in a section of vacant lots and old buildings, are isolated groups of attractive houses. In 1938 the Federal Housing Administration allotted $280,000 to replace old houses with new. At the refinery are extensive feeding pens where cattle and sheep are fattened on potent smelling beet pulp, molasses, and alfalfa.

In this section of town live many of the Mexicans employed in the sugar industry. Others live in a village of about 50 white adobe buildings on a ten-acre area of alkali flats southeast of the refinery. Often, one small house accommodates two families. A Mexican fiesta is held in mid-September, with English translation of program numbers for visitors.

Billings shows its agricultural origin in many ways. The easy friendliness of its citizens is that of a farming community; sometimes fully half the people on the streets have the unmistakable air of the land about them. Cowboys, especially numerous on the days when sales are on at the stockyards, click down the sidewalks in high-heeled boots and broad-brimmed hats.

Descendants of Irish, English, Scottish, and Scandinavian settlers predominate. The foreign-born are but a small part of the population.

It is told that when the town was only two or three months old, one Seth Bullock, approaching over a miserable trail on a dark, rainy night, asked a citizen the distance to Billings. "You're in Billings now," said the citizen. "The devil I am!" said Seth. "Can you tell me where Star, Bullock and Company's store is?" "Keep right on this street," said the citizen. "The store is on the left-hand side, 26 miles from here." This trait of reckless affirmation is more than booster spirit. It not only inspires Billings' claim to be the capital of a vague tributary region called the "Midland Empire," but has promoted its actual growth, in a brief half century, from a tiny frontier trading post and cowtown to the metropolis of an area as large as New York State.

An Indian trail once crossed the site, passing southwest along the river from a gap in the Rimrock. Here François Larocque came in September 1805, looking for beaver. Ten months later Capt. William Clark and his party, returning from the Pacific *(see HISTORY)*, came down the trail on their way to rejoin Lewis at the mouth of the Yellowstone. Then for years only trappers, traders, and adventurers who left little or no record of themselves visited the region.

From 1853 to 1873 surveys of the valley were delayed by trouble with the Sioux. In June 1876 the news of the Custer Battle drew Nation-wide attention to the region. More troops were sent; the Sioux were subdued; what had been a wild and little-known land was opened to the stockman and land seeker. Soon small settlements were grouped around stage stations and post offices.

When the Northern Pacific Railway entered the valley in 1882, Coulson, founded in 1877 at the eastern edge of the bowl, assumed it would be selected as the site of the city the railroad company ordered built. Refusing, however, to pay the exorbitant prices Coulson landowners asked for their property, the company laid out the new city two miles up the river, and named it Billings in honor of Frederick Billings, its president. Soon Coulson was receiving mail as East Billings.

In a few months Billings became a thriving city with schools, churches, newspapers, and a street railway capitalized at $40,000, though composed of only two 15-foot yellow cars drawn by Indian ponies. The "two-bit" fare to Coulson also paid for two glasses of beer at the Coulson brewery. The trip became the joy-ride de luxe for Billings beaux and their girls. When huge Custer County, whose affairs were administered at Bozeman because it had no county seat of its own, was divided in 1883, Billings became the seat of Yellowstone County.

Then the boom collapsed. Three large fires, two of them fought without adequate water, destroyed many of the makeshift wooden buildings. The disastrous winter of 1886–87 crippled the stock business, and by 1890 the population had shrunk from more than 1,500 to 836. With its first reckless growth dramatically ended, Billings settled down. When prosperity came again, it was based on the solid foundation of a growing cattle industry and agriculture under irrigation.

In 1874 Addison Quivey reported the Yellowstone Valley "valuable for neither agriculture, grazing, nor minerals, but . . . interesting . . . as the last home and burial place of the horrible monsters of the earliest animal creation." Five years later an irrigation ditch was dug near Coulson and the valley began its magnificent refutation of Quivey's judgment. In 1938 irrigated land around Billings exceeded 600,000 acres.

Irrigation early encouraged experiments in sugar-beet growing that led to the establishment of a refinery in 1906. The first beet field workers were Japanese, but the sugar company found them unsatisfactory. They were replaced after one season by industrious Russian-Germans who had heard of the new jobs and were willing to work by the "Dutchman's lantern" (the early morning moon) to make their way in America. Even the babies were carried to the fields, where their mothers were hoeing or thinning the long rows. Soon these people bought land and adopted the American way of life; many settled on the Huntley Irrigation project, 15 miles outside of Billings, where they make up a third of the population. Mexicans imported in 1918 took their place in the beet fields.

The installation in 1933 of pulp-drying equipment at the refinery en-

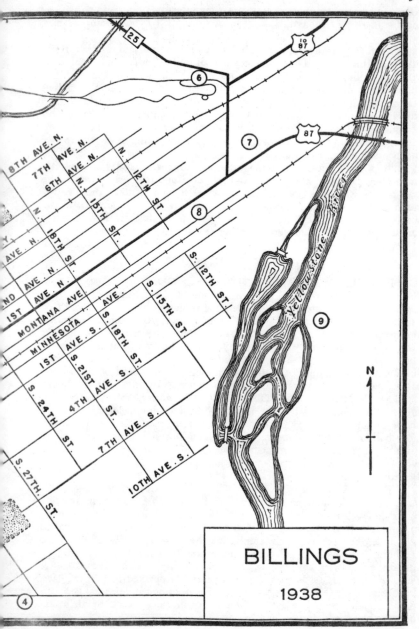

8TH AVE. N.
7TH AVE. N.
6TH AVE. N.
N.
N. 12TH ST.
15TH ST.
18TH ST.
AVE. N.
1ST AVE. N.
MONTANA AVE.
MINNESOTA AVE.
1ST AVE. S.
S. 21ST ST.
S. 24TH ST.
4TH AVE. S.
7TH AVE. S.
S. 27TH ST.
S. 18TH ST.
S. 15TH ST.
S. 12TH ST.
10TH AVE. S.

Yellowstone River

N

BILLINGS

1938

couraged an industry subsidiary to sugar manufacture: the rapid conditioning for market of thousands of head of livestock by the feeding of beet pulp.

Hay, chiefly alfalfa, outranks beets in cash value and finds a ready market in the dry-land areas. The value of milk, butter, and wool marketed in Billings exceeds $8,000,000 a year. Milk is far in the lead, but Billings was once the largest inland wool shipping point in the United States. The city is an important cattle and horse marketing center. Industries include flour milling, meat packing, and canning. The labor of 300 persons is required to process the bean crop after it reaches the cleaning mills. Oil refining and woodworking are the most important enterprises independent of agriculture.

Billings is a convenient transportation crossroads, and its wholesale trade flourishes. The planes of two air lines drone regularly down to the port on the Rimrock. Good motor roads reach up and down the Yellowstone Valley, north and east across the plains, over the mountains to the west and southwest. Billings is Montana's only plains city having direct rail connections with Denver and other cities to the south.

POINTS OF INTEREST

1. EASTERN MONTANA NORMAL SCHOOL *(open 8:30-5 Mon.-Fri.; 8:30-1 Sat.)*, 1500 N. 30th St., is one of the six units of the State University. First housed (1927) in rented rooms, it was soon moved to a building of Gardiner travertine and Montana-made brick on an elevation that permits a fine view of the city. The design is modern; a central tower rises two stories above the four-story wings. The registration (resident students) in 1936–37 was 55 men and 258 women. Courses in art, English, mathematics, music, physical education, science, and social science are supplemented by actual teaching experience in Billings' public schools.

2. ST. VINCENT HOSPITAL-SCHOOL *(open)*, 1st Ave. N. and Division St., founded after the 1916 epidemic of infantile paralysis as a single orthopedic ward in the old St. Vincent Hospital, occupies the three-story building and the third floor of the new hospital. Special courses are given in stenography, dancing, drawing, and modeling. In connection with the school, the Billings Rotary Club sponsors a summer camp in the Beartooth Mountains, six miles south of Red Lodge.

3. PARMLY BILLINGS MEMORIAL LIBRARY *(open 9-9 weekdays; 1-9 Sun.)*, Montana Ave. and 29th St., was given to the city in 1901 by Frederick Billings, Jr., in honor of his brother Parmly, who had lived in Billings. It is housed in a towered Romanesque building of native sandstone. The appointments emphasize the local atmosphere; the walls are hung with western paintings and relics. In 1922 Elizabeth Billings added the Frederick Billings, Jr., Memorial Wing to house the MUSEUM *(open during library hours)*. There are sections devoted to pioneer days, the Custer Battle, Montana birds, and paleontological finds; a gun collection contains two six-foot Hudson's Bay flintlocks, each worth a six-foot pile of furs to an old-time Indian.

4. The SUGAR REFINERY *(open 1:15-3 weekdays; 1:15-2:45 Sun., during Sept.–Feb.)*, S. 31st St. and State Ave., is the first and largest Montana refinery, and one of the largest in the world. Capable of slicing 3,000 tons of beets daily *(see INDUSTRY AND COMMERCE)*, it covers about three city squares, employs 700 men in season, and makes sugar refining Billings' foremost industry.

The central plant of red brick rises four stories and is topped with an attic story of whitewashed steel surmounted in turn by two smokestacks. Glistening steel pipes and ventilators sprout from the roof. Box-like smaller buildings, chiefly of brick, stand about the grounds. To one side, six cylindrical gray storage tanks, like those of a modern flour mill, rise above the roofs of the buildings. A silvery water tank on great stilt-like legs rises nearly to the height of the smokestacks. Railroad tracks extend westward from the plant on multiple trestles; beets are dumped from the cars into huge washing troughs under the trestles. Behind the plant are great mounds of limestone and of the dark waste products of sugar manufacture.

RIMROCK DRIVE TOUR—4.3 m.

This loop trip above the city on the north goes northwest on N. 27th St. into Lindbergh Blvd., which climbs steeply up the Rimrock to the airport. Swinging east at the airport, the road follows more or less closely the edge of a sheer cliff. The drive is fascinating at night for its view of the lighted city.

5. The RANGE RIDER OF THE YELLOWSTONE overlooks the city from the airport. The bronze life-size group (unveiled July 4, 1927) of a cowboy and his mount, posed by William S. (Bill) Hart and his horse, Paint, is the work of Charles Christadora. It was placed originally at the edge of the Rimrock several hundred yards east of the airport, but was moved in February 1938 because the flood waters of June 1937 damaged the cliff beneath and made its position unsafe.

R. from Lindbergh Blvd. on Rimrock Dr.

6. BOOTHILL CEMETERY, E. end of Rimrock Dr., was the first burial place used by Billings pioneers, many of whom died "with their boots on." Bad men, peace officers, and Indian skirmishers lie side by side in shallow graves. A shaft built of small stones marks the site. Of the original markers, only a wooden cross·and a weathered sandstone slab remain.

R. from Rimrock Dr. on US 10; US 10 turns R. into 1st Ave. N.

7. MIDLAND EMPIRE FAIRGROUNDS, entrance at E. end of 1st Ave. N. has a half-mile track and permanent buildings including a large T-shaped main building with a barrel-vaulted roof and an auditorium seating 10,000. The fair features extensive agricultural and livestock exhibits, racing with pari-mutuel betting, and a rodeo in which ranking performers compete.

8. BILLINGS STOCKYARDS (212 pens), entrance at 1st Ave. N. and N. 10th St., cover 7½ acres. Here, amid the dust and smell of auction day, the shrill yells of punchers and the shouts of buyer and seller rise above the bawling of cattle and the startled snorting of horses as the herds are hustled through long rows of corrals and chutes. As many as 3,000 cattle and 500 horses have been shipped out in one day.

POINTS OF INTEREST IN ENVIRONS

9. SACRIFICE CLIFF, 1.5 m. on E. side of Yellowstone River, visible from downtown Billings, is a 200-foot nearly vertical escarpment from which, more than 100 years ago, Crow Indians afflicted with smallpox leaped to death to appease their gods. Scores of bodies were once fastened to the trees on top of the cliff, though common Indian practice was to place only a few in any one burial ground.

10. BILLINGS POLYTECHNIC INSTITUTE, 3 m. NW. on Polytechnic Dr., was founded in 1908 by Lewis and Ernest Eaton. The entire job of designing, building, and equipping the school plant, including the quarrying of sandstone for the nine buildings, was done by student labor under faculty supervision. Student industries operated with student-built machinery include manufacture and marketing of flour and cereals; printing and binding of books and periodicals; woodworking; radio, electric, and automotive servicing. Work in the plants pays for the education of many students. With the exception of the square red brick Science Hall (1909) the buildings are of gray rimrock sandstone in various adaptations of medieval English architecture. One of the dormitories has battlements and square towers.

Huntley Irrigation Project, *15.4 m.*, Pompey's Pillar, *29.8 m. (see Tour 1, sec. a).* Horsethief Cache and Home of Calamity Jane, *24 m. (see Tour 1, sec. b).* Inscription Cave, *7.8 m.,* Custer Battlefield National Cemetery, *65.7 m. (see Tour 3, sec. b).*

CONSERVATORY OF MUSIC, BILLINGS POLYTECHNIC INSTITUTE

Butte

Railroad Stations: Front and Utah Sts. for Northern Pacific Ry. and Union Pacific R.R.; 2nd and Montana Sts. for Milwaukee Rd. and for Butte, Anaconda & Pacific R.R.; Arizona and 3rd Sts. for Great Northern Ry.

Bus Stations: 101 West Broadway for Intermountain Transportation; Broadway and Wyoming Sts. for Greyhound, Washington Motor Coach, Deer Lodge Transportation, and Northern Pacific Transport; 109 E. Broadway for Butte—Wisdom Mail Stage.

Airport: 4 m. S. on US 10 for Western Air Express and Northwest Airlines; taxi, $1.

Street Busses: Fare 10¢, or 4 tokens for 25¢.

Taxis: Minimum 50¢; further fees depending on distance, grades, and the like.

Traffic Regulations: No left turns at Park and Main or Broadway and Main. No U-turns at stop light. Parking restrictions indicated on streets. Cars going up or down hill have right of way.

Street Numbering: Park St. is dividing line for streets running N. and S., Main St. for streets E. and W.

Accommodations: More than 40 hotels. Many rooming houses and tourist camps.

Information Service: Chamber of Commerce, 62 W. Broadway.

Radio Station: KGIR (1340 kc.).

Motion Picture Houses: Four.

Golf: Municipal course, Rowe Rd., 18 holes; greens fee 35¢.

Tennis: 1300 Harrison Ave.

Athletics (incl. baseball and football): Opposite tennis courts, 1300 Harrison Ave.; Clark Park, Grand and Texas Aves.; the Cinders, Alabama and Silver Sts.; Emmett St. field, Excelsior and Gold Sts.

Riding: 1718 Yale Ave.; $1 per hour.

Annual Events: Balkan pre-Lenten festival *(Mesopust)*, February. Miner's Union Day celebration, June 13. Rodeo, usually second week in July. Miner's field day, August 2. Football game, State University vs. State College, late October.

BUTTE (5,755 alt., 39,532 pop.), Montana's largest city, lies against a bare southward-sloping hillside, like a vast page of disorderly manuscript, its uneven paragraphs of buildings punctuated with enormous yellow and gray copper ore dumps and with the gallows frames that mark mine shafts. At the foot of the hill Silver Bow Creek—otherwise Clark Fork of the Columbia—flows westward through a flat and almost treeless valley between barren mountains. To the northwest is Big Butte, the volcanic cone from which the city takes its name, identified by the white "M" placed near its summit by students of the State School of Mines. From a distance Butte seems to straggle all over the hill, but this impression is lost within the city itself, which has a lively up-to-date air unlike that of the average mining camp.

The present-day miner, "coming down the hill," leaves his digging clothes in a locker in the dry-room near the shaft. He takes his shower, shaves, and appears on the street dressed like the average business man.

MEADERVILLE

Often he stops for a "John O'Farrell" (whiskey with a beer chaser), as in the old days, before going on to other entertainment.

All ore is now smelted at Anaconda, 26 miles to the west, and the sulphurous smoke that once made it necessary to keep plants under glass, and street lights burning even by day, no longer blankets the town. The air is clear, flowers bloom in trim gardens, and trees soften the outlines of utilitarian structures.

Beneath the city is one of the richest mineral deposits in the world— an area less than five miles square that has produced between two and three billion dollars in mineral wealth since 1864. There are 253 miles of streets on the surface of Butte Hill. Under the surface the corridors and tunnels, which are being extended at the rate of 35 miles a year, total more than 2,000 miles. The deepest mine, the Steward, drops a distance of 3,633 feet—from near the Continental Divide to a point within 2,000 feet of sea-level.

Though it is by no means a gross and lurid place, as commonly reported, Butte, in good times, is a prodigal, gay-living, rough-and-ready town. Saturday, when the miners are paid, offers an especially gay spectacle. Theaters are crowded from noon to midnight; cocktail lounges and beer parlors do a lively business; night clubs and specialty cafes are filled. Gambling houses operate openly, and are about as common as pool halls; keno players sit absorbed in their numbered cards, in the little heaps of corn or beans with which they mark the numbers drawn, and in the electric panel that announces the numbers.

But to the discerning the city reveals another side, gallant and warm-hearted and perhaps equally reckless, for Butte is capable of "giving its shirt" when occasion arises. It is a cosmopolitan city, early settled by Irish, Welsh, and Cornish miners, later by representatives of many countries, notably the Balkan States. There is a small Chinatown, an Italian colony in Meaderville, and a Finnish district on East Broadway and Granite Street. National organizations range from German singing societies to a chapter of the Chinese Bing Kong Tong; several restaurants specialize in foreign foods. A few folk customs of the various groups have been preserved, the best known being the Mesopust *(see ETHNIC GROUPS)*. The old custom of singing carols on Christmas Eve was brought over by English miners. For more than 40 years male choruses sang on the principal street corners; then the singing began to attract such throngs as to cause dangerous traffic tie-ups, and the singers, organized as the Butte Male Chorus, forsook the streets in favor of the radio.

Cornish (Cousin Jack) miners of earlier days contributed the pasty, or meat pie, to Butte cuisine. They called it "a letter from 'ome." Saffron buns or "nubbies" are another Cornish food. The favorite sport of the Cornishmen is coursing—greyhounds pursuing rabbits. Their coursing tracks southeast of the city on Harrison Avenue are known as "Cousin Jack race tracks."

Butte's history goes back to 1864, when G. O. Humphrey and William Allison arrived from the gold camp at Virginia City and found placer deposits in Silver Bow Creek. They also found a prospect hole four or five feet deep, and near it, a pair of elk horns apparently used in digging. Beyond that the earlier prospector had left no record of himself. Humphrey and Allison opened what they called the Missoula lode, and a few other prospectors drifted in and staked out claims. Two years later, when the first house was built on the present Quartz Street, 40 men and 5 women were living in tents in Buffalo Gulch, near the site of Centerville. In 1867 the placer camp had between 400 and 500 inhabitants. But water was scarce and by 1870 half the people had left.

In 1874 William L. Farlin, one of the first prospectors in the area, returned from Idaho, and quietly claimed several outcrops of quartz from which he had previously taken samples for assay. Word soon spread that the black ledges of Butte were rich in silver, and a period of claim staking and claim jumping followed. Miners swarmed to the camp; the silver boom began.

The excitement brought Marcus Daly (1841–1900) to Butte. Daly, who was an immigrant from Ireland at the age of 15, "landed in America

MINE AND ORE DUMP

with nothing in his pockets save his . . . Irish smile." He learned about mining in the Nevada silver camps and was known as a shrewd judge of silver properties. After some highly profitable preliminary operations in Butte, on behalf of Salt Lake City bankers, he sank a shaft on a claim of his own previously ignored as valueless. Experts laughed at him, and, when he began to strike copper instead of silver, even Daly was disappointed. He persisted, but instead of reaching silver he found increasingly rich copper ores. At 400 feet he reached a vein 50 feet wide and of unparalleled richness. In less than 20 years he became the head of one of the world's most powerful monopolies, and a founder and builder of cities (see Tour 18).

A townsite patent was issued in 1876, and the city was incorporated in 1879. Two years later, when the Utah & Northern Railroad provided an outlet to the Union Pacific main line at Ogden, the copper boom was on. By 1885 Butte had a population of 14,000. There were several banks, churches, and schools, a hospital, a fire department, a water company, and a "committee of safety" composed of 200 citizens, who kept a sharp lookout for troublemakers. A second railroad was built, connecting with the newly completed Northern Pacific at Garrison. The Great Northern reached Butte (1889); the Butte, Anaconda & Pacific, which hauls ore to the Anaconda smelter, was completed (1894); and in 1908 the Chicago, Milwaukee, St. Paul & Pacific ran its first trains through the city.

In 1900, the Montana School of Mines was opened in Butte, which is fortunately situated for the study of mining.

Butte labor is strongly organized, with more than 12,000 workers in active unions. The Mine, Mill and Smelter Workers' local union is the largest, and it greatly influences the State's labor policy. Most of the strikes that occurred during the development of the mines were settled quietly, but a few were long-drawn and bitter (see LABOR).

Butte's rise to the status of copper metropolis of the Americas is the most dramatic page in Montana's story (see HISTORY). Feverish activity in boom times alternated with unemployment and suffering during slumps. Wars between copper kings alternated with labor fights. But the power of copper grew throughout. The present-day Butte industry influences more or less directly every important industry in the State, and has powerful connections in other States and many foreign countries. Production is geared to large consuming operations (for example, brass fabrication) in other parts of the Nation, and a campaign of education promotes the use of copper products. Butte copper has a greater tensile strength than any other, and is used in products intended to withstand great strain. It is claimed that there are reserves of this metal sufficient to last for a hundred years without the development of new ore bodies.

POINTS OF INTEREST

1. MARCUS DALY STATUE, center of N. Main St. between Copper and Gagnon Sts., by Augustus Saint-Gaudens, erected by popular subscription in 1906, is a bronze of the copper king standing at ease, coat on arm and battered hat in hand, a picture of the self-assurance that helped make him master of the State's copper industry.

2. SMITHERS HISTORICAL PHOTOGRAPH COLLECTION (open 9-6 weekdays), 21 W. Granite St., contains many reproductions of faded originals owned by pioneers. About 400 depict the life of Montana Indians during the past century.

3. The W. A. CLARK HOUSE (private), W. Granite and N. Idaho Sts., is a three-story red brick mansion in the style of the 1880's, with white stone ornamentation. Small porticoes with slender columns and elaborate gingerbread decorations face the street on two sides. The walls have many angles and the lines of the steep roof are broken by numerous gables and dormer windows. Because the grounds slope toward Granite Street, the building seems higher in front than in the rear. William Andrews Clark (1839–1925) was president of the Montana State Constitutional Conventions of 1884 and 1889. In his efforts to control the Democratic party in Montana, he was constantly opposed by Marcus Daly. He was twice refused the seat in the U. S. Senate to which he claimed election, but after a third election in 1901 he was at length seated. He served throughout his term, and then retired.

4. The ART CENTER (open 2-4 and 7-9:30 daily), 2nd floor School

Administration Bldg., 111 N. Montana St., was begun early in 1938 by the Federal Art Project. Exhibits vary from time to time, but always include representative works by Montana artists.

5. The PUBLIC LIBRARY *(open 9-9 weekdays; 1-9 Sun.)*, W. Broadway and Dakota St., contains about 50,000 books, and the current periodicals. Special cases of Montaniana, art reproductions, and old or rare books are in the librarian's office. The building is of deep red brick with gray sandstone facings. The pediment at the top of the north wall is three stories above the arched double entrance. At one corner a round tower, of narrow red brick piers and glass is topped with a flaring crown, and is decorated with bands of carved brick and sandstone. The fenestration on either side of the entrance is asymmetric; on one side is an arched window and a deeply recessed circular one; on the other side is a large rectangular window. The window treatment on the east side of the building is more regular, with all the upper windows arched, the lower ones rectangular, but the corner opposite the tower has an almost jocular note, for under a second pediment at the roof level is a circular window set in a sandstone horseshoe.

6. SITE OF MAGUIRE'S OPERA HOUSE, 54 W. Broadway, is occupied by the Leggat Hotel. Here, from 1885 to 1902, John Maguire, an Irish minstrel turned impresario, made theatrical history on the frontier. "The Grand Opera House at Butte," said the August 1885 issue of *West Shore*, a magazine published at Tacoma and Portland, "is the finest . . . on the Pacific Coast outside of San Francisco." It must indeed have been good, to make the Coast magazine class Butte, 700 miles inland, as a Coast city. Maguire's presented such operas as *The Bohemian Girl, Tannhäuser,* and *Carmen,* with some of the best operatic stars of the period. In 1888 the house was burned, but was soon rebuilt. In 1895 Mark Twain lectured from its stage. A few years later Maguire sold it, and it became a vaudeville theater until torn down to make room for the hotel.

CHINATOWN occupies the single square formed by Main, Galena, Colorado, and Mercury Sts., and is divided by China Alley. The buildings, mostly of brick, are old and shabby. Except for the names on one or two electric signs, bulletins in Chinese characters posted on some of the walls, and a single building with weird carved ornaments on its facade, there is no external evidence that the quarter is Chinese.

Tong wars in other cities have occasionally found echoes in Butte, and hatchet men have not been unknown. In 1881 the *Miner* reported the following notice in Chinese posted on several buildings in Chinatown: "The sign of the firm is Lun Han Tong. Three men at Walkerville keep a wash house against the law, and the man that goes and kills those three will be paid . . . $1,500." The newspaper said a Chinese lawyer testified under oath that the translation was correct, but added doubtfully: "No one can tell. The . . . document may be even more diabolical than it looks."

Another 1881 item tells how Gong Sing, being refused what he regarded as a fair price for a woman named You Kim, seized a hatchet and chopped her "at about the point where President Garfield was shot."

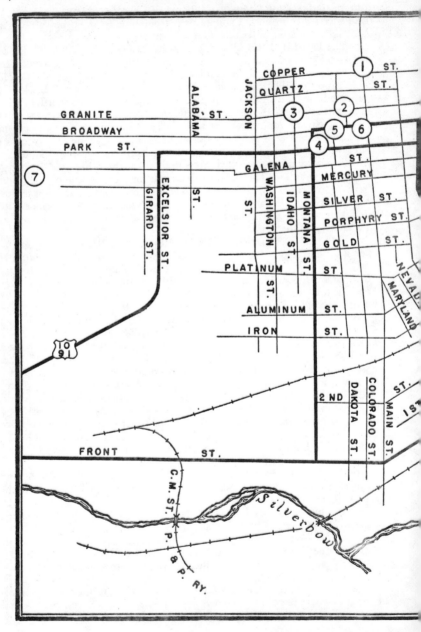

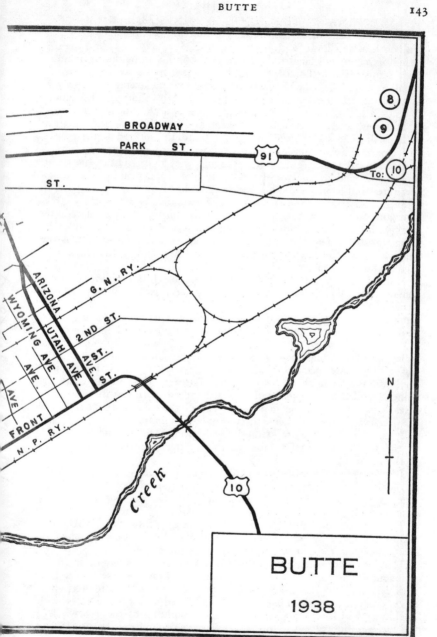

BUTTE

1938

7. MONTANA STATE SCHOOL OF MINES *(open 8-5 Mon.-Fri.; 8-12 Sat.)*, W. end of Park, Galena, and Mercury Sts., occupies the southern bench of Big Butte, with a commanding view of the city and the surrounding mountains. Since its opening in 1900, this school has maintained high standards of scholarship and has done notable work in mining, metallurgy, and geology. The student body, which averages about 450, includes men from every State and a dozen foreign countries. The campus of 11½ acres is beautified with lawns, trees, and shrubs. To plant some of the trees, workmen had to blast large holes in the rock and fill them with earth. The six modern, fire-proof buildings, of red pressed brick with concrete bases and white stone facings, are connected by underground passageways, a great convenience in winter. In front of the buildings the ground drops away by steep terraces to Leonard Field, where there are tennis courts and other sports facilities.

RESIDENCE HALL (1935), W. end of Park St., is a four-story structure with two-story wings, built, in modern functional style, of tapestry brick with terra cotta facing. Three long flights of concrete steps lead up from the street. The hall is governed by an organization known as the Mavericks, in cooperation with the house mother, and by the fraternities Sigma Rho and Theta Tau.

MAIN HALL, W. end of Galena St., the original building (1896), contains the administrative offices, library, and lecture rooms. It is a Renaissance building of red brick, with base and facings of granite and sandstone. Above the entrance are bas-relief portraits of leaders in physics, geology, mineralogy, metallurgy, and chemistry. The LIBRARY *(open 9-5 and 7-9 Mon.-Fri., 9-12 Sat.)*, in the south wing, houses a notable collection of scientific books and documents pertaining especially to mining, geology, and metallurgy, and virtually complete sets of the technical publications of schools and government bureaus. The W. A. Clark III Mineral Collection, consisting of several hundred specimens in seven large cases, is displayed on the first floor. The GEOLOGICAL MUSEUM *(open 8-5 weekdays)*, in the basement, has 10,000 or more specimens of carefully classified minerals, rocks, and fossils from Montana and other parts of the world. A special exhibit of mine models portrays underground workings of all types.

The METALLURGY BUILDING (1923), facing S. at W. end of Mercury St., houses laboratories, offices, a water distillation plant, and ventilating equipment. It is designed in a modified Renaissance style with ample fenestration and a carved stone entrance.

The northern and northeastern suburbs of CENTERVILLE, WALKERVILLE (reached by N. Main St.), and MEADERVILLE (reached by US 91) contain most of the Butte mines and miners' homes.

The outstanding characteristic of Centerville and Walkerville is an impression of age that seems almost incredible in a town whose history goes back less than 80 years. Weathered frame buildings cling to steep hillsides. Scattered among them are old-fashioned red brick houses with double bays in front, and here and there a building of rough-hewn logs has survived the years. Sagging picket fences surround grassless yards, and

AFTER BLASTING

many of the houses are reached by broken stairways leading from the street. The streets themselves, striving to maintain a fairly consistent grade, run sometimes above, sometimes below, the floor level. The sidewalks and battered boardwalks often give up the struggle and rise or descend by means of wood or concrete steps.

The whole tenement area is trade-marked with the random upthrust of the surface workings of the world's richest copper mines. Rarely are all or nearly all of these mines in operation at one time. Of those in operation, some move almost without sound; others, with more of their machinery exposed, roar and rumble like vast threshing machines. About some of them the huge piles of waste resemble ash heaps; around others a yellowish tinge to the ore increases the impression of a threshing operation, making the dumps look like overgrown strawstacks. In the background are the tremendous crags of the Continental Divide. Walkerville is inhabited mostly by Cornish miners and their descendants. The town holds an election only if and when a candidate files for office.

Meaderville, farthest east of the three suburbs, is separated from the others by an area that includes such famous old mines as the Badger State, the Speculator, the High Ore, and the Anaconda. It has a more modern appearance than Centerville or Walkerville, and stands on a more level site. The Leonard Mine in Meaderville is the only copper mine open to the public.

8. The LEONARD MINE *(open; tour 1-3 weekdays, by advance arrangement at Chamber of Commerce, 62 W. Broadway),* off US 91 at Noble St., Meaderville, is a representative copper mine employing the deep mining methods used in the Butte mines. The greater part of the ore from these mines is brought to the surface through three shafts equipped with electric hoists capable of handling 24,000 tons every 24 hours. Scores of other shafts are used only for ventilation and for lowering and raising the 7,000 men required under normal operating conditions. The ores occur in faulted and complex fissure vein systems inclosed principally in granite. In mining, holes made with machine drills operated by compressed air, are loaded with explosives, and blasted; the broken ore is shoveled into chutes leading to ore trains; the opening made by the blast is timbered; finally the chamber (or stope) is filled with waste rock from other parts of the mine. Chambers average perhaps 20 feet in width. Trains carry the ore from the chutes to the shaft, and cages ("skips") hoist it to huge bins at the surface. Electric trains haul it to the smelter at Anaconda.

A miner going to work in the Leonard Mine changes into digging clothes at the locker building near the shaft, and waits for his turn in the "chippy"—the cage used to raise and lower men. Since only eight, tightly packed, can ride on each of the cage's three decks, it often takes 30 minutes to convey a shift to work. The cage, suspended by a heavy cable that winds on winches operated by compressed air, bumpingly descends a timbered fireproof shaft at the rate of 800 feet a minute, passing a mine level at every 100 feet or so, until the miner reaches the "station" on the level where he is to work. Here are deep skip pockets for storage of ore; converging lines of rails for ore trains; great pumping plants for disposal of mine water; and all the complex machinery necessary to deep mining. The miner goes down a gallery to the main drift (lateral tunnel) on the vein, and then to his stope (work chamber), which usually has two or more floors 10 feet apart, reached by ladders up a manway. On his way he normally passes long trains of ore cars shuttling about on the lower levels of the mine. Streams of warm, green water containing copper sulphate in solution rush down channels under the sloping tunnel floors. The sound of the pumps that force the water up from the lower levels of the mine to the precipitating plant at the surface is like a great, steady pulsebeat deep in the earth.

9. The PRECIPITATING PLANT *(open day and night),* off US 91 at Colusa St., Meaderville, is a system of flumes and settling tanks extending for hundreds of yards back and forth, in which pure copper is recovered from water pumped out of the mines. The tanks are filled with scrap iron and tin cans. The iron replaces the copper in the water and forms iron sulphate, leaving the copper precipitated in the tanks. The plant recovers about 6,000,000 pounds of copper annually. Oldtimers say that a German, Frederick Mueller, discovered the process, but that another

man whose name does not survive obtained his lease on the mine overflow and for many years reaped the profits.

The FLAT, a suburb in the valley at the foot of the hill, has an estimated population of 10,000, many of whom are Jugoslavs. It is somewhat shabby, but newer than the northern suburbs. The southern extension of Montana Street called the Boulevard, is well lined with road houses. Near its end are several Butte cemeteries. Funerals in the old days meant big business for the tavern keepers along the route, since those ·attending usually stopped at one or more of the "oases" both going and coming. Many were the exciting horse races along the Boulevard. Not all livery stable patrons were good drivers, but the standard order was "a fast horse and a couple of buggy whips."

10. COLUMBIA GARDENS *(open)*, 3 *m*. E. on Park St. and R. on dirt road at city limits, is Butte's principal outdoor amusement resort. Created in 1898 by W. A. Clark, who spent a million dollars to change it from a barren area to a park, it was the only picnic place available to Butte residents before the advent of the automobile. In summer, dances are held every evening at the pavilion, which accommodates 1,000 couples. The park has a well-equipped children's playground, and such mechanical amusement features as a roller coaster. There are landscaped stretches of lawn and flowers, a grove provided with tables and benches and fireplaces. Summer houses and pagodas furnish shelter. Every Thursday during summer vacation, city busses transport children under 12 to the park without charge. On these days little girls may pick flowers from the mammoth pansy bed, which contains 85,000 plants.

POINTS OF INTEREST IN ENVIRONS

Thompson Park, *10.2 m.*, Summit of Continental Divide at Pipestone Pass, *13.8 m.*, Gregson Hot Springs, *14.8 m.*, Lewis and Clark Cavern, *50.1 m. (see Tour 1, sec. c).*

Great Falls

Railroad Stations: W. end of 1st Ave. S. for Great Northern Ry. and Burlington R.R.; 1st Ave. N., R. of viaduct to 1st Ave. bridge over Missouri River, for Milwaukee R.R.
Bus Stations: Falls Hotel, 402 1st Ave. S., for Greyhound; 309 1st Ave. N. for Intermountain; Milwaukee R.R. station and Falls Hotel for Milwaukee; interurban, fare 10¢, 30-min. schedule.
Airport: Gore Hill, 3 m. SW. on US 91 for Western Air Express and Wyoming Air Service; taxi 50¢.
Taxi: 25¢ for 12 blocks, 35¢ for 20, elsewhere 50¢; extra passenger 25¢; special sightseeing rates.
Traffic Regulations: Semaphores and lights on the R. at intersections. No U-turns on Central Ave. between Park Drive and 10th St. from 7 a.m. to 11 p.m. All-night parking prohibited unless front and rear lights are displayed.
Street Numbering: Avenues run E. and W., and are numbered from Central Ave. Streets numbered eastward from the river.

Accommodations: Eleven hotels; extensive tourist and convention facilities.

Information Service: Chamber of Commerce, Rainbow Hotel, 20 3rd St. N.
Radio Station: KFBB (1,290 kc.).
Motion Picture Houses: Four.
Swimming: Mitchell Pool, Municipal Park on River Dr. near 1st Ave. bridge; Morony Natatorium, 12th St. N. and 2nd Ave.; Y.M.C.A. pool, 1st Ave. N. and Park Dr., 25¢ for nonmembers.
Golf: Riverview public course, 18 holes, N. of Missouri River near 9th St. bridge; greens fee 50¢.
Tennis: Concrete courts, high school, 2nd Ave. and 19th St.
Athletics (incl. baseball and football): 7th Ave. S. and 16th St.; 4th Ave. and 20th St. N.; 6th St. near fairground; high school stadium, 2nd Ave. and 19th St.; American Legion, 28th St., S. of River Dr.

Annual Events: Scottish New Year celebration, Jan. 1. Balkan Christmas festival, Jan. 6. Winter carnival, February. North Montana fair, early August. Labor Day parade, September.

GREAT FALLS (3,330 alt., 28,822 pop.), seat of Cascade County and second largest city in the State, is on a gentle slope of sandy plain within a bend of the Missouri River, opposite the mouth of the Sun River. In the distance four mountain ranges rise, the Highwoods and Little Belts to the east and southeast, the Big Belts to the south, and the main range of the Rockies to the west. One section of the city spreads westward across the river, and a town called Black Eagle, or Little Chicago, has grown up around the metal reduction works on the north side.

Great Falls owes its growth largely to the development of hydroelectric power at the falls on the Missouri for which it is named. The city is well lighted and clean; its factories use few dust- and smoke-generating fuels. A zoning system helps to maintain high standards of construction. Most buildings are modern. The largest of 17 parks lies along the Missouri

River, and smaller ones are scattered throughout the city. In the residential area the wide shaded streets run straight from end to end of the city, bordered in most places by green lawns planted with trees, shrubs and flowers. Industrial plants are landscaped wherever possible. If its size be overlooked, the city bears resemblance to Minneapolis, Minnesota, from which many of its people came.

The importance of Great Falls lies mainly in its industries, especially the refining and fabrication of copper and zinc, but it is also a banking, commercial, and agricultural center. Development of irrigation, of oil and gas production, and of coal and silver-lead mining in the country around has built industries and given added importance to old ones.

Great Falls has several active literary societies and a conservatory of music.

Admiration of Charlie Russell, the cowboy painter and sculptor, persists at all levels of Great Falls society; people who make no pretense of any knowledge of art understand and try to be like him. Largely, perhaps, because of his influence, Great Falls has kept the hospitality and other old-time virtues that have tended to wear thin in so many western cities.

Capt. Meriwether Lewis first saw the Great Falls of the Missouri on June 13, 1805. The following day, while exploring alone above the falls, he was chased by a grizzly bear. To escape, he plunged into the river up to his waist and "presented the point of his espontoon," a sharp spearlike weapon then used in the army. The bear "retreated with as much precipitation as he had pursued." Returning toward camp late in the day he fired at an animal he thought "to be of the tiger kind" (probably a mountain lion). "He then went on, but as if the beasts of the forest had 'conspired against him, three buffaloe bulls . . . left their companions and ran at full speed towards him." When he stopped and faced them, they "retreated as they came." The next morning he discovered a large rattlesnake coiled on the trunk of a tree under which he had slept. He killed it and found that it had "one hundred and seventy-six scuta on the abdomen, and seventeen half-formed scuta on the tail."

The party spent a month (June 15 to July 15) in making the 18-mile portage around the falls and rapids, using a rude cart with a mast from one of the boats as an axle, and sections of a large cottonwood tree as wheels. During this period Capt. William Clark made a map of the falls. On June 19 Captain Lewis discovered the Giant Springs. On the evening of July 4 he doled out their small remaining store of liquor, and the men sang and danced until interrupted by a brisk thunderstorm.

Returning from the Pacific a year later, the party camped near the falls again. "I sincerely believe," wrote Lewis in his journal, "that there were not less than 10,000 buffalo within a circle of two miles."

There is no record of other white visitors until 1822, when Jim Bridger passed, on a solitary trip up the Missouri. The following spring Andrew Henry's fur trading party was turned back by the Blackfeet. From 1838 to 1842 a Federal scientific expedition under Capt. Charles Wilkes, guided by Bridger, mapped the region.

The site of the future city was in the country of the Blackfeet, who were inclined to be troublesome. In April 1849 a war party of 400 attacked Jim Bridger and 83 white trappers near the mouth of Sun River, and killed three men. Then in 1853 Gov. Isaac I. Stevens came out with his railroad surveyors *(see HISTORY)*, and two years later concluded treaties with the important tribes. By the time the Mullan Road, which passed a few miles to the north, was completed, travel was comparatively safe.

Unlike such centers as Butte and Helena, which came into being overnight upon the discovery of important mineral resources, Great Falls was, from the start, a planned city, a fulfillment of the dreams of its founder, Paris Gibson (1830–1920). Gibson, a Minneapolis man, first visited the spot in 1880, and was impressed by its possibilities as an industrial site. He returned in the spring of 1883, with Robert Vaughn, a surveyor, and H. P. Rolfe, an attorney. They platted the townsite and named it Great Falls. The first resident was Silas Beachley, who lived there that winter, and suffered great privation when his food supplies and blankets were confiscated by Indians.

Gibson enlisted the aid of James J. Hill of the Great Northern Railway, C. A. Broadwater of Helena, and others in building the city. A few houses, a store, and a flour mill were set up in 1884, a planing mill, a lumber yard, a school, a bank, and a newspaper the following year. In October 1887 the young city's 1,200 people celebrated the arrival of the Great Northern Railway.

Incorporated as a city November 28, 1888, Great Falls elected Paris Gibson its first mayor. A silver smelter was built near the Giant Springs the same year, but the venture was short-lived because of the demonetization of silver.

In 1890 the meat-packing industry, which later became the largest between St. Paul and Spokane, was organized. A railroad to the mining towns of Neihart and Barker opened a rich tributary district to the south. Black Eagle Dam, generating 9,000 (later 25,000) horsepower, was completed—the first of the four hydroelectric units near Great Falls. The population increased to nearly 4,000; the town's real growth began.

The original copper reduction plant above Black Eagle Falls was completed in 1892, and operated until 1916, when it was replaced by the modern electrolytic copper and zinc refineries, with a wire and cable factory added.

By 1912 two new hydroelectric plants, the Rainbow and the Volta, were together generating 140,000 horsepower. John D. Ryan organized a company with offices in Great Falls that acquired control of these and other power sites in the State. A year later the Chicago, Milwaukee, St. Paul & Pacific Railroad connected the city with Harlowton and Lewistown in the rich agricultural Judith Basin.

Through the war years Great Falls expanded as new dams were built and war uses called for more and more copper. During the 1920's the use of copper decreased generally, but Great Falls retained its growth and prosperity because of its position as the center for a large agricultural area.

POURING ANODES

The early 1930's saw the completion of such projects as the 70,000-horsepower Morony dam and power plant; the million-dollar high school and athletic stadium; the Presbyterian church; and the Columbus Hospital, another million-dollar institution. The North Montana Fair, organized in 1931, attracts thousands of visitors annually. Beginning in 1935, a program of park development and other improvements were carried out with WPA labor.

In 1936 and through the summer of 1937 the metal refineries and wire and cable mill operated at capacity, employing more than 2,500 men. The city benefited from increases in farm and ranch income in tributary districts. The demand for lead and silver caused old mines to the south to become active, and there was renewed development of oil and gas fields in the Cut Bank area. In the fall of 1937, however, employment declined in several industries.

Before 1910 the city had two central labor bodies, one affiliated with the American Federation of Labor, the other (made up entirely of industrial unions) independent. In that year, however, it became clear in Great Falls, as it did nationally in 1937, that harmony was a prerequisite to effective labor action. A conference was held, and the groups united in a single council, the forerunner of the present strong Cascade County Trades and Labor Assembly.

A city-wide lockout that began in 1916 and lasted until the United States declared war on Germany (April 6, 1917) left labor in Great Falls seriously weakened. Four years later an 18-month strike of cooks and waiters almost destroyed the assembly, but ended in recognition of the right to organize. With this victory, membership began to grow and unions that had kept their charters only by paying a per capita tax on "dummy members" regained their power.

In 1933 a resurgence of organizing brought several new unions into Great Falls, among them one of the first Newspaper Guild locals in the Northwest. Union membership increased until it included at least two-thirds of the city's employed workers. The 1934 strike of mine, mill, and smelter workers was settled on the basis of a 40-hour week, return of the closed shop, and a basic wage of $4.75 per day, with a sliding scale of increases depending on the price of copper. With its own position made secure, labor is turning more and more to public business, specifically to campaigns for public improvements.

Most of the city's people are natives of Montana or nearby States, but among the workers in the several industries are considerable groups of foreign-born. Many of them keep alive distinctive national customs. As in Butte and Anaconda, the Jugoslav laborers celebrate the *Mesopust* and the charming Balkan Christmas rites *(see ETHNIC GROUPS)*. The Scots have a New Year celebration called *Hogmanay,* which includes public performances of Scottish folk dances. The heart of it, however, is the ceremony of "first feasting," which takes place in the homes. A table is set for guests, who arrive immediately after the beginning of the New Year. A blond man must partake of the food first, and unless such a man is present visitors may not enter.

POINTS OF INTEREST

1. CHARLES M. RUSSELL MEMORIAL MUSEUM *(open 2-8 daily, July-Aug.; other times by appointment),* 1217 4th Ave. N., is the log cabin studio of the late cowboy artist, who lived in Great Falls for many years *(see THE ARTS)*. The cabin, his home on an adjoining lot, and an addition built by the city, were opened to the public in 1930. In the museum are preserved his cowboy accouterments and other relics, including gifts he received from his many Indian friends. Examples of his work with pen, brush, and pencil are shown with a brief description of each. Models he made for use in painting include figures of horses, native animals, and other subjects. Copies of his illustrated books are prominently displayed.

2. The PUBLIC LIBRARY *(open 9-9 weekdays, 2-9 Sun.),* 203 3rd St. N., consists of 47,000 volumes housed in a low buff brick building which is surmounted by a dome and has a two-columned portico. Its notable collection of northwest Americana contains a copy of the official report of the Lewis and Clark expedition published in 1815. Collections of rocks, minerals, fossils, mounted birds, and butterflies are housed in the building.

3. STATE SCHOOL FOR THE DEAF AND BLIND *(open)*, 38th St. between Central Ave. and 2nd Ave. N., a long, plain, rectangular yellow stucco building, has full modern equipment, including shops and laboratories for vocational training, gymnasium, tennis courts, and football and baseball fields. The enrollment in 1936 was 86 deaf and 21 blind.

4. COLUMBUS HOSPITAL *(open)*, 1601 2nd Ave. N., is a six-story crescent-shaped structure of reinforced concrete and dark brown tapestry brick, with a taller central section surmounted by a series of small pinnacles. The long narrow wings that extend across the entire front of a city block admit maximum sunlight and air. The building is arranged for convenience and speed of communication and is regarded as an outstanding example of American hospital design. George Shanley was the architect.

5. ST. ANNE'S CATHEDRAL (1906), 701 3rd Ave. N., is the Roman Catholic diocesan headquarters for eastern Montana. It is built of gray-brown stone in the Gothic style. The rear of the building consists of several boxlike structures seemingly added without special regard for the original plan. On the cathedral grounds is St. Mary's Institute (1915), a junior college for women.

6. The PRESBYTERIAN CHURCH (1931), 1317 Central Ave., except for a brick memorial wing, is built entirely of light gray sandstone blocks of varying shapes and sizes, which give the walls a strange but effective patchwork appearance. The design is a modern adaptation of Gothic, with a high vaulted nave, stained glass windows, and small recessed windows beside a deep entrance arch.

7. URSULINE ACADEMY (Mt. St. Mary's), 2300 Central Ave., was built in 1911 of brick and stone, with terra cotta trim in geometric designs. The façade has a semi-military air, with stepped parapets on both central tower and wings. Grade school, high school, and junior college departments are conducted; the attendance is about 500. The academy is the center of parochial education in the city.

8. CITY HIGH SCHOOL (1930), 2nd Ave. S. between 18th and 20th Sts. and extending to 4th Ave. S., is the outstanding high school plant in the State. The many-windowed three-story building, of modern design, is built of tapestry brick and Bedford stone over a frame of concrete and steel, and is divided into north and south wings and a central section with a large extension to the rear. The interior is finished in oak, with fixtures in streamlined modern designs. The attendance is nearly 2,000. Laboratories for vocational training add greatly to the scope of the curriculum. The athletic stadium seats 10,000. Floodlighting is provided for evening games.

9. COLLECTION OF ORIGINAL RUSSELL PAINTINGS *(open)*, 220 Central Ave., is housed in a cigar store. Large cases along the walls contain many of his letters, bits of sculpture, and pen and ink sketches. This store and bar is typical of the places where the artist liked to lounge and met men of his own plain and friendly kind; like the other places where he is well remembered, the store has kept something of the impress of Russell's personality.

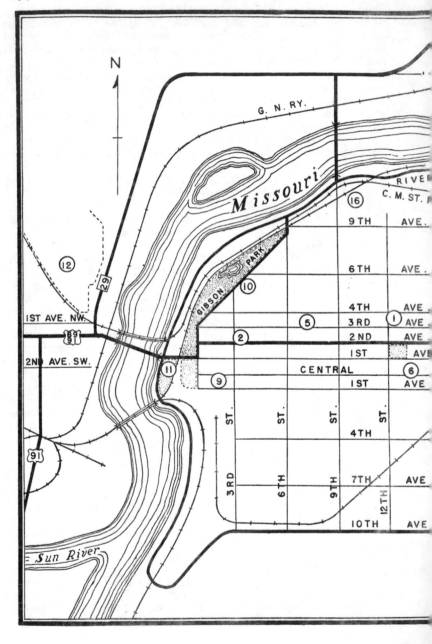

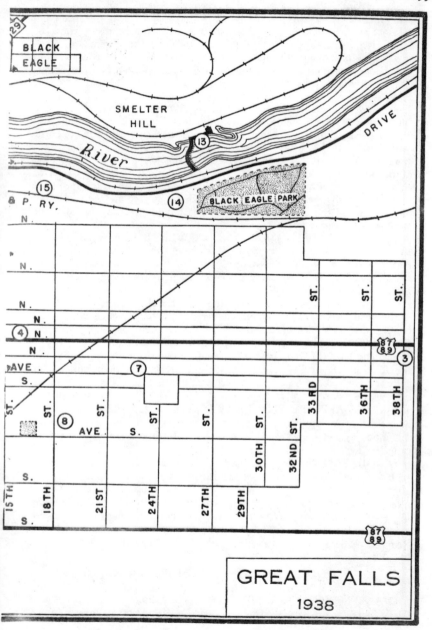

GREAT FALLS

1938

10. GIBSON PARK, Park Dr. between 1st Ave. S. and 8th Ave. N., extending to the Great Northern Ry., is within easy walking distance from the shopping district, with the Missouri River flowing by just beyond the tracks. It has a children's playground and a lake where swans and wildfowl live. In summer the municipal band gives a weekly concert from the Cooney memorial bandstand near Fourth Avenue N. The PARIS GIBSON STATUE, a bronze dedicated in 1926 to the founder of Great Falls, stands in Flower Circle at the head of Central Ave.

11. MUNICIPAL PARK, E. end of 1st Ave. bridge, extends south to Broadwater Bay, a widening of the Missouri River. A swimming pool with a capacity of about 1,000,000 gallons was completed in 1934 by WPA labor. At the bay are docks and a boathouse.

12. NORTH MONTANA FAIRGROUND, W. of the river and N. of the junction of 1st Ave. NW. and State 29, is a landscaped tract of about 40 acres, with a group of 12 modern exhibit buildings, a half-mile race track, and a grandstand seating 7,000. Organized in 1931, the fair has superseded the State fair at Helena, last held in 1932. In 1936 the attendance exceeded 200,000.

13. BLACK EAGLE DAM AND POWER-HOUSE, visible N. of River Dr. near NE. city limits, is just above the bare rock ledges that mark the site of the old Black Eagle Falls. South of the road a large space covered with trees is set aside as Black Eagle Park. Capt. Meriwether Lewis told how the site was named:

"Below this fall is a beautiful little island well timbered . . . On a cottonwood tree an eagle has placed her nest; a more inaccessible spot I believe she could not have found; for neither man or beast dare pass those gulphs which separate her little domain from the shores."

14. The REX FLOUR MILL (*open on application at office*), SW. of the falls and S. of River Dr. at 25th St., the largest flour mill in the State, employs about 90 men. The elevators have a capacity of 2,250,000 bushels.

15. The SAPPHIRE FLOUR MILL (*open on application at office*), S. of River Dr. at 17th St., employs about 35 men. Its elevators hold 1,000,000 bushels of wheat. The neon sign atop the double row of great cylinders has letters 15 feet high.

16. OIL REFINERY (*open by permission; no matches or smoking*), 10th St. N. near River Dr., was established in 1931 as a topping plant; in 1935 a modern cracking plant was added. At the topping plant is a tower, fitted with a series of pipes, that resembles a huge bottle magically pouring a stream of clear gasoline from the topmost pipe; naphtha from one a few feet lower; kerosene from the next; and from the next, fuel oils. Reduced crude oil for the cracking plant is drawn from the lowest level.

POINTS OF INTEREST IN ENVIRONS

GIANT SPRINGS, 3 *m*. NE. on River Dr., discovered by Lewis and Clark in 1805, discharges, every 24 hours, 388,800,000 gallons of water

GIANT SPRINGS

at a constant temperature of 52° F. the year round. Its source has not been established, and the water has never been used commercially.

Piegan Indians had a legend to explain the mysterious spring. They offered sacrifices to the Sun here in the belief that the waters gushed from a lake in the skies on the shores of which the Sun had his tepee.

A park around the spring has picnic tables, good fishing, and a fish hatchery *(open)* showing trout in various stages of growth. The site is a favorite picnic spot for Great Falls residents.

Fort Shaw, *26.4 m.,* Lewis and Clark National Forest, *47.5 m. (see Tour 4);* Ruins of St. Peter's Mission, *42.9 m. (see Tour 6);* Rainbow Falls, *7.6 m.,* Volta Dam *12.8 m.,* Great Falls, *16.2 m.,* Morony Dam, *19.8 m. (see Tour 14).*

Helena

Railroad Stations: Neill Ave. at N. end of Fuller Ave. for Great Northern Ry.; Helena and Railroad Aves. for Northern Pacific Ry.
Bus Station: 313 N. Main St. for Greyhound, for Washington Motor Coach, and for Intermountain Transportation Co.
Airport: 2 m. NE. on US 91 and Airport Road (R) for Northwest Airlines and Western Air Express; taxi 50¢.
Street Busses: Fare 10¢; 15¢ to Fort Harrison and East Helena. All lines start from 6th Ave. and Main St.
Taxis: 25¢ per person, $3 an hr.
Traffic Regulations: 30-min. parking on Main St. and 6th Ave. during business hours. No all-night parking downtown. No U-turns on Main St., Rodney St., or 6th Ave.
Street Numbering: Most streets are named, with Broadway the division between N. and S.; Main St. between E. and W. Numbered avenues on E. side; numbering begins near S. city limits, but, N. of 3rd Ave., is interrupted for several blocks by named avenues on both sides of Broadway.

Accommodations: Six hotels, five tourist camps.

Information Service: Montanans, Inc., Montana Club Bldg., 6th and Fuller Aves.; Commercial Club, Placer Hotel, Main and Grand Sts.; Montana Auto Association, 19 N. Main St.
Radio Station: KPFA (1210 kc.).
Moving Picture Houses: Three.
Swimming: Broadwater Natatorium, 3 m. W. on US 10; adm. 25¢, suits 25¢.
Ice skating, boating, swimming: T.O.K. Park on shore of Lake Hauser, 12 m. NE. on York-Nelson Rd.; swimming suits and rowboats for rent.
Golf: Country Club, 7 m. W. on US 10, 18 holes, greens fee 75¢.
Tennis: Beattie Park, 1 block W. of Great Northern Station on Neill Ave.; Hill Park, Fuller and Placer Aves.

Annual Events: State legislature convenes in January of odd years. Vigilante parade, May. National Guard encampment, June 1 to 20.

HELENA (4,124 alt., 11,803 pop.), Montana's capital, with its back against low, rounded Mount Helena and Mount Ascension, looks out over the flat and almost treeless Prickly Pear Valley, stretching away golden brown to the foothills of the Big Belt Mountains on the east and to spurs of the Rockies on the north and west. Main Street runs along the bottom of historic Last Chance Gulch, and is somewhat hemmed in; but from almost anywhere else in the city the view is far-sweeping and memorable. On a summer morning, when the sun rises over the wooded Big Belts, the yellow-brown plain, stippled with green fields and ditches, is suddenly washed with light, and the lakes along the Missouri River, a dozen miles away, glow and glisten with color.

One of the first cities in the State, Helena is a blend of old and new, with rather more of the old, as age is understood in Montana. Its busi-

STATE CAPITOL

ness streets, narrow and crooked, are adapted to the contours of mountain slopes and furrowed gulches. Many of the buildings have stood as they are for more than 50 years. In the early 1870's the population was nearly what it is today; in the 1890's, when the silver mining boom was at its height, it was larger by several thousand. The demand for new building, except to replace fire losses, has not been great. Some effects of the 1935 earthquakes—cracked and reinforced buildings—are visible, especially on the east side of the city and near the Northern Pacific station.

Many of the residents are employed by governmental agencies—Federal, State, county, and city; industrial workers are in the minority. Though Helena, as the seat of State government, with a commission government of its own, is the political center of Montana, it has a tendency to go quietly about its everyday affairs, but business picks up and the streets are thronged on Saturday afternoons when the farmers come to town. In odd years, however, the pattern is violently varied. When the legislature is in session, business booms. Lawmakers, lobbyists, and job hunters crowd the hotels. Restaurants, bars, gambling houses, and night clubs do a land-office business. Helena is "all dolled up," dazzlingly lighted, and gay. Wags try to invent new stories to tell about the legislature, and end by telling the old one about the senator who explained his unaccustomed possession of a large roll of bills by saying that someone pushed it over the transom while he slept. The expression "It came over the transom," to explain any unusual good fortune, is a part of local folklore.

As a supply center the city serves the surrounding mines, the cattle and sheep ranches to the north, the farms of the Prickly Pear Valley, and, to a lesser extent, of the Missouri Valley to the south. The industries include brick, tile, and cement pipe manufacturing. Mining operations employ about 1,000 men; dairy farms and other agricultural activities a few hundred. Labor is well organized, and union membership is growing. Except for a printers' strike that stopped publication of the two dailies for five months in 1934 there have been only minor disputes with employers; businesses are not large enough for management and labor to grow far apart.

There are few foreign-born people in Helena. The original settlers were mainly of English, Irish, Scottish, and German descent, and the pioneer families and their descendants still form more than half of the population. Many of the newer arrivals are of Scandinavian ancestry.

The Helena region was never the regular abode of any Indian tribes, though the presence of stone arrowheads and other relics found in the vicinity indicate that it was occasionally visited by Blackfeet and Salish hunting parties. Members of the Lewis and Clark Expedition were the first white men to see the place. On July 19, 1805, the day they discovered the Gates of the Mountains, Captain Clark and a scouting party reached the Little Prickly Pear, where Clark was compelled to stop and pull 17 cactus spines from his feet—reason enough for naming the creek and valley Prickly Pear. In the fall of 1862, an immigrant train on the Mullan Road halted near what was known as the Three Mile House, about 14 miles north of the present site of Helena. After some discussion and looking around, the newcomers decided to go south into the Prickly Pear Valley and build houses for the winter. Though their "settlement" was only temporary, they were the first people actually to dwell for a time on or near the site of the future city.

Helena owes its existence to the gold discoveries in Last Chance Gulch late in the summer of 1864. As word of the strike spread, the miners, between their stints of panning and sluicing, pitched tents and built hasty cabins against the slopes of the gulch. Crude business buildings began to appear. Among the boulders between the uneven lines of shacks, washed by the tailings from the sluices, was "Main Street," the trail by which bull and mule team freight outfits entered the lusty young city. Soon new streets were laid out, and as they spread away from the gulch they became straighter, more orderly.

In October 1864 it was decided that Last Chance was not a suitable name for the rapidly growing camp. A certain John Somerville dominated a meeting to decide upon a more dignified name and obtained the adoption of Helena (He-le′-na), the name of his home town in Minnesota. The miners and bullwhackers, however, did not like his way of pronouncing the name; to them "h-e-l" spelled hell, whatever Minnesotans might say. They accordingly shifted the emphasis to the first syllable, and pro-

MAIN STREET OF HELENA IN THE 1870's

nounced the name with the second *e* almost silent (Hel'-e-na). Their
pronunciation became the accepted one.

Here, as in other gold camps, the vigilantes were organized, and several
undesirables were hanged or banished. In a few cases, however, it was
charged that prejudice had been allowed to outweigh facts in the scale of
vigilante justice, and their summary methods fell into disrepute.

It was not until 1870, when Helena was the most important town in
the Territory, that a patent for its town-site was issued. Despite a bad
fire the previous year, buildings valued at nearly $2,000,000 then stood on
the site. In the 1870's its growth was accelerated by discovery of rich
deposits of placer gold in the gulches east of the Missouri; of quartz gold
to the south; of more quartz gold at Marysville to the west; and of silver
and lead at Rimini, to the southwest *(see Tour 1A)*. In the late 1870's and
the 1880's it was further stimulated by development of the rich silver and
lead deposits at Wickes, Corbin, and Elkhorn. The city was incorporated
in 1881, and was reached by the railroad two years later. In 1888, when
the East Helena smelter replaced that at Wickes, Helena was a great
mining center and was said to be the richest city per capita in the United
States, numbering among its residents some fifty millionaires.

In 1875 Helena became the capital of the Territory, though Virginia
City made a strenuous campaign to retain the honor. After 1889, Helena

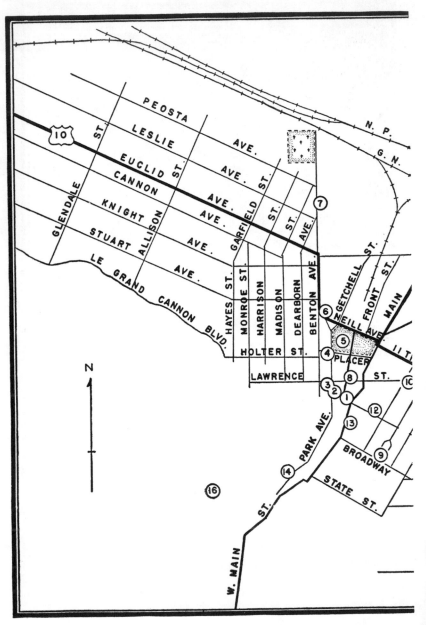

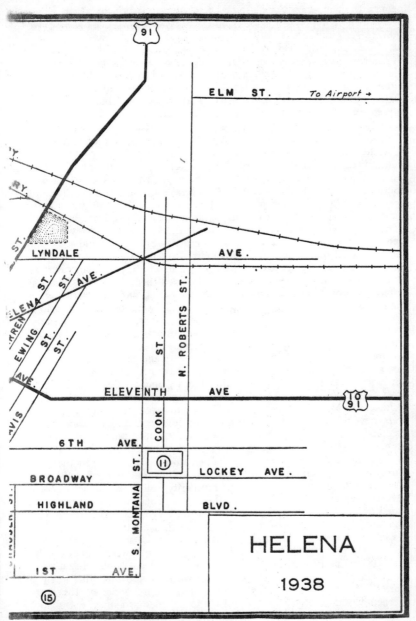

became the temporary State capital, pending an election in which almost every town of importance was a candidate. Helena won, but the first election (1892) did not satisfy Anaconda, the runner-up, and in 1894 a second election was held. Helena was backed by W. A. Clark, Anaconda by Marcus Daly *(see Tour 18)*, its founder. After a fierce campaign Helena again won, but its majority was less than 1,000. Much of the bitterness of the contest came from the intense rivalry between Clark and Daly, both engaged in developing the Butte mines, and both striving for supremacy in politics. Daly was more popular in Butte and Anaconda, but Clark had more influence in the State as a whole.

In the 1880's and early 1890's there was an orgy of display on the part of Helena's parvenus. Onetime prospectors, flush with the profits of the mines, became what they regarded as aristocratic, and not only "kept up with the Joneses" but surpassed them. Sure that the city's growth would continue indefinitely, they platted lots several miles out in the valley, and even built a streetcar line to serve these "outskirts." While waiting for the city to catch up with its transportation system, they lived in pretentious mansions on the West Side and in the suburbs of Kenwood and Lennox, first in coaches driven by top-hatted and swallow-tailed coachmen, and later in electric coupes that moved at a dog-trot on the level and stalled on the hills. A small army of maids, butlers, and other servants waited on them, and served them foods and wines as different as possible from the sour-dough, beans, and raw firewater of their prospecting days. The houses they built were ornate affairs in a variety of designs, with exteriors featuring turrets, cupolas, and porte-cocheres; interiors decorated with hand-carved mahogany, oak, and maple, with a fireplace in nearly every room; spacious grounds within stone walls or iron fences, with iron deer on the lawns and stone lions or other figures at the entrances. Some lawns were further adorned with fountains, lead statuary, granite mounting blocks, and carved stone hitching posts. The fall in the price of silver in 1893 ended this florid period of architecture. Many of the people who had invested their money in elaborate new houses departed. The spacious, high-ceilinged mansions were occupied by middle-income folk to whom adequate heating was a prime problem.

Building of the Canyon Ferry, Hauser, and Holter dams on the Missouri River between 1900 and 1910, and the gold mining activity at Marysville, brought a brief return of prosperity, since many Helena people were employed on the dams and in the mines. Then came another slump, ended by the war years 1914–1918, when the mines, especially those with lead, zinc, and copper ores, again hummed with activity.

Business waned in 1919 and for years the biennial sessions of the legislature were the principal events. In 1931 pipe lines were laid from the gas field at Cut Bank through Helena, Butte, and Anaconda. Installation of gas in Helena and East Helena gave work to 500 men for nearly a year. With this flurry over, the depression set in. Some of the more energetic residents took to the hills and gulches around the city and found placer ground rich enough to yield fair wages.

In the fall of 1935 a series of earthquakes caused four deaths and property damage estimated at $4,000,000. Within a year, however, most of the ruins were removed and damaged structures repaired or rebuilt. In some cases the buildings had to be "tied" together with long rods run through from wall to wall. The business section was outside the zone of severe early shocks, and suffered only moderate damage. Shocks of less intensity came at intervals through 1936 and 1937, but did no damage. Various theories were advanced to explain the long continuance of the quakes. According to one of them several faults underlie the district, and a slip along one fault places stress on the others, forcing them to slip in turn.

The Civil Works Administration in 1933–34 employed hundreds of Helena people, extensively repaired the capitol and the county courthouse, and landscaped a city park. In 1935 the State headquarters of the Works Progress Administration gave office employment to more than 200 people, and employed 275 on various projects in the city. Federal monetary policies, by increasing the price of gold and silver, stimulated mining, and restored it to an important place in the life of the city. In 1937 the Public Works Administration offices were closed, and WPA headquarters removed to Butte.

POINTS OF INTEREST

1. The MONTANA CLUB *(open on application)*, 6th and Fuller Avenues, stands on the site of the first gold discovery in Last Chance Gulch in 1864, an event commemorated by a bronze tablet on the Fuller Avenue side of the building. The seven-story brick and stone structure was designed by Cass Gilbert in early Italian Renaissance style. The rooms are richly furnished and decorated with mahogany woodwork and many murals and other paintings. On the membership rolls of the club, a social and recreational organization, are the names of some of the State's most distinguished citizens.

2. The FEDERAL BUILDING, Park Avenue at West end of 6th Avenue, is a four-story Romanesque structure of granite and sandstone. A wide flight of stone steps leads to the main floor. In 1932–33 the building was enlarged and remodeled, but the original lines were left unchanged.

3. HELENA PUBLIC LIBRARY *(open 9-9 weekdays; reference room only, 2-6 Sunday and holidays)*, Park Avenue and Lawrence Street, is housed in a small stone building of Tudor design, originally a church, but given to the city in 1933 by the Unitarian congregation, which also gave a fund of $20,000 for remodeling the building. The structure has some excellent woodwork, especially in the exposed walnut trusses that support the roof. The library has about 60,000 books and many newspapers and magazines. The founding association was formed in 1866.

4. ST. JAMES PRO-CATHEDRAL, Park Avenue and Placer Street, is designed in the manner of an English church of the Tudor period. It is cruciform in plan, with the nave constructed of red porphyry, the wings of dark red brick. It is the only Episcopal church in Helena.

5. HILL PARK, Neill Ave. between Park Ave. and Main St. and extending to Placer St., is cut in two by Fuller Ave. About seven acres in extent, it was given to the city in 1912 by the Great Northern Railway and was named for James J. Hill, its founder. It has walks and benches, drinking fountains, a wading pool, a rustic bandstand, and sloping lawns planted with trees and shrubs.

6. ALGERIA SHRINE TEMPLE *(open on application at Shrine offices, 4 N. Jackson St.)*, Neill Ave. at Park and Benton Aves., was built in 1920. It is of Moorish design, with a slender minaret, white barrel-vaulted roof, small grilled windows, and a mosaic entrance of black and white stone. It is in two sections connected by a series of halls; one section contains a ballroom, the other an auditorium seating 4,000. The walls are of tapestry brick, trimmed with stone. Lawns, trees, shrubs, and flower beds adorn the grounds.

7. CARROLL COLLEGE, Benton Ave. between Leslie and Peosta Sts., is the only Catholic men's college in Montana. The cornerstone was laid in 1909 by Bishop John P. Carroll, in the presence of President William H. Taft. Originally Mount St. Charles College, the institution was renamed in honor of Bishop Carroll, who was responsible for its founding and development. The main building (1911), the north wing (1918), and the south wing (1924), all built of red Montana porphyry trimmed with gray granite, appear to form a single four-story structure. It is designed in the Collegiate Gothic style. The library contains 11,000 volumes. There are well-equipped laboratories, an athletic field, and a gymnasium. The attendance averages about 270. High school, college, and pre-professional courses are offered.

The site of the college is one of the most commanding in the city; residents have come to know it as Capitol Hill, and strangers often mistake the college buildings for the capitol. The hill was offered as a capitol site in 1895, but was rejected by the capitol commission because of its price ($7,000).

ROCOCO HOUSES of the "golden era" stand vaingloriously along Dearborn Ave., which passes through a part of the West Side residential district. On either hand are choice examples of the "castles" which Helena, in the 1880's and 1890's, regarded as the last word in fine houses. Most of the original owners have long been dead, and later occupants have converted many of the old homes into apartment houses.

8. MONTANA LIFE BUILDING *(open 9-5 Mon.-Fri.; 9-1 Sat.)*, Fuller Ave. and Lawrence St., is a three-story neoclassic building of white terra cotta block tile, with a four-columned Doric portico and a frieze of floral designs.

9. LEWIS AND CLARK COUNTY COURTHOUSE (1885), Broadway between E. and W. Ewing Sts., was designed on old Norman lines by Wallingford and Stern, St. Paul architects. The walls are of gray granite, trimmed with red sandstone. The grounds, planted with grass, trees, and flowers, have the appearance of a small park. Because of earthquake damage, the tall clock tower was removed, and repairs made in 1936 otherwise altered the original roof pattern. A heavy stone coping, in par-

ALGERIA SHRINE TEMPLE

ticular, was eliminated, as being too great a hazard in the face of repeated quakes.

The OLD PLACER DIGGINGS in Dry Gulch, S. end of Davis St., are worked to some extent in spring and summer. Miners raise "pay dirt" from the old shafts to the surface by hand windlass. No water is available for sluices and they use a hand-operated "dry-washer," which screens out the coarse material and saves the fine sand that carries the gold values. When a good deal of the finer material has accumulated it is panned in the usual manner with water brought in barrels. It is said that the placer workers average about $5 a day by these crude methods.

10. ST. HELENA ROMAN CATHOLIC CATHEDRAL, Warren St. at E. Lawrence St., is modeled after the Cologne Cathedral in Germany. There are considerable variations in detail, such as the clover leaf window over the middle front doorway arch, but the purity of the Gothic design is faithfully preserved. The plans were drawn by Von Herbulis, a European architect who aided in designing the Votive Church in Vienna.

The cathedral is built of Bedford limestone in the form of a Latin cross 246 feet long and 150 feet wide. Twin spires rise 218 feet above the ground. The north, or Thomas Cruse spire, houses a set of 16 chimes operated from a keyboard. Stained glass windows made in Munich, Germany, bear representations of the patron saints of various nations, and depict scenes from the life of Christ and from church history. The nave has a seating capacity of 1,000. Marble clustered columns support the ceiling vaults which are 65 feet above the floor. The main altar and communion rail of white marble were made in Italy. A pipe organ was installed in 1914. Construction of the cathedral, costing about $1,000,000, was made possible by gifts from the late Thomas Cruse and his heirs, and by contributions from members of the parish. Financing and building were supervised by Bishop John P. Carroll, who laid the cornerstone in 1908 and consecrated the finished edifice in 1924.

11. The STATE CAPITOL *(open 9-5 Mon.-Fri.; 9-4 Sat.; custodian acts as guide)*, 6th Ave. between S. Montana and S. Roberts Sts. and extending to Lockey Ave., is built on the crown of a gently sloping hill surrounded by extensive grounds. The site, with $4,000 for landscaping, was given to the State in 1895 by promoters of the Lennox residential area.

The massive three-story structure, neoclassic in style, is built on a symmetrical plan with a wide central section, broken by central and end pavilions and impressive colonnaded wings. The building is raised on a rusticated first story and topped with a classic cornice and balustraded parapet. The dominant external feature is the lofty central dome, surfaced with copper and surmounted by a small reproduction of the Statue of Liberty. It is raised on a heavy square base embellished on each face with a pedimented central motif. Light is admitted to the rotunda beneath the dome through triple windows in the base and through a series of bull's-eye windows in the collar of the dome. The building is 464 feet long and 130 feet wide, with an average height of 90 feet. The dome rises 165 feet. The central, or original, section of the building, is 250 feet by 130 feet; it was built of sandstone, but in 1933 CWA workers faced it with Montana granite to conform with the exterior finish of the two wings.

The main entrance, set in a massive central pavilion and designed in the manner of a Roman triumphal arch adorned with four fluted Ionic columns, is approached by a long flight of marble steps. Four scrolled consoles rest upon the cornice; the whole is topped with a central pedestal, with flanking urns. The end wings, completed in 1911, have Ionic colonnades, two stories high, in harmony with the design of the original structure.

The interior of the capitol, in French Renaissance style, has flaring marble stairways, wide corridors, spacious chambers, and numerous statues and murals. The interior decorations and the murals in the senate chamber are the work of Charles A. Pedretti.

On the ground floor are the historical library and some of the State offices.

On the main or second floor are the executive offices. The Governor's reception room in the east wing, is decorated in brown, tan, and ivory; the walls are paneled in English oak; marble mantels and silver chandeliers complete the decorative appointments. The corridors on this floor, leading east and west from the central rotunda, are decorated in tones of deep green, brown, and gold with marble wainscoted walls, columns, and pilasters. The rotunda, with the dome 100 feet above the floor, is painted in shades of red, blue, and old ivory. Gold is freely used to enrich the plaster ornament. On the walls of the rotunda are four paintings depicting early pioneer characters—an Indian, a cowboy, a miner, and a trapper said to resemble Jim Bridger, explorer and teller of tall tales. In the base of the dome are 16 stained-glass windows. On the ribbed soffit of the dome are ornamental bas-reliefs.

The stairway from the main to the third floor is of white marble, with newel posts and balustrade of bronze. Above it is a stained-glass ceiling. At the head of the stairway, above a stained-glass window, is a painting of the driving of the last spike at Gold Creek, upon completion of the Northern Pacific Railway in the fall of 1883. It is the work of Amadee Joullin of San Francisco.

On the third floor, the west wing of the central section contains the offices of the two houses of the legislature and their committee rooms. The eastern half of this floor houses the supreme court chambers and offices of the justices, and the law library of Montana.

The house of representatives in the west end wing is a large rectangular chamber with a ceiling skylight. The walls are wainscoted with marble and have ornamental columns. Directly over the speaker's desk is the largest painting in the house: a picture, valued at $30,000, of Lewis and Clark meeting the Indians at Ross Hole. It is the work of Charles Russell. In the house lobby are six large historical paintings by E. S. Paxson. The first, just left of the entrance, shows Indian messengers on their way to St. Louis to obtain the "white man's book" (the Bible). The next picture, *The Border Land,* shows settlers with their wagons on one side of a stream, Indians on the other. *Lewis and Clark at Three Forks* is a large panel depicting the explorers with their Indian woman guide Sacajawea at the spot where she identified her own country. Opposite are paintings of Lewis at Black Eagle Falls, of Pierre de la Verendrye, and of the surrender of Chief Joseph.

The senate chamber in the west wing of the original section is similar to the house in design. The floor is blue-carpeted and the furnishings are of mahogany. Around the room just below the skylight is a cove twelve feet deep containing paintings. One of the two largest, directly over the president's desk, commemorates the Louisiana Purchase. Opposite is a depiction of Custer's last fight. To the left of the president's desk is a painting of the early fur traders Dawson (standing) and Chouteau (sitting), with bundles of furs and pelts heaped around them. Next to this work is another painting of Lewis, Clark, and Sacajawea. Left of the Custer picture is a panel that represents Fathers Ravalli and De Smet bringing Christianity to the Indians. The last panel is a scene in Nelson's Gulch near Helena.

In the supreme court chamber, with its green-carpeted floor and mahogany furnishings, are other paintings by Charles A. Pedretti. Above the rostrum are three of his paintings—(left to right)—an emigrant train being attacked by Indians, Lewis's first glimpse of the Rockies, and President Cleveland signing the act that admitted Montana to the Union. Other paintings to right and left of this group are *The Gates of the Mountains, The Last of the Buffalo,* and *The Buffalo Chase.* In the law library are several landscapes by Ralph de Camp.

The 12½-acre landscaped capitol grounds are set with trees and shrubs native to Montana. In front of the building is a paved plaza about 40 feet long and 35 feet wide; from Lockey Avenue a circular driveway leads to the south entrance of the building; winding walks cross the grounds. Near the west entrance is a bronze equestrian statue of General Francis Meagher, acting Territorial Governor, who was drowned near Fort Benton in 1867. The statue is the work of Charles J. Mulligan, a pupil of the sculptor Lorado Taft.

The legislature of Montana first met in a log cabin with a dirt floor, at Bannack, on December 12, 1864. Thereafter, for a time, it met in buildings that were either rented or donated. As the need for a State-owned capitol grew, a commission consisting of the Governor and four qualified electors was appointed to plan the erection of a permanent building. In 1896 one million dollars was appropriated for the State Capitol, and an open competition was held to select a design. Forty-nine firms and individual architects submitted plans, and George R. Mann of St. Louis won. Second prize was awarded to Cass Gilbert.

The cornerstone was laid July 4, 1899, under the auspices of the Grand Lodge of Masons with all the formality and solemnity of Masonic ritual. People from all parts of the State attended the ceremony. Helena was thrown wide open—fireworks were discharged, people danced in the streets, and there was a shooting scrape or two.

In 1909 the legislature voted to enlarge the capitol by adding wings. The firm of F. M. Andrews of New York was selected as architects with Link and Haire of Helena as associates. The wings were completed in 1911.

The STATE HISTORICAL LIBRARY *(open 9-5 Mon.-Fri.; 9-4 Sat.),* first floor, east wing of the capitol, is Montana's outstanding historical museum and preserves souvenirs of every phase of the State's development. There are grim mementos of vigilante activities, of several wars, and of Indian history. One cabinet holds a collection of Indian curios gathered by Peter Ronan and presented to the historical society by Senator W. A. Clark. Relics of the Custer Battle include the officers' swords, pictures of the participants, and copies of the first newspaper accounts of the disaster. The State's industries are represented by exhibits of wood, ores, metals, and refining and manufacturing processes. The natural history section has dinosaur bones and other fossil remains, mounted specimens of buffalo, deer, elk, mountain goats, bears, and native birds.

The library shelves contain several thousand volumes dealing with the history of Montana, the Northwest, and the Nation. There are complete files of all Montana newspapers, and some rare copies of Colonial pamphlets. Another rarity is a large volume of Audubon prints, of which only 25 copies were made before the plates were destroyed by fire. On the wall of the library are pictures of Montana pioneers and pioneer scenes.

12. A STONE BARN *(private)*, 320 E. 6th Ave., back of the Christian Science church, was the studio of Charles M. Russell during his winters in Helena in the 1880's and early 1890's. The artist used to drift in from the range late in the fall, and stay until there was sufficient new grass in spring to feed his horse. He also painted in a hen house nearby. In such humble quarters he did some of his best-known work. The barn is used as a dwelling.

The OLD BUSINESS DISTRICT, S. Main St. between Broadway and State St., is occupied by buildings erected in the 1870's. Log and brick structures in various states of repair line the street on both sides. Here the richest placer deposits were found. It is said that the early-day miners did not reach true bedrock at this point; the older buildings rest on unworked sands and gravels that are probably much more valuable than the buildings themselves.

13. PLACER HOTEL, W. Main and Grand Sts., is on the site of an old placer working. When the basement was excavated in 1911, the deeper sands yielded enough gold to pay the cost of the work.

14. HELENA'S OLDEST BUILDING *(open by permission)*, 208 S. Park Ave., is a low two-room log cabin. It was built in 1865 by a man named Butt, who lived there only a short time. Two large black locust trees in front of it were planted in 1870. It is in fair condition, and is occupied as a residence.

POINTS OF INTEREST IN ENVIRONS

15. MOUNT ASCENSION (5,360 alt.) is S. of the city's East Side (footpath at 1st Ave. and Chaucer St.). The trail is not steep, and this mountain is the most convenient place for a night view of Helena.

16. MOUNT HELENA (5,462 alt.), just beyond the SW. city limits, is reached by a footpath from W. Lawrence St. The ascent is steep in places, but not difficult or dangerous. The trail winds through timber along the north slope of the mountain, past a cavelike shelter. Near the summit it rises sharply. The view embraces the Continental Divide and Ten Mile Canyon to the west; the Prickly Pear and Missouri Valleys, and the Elkhorn and Big Belt Mountains to the east. For years the State fair featured a run up the mountainside that was no sport for a weakling.

UNIONVILLE, 4 miles S., is reached by either of two roads that begin at the south end of W. Main St. and wind up Grizzly and Oro Fino Gulches. The roads join before reaching Unionville. In and about the town are several old gold mines, including the Spring Hill and Whitlatch-Union, the ruins of an early stamp mill, and a modern flotation mill. Many Helena people own summer homes in the neighborhood.

Lead Smelter and Zinc Recovery Plant, *5.5 m.,* Broadwater Resort, *3.4 m.,* Fort Harrison Veterans' Hospital, *4.3 m.,* McDonald Pass on the Continental Divide, *15.9 m., Rimini, 17.1 m. (see Tour 1A).* Alhambra Hot Springs, *14.6 m.,* Gates of the Mountains, *19.4 m. (see Tour 6, Sec. b).* Marysville, *20.7 m. (see Tour 8).*

Missoula

Railroad Stations: N. end of Higgins Ave. for Northern Pacific Ry.; S. end of Higgins Ave. bridge for Milwaukee R.R.

Bus Stations: 238 W. Main St. for Intermountain Transportation and Meisinger's Stages; 118 W. Broadway for Washington Motor Coach (Greyhound); Northern Pacific Ry. station for Northern Pacific busses.

Airport: 2 m. SW. on US 93 for Northwest Airlines; taxi 50¢.

Street Busses: Fare 5¢.

Taxis: Fare 25¢ a person for first mile; then 10¢ a mile.

Traffic Regulations: No U-turns on Higgins Ave.; no all-night parking on paved downtown streets; 1 hr. parking limit downtown, 8 a.m. to 6 p.m.

Street Numbering: Streets are numbered from Higgins Ave. E. and W.; from Front St. N. and S.

Accommodations: Four hotels; 6 tourist camps.

Information Service: Chamber of Commerce, 207 E. Main St.

Radio Station: KGVO (1260 kc.).

Motion Picture Houses: Five.

Swimming: Municipal pool, Pattee and Front Sts.; free.

Tennis: University courts, Connell and John Aves.; fee 25¢ an hr. for nonmembers.

Golf: Municipal course, 18 holes, 400 South Ave. E.; greens fee 50¢.

Athletics (incl. baseball and football): Dornblaser Field, university campus; ball park, Higgins and South Aves.; Kiwanis Park, 300 E. Front St.

Annual Events: Interscholastic track and field meet, May. Western Montana fair, August. Fish and game banquet, no fixed date.

MISSOULA (3,223 alt., 14,657 pop.), stands on the level bed of a pre-historic lake, at the mouth of Hell Gate Canyon. The Sapphire Mountains extend southward; the Bitterroots, with Lolo Peak prominent among them, loom on the southwestern horizon. From the high country to the north, icy Rattlesnake Creek rushes down to empty into Clark Fork of the Columbia (locally called the Missoula River) near the city's eastern limits. The narrow entrance to Hell Gate Canyon is guarded by Mount Jumbo on the north, Mount Sentinel on the south. In the northwestern distance rises the symmetrical top of Squaw Peak, glistening white in winter, smoke-blue in summer. Clark Fork, which cuts the city in two, is shallow but swift, its current split by a series of islands. Three bridges unite the north and south parts of Missoula: the old-fashioned iron-and-plank Van Buren Street bridge near the east end of town, the Higgins Avenue bridge at the center, and the modern concrete Parkway bridge near the west end.

The city itself is neat and attractive, and gives an impression of compactness in its business district and in such residential areas as the one west of the university. South of the river the residential section merges imperceptibly with the environs of the university, where the homes of many faculty members are interspersed with fraternity and sorority houses that are distinguished from other residences only by occasional groups of loitering students. Student life in these houses, while not marked by restraint, has closer ties with the faculty than is generally the case in such institutions. The city has a tendency to straggle away with little apparent plan. One section extends far northeastward between Rattlesnake Creek and Mount Jumbo, and ends as a huddle of summer cabins in a grove of pines. Another, somewhat grimy and smoke-stained, is crowded between the Northern Pacific Railway and the base of Waterworks Hill. On its wide western edge where it meets no natural barrier, the city advances on the river flat seemingly at random.

In general, Missoula is characterized by broad avenues lined with maple and cutleaf birch, handsome residences, well-kept lawns, and gardens of great variety and richness. Because of its comparatively low altitude and its situation on the Pacific slope of the Continental Divide, Missoula has —for Montana—a mild climate and generous rainfall. Cherry and apple trees, fragrant with blossoms or rosy with fruit according to season, adorn nearly every good-sized yard in the residential sections.

In addition to being Montana's chief educational center as home of the State university, Missoula is headquarters for Region One of the U. S. Forest Service *(see FORESTS)* and a trading center for the agriculture of four fertile valleys: the Flathead, the Bitterroot, the Blackfoot, and the Missoula. Its location to a large extent determines the nature of its industries; flour milling and sugar refining are most important. A brewery, a meat packing plant, and several creameries handle large quantities of farm and ranch products. The largest sawmill in Montana is at Bonner, seven miles east of Missoula, and lumber and finished wood products are made within the city.

Missoula takes its name from the Salish Indian word *Im-i-sul-a (by the chilling waters)*. Some interpretations refer to its site as a place of bad omen, rather than to the temperature of the river, which is essentially that of any mountain stream. But if the name is one of darkness and foreboding it does not describe the city. Missoula's bright, youthful optimism, heightened by the presence of 2,000 university students, is, on the contrary, perhaps its most definite characteristic.

Long before the white man came, the site of Missoula was familiar to both Salish and Blackfeet Indians. The Salish had to pass through Hell Gate Canyon to reach the plains on their periodic buffalo hunts. At the entrance to the canyon, an ideal spot for ambush, the Blackfeet would attack them. The reputation of the place caused French-Canadian trappers to call it "Porte de l'Enfer," or "Gate of Hell."

The first white men were not molested. Capt. Meriwether Lewis and his party camped briefly at the confluence of Rattlesnake Creek and Clark Fork on July 4, 1806 *(see HISTORY)*, then proceeded safely up Hell Gate Canyon. David Thompson visited the site of Missoula in 1812, climbed Mount Jumbo, and from there mapped the surrounding country. But the first settlers in the region, the Jesuits who founded St. Mary's

Mission, 30 miles to the south, met with Indian troubles that forced them to abandon the mission for a time.

Gov. Isaac I. Stevens led his railroad survey party into the region in the fall of 1853. With him was Capt. C. P. Higgins, one of the founders of Missoula. In 1855 Stevens met the Flathead, Pend d'Oreille, and Kootenai Indians in council at a cottonwood grove nine miles west of Missoula, and concluded a reservation treaty with them.

By that time there was considerable traffic through Hell Gate Canyon, and the valley became a stopping place for pack trains. In 1860 Frank L. Worden and Captain Higgins built a log trading post four miles west of the present townsite, and called it "Hell Gate Ronde"; other cabins were built around it. In the winter of 1860–61 William Hamilton erected a small log cabin at the mouth of Rattlesnake Creek, the first building on the site of present-day Missoula. The legislature of Washington Territory established Missoula County, including in it a large part of what later became western Montana, and Hell Gate became its seat. Montana's first county election was held there in 1861.

Next year the Mullan military road approached Hell Gate, the crews working throughout the winter to complete the grades through the canyon. In the summer of 1863 hundreds followed this road from Idaho to the gold mines at Alder Gulch.

In 1865 Worden and Higgins built a sawmill and a flour mill at almost the exact present-day center of the city, and started a new store near the mills. The handful of settlers at Hell Gate Ronde moved to the new site, which was at first known as Missoula Mills.

Up to 1872 the district was served by five toll roads from Deer Lodge. The toll was 50 cents for horse and rider, $1 for a team, and 25 cents a head for cattle. That year the county bought the roads, and there was a great celebration. The following April several Sisters of the Charity of Providence opened a hospital and school in a small frame building near the site of St. Patrick's Hospital. The small chapel in the building was Missoula's first place of worship.

When the Nez Perce Indians, under Chief Joseph, went on the warpath in 1877 (see HISTORY), the people of Missoula became alarmed and asked for troops. They were not molested, but the incident led to the establishment of Fort Missoula, two and one-half miles southwest of the city.

Missoula's principal growth dates from the arrival of the Northern Pacific Railway in 1883, when it became a division point with repair shops. On March 12, 1885, it was incorporated as a city. Growth was further stimulated by the building of the Chicago, Milwaukee, St. Paul and Pacific (1908).

The State university, established in 1895, has greatly influenced the economic and cultural life of the city. The accommodation of students amounts to an industry that helps tide the community over lean years; culturally, its most immediate effect has been to make higher education available to a far greater share of the young men and women of Missoula than of other communities in the State, some of which are separated from it by a distance equal to that from New York to Quebec or Chicago to Memphis.

Missoula experienced a slow but steady growth during the first third of the twentieth century. The State university began to take a larger place in community life, the regional office of the U. S. Forest Service was installed at Missoula in 1908, there was a steady increase of civic groups common to most cities, and the city planning board was organized in 1934. Even so, Missoula emerged but slowly from its status as a frontier town. As late as the early thirties, Indians still camped on the flats around the city to dig camas roots.

In 1936 and 1937 Missoula grew rapidly, and estimates of population ranged from 18,000 to 25,000 at the end of the latter year. The largest single factor in this growth was perhaps the westward movement of thousands of people from the eastern drought areas.

MONTANA STATE UNIVERSITY

The University is at the E. end of University Ave., and consists of 19 buildings on a 100-acre campus at the base of Mount Sentinel. An additional 520-acre tract extends up steep, grassy slopes to the summit, 2,000 feet higher, a campus feature appropriate to this mountainous State. The modern buildings vary in architectural style, each showing the influence of the period when it was designed. Seen from the University Avenue approach in summer, the whole campus is dressed in vivid green; the red-brick Main Hall, standing in an open space at the head of the great area of greensward called the Oval, is the first object of a contrasting color to catch the eye. The other structures are revealed by green roofs rising among the trees.

The first step toward founding Montana State University was taken in 1881, when Congress set aside 72 square miles of public land with the provision that the income from its sale or lease be used for the support of such a school. The campus site was given to the State by Frances G. Higgins and Edward L. Bonner of Missoula.

In 1895 the University was established, with Oscar J. Craig as its first president. There was little equipment, and classes were held in temporary quarters until 1899 when the first buildings were ready for occupancy. Many buildings have been added; in 1937 the group on the campus represented an investment of $3,000,000. The schools of forestry and journalism were added about 1912 to round out the curriculum. The forestry school, in particular, has distinguished itself. Nearly all its graduates are employed by the U. S. Forest Service in Region One.

Harold Clayton Urey, who was awarded the 1934 Nobel prize in chemistry, for his discovery of heavy water, was a student and later an instructor at Montana. H. G. Merriam, whose *Frontier and Midland (see THE ARTS)* is recognized as one of the Nation's important magazines of regional literature, is professor of English and chairman of the division of the humanities. The Montana Masquers, a university dramatic group, have a distinguished record of productions. On December 16, 1921, they gave the first performance in English of Leonid Andreyev's

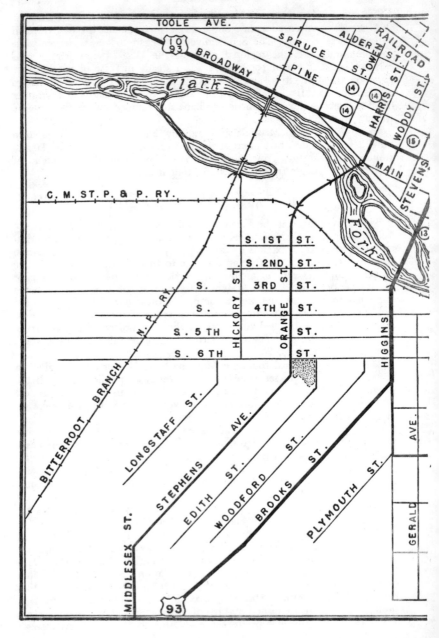

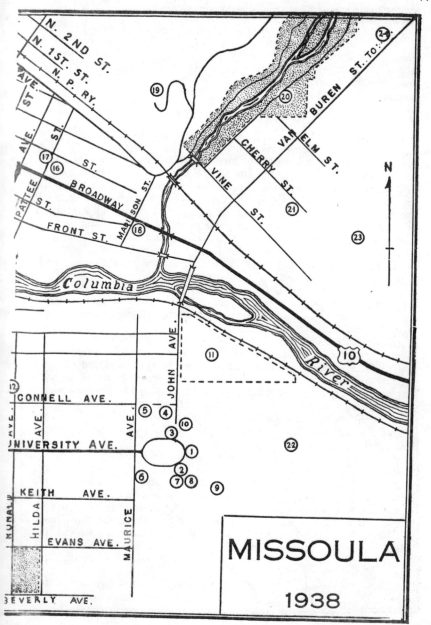

MISSOULA

1938

He Who Gets Slapped, anticipating the Theater Guild's New York opening by 24 days.

The University is co-educational. Most of the 2,000 undergraduates register in the College of Arts and Sciences, which has four major divisions: humanities, biological science, physical science, and social science. About 460 take forestry and journalism. There are also schools of business, education, law, music, pharmacy, military science, and religion, a summer school, and extension courses.

POINTS OF INTEREST

1. MAIN HALL *(open 7:45-11 weekdays; 9-6 Sun.)*, head of Oval opposite end of University Ave., one of the oldest buildings (1898) on the campus, houses the administrative offices and has classrooms and a small auditorium on the second and third floors. It is designed in a modified Romanesque style with an impressive entrance and clock tower. In the entrance hall is a topographic map of the State, 7 by 12 feet, with geological structure indicated by coloration; relief maps and an exhibit of Montana petroleum products are near it. In the basement are cases of minerals and rocks gathered by the geology department.

2. SCIENCE HALL *(open 8 a.m.-10:30 p.m. weekdays; 8-1 Sat.)*, just S. of Main Hall, was built in 1898. It is an old red brick structure with high-ceiled classrooms and small laboratories.

3. The LAW SCHOOL *(open 8 a.m.-10 p.m. Mon.-Fri.; 8-12 Sat.; 3-6 Sun.)*, N. of Oval and W. of John Ave., was built in 1908 to house the library. Its two-columned and pedimented entrance portico is designed in the classic tradition.

4. The LIBRARY *(open 8-12 and 1-5 Mon.-Fri.; also 7-9:30 Mon.-Thurs.; 9-12 and 2-5 Sat.; 2:30-5:30 Sun.)*, back of Law School at N. end of Hello Walk, is a three-story structure of reinforced concrete and tapestry brick erected in 1921. It is the largest library in the State, with 125,000 books and 35,000 pamphlets. Stacks, protected by fireproof walls, extend through all three floors on the north side of the building. The Treasure Room on the third floor has an extensive collection of source material on the Northwest. Paxson's painting *Sacajawea* and a western scene by Irvin Shope hang on its walls.

5. The modern STUDENT UNION BUILDING *(hours vary; visitors welcome)*, SE. corner Maurice and Connell Aves., is the students' social center. Built in 1935, it is highly functional in design, with long simple lines and sparing use of ornamentation. A bookstore and a restaurant occupy the first floor; offices of student organizations and athletic board, the second floor; a lounge extends the entire length of the third floor; a large ballroom, the Gold Room, and two smaller ones, the Copper and Silver Rooms, are on the fourth floor. The auditorium (seating 1,500) and the stage occupy the entire north side of the building up to the Gold Room level.

6. The low, square ART MUSEUM *(open 1-5 weekdays except during meetings in auditorium)*, S. of Oval on Maurice Ave., was dedicated in 1937. It is the first art museum in Idaho, Montana, Wyoming, or the

Dakotas—an area once described by a magazine as "from the standpoint of art a cultural air pocket . . . with a nostalgia for national prominence in the arts. . . ." Handicapped by lack of funds, the museum was obliged to begin its art collection with a group of 47 collotype facsimiles stressing artistic quality rather than "price tag aesthetics." The facsimilies, carefully chosen for their faithfulness to the originals, included copies of works by such masters as Monet, Rembrandt, Van Gogh, Degas, Gauguin, Kent, Cézanne, and others. A set of lantern slides is used chiefly by study groups to illustrate architecture, painting, and sculpture.

7. The JOURNALISM BUILDING *(open 8 a.m.-10:15 p.m. Mon.-Fri.; 8-6 Sat.)*, directly S. of Science Hall, is a simple three-story brick structure built in 1936, which houses the school of journalism and the publishing plant of the student newspaper, the *Montana Kaimin.* The entrance is distinguished by five sandblasted glass panels depicting the history of printing.

In this school instruction and practical experience are carried on together. The publishing plant is similar to that of a commercial newspaper; students help to operate a university news service for the Montana Press Association, and the association has an advisory board for the school.

8. The FORESTRY BUILDING *(open 8-10 Mon.-Fri.; 8-6 Sat.)*, directly S. of Main Hall, was erected in 1921. The walls of tapestry brick are ornamented with pine trees and other figures in terra cotta, which form a decorative band encircling the building between the second and third floors.

The school has its own nursery and its own 2,000-acre laboratory forest. Large forests and lumbering operations within a few miles of the campus provide opportunities for study of timber stands and conditions prevalent in northwestern forests. Regional headquarters of the U. S. Forest Service cooperates with the school. Practice in the field supplements instruction, and insures a working grasp of forest care and wild-life management. Enrollment is limited, and only students who show marked ability are permitted to take the full course.

9. The GYMNASIUM *(open 7:30-6 weekdays)*, SE. of the Forestry Bldg., S. end of Dornblaser Field, is a spacious building designed (1921) in the modern style. Its facilities include a swimming pool *(open to men 8-6 Mon., Wed., Fri.; to women 8-6 Tues., Thurs.)* and an indoor running track. Over the entrance is a copy in bronze of the *Discobolus* of Myron.

10. The NATURAL SCIENCE BUILDING *(open 8-11 Mon.-Fri.; 8-6 Sat.; 9-6 Sun.)*, John Ave., N. of Oval, erected in 1918, is of functional design. Edgar S. Paxson's canvas, *Custer's Last Stand,* measuring 6 by 9 feet, hangs (R) just inside the entrance. The BIOLOGICAL MUSEUM *(open whenever a staff member is in the building, usually 8-6)*, on the second floor, contains an extensive collection of Montana plants, animals, and insects.

11. The FORESTRY SCHOOL NURSERY, entrance at John Ave. and S. 6th St. E., can grow as many as 1,000,000 trees a year. At its south end are breeding pens for pheasants.

OTHER POINTS OF INTEREST

12. The BONNER HOUSE *(private)*, 910 Gerald Ave., is a notable example of the Victorian gingerbread style of architecture. Well preserved and set in spacious grounds shaded by tall trees, it is designed with a round tower at one corner, and elaborately decorated with every style of ornament known to the builder of that period.

13. The SITE OF THE FIRST MILL AND FIRST STORE, below N. end of Higgins Ave. bridge, is occupied by a power plant. The flour mill was a two-story frame building on a stone foundation. Power was supplied by an overshot wheel driven by water brought in a wooden flume from Rattlesnake Creek.

14. The ROMAN CATHOLIC GROUP, on both sides of W. Pine St. between Harris and McCormick Sts., consists of a half-dozen institutions. St. Francis Xavier Church (1891) is designed in a modified Romanesque style, with elaborate paintings and mural decorations by Joseph Carignano, S. J. The Sacred Heart Academy (1873), Loyola High School (1907), and St. Francis Xavier Parochial School (1927) have several hundred students enrolled. The latter has a large modern gymnasium and auditorium. St. Patrick's (1873), western Montana's best equipped hospital, originally shared a small building with the academy. The unused St. Michael's Mission (1863) was originally at Hell Gate Ronde as the first church for white men in western Montana; it was later moved to its present situation.

15. MISSOULA COUNTY COURTHOUSE (1908), W. Broadway between Woody and Stevens Sts., and extending to W. Pine St., is a three-story structure of light gray terra cotta surmounted by a clock tower. Eight murals by Paxson hang above the stairs just inside the Broadway entrance. The panels depict a Montana roundup, an Indian buffalo hunt, early methods of transportation, and events in Montana history.

On the tree-shaded grounds are a concrete bandstand used for concerts by the municipal band, a World War memorial (1921) in bronze, depicting a doughboy, and the gray stone county jail built in 1886.

16. The FEDERAL BUILDING, NE. corner of Broadway and Pattee St., is a three-story structure of classic design. The east wing and the spacious addition in the rear are occupied by the U. S. Forest Service.

17. The PUBLIC LIBRARY *(open 10-9 weekdays during school year; 9-6 July–Aug.)*, SW. corner of E. Pine and Pattee Sts., contains 50,000 volumes. The Ryman collection of more than 300 volumes emphasizes Northwest history and Montana subjects. There is a special Montana collection of 300 volumes. A painting of Chief Charlot of the Flathead Indians, by Edgar S. Paxson, hangs in the reading room on the second floor. In the basement is the CHILDREN'S DEPARTMENT *(open 12-6 Mon.-Fri.; 10-6 Sat.)*.

The two-story building is of reddish brown brick and gray stucco with white-trimmed windows. Wide concrete steps lead up to the entrance, between brick piers and concrete columns supporting a pediment.

18. The RANKIN HOUSE *(private)*, 134 Madison St., the former

GREENOUGH PARK

home of Jeannette Rankin, first woman member of Congress, is one of the oddities of Missoula. The building is a simple two-story boxlike brick structure, but the cupola of wood and glass is roofed like a Burmese temple. It was built in the 1880's.

19. WATERWORKS HILL, N. of Northern Pacific Ry. tracks, is reached by a dirt road L. from oil paved Madison St. From this point there is an excellent view of the city.

20. GREENOUGH PARK, entrance at Vine and Madison Sts., extends along Rattlesnake Creek at the foot of Waterworks Hill. It was given to the city by Mrs. Tennessee L. Greenough, whose gingerbread period house, with its spacious grounds, is opposite the park entrance. Most of the 17-acre park is heavily wooded. Tables for picnic parties are provided in cleared spaces, but in the main the wild natural beauty has not been disturbed. A one-way road circles the park ravine, and there are numerous foot trails and bridges.

21. The SITE OF THE CHINESE CEMETERY, SE. end of Cherry St. between Harrison and Fillmore Sts., has known few Chinamen, dead or alive, for a generation. In 1865 many Chinese came in from the Cedar Creek placer diggings, but left after four of their number were killed by white laborers in 1892. The cemetery was used only temporarily, the bones of the dead being exhumed after 12 years and shipped to China, in accordance with custom. A newspaper item (1891) tells of a funeral in which 500 Chinese took part while most of the white population

watched. Mourners were so adorned with festival draperies that they frightened horses; band music mingled with the beating of drums. The dead man's personal effects were burned, to prevent wrangling by the heirs. There was plenty of food and drink, and what remained after the burial was devoured by hungry Indians.

In October 1937 WPA workmen engaged in leveling Cherry Street found a silver-handled casket containing a silk kimono, trousers, and a pair of shoes. A burial brick inscribed in Chinese explained that "Lee Foo Lim is buried here."

POINTS OF INTEREST IN ENVIRONS

22. MOUNT SENTINEL, reached by trail from the university campus, is a strenuous but short climb, and the view from the top embraces the whole sweep of the mountain-rimmed Missoula Valley and extends far down the Bitterroot. On the north is a steep drop into Hell Gate Canyon; on the east are gentle forested slopes.

23. MOUNT JUMBO, reached from Vine St. or Cherry St., is somewhat easier to climb than Sentinel. The view is excellent. A single pine stands guard about halfway up the grassy western slope.

24. MONTANA POWER PARK, 3 miles N. on the Rattlesnake Rd., a continuation of Van Buren St., is in a shady grove, with piped running water, stoves for outdoor cooking, tables and benches, volley ball courts, and a baseball field.

West end of Hell Gate Canyon, *1 m.* Sugar Refinery, *1.7 m.,* Hell Gate Store, *4.4 m.,* Council Grove, *9 m.,* Frenchtown, *16.3 m. (see Tour 1, Sec. d);* Fort Missoula, *2.5 m.,* Flathead Indian Reservation, *42 m.* Stevensville *29.5 m. (see Tour 7);* Bonner Sawmill, *7.8 m. (see Tour 8);* National Bison Range Headquarters, *47.3 m. (see Tour 12).*

PART III
Tours

Tour 1

(Beach, N. D.)—Wibaux—Glendive—Miles City—Billings—Bozeman—
Three Forks—Butte—Garrison—Missoula—Saltese—(Wallace, Idaho);
US 10 and US 10 S.
North Dakota Line to Idaho Line, 741.8 m.

Intermountain Transportation Company and Northland Greyhound Bus Lines pro-
vide transportation throughout; route paralleled by Northern Pacific Ry. between
Glendive and Missoula; by the Chicago, Milwaukee, St. Paul & Pacific R.R. between
Three Forks and the Idaho Line; and throughout by planes of Northwest Airlines.
Hotels in cities; tourist cabins and campgrounds at short intervals.
Roadbed oil-surfaced throughout. In the mountains, snow and ice sometimes create
hazards in winter, but road is kept open.

Section a. NORTH DAKOTA LINE *to* BILLINGS, 271 *m.,* US 10.

This section of US 10 traverses the "boots and saddle" country of eastern Montana, once a limitless sweep of grassland and sagebrush, now
largely broken up into fenced rectangles of field and pasture. The Yellowstone River, paralleling the highway and providing water for irrigation,
has determined the character of development here: a large part of the
land is now farmed and the towns along the main highway are largely
farmers' trade centers; out on the side roads, however, are communities
rich in the atmosphere of the old cattle country. Here the cowpuncher
lingers; the man who cannot travel fifty miles in the saddle without discomfort is felt to have missed the most important part of a citizen's
education.

The landscape varies greatly. For long distances there is only rolling
plain—the rugged sort of country that passes for level land in Montana.
At other places the road runs for miles under high banks that shut off
the view to one side or the other, then rapidly rises to a bench, with
buttes and eroded cliffs between itself and the river, while in the farthest
distance loom hills that are unmistakably hills even by western standards.
In spring most of the hillsides are green; later they vary from sober gray,
through yellows and browns, to deep red. Many of them are marked with
black bands, exposed veins of lignite, from a few inches to many feet
in thickness. In some places, the roadbed itself is partly coal.

The first known white party to travel along the Yellowstone was that
led by Lt. William Clark in 1806 *(see HISTORY).*

US 10 crosses the North Dakota Line, 0 *m.,* 2 miles west of Beach,
N. D.

WIBAUX (pronounced Weebo), 11 *m.* (2,634 alt., 619 pop.), the
seat of Wibaux County, is in a deep coulee (valley) on the banks of
Beaver Creek. This otherwise leisurely stream in spring becomes a flood.

Several times its waters have partly submerged the town. The atmosphere of the town is reminiscent of the days when bawling cattle and hard-riding cowboys raised clouds of dust in its narrow streets.

The stories of "shooting-up-the-town" that persist in many western places have real foundation here. Cowhands in from the range for a spree often amused themselves and disturbed the peace of less high-spirited citizens by reckless exhibitions of skill with firearms. It is said that a Wibaux storekeeper once built an excellent sidewalk in front of his store by driving into the ground the empty cartridge-shells he picked up where the boys "broke their guns."

Both town and county were named for Pierre Wibaux, who settled here in 1883. His humor and sagacity are remembered in local legend. According to one tale, a Chicago packing plant once contracted with him for a fall shipment of cattle at a specified price. By roundup time the price had dropped, and the company refused to live up to its agreement.

Certain that the contract was binding, Wibaux shipped his cattle to Chicago, sold to other buyers at the prevailing market price, and sent the packer a bill for the deficit. Payment was refused. Wibaux brought suit, and took a coachload of cowboys to Chicago to appear as his witnesses. "Have a good time, boys," he said. "Spend as much as you like. That company will pay for your entertainment." The boys needed no urging. They painted Chicago a rich cattle country red. Wibaux won the suit and the packing company was compelled to pay a large bill for "expense of plaintiff's witnesses."

The blizzards of 1886–87 wiped out Pierre Wibaux's herds but he found new backing in France, and lived to see the day when he owned 75,000 head.

Ranchers far distant from the railroad used Wibaux for a shipping point. Theodore Roosevelt drove his stock here from Medora, N. D., because of the town's large loading pens. In a single year, 1,500,000 head of sheep were shipped from here.

1. Left from Wibaux on State 7 to the BRUGHARD PLACE, 20 *m.*, landscaped in the manner of an English country estate. Formerly known as Edgehill Ranch, it was the show place of the region.

2. Right from Wibaux on Beaver Creek Road, a dirt road, to the old PIERRE WIBAUX RANCH, 13 *m.*

3. Left from Wibaux on a saddle trail to ANVIL BUTTES, 11 *m.*, in badlands. The coloring of the buttes is most unusual at dawn and in the early evening. *(Guides and horses arranged for at office of the County Superintendent of Schools.)*

GLENDIVE, 38.6 *m.* (2,071 alt., 4,629 pop.), seat of Dawson County, was named for nearby Glendive Creek (a corruption of Glendale), the name given it by Sir St. George Gore *(see HISTORY)*. Formerly the metropolis of a cattle empire, Glendive is now the trading and shipping center of an area that produces sugar beets, grain, and forage crops. The shops and division offices of the Northern Pacific Ry. provide an industrial pay roll. Lignite coal from nearby mines and natural gas piped from wells in the Cedar Creek anticline (arch of stratified rock) 20 miles south, supply the town's fuel.

RETURNING FROM THE FIELD

There is a free municipal swimming pool on Prospect Heights, N. Meade Ave.

LARIMER'S AGATE SHOP *(open weekdays 8-6)*, 225 N. Merrill Ave., contains an exhibit of moss agates, fossils, and Indian artifacts. THE DELL LEWIS COLLECTION *(open weekdays 9-5)*, 308 River Ave., displays many pieces of Indian pottery, utensils of unknown age, and arrowheads showing skilled craftsmanship.

HUNGRY JOE (L), a massive butte, was named for an old prospector who once lived on or near it. Its summit, accessible by an easy hike over an old road, provides a view across the weird and bright-colored distortions of the badlands to the south.

US 10 turns R. on Bell St. and crosses the YELLOWSTONE RIVER, 38.8 *m.*

At 39.5 *m.* is the junction with State 14 *(see Tour 9)*.

At 40.3 *m.* is the junction with State 18 *(see Tour 9)*.

Between Glendive and Fallon, US 10 runs through range land and wheat country. Here in the early 1880's occurred the last great buffalo hunt. Robe hunters brought in as many as one million hides in a season. The slaughter was carried on in winter by hunters, who spent their summers cutting wood for river steamers.

BADLANDS BUTTE (L) rises prominently beyond the Yellowstone, with the white sandstone bulk of EAGLE BUTTE behind it.

FALLON, 69.7 *m.* (2,251 alt., 200 pop.), was named for Benjamin O'Fallon, Indian agent and army officer, nephew of William Clark, the explorer. His report of the slaughter of 29 members of the Jones-Imenell party of the Missouri Fur Company by 400 Blackfeet, in May 1823, presents one of the most vivid pictures of Indian warfare in the West.

About 1900 grain raising became important in this area, gradually increasing until the late 1920's, when mechanized farming was at its peak. Some farmers planted 1,200 acres of wheat yearly. Diversified farming replaced specialized grain production in the early 1930's.

Buffalo grass, which once nourished millions of bison, is the natural vegetation of the region. Its destruction began when cattle and sheep replaced the buffalo, and was completed when the rich topsoil, no longer held by fibrous, slow-spreading roots, blew away during the drought years.

TERRY, 79.5 *m.* (2,250 alt., 779 pop.), seat of Prairie County, was named for Gen. Alfred H. Terry, who commanded an expedition against the Sioux and Cheyenne in the campaign of 1876.

Terry is the home of Berny Kempton, a former bronco buster and rodeo champion, who entertained Europeans with his roughriding, and astonished Australians by lassoing kangaroos. The rowdy vigor of the West is manifest here in the banter of cowpuncher, townsman, and farmhand, as they meet on the streets or congregate in the poolrooms and drinking places.

For a dozen miles the highway crosses a dry upland, parched by repeated years of drought. Only the scavenger magpie is at home in this waste.

POWDER RIVER, 86.6 *m.,* a tributary of the Yellowstone, named the Redstone by Clark in 1805, acquired its present name because the fine black sand along its banks resembles gunpowder. Generals Terry and Custer camped at this crossing June 10, 1876, during their ill-fated campaign against the Sioux and Cheyenne. Powder River is well known in cattle country fiction, and during the World War was the battle cry of the Ninety-first Division.

At 92.3 *m.* the road leaves the upland, and winds through the breaks of the Yellowstone Valley. Many of the trees along the coulee bottoms are twined about with a luxuriant growth of clematis, which, when in seed, gives a sheen resembling hoarfrost to the thick-set boughs. Sage hens, Chinese pheasants, and other game birds nest along the grassy banks of the river.

LEON PARK, 116.8 *m.* (R), has a free campground and swimming pool, a nine-hole golf course *(fee 35¢),* and a boat course *(boats 25¢ an hr.).*

At 117.3 *m.* is the junction with US 12 *(see Tour 17).*

The HORSE ABATTOIR, 117.8 *m.* (R), was established to make profitable use of the thousands of horses that cluttered the range after farm mechanization and other causes had reduced the market for horses. It was fully equipped with modern slaughterhouse machinery. Horses were driven in from large corrals, shot, skinned, boned, and converted into a kind of inspired corned beef, much of which was shipped to Belgium.

MARKET DAY

When, thanks to this demand, the local price of horses soared, the plant was closed. The FERA established a tannery here. Hides and pelts tanned here were displayed by the Department of Agriculture as examples of fine work. When a cry went up against Government competition with private industry, tanning was abandoned and the plant became a repair shop, despite an offer from the tannery workers, backed by the Farmers' Union, to run it as a cooperative enterprise.

MILES CITY, 118.8 *m.* (2,364 alt., 7,175 pop.), named in honor of Gen. Nelson A. Miles, commander of the Fifth U. S. Infantry at Fort Keogh for several eventful years, is the seat of Custer County.

Much of Custer County is still devoted to grazing. Although fences have reduced the range and brought changes in the operation of large cow outfits, the ten-gallon hats and high-heeled boots of puncher tradition are often seen on Miles City streets. The town, whose name was once synonymous with the "wild and woolly," has lost much of its old "toughness." Many of the riders and wearers of spurs are mounted farmhands who hope to be mistaken for the punchers they admire. But the town nevertheless retains something of the color of the days when a long Texas cattle trail ended here. A rodeo is held every year, usually on or near July 4th. A cow-country flavor is noticeable also in the Eastern Montana Fair, held in September.

In the old rough days, the south side of Main St. was a solid block of saloons, gambling dens, and brothels, while the "decent" element (composed of buffalo buyers, bankers, and pawnshop keepers) lived on the north side. On one occasion, it is said, a member of the respectable group hit a gambler on the head with a singletree, and killed him. To save the good man embarrassment, his friends hastily hanged the dead man as a dangerous character.

The town, once part of the hunting and camping grounds of the Crow, is visited occasionally by Cheyenne from the Tongue River Reservation.

The city is a livestock market, and has a packing plant, as well as one distinctive cow-country business—the manufacture of saddles.

The first settlement, Milestown, sprang up on the eastern boundary of Fort Keogh Military Reservation (see HISTORY), south of the Yellowstone, but was abandoned when the Government gave up that part of the reservation east of Tongue River. The present community is on the level bottom land at the confluence of the Tongue and Yellowstone Rivers.

General Miles arrived at the mouth of Tongue River in August 1876, with instructions to reduce the possibility of war by compelling the Sioux and Cheyenne to return to their reservations. He established a cantonment, which the troops occupied during the winter, and arranged for the building of Fort Keogh at the mouth of Tongue River in the spring. Miles encountered Sitting Bull north of Terry in October 1876, and defeated him in a running battle at Cedar Creek. Early in January he defeated Crazy Horse near the present site of Birney. In May he defeated Lame Deer, and in the fall of 1877 he caught Chief Joseph near Chinook (see Tour 2, Sec. a).

In the days of steam boating on the Missouri, this town was a river port that received much freight, chiefly during the June rise of the Yellowstone.

SADDLERIES (open to public), 423 Main St. and 506-508 Main St., sell their wares throughout the world. Together they employ from 12 to 18 expert craftsmen, who make everything from the ordinary saddle sold by catalog advertising up to the $5,000 silver- and gold-mounted "work of art" ordered by some cinema cowboy. They also make bags, pocketbooks, and other leather articles.

PHOTOGRAPHS BY L. A. HUFFMAN, who came to Fort Keogh in 1877, are displayed in the lobby of the Olive Hotel, in the Miles City Club and other public places. The pictures show Indian friends of the photographer, roundup and frontier dance-hall scenes, and wild and domestic animals. Huffman made his first pictures with a home-made camera and developed them by a process of his own.

The D. F. BARRY COLLECTION OF PHOTOGRAPHS, also of interest, is on view in a room at the plant of the Miles City Star. Hailed by Charles M. Russell as a master photographer, Barry posed few of his subjects, who were ordinary people doing everyday things. The Star plant also has The First Newspaper, a painting by Russell depicting an Indian reading hieroglyphics that another is weaving into a blanket.

RIVERSIDE PARK, at the western city limits (R), has a swimming pool *(free for those who bring their own suits)*.

Miles City is at the junction with State 22 *(see Tour 10)*.

FORT KEOGH, 120.8 *m.* (R), was built in 1877 as a base for troops engaged in subjugating Indians who rebelled against the white man's wanton destruction of their food supply. Gen. Nelson A. Miles commanded it up to 1880, when all the buffalo and a great many of the Indians had died. But it remained an army post until 1900, and then became a remount station where horses were trained for the U. S. Army. Later the fort and military reservation was converted into a livestock experiment station. Here studies are being made of range conditions in an effort to make grass grow as it did in the days of the bison.

Seven of the log buildings of the original fort stand but they have been rebuilt, and siding has been nailed over the logs. The old parade ground is covered with weeds.

SIGNAL BUTTE (L) was used by officers at Fort Keogh for relaying messages by heliograph to the Black Hills, 175 miles southeast.

HATHAWAY, 140 *m.* (2,451 alt., 50 pop.), has a post office and gasoline station.

ROSEBUD, 152.5 *m.* (2,501 alt., 250 pop.), was named for the wild roses that blossom profusely in the meadows around it.

At 157.9 *m.* is the junction with State 45.

Left on this graveled road along Rosebud Creek to a junction with State 8, 53 *m.;* L. on State 8, 4 *m.* to LAME DEER (3,700 alt., 69 pop.), the agency of the Tongue River Indian Reservation (442,840 acres; established 1884), the home of 1,561 Northern Cheyenne. A few of the old braves who fought in the Indian wars of the 1870's remain.

The reservation lies between the Crow reservation and Tongue River. Most of it is rolling grassland, but there are some forests. Tribal lands total 209,720 acres. Some property, individually owned, is leased to white farmers. Agricultural advisers and a livestock association help the Cheyenne to obtain a fair income from their land and stock. Part of the land is irrigated.

The Cheyenne still use tepees occasionally in summer, but have adopted the easily prepared canned food of the white man. A school at Busby not only gives courses in modern cooking, but also produces beef, vegetables, and milk to feed its pupils. There are Roman Catholic and Mennonite congregations among the Indians, and a "peyote" cult of unknown strength *(see Tour 3, sec. b)*.

The Cheyenne were in general too nomadic to do much craftwork, but their bead-work is excellent. In the office of the county superintendent of schools at Forsyth are some fine examples of this work, with the beads strung on finely drawn sinews through punched holes.

The Cheyenne call themselves Tsis-tsis-tas *(similarly bred)*. "Cheyenne" is from the Sioux Shahiela or Shahiena, though sometimes said to be derived from the French chien (dog). The Dog Soldiers are a Cheyenne society.

White men first met the tribe in the Dakotas, but had no trouble with them until the northern (Montana) group split off. The first fight (1857) grew out of an argument over horses. A series of clashes followed; the Indians steadfastly refused to go on a reservation.

On March 17, 1876, Colonel Reynolds with about 500 men routed them on Powder River. On June 17 Sioux and Cheyenne forces held back General Crook on the Rosebud, near the present reservation, and eight days later they wiped out Custer. But the power of the whites was too great for them. By the end of October 3,000 Indians were taken; many others fled to Canada. After one more fight the Cheyenne surrendered. One thousand were taken (1877) to a reservation in Indian

Territory. A year of malaria and ill-treatment sent some back toward Montana, burning, killing, and stealing. They fought three battles against heavy odds, with a loss of but 15. Captured in October 1878, they were taken to Fort Robinson, Neb., only to make an attempt at escape in which many were killed. In the end they won their right to live in Montana. As it was evident they preferred death to returning south, they were given this reservation in 1884.

Before it split, the tribe was governed by a council of 44 chiefs. The four oldest members among them could delegate authority to a single chief. At present the council deals only with intra-tribal affairs; a superintendent enforces Federal rules. The O-mis-sis, largest and most important of the tribe's ten divisions, includes most of the Northern Cheyenne.

"Medicine" is at once a symbol and an invocation of what white men call luck. Places, things, or actions that have brought misfortune are "bad medicine." Tribes have a big medicine, families and individuals lesser ones.

The sacred cap is big medicine that honors the buffalo, once the chief source of food. The cap is made of the skin of a buffalo cow. Attached to it are two carved and painted horns. The keeper of the cap, like the medicine arrow keeper, is one of the most important men in the tribe.

A Cheyenne myth says that the Great Medicine (Creator) made three kinds of people: men covered with hair; white men with hair on their heads, faces, and legs; red men with long hair on their heads only. The hairy men were strong, the white men cunning, the red men swift. Long ago the hairy men left their home in the north, and the red men followed. The hairy ones disappeared, and when the red men returned the white men were gone. Included in the story are descriptions of great floods, earthquakes, volcanic eruptions, and climatic changes—in effect a history of North American geology in legendary form.

FORSYTH, 164 m. (2,515 alt., 1,591 pop.), the seat of Rosebud County, was named for Gen. James W. Forsyth, who landed here from a river steamer before there was a town and later wrote *A Report of an Expedition up the Yellowstone River in 1875.* Indians from the Tongue River reservation come here to trade and visit.

At 170.5 m. is the junction with an improved road.

Left on this road is COLSTRIP, 36 m. (2,540 alt., 160 pop.). The coal-mining operations here are very impressive. A 30-foot vein of lignite lies only a few feet underground. A gigantic dragline scrapes the overburden, then a steam shovel takes up the coal at the rate of five to seven tons at each "bite." The machinery is electrically operated, and all the coal is dumped directly into railroad cars as it comes from the vein. If this work were done by ordinary coal-mining methods, an army of men would be employed. Colstrip supplies much of the coal used for operation of Northern Pacific locomotives.

SANDERS, 185.1 m. (2,678 alt., 50 pop.), consists chiefly of stock-loading pens on the wide flat along the Yellowstone.

HYSHAM, 191.5 m. (2,667 alt., 258 pop.), seat of Treasure County, was named for Charles Hysham, owner of the Flying E brand, whose cattle range extended more than 70 miles across the county.

Large fossil beds lie on both sides of the river here. Moss agates found in the vicinity are for sale in the town.

US 10 now winds through lonely badlands. Under an uncompromising sun the sides of the buttes are mottled with brown, buff, and gray. After sundown, as twilight shades into dusk, the masses of guttered rock take on eerie tones of purple and black. Only the bark and scurry of prairie dogs by day, and the dismal howl of coyotes by night, indicate the presence of living things.

BIG HORN, 208.1 m. (2,712 alt., 50 pop.), is on ground occupied

almost continuously by white men since Lt. William Clark camped here
on July 26, 1806. Manuel Lisa built a trading post here in 1807. In 1822
Col. W. H. Ashley built another post, Fort Van Buren, two miles below
the mouth of the Big Horn River *(see HISTORY)*. Many who followed
the old trails or wore new ones to the "Shining Mountains," stopped to
rest at this settlement, which remained small but contributed much to the
comfort of travelers and adventurers who came by waterway and trail.

General Gibbon with 450 men crossed the Yellowstone at this point in
June 1876, as he hurried south to aid General Custer in a battle that had
already been lost.

The BIG HORN RIVER, 209.5 *m.*, a tributary of the Yellowstone,
rises in the Big Horn Mountains of Wyoming. Both the river and the
mountains were named for the bighorn or Rocky Mountain sheep.

CUSTER, 214.4 *m.* (2,749 alt., 150 pop.), was named for Gen. George
A. Custer, killed in the Battle of the Little Big Horn *(see Tour 3)*.

Junction, a former village on the left bank of the Yellowstone, was
washed away by the river. It was a freighting station for the Crow Indian
Reservation. Earlier, it had been a campground for those traveling to and
from Fort Custer at the mouth of the Little Horn.

Several years ago the skeleton of a Triceratops, a giant dinosaur, was
found in the Lance formation that forms the bluff on the left riverbank.

The D R RANCH, 226.2 *m.* (R), is a typical modern "spread" (cattle
ranch).

POMPEY'S PILLAR, 238.7 *m.* (2,849 alt., 130 pop.), a valley village, was named for the nearby natural monument.

POMPEY'S PILLAR, 241.2 *m.* (R), is an isolated rock 200 feet high on
the south bank of the Yellowstone River. Clark climbed it, July 25, 1806,
and carved his name on it. He named the rock in honor of little Pomp,
son of Charbonneau and Sacajawea, chief guides and interpreters of the
Lewis and Clark expedition. It had long been used by the Indians as a
lookout and as a point from which to send up smoke signals.

WORDEN, 247 *m.* (2,971 alt., 250 pop.), is a shipping point for
sugar beets, Great Northern beans, seed peas, and vegetables.

Between Worden and Huntley on both sides of the highway are productive farms watered by the HUNTLEY IRRIGATION PROJECT *(see AGRI-
CULTURE)*. Crops yielding more than $100 net profit an acre have been
harvested year after year. The project has been a material factor in the
expansion of the sugar-beet industry.

HUNTLEY, 255.6 *m.* (3,038 alt., 150 pop.), is the administrative
center for the Huntley Irrigation Project.

US 10 crosses the Yellowstone; the BIG HORN MOUNTAINS are
visible (L); southwest are the BEARTOOTHS.

At 266.1 *m.* is the junction (R) with US 87 *(see Tour 3)*. Between
this point and 270.5 *m.* US 10 and US 87 are one route.

Vertical SACRIFICE CLIFF *(see BILLINGS)*, 269.3 *m.* (L), rises 200
feet above the river. Back of Sacrifice Cliff is SIGNAL POINT, where Indians built their signal fires.

At 270.5 *m.* is the junction (L) with US 87 *(see Tour 3)*.

BILLINGS, 271 m. (3,117 alt., 16,380 pop.) *(see BILLINGS)*.

Points of Interest: Normal School, Polytechnic Institute, Orthopedic Hospital-School, Parmly Billings Memorial Library, Sugar Refinery, and others.

Billings is at the junction (L) with US 87 *(see Tour 3)*.

Section b. BILLINGS *to junction* with US 10 N and US 10 S,
178 m., US 10.

Between Billings and Livingston US 10 follows the tortuous course of Yellowstone River between mountain ranges. A large part of the valley is irrigated. The road swings northwest through some of the highest and most rugged of the northern Rockies.

West of BILLINGS, 0 *m.,* at 10 *m.* is the junction with an unimproved road.

Right on this road to BASELINE SCHOOL, 5 *m.;* L. over a very narrow dirt road that rises sharply *(dangerous R.R. crossing at 7 m.)* to an abandoned schoolhouse, 11 *m.,* at the base of an unnamed timbered butte; L. across Canyon Creek on a narrow bridge, 11.5 *m.;* R. at 12 *m.* to a bend in the road where stands (L) a vacant house with pointed roof, 14 *m.* Back of this building is the SITE OF THE "HOLING-UP" SHANTY of Calamity Jane—Martha Canary.

Born in Princeton, Mo., May 1, 1852, she came with her parents to Virginia City in 1865 at the height of the Alder Gulch stampede. Few women took any part in the roaring, dangerous life of these camps. The woman who could engage in it actively, and not only compete with men in their own field but actually surpass many of them, gained their unstinted admiration. Calamity Jane became a scout for the U. S. Army in Indian campaigns, a prospector, a crack shot, and an expert horsewoman. No chronicler has drawn Calamity as a great lover, though sentimental journalists have tried to make something of her friendship with Wild Bill Hickok. Certainly she was not the "calico cat" type of female camp follower. She was given to shooting up saloons, and to raising hell with tongue and quirt. Old-timers in Castle, where she kept a restaurant in her later years, and in Harlowton, Big Timber, and other towns, remember little good of her. But in fiction she lives on as the keen-eyed, courageous, riproaring daughter of the old West.

HORSETHIEF CACHE, a high tableland surrounded by steep bluffs, is on the south side of the canyon, across from the site of Calamity Jane's house. It has but one approach, and that is well concealed.

In this hide-out cattle rustlers of the 1880's corraled stolen stock while waiting for a market. The lusty outlaws Charles (Rattlesnake Jake) Fallon and Edward (Longhair) Owen used it for a long period. Both were killed in a Lewistown gun battle in 1884 *(see Tour 3).*

LAUREL, 15.1 *m.* (3,311 alt., 2,558 pop.), straggles on both sides of an intricate pattern of railroad tracks. Products from many parts of the world pass over the joint trackage here of the Northern Pacific, the Great Northern, and the Chicago, Burlington & Quincy. From here much of Montana's wheat, hay, copper, zinc, livestock, wool, lumber, poles, and other products are routed directly east to midwestern towns; southeast to St. Louis, Kansas City, and Gulf points; and west for ocean shipment. Long drags (ordinary trains, or strings of empty cars), redballs (special merchandise trains, with sealed cars), and hotshots (trains that travel at excess speed from terminal to terminal) arrive here, are "broke up" and "made up," and depart at all hours of the day and night.

The large ASSEMBLY YARDS and CAR REPAIR SHOPS of the Northern

CALAMITY JANE

Pacific Ry. are L. The Beartooth Range and the Pryor Mountains are visible beyond them.

At Laurel is the junction with US 310 *(see Tour 13)*.

KLAN BUTTE, 21.1 *m.* (R), is 200 yards from the road, its top accessible by two narrow trails. Some years ago members of the Ku Klux Klan used it as a meeting place. Rumor has it that Klan ceremonials on the high rock came to a sudden end when, in the course of an evening's ritual beneath a fiery cross, a rattlesnake bit the Grand Kleagle.

A CLARK CAMP SITE is at 22.1 *m.* (L). Here on the riverbank the explorer and his followers camped from July 19 to July 24, 1806.

PARK CITY, 23.9 *m.* (3,410 alt., 350 pop.), was first called Rim Rock. Settlers planted elm, maple, and evergreens on the prairie, to the north of the town; the grove is used as a tourist camp. Farmers from surrounding ranches sell fruits and vegetables at roadside stands near the village throughout the summer.

COLUMBUS, 41.9 *m.* (3,624 alt., 835 pop.), seat of Stillwater County, began as a stage station on the Yellowstone Trail. Lying between the large sheep and cattle ranches to the south, and the wheat farms to the north, it developed as a trade center and shipping point.

This is the railroad station nearest to a comparatively uncommercialized mountain recreational region on the headwaters of the Stillwater River.

Left from Columbus on an improved road is ABSAROKEE, 14 *m.* (4,000 alt., 353 pop.), in a dude ranch area. There is fine trout fishing in Stillwater River and in mountain streams nearby. Country dances are held every Saturday night in summer. The town and the Absaroka Range bear the Crow's own name for themselves, the exact meaning of which is not known. According to some interpretations, early French traders erred in translating the Crow word "Apsaruke" as *gens de corbeaux* (the raven people). The older Crow declare it was their enemy, the Sioux, who perpetuated this error and fastened the name "Crow" on them.

REEDPOINT, 58.8 *m.* (3,767 alt., 158 pop.), lies below the point of a ridge named for a family that homesteaded here. The Absaroka Range is visible (L), tinted at sunset with rose and gold, its foothills touched with purple shadows cast by the CRAZY MOUNTAINS (R).

GREYCLIFF, 72 *m.* (3,980 alt., 85 pop.), is named for a gray-tinted cliff 3 miles east.

BIG TIMBER, 82.3 *m.* (4,072 alt., 1,224 pop.), seat of Sweet Grass County, was named for the creek that rises in the Crazy Mountains and flows into the Yellowstone opposite the town. Little remains of the timber, chiefly large cottonwoods, that at the time of settlement grew in the Yellowstone Valley near the old stage station at the mouth of Big Timber Creek. The point was called Rivers Across by Lieutenant Clark, because not only Big Timber Creek but Boulder River flow into the Yellowstone here.

Almost dormant in winter, Big Timber bustles in summer, its wide streets thronged with tourist cars, for it is the center of one of the principal recreational regions in the State. Montana's first dude ranch was started at the base of the Crazy Mountains about 1911.

The abundance of sweet-scented grasses and flowering plants in the valley spurred the development of livestock ranches and made honey production profitable. In the 1890's Big Timber was one of the largest wool-shipping centers in the United States. From the vast ranges that extend northward, ox teams brought load after huge load to town. In 1901, Montana's first woolen mill was established here in a stone building that stands on McLeod St.

In early Big Timber, as in other frontier towns, justice was informal but effective. A character remembered only as the Bad Swede, a chronic disturber of the peace, was once sentenced to spend three days in jail. The nearest jail was at Bozeman. As the sheriff had no desire to ride 60 miles with his cantankerous prisoner, he lowered him into a 30-foot prospect hole. Bad Swede, it is said, emerged from this form of "solitary" a changed man.

The FISH HATCHERY *(open)* produces annually more than 3,500,000 fingerlings—native, rainbow, and Loch Leven trout, and silver salmon.

Left from Big Timber on McLeod St., which becomes a dirt road, to MCLEOD HOT SPRINGS *(recreation hall and warm-water plunge, open May 15–Sept. 15)*, 17 *m.*

At 20 *m.* is a junction with a dirt road; R. 15 *m.* on this road to ANDERSON HOT SPRINGS, where is a warm lithia-water plunge.

CONTACT, 27 *m.* (5,400 alt.), on the main dirt road, was once a stage station notorious in its day for the gambling that went on there. It was named for its position at the point of contact between a limestone formation and quartz lodes.

INDEPENDENCE, 40 *m.* (8,800 alt.), was a booming camp in the last years of the nineteenth century. Its boom is said to have been based largely on a stock-promotion scheme. It had 500 inhabitants when the crash came in 1893. Nothing remains but a few wrecked buildings and pieces of rusted machinery. In winter trappers live in the deserted buildings, and run their lines into the nearby hills.

West of Big Timber the highway is hemmed in by mountains—the Absarokas (L), the high Crazy Mountains (R), the Bridger Range straight ahead.

The foothills and higher valleys provide feed for large bands of sheep. Some belong to ranchers in the dry lower valleys who must drive their herds to the national forests every summer for green forage, cool weather, and pure, fresh water.

At shearing time—late May and early June—the big sheds on sheep ranches are busy places. In preparation for the shearing, the rancher builds jugs (pens) of boards wired together, and arranges a runway through which a few sheep at a time are passed on their way to and from the pens. Large ranches use power-driven clippers, which shear the sheep more closely and rapidly than do hand shears. On the average small ranch, however, hand shears continue in favor.

Professional shearers travel in crews from ranch to ranch. Many start out early in the year and follow the season from Mexico to Montana.

Shearing weather is usually hot, and the wool is oily and heavy. Wranglers shove, tug, and whoop as they drive five or six sheep at a time down the runway to each pen. Sometimes the frightened creatures resist so stoutly that they have to be dragged or half carried; sometimes wranglers "fox" them by leading a trained wether before them down the runway.

As the sheep enter the jug, each shearer catches a ewe by a hindleg and hauls her to a sitting position. He begins shearing at the head, going down the throat or between the ears. If the ewe is a yearling, she is apt to struggle and to be nicked by the shears. If old, she sits quietly, knowing what a great relief it is to be sheared. Rams always fight, and shearers receive extra pay for working on them. Only the most expert shearer can take fleece after fleece without nicking a sheep. A man in a hurry occasionally kills one that plunges. The sheared sheep are cleared out and the pen refilled while the shearer has his last ewe on the floor. At times almost all the pens are empty at once; shearers call for more woolies while they briefly hone their shears; wranglers sweat and whoop and curse.

As the dirty gray fleece folds off, leaving the sheep a clean white or whitish yellow the shearer bunches the wool with his feet and hands, ties it with a string, drops it over the side of his jug, with almost a single motion. At the end of the day he knows how many sheep he has sheared and how much he has earned by the number of strings remaining in his belt. A shearer who can clip 200 sheep a day with the power shears, or 100 with the hand shears, is the object of considerable admiration to neighbors, buyers, idle herders, and other spectators.

While the shearer straightens his back and smokes a cigarette, his helper sweeps the tags out of the pen. The tags—fragments of wool matted with dirt and manure—follow the fleeces into an 8-foot wool sack suspended from a 12-foot platform, and packed solidly—but not too solidly—by a "stomper" who emerges from the sack as it fills. His is very hard work, for the wool, full of dirt and ticks, rolls in on him; his spot is the hottest and grimiest place in the shed. When the sack is full, he sews the mouth with twine; it is then loaded on a truck or placed in a warehouse to await the buyer's inspection.

In the heat the odors of men and sheep blend into one master stench compounded of sweat, oily wool, sheep manure, and tobacco.

The denuded sheep are lank and awkward, many of them bloody; a glance at them explains why "homelier'n a sheared sheep" has become an everyday westernism. They are run through a tank of creosote solution for disinfection, then marked with the owner's symbol in red, green or black paint, and taken to the summer range.

SPRINGDALE, 97.5 *m.* (4,324 alt., 75 pop.), is near the point where Indians stole Clark's horses in 1806, and forced him and his party to travel down the Yellowstone in bullboats.

Right from Springdale on a dirt road to HUNTER'S HOT SPRINGS, 1 *m.*, which flow at the rate of 90,000 gallons an hour. J. A. Hunter, a physician, came here in 1864, on his way to the gold fields in Emigrant Gulch, and decided to stay. The springs had long been a popular bathing place of Indians, who tried to drive Hunter away. On several occasions soldiers were sent to help hold the springs against their attacks. The buildings were destroyed by fire in 1930.

The SITE OF THE SLAYING OF JOHN M. BOZEMAN, 103.2 *m.*, is (R) in a narrow part of the valley. Bozeman was killed by Piegan Indians in April 1867 *(see HISTORY)*, and buried here. In 1870 his body was removed to the city that bears his name.

At 115.7 *m.* is the junction (R) with US 89 *(see Tour 4)*. Between this point and Livingston, US 10 and US 89 are one route.

LIVINGSTON, 116.5 *m.* (4,490 alt., 6,391 pop.), lies near the point where the Yellowstone, flowing northward from its source in Wyoming, makes a great bend eastward. As a railroad and trade center in a farming and stockraising county, the town has an air of bustle and enterprise. Stockmen and farmers in work clothes walk its streets; many trucks and trailers loaded with pigs, sheep, calves, or horses are seen in the streets, on their way to market or from one ranch to another.

Livingston is also the outfitting point in a large recreational area and its citizens try to keep alive the spirit of the old West for visitors. Its hotels and cafes display copies of the paintings of Russell and other western artists, and photographs of ranch life, rodeos, and Indians in parade dress. The automobiles on its streets bear license plates from half the Union. In January when herds of elk come down from the snow-bound high country to the south, the town is filled with hunters.

Like all Montana cities founded during the frantic boom days of the 1870's and 1880's, Livingston has its share of old houses with Gothic and Romanesque windows and gingerbread ornamentation.

At the annual Frontier Celebration, held early in July, riders from every part of the stock country compete in bronco-busting and other rodeo activities, and Indians stage the "celebration of the conqueror," which consists largely of dances and races. In keeping with the city's consciousness of its position as host and entertainer to easterners, a touch of Hollywood is usually present in the atmosphere of the Wild West show.

The history of Livingston is studded with the names and deeds of such pioneers and pathfinders as John Bozeman and Jim Bridger *(see Tour 13)*. Many an old-timer has settled down here to pass his remaining days remembering the life that was. Such a veteran was the late Patrick T. (Tommy) Tucker, dean of cowpunchers and author of *Riding the High Country (see LITERATURE)*. Tucker was an expert yarn spinner and sold many copies of his book by starting a tale of "way back when," and then producing the volume, with the explanation that the rest of the story could be found there.

Lieutenant Clark and his men came down Billman Creek and arrived at the Yellowstone, just south of town, on July 15, 1806. The first settlement in the vicinity was made about 1873, when Benson's Landing came into being at a ferry crossing 4 miles north of this place. Livingston began its existence on July 14, 1882, when railroad surveyors camped on its site and called it Clark City for William Clark. Late in the same year Northern Pacific rails reached the town. Throughout its development it has depended greatly upon the railroad. Even its name was changed to honor a director of the Northern Pacific, Crawford Livingston of St. Paul.

During the railroad strike of June and July 1894, when service was interrupted for two weeks, Federal troops were brought in to protect railroad property. A drunken captain stabbed a townsman with a sword, and President Cleveland declared martial law to maintain order. The strike was unsuccessful.

MILES and SACAJAWEA PARKS are on islands in the Yellowstone River. A third park, STERLING PLAZA, is near the river on S. Main St. Band concerts are given here in summer.

On McLEOD ISLAND, opposite Sacajawea Park, is a 9-hole golf course *(open)*.

The HARDING COLLECTION OF INDIAN RELICS *(open on request)*, 107 Eighth Ave. N., consists chiefly of objects recovered from burial places and from piskuns *(see BEFORE THE WHITE MAN)*.

The old BUCKET OF BLOOD, 113 Park St., one of many old-time Montana saloons so named, was probably a little rougher than most. It was not only a tough place in its own right but was the center of a group of resorts of the same kind including a gambling dive run by Tex Rickard, Kid Brown, and Soapy Smith until the Klondike rush took them off to the Yukon. Madame Bulldog, once Kitty O'Leary, ran what was euphemistically known as a dance hall. Her joint, she said, was a decent one. Announcing that she would stand for no damfoolishness, she saved the wages of a bouncer by polishing off roughnecks herself. Her dimensions, like her sensibilities, were pachydermal; she tipped the scales at 190, stripped. And stripped she was most of the time. Calamity Jane was one of her associates for a time, but legend has it that they fell out, whereupon Madame Bulldog tossed Calamity into the street, "as easy as licking three men." When asked whether Calamity Jane really tried to fight back, one who knew both women replied succinctly, "Calamity was tougher'n hell, but she wasn't crazy!"

The SITE OF CALAMITY JANE'S CABIN, 213 Main St., is in a weed-grown square called the Plaza, which contains a bandstand. She lived here several years, suffering increasing poverty and unhappiness with the years. *(See above.)*

At 117.3 *m.* (7th St. N.) is the junction with US 89 *(see Tour 4)*. US 10 follows Globe St. (R).

Between Livingston and Bozeman the route roughly parallels the old BOZEMAN TRAIL *(see HISTORY)*.

OLD BALDY (8,640 alt.), visible (L) at 118 *m.*, is a prominent mountain in the Absaroka Range known to immigrants and early settlers as Crow Test Peak. Young Crow braves proved their strength and endurance by keeping lonely winter vigils on its summit. Naked and weaponless, they spent their days in sacrifice and prayer to the Great Spirit. Those who endured the test were admitted to the tribal council.

Behind and above Old Baldy tower EMIGRANT PEAK (10,950 alt.) and MOUNT COWAN (11,190 alt.), irregular pyramids streaked with snow.

At 123 *m.* the highway crosses the eastern boundary of the GALLATIN NATIONAL FOREST. The cover is largely lodgepole pine and Douglas fir, with limited numbers of Engelmann spruce.

A series of sharp switchbacks begins at 128 *m.*, and continues to the summit of BOZEMAN PASS (6,003 alt.), 130 *m.* The high mountains (R) are the BRIDGER RANGE, named for Jim Bridger *(see Tour 13)*.

The highway descends the narrow, rocky canyon of the East Gallatin River into the Gallatin Valley.

At 141.8 *m.* is the junction with a graveled road.

Left on this road to SUNSET HILLS CEMETERY, 0.3 *m.*, which overlooks the city. Its use as a burial ground dates back to 1864. In 1872 Lord and Lady Blackmore, English visitors, stopped in Bozeman on their way to the Yellowstone geyser region with a party of geologists. Lady Blackmore died. Her husband bought five acres of land here and gave it to the city as a cemetery. Here he buried his wife, and placed a pyramidal monument over her grave. MOUNT BLACKMORE (10,196 alt.), which rises in the distance, directly south, is said to have been so named because its form resembles that of the monument.

When the body of John M. Bozeman was brought here in 1870, the grave was marked with a pine headboard. Cattle grazing on the burial ground leveled the board, and the grave remained unmarked until 1883, when a marble monument was erected.

Nearby is the grave of Henry T. P. Comstock, who committed suicide on September 27, 1870, after he had run through the $10,000 he received as his share in the discovery of the Comstock Lode of Nevada. In Lot 71, Block 31, is the unmarked grave of Prof. Willis G. Nash, Montana State College music instructor who had been the prototype of the lame boy in Dinah Maria (Mulock) Craik's *The Little Lame Prince.*

BOZEMAN, 142.6 *m.* (4,754 alt., 6,855 pop.), seat of Gallatin County, is, for Montana, an old and decorous town. Local ordinances prohibit dancing anywhere after midnight and in beer halls at any time. It is illegal to drink beer while standing, so all Bozeman bars are equipped with stools. On the city's wide streets, shaded by cutleaf birch, there is little of the restless activity of industrial centers. Its quiet reflects a sense of security based on the prosperity of the surrounding farms. Yet its rural characteristics are modified by the thousands of visitors who every year pass through Bozeman on their way to Yellowstone Park. An air of youthful liveliness is contributed by the students of Montana State College.

The Gallatin Valley extends westward from the town. It is one of the most productive agricultural and stock-raising regions in the State. To the south the snow-capped Gallatin and Madison ranges rim the narrowing valley. On the north the Bridger and flanking ranges of the Rockies protect it from severe cold winds.

In 1864 John M. Bozeman, traveling the trail he had blazed from Wyoming *(see HISTORY)*, guided the first train of immigrants into the Gallatin Valley. Jim Bridger guided another train in the same year. The passes the leaders used now bear their names. US 10 follows Bozeman's route. Bridger's trail passes through the Bridger Canyon and Range to the north *(see below)*. Trappers of the middle nineteenth century apparently preferred Bridger's route. Bridger and Bozeman were friends and rivals. A story often told relates how they once led wagon trains through their respective passes in a race to Virginia City, and arrived within a few hours of each other.

Six cabins and a two-story hotel huddled at the eastern end of Gallatin Valley by the end of 1864. During a flour famine that winter, the settlers lived on "meat straight." Bozeman gave his name to the settlement, but for many years it was known locally as Missouri from the number of Missourians among the settlers. The city has never depended on mining booms for its growth, except insofar as the mining camps provided markets for foodstuffs.

In 1867 it became the seat of Gallatin County, one of the nine Territorial counties of Montana.

MONTANA STATE COLLEGE, Harrison St. and 8th Ave., established February 16, 1893, is the oldest operating unit of the University of Montana (see EDUCATION). It shares its 95-acre campus and buildings with the U. S. Bureau of Entomology, the Agricultural Extension Service, and the State Agricultural Experiment Station. It offers courses leading to the Bachelor of Science degree, and carries on wide research in agriculture and engineering, doing agricultural extension work through county agents. The student enrollment averages 1,200.

The LIBRARY of 30,000 volumes (weekdays 9-5) is on the second floor of MONTANA HALL, a three-story brick structure of Tudor design. The BIOLOGICAL MUSEUM (open 8-5 daily) in LEWIS HALL has a collection of 50,000 plant specimens, large groups of fossils, and many mounted birds and animals. A GREENHOUSE, devoted to experimental work with flowers and vegetables, contains many tropical and subtropical plants. An OUTDOOR MUSEUM, in the southwest corner of the campus, has petrified stumps 4 feet in diameter, and a spring-fed pool stocked with mutant rainbow trout.

BEALL PARK, Bozeman and Villard Sts., a pleasant village green, has tennis courts and a playground, as well as MILLSTONES of Bozeman's first flour mill (1865).

The CITY HALL, Main and Rouse Sts., was once the Opera House, as the name over the entrance indicates. As such, it opened in 1890 with the Mendelssohn Quintette of Boston. For years it was one of a chain operated by John Maguire, pioneer impresario of Butte. The walls of the stage and auditorium on the second floor display advertisements, cobwebbed and yellow, and faded posters announcing Joseph Jefferson in *Rip Van Winkle*, Eddie Foy in *A Night in Town*, Clay Clement in *Faust*.

The SEED PEA WAREHOUSES, Babcock and Wallace Sts., are among the largest of their kind in the West. Here seed peas produced in the Gallatin Valley and elsewhere in Montana and the West, are sorted for quality and size, packed, and stored to await shipment.

Bozeman is at the junction with US 191 (see Tour 5).

1. Right from Bozeman on Rouse Ave., which skirts the Gallatin County Fairgrounds (L), to a CANNERY, 1.9 m., where about 250,000 cases of canned goods (mostly peas and string beans from Gallatin Valley farms) are annually packed.

2. Right from Bozeman on State 187, which follows Wallace Ave. and becomes a dirt road, to a junction with an unimproved road, 2 m.; R. here 1 m. to the SITE OF FORT ELLIS. Here William Clark and his party camped on July 14, 1806; and here, on August 27, 1867, Fort Ellis, named for Col. Augustus Van Horn Ellis of the 124th New York Volunteers, was established. For 19 years it played an important part in the taming of the Gallatin frontier. The Washburn-Langford expedition, whose report of the geysers, hot springs, terraces, paint pots, and other marvels of the Yellowstone region led to the creation of Yellowstone National Park, outfitted at Fort Ellis in August 1870.

At 5 *m.* State 187 enters BRIDGER CANYON. The granite pinnacle above the road (L), known locally as the Stone Maiden, is the subject of a Crow legend. Black Eagle, the lover of comely Evening Star, once led a war party to drive off an enemy of the tribe. Evening Star came daily to this point to watch for his return. He came back with honor but without life, and grief turned Evening Star to stone. The stars of evening are said to linger in compassion over her.

Between Bozeman and Three Forks, US 10 follows an almost straight course through the lower Gallatin Valley.

BELGRADE, 153.3 *m.* (4,467 alt., 533 pop.), a milling cénter with towering grain elevators, was named by a Serbian who was on the special train that took President Villard of the Northern Pacific to Gold Creek for the ceremony of driving the last spike.

MANHATTAN, 162.4 *m.* (4,258 alt., 501 pop.), is a one-street town with a few business buildings facing a tree-enclosed park. It was named by a group of New Yorkers who operated under the name of the Manhattan Co. and owned land here. The George Sinton ranches, one of the largest cattle spreads north of Texas, has headquarters here.

The outline of the Continental Divide comes into view straight ahead at 164 *m.*

LOGAN, 167.9 *m.* (4,114 alt., 126 pop.), formerly a stage station known as Cannon House, was renamed after the Northern Pacific Ry. acquired the right-of-way from Odelia Logan in 1885.

The steep cliff, 168.4 *m.* (L), was once a piskun *(see BEFORE THE WHITE MAN).*

At 172.2 *m.* is a junction with a graveled road.

Right on this road to the THREE FORKS OF THE MISSOURI 3.5 *m.,* where the Gallatin unites with the Madison and Jefferson Rivers. Lewis and Clark named the forks in 1805. The actual point of confluence of the Madison and Jefferson is obscured by thick willow growth.

THREE FORKS, 174.4 *m.* (4,081 alt., 884 pop.), has an air of order and dignity. The homes and business houses are particularly well kept and many have been painted white.

The site of Three Forks, an ancient battleground of Crow and Blackfeet, was visited by Lewis and Clark on July 27, 1805. It was here that Sacajawea felt she was at last in the land of her own people, from whom she had been stolen in childhood.

Trappers sent out by the Missouri Fur Company made the first attempt to establish a trading post here in 1810. They built a stockade on a neck of land between the Jefferson and Madison Rivers about 2 miles above the confluence, but the Blackfeet drove them out with severe losses before the year ended *(see HISTORY).* Father De Smet spent a short time in the Three Forks region in 1840. No attempt to establish a town near here was made until 1864, when a group of Missourians laid out Gallatin City at what they believed was the head of navigation on the Missouri. When they learned that the Great Falls of the Missouri stood between their site and the head of navigation, they abandoned it. In 1908 the railroad came through and established a town here as a division point.

At 178 *m.* US 10 divides into US 10 S and US 10 N *(see Tour 1A),* alternate routes between this place and Garrison.

Section c JUNCTION US 10 S-US 10 N *to* GARRISON, *109.6 m.,*
US 10 S.

Much of US 10 S winds among mountain ranges and through canyons, in many places both deep and narrow. It crosses the Continental Divide through Pipestone Pass, offering spine-tingling views of forested mountains and boulder-strewn valleys. In its western descent it passes through Montana's richest mining region, skirting the thousand smokes of Butte. At the western end, in Deer Lodge Valley, though never out of sight of lofty mountains, it traverses rich fields and grazing lands.

US 10 S runs southwest from the junction with US 10 N *(see Tour 1A),* 0 *m.,* along the Jefferson River (L).

At 9.3 *m.* is the junction with State 1 *(see Tour 15).*

At 14.4 *m.* is the junction with a dirt road.

Right on this road to its end, 3.3 *m.;* straight ahead from here 0.6 *m.* on a foot trail to LEWIS AND CLARK CAVERN *(guides),* a National Monument in Jefferson Canyon. The cave is in the Madison limestone formation at the base of a high cliff. It was discovered and partly equipped with stairways in 1902 by Daniel Morrison, a surveyor, and is known locally as Morrison Cave.

Exceeded in size in the United States only by Mammoth Cave in Kentucky and the Carlsbad Caverns in New Mexico, this cavern is a succession of vaulted chambers and passageways thickly hung with stalactites and studded with stalagmites. Surface water seeping down the bedding planes of the Madison limestone, here tilted about 53°, hollowed out the cave by gradually dissolving the limestone at successive levels. The cave is dry, except at its lowest point, about 300 feet below the entrance. But the dripping of water during past centuries has carved out crypts and corridors curtained in places with translucent stone that varies in color from pure white to deep amber.

The entrance from the trail is an artificial one made by the former owner. From it a wooden stairway mounts a 20-foot rise in the rock floor of the passage. Beyond the stairway is the natural entrance, 25 feet above the trail and about 60 feet northwest of the newer entrance. It can be reached only with the aid of a rope. Three hundred and eighty-five steps are descended to reach the FIRST LARGE CHAMBER. Here stalagmites and stalactites, opaque and almost flawless, form fluted pillars. A form of stalactite with curved and branching arms (helictite) is beautifully developed.

From this large room a tortuous path descends to the DEEPEST ROOM. A great number of stalactites, fallen to the floor and cemented to it by flowstone, furnish toeholds for scrambling up and down the steep incline. In this room is one large stalagmite in process of formation, with water dripping onto it. A spring makes a clear pool in the center of the floor, and, above, the ceiling rises to a dome that looks like rough mosaic work.

From the foot of the stairway narrow corridors lead to other chambers, of which the first is the CATHEDRAL ROOM. From its ledged floor great spires rise toward the domed ceiling, in sepia hues and lighter shades of brown.

Beyond and below is the BROWN WATERFALL. From a rocky ledge above the floor a cascade of rock seems to spill down the chamber wall like a plunging brown river.

A rough corridor known as HELL'S HIGHWAY is traveled with the aid of ropes and leads into the ORGAN ROOM. The stillness of this room, with its mass of pipelike columns, faintly golden, gleaming amber, and rich brown, is impressive. The columns give off musical sounds when struck with pieces of broken rock, as do many of the stalactites and stalagmites in other chambers.

The smaller corridors and chambers vary in formation and coloring. The walls of some are intricately filigreed, others seem hung with draperies of weird pattern. At one place a COFFIN is surmounted by a stalagmite candle; the LION'S DEN, enclosed

JEFFERSON CANYON

by joined tites and "mites," is strewn with pieces of fallen stalactites that suggest the bones of victims.

The full journey requires vigor, sure-footedness, and a readiness to cling and sometimes to crawl by the light of a miner's lantern. The air is good.

At 15 *m.* is the Canyon of the Jefferson River, known locally as Sixteenmile Canyon. The TOBACCO ROOT MOUNTAINS are L. in the Gallatin National Forest, the Bull Mountains R. in the Deer Lodge National Forest.

WHITEHALL, 28 *m.* (4,371 alt., 553 pop.), is a long, narrow, quiet town, the trading center for the southern part of Jefferson County, one of the original Territorial counties. It is apparently merely a line of stores and houses strung out along US 10 S but actually, most of it sits back among shade trees and shrubbery. Before 1863 fur traders were the only white inhabitants in this region. About that time Thomas Brooks built a stage station 4 miles north of this place on the route between Virginia City and Fort Benton, naming it Old Whitehall for his former home in England. The number of settlers in the region increased slowly but Whitehall did not have much importance until 1889 when the Northern Pacific branch between Logan and Garrison was built.

At 33.5 *m.* is the junction with a dirt road.

Right on this road to PIPESTONE HOT SPRINGS, 4 *m.* (*hotel, cabins, free campgrounds; vapor baths; large plunge, adm., children 25¢, adults 35¢; saddle horses*). Marine shells and bones of prehistoric animals have been found in a mixed shale and limestone deposit nearby.

At 37.8 *m.* is the junction with State 41 (*see Tour 16*).

US 10 S here begins the gradual climb to Pipestone Pass, following the course of Pipestone Creek. The eastern slope is arid, with much sagebrush and prickly pear, interspersed in early summer with the brilliant blossoms of Indian paintbrush, larkspur, bitterroot, lupine, and yellow monkeyflower.

At 47.4 *m.* the highway crosses the CONTINENTAL DIVIDE (6,418 alt.) through PIPESTONE PASS. At the summit, only a few yards from the source of Pipestone Creek, are the beginnings of small spring-fed streams that flow down the west slope into Silver Bow Creek.

THOMPSON PARK (*trail picnicking facilities, campgrounds*), between 47.9 *m.* and 51 *m.* (L), is an attractive 3,400-acre mountain playground covered with lodgepole pine and Douglas fir. Near timber line are alpine fir and limber pine. In part a gift to the city of Butte from William Boyce Thompson, the park was rounded out by the addition of several thousand acres of Deer Lodge National Forest land. There is an amphitheater in a natural bowl, and also a toboggan slide, a bobsled run, and a ski jump 610 feet long, with a descent of 229 feet.

West of Pipestone Pass US 10 S is known as Harding Way. At one of the wider curves, 84.4 *m.*, is a view of Butte, especially spectacular at night when the lights glow against the mountain behind the city.

From this highway is seen BIG BUTTE (6,310 alt.), for which the mining city was named; the large white "M" on it is the work of students at the Montana School of Mines. Indians called this Evil Mountain, saying that long ago Big Butte was the highest peak of the main range. One time a young chief was killed there by an enemy and the medicine man of his tribe cursed it, and ordered it removed. During the night the great mountain was torn apart and the largest piece was hurled toward the valley. It struck where Walkerville stands (*see BUTTE*) and slid along to its present position, leaving in its path the ridge that connects it with the high ground at Walkerville. No trees grew on it thereafter. Indians intent on suicide often took their last view of earth from its summit.

At 49.8 *m.* is the junction with Roosevelt Drive.

Left on Roosevelt Drive through Thompson Park, 4 *m.;* L. on a dirt road to HIGHLAND CITY, 21 *m.* This ghost gold camp at the base of RED MOUNTAIN (10,000 alt.) was once larger than Butte, crude in appearance and equally crude in its way of life. For diversion, men quarreled and killed; then others banded together to hunt down and kill the killers.

After seven years the stream of gold came suddenly to an end; in another year the town was almost deserted. Most of the 600 log structures, many of them two stories high, rapidly decayed. Trees took root where hearth fires had burned, and dropped their needles over the debris. Streets were obliterated by the cross trails of later prospectors. A few buildings still stand, the cellars of others are buried in the sagebrush. Though few people stayed here long, the graveyard is the most tangible of the city's remains. Here is buried Shotgun Liz, sharpshooting hurdy-gurdy girl of frontier dance halls.

Much gold came out of Highland Gulch. Evidence of large placer workings remain, and in adjacent gulches men still scrape a scanty existence from reluctant gravel. Occasionally someone finds a pocket or a nugget, and hopes briefly to see a new Highland City on the ruins of the old. In 1916 John Kearn, sole resident at that time, picked up a nugget worth $1,200.

US 10 S approaches Butte from the south.

At 58.1 *m.* is the junction with an oiled road (Holmes Ave.).

Left on Holmes Ave. for an alternate route that skirts the city on the south. Holmes Ave. runs west to the Milwaukee tracks; R. here on Rowe Road to Montana St.; R. on Montana St. to Front St.; L. on Front St., which crosses the Milwaukee tracks and bends R. to join the combined route of US 10 S and US 91, 3.6 *m.*

BUTTE, 61.2 *m.* (5,755 alt., 39,532 pop.) *(see BUTTE).*

Points of Interest: Marcus Daly Statue, Smithers Historical Photographs Collection, Chinatown, Meaderville, Leonard Mine, State School of Mines, Columbia Gardens, and others.

In Butte is the junction with US 91 *(see Tour 6, sec. b);* for 5.7 miles US 10 S and US 91 are one route.

ROCKER, 65.1 *m.* (5,395 alt., 96 pop.), virtually a suburb of Butte, is an industrial town through which pass long trains of gondola cars loaded with ore bound for the reduction works at Anaconda *(see Tour 18).* Oil refineries and a plant for treating mine timbers are here.

SILVER BOW CREEK (L), named in 1864 when three prospectors saw the sun shining on it through a rift in the clouds, is muddied with the refuse of Butte mines, though in places it is intensely blue from dissolved copper salts.

Between Rocker and Garrison the southern horizon (L) is banked with the dramatic, barren peaks of the highly glaciated Anaconda Mountains. Streams rise in broad amphitheaters with steep, rocky back walls and level floors on which lakes and parklike meadows alternate with stands of spired evergreens. MOUNT EVANS (10,630 alt.), the highest summit, rises bare and deeply furrowed above a host of lesser peaks.

At 66.9 *m.* is the junction (L) with US 91 *(see Tour 6).*

At 74 *m.* is the junction with a graveled road.

Left on this road to GREGSON HOT SPRINGS, 2 *m. (campgrounds, natural steam baths, dance pavilion; warm plunge, adm. 40¢).*

At 76 *m.*, the junction with US 10 A *(see Tour 18)*, the high smoke-stack of the Anaconda smelter is visible (L).

At 84 *m.* is the junction with a dirt road.

Left on this road 0.2 *m.* to WARMSPRINGS (4,852 alt., 110 pop.), in which is the STATE HOSPITAL FOR THE INSANE *(open 9-11 and 1-4 daily)*. Its trim brick build-ings, in modern functional style, and its neatly kept grounds contribute much to the air of sanctuary that characterizes the town.

Just south of the hospital buildings are the springs for which the place was named. A conical mound, built up by the springs' mineral deposits, resembles an Indian lodge with smoke ascending from it. Here came herds of white-tailed deer to graze on the abundant grass around the mound, and obtain salt by licking the rocks at its base. Indians named it It-soo-ke-en-car-ne *(lodge of the white-tailed deer)*. Poetic French *voyageurs* called it la loge du chevreuil *(the lodge of the roe-buck)*; this the laconic ranchers of a later day contracted to Deer Lodge *(see below)*.

South of the State Hospital is the 15-acre STATE GAME FARM *(open)*, estab-lished in 1929. Small herds of elk and buffalo are maintained here; propagation of Chinese pheasants, Hungarian partridges, California quail, and Oregon mountain quail is carried on. Showbirds of brilliant plumage include the melanistic mutant, and the golden, silver, Reeves, and Lady Amherst pheasants.

At 90 *m.* is the junction with an oiled road.

Left 1 *m.* on this road to GALEN, the STATE TUBERCULOSIS SANITARIUM *(open daily 3:30-5:30)*. This plant, founded in 1912, has grown slowly until it consists of ten main buildings and six cottages. Preference is given to county charges and ex-service men, and, because of the limited facilities, they are almost the only per-sons admitted. More than half the patients are women. One-fifth of the men ad-mitted are victims of silicosis.

DEER LODGE, 98.8 *m.* (4,530 alt., 3,510 pop.), seat of Powell County, is bisected by Clark Fork of the Columbia, here called the Deer Lodge River. On the west side of the town are the somber stone walls and guard towers of the State penitentiary, and the yards and shops of the C.M. St. P & P R.R., the town's leading industrial unit, which employs 250 men. On the east side, which has broad streets, are many sturdy square houses popular in the West during the 1870's and 1880's. Castles built with the wealth of mines and ranches and log cabin homes survive almost side by side.

In 1862, when the first important gold strikes in this area attracted at-tention *(see HISTORY)*, a shack town sprang up here, called variously, Cottonwood, Spanish Forks, and La Barge. Deer Lodge was the name offi-cially adopted in 1864. An important stop on the Mullan Wagon Road, it was listed by Captain Mullan in his *Miner's and Traveler's Guide*. It was one of the few places along the route where immigrants could obtain fresh beef and vegetables, and the services of a blacksmith. Prospectors coming up from the south called it the "good little town on the road to Bear" because it was a pleasant place to break the journey on the trail to Bear-mouth, a mining camp 50 miles farther down the Clark Fork *(see Tour 1, sec. d)*.

The W. A. CLARK HOUSE *(open)*, 311 Clark Ave., once the residence of W. A. Clark *(see HISTORY)*, dates from the 1860's. The front of the T-shaped one-story structure is frame with a wide porch. The shank of the T is built of logs.

The STATE PENITENTIARY *(open 2-4 Fri.)*, south end of Main St., was built in 1871. Its walls and older buildings are constructed of stone, the newer of brick and reinforced concrete. More than one-fifth of the 600 convicts are employed on ranches and in other work outside the walls. Those inside work in a sawmill, weave rag rugs, or manufacture automobile license plates. The prison has a bakery and a laundry, and conducts barber, carpenter, shoe repair, plumbing, and vulcanizing shops. Much of the food is produced on prison farms.

The WARDEN'S RESIDENCE is directly opposite the penitentiary. The outside is finished with varnished Oregon spliced fir, the inside with oak, curly birch, and Circassian walnut. The living room and dining room floors are bordered with zigzag inlay.

A GOLD NUGGET COLLECTION *(open on application),* Main St. and Milwaukee Ave., contains specimens taken from the streams of Powell County, including Gold Creek, site of the earliest placer finds in the State. The nuggets have an aggregate weight of 140½ ounces, and are worth $3,707. The largest has a Troy weight of 23.18 ounces.

MOUNT POWELL (10,300 alt.), visible (L) at 104.6 *m.,* was named for John W. Powell, a rancher who homesteaded at its base and was the first white man to scale it.

The SITE OF THE GRANT HOUSE is commemorated by a monument at 109.3 *m.* (R). This log structure was erected by John F. Grant, a rancher, about 1855, near the mouth of the Little Blackfoot River. It became known far and wide as a stop-over for prospectors and as a place to trade, gather news, and forget frontier hardships in fiddle-inspired revelry. If a blizzard swooped down while a dance was in progress, hospitable Johnny Grant would tell his visitors to stay until it was over. They usually danced all night, slept on buffalo robes on the floor, and awoke to eat and dance again. As Johnny was a squaw man, the cabin was also frequented by Indians, many of whom claimed relationship with their host.

At 109.6 *m.* is the western junction US 10 N *(see Tour 1A).* Near this point (L) the Little Blackfoot River flows into the Clark Fork of the Columbia.

Section d. GARRISON to IDAHO LINE, *183.2 m.,* US 10.

Between Garrison and the Idaho Line US 10 winds through the canyons of the Clark Fork and the St. Regis River. At Missoula, where the Bitterroot, Flathead, Blackfoot, and Clark Fork Valleys meet, horizons recede to distant peaks and ranges; but they soon narrow again. In many places the Clark Fork is broad and calm, and, except after heavy rains, green; in other places it spills violently through rocky channels. In the St. Regis Valley, near the Idaho Line, the mountain slopes are steep and rocky, denuded by forest fires.

Pioneers bound for the Washington Territory followed the Mullan Wagon Road *(see HISTORY),* which entered the valley of the Clark Fork not far from its junction with the Little Blackfoot River. Its course between Garrison and Lookout Pass on the Idaho Line was roughly that of US 10. The building of the road from Fort Benton to Walla Walla took four years though it was never more than a crude trail. Loaded wagons required 47 days to make the 624-mile journey, pack animals 35 days.

US 10 goes northwest from the junction of US 10 S *(see Tour 1, sec. c)* and US 10 N *(see Tour 1A),* 0 *m.*

GARRISON, 0.6 *m.* (4,344 alt., 100 pop.), named for William Lloyd Garrison, is a grimy railroad town on the bank of Clark Fork, sheltered on the north by a high bluff.

A PHOSPHATE MILL (R), 4.5 *m.*, of 100 tons capacity, grinds rock of high phosphate content brought by truck from several small mines in the nearby mountains. The product is used for fertilizer.

At 9.3 *m.* is a junction with a dirt road.

Left on this road is the village of GOLD CREEK, 0.2 *m.* (4,201 alt., 35 pop.). Just L. of the settlement is the confluence of Clark Fork and Gold Creek. Near the source of the latter gold was first discovered in Montana *(see HISTORY).* Gold Creek village was the scene of the ceremony celebrating completion of the Northern Pacific Ry. in 1883 *(see TRANSPORTATION).*

A MINING DREDGE *(visitors' passes obtainable except Mon. at offices in Gold Creek)* 5 *m.*, operates to bedrock, with a daily capacity of 5,000 cubic yards of gravel. The operators control seven miles of the stream between Gold Creek and Pioneer.

PIONEER, 9 *m.*, is the small group of cabins built in the spring of 1862 just before the Gold Creek diggings were abandoned for those at Bannack. Because of the lack of transportation, the miners had trouble in obtaining tools with which to work, and yields of metal were low; James and Granville Stuart made only $17.60 on their best day here.

At 19.3 *m.* is the junction with State 31 *(see Tour 8).*

DRUMMOND, 20.9 *m.* (3,967 alt., 300 pop.), scattered on both sides of US 10, is on the site of a trapper's camp. The Northern Pacific water tank seems to dominate the town. In the SAPPHIRE MOUNTAINS (L) are valuable deposits of silver, sapphire, and phosphate.

At Drummond is the junction with US 10 A *(see Tour 18).*

At 32.6 *m.* is a junction with a dirt road.

1. Left on this road, crossing a bridge, to BEARMOUTH, 0.5 *m.* (3,813 alt., 510 pop.), formerly Bear's Mouth, a stage stop on the Mullan Road. Prospectors turned off here to reach the Blackfoot River country (R). It is the main shipping point for ore trucked down from the Garnet region.

2. Right over a narrow mountain road that winds up Bear Gulch to BEAR-TOWN, 6 *m.* (4,583 alt., 3 pop.). Stamping ground of the notorious "Beartown Roughs," and one-time runner-up for State capital, Beartown is said to have yielded $1,000,000 in silver and gold in 1866 and 1867.

At 9 *m.* is the base of the steeply rising "Chinee Grade." In this vicinity is supposedly a Chinaman's cache of considerable amount. Many have searched in vain for the 5-pound baking-powder can filled with gold that is said to have been buried under a tree.

GARNET, 11 *m.* (5,904 alt., 25 pop.), a few years ago a ghost town, is a busy mining camp. Many of the old-timers are still here, prospecting and spinning yarns. One of the yarns is of a winter when, because of deep snow, supplies could not be brought in and men could not get out. At length one man, equipped with a miner's lamp and laden with carbide, worked his way down to Bearmouth through the mine tunnels and arranged for supplies to be brought in.

GOLD DREDGE AT GOLD CREEK

BEAVER DAM

At 35.6 *m.* is the eastern end of HELL GATE CANYON, through which Clark Fork flows for 36 miles. High timbered slopes rise steeply beside the road. The·canyon was named *La Porte de l'Enfer* by French trappers, who knew it as a place of ambush.

NIMROD HOT SPRINGS, 39.8 *m.,* has an outdoor plunge *(adm. 25¢).* In the river swamps (L) large beds of tender watercress are kept green throughout the winter by the warm spring water.

At 50.7 *m.* is the junction with the Rock Creek Road.

Left on this forest road through a winding canyon along Rock Creek to ROCK CREEK LAKE, 40 *m.,* the source of the creek. There is good trout fishing throughout the length of the stream, and several improved campgrounds lie near its banks.

CLINTON, 56.3 *m.* (3,490 alt., 50 pop.), rests like a red and gray bird in the middle of a neat landscape.

At 66.1 *m.* is the junction with State 20 *(see Tour 8).*

MILLTOWN, 66.4 *m.* (3,521 alt., 552 pop.), exists chiefly because of the sawmill *(see Tour 8)* whose yards stretch along the highway and give the town its character. When the mill is in operation, a clean smell of freshly sawed timber re-enforces the visual impression.

At 71.1 *m.,* near the western end of Hell Gate Canyon, is a curved underpass on a hill *(drive with great care).* In winter northeasterly storms sometimes sweep down through the "wind tunnel" here and burst upon

Missoula with the force and penetrating power of Arctic blizzards. The bald knob (R) is MOUNT JUMBO which, viewed from the west—by persons with sufficiently vivid imaginations—has the appearance of a recumbent elephant. The rocky, forested slope of MOUNT SENTINEL (L) rises above the winding river and the campus of Montana State University *(see MISSOULA).*

MISSOULA, 73.4 *m.* (3,233 alt., 14,657 pop.) *(see MISSOULA).*

Points of Interest: Montana State University, Missoula County Courthouse, Catholic Group, Free Library, Bonner House, Greenough Park, Waterworks Hill, and others.

In Missoula is the junction with US 93 *(see Tour 7);* between Missoula and a junction 9.5 miles west US 10 and US 93 are one route.

At 74.5 *m.* is the junction with the old Yellowstone Trail.

Left on this improved road to the SUGAR REFINERY *(open on application at office anytime except Oct. 1-15),* 0.6 *m.* (R). This plant, completed in 1928, produces more than 300,000 hundredweight of sugar annually and employs 200 persons when operating at capacity. The two-story mill of pressed brick and steel rises to four stories at the east end. The eight other buildings, all of brick, steel, and concrete, are shops, warehouses, and the like. The operating season—"campaign" in refining jargon—begins in October, and lasts 85 to 100 days, each day divided into three eight-hour shifts. On the factory grounds are several small plots devoted to experimental beet growing.

At 3.1 *m.* is a junction with a dirt road; L. 0.2 *m.* on this road to the old HELL GATE STORE, a small log cabin used as a chicken house and surrounded on three sides by pigpens. It sheltered Montana's first mercantile establishment not classified as a trading post. In August, 1860, Frank L. Worden and Christopher P. Higgins brought a pack train of merchandise for this store over the new Mullan Road from Walla Walla. Loaded on one of their mules was the first safe brought into the region. A little settlement that grew up around the store was called Hell Gate Ronde; Mullan listed it in his *Miners' and Travelers' Guide:* "28th day (from Walla Walla). Move to Higgins' and Worden's store at Hell-gate, distance 12½ miles. Road excellent; wood, water and grass here. Good place to rest animals for a day or two; blacksmith shop at Van Dorn's and supplies of all kinds can be obtained, dry goods, groceries, beef, vegetables and fresh animals, if needed." But the "supplies of all kinds" were extremely expensive at Hell Gate. Sugar was 60 cents a pound, coffee 80 cents, and whiskey $8 a gallon.

In the winter of 1863–64 several of Henry Plummer's gang of road agents, led by Cyrus Skinner, began a reign of terror in Hell Gate. They loafed in the store, where Skinner preferred to sit on the safe. Worden, Higgins, and everyone in the village believed the gang was intent on rifling the safe, which contained $65,000 in gold dust.

On the night of January 27, 1864, a posse of 21 citizens from Alder Gulch rode into town, and rounded up the gang. Brief trials were held in the store; Cyrus Skinner sat on the safe as usual during the proceedings. Six men were sentenced to hang, and died with the password of Plummer's gang, "I am innocent," upon their lips.

George Shears, Skinner's lieutenant, was hanged in a barn near the store. The rope was thrown over a beam, and he was asked to walk up a ladder to save the trouble of preparing a drop for him. "Gentlemen," he said, "I am not used to this business. Shall I jump off or slide off?" He was told to jump.

Whiskey Bill Graves was led outside. One end of a lariat was fastened about his neck, the other thrown over a stout limb. One of the vigilantes mounted a horse and Graves was lifted up behind him. "Good-bye, Bill," said the rider, and drove his spurs into the horse's flanks.

Hell Gate survived five years; then Worden and Co. moved the store four miles east, and erected a sawmill and flourmill *(see MISSOULA).*

COUNCIL GROVE, 7.9 *m.* (L) on the old Yellowstone Trail, is the poplar and cottonwood thicket in which Gov. Isaac Stevens of Washington Territory in 1855 negotiated the first treaty with the Flathead Indians. By this treaty the Jocko Reservation, carved out of the Mission Mountains and the Flathead Valley, was set aside for the Confederated Tribes of the Flathead *(see Tour 7).* All other lands occupied by the tribes were ceded to the Government. The treaty authorized the Salish to occupy the Bitterroot Valley, their long-time home, for an indefinite period. The concession was temporary, and Chief Victor, the spokesman for the Salish, probably did not fully understand its terms. It was the cause of later misunderstandings. Remnants of the Salish continued to live in the Bitterroot Valley until 1891.

DESMET, 79.4 *m.* (3,237 alt., 25 pop.), a shipping point for Grass Valley stock, has large loading pens (R). The town was named in honor of Father Pierre Jean De Smet, the first missionary in this region *(see HISTORY, RELIGION).*

Northwest of Desmet the Northern Pacific Ry. turns sharply R. and passes through the CORIACAN DEFILE, the gateway between the Missoula and Flathead Valleys.

In the distance (R) conical SQUAW PEAK (7,978 alt.) points its impudent mammilla at the sky. Known locally as Squaw Teat Peak, it is the most symmetrical of the mountains visible in this area.

At 82.9 *m.* is the junction (R) with US 93 *(see Tour 7, sec. b).*

FRENCHTOWN, 89.7 *m.* (3,027 alt., 187 pop.), lies (L) in a rich valley. The spire and cross of its weather-beaten old church are its most prominent landmarks. It has an appearance of calm that is belied by the vigor and aggressiveness of its inhabitants, who are mostly of French-Canadian descent. Local children still begin their schooling with little understanding of the English language. St. Jean is the patron saint of the parish, and his day, June 24th, is noisily celebrated.

At 95.8 *m.* US 10 climbs over sharp curves to a bench, from which is a view of the Clark Fork Valley. An observation point at 97.3 *m.* provides an equally good view westward. The rugged slopes of the Bitterroot Mountains are L.; the Coeur d'Alenes are on the opposite side.

The highway descends into a narrow canyon lined with outcroppings of rock—rusty red, yellow, and brown. Above, the receding green hills and gulches are topped with pine, larch, and Douglas fir.

ALBERTON, 104.3 *m.* (3,040 alt., 278 pop.), a railroad men's town, is named for the pioneer family of Alberts, who homesteaded here when Indian trails were the only routes of travel.

Between Alberton and St. Regis the route is through the LOLO NATIONAL FOREST.

At 106 *m.* is a junction with a dirt road.

Left on this narrow mountain road to LOLO HOT SPRINGS, 26 *m.* (4,171 alt.) *(see Tour 7, sec. c).* This route is part of a popular loop-trip from Missoula.

ELK LODGE, 113.3 *m.* (3,000 alt.), consists of cabins, a store, and a service station. Furrowed cliffs (R) present purple and gold faces in striking contrast with the predominating greens and browns of the surrounding country.

At 114.4 *m.* the Clark Fork flows through a deep and narrow gorge. The highway crosses SCENIC BRIDGE.

SUPERIOR, 133.9 *m.* (2,725 alt., 350 pop.), is divided by the Clark Fork. The log and frame buildings of the 1870's and 1880's, mostly abandoned, lie at the base of a steep grade on the right bank. On the flat across the river are the buildings of the newer town.

The town's name was used in 1869 by a settlement at the mouth of Cedar Creek, 1 mile east, whose first citizen came from Superior, Wis. When this settlement was abandoned, the name was appropriated by the new town.

The ORDEAN HOTEL, with gabled roof and a two-story veranda, was once a favorite stopping place of prospectors who came in from the gulch with a "load in their pokes." They felt that its plush and gilt, mirrors and marble, justified the high cost of the otherwise meager accommodations. The drunker a man became, the more elegant the place seemed.

1. Left from Superior to the old Yellowstone Trail; 1 *m.* L. on this graveled road to Cedar Creek Road, 2 *m.*; R. on Cedar Creek Road to LOUISVILLE, 16 *m.* (4,100 alt.), a ghost town that was a roaring gold camp in the 1870's.

In 1869 a French Canadian named Barrette, drawn by the lure of gold, was traveling overland from California to St. Joe, Idaho. Pickings were poor there, however, and he swung over the Bitterroot Divide and struck the Mullan Road. In the fall he reached the rocky defile of a creek and noted a basin that appealed to him as a good place to prospect. He went to Frenchtown for supplies, and returned to the basin with a partner, B. Lanthier. They camped on a small tributary of Cedar Creek, 15 miles upstream from the confluence of the latter with the Clark Fork. Barrette named the small stream Cayuse Creek. While Lanthier cooked supper, Barrette panned $4 in gold.

The pair immediately staked claims. Short rations compelled them to return to Lozeau's Ranch on the Clark Fork, where they intended to spend the winter. Lanthier went into Frenchtown to arrange for supplies, and the news of the discovery leaked out. Although it was mid-January, a stampede broke for Cayuse Creek. Within 2 days the frantic gold seekers staked more than 200 claims, and started panning the stream despite bitter cold weather. Few heeded the practical need of supplies; even after scurvy struck the camp, the next load of freight to come in on pack mules was whiskey. Ten thousand people were drawn to the camp in the first year, but the boom continued only until 1871. Interest then shifted upstream and a new camp, Forest City, was made. By the winter of 1872 Forest City was deserted in favor of Mayville, still farther up Cedar Creek. In two years Mayville also played out; but this time, because of the difficulty of moving equipment by pack train, the residents simply walked away, leaving tools, stoves, billiard tables, pianos, bar fixtures, and all the other things that they could not conveniently carry. After they had deserted Cedar Creek, Chinese miners drifted in to live in the crumbling shacks of Louisville, content to glean what the white men had passed by.

2. Right from Superior on the unimproved Flat Creek Road to IRON MOUNTAIN MINE, 3 *m.* Ore was discovered here in 1886, and soon the town of Pardee sprang up around it. The surface gold and silver ores were rich enough to justify packing them on mules over high mountain passes to Paradise, on the Northern Pacific Ry. When the Coeur d'Alene branch of the Northern Pacific was built through Superior in 1891, the mine began to operate on a large scale. A mill was erected at Iron Mountain, as the station at Superior was then called, and an aerial tram connected it with the workings. Except for occasional operations by lessees, the mine has been idle for many years, and Pardee abandoned.

ST. REGIS, 141.4 *m.* (2,678 alt., 300 pop.), is composed of straggling clumps of buildings amid convergent railroad tracks. Its center is a bridge across the Clark Fork. Once an important sawmill town, it dwindled to a supply point for small logging operators after the great forest fire that swept western Montana in August 1910.

The St. Regis River, which comes from the west to join the Clark Fork here, was named by Father De Smet in 1842, in honor of St. Regis, a brother Jesuit.

At St. Regis is the junction with the St. Regis Cut-Off *(see Tour 12)*. US 10 goes west along the St. Regis River. At 150.7 *m.* US 10 enters the CABINET NATIONAL FOREST and begins the ascent of the Camel's Hump through dense stands of virgin white pine, feathery tamarack, and fir.

CAMEL'S HUMP, 155.4 *m.* (3,951 alt.), is supposedly named for its form. Coincidentally, camel pack trains were once briefly used on the Mullan Road, which followed this route *(see TRANSPORTATION)*. The first camel train to freight goods into Montana came toiling out of the Nevada desert in the summer of 1864. It was a source of wonder to whites and Indians alike. Each camel carried 1,000 pounds, twice the load of a mule, found his own forage, and ate food a mule would reject. But mules and horses became unmanageable when they scented the strange beasts, and the men who handled them did not like them much better.

The road descends the west slope by a succession of curves and turns.

CABIN CITY, 158.8 *m.* (3,100 alt.), is a post office, restaurant, store, and service station.

At CANTONMENT JORDAN, 161.9 *m.,* Capt. John Mullan camped during the winter and spring of 1859–60, while the difficult grade over the Camel's Hump was built. It was mentioned in Mullan's *Guide:* "21st day (from Walla Walla). Move to Cantonment Jordan, 5½ miles distant. Grass one-half mile above camp; wood and water everywhere."

DEBORGIA, 162.5 *m.* (3,035 alt., 125 pop.) named for St. Francis De Borgia, clings to the rocky land.

The SAVENAC FOREST NURSERY (L), 167 *m.,* the largest in the United States for the development of trees for reforestation, was established by the U. S. Forest Service in 1909. Its annual capacity is 6,000,000 trees; the major species grown from seeds include western white and yellow pine, and Engelmann spruce. Many small plots are used for experimental work. The trees remain in the seed beds from 1 to 2 years, are transplanted once, and kept until they reach a height of 6 to 10 inches. They are then shipped for permanent planting on Montana and Idaho forest lands, usually in areas that have been twice swept by fires. On such "double burns," natural reforestation is improbable.

SALTESE, 172.1 *m.* (3,476 alt., 200 pop.), strung out along the highway and railroad tracks in a narrow canyon, is a supply point for small silver and gold mines in the nearby mountains. During the World War, copper mines to the southwest were very active. High above the town the electrified Milwaukee Road clings to a narrow, winding shelf carved from the rocky mountainside. With old-fashioned western hospitality, Saltese keeps the door of its small jail (R) always open, a gesture of welcome to weary hoboes.

The town, first known as Silver City, was renamed in 1891 to honor a Nez Percé chieftain. Its site was earlier known to packers, trappers, and prospectors, who called it Packer's Meadow, as a good campground on the difficult trail; later it became a stop for west-bound travelers on the Mullan Road, for Lookout Pass, 12 miles W., could hardly be crossed before nightfall.

BOOTHILL (R) is a cemetery in which are buried 9 men and women who died with their boots on. The first was Chris Daggett, who froze to death on the trail while carrying the mail to Mullan, Idaho. The others met death in more turbulent ways in the days before Silver City had any other law than a quick draw and an easy trigger. Burials on Boothill were informal and not very solemn. Graves were usually dug after the coffins, rude boxes hastily made, had been carried to the plot. The gravediggers amused themselves by pitching pennies at the chinks between the rough pine boards. Once the sport was begun, the digging could not proceed until he who made the fewest hits walked back to town to fetch beer for the others.

TAFT, 176.6 m. (3,625 alt.), is a ghost camp of 3 or 4 unoccupied frame buildings. In 1908, when the Milwaukee Road was driving its St. Paul Pass Tunnel through the Bitterroot Mountains (see TRANSPOR-TATION), it was a town of 2,000 inhabitants whose many saloons, gambling houses, dance halls, and flimsy buildings crowded the narrow valley. In the winter of 1909–10 the town was almost entirely destroyed by fire. When Idaho and Washington were dry and Montana wet, Taft was one of the supply points for bootleggers operating in the dry States, and was visited frequently by residents of such towns as Mullan, Wallace, and Kellogg, Idaho. But even that could not keep it alive. It saw its last real activity in 1916, when an electric power line was built across the Coeur d'Alene Mountains (R) to connect the railroad substation at East Portal, 2 miles west with Thompson Falls.

West of Taft the gulch divides. US 10 keeps to the R., along the North Fork of the St. Regis River.

At 179.5 m. the winding ascent through Lookout Canyon begins. There is a sharp curve and underpass at 181 m., and near the summit are further sharp curves, some without guard rails (drive carefully).

At LOOKOUT PASS SUMMIT, 183.2 m. (4,738 alt.), US 10 crosses the Idaho Line, 13 miles east of Wallace, Idaho (see Idaho Tour 10).

<<<<<<<<<<<<<<<<<✿>>>>>>>>>>>>>>>>>>>

Tour 1A

Junction with US 10 S—Townsend—Helena—Garrison; US 10 N. Junction US 10 S to Garrison, 107.1 m.

Route roughly paralleled by Chicago, Milwaukee, St. Paul & Pacific R.R. between

Three Forks and a point south of Toston; by Northern Pacific Ry. between Toston
and Garrison; and by Northwest Airlines throughout.
Many tourist camps and hotels.
Oiled roadbed throughout, open all seasons. MacDonald Pass dangerous during wet
or icy weather; in winter occasionally closed a few hours while snow plows work.
Good route for trailers.

Between Three Forks and Helena US 10 N runs through the broad
valley of the upper Missouri River, a fairly level, thinly populated area.
From dry uplands it descends to irrigated fields and meadows. On both
sides rise mountains, brown and purple in the clear air.

In 1805 Lewis and Clark made a careful report of what they saw along
the Missouri but, careful as they were to report on the presence of fur-
bearing animals and other sources of wealth they apparently saw nothing
to indicate the mineral wealth revealed half a century later in Confederate, Last Chance, and other gulches.

West of Helena US 10 N runs through narrow valleys, thickly forested with pine and pointed fir. It crosses the Continental Divide through
MacDonald Pass.

US 10 N branches north from the point, 0 *m.*, where US 10 divides
into alternate routes, 3.6 miles west of Three Forks.

From the hill (R) just north of the junction is a bird's-eye view (L)
of the cottonwood bottoms in which the Jefferson, Gallatin, and Madison
Rivers join to form the Missouri *(see Tour 1, sec. b).* Some authorities
say that the Missouri was named for a tribe of Sioux living near the river
whom the Illinois called Emessourita *(dwellers on the Big Muddy).* On
early French maps it appears as "Emossouritsu," "Oumossourits," and
even "le Missouri ou R. de Peketanoui."

The range along the road, unfenced and bare of any vegetation other
than sparse grass and sagebrush, is dull sepia and brown.

At 6.9 *m.* the foothills of the main range of the Rockies are visible
(L). Straight ahead are the Big Belt Mountains, so named because of a
prominent girdle of outcropping limestone.

TOSTON, 20.2 *m.* (3,925 alt., 200 pop.), is a farmers' town on the
riverbank, shaded by cottonwoods and surrounded by irrigated bottoms
planted with alfalfa and timothy. Cattle graze on the low hills.

Left from Toston on a dirt road to PARKER, 8 *m.*, a ghost mining camp.
RADERSBURG, 13 *m.* (4,567 alt., 152 pop.), is an old mining town that to some
extent came back. It sprang up in 1866, when John Keating opened the Keating
Mine, and boomed the following year, when the East Pacific claim was discovered
north of town. The two mines together produced more than $3,000,000 in gold and
silver up to 1904, but were worked only intermittently during the following thirty
years. Rising prices after 1933 brought a brisk revival of activity.
Radersburg is the birthplace of Myrna Loy, christened Myrna Williams, the movie
actress.

TOWNSEND, 30.5 *m.* (3,833 alt., 740 pop.), the seat of Broadwater
County and once a busy place, lost much of its liveliness when automobiles and good roads brought Helena within easy travel distance of the
inhabitants of the valley ranches. There are only a few business establish-
ments, and drab frame and log buildings are neglected and weather-

beaten. A few well-kept dwellings still face the wide tree-shaded streets. At Townsend is the junction with State 6 *(see Tour 11)*.

1. Left from Townsend on a dirt road is HASSEL, 5 *m.,* the ghost of a noted mining camp of the 1890's. A few lessees still work the gold and silver properties of the district. Though unusual faulting makes Hassel ore veins hard to follow, the mines are credited with a production of about $100,000 since 1934.

2. Right from Townsend on a dirt road to another road, 15 *m.;* R. here to DIAMOND CITY, 23 *m.* (4,000 alt.), formerly one of the richest camps in CONFEDERATE GULCH.

Confederate soldiers captured in Civil War battles near Lexington, Mo., were banished up the Missouri by the Union commander. Two of the exiles, Washington Baker and Pomp Dennis, intent on staking claims in Last Chance Gulch, came up from Fort Benton in the autumn of 1864, prospecting as they went. Here at the mouth of one of the gulches in the Big Belt Mountains, they found unusual amounts of detritus and wash. The first pans yielded 10¢ each, but later returns were greater.

By spring a double line of houses straggled along the single street which followed the bends of the gulch. Prospectors of all kinds poured in—veterans of the gold rushes to California, Colorado, and Idaho, and amateurs who did not even know how to begin to hunt for the precious metal. One of the amateurs naively asked an old-timer to suggest a place where he could "do some digging." The older man, in true frontier style, pointed out the most unpromising spot in sight and suggested, "Try that bar up there; you might find something." The novice, following the advice, staked the claim. His MONTANA BAR, placer ground covering less than 2 acres, was one of the richest ever found. Occasional yields of $180 a pan on other claims seemed small when compared with the incredible recoveries made on Montana Bar, where pans worth $1,000 were common. The last of the pay dirt on the bar was sluiced off in one big clean-up that yielded two and one-half tons of gold, worth more than $1,000,000.

During the boom years the streets seethed with excitement and activity. Crews labored night and day to build a flume that brought water 7 miles for hydraulic work. Houses had to be raised 15 feet to save them from burial beneath the avalanche of tailings and boulders that was washed down the gulch. For a time Diamond City had a population of more than 10,000. But as soon as the cream had been skimmed, the prospectors who had not struck it rich moved on. In 1870 the town had 255 people; in another 12 months, 64; by 1883 four families remained. At length these, too, departed, and only a few foundations remain among mounds and ridges of sifted tailings. The total yield of Confederate Gulch is estimated to have been 15 to 17 millions, of which 90 percent was produced before 1870.

Much of the irrigated land between Townsend and Helena is used for growing grain and hay. There are also stock ranches here, some with international reputations as producers of fine horses. Local sales of registered stallions bring buyers from the important markets of the United States, Canada, and Europe.

The highway crosses numerous tributaries of the Missouri; along them are thick growths of huckleberries, chokecherries, gooseberries, serviceberries, and, in places, wild strawberries and raspberries. Rattlesnakes inhabit the rocky slopes of the hills, but are seldom encountered at elevations of more than 4,500 feet. Snake stories with a Paul Bunyan flavor are often heard in this neighborhood.

At 31.7 *m.* US 10 crosses the Missouri River, veers L., and follows easier grades.

OLD BEDFORD MILL (L), 33.9 *m.,* is on the site of the Bedford stage station of the old Helena-Virginia City line. The mill was active when more grain was grown in this valley. A hot spring is near the mill.

Confederate Gulch *(see above)* is visible (R) at 35.2 *m.* The Elkhorn Range looms (L) above the broad expanse of grass and sage. Threaded with gullies and canyons that once contained active placers, it still lures prospectors. Like the Big Belts (R), it is in the Helena National Forest.

WINSTON, 42.8 *m.* (4,375 alt., 165 pop.), is a group of small buildings, dull red and brilliant yellow, against barren, grayish brown mountains.

MOUNT HELENA (5,462 alt.) dominates the western sky line at 54.7 *m.* ahead.

At 55.3 *m.* the high smokestack of the East Helena smelter is visible (L).

EAST HELENA, 57.6 *m.* (3,901 alt., 1,039 pop.), is a smelter town with many foreign-born inhabitants, most of whom came from the Balkans shortly after 1900. During prohibition many turned to the home-brewing practiced in their native lands; their products became so popular that a number left their jobs at the smelter to devote their entire time to easing the dry throats of the nearby capital. Legislative sessions brought miniature booms. With the repeal of prohibition, however, smelting again became East Helena's chief industry.

The LEAD SMELTER and the ZINC RECOVERY PLANT *(both open on application at office)*, connected by a slag conveyor, are operated jointly. Zinc, lead, gold, and silver ores from Idaho and Montana are reduced in 4 furnaces whose united annual capacity is 300,000 tons of ore and concentrates.

At 59 *m.* (L) the twin spires of St. Helena Cathedral and the dome of the State CAPITOL are seen. Mount Helena, straight ahead, is identified by the H of white painted rocks on its eastern slope.

At 61.2 *m.* is a junction with US 91 *(see Tour 6)*, which unites briefly with US 10 N.

HELENA, 63.1 *m.* (4,214 alt., 11,803 pop.) *(see HELENA)*.

Points of Interest: State Capitol, St. Helena Cathedral, Lewis and Clark County Courthouse, Public Library, Carroll College, Algeria Shrine Temple, Hill Park, placer diggings.

Helena is at the western junction with US 91 *(see Tour 6)*.

At 66.4 *m.* is the junction with a graveled road.

1. Right on this road to FORT HARRISON *(open daily 9-7)*, 1 *m.* (4,006 alt.), abandoned in 1910, but reopened as a training camp for Montana troops during the World War. The earthquakes of 1935–37 seriously damaged 10 of the 41 brick buildings. About 20 of those remaining are used by the National Guard, the rest belong to the Veterans Administration Facility. The main building has been made earthquake-resistant.

2. Left from US 10 N on the one-way road, which circles Mount Helena as Le Grand Cannon Blvd. and enters Helena at the head of Holter St., 4 *m.* The route provides far-reaching views and along it are several picnicking spots.

BROADWATER RESORT (R), 66.5 *m.*, built in 1889 by Col. C. A. Broadwater, is a rambling two-story frame structure with wide porches. The large pool *(open June 1–Sept. 1; adm. 25¢)* is sheltered by a wooden structure of Moorish design; water is piped to it from hot springs nearby. The spacious grounds are landscaped. In the 1890's Broadwater was fre-

A THRESHER

quented by the local elite but in the following decades it had a checkered career. For long periods it stood unused; several hopeful lessees found it unprofitable; but after 1935 it again became a popular roadhouse in Montana.

Right from Broadwater on an unimproved road to GREENHORN GULCH, 11 *m.*, which many years ago held a populous, important, and somewhat excitable placer camp. In April 1883 the Territorial Governor telegraphed the postal authorities at Washington: "Vigilantes at Greenhorn, Montana, have removed postmaster by hanging . . . Office . . . now vacant . . ." The Northern Pacific flag station, AUSTIN (4,771 alt., 78 pop.) is all that remains of the settlement.

The GREENHOUSES AND NURSERY *(open to public)*, 67.2 *m.*, specialize in the development of flowers, shrubs, vegetables, and ornamental trees suitable for use in high land. Plants bloom in the greenhouses the year around.

By the nursery is Tenmile Creek, which provides most of Helena's water supply.

The HELENA TOWN AND COUNTRY CLUB *(visitors' cards obtainable at Placer Hotel; greens fee $1)*, 71.7 *m.*, has a clubhouse and an 18-hole golf course.

At 73.2 *m.* is the junction with an improved road.

Left on this gulch road into the heavily timbered TENMILE CANYON, dotted with the summer homes of Helena residents. Some of the houses are hidden by thick growths of fir, tamarack, and lodgepole pine.

At 3 *m.* is an improved public campground (R).

RIMINI, 7 *m.* (5,192 alt., 85 pop.), is the trade center of a district that has produced gold, silver, and lead to the value of $3,000,000. A few mines are still worked by lessees.

Shortly after the discovery of its silverlead lodes in the early 1880's, the citizens saw the drama of Paolo and Francesca da Rimini performed by a road company; they recorded their approval in the new camp's name. Montanans pronounce it "Rim'-in-eye."

Left 2 *m.* from Rimini on a trail to CHESSMAN RESERVOIR, a part of the Helena water system. In early summer the trail is bordered with a mass of wild flowers— lupine, bluebell, shooting star, phlox, aster, wild rose, and many others.

The MONTANA LEAD MINE, 7.5 *m.*, owned by the estate of James J. Hill, the railroad builder, now makes only occasional shipments to the East Helena smelter. The manager's residence, a log chalet with charming grounds bordering the creek, is one of the show places of the Helena region.

The road ascends a steep grade to a bench between tall walls of lodgepole pine. Red Mountain rises impressively in the southwest.

The PORPHYRY DIKE MINE, 12 *m.*, is in a region where great rhyolite flows hold low-grade gold ore. Only large-scale milling is profitable.

Right 0.5 *m.* from the Porphyry Dike on a footpath to the summit of RED MOUNTAIN (8,802 alt.), which gives a sweeping view westward of a rugged, uninhabited wilderness that rises to the Continental Divide.

MacDONALD PASS in the Continental Divide, 79 *m.* (6,323 alt.), was named for Alexander MacDonald, who until 1885, maintained a toll road there. He had to employ a full-time crew to keep the road in condition; where underground seepage created bogs, he found it necessary to corduroy considerable stretches. The stages between Helena and Deer Lodge used this pass and it was the scene of several bold mail robberies.

A spring of clear, cold water is near the summit (R) on the east slope. Both slopes are long and steep *(drive with care)*. The views are dramatic.

Left from MacDonald Pass on a dirt road to MACDONALD CAMPGROUND *(stoves, picnic tables, water)*, 0.5 *m.*, in a forest clearing.

ELLISTON, 85.5 *m.* (5,061 alt., 225 pop.), is a trade town in a gold quartz- and placer-mining district. A lime quarry and a mill are at the base of a high hill near the eastern limits of town. MOUNT BISON (8,018 alt.) rises (L) in the distance.

Between Elliston and the junction with US 10 S, the route follows the Little Blackfoot River.

AVON, 94.1 *m.* (4,702 alt., 162 pop.), is a supply point where cattle and sheep ranchers rub elbows with prospectors and miners.

Right from Avon on a graveled road is FINN, 14 *m.* (4,691 alt., 17 pop.), whose small general store sells almost entirely to miners; for the most part they pay in gold dust.

The road skirts the southern end and southeastern slopes of the Flathead Range.

HELMVILLE, 23 *m.* (4,305 alt., 202 pop.) *(see Tour 8)*, is at the junction with State 31 *(see Tour 8)*.

At 107.1 *m.* US 10 N and US 10 S join to become US 10 *(see Tour 1)*, on the eastern outskirts of GARRISON *(see Tour 1, sec. d)*.

‹‹‹‹‹‹‹‹‹‹‹‹‹‹‹‹‹‹‹‹ ✿ ›››››››››››››››››››

Tour 2

(Williston, N. D.)—Glasgow—Malta—Havre—Shelby—Glacier Park Station—Kalispell—Libby—(Bonners Ferry, Idaho); US 2. North Dakota Line to Idaho Line, 701.7 m.

Great Northern Ry. parallels route between North Dakota Line and Columbia Falls, and between Libby and Idaho Line.
All types of accommodations in larger towns. Modern tourist-cabin camps and camp-grounds at long intervals.
Oiled roadbed between North Dakota Line and Kalispell; between Kalispell and Idaho Line some untreated stretches where travel is difficult in winter and early spring. Marias Pass between Glacier Park Station and Belton sometimes closed by drifted snow in winter; dangerous in all weather because of sharp curves and pre-cipitous, unguarded edges.

Section a. NORTH DAKOTA LINE to HAVRE, 293 m., US 2.

US 2, following the Missouri and Milk Rivers across the windswept glaciated plains and shallow valleys of northern Montana, is locally known as the High-line, and semiofficially as the Roosevelt International Highway. It crosses what was the open range in Montana's spectacular cattle-raising days. In recent decades some high-grade wheat and other grain have been grown here, but this is still primarily a grazing region. The impressiveness of the landscape comes from its sweep of vast plain, from which low buttes rise here and there with sharp silhouettes.

Between the towns few dwellings are seen.

US 2 crosses the North Dakota Line, 0 m., 19 miles west of Willis-ton, N. D.

BAINVILLE, 8.7 m. (1,962 alt., 400 pop.), in earlier days was merely a trading post. The town, which was platted in 1906, is a cluster of dusty frame houses and a brick structure or two. It, like many other towns of the region, has suffered severely during the years of drought and de-pression.

SIGNAL BUTTE (L) is an observation point that has been used by Indians, trappers, and stockmen.

Left from Bainville 11 m. on a dirt road to the SITE OF FORT UNION, near the junction of the Missouri and Yellowstone Rivers. In 1805 the Lewis and Clark ex-pedition passed this point in pirogues. Twenty-three years later the American Fur Company built Fort Floyd, later known as Fort Union, as a center for its trade with the Assiniboine. The Indians came long distances by trail and water to exchange beaver, mink, marten, and other pelts for whiskey, beads, calico, tobacco, and—most prized of all—smooth-bore rifles and black powder. The liquor was sold to them in defiance of Federal law, but greatly helped to win the trade that might otherwise have gone to the Hudson's Bay post in Canada. For protection against drunken or marauding tribesmen, Fort Union's great log buildings were enclosed by a 20-foot stockade with blockhouses at two corners.

Until the great days of the fur trade had passed, Fort Union was eminent among frontier outposts. From it Kenneth McKenzie, its first factor, developed and directed activities covering a large region; here, on June 17, 1832, the *Yellowstone,* first steamboat to come this far up the river, arrived from St. Louis. Prince Paul of Württemberg; Maximilian, Prince of Wied; Audubon, the naturalist; Jim Bridger, the scout; and Father De Smet, the Jesuit missionary, were among those who visited the populous post. In 1868 the U. S. Government purchased and dismantled it, using its materials in the construction of Fort Buford, 8 miles down the Missouri River.

West of Bainville massive gray buttes rise from the river flat, but they are often hidden by low mists from the Missouri. Sunlight is bright and winds are strong in this region. A breeze that makes a long chain stand out like the tail of a kite isn't so bad, say old-timers; but when the end links start snapping off, one after another, it is safe to assume that a good, stiff blow is about to begin. During the World War the prairie here produced enormous crops of wheat. Some farms were so mechanized that they had not a single animal. Huge unwieldy tractors were brought in to make their slow, grinding, and explosive ways across the land, plowing, harrowing, and sowing in one operation. The farmers, too busy with their hundreds of acres of grain to keep cows or to garden, bought their milk and vegetables in cans. When grain prices fell after the war, the use of the huge tractors was discontinued. Later smaller and more efficient ones were acquired.

CULBERTSON, 22.7 *m.* (1,921 alt., 536 pop.), is a grain-shipping point, as its large elevators indicate to newcomers. It is named for Alexander Culbertson, who in 1839 succeeded Kenneth McKenzie as factor at Fort Union *(see above).* In 1879 his son Jack established a ranch near here. Just when or how the town came into existence is not known, but the theory that there was a town gained currency between 1888 and 1892. In the latter year, however, a certain Lucy A. Isbel stepped off the train and spent some time looking for it. Two log buildings were not regarded as a town where she came from.

At the western edge of the village is a junction with State 16.

1. Left on State 16 to the MISSOURI RIVER BRIDGE (1934), 2.7 *m.* From this steel structure 1,169 feet long and one of the finest in the State, is viewed a great bend of the tree-lined river, with typical breaks along the edges of the river flat.

2. Right on State 16, a graveled road that parallels Big Muddy Creek, is FROID, 13 *m.* (2,026 alt., 434 pop.), formerly the home of John W. Schnitzler, whose wheat fields covered thousands of acres. His enthusiasm for aviation obtained an excellent landing field for Froid and the honor of being the only small town formally visited by the great group flight around the Nation in July 1928. He was killed, in 1932, when his private plane crashed against a high butte near Glasgow.

MEDICINE LAKE *(boats available),* 24 *m.* (R), is a Federal migratory waterfowl reserve. The village of MEDICINE LAKE, 26 *m.* (1,948 alt., 384 pop.), was once Plentywood's rival for the business of Sheridan County.

At 34 *m.* is the junction with a dirt road; R. here 10 *m.* is DAGMAR, the trade center of a Danish community that has for a long time successfully conducted various cooperative enterprises. These include a store, a coal mine, a telephone exchange, a fire insurance company, and a burial association providing funerals for $45.

PLENTYWOOD, 49 *m.* (2,024 alt., 1,226 pop.), seat of Sheridan County, is said to have been named, before it was settled, by the foreman of a cattle outfit who found an unexpected hoard of wood on the bare prairie. No wood grows near here except small boxelder and poplar.

Plentywood is the capital of a grain-producing area whose development has been

FARM FAMILY, NORTH OF MEDICINE LAKE

rapid and boisterous. It has experienced prosperity, drought and starvation, prosperity, and drought again.

The people here have been notably independent in politics. They began, mildly enough, by supporting the Bull Moose ticket in 1912. In 1918 the Non-partisan League established the *Producers News* here, which under the editorship of Charles E. Taylor, helped to build up an organization that on several occasions attracted national attention. From 1920 to 1926 nearly the entire population of Sheridan County belonged to the Farmer-Labor Party; in 1922 and 1924 its ticket filled the county offices. The *Producers News* had a staff of editors, contributors, and collaborators that at one time included such people as Ella Reeve (Mother) Bloor and Tom O'Flaherty, brother of Liam O'Flaherty, the Irish author. Between heated political campaigns it found time to discuss contemporary cultural issues, and made Plentywood for several years one of the best-informed small towns in the Northwest; but it gathered its opposition as it went along. The Republicans and the Democrats consolidated their forces and in 1926 took advantage of the theft of $106,000 from the county treasurer's office to throw suspicion upon those in office. In the 1928 elections the Farmer-Labor ticket was defeated; conservatives have controlled the county since then. Nevertheless, the non-conformist minority has been active from time to time through the depression years. In 1930 about 500 citizens of the county voted the Communist Party ticket straight; in the winter of 1932–33 a group of militant malcontents took clothing by force from the Red Cross headquarters here. Partly because of such occurrences, Alfred Miller, an editor of the *Producers News*, was later arrested and threatened with deportation to Germany, his birthplace. In 1937, after the *Producers News* suspended publication, many of the former leaders left.

Left from Plentywood (straight ahead) on State 5, crossing the Big Muddy Flat and passing fantastically carved badlands (R) near ARCHER, 63 *m.* (2,064 alt.,

22 pop.). The EAGLE'S NEST (L), 82 *m.*, is a low basin below a piskun *(see BEFORE THE WHITE MAN).*
State 5 continues through level farmland.
SCOBEY, 94 *m.* (2,450 alt., 1,259 pop.), is the seat of Daniels County. Six large grain elevators rising from the prairie are evidence of the fertility of the surrounding country. During the World War and the following boom times, especially the years 1927–28, Scobey was one of the most important primary wheat markets in the Northwest. Since the drought began the lines of wagons waiting by the elevators have been much shorter than formerly.
Left from Scobey on State 13, an oiled road traversing grain- and cattle-raising country with many good duck-hunting areas.
At 141 *m.* is a junction with US 2, 7 miles east of Wolf Point *(see below).*

At 28.5 *m.* is the eastern boundary of the Fort Peck Indian Reservation, home of the Assiniboine and the Yankton Sioux. The road here runs along the Missouri River bottom lands, in springtime fragrant with the scent of chokecherry blossoms and in summer shaded by cottonwoods.

BROCKTON, 42.9 *m.* (1,955 alt., 300 pop.), is a wind-swept village on the prairie.

POPLAR, 56.7 *m.* (1,963 alt., 1,046 pop.), grew up around Fort Peck, which was maintained until 1887 to protect cattle ranchers from hostile Indians. The town and the river that skirts it were so named because of the trees along the banks of the stream. Before a bridge spanned the river, swains from the town swam their horses through the spring ice floes, when going to court girls living on the northern ranches.

In Poplar is the agency of the FORT PECK INDIAN RESERVATION of 1,525,537 acres, created in 1872. Subagencies are at Frazer and Wolf Point.

The Assiniboine, though they are now only two-fifths of the population, were the owners of the original reservation. Of Siouan stock, they were separated from the Sioux after a battle near Devils Lake in legendary times. The Assiniboine hunted from the Missouri River to the Saskatchewan, and from the Assiniboine to the Milk. They felt that the Yankton Sioux, who arrived from South Dakota in 1886, were intruders, and fought them fiercely.

Gauche *(Left Hand)*, chief of the Assiniboine, described by Father De Smet as "crafty, cruel, deceitful," kept his people at war with all their neighbors. They were not unfriendly to the whites. Under Left Hand's leadership the Indians burned Fort Piegan in the course of hostilities with the Blackfeet, but Gov. Isaac Stevens, during his railroad survey, found them friendly and helpful. The Indians said Stevens "talked straight."

The Sioux, on the other hand, were always enemies of the whites. They murdered settlers, harassed river boats, and shot woodcutters along the Missouri and the Yellowstone. In its last years, they avoided Fort Union as "bad medicine" and prevented other tribes from trading there. Under their great chiefs, Sitting Bull and Gall, they were continuously on the warpath until the United States finally forced them to surrender.

Of the 2,900 Indians on the reservation half are full-bloods. The members of the two tribes live in separate communities, and their languages are so different that intertribal communication is in English.

For years the Assiniboine filed claims against the Government for tak-

AN EASTERN MONTANA FARMER

ing their land and were eventually awarded $4,000,000. Both tribes are moderately well-to-do and progressive. Their chief income is rental from grazing lands. Under the original allotments each Indian received 320 acres of grazing land, 40 of irrigable land, and 20 of timber, mostly along streams. When the reservation was opened to settlers, homestead fees went into the tribal funds. About 150 earn money by making moccasins, beadwork, baskets, willow canes, and the like. About 900 children are (1939) in the public schools, and 25 youths are in college.

In 1935 the Sioux and Assiniboine rejected the Wheeler-Howard self-governing act, preferring the rule of an executive board under the direction of the Indian agent. Two board members are elected from each of six districts, a chairman and other officials at large.

The Assiniboine, like other Indians, have suffered seriously from white men's diseases. In 1837–38 an epidemic of smallpox nearly wiped out the tribe. It is said that the infection was carried to them by a blanket a tribesman stole from a white sufferer on a river steamer. Today less than 5 percent have tuberculosis (about 1890 the most dreaded disease) but badly balanced diets, composed chiefly of "store food" have lowered the resistance of many. A Government hospital and two physicians furnish medical care.

The ancient grass, victory, and rain dances are performed whenever the council decides, but the sun dance is held annually, June 30–July 4. Like all Indian dances *(see sec. b)*, this one has religious significance. Most of the dancers wear the feathered headdress and beaded garments, but a few, brightly painted, wear only a G string. They dance facing the sun and a pole carved with symbols of forked lightning, sunrays, and moonbeams. Nearby are the sun-dance poles of past years. The Federal Government has forbidden the extreme self-torture formerly indulged in, but the participants still dance all day without taking food or water. *(Visitors with cameras permitted to witness dance; no set admittance fee, but gifts of money are expected.)*

At 71.5 *m.* US 2 intersects State 13 *(see above)*.

WOLF POINT, 78.6 *m.* (2,004 alt., 1,539 pop.), seat of Roosevelt County, still exhibits the vigor of its early days, when it was a cattle town. It was named for a high hill (R) that was a landmark for steamboat pilots. The Wolf Point Stampede, a first-rate rodeo, is held each year in July. The town has a radio broadcasting station, KGCX (1310 kc.).

West of Wolf Point US 2 traverses rolling moraines, debris left by the Wisconsin ice sheet *(see NATURAL SETTING)*.

OSWEGO, 90.6 *m.* (2,026 alt., 150 pop.), was named by early settlers from Oswego, N. Y. It consists of scattered buildings that escaped the flames of a devastating fire. Old-timers' reunions are popular summer events here. The oldsters, wearing the garb of the 1880's and 1890's, mingle with members of the third generation. In the evening all dance the lively two-step and polka, to music furnished by local fiddlers. Between dances the settlers swap yarns of the days when they rode the range.

Just west of Oswego is an INDIAN CEMETERY with graves above the ground.

By day, FRAZER, 98.2 *m.* (2,068 alt., 300 pop.), is announced by tall grain elevators that indicate the reason for its existence. At night a few neon signs break the intense darkness of the prairie. Ancient horse-drawn rigs move down the street beside streamlined automobiles.

The observation tower above Fort Peck Dam is visible (L) at 107 *m.* US 2 here leaves the Missouri to follow Milk River, the most important stream of north central Montana. It was so named by Capt. Meriwether Lewis because of the whiteness of its waters.

NASHUA, 114.5 *m.* (2,068 alt., 351 pop.), is sheltered by a high butte (R) that in winter provides excellent opportunities for skiing and tobogganing. The town, at the confluence of Milk River and Porcupine Creek, is at the western boundary of the Fort Peck Indian Reservation. Its population has doubled since 1933 because of construction work on Fort Peck Dam.

Nashua is the junction with the improved dirt Fort Peck Dam road *(see Tour 10A).*

GLASGOW, 129 *m.* (2,095 alt., 2,216 pop.), the seat of Valley County, is one of the oldest communities in northeastern Montana; since the beginning of construction at Fort Peck Dam, it has been one of the busiest. Everywhere is evidence of prosperity; the population more than doubled between 1933 and 1937. Streams of people arrive and depart daily on business connected with the dam development. Hotels and tourist cabins are crowded.

The town came into existence in 1887 during the building of the Great Northern Ry., which at first called it Siding 45—it had the forty-fifth siding west of Minot, N. D. When it was platted in the following year it was named in honor of Glasgow, Scotland. By July 1888 it consisted of 8 saloons, 3 restaurants, and 1 store—all but 2 housed in tents. During this rather feverish period Charles Hall, the first settler, sold most of the town site without the formality of ownership.

In time Glasgow became the cattle-, sheep-, and grain-shipping center of an extensive area but it did not have much other importance until September 1932. when two U. S. Army engineers took its mayor out along the Missouri River, and spoke casually about building a dam. "Why, it would cost a million dollars!" gasped the mayor. "Yes," said the engineers, "probably 75 million." The project was approved, a half dozen shanty towns mushroomed nearby. and Glasgow shook itself awake to the fact that it was to be, for a few years at least, a small metropolis. The life that immediately began fermenting in and around it almost put to shame the hell-roaring activities of its frontier days. The magazine *Life,* in its first issue (1936), presented a pictorial record of the revival of a wild west atmosphere. *(Frequent bus service to dam; two planes make flights over dam area.)*

At Glasgow is the junction with State 22 *(see Tour 10).*

HINSDALE. 158.8 *m.* (2,182 alt., 359 pop.), like many High-line towns, has a brick school on Main St. that is its most imposing structure and the center of civic and social activities.

SACO, 172.7 *m.* (2,184 alt., 500 pop.), owns its own natural gas system. Its gas rate is the lowest in the State.

The irrigated loam of Milk River Valley produces sugar beets, alfalfa, bluejoint hay, and small grains.

LAKE BOWDOIN (L), 184.7 *m.,* is in a widespreading area of swamps and pools that formerly provided the best duck-hunting in the State. In 1936 it became a Federal refuge for migratory birds.

The brushlands of Milk River Valley shelter Chinese pheasants, Hungarian partridges, grouse, sage hens, and cottontail and snowshoe rabbits. Deer live in the breaks of the larger streams and antelope range on the south side of Milk River. Jack rabbits and prairie dogs are so numerous that they are farm and ranch pests; coyotes maintain their number despite a bounty offered for their destruction.

At 186.7 *m.* is the junction with a dirt road.

Right on this road to the AMERICAN LEGION HEALTH POOL, 4 *m.*, on the storage grounds of the Milk River irrigation project. It has a warm plunge, 60 feet wide, and 80 long, and hot baths *(open 8 a.m. to midnight; adm. 10¢)*. While drilling an oil well in 1924, workmen struck highly mineralized water at 3,200 feet; gas bubbling up through the water became ignited; and for 6 years visitors saw "burning water." In 1930 the local American Legion post obtained authority from Congress to use the water for curative and recreational purposes.

Throughout this region the "sodbuster" tradition is of relatively recent origin. As late as 1916 homesteaders arrived with horses, wagons, plows, stoves, bedding, and small grubstakes. Since there was no timber and they could not afford to buy lumber, the newcomers plowed up sod and laid slabs of it in tiers over pole frameworks to form dwellings. Some sod huts still stand in outlying districts, though they are seldom used for human habitation.

MALTA, 200.6 *m.* (2,254 alt., 1,342 pop.), seat of Phillips County, was named for the island in the Mediterranean. Its present drabness and apathy give no hint that from 1870 to 1900 it was the center of a cattle empire that reached from Glasgow to Havre, and from the Missouri River breaks to the Canadian Border. Owners of four famous brands—Phillips, Coburn, Matador, and Phelps—controlled this range and the Bearpaw pool.

A ranch at Brookside, about 30 miles southwest of Malta, was the home of two brothers, Wallace and Walt Coburn. Wallace, a friend of Charles M. Russell *(see THE ARTS)*, published a book of cowboy poems that Russell illustrated. Walt is a writer of western yarns.

The large boulder in Malta's city park, opposite the Great Northern Ry. station, resembles a sleeping buffalo. Until 1934 it was a prominent landmark of a place 25 miles northeast of here. Generations of Assiniboine revered it; the curious markings on it played a part in their tribal ritual.

Many of Charles M. Russell's pictures were produced in and near this town.

DODSON, 219.9 *m.* (2,291 alt., 249 pop.), was named for a merchant who conducted a well-patronized trading post and saloon here, before the building of the Great Northern Ry. Local legend commemorates "Peanut" Parson, a bachelor who ate his peas with a knife ground to the keenness of a razor blade. An easterner who spent two weeks with Peanut in 1911, was about to object to this dangerous habit, when Peanut leaned apologetically across the table: "Pardner," he protested mildly, "every time you put that there fork in your mouth I shiver in my boots for fear you'll punch a hole plumb through your tongue."

Between Dodson and Fort Belknap, US 2 traverses the northern end of the FORT BELKNAP INDIAN RESERVATION (620,330 acres; created 1887). At 245.2 m. (L) is the FORT BELKNAP AGENCY. The Gros Ventre and the Assiniboine, formerly enemies, have lived amicably together for many years on this reservation, and have had no external conflicts since 1887, when they made peace with the Canadian Bloods. The 758 Gros Ventre *(Big Bellies)* and 672 Assiniboine, or Mountain Sioux, are thrifty and industrious.

The present Gros Ventre are remnants of the Gros Ventre of the Prairie, a branch of the Arapahoe that came into Montana in the early nineteenth century. They lived along the north bank of the Missouri River until driven across it by the Cree in 1872. The Assiniboine take pride in their Sioux origin, but intermarry with the adaptable Gros Ventre.

Members of both tribes raise excellent cattle, including some blooded stock, and are among the most successful Indian stock growers in Montana. Surplus grazing land is leased to sheep-growers. Late June is shearing time *(see Tour 1)*. Some communal activities are carried on, though the land is held and exploited under individual allotments.

Fort Belknap Indians have abandoned such ancient customs as arbitrary rule by a chief, and the servitude of women. They are deeply religious and, though many are Protestants or Roman Catholics, they continue to perform a modified Sun Dance annually at the agency *(July 1-2; visitors permitted)*. At their annual fair, usually held in September at Hays *(see Tour 2A)* these Indians exhibit splendid horsemanship.

About 300 Chippewa-Cree who have never surrendered their land rights to the Government, live on and near the Fort Belknap Reservation. Poor, unrecognized as a tribe, a perplexing problem to social and relief agencies, these Indians are making a claim of usurpation against the Government and asking compensation for the loss of their lands. Smaller remnants of various tribes are scattered over the State; some have been given homes on the Rocky Boy Reservation *(see Tour 14)*.

A favorite among Fort Belknap Indians is Coming Day, who in 1937 was more than eighty years old and still maintained his reputation for fearlessness. In his prime he rode joyously in the white man's "devil-bug," that sputtered and smoked and traveled like wind without the use of ponies. In August 1936 he boarded the white man's "thunder bird" during the reservation fair and waved gaily to his quaking comrades. When the plane was at an altitude of several thousand feet he exhorted the pilot in the Gros Ventre tongue to go higher. "As yet," he shouted scornfully, "we are not to the height where flies the common magpie!"

At Fort Belknap Agency is the junction with the Zortman Road *(see Tour 2A)*.

HARLEM, 249.4 m. (2,371 alt., 708 pop.), lies in a coulee (valley) shaded and sheltered by cottonwoods. Modern brick buildings intrude among the wooden structures of pioneer times. It is said that its first post office was a shoe box on the counter of a general store. When the volume of mail became too great for the shoe box, an empty beer case fitted with pigeonholes took its place.

Harlem is the trading center for the Fort Belknap Reservation, and its streets are often enlivened by the presence of Indians in bright and complicated mixtures of white and native dress. Under an unbuttoned vest, a buck may wear a rose-decorated corset with dangling straps and buckles. Some squaws drape their shoulders with yards of brilliant calico. These, however, are the costumes of individualists. A buck usually wears a broad-brimmed hat over his braids, a faded shirt, corduroy trousers, and boots, shoes, or moccasins. Bright hair ribbons are worn by both buck and squaw.

Formerly a sheepherders' convention was held here annually. At the last one (1922) the herders organized a union.

ZURICH, 261.3 m. (2,410 alt., 305 pop.), is a small trading center and shipping point in the sugar-beet area.

The CHINOOK SUGAR REFINERY, 270.3 m. (L), the fourth largest in Montana, has, since 1925, introduced a thriving industry into this region *(see INDUSTRY AND COMMERCE)*. The Mexican and Filipino laborers employed in the beet fields as thinners and toppers gather about the nearby shacks after the day's work to play guitars and sing.

CHINOOK, 271.3 m. (2,310 alt., 1,320 pop.), seat of Blaine County, bears the Indian name for the winds that, by melting the snow in January or February and letting cattle through to the rich bunch grass, have saved many a stockman from disaster. It was Charles M. Russell's postcard picture of a starving range cow, *Waiting for a Chinook (The Last of Five Thousand)*, that first won him recognition as an artist *(see THE ARTS)*.

The PUBLIC LIBRARY, Ohio Ave. and 6th St., contains reproductions of several Russell sculptures.

The MUNICIPAL SWIMMING POOL *(open July-Aug.)* is at Pennsylvania Ave. and 8th St.

Left from Chinook on Central Ave., which becomes a dirt road, to the NEZ PERCÉ BATTLEGROUND, 16 m., north of the low, isolated Bearpaw Mountains. A granite monument marks the spot where Chief Joseph, the Indian military genius, surrendered to Gen. Nelson A. Miles after the Battle of the Bear's Paw (October 1877).

Joseph had led his followers in a masterly retreat from Idaho *(see HISTORY)*. Here in the Bearpaw country, which they thought was in Canada, they made camp with their wounded. The mistake was discovered when General Miles attacked on September 30. A 4-day battle forced Joseph to make a decision—he must either surrender, or abandon the wounded, the old women, and the children.

"Hear me," he said to the white commander. "I am tired. My heart is sick and sad. Our chiefs are dead; the little children are freezing. My people have no blankets, no food. From where the sun stands, I will fight no more forever."

The surrender marked the end of the major Indian wars in the United States. The remaining Nez Percés were taken first to Bismarck, N. D., then to Leavenworth, Kans. In 1884 they were placed on the Colville Reservation in Washington.

LOHMAN, 279.4 m. (2,445 alt., 63 pop.), is a section where nat·

ural gas is plentiful and where the seepage near springs is often ignited. Indian superstition once made much of the "fire that comes out of the ground."

HAVRE, 293 m. (2,486 alt., 6,372 pop.), seat of Hill County, shows what careful planning went into its rebuilding after a great fire in 1892. The presence of the students of Northern Montana College give it an air of youth and sprightliness.

The town came into existence in 1887, when James J. Hill, for whom Hill County is named, sent his railroad-construction camp westward to this point; finding plenty of good water here, he decided to build a branch southward to Great Falls from this point rather than from one in the dry region to the west, as he had planned. Great Northern officials named the town for the French city Le Havre, but its citizens have always pronounced it Hav-ver. It developed as a railroad division point and stock-shipping center.

Havre is popularly known as the coldest place in the United States, but local patriots declare this a misconception arising from the publicity given to the readings of the U. S. Weather Bureau station here. The climatic extremes of the region, coupled with the distances between towns, make it easy to understand the development of a tradition of hospitality. In early days neighborly cooperation was essential to survival.

NORTHERN MONTANA COLLEGE (1929), along State 29 in the southwestern part of the city, is a junior college and a unit of the University of Montana. It offers two-year courses in the liberal arts and in preprofessional studies. First housed in the high school, in 1932 it was moved to a remodeled building on a 60-acre campus. Between 1932 and 1937 three buildings were added and the grounds were landscaped, partly with relief labor. The new buildings, of modern functional design, are constructed of brick made in Havre. The school has a stadium seating 7,000, and an open-air theater with a large stage.

At the annual Music Festival in May more than 50 bands and 1,500 musicians from all parts of the State compete. The event culminates in a concert held in the stadium.

The MUNICIPAL SWIMMING POOL *(open 10-8:30; suits 25¢)* is on 4th St. between 7th and 8th Aves.

The HILL COUNTY FAIRGROUNDS *(fair in August)* are 1 mile northwest of town on State 29. The race track, one of the best in Montana, is the scene of races between fast horses from several western States and from Canada

At Havre is the junction with State 29 *(see Tour 14)*.

Section b. HAVRE *to* BROWNING JUNCTION, *177.7 m.,* US 2.

Between Havre and Browning Junction US 2 traverses plains that are for the most part bare and, in dry years, desolate. Stock range and wheat farms fill the area east of the sudden upthrust of the Rocky Mountains.

In general, towns along the route present hybrid appearances, with, side by side, the weather-beaten buildings of the old range days and the cheap modern structures holding chain stores and filling stations. On spurs near the railroad depots are grain elevators and cattle-loading pens. Homes scatter away from a single short business block, or from the general store, the school, and the church clustered at a cross road.

West of HAVRE, 0 *m.*, at 4 *m.* is (L) the HAVRE COUNTRY CLUB *(greens fee weekdays 50¢, Sun. $1).*

FRESNO, 13.9 *m.* (2,690 alt., 12 pop.), is, in the Montana vernacular, "a wide spot in the road." It consists of a general store, a railroad station, and a few houses. In the store is a collection of relics of pioneer Montana.

KREMLIN, 19.4 *m.* (2,832 alt., 85 pop.), is said to have been so named by Russian settlers because they saw the citadel of Moscow in the mirages that appear on the surrounding prairie. On the unplowed lands along the highway grows short but highly nutritious buffalo grass. Some of the more prosperous ranchers of the vicinity lease their idle lands; others in the fall buy up as many cattle and sheep as they can afford to winter on the prairie. Thus when grain crops are poor, or prices low, they are assured of a moderate cash income.

GILFORD, 30.9 *m.* (2,830 alt., 250 pop.), and HINGHAM, 35.9 *m.* (3,036 alt., 251 pop.), are storage and shipping points for stock and grain.

At 41.9 *m.* is the junction with a graded road.

Right on this road is RUDYARD, 0.1 *m.* (3,112 alt., 165 pop.), named for Rudyard Kipling.

At 48.1 *m.* is the junction with a graded road.

Right on this road is INVERNESS, 0.1 *m.* (3,306 alt., 137 pop.), named by "Scotty" Watson, pioneer stockman, in memory of his native town in Scotland.

CHESTER, 61.7 *m.* (3,283 alt., 387 pop.), seat of Liberty County, is on the bank of Cottonwood Creek at the place where ranchers of the 1880's paused to rest on the long drive to the railhead at Minot, N. D.

West of Chester the Sweetgrass Hills *(see Tour 6, Sec. a)* are prominent (R) on the horizon.

LOTHAIR, 74.9 *m.* (3,308 alt., 150 pop.), is in the midst of undeveloped oil and natural-gas fields.

GALATA, 81.7 *m.* (3,096 alt., 75 pop.), a trading point and cattle-shipping station, has a history somewhat similar to that of many small High-line towns. In 1901 David R. McGinnis, first immigration agent of the Great Northern Ry., impressed by the beauty of the spot where Galata Creek, a dry wash (stream bed without water) crossed the railroad tracks, filed claim to the land, and engaged a surveyor to lay out a town. A year later he brought carpenters and lumber from Kalispell, and built a two-room house. Until 1904, when it burned, stock shippers were glad to crowd into the tiny rooms during cold winter days, but no one followed the lead of the city's founder by buying land or building houses. In 1905 McGinnis began an earnest effort to make Galata's urban existence a reality. He built a two-room real estate office and an eight-room hotel; he induced a storekeeper to come here and, when the man lacked funds to erect a store, allowed him to use a room in the real estate office. In those days a rancher would drive in with a chuck wagon, load up $500 or $1,000 worth of supplies, pay in cash, and return home grubstaked for a long winter. Only a few customers were necessary to maintain a thriving business. Nevertheless, Galata's merchant closed his shop within a few years and the hotel was abandoned.

One day McGinnis, living in Kalispell, was astonished to receive a check for back rent on the store. A cowhand had moved in, and was doing a fair business among the dry-land farmers who had settled on the former range. In 1910 Galata had four lumberyards and five stores. During the wartime boom settlers came into the area in droves, but with its collapse many of them went away.

In 1925 the town made an effort to ride to importance on the oilfield band wagon. A full-page advertisement in the achievement edition of the Shelby *Promoter* extolled Galata as the center of an agricultural paradise, and pointed out that it was the "city" nearest the new Liberty oil dome. Unfortunately, the Liberty dome was far out on the east flank of the Sweetgrass Arch, and all the wells drilled into it were dry.

US 2 winds down a steep descent into Shelby Coulee, a preglacial valley.

SHELBY, 106.8 *m.* (3,283 alt., 2,004 pop.), seat of Toole County, is strung out along a narrow main street that parallels the Great Northern Ry. tracks. It has developed through a succession of booms—the cattle boom of the 1880's, the dry-land boom of the early 20th century, and the oil boom of the 1920's.

The town came into existence in 1891, when the builders of the Great Northern, forging across the prairies toward Marias Pass, threw off a boxcar at the cross trails in the coulee and named it Shelby Junction for Peter P. Shelby, general manager of the Great Northern in Montana. The manager, thus honored, is said to have remarked: "That mudhole, God-forsaken place, . . . will never amount to a damn!"

But Shelby became the distributing center for a trade area extending 50 to 75 miles in every direction. Chuck wagons drove in from the south, from points up and down the Marias River, and from the Sweetgrass Hills to the north, and went out loaded with supplies. Cowboys and sheep-herders, after months on the range, rode in for a fling at the honky-tonk night life. In the late 1890's Shelby was the sort of town that producers of western movies have ever since been trying to reproduce in papier-mâché. Yet this wild and woolly place with its spurs and chaps and ten-gallon hats never had any stockyards. Stock was loaded a few miles down the track near Galata—at a safe distance from Shelby.

In 1893 the town playboys were featured in the *Police Gazette* after holding up an opera troupe passing through on a railroad train. The various versions of the story agree that they shot out the engine head-light, the car windows, and the red signal lights, and forced the conductor to execute a clog dance.

In 1921 Gordon Campbell, the geologist who discovered oil in Montana, drilled successfully near Kevin, about 8 miles north of the town *(see Tour 6)*, and before long the Kevin-Sunburst field, reaching from

Shelby to the Canadian Border, was notable. Shelby's population increased by leaps and bounds and money flowed freely. Some citizens, yearning for more front-page publicity, suggested the promotion of a heavyweight championship fight between Jack Dempsey and Tommy Gibbons. The idea, first put forward as a joke, struck Shelby's fancy. Negotiations were opened, and at length the fight was scheduled for July 4, 1923. The town built an arena designed to hold 45,000 cash customers; unfortunately only 7,000 attended. The local promoters took it on the chin, along with Gibbons, who didn't get a nickel for the beating. A gaudy signboard marks the spot where the arena stood.

At Shelby is the junction with US 91 *(see Tour 6).*

Stockmen of this area once boasted of driving cattle from Shelby to the North Dakota Line without cutting a fence. The dry-land settlers, with their 320-acre tracts, changed this; the remaining unfenced ranges are few and relatively small.

The large ABSORPTION PLANT *(not open to visitors),* 126.2 *m.,* extracts high-test gasoline from natural gas. Gas enters the plant at pipe-line pressure—350 pounds to the square inch—and is heated in great tanks and coils to 700 pounds pressure, at which point the gasoline is precipitated.

CUT BANK, 130.2 *m.* (3,740 alt., 845 pop.), seat of Glacier County, is the booming center of Montana's youngest oil and gas fields. Great steel drums and stilted tanks tower above it. Gas piped from this region is used in the homes of Great Falls, Helena, Butte, and Anaconda, and has replaced pulverized coal in the copper-reduction plants. The Blackfeet described the stream that flows through the town as "the river that cuts into the white clay banks." From this, white men derived the name Cut Bank.

Right from Cut Bank on a dirt road to the CUT BANK OIL AND GAS FIELD *(see INDUSTRY and COMMERCE).* Wells, oil derricks, and pumps are scattered over the prairie for 16 miles. Gas comes out of the ground so cold that it forms inch-deep ice on the piping. The flow is registered by large meters. Oil must be pumped into feeder lines; as many as 6 and 7 wells are pumped from one power plant. One 4-inch pipe line leads to Sweetgrass *(see Tour 6, Sec. a)* on the Canadian Border, where the oil is sold for export to Canada.

US 2 crosses Cut Bank Creek, 130.9 *m.,* the eastern boundary of the Blackfeet Reservation.

At 131 *m.* is the junction with a poor dirt road.

Left on this road to the top of a hill, 0.3 *m. (climb in low gear),* an excellent point from which to view the oil field, Cut Bank Canyon, and the distant mountains.

At 131.1 *m.* a rocky gulch (R) opens toward the highway.

Right on foot up this gulch 200 feet to a flat rock (L) from which the bones of a small dinosaur were taken. The imprint of backbone and ribs is visible. The skeleton is in the Smithsonian Institution, Washington, D. C.

The sandstone shaft (R) 100 yards from the highway, 152.8 *m.,* marks the most northerly. point reached by Captain Lewis on his scouting trip up the Marias River, July 26, 1806 *(see HISTORY).* The shaft is 4 miles from the grove on Cut Bank Creek where Lewis and his party camped for two days. In late summer great blue fields of blossoming flax *(see AGRICULTURE)* in this area seem to reflect the cloudless sky.

At 161.8 *m.* is a junction (L) with US 89 *(see Tour 4)*. Between this point and Browning Junction, a distance of 14.9 miles, US 89 and US 2 are one route. The mountains in Glacier National Park are visible straight ahead. Outstanding is Chief Mountain (9,056 alt.).

BROWNING, 165.4 *m.* (4,462 alt., 1,172 pop.), is a tourist town named for a U. S. Commissioner of Indian Affairs. Roads from all parts of the Blackfeet Reservation converge at this town, where is the AGENCY OF THE BLACKFEET RESERVATION.

The Indians, the chief year-round patrons of the stores here, in summer provide the local color relished by tourists. They carry themselves with dignity and a gravity that hides considerable amusement over their roles as entertainers. Many a patronizing eastern visitor would be shocked by the natives' private comments on his antics. Since most of the Blackfeet have been educated in Government schools, and speak good English, attempts to address them in pidgin English may result in embarrassment.

The reservation, which now covers only 2,343 square miles, extended from the Continental Divide to the Dakotas when it was established in 1855. Sales and cessions to the Government reduced it to the area that lies between Glacier National Park and the Cut Bank meridian. The eastern part of the park, the last section sold, was acquired by the Government in 1919 for $1,500,000. The Blackfeet invested some of the money received from the sale of lands in livestock and irrigation canals; some of it was spent less wisely. The houses of their 400-acre tracts are, with few exceptions, small, poorly furnished, and ramshackle; to remedy this, the Government has inaugurated a housing program. The Blackfeet have been given several thousand cattle and they derive a fair royalty from some of the Cut Bank oil wells. In recent years the Court of Claims allowed the tribe $450,000 for lands taken by executive orders of Presidents Grant and Hayes.

Under the Reorganization Act of 1934 the Blackfeet are governed by an elected council of 13 members. They were among the first Indians to adopt a constitution for tribal self-government.

The Blackfeet have several large community gardens, and a few private ones. They now depend little on game though *isapwotsists* is still a favorite food; it consists of the small intestine of game-animals—or beef —stuffed with tender meat, broiled, and then boiled.

The old-time Blackfeet were known and feared by other tribes as fierce and cruel warriors, and far-ranging hunters. They were true nomads, following the buffalo up and down the plains. They were intensely hostile toward the white usurpers, who in later years kept them drunk and on the verge of starvation. (In the winter of 1883–84, Government rations were reduced and 600 died.) Their hostility was not lessened by such occurrences as Major Baker's destruction of a camp quarantined for smallpox in 1870.

About one-fourth of the Blackfeet adhere to the old Sun faith. Each summer they hold the O-Kan celebration *(see BEFORE THE WHITE MAN)*.

Blackfeet legend accounts for the tribal name. It tells how an old man with three sons had a vision that caused him to send them to the far plains of the North Big River (Saskatchewan) in search of game. There they saw great herds of buffalo, but could not approach to kill them. In another vision, Sun told the old man to rub the feet of the eldest with a black medicine, which Sun provided. With this aid, the young man easily overtook the fleeing buffalo and his father decreed that this son's descendants should be called Blackfeet. When the other sons demanded some of the medicine, the old man instead sent them east and south to seek enemies. The first, returning with many scalps, was named Akhaina *(Many Chiefs);* his descendants painted their lips red, and were called Bloods by white men. The other, because he brought home the garments of his enemies, was named Pikuni *(Far-off Clothing)*, mispronounced "Piegan." It is a more recent tradition that the Blackfeet were given their name because their moccasins were blackened in crossing the burnt prairies between Lesser Slave Lake and the Montana plains.

To obtain Sun's assistance for a person ill or in danger, a virtuous woman relative of the afflicted must vow to build a medicine lodge during the berries-ripe moon; other women may become her assistants. From the chief vow-woman of the previous summer (who becomes her "mother") she must buy the Natoas *(Sun-turnip)* bundle, and learn the rites and sacred songs. The vow-women's lodge, in the tribal circle, is painted the Sun's color, red, and decorated with a symbol of the butterfly, giver of good visions. A hundred beef tongues (formerly buffalo) are brought here to be cut up for sacrificial food and purified in a nearby sweat lodge. Vow-women fast 4 days, in the red lodge, learning the rituals, while medicine pipe-men sit with them and sing a hundred songs to Old Man (Sun), Old Woman (Moon), and their son, Morning Star; all purify themselves with grass smoke.

During this period there is much singing, dancing, praying, visiting, and storytelling throughout the camp. Guns, blankets, medicine pipes, and tobacco are traded and sold—the pipes for as much as forty horses. Each day a group belonging to the All Friends society dances.

On the fourth day the vow-women open the Natoas bundle, which contains among other things, a red moose-claw digging stick, and the vow-woman's headdress. This is a lizard-shaped piece of buffalo leather colored red-and-blue and decorated with feathers and strips of white weasel skin. On its front is a small human image and a weasel skin containing an enemy's hair; on its back is the tail of a lynx. The new vow-woman, carrying the headdress and the digging stick, leads the way to the spot selected for the building of the medicine lodge, while the All Friends, mounted and in war costume, go to select the center post. At a forked tree, two old men count 4 brave deeds each, striking the tree once for each deed, and pray that the tree will not fall on others or split its fork when it falls. Young men cut and drag it to the camp, and lay its base by the hole that

has been dug, the forked end westward. Seated on a hide before the red lodge, a warrior, counting 4 brave deeds, cuts strands for binding the roof to the wall. The vow-woman, standing on a buffalo robe with the one being helped, holds up a piece of dried tongue and prays. She breaks off a piece of meat and buries it, eats the rest, and gives pieces to others, who do likewise. She then faces the post, on which a member of the All Friends, painted black, is stretched full length. Hidden by robes, medicine pipe-men perform ceremonies over him. He rises, and in his place they attach gifts to the Sun. All Friends approach from four directions bearing lodgepoles tied in pairs, like tongs, with which they raise the post. This climaxes the celebration; the lodge is then hurried to completion.

BROWNING JUNCTION, 177.7 *m.*, is at the junction (R) with US 89 *(see Tour 4)*.

Section c. BROWNING JUNCTION *to* IDAHO LINE, *231 m.*, US 2.

The beauty of the rugged landscape along this section of US 2 is excelled in few parts of the world. The flanks of the snow-capped peaks are wrapped in dark-green forests. Between the ranges are broad fertile valleys or shadowed canyons in whose bottoms flow swift icy streams. Clear lakes reflect the sky, the mountains, the bold headlands that thrust out into the water, and their own forested shores.

Between Browning Junction and Belton the route skirts the southern boundary of Glacier National Park, and crosses the Continental Divide.

Between Belton and Kalispell, it runs through the canyon and valley of the Flathead. West of Kalispell it crosses the Cabinet Mountains, whose slopes bear a generous part of the State's timber.

US 2 winds southward from BROWNING JUNCTION, 0 *m.*, to the summit of Two Medicine Ridge, known locally as Looking Glass Hill, 3.9 *m.* At 5.2 *m.* it overlooks Lower Two Medicine Lake (R) with Rising Wolf Mountain (9,505 alt.), the central of three peaks *(see GLACIER NATIONAL PARK)*, behind it.

At 8.1 *m.* is the junction with an unnumbered oil-surfaced road.

Right on this road to TWO MEDICINE LAKE, 8 *m.* *(see GLACIER NATIONAL PARK)*.

GLACIER PARK STATION, 11.9 *m.* (4,806 alt., 200 pop.), is the principal rail station used by visitors to Glacier National Park. During the tourist season (June-Sept.) thousands of the pleasure seekers throng through here. The variety of people and costumes sometimes seen on the station platform is astonishing. During the other 9 months of the year the town lies dormant, most of the time under many feet of snow.

The interior of large GLACIER PARK HOTEL, built of smooth logs in a free adaptation of Alpine hotel architecture, is decorated with western trophies and Indian curios. The tall unpeeled log columns of the lobby have rude Ionic capitals. Costumed Indians and cowboys sing, dance, and tell stories here.

The woodcarvings and sculptures of John Clark, Indian deaf-mute, are exhibited in his curio shop just north of the hotel, on the main street. Indian-made goods are for sale in several shops; fine beadwork is a Blackfeet specialty.

SUMMIT, 23.3 *m.* (5,212 alt., 10 pop.), in Marias Pass, is on the Continental Divide. North of the railroad tracks on the brow of the hill (R) is a STATUE OF JOHN F. STEVENS, who discovered the pass *(see GLACIER NATIONAL PARK)*.

The tall limestone shaft in the center of the highway, 23.6 *m.*, is a MONUMENT TO THEODORE ROOSEVELT.

US 2 winds down the western slope of the Divide, following Bear Creek, through heavy forests of fir and pine, to its confluence at Walton with the Middle Fork of the Flathead. Flowers bloom luxuriantly along the highway. *(Drive with care; narrow road with sharp curves and unguarded edges.)*

At 41 *m.* is the junction with a dirt road.

Left on this road is ESSEX (Walton), 0.2 *m.* (3,871 alt., 150 pop.), which, like many mountain towns, has two names. Essex is the post office; Walton is the Great Northern Ry. station.

At NYACK (Red Eagle), 58.1 *m.*, those who wish may cross the Middle Fork in a basket hung from a cable.

BELTON, 68.9 *m.* (3,219 alt., 180 pop.), is the western entrance to Glacier National Park, is a service town of brisk modernity amid snow-capped mountains and vast evergreen forests. There is usually good fishing in the Flathead River within 100 yards of the town. On the National Park side no license is needed.

YOUNG MOOSE

At Belton is the junction with Going-to-the-Sun Highway *(see GLA-CIER NATIONAL PARK).*

CORAM (Citadel) is at 76.8 *m.* (3,158 alt., 200 pop.). *(Guides available for pack trips into the primitive areas to south.)*

At 78.5 *m.* is the junction with a narrow, graded dirt road.

Left on this road along the valley of the South Fork of the Flathead, between the Flathead and Swan Ranges, to HUNGRY HORSE CREEK, 8 *m. (public campground, stoves, tables, and sanitary facilities).*

The road leads into the South Fork wilderness, which covers about 1,640 square miles in the FLATHEAD NATIONAL FOREST. Many of its parks, streams, and ridges may never have been seen by man.

The 10-mile stretch between Hungry Horse Creek and RIVERSIDE, 17 *m.,* was burned over in the great fire of August 1926. It is the only bare country in the South Fork area. The virgin forests seem limitless; large stands of larch, western white pine, yellow pine, Engelmann spruce, Douglas fir, and other valuable species have never resounded with the lumberman's ax.

GREAT NORTHERN MOUNTAIN (8,700 alt.) is a towering pile of naked rock (L).

FELIX CREEK, 25.1 *m.,* has a campground. Impressive views open at 27 *m.,* where TROUT LAKE lies R.

Near ELK PARK, 37.2 *m.,* are numerous excellent camp sites.

SPOTTED BEAR, 50 *m.,* is at the end of the road. Here is a ranger station. A small lodge accommodates 15 persons. *(Cabins; horses, guides, and packers available for short or long trips.)*

The SPOTTED BEAR GAME PRESERVE, 200 miles square, is south of the ranger station. All through this area game is almost as abundant as it was 150 years ago. Deer, elk, moose, mountain goats and sheep, black and grizzly bears, lynxes, mountain lions, beavers, martens, and other animals are here. Lakes and streams offer cutthroat, rainbow, and Dolly Varden trout. A network of horse and foot trails gives access to rough, wild country.

At 80.9 *m.* US 2 crosses the South Fork of the Flathead River just above its junction with the stream formed by the union of the North and Middle Forks of the Flathead. The united river has cut BAD ROCK CANYON, 82 *m.,* between the Whitefish Range (R) and the Swan Range (L).

The highway follows the old Indian trail used by the Flathead to reach the buffalo range east of the mountains. At 84 *m.* it enters Flathead Valley, one of the most productive farming areas in the State.

At 85.4 *m.* is the junction with an improved road.

Right on this road is COLUMBIA FALLS, 2 *m.* (3,099 alt., 637 pop.), planned as a division point on the Great Northern Ry., and platted on a scale that proved too generous when Whitefish *(see Tour 7, Sec. a)* became the division point. Excellent sidewalks extend some distance beyond the built-up area.

At 93.4 *m.* is the junction with State 35, and with an unnumbered road.

1. Left on the unnumbered road to LAKE BLAINE, 6.6 *m.* *(tourist cabins, grocery store, sandy beach, bathhouses, boats).* The lake contains bass and silver salmon. Trails lead to fishing streams and over impressive ridges and mountains.

2. Left on State 35, an improved road, through farming country subirrigated by an underlying layer of quicksand and water, 8 to 15 feet thick.
CRESTON, 3.8 *m.* (3,000 alt., 20 pop.), consists of a general store, a post office, a restaurant, and a filling station.

At 9.3 *m.* is the junction with a dirt road; L. 4.8 *m.* on this to ECHO LAKE *(boats available),* in the foothills of the Swan Mountains. The lake is dotted with small islands; its shores are thickly wooded. The only outlet is a subterranean stream. Black bass and whitefish are taken with rod and fly. There is good swimming in front of a sandy beach.

BIGFORK, 14.3 *m.* (3,989 alt., 250 pop.), is a huddle of little gray houses in a hollow just below the dam and powerhouse (R) that supplies electricity to Kalispell and much of Flathead County. Below the town the Swan River flows into Flathead Lake.

At Bigfork is a junction with State 31 *(see Tour 8).*

FLATHEAD LAKE (2,892 alt.) *(see Tour 7, Sec. b)* is R. at 16 *m.* Foothills of the Cabinet Mountains rise from its western shore. State 35 closely follows the eastern shore.

At 17.9 *m.* the road enters the FLATHEAD NATIONAL FOREST. The Swan Range is visible (L). These mountains have not been made the subject of legend, as have the austere Missions *(see Tour 7, Sec. b),* but the sheerness and remoteness of their naked granite tops, showing through perpetual snow, rouse the imagination. The clarity of the atmosphere surrounding them and the play of light and cloud-shadow on them add to the effect.

BEARDANCE CAMPGROUND *(stoves, tables, spring water),* 23 *m.,* is maintained by the U. S. Forest Service.

GLEN, 23.5 *m.,* is a general store and service station. Near here, and at numerous points along the eastern shore of Flathead Lake, summer cottages can be rented. Several very attractive summer homes are scattered along the shore.

At intervals between 26.1 *m.* and 35 *m.* are dead cherry orchards, killed in October 1935 by early storms. The raising of sweet cherries, begun 40 years before, had just begun to be an important industry. About 50,000 trees were destroyed after yielding only one mature crop.

At 27.1 *m.* the road leaves the Flathead National Forest.

At YELLOW BAY, 27.6 *m.,* is Montana State University's BIOLOGICAL EXPERIMENT STATION and SUMMER LABORATORY (R). The station was established in 1899 by Dr. M. J. Elrod of the university's biology department for the purpose of studying the plant and animal life of Flathead Lake. Faculty members and graduate students of biology work here, mostly in summer.

The road winds around the bay through a dense forest.

BLUE BAY, 31.3 *m.*, is popular with fishermen who come to snag the landlocked salmon that spawn along the east shore. This fish was once disregarded by anglers, many of whom sought to have the species removed from the lake. Now, during a short period, roughly late November and early December, Blue Bay's sandy beach is crowded with shivering fishermen, some of whom have driven 100 miles to join the swarm along the water's edge, jostling one another for places to stand. Many fishermen consider the flesh unpalatable and give or throw away their catch. The snag usually employed, three fishhooks bound back to back, is hurled into the deep offshore waters among the spawning fish.

The joy found in this form of sport is a mystery to non-fishermen. There is nearly always a cold raw wind; nearly everyone becomes drenched. Snags, hurled toward the water, often lodge in a sleeve, a trouser seat, or an exposed part of someone's anatomy. Tempers are short; quarrels over which fish is whose are frequent. Many go away empty-handed, though thousands of pounds of fish are taken by the fortunate. In 1934 and 1935 the Montana Relief Commission was permitted to seine and can the salmon for distribution among the needy. About 21,000 cans were packed in 1935.

STATION CREEK FISH HATCHERY, 36.7 *m.*, raised rainbow and blackspot trout for planting in Montana waters.

The KNIGHTS OF COLUMBUS PARK, 37.3 *m.*, is a recreational area for members of the order.

The highway swings away from the lake at 39.7 *m.* through a dark forest of fir and tamarack. At 44.7 *m.* is the junction with US 93 *(see Tour 7, Sec. b).*

KALISPELL, 99.2 *m.* (2,959 alt., 6,094 pop.), seat of Flathead County, is a farmers' trade center and tourists' headquarters. *(Guides and horses available for mountain trips.)* Many of the buildings on the broad, tree-lined streets are modern in design; the four delightful parks, covering 40 acres, were landscaped as a W.P.A. project. Kalispell's porgressive planners have produced a city that fits well into the awesome beauty of its setting. The Whitefish Range is on the north, the Swan Range rises sheer on the east.

The Flathead Valley appealed highly to Indians of the Salishan tribes, who called it "the park between the mountains." Until 1809, when David Thompson of the Canadian North-West Company explored it, no white man had been here. As it was accessible only by hazardous travel over the old Tobacco Plains Trail, no permanent settlement was made until 1881; the post established by Angus McDonald for the Hudson's Bay Co., and the post office at Dooley's Landing on the Flathead River, had been the only trading points.

When in 1891 the Great Northern completed its track to this point, the little settlements at Demersville, a steamboat landing on the Flathead River, 4.5 miles southeast, and Ashley, 0.5 mile west, were moved here piece by piece and became Kalispell.

The city has grown steadily with the development of lumbering and agriculture in the Flathead country, which produces 40 percent of Montana's lumber and has never known a crop failure.

There are several dude ranches nearby, and numerous lakes and streams provide opportunities for bathing, boating, and fishing.

The S. E. JOHNS COLLECTION *(open; free),* 128 Main St., contains fire arms, Indian weapons and relics of pioneer Montana. The F. A. ROBBIN COLLECTION, 1st Ave. E. and 2nd St., contains 100 obsolete weapons.

Kalispell has a radio station, KGEZ (1310 kc.).

Here is the junction with US 93 (see Tour 7).

At 117.8 m. is the junction with State 24.

Right on State 24, an improved dirt road, is MARION, 0.3 m. (3,947 alt., 10 pop.). LITTLE BITTERROOT LAKE (L), 1 m., has cabins and a campground on its shore. Between it and ISLAND LAKE, 22 m. (R), the road passes through Pleasant Valley. LAKEVIEW, on Island Lake, and JENNINGS, 41.8 m., offer good fishing and camp sites.
State 24 leads through little-visited parklike country.

Between 131 m. and 136 m. US 2 skirts the shore of McGREGOR LAKE (L). In spring and fall, fishing for silver salmon and cutthroat trout is good. At 142.4 m. the road crosses the Flathead-Kootenai watershed. Both Flathead and Kootenai Indians visited the lake country on both sides of this low divide to hunt and fish, but it was never the permanent home of any tribe. The old Kootenai Trail, the one most often used by these friendly tribes, passed THOMPSON LAKE, 143.5 m. (L), on its route between the Kootenai River and Clark Fork of the Columbia.

HAPPY INN, 151.2 m. (3,768 alt., 10 pop.), a resort with tourist cabins, is by CRYSTAL LAKE (boats available).

LOON LAKE (L), 154.2 m., close to the highway, is a good spot for fishing.

At 158.7 m. the road swings north, and runs for a short distance down the heavily forested valley of the Fisher River, whose source is in the Cabinet Mountains (L). At 160 m. is the RAVEN RANGER STATION in the KOOTENAI NATIONAL FOREST; in LIBBY CREEK, nearby (R), is exceptionally good fishing for cutthroat trout. Libby Creek Valley is the scene of commercial logging operations.

LIBBY, 193.7 m. (2,053 alt., 1,752 pop.), is a lumberjacks' town. They come in from nearby logging camps for supplies and occasional celebrations that are vastly exaggerated in legend and fiction. The lumberjacks have a style all their own, and a swaggering vitality that seems to be increased rather than diminished by their exhausting and dangerous work. Though they do not invariably appear in brilliant checked shirts and mackinaws, stag pants, calked boots, and wiry black beards, the streets of Libby nevertheless give evidence that this is Paul Bunyan's country. Libby's sawmill, second largest (1938) in Montana, saws between 60 and 80 million board feet of lumber annually.

Libby, named for the daughter of one of a group of prospectors who discovered gold on Libby Creek in 1862, is the seat of Lincoln County, one of the most mountainous and heavily wooded areas in the State. Much of the region is not readily accessible, but its scenery and fine fishing repay the effort to reach it. Near the town the rare mineral, vermiculite, is mined (see INDUSTRY AND COMMERCE).

In the PUBLIC LIBRARY, left wing of the courthouse, is a photostatic copy of a map of the Kootenai region drawn in 1813 by David Thompson (see HISTORY). The original is in the British Museum.

LOADING LOGS

Right from Libby on State 37, a partly improved road, up the primitive Kootenai Valley to a junction with an unimproved dirt road, 54.6 m. Left here, 34 m. up Dodge Creek, a tributary of the Kootenai River, to the UPPER FORD RANGER STATION; L. down the narrow valley of the Yakt River between the YAKT MOUNTAINS (R) and the PURCELL MOUNTAINS (L) to YAAK, 38 m., a general store. South of Yaak a dangerous 31-mile-long road back to Libby, crosses the Purcell Mountains through a wild region of deep canyons, small waterfalls, and snow-capped peaks. Tiny settlements and ranger stations on this route are outposts in the truest sense. The area traversed is the wildest and most rugged in Montana, many of its sudden revelations of grandeur more exciting than those on main roads.

West of Yaak the dirt road continues through rugged, heavily timbered country. GRIZZLY PEAK (9,700 alt.) is seen (L). The fishing here, as in most remote districts, repays the enthusiast for many difficulties encountered in reaching it. SYLVANITE, 57 m., is headquarters of the Keystone Gold Mining Co., whose mines are in nearby gulches. The tiny town also boasts a ranger station, a C.C.C. camp, and a general store and post office.

At 68 m. is the junction with US 2, close to the Idaho Line.

REXFORD (2,568 alt., 200 pop.) is 55 m. from US 2 on State 37. East of it, at EUREKA (2,315 alt., 860 pop.), 64 m., is a junction with US 93 *(see Tour 7)*.

US 2 follows the KOOTENAI RIVER (R), named for the tribe of Indians *(the Deer Robes)* formerly living in this region. They were credited with being the finest deer hunters and tanners of hides among western Indians. The remaining Kootenai live on the Flathead Indian Reservation *(see Tour 7)*.

Close to the point where Pipe Creek flows into the Kootenai River, 198.5 *m.*, is (R) the SITE OF THE KOOTENAI CEREMONIAL SWEAT BATHS, indicated by thousands of pieces of rocks, broken when thrown red hot into shallow pits 6 to 8 feet square to heat the water. The bather covered the pit with hides and steamed himself in the nearly blistering water. When he emerged, shining with perspiration, he plunged into the icy waters of the Kootenai to close his pores.

Nearby the Kootenai obtained a fine white sandstone from which they made pipe bowls.

KOOTENAI FALLS (R), 205.3 *m.* (1,998 alt.), is about 300 feet from the highway. There is a spring, a rock fountain, and a U. S. Forest Service campground nearby. The water descends more than 200 feet in a series of cascades. David Thompson made the difficult portage around the falls in 1808 and named them the Lower Dalles. In his journal he recorded: "To this date we had meat of a few small antelope, but by no means enough to prevent us eating moss bread and dried carp, both poor, harsh feed . . . We met two canoes, from which we traded twelve singed muskrats and two shoulders of antelope, thankful for a change from the moss bread which gave us the belly ache."

KOOTENAI GORGE is viewed over the iron railing of the railway at 205.8 *m.* A hollow, offstage roar is heard before the place is reached; this becomes a welter of undifferentiated noises that is at first deafening; then the sounds tend to separate into distinct motifs.

At 209.6 *m.* is the junction with an improved dirt road.

Left on this road to SAVAGE LAKE, 2.9 *m.* *(cabins and boats available; good fishing)*. Deer graze on adjacent meadows. Excellent Forest Service trails lead into the wilderness.

The road follows a trail first used by Indians, and then by smugglers bringing Chinese from Canada to do construction work on the Northern Pacific Ry. *(see TRANSPORTATION)*. It approaches the spectacular CABINET PRIMITIVE AREA, accessible only on foot or horseback *(see RECREATION)*, and winds through an extensive forest of white pine.

BULL LAKE, 16.5 *m.* (R), is in the thickly wooded foothills of the Cabinet Mountains. According to Indian history, a landslide dammed the stream that formed this lake, destroying a camp in the process. Evidence of the slide is visible at the foot of the lake.

The road winds down through Bull River Valley and several times crosses the stream, which is known for its fine fishing. A severe forest fire occurred in this area in 1910.

At 30.1 *m.* is a trail (L) to a lookout station on top of BERRAY MOUNTAIN.

At 38.4 *m.* is the junction with State 3 *(see Tour 12)*.

TROY, 213.2 *m.* (1,892 alt., 498 pop.), is on the dividing line between Mountain and Pacific Standard time *(west-bound travelers set watches back 1 hour)*. Troy is a freight division point on the Great Northern Ry., and headquarters of silver mining outfits working in the Cabinet Mountains.

1. Left from Troy on a dirt road to the SNOWSTORM MINE *(open to visitors)*, 5 *m.*, on Callahan Creek, a heavy producer of ore containing gold, silver, lead, zinc, and copper.

2. Left from Troy on a forest road to the LOOKOUT STATION on KEELER MOUNTAIN (4,949 alt.), one of the few peaks in Montana with a roadway to

the top. The Purcell Mountains (north) and the Cabinet Mountains (south) are plainly visible across far-sweeping, heavily timbered areas.

For nearly a mile the road winds along a narrow shelf cut from the mountain side, with the river below. Many cuts are in deep shadow. *(Watch out for trucks bearing logs.)*

A SILVER FOX FARM is (R) at 216.5 *m.*

At 225.3 *m.* is the junction with an improved road *(see side tour above from Libby).*

US 2 crosses the Idaho Line, 231 *m.,* 27 miles east of Bonners Ferry, Idaho.

‹‹‹‹‹‹‹‹‹‹‹‹‹‹‹‹‹‹‹‹☒››››››››››››››››››››

Tour 2A

Junction with US 2 (Fort Belknap Agency)—Hays—St. Paul's Mission —Landusky—Zortman; unnumbered road and State 19.
Junction US 2 to Zortman, 46.6 m.

Graveled roadbed between Fort Belknap Agency and St. Paul's Mission. Remainder of route unimproved, narrow, and winding, impassable except in dry weather.
Hotels at Zortman and Landusky; tourist cabins at Hays; camp sites along road. Visitors should carry coats, campers warm blankets.

This route traverses rolling grassland, little changed by the advent of white men, runs through fire-swept, spectacular mountains, and into old, nearly abandoned mining towns. Most of the route lies within the boundaries of the Fort Belknap Indian Reservation *(see Tour 2, Sec. a).* Large herds of grazing cattle are seen.

The unnumbered road branches south from US 2 *(see Tour 2, Sec. a)* at FORT BELKNAP AGENCY, 0 *m.*

SNAKE BUTTE, 5.1 *m.* (R), is the site of a Government quarry, from which stone is being taken for construction use at Fort Peck Dam. The road turns L. here. Straight ahead are the LITTLE ROCKY MOUN-TAINS, an isolated gray-green range that rises like an island above the prairie.

In 1912 THREE BUTTES (R), 22.2 *m.,* sheltered robbers of a Harlem bank. Near the summit of the highest butte, the robbers held off the sheriff and his men until lack of food and water forced them to surrender.

A FORT BELKNAP SUBAGENCY is (L) at 32.2 *m.*

At a fork, 32.7 *m.,* the road turns R. and at 34.8 *m.* is in the foothills of the Little Rockies.

HAYS, 37.1 *m.* (3,550 alt., 20 pop.), is an Indian town. It comes to life once a year—in September when the Indians hold their fair. Then dancing and singing goes on in the street, games are played and races run. Gay native trappings vie with the gaudiest products of white man's manufacture. Intricate beadwork is often seen.

ST. PAUL'S MISSION *(open)*, 38.2 *m.*, on People's Creek, was founded in 1886 by a Jesuit, Father Frederick Hugo Eberschweiler, who is said to have gained the respect of the Gros Ventre by learning their language more rapidly than any other white visitor. Finding that men from Fort Benton were unwilling to come to the Little Rockies to build his mission because of warfare between the Gros Ventre and the Canadian Bloods, he sought aid in the settlement that later became Landusky; a crew of prospectors responded. The work proceeded swiftly, and early in 1887 Father Eberschweiler, assisted by some Ursuline Sisters, began instruction.

One of the early log houses still stands, but the main building, which contained paintings, used by the priest in teaching the natives, has been destroyed by fire. Two newer buildings are of stone.

At 39.1 *m.* the road enters a narrow canyon, and becomes rough, narrow, and winding; when two vehicles meet in some sections, one must back for a considerable distance to make passing possible. Truckloads of logs are a particular bane to motorists here. The canyon walls are steep and awe-inspiring in places, sculptured by wind, and stained by lichens, which in spring renew their green and bronze and yellow colorings. The road repeatedly fords People's Creek which has a firm gravel bed.

At 39.4 *m.* is the junction with a trail.

Right on this trail 200 yards to a NATURAL BRIDGE, a perfectly formed limestone arch, 50 feet wide, and, at one point 60 feet above the canyon floor.

At 39.8 *m.* is a natural campground. Until some of this region was burned over in 1936, it had much rugged beauty.

LANDUSKY, 44.9 *m.* (4,500 alt., 120 pop.), clings precariously to a mountain side. It is now almost abandoned, though its slumber of more than three decades was broken after 1933 by a modest production of gold from the nearby August mine, which is said to have yielded $2,000,000 since its boom days in the early 1890's.

Powell Landusky, for whom the town was named, was a violent product of a violent time. A raw kid at Alder Gulch in the late 1860's, he was nicknamed "Pike" because he boasted that he "came from Pike County, Missouri, by God." He won a reputation as the toughest rough-and-tumble fighter in the West. In 1868 he went to the mouth of the Musselshell to trap and trade with the Indians; captured by a war party of Brûlés, he angrily beat one of the braves with a frying pan, then whipped off the warrior's breechclout to continue the lashing. The awed Indians withdrew, and left two ponies to propitiate the demoniac captive.

At his trading post, Lucky Fort, on Flatwillow Creek in what is now Petroleum County, Landusky was shot by a Piegan. His jaw shattered, he simply tore out a loose fragment containing four teeth and threw it away.

In August 1893, Landusky and Bob Orman discovered the mine in the Little Rockies that they named for the month of discovery. At first they packed out their quartz by night, because they thought the claim was on the Fort Belknap Reservation, and feared governmental interference. Other prospectors and miners poured in and in 1894 the settlement here was organized.

Five miles south was the ranch of the tough Curry brothers, who were said to have Indian blood. It was local gossip that these prosperous ranchers sometimes branded cattle not their own. In order of age, they were: Harvey (Kid), Johnny, and Loney. They and their like were the two-gun riders sketched by Charles M. Russell as they thundered up and down the street of this town, strewing lead. After a typical fray a gambler remarked that he could go out with a pint cup and gather a quart of bullets.

Pike Landusky built a saloon for Jew Jake, who had drifted over from Great Falls after one of his legs had been shot away by a deputy sheriff. Jake liked to show off by using a Winchester rifle for a crutch. His saloon was the hang-out of the Curry boys and their friends and enemies.

In 1894 Johnny and Kid Curry were arrested on some minor charge and placed in the custody of Pike Landusky. Loney, something of a ladies' man, had been making a play for one of Pike's stepdaughters, to the old fighter's rage. Pike took advantage of the arrest to taunt and abuse Loney's brothers. At this time the town was preparing for a big Christmas celebration. Johnny Curry lent his new log barn for the big dance. Loney tuned up his fiddle and whipped the home-talent orchestra into shape. A "dead ax" wagon was sent 10 miles to borrow a small portable Mason and Hamlin organ. Only one plan was frustrated: someone had told Lousy, the stage driver, to order four dozen quarts of big juicy oysters from Baltimore, but Lousy, no authority on oysters, had ordered canned ones from Minneapolis.

On the evening of December 28, when the celebration was nearing its end, the Kid rode into town and entered Jew Jake's place. Perhaps a dozen men were in the room, among them Pike, wearing a heavy fur-lined overcoat. The Kid knocked him down, and took advantage of the coat, which impeded his enemy's movements, to beat him unmercifully. Landusky at length managed to draw his automatic, but it jammed; the Kid's .45 revolver did not.

The Curry gang left the country with haste. Seven years later the Kid held up a Great Northern passenger train at Exeter Siding, west of Malta, and carried $80,000 into the hills. He was captured, but escaped and vanished from Montana. Johnny was killed by a rancher whom he tried to intimidate. Some say that he and Pike Landusky are buried side by side in the tiny graveyard at Landusky but old-timers believe that Pike was buried on a ranch about 1 mile from town.

At 46 m. is a junction with State 19; L. on this improved road.

ZORTMAN, 46.6 m. (4,000 alt., 70 pop.), is not quite a ghost town, but has the forlorn, time-bleached appearance common to abandoned camps. Many cabins, built by hopeful prospectors in the 1890's, stand windowless and lonely among the trees.

Pete Zortman, who came to the Little Rockies in the 1880's, discovered a mine he named the Alabama, which is said to have produced $600,000. In the early 1890's Charles Whitcomb discovered what became the Ruby

Gulch mine, 2 miles north of Zortman, credited with $3,500,000. What was asserted to be the world's second largest cyanide mill was erected here, and for several years wagonloads of gold bricks were freighted out of town to Malta and Dodson.

Zortman's story was very like Landusky's. It is said that there was a saloon entrance every 40 feet along the street and a badman on every corner. One of its legendary characters was Joe Mallette, a freighter whose skill earned him the most difficult jobs in a difficult trade. He rigged a boom on the uphill side of his wagon, and perched on it to steady his loads on the primitive mountain trails. Once the slant became too great for his weight to offset and his load of bottled stuff turned over, tossing him down the slope in a cascade of glass and foaming beer. On another occasion when he was attempting to haul a large boiler over the alkali flats to the Ruby Gulch mine, his wagon sank to its axles. Mallette rigged a rolling hitch and rolled the boiler, a few feet at a time, across three miles of mud.

Shortly after 1900, when all the easily accessible ore had been removed, Zortman's mill burned down and in 1929 a fire destroyed four buildings on the main street, virtually wiping out the town.

<<<<<<<<<<<<<<<<<<<<<<<✷>>>>>>>>>>>>>>>>>>>>>>>

Tour 3

Junction with US 89 (Armington)—Lewistown—Grass Range—Roundup —Billings—Hardin—(Sheridan, Wyo.) ; US 87.
Junction US 89 to Wyoming Line, 325.5 m.

Route paralleled by Great Northern Ry. between junction with US 89 and Lewistown; between Billings and Wyoming Line by Chicago, Burlington & Quincy R.R. and Great Northern Ry.
Hotels in larger towns; tourist camps on outskirts of towns.
Oil-surfaced roadbed with exception of a 22-mile graveled stretch between Lewistown and Grass Range; open all year.

US 87, the Custer Battlefield Highway, traverses central Montana in a zigzag diagonal course.

Section a. JUNCTION US 89 *to* BILLINGS; *217.7 m.,* US 87.

This section strikes through the Judith Basin, a large fertile valley in Fergus and Judith Basin Counties, once buffalo country that was prized and fought over by Indians. This flat or gently rolling region is extensively irrigated and subirrigated; the green of hay and grain fields alternates with the rich black of fallow strips. Its horizons are the crescent of the Little Belt Mountains on the west; the Highwoods, Bearpaws, and Little Rockies on the north; the Moccasins and Judiths on the east; and the Big Snowies on the south., As a productive agricultural area, it compares favorably with the Gallatin Valley.

South of Grass Range the route runs through rough grazing country on the border line between foothills and plains. It descends into the Musselshell Valley, traverses a coal mining area in the low, scrubby Bull Mountains, and descends into the Yellowstone Valley.

US 87 branches southeast from its junction with US 89 *(see Tour 4)*, 0 *m.*, 1.5 miles south of Armington *(see Tour 4, Sec. b)*.

From the crest of a ridge, 7.1 *m.*, in the foothills of the Little Belt Mountains there is a panorama of Judith Basin.

The highway emerges from the foothills of the Little Belt Mountains into the Judith Basin at 19.3 *m.* The river draining this basin was named by Lieutenant Clark in 1805 in honor of Miss Judith Hancock of Faircastle, Va., who later became his wife. Because of its encircling mountains, Judith Basin receives slightly more rainfall than other parts of central and eastern Montana. Its chocolate loam, well supplied with lime, is fertile. Even dry farming yielded bountiful crops of hard red milling wheat before the drought of the 1930's.

GEYSER, 21.9 *m.* (4,159 alt., 175 pop.), blends into the drab hills around it. As a railroad point and a trading town of farmers, it has a stable if monotonous existence. In 1925 an earthshock brought to the surface a stream of water in a theretofore dry coulee nearby.

SQUARE BUTTE (L), an almost rectangular flat-topped mountain, is the principal landmark of the Judith Basin. Charles M. Russell liked to include it in his pictures.

STANFORD, 37.2 *m.* (4,200 alt., 509 pop.), seat of Judith Basin County, is a stockmen's town, neat and brisk, with broad streets, pleasant white-painted houses, and a handsome brick high school (L). Though it is still active as a shipping point for livestock and grain, it had greater importance in the days when it was the most important freighting station in the basin.

The town began as a station on the Fort Benton-Billings stage route. It was often visited by Charles M. Russell when he worked on ranches in the vicinity. One employer set him to herding sheep. To relieve his boredom he began making images of Indians and horses out of the richly tinted mineral clay. He became so absorbed that he forgot his charges, who wandered off over the hills. Returning to ranch headquarters, he said to his boss, "Jack, if you want me to herd sheep, you'll have to get me another band."

For years stories of white wolves of prodigious strength and cunning grew and multiplied among the folk of this region. A huge one known as Old Snowdrift became a legendary monster, described variously in many places in central Montana. He had a fit mate, Lady Snowdrift. In 1921 it was reported that he was in the Highwoods killing sheep, cattle, and wild game. Stacy Eckert, a Forest Service ranger, spent much time on his trail. He did not catch Old Snowdrift, but he did find his den, and with the help of a rancher took seven puppies. One of these, called Lady Silver and trained by Eckert, played in motion pictures with the dog Strongheart. In two months of 1922 Old Snowdrift and his mate killed 21 cattle. In October Don Stevens, a Government hunter, set a trap that caught Lady Snowdrift. She dragged the heavy trap, and the 20-pound rock to which it was attached, to her den, where Stevens found and shot her. Early in 1923 he caught Old Snowdrift, whose pelt was the largest ever taken in the Highwoods. These wolves were not pure white, but a very light silver gray.

WINDHAM 45 m. (4,266 alt., 115 pop.), serves nearby cattle and wheat ranches as a trading center.

Well known in this country was "Liver-eating" Johnson, an old frontiersman, who hated Indians implacably. Johnson received his name because of an often repeated threat to eat the liver of the first Indian who came near his place; some old-timers insist that he did eat it.

The MOCCASIN MOUNTAINS, whose low, rounded summits are densely forested with lodgepole pine, are visible (L).

The BIG SNOWY MOUNTAINS are visible ahead (R), a chain of rounded summits. Geologists call them laboratory mountains, because they are old geologically and their gentle contours illustrate the history of mountain building.

At 61.4 m. is the junction with a graveled road.

Right on this road is HOBSON, 0.4 m. (4,073 alt., 240 pop.), an old and rather faded town that has long been a trading center for wheat ranchers along the Judith River.

In the 1880's UTICA, 12.5 m. (3,940 alt., 62 pop.), was headquarters for the great Judith roundup, described and painted by Charles M. Russell, who participated in it for several years. All the brands on the Judith River drainage were seen in this roundup.

The YOGO SAPPHIRE MINES, 25 m., in Yogo Gulch of the Little Belt Mountains, are important regular producers of sapphires; they and mines in Siam and Australia produce almost the entire world output. It is said that the first discovery of sapphires here was made in February 1896 by Jim Ettien, a sheepherder, who for $1,600 sold the claims that have since produced $10,000,000 worth of gems. A chain of 18 lode claims, comprising 1,550 acres, is owned by a British firm. Only two of the claims have been extensively worked.

The sapphires occur in a pipe as do the diamond-bearing clays of Africa. This is about 8 feet wide, 3½ miles long, and of unknown depth. The principal workings are now below the 250-foot level. The clay is mined from shafts; in the beginning it was brought up in buckets from narrow trenches that were continually caving in.

The sapphire-bearing clay, which appears to be hard blue rock slightly tinged with green, is washed with water and slaked in the open air. Nearly four years' slaking is required before the sapphires can be sifted from the clay. They are shipped to London for classification, then to France and Switzerland for cutting and polishing. Very small and imperfect sapphires have a wide market for use in watches, meters, and other delicate mechanical devices, and for the manufacture of phonograph needles. Purity, clarity, and beauty have given Yogo sapphires their high place in the world market.

At 70.3 m. is the junction with State 19; R. on this graveled road is MOORE, 0.4 m. (4,165 alt., 288 pop.), which proclaims its name on a water tank. Moore has a neat, prosperous appearance; its grain elevators handle the generally abundant wheat crops of the Rock Creek bench, which extends southward to the Snowy Moun-

CROSSING THE BARBWIRE

tains. The decline that came with the drought of the 1930's affected Moore less than many other towns.

Summer-fallowed fields in this vicinity often lose their topsoil during high winds in summer. From the northwest appears a great black cloud a hundred feet or more high that stretches across the entire basin. There is a scurrying of tumbleweeds, then a stinging blizzard blots out the sun, buries miles of fences and roads, stalls cars, and obliterates small ponds.

GARNEILL, 15 *m.* (4,415 alt., 160 pop.), at first seems to consist of a single brick store. Beyond this building, however, are a church, a school, and scattered dwellings, then abandoned buildings, faded, rickety, and near collapse. Garneill was named for Garnet Neill, the wife of an early rancher; it was a trading post when the Central Montana R.R. established a station here in 1903. The railroad named its station Ubet, in honor of an old stage station, 3 miles west. Three towns were laid out, because of a division of sentiment on moral issues. There was Ubet around the railroad station; there was North (or dry) Garneill, which survives; and there was South (or wet) Garneill, which consisted of the pretentious hotel, saloon, blacksmith shop, and stores that burned in recent years. The railroad company in time changed the name of its station to conform to local wishes.

At Garneill is the UBET AND CENTRAL MONTANA PIONEERS MONUMENT (R), a two-and-one-half-ton granite rock; in its concrete base are embedded pieces of ore, Indian relics, petrified wood, and other objects—between the names of important pioneers and the dates of their arrival in Montana. On each side of the monument are pear-shaped sandstones, molded seemingly by human hands. They were found on Blood Creek in Petroleum County.

1. Right 3 *m.* from Garneill on a dirt road to the SITE OF UBET, at one time the best-known stage station in Montana Territory. One or two of the old log buildings remain, used in the early 1930's by sheepherders. The story of Ubet is told in a

book of that name by John R. Barrows, whose father, A. R. Barrows, established the post in 1880. There was a two-story log hotel—elaborate for the time—a post office, a blacksmith shop, an ice house, a saloon, a stage barn, and a stable. The name was a frontier improvisation inspired by the "You bet!" given by the elder Barrows when asked if he could think of a good name for the post office.

At that time there were hardly half a dozen human habitations along the stage route between Billings and Ubet. Ubet, with Mrs. Barrows' cooking and the comfort of the hotel, was therefore important. It endured until advancing railroads ended the need for stage service. Some measure of the settler's esteem for the post is found in the fact that both Garneill and Judith Gap were first named for it. Many pioneers are buried on a hill to the north, but the graves are unmarked.

2. Left 10 *m.* from Garneill on a dirt road to the old Neill ranch; L. up Neill Canyon to the foot of the mountains, 13 *m.;* from here a steep one-mile marked Forest Service trail leads to the OLD ICE CAVE, just under the brow of the mountain in a limestone formation. From a narrow opening in the cliff wall a trail drops steeply into the cave over about 50 feet of rubble and snow. The ceiling, 30 feet high at the entrance, slopes to meet the floor 100 feet away. The floor is ice, several feet thick. At the base of one of the many ice pillars formed by the water that drips from the ceiling, a generous, never failing spring bubbles up, flows along the ice to the end of the cave, and disappears. There is some danger from jagged icicles that now and then drop from the ceiling, and from rock fragments loosened by the seeping water. From the mouth of the cave is a view that on clear days extends over the green and brown checkerboard of central Montana to the Pryor, Beartooth, Absaroka, Crazy, and Little Belt Mountains. Just over the brow of the mountain, 0.4 *m.,* is the NEW ICE CAVE. After a steep initial descent into a rocky pocket, a narrow tunnel which must be traveled on hands and knees leads into a low-ceiled room 200 feet long and 50 feet wide. The floor is solid ice of unknown depth.

At 20 *m.* on State 19 is JUDITH GAP (4,582 alt., 288 pop.), built around a hill. On the summit are a church, a school, and water tank. Many of the town's buildings have been removed or abandoned. The village looks faded and tired, and it may well be tired, for it is buffeted perpetually by winds and scorched intermittently by drought. It was once a busy grain-shipping center; and its roundhouse, coal chute, and water tanks are reminders of the time when it was a busy division point on the Great Northern Ry. The roundhouse and shops were closed in 1922.

Judith Gap, in which it sits, is a funnel that attracts northern blizzards of a ferocity unsurpassed in Montana, and then lets them blow back, seeming colder than before. The gap makes a pass between the Snowy Mountains (L) and the Little Belt Mountains (R) that was important in the days when freighters, prospectors, cattle drivers, hunters, and settlers passed northward into the Judith Basin, or southward toward the Yellowstone or Musselshell Valleys. These travelers followed a path made by Indian hunting and war parties seeking or defending the rich hunting grounds of the Judith Basin.

Before the World War the gravel benches around Judith Gap produced wheat that won prizes at big expositions; the few surviving old-time farmers wonder why such wheat has never grown since then.

LEWISTOWN, 85.7 *m.* (3,960 alt., 5,358 pop.), in the pleasant Spring Creek Valley, is sheltered by a bluff on the northwest. Because of this and its abundant shade trees, it is almost invisible until the highway descends to it. Then, in the deceptively clear air, some of its residential streets seem to extend almost to the base of the Judith Mountains (R). To the north rise the blue mounds of the Moccasins.

US 87 passes the FERGUS COUNTY COURTHOUSE (L), whose delightful well-kept lawn and skillfully arranged shrubs and flowers advertise the taste of the community. Lewistown is a planned city; its people proudly describe it as a city of homes. It is the capital of the agricultural interests of the Judith Basin, though mining activity in the mountains to the north and drilling in the Cat Creek oil field in the east add to its prosperity.

The inhabitants are increasingly aware of the recreational attractions of the region, and are taking steps to exploit them.

Lewistown, first called Reed's Fort for Maj. A. S. Reed, who opened the first post office in 1881, began as a small trading post on the Carroll Trail between Helena and Crow Island at the mouth of the Musselshell. When it was incorporated in 1899 the name was changed to honor a Major Lewis who in 1876 established Fort Lewis two miles to the south. Until the arrival of the Central Montana (Jawbone) R.R. in 1903 *(see TRANSPORTATION)*, which brought homesteaders to the Judith Basin, Lewistown was merely a freighting and trading center for cattlemen and miners.

An incident of the settlement's roaring days is related in the *Journal* of Granville Stuart. Large scale rustling was causing so much trouble for central and eastern Montana that in April 1884 the Montana Stock Growers' Association, in convention at Miles City, was forced to consider the situation. Afraid of precipitating a range war, the majority voted to take no action against the cattle thieves, despite vigorous protests from Theodore Roosevelt and the Marquis de Mores. The rustlers extended their activities. Groups of desperate ranchers united and took matters into their own hands, catching and hanging a few of the thieves.

On July 4, 1884, a couple of suspected ringleaders, Edward (Longhair) Owen and Charles (Rattlesnake Jake) Fallon, who were more villainous-looking than even their motion-picture successors, rode into town. After they had lost most of their money on a horse race, and had become very drunk, they thrashed one citizen and started to shoot up the town. Local men, armed with Winchesters, quickly took positions in stores and saloons along the single street. Rattlesnake Jake started to leave town, but, seeing Longhair wounded, fought his way back to him; the two continued firing until they could no longer pull a trigger. Rattlesnake Jake received nine wounds, Longhair eleven. Their last stand was made in front of the tent of an itinerant photographer, who photographed the bodies where they fell, to his profit. The aroused ranchers continued the clean-up until large-scale cattle thievery in Montana ended.

Though Lewistown today is a peaceful place, the two-gun man Ed McGivern, for many years the world's champion all-around pistol shot, is one of its special deputy sheriffs and a police deputy whose duty it is to teach local policemen to handle pistols. In his early barnstorming years he shot pieces of chalk from between his wife's fingers at 25 feet and targets from her head, aiming over his shoulder while looking into a mirror. Later he perfected an electric device to measure his speed. Records of his feats are on file in Smith & Wesson laboratories. At 12 feet, with a .38 special double-action revolver he can put five shots in a playing card in two-fifths of a second, or drawing from the holster, in one and one-fourth. He can shatter five charcoal balls tossed in the air by two men in from one and four-fifths to two and four-fifths seconds. He shoots with either hand or with both, and from every imaginable position. He is also an expert in the use of the shotgun and the high-powered rifle.

1 Right from Lewistown on Sixth St., which becomes a dirt road, to the junction

with a side road, **4** *m.;* R. here **0.2** *m.,* crossing railroad tracks to·BIG SPRINGS, the source of Lewistown's water supply. The springs discharge 62,700 gallons of water a minute. The water supply and the charm of the surroundings made this a favorite Indian campground.

Adjacent is the STATE FISH HATCHERY, established in 1921 by the Montana Fish and Game Commission; its capacity is 1,000,000 rainbow, brook, and blackspot trout each season. The fish are used to stock central Montana streams.

The dirt road goes on to HEATH, **9** *m.,* where is the HANOVER GYPSUM AND CEMENT PLANT (L).

Right from Heath on State 25 to the DUNLAP DUDE RANCH, **14** *m.,* on Half Moon Creek. Horse trails lead from this ranch into remote sections of the Snowy Mountains.

2. Left from Lewistown on State 19 to a junction with a dirt road, 1 *m.;* R. here to NEW YEAR, 13 *m.* (3,980 alt.), a ghost camp. New Year sprouted brashly along with other camps of the Judiths and Moccasins after the discovery of gold at Maiden *(see below)* in 1880. Its mill used the cyanide process of extracting gold that made the Judith and Moccasin mines so profitable.

CRYSTAL CAVE *(guide and light necessary)* opens off the main shaft of the New Year Mine. It has been only partly explored. In the main chamber, 300 feet across and about 100 feet high, dripping water saturated with calcites and various minerals has created a sparkling showroom full of endlessly varied rock crystals.

MAIDEN, 18 *m.* (4,063 alt.), also a ghost camp, witnessed the first fortune-making in the Judith and Moccasin fields. Perry McAdow, a veteran of the Virginia City boom, took two out of the Maiden diggings. At the World's Fair in Chicago in 1893, he exhibited a gold and silver statue of the actress Ada Rehan, and caused a stampede to the Judiths that brought the Giltedge, New Year, Kendall, and Barnes-King camps into being. It has been estimated that $18,000,000 in gold was taken from the Maiden, Giltedge, and Kendall mines alone.

GILTEDGE, 21 *m.* (4,170 alt.), is another ghost camp; L. here on a dirt road to the SITE OF FORT MAGINNIS, 25 *m.* (4,265 alt.). The fort, named for Maj. Martin Maginnis, Territorial delegate to Congress, was established in July 1880 by Capt. Dangerfield Park to protect settlers and stockmen from Indian attacks. It was built on the hay pasture of a ranch, laid out that summer by Granville Stuart. Stuart found it more trouble than protection. When cattle and horses were stolen by Indians, the soldiers, through ignorance, indolence, or official delay, often made their recovery impossible and allowed the thieves to go unpunished. Other ranchers shared Stuart's disgust, and in 1890 the fort was abandoned; ranchers and Lewistown citizens later carried off the buildings.

Granville Stuart was important in Montana history. A Virginian of Scottish descent who had in 1852 learned the ins and outs of gold mining in California, he came to Montana, and in 1858 helped find gold on Gold Creek *(see Tour 1, sec. d.).* There, besides prospecting, he raised grain and vegetables, trapped, traded, read Byron, married a squaw, and mended Henry Plummer's shotgun when that bright young man came through on his way to Bannack. At Virginia City during the feverish 1860's and later he mined and traded again, and continued educating himself by reading law when he could—and Shakespeare, the Bible, and Adam Smith.

He became manager of the Davis & Hauser Co. in 1879; it was soon reorganized as Davis, Hauser, & Stuart, with the brand DHS (D-S). With such men as James Fergus, Conrad Kohrs, D. A. G. Floweree, John T. Murphy, P. H. Poindexter, and W. C. Orr, he helped change the Montana range from a wilderness into a highly profitable cattle country.

As secretary of the Montana Stock Growers' Association, Stuart urged peaceful means of wiping out rustlers; but when these failed, he helped engineer orderly hangings. Under his leadership the stockmen dealt with Indians, prairie fires, stampedes, blizzards, drought, and stock diseases—and brought the Montana cattle business to a value of many million dollars. His plan for solving the Indian problem, endorsed in 1885 by the National Stock Growers' Association, showed his common sense and social values. He favored (1) disarming and dismounting the Indians; (2) granting them land in severalty, with inalienable title, and selling their surplus land; (3) giving them the privileges and responsibilities of full citizenship.

Stuart, like most other Montana ranchers, saw his herds wiped out by the winter of 1886–87. In 1891 he was appointed State Land Agent; three years later he became a special United States Envoy to Uruguay and Paraguay. From 1904 to his death in 1918, he was librarian of the Butte Public Library. His journals and historical writings are regarded as valuable source material.

At 102 *m.* sage plains succeed the low hills; ranch homes are few and far apart.

At 117 *m.* is the junction with State 18 *(see Tour 9).*

GRASS RANGE, 117.9 *m.* (3,488 alt., 212 pop.), is a prairie town, spread out, in the words of one resident, "most as big as Chicago." Here, as in many other Montana towns, it is not unusual to see a rancher driving a late-model automobile with a sheep dog, a ewe, or even a calf in the back seat. Livestock paid for the car—livestock ride in it if the need arises. Most ranchers prefer the "pick-up" or station-wagon type of automobile, which can haul a load of salt, supplies for camp tenders, a ewe with lambs, or a barrel of water without difficulty. The typical Montana rancher puts the modern high-powered car to tests never thought of on the proving grounds; he drives wherever there is a track for one wheel, climbing rocky ridges that, a few years ago, he would have negotiated on foot leading his horses and wagon.

The SPRING, 123.8 *m.* (R), was a regular watering hole on the old cattle trail north of Roundup before any towns existed on the range. The water, though alkaline, is fit to drink.

Three deserted shacks are all that remain of the town of BATTRICK, 128.8 *m.* (3,924 alt.).

At 150.5 *m.* the highway enters DEVILS BASIN, a shallow pocket rimmed in part with sharply eroded bluffs. Drillers found signs of oil here in 1919, a year before the Cat Creek discovery, but the field was not developed. According to a local story a geologist asked drillers at Devils Basin if there were any areas more worth prospecting nearby. When they replied carelessly that there might be one farther east, the geologist went on into the Cat Creek area, and almost immediately brought in a shallow well of high-grade oil that started a succession of booms *(see Tour 9, Sec. b).*

At 165.3 *m.* is a junction with State 6 *(see Tour 11).*

ROUNDUP, 165.8 *m.* (3,184 alt., 2,577 pop.), lies among rolling hills clad sparsely with yellow pine and dotted with granite boulders. It is neatly laid out, with well-shaded streets, and its houses, many of which stand on high terraces, are surrounded by gardens. At the southern end the main street runs straight toward a partly bald bluff that forces it to turn L. and down a hill. It ends at the railroad station.

As seat of Musselshell County, Roundup is the educational, social, and business center of its region, and the trade center of the State's leading coal-mining region; mining operations are seen to the east and west.

As its name suggests, the town was once the gathering point for great herds that grazed up and down the valley. It remained a cowtown until 1903, when homesteaders arrived, fenced the range, and crowded the stockmen behind barbwire. In 1907, when the Milwaukee Road was built across the State, Roundup began to develop. The former rough-and-ready town is now so staid that a sign in front of one of the motion picture houses advises passers-by: "Go to the movies often; nowhere else can you get so close to life for so little."

The western tradition of tall yarning long survived here. An eastern visitor once wrote in a bread-and-butter letter to a Roundup newspaper editor: "Out there every prairie dog hole is a gold mine; every hill a mountain; every creek a river; and everybody you meet is a liar." A still popular local story declares that sheepherders' dogs, once having known the lure of Roundup's lampposts, never return to their masters. Sheepherders themselves are attracted to Roundup when they have money, but perhaps for different reasons.

Temperatures in this area vary from — 50° in winter to 110° in the shade in summer, with nights usually cool. In winter the variation is sometimes as much as 70° in a few hours. A chinook may bring the mercury far up out of subzero, but in a day or two a northwester may send it plummeting again. The topsoil, fertile and of good depth, is of the gumbo type; in rainy weather dirt roads are both sticky and slippery, almost impassable for cars. There is a local story that after a circus held on the edge of town during wet weather, two wagonloads of spectators' rubbers were picked out of the mud.

The highway crosses the Musselshell River, 167.8 *m.*, a shallow, winding tributary of the Missouri, so named by Lewis and Clark because they found fresh-water mollusks along its lower reaches.

KLEIN, 170.4 *m.* (3,224 alt., 850 pop.), a scattered coal-mining settlement in the foothills of the Bull Mountains, has a grimy, haphazard appearance. The Republic, one of the larger coal mines of the district, supplies the coal used by the Milwaukee's locomotives and shops in this part of the State. Production averages 62,500 tons a month.

At 177.4 *m.* is the junction with a dirt road.

Left on this road into the hunting area of the BULL MOUNTAINS, 20 *m.*, through yellow-pine forest and over rough eroded sandstone formations. In the lower country the warning buzz of rattlesnakes is often heard. On the upper slopes blue grouse and big game are abundant. Wild horses graze on the more open, higher stretches. The mountains here are low and isolated, characterized by caves, sharp ridges, pinnacles, and blind canyons. In places they are covered with scrubby growths of jack pine, buffalo bushes, and sage.

The road crosses the summit of the Bull Mountains, at 180.3 *m.*, then winds down through rocky, sparsely timbered country into the Yellowstone Valley.

At 213.3 *m.* is a junction with US 10 *(see Tour 1)*. Between this point and Billings US 87 and US 10 are united.

BILLINGS, 217.7 *m.* (3,117 alt., 16,380 pop.) *(see BILLINGS)*.

Points of Interest: Eastern Montana State Normal School, Billings Polytechnic Institute, Orthopedic Hospital-School, Parmly Billings Memorial Library, Sugar Refinery, and others.

Billings is at a junction with US 10 *(see Tour 1)*.

Section b. BILLINGS *to* WYOMING LINE, *107.8 m.,* US 87.

This section of US 87 passes through a region of minor mountains into the rugged Big Horn country, the home of the Crow Indians, a land of plains and distances with snowy peaks at their southern end. The Crow called it the "good country" because they fared well in it. Here also ranged the fighting Sioux and Cheyenne who destroyed Custer. South of Hardin the highway follows the Little Horn River, crossing it several times.

US 87 turns L. from the junction with US 10, 0 *m.,* in BILLINGS.

US 87 crosses a boundary of the CROW INDIAN RESERVATION at 7.7 *m.*

INSCRIPTION CAVE (L), 7.8 *m.,* has walls covered with Indian hieroglyphics of unknown antiquity, now badly defaced by vandals and erosion. About 200 feet west of it is GHOST CAVE, so named for no apparent reason. Below the caves is a small picnic grove.

At 12 *m.* is a junction with an improved road.

Right on this road is PRYOR, 25 *m.* (4,140 alt., 150 pop.), with a SUBAGENCY OF THE CROW RESERVATION. It was name for Sergeant Pryor of the Lewis and Clark expedition. Here, besides the trader's store, is a two-story log cabin, the FORMER HOME OF PLENTY COUPS, the last of the great Crow war chiefs; he always maintained friendly relations with the whites. In 1921 Plenty Coups represented the Indian tribes of the United States at the dedication on Armistice Day of the Tomb of the Unknown Soldier in Arlington Cemetery, Va. His short speech on war and peace has been regarded as a masterpiece of Indian oratory. Plenty Coups died in 1933 at the age of 84.

Pryor and its vicinity give the impression of a lazy backwater, where only the arrival of a stranger creates an occasional ripple of interest, and community gossip is exchanged almost without words. A familiar figure in its streets is Will James, the cowboy author and artist *(see THE ARTS).*

The road continues as an ungraded trail, little changed since the old ranching days.

The WILL JAMES RANCH, 35 *m.,* embraces more than 4,000 acres of range. Among the herds that graze here are several famous old horses. The ranch buildings are small, simple log-and-frame structures, with a few trees around them. A low rim of red sandstone cliffs surrounds the place, with Crown Butte L. and West Pryor Mountain R. James used the local setting in several books.

The unfenced rangeland of the Big Horn country is a greatly eroded plateau. The walls of the deep gulches expose ancient sedimentary rocks containing fossilized remains of prehistoric animals.

The highway again crosses the Crow Indian Reservation at 21.1 *m.* to skirt its northern boundary for about 28 miles.

From the top of a low ridge at 25.5 *m.* the BIG HORN MOUNTAINS, a range reaching into Montana from northern Wyoming, are visible straight ahead. They may have been the "shining mountains" reported by the Verendryes in 1743 on their unsuccessful attempt to reach the Pacific *(see HISTORY).*

In the neighborhood of FLYINN, 26.2 *m.* (2,510 alt., 7 pop.), a prairie post office, paleontologists have unearthed many fossilized skeletons *(see NATURAL SETTING).*

HARDIN, 49.8 *m.* (2,966 alt., 1,169 pop.), seat of Big Horn County, is the trading center of an area opened to white settlement in 1906. A farmers' town, chiefly serving the Crow Reservation, Hardin takes on life in summer, when it is much frequented by the beaded and beribboned Indians who make up one-fourth of the county's population. On the southern outskirts is a colony of Mexican beetfield workers.

The MUSEUM in the BIG HORN COUNTY LIBRARY, Custer Ave. and 5th St., contains mementos of the Custer battle and of General Custer.

Right from Hardin on State 47, an improved dirt road, is ST. XAVIER, 23 m. (3,033 alt., 62 pop.), largest settlement on the Crow Reservation. In 1887 Father Prando, a Jesuit missionary, and two companions founded a mission here. At first they used their single tent as church, reception room, storehouse, kitchen, and dormitory. In the following year a frame schoolhouse was completed.

One of the leaders of the Crow, who were very restless at the time and eager to fight troops stationed at Fort Custer, was a medicine man who brandished a rusty saber when proclaiming his ability to exterminate every paleface. One evening three Ursuline nuns accompanied by a priest arrived at the mission and shortly afterward the Indians fired several shots into the agency buildings. The next morning the four proceeded to the mission school but were not molested. A Crow scout ended the incipient rebellion a few days later by shooting the medicine man.

The RUINS OF FORT C. F. SMITH, 38 m. (4,570 alt.), are on a bluff 500 yards from the Big Horn River. Fort Smith was established August 12, 1866, to protect Bozeman Trail travelers from the resentful Sioux. Its stockade, of logs and adobe, 125 yards square, was an impregnable haven; from its lookout tower riders three miles distant could be watched. The fort was manned by the 27th Infantry, whose colonel had irritated Secretary of War Stanton by continually asking for a transfer to some easy post. Stanton at length asked his clerk, "Which next to hell is the worst place to send a regiment?" The clerk replied, "To the Powder River country." Stanton sent the 27th Infantry to this place; events proved that the clerk had been right. From the beginning the fort was besieged by Red Cloud's Sioux. It was abandoned in 1868, after several bloody encounters, notably the Hayfield fight in which 11 soldiers and 8 civilians fought off 600 Sioux, sustaining only 4 losses, and the annihilation of Capt. William T. Fetterman's command of 82 men near Fort Phil Kearny, Wyo.; the fort site was included in land set aside as the Crow Reservation (see HISTORY). The old tower has fallen in a heap and the wall is a mass of debris.

Midway between the ruins and the Big Horn River was the post's burial ground. In 1892 the remains of 17 soldiers and civilians were removed from this place to the Custer Battlefield National Cemetery (see below).

The DE SMET TREE, an ancient cottonwood under which the priest (see HISTORY) in 1840 celebrated the first Christian mass in the Big Horn country, stands near the ruins. Two and one-half miles south, on Warrior Creek, is the site of the Hayfield fight.

At 39 m. is the mouth of BIG HORN CANYON, which winds through the Big Horn Mountains. Rust-colored cliffs rise almost 3,000 feet above the river. The bighorn sheep are native to this country, but they seldom appear near the highway.

The TOWER, 53 m., is a knife-edged formation of sandstone, 700 feet high, around which the river sweeps in a horseshoe. In 1935 a herd of 300 bison and several hundred elk from Yellowstone Park were liberated nearby.

At 51.6 m. is the junction with a dirt road.

Left on this road to the SITE OF FORT CUSTER, 1.4 m. (3,041 alt.), on the bluff above the confluence of the Big Horn and Little Horn Rivers. It was built by Lt. Col. George P. Buell in 1877, the year after the Custer battle. Since there were no further uprisings in the vicinity, the soldiers had plenty of time for entertainment. John Maguire, pioneer impresario (see BUTTE). occasionaly visited the fort on his tours of the settlements. In March 1880 he presented Captain John Smith, using Crow in the cast. At the point where Pocahontas was pleading for the life of John Smith, a Crow burst into the theater, shouting that a band of Sioux had stolen the

CROW TEPEES

Crow horses from the hitching rack outside. While the bugler blew boots and saddles Chief Plenty Coups called a hurried war council and the Indians joined the
cavalry in pursuit of the thieves.

CROW AGENCY, 63.1 *m.* (3,041 alt., 350 pop.), is the administrative
headquarters of the Crow Reservation. The administration buildings, Indian park, and Baptist mission are L.

The Crow Indian Reservation, containing 3,700 square miles, created
1851, is the home of 2,112 Indians and as many whites. Each of its six
districts has a subagency, with a field nurse, field agent, or other responsible officer.

The Crow cut three crops of alfalfa during the summer, and raise oats,
barley, and wheat. Sugar beets yield up to 19 tons an acre in the irrigated
Big Horn Valley. On leased reservation land is Thomas Campbell's
80,000-acre dry-land wheat ranch, largest in the United States. Grassy
slopes provide excellent summer and winter range; 34,000 acres of national forest land reserved for Indian-owned livestock contain several
hundred buffalo and elk.

Most of the Indians own fairly modern homes, but in summer their
lands are dotted with tepees. Tribal laws conform to the Department of
Interior regulations; the council of two is elected by popular vote; the

superintendent (1938), Robert Yellowtail, is the first Indian to administer a western reservation. Individual rather than communal ownership is traditional among the Crow but they have fine tribal unity.

Though trachoma and tuberculosis were formerly somewhat prevalent, the Crow are relatively healthy.

Widespread membership in the forbidden "peyote" societies continues among the Crow. Peyote ("button" of the mescal plant, a cactus), drunk in an infusion or chewed, brings happy visions.

The Crow were rovers with no interest in any craft but the making of fine beadwork, originally quill work.

During the Crow Agency fair in August these Indians exhibit beaded articles and a few others they are now learning to make, but their real interest is in fancy riding, horse racing, arrow throwing, and ceremonial dancing.

The Crow call themselves Apsaruke, or Absarokee *(people of the raven)*. They have lived here since long before the white man came and are possibly the people described as "les beaux hommes" in the Verendrye journal. Some of the Crow, enemies of the Sioux and Cheyenne, served General Custer as scouts. The Indian attitude toward the land was expressed by a Crow named Curly: "The soil you see is not ordinary soil—it is the dust of the blood, the flesh, and the bones of our ancestors. You will have to dig down to find Nature's earth, for the upper portion is Crow, my blood and my dead. I do not want to give it up."

Many Crow have adopted white family names but many land titles are registered under school or church-given white names plus Anglicized Indian names. Among them are Aloysius Child-in-his-mouth, Frank He-does-it, Chief Bull-dog-falls-down, Mary Takes-a-wrinkle, Montgomery Ward Two Bellies, Michael Bull-chief, James Medicine Tail, Ben Long Ears, Rides Pretty, and Oscar Other Medicine.

Many borrowed stories are told in Crow lodges on winter evenings, for the Crow adopted much of the culture of their neighbors. Typical is a version of the Creation myth:

"Old Man Coyote was walking round and round, as was his habit. 'That I am alone is bad,' he said. 'If I looked at someone now and then, and talked with him, it would be well.'

"He urged two small red-eyed ducks to dive into the water and, if they reached something, to bring it up. After repeated trials, the ducks brought a little mud. Coyote said: 'Well, my younger brothers, this we will make big, we will make our abode.' He blew on it, and made the earth. Then he took a little root; he made the grass, the trees, and other plants.

"One of the ducks spoke: 'It is fine, but its being level is too bad. If there were rivers and little coulees and hills, it would be well.'

"He traced rivers, he made hills, he went around. Then, from some of the dirt, he made companions for himself and the ducks: first men, then women. That's the way it was." The myth goes on to the creation of animals and other things.

It was Crow custom to bury the dead upon a height, supposedly nearer the spirit world, with their belongings beside them; often their lodges were destroyed. White blankets were worn by the mourners as symbols of the star trail the dead were believed to be traveling; the mourners sometimes mutilated themselves.

Formerly Crow marriage rites were simple; after an exchange of presents, the squaw moved into her husband's lodge. It was sometimes harder to get rid of a squaw than to obtain one; a white man, who won a Crow woman at a horse race, had to give the tribe fifty dollars to take her back.

At 64.7 m. is the junction with a graveled road.

Left on this road 1 m. to the CUSTER MONUMENT in the CUSTER BATTLEFIELD NATIONAL CEMETERY (custodian acts as guide) (3,029 alt.), one mile square; the area was set aside by the Federal Government, December 7, 1886. The monument, a sandstone obelisk surrounded by an iron fence, lists the names of 265 men killed on the battlefield, but only 209 marble slabs have been set up, supposedly marking the spots where men fell. When General Terry arrived on the field two days after the battle (see HISTORY), his troops and Reno's were too busy caring for their wounded to have much time for burying the dead. Four days after the battle Terry sent a detail that buried the bodies of officers in graves a few inches deep, but only partly covered those of the enlisted men. Capt. H. L. Nowlan charted the officers' graves. A year later a detail from Fort Keogh arrived to exhume the remains of officers. The covering earth had been blown and washed away, and many skeletons were above ground. Wolves and coyotes had been busy. The skull, one femur, and a few small bones of Custer were found and taken to West Point for burial. In 1885, when all bones found on the surface were buried in a square pit at the base of the sandstone monument, wooden stakes were placed on the places where the bones were found. Years later a commission arrived to replace the stakes with stone markers but so many of the bits of wood had rotted away that the slabs were set up largely by guesswork. Those in charge of the marking hunted for spots where grass grew rank, on the assumption that the soil under them had been enriched by animal matter. Large rank areas were passed over on the theory that they represented places where horses had died.

Nevertheless, these irregularly grouped markers along a hilltop, with a few scattered along the edges of the field, give a better picture of what happened here on the afternoon of June 25, 1876, than the thousands of controversial words that have been published about the fight. Academicians still ask how it was that the Sioux and Cheyenne were armed with Winchesters, superior to the arms of the Seventh Cavalry; why Custer divided his command into four parts; why Custer was in such a hurry; why Benteen did not come to his assistance. Authors, such as Thomas B. Marquis, continue to assert that many of Custer's command committed suicide.

This cemetery, covering 7.5 acres, has become a repository for the dead of various battles and forts of the Northwest. In 1931 the bones of 1,421 soldiers and civilians from Forts C. F. Smith, Phil Kearny, Maginnis, Abraham Lincoln, Custer, Keogh, and others, had been reburied there.

GARRYOWEN, 69 m. (3,080 alt., 50 pop.), is a crossroads settlement. Its name commemorates the ancient Irish air, Garryowen, that was the battle song of Custer's cavalry.

The EXPERIMENTAL RANGE REVEGETATION PLOT (R). 73.5 m., is one of several where work is being carried on by the U. S. Department of Agriculture to determine types of grass most suitable to the soil. Other grass plots are seen at intervals along the highway.

The Rosebud Mountains (L), a low, sparsely timbered range, parallels the Little Horn River.

LODGE GRASS, 84.2 m. (3,056 alt., 373 pop.), is a trade town of the ranchers whose herds graze on the rich grass-covered uplands that were formerly covered with buffalo. Before the white man came, the

Crow made their summer hunting camps here, and knew the place by a name that probably meant "rich grass," but was sometimes interpreted as "greasy grass." The Crow words for "lodge" and "grease" were so similar that by further misinterpretation this place became Lodge Grass.

The low barren summits (L) at 86.2 *m.* belong to the WOLF MOUNTAINS. Only a narrow valley separates the Rosebud and Wolf Ranges, and on maps they seem one chain.

The valley of the Little Horn narrows into a canyon between the Wolf Mountains and the foothills (R) of the Big Horn Mountains.

WYOLA, 97.9 *m.* (4,100 alt., 125 pop.), is a shipping point for cattle ranches in the valley. Here the Montana Highway Commission maintains a port of entry during the tourist season.

At 107.8 *m.* US 87 crosses the Wyoming Line, 30 miles northwest of Sheridan, Wyo. *(see Wyoming Tour 3).*

⤙⤙⤙⤙⤙⤙⤙⤙⤙⤙⤙⤙⤙⤙⤙⤙⤙✸⤚⤚⤚⤚⤚⤚⤚⤚⤚⤚⤚⤚⤚⤚⤚⤚⤚⤚

Tour 4

(Calgary, Alberta)—Browning—Great Falls—White Sulphur Springs—Livingston—Gardiner—(Mammoth Hot Springs, Wyo.) ; US 89.
Canadian Border to Wyoming Line, 420.5 m.

Route paralleled by branches of Great Northern Ry. between Pendroy and Neihart, of Chicago, Milwaukee, St. Paul & Pacific R.R. between White Sulphur Springs and Ringling, of Northern Pacific Ry. between Wilsall and Gardiner.
Accommodations of all kinds in cities, limited but comfortable in villages and towns, tourist homes at intervals between towns.
Oil-surfaced roadbed most of way; remainder graded and graveled. Mountainous stretches have usual mountain hazards—small landslides in wet weather and occasional heavy snows in winter.

Section a. CANADIAN BORDER *to* GREAT FALLS, *185.8 m.,* US 89.

This section of US 89 cuts across the low divides between tributaries of the St. Mary, Milk, and Marias Rivers, and runs along the abrupt eastern slope of the Rockies. It is part of a direct route between Glacier and Yellowstone Parks, sometimes known as the Yellowstone Glacier Beeline. The rolling grassland it traverses is the western extremity of the Great Plains, still to some extent an open cattle and sheep range. Almost half its course lies in the relatively fenceless Blackfeet Reservation, just east of Glacier National Park. Most of the streams that flow eastward from the Rockies in this area offer good fishing, especially at the points where they emerge from the hills.

US 89, a continuation of Alberta 1, crosses the Canadian Border, 0 *m.*, 0.1 mile south of Carway, Alberta, a customs station and port of entry 158 miles south of Calgary.

It runs along the western edge of the Blackfeet Indian Reservation, with the mountains of Glacier National Park R.

All the country east of the Rocky Mountains and north of the Yellowstone River, far into Canada, was once the buffalo range and hunting ground of the Blackfeet, who jealously defended it from invasion by other tribes and stubbornly resisted white occupation until subdued by superior force.

A legend common to many tribes is that the first buffalo came out of a hole in the ground, and when the buffalo began to disappear because of the whites' uncontrolled slaughter, the Indians believed that the white men had found the hole and had rolled a large boulder over it.

At 10.7 *m.* is the junction with the Chief Mountain International Highway.

Right on this graveled road, locally called the Kennedy Creek Cut-off, around the base of CHIEF MOUNTAIN (9,056 alt.), the isolated yellow-and-tan colossus of hard limestone that rears up on the boundary of Glacier National Park and marks the eastern limit of the Lewis overthrust. The irregular wedge of the mountain provides an excellent opportunity for study of the geological structure of the northern Rockies *(see GLACIER NATIONAL PARK)*. Part of the roadbed is composed of the glacial debris that surrounds the mountain.

At 13 *m.* is the junction with a crude trail; L. here 1 *m.* to BELLY RIVER, a fishing stream of unusual reputation. In Glacier Park it flows along the eastern side of the mountains, with only foothills and a few detached peaks between itself and the Great Plains.

At 14 *m.* the road and river cross into Canada, 14 miles southeast of Maskinonge Lake in Waterton Lakes National Park.

BABB, 15 *m.* (4,460 alt., 25 pop.), has tourist cabins, a general store, and a post office. It was settled in 1912 as headquarters for the Reclamation Service project that diverted water from St. Mary River, which drains into Hudson Bay, across the Hudson Bay Divide to the Milk River for irrigation purposes.

At Babb is the junction with an oiled road *(see Park Tour 4)*.

South of Babb the highway parallels the shore of LOWER ST. MARY LAKE, approaching it closely at several points.

ST. MARY, 24.1 *m.* (4,480 alt., 103 pop.), is at the foot of UPPER ST. MARY LAKE, just within Glacier National Park. Here is the junction with Going-to-the-Sun Highway *(see Park Tour 1)*.

Opposite St. Mary rises the steep Hudson Bay Divide, which US 89 crosses at 30.7 *m.* (6,076 alt.). Waters north of the ridge flow into the Saskatchewan River; south and east, into tributaries of the Missouri. The first of these, the South Fork of the Milk River, is crossed at 35 *m.* The road crosses the Milk River Ridge, 36.3 *m.*, which offers a far view (L) over the plains. There are only occasional glimpses of the mountains of Glacier Park; the road goes through dense growths of aspen and stunted cottonwood.

At 38.8 *m.* is the junction with a narrow dirt road *(see Park Tour 3)*.

BROWNING JUNCTION, 43.2 *m.* *(see Tour 2)*, is at the junction with US 2 *(see Tour 2)*. Between this point and a junction at 59.1 *m.* US 89 and US 2 are one route *(see Tour 2, Sec. b)*.

At 59.1 *m.* is the junction with US 2 *(see Tour 2)*.

Between Browning and Great Falls US 89 skirts the western edge of the Sweetgrass Arch *(see RESOURCES AND THEIR CONSERVA-TION)*, one of the important oil-bearing geologic formations in the world. Through much of this area exploratory drilling goes on almost constantly.

A high open place at 63.2 *m.* affords a view (L) of the plains, and (R) the Continental Divide. During intertribal warfare on these plains, the Indians often started fires that swept the prairie for hundreds of miles.

The road crosses Two Medicine Creek, 67 *m.*, and runs through the irrigated lands of the Blackfeet *(see Tour 2, Sec. b)*. Outside the small valley, the visible area is mostly sheep pasture.

The TEPEE RINGS (R and L), 70 *m.*, are circles of small stones marking the site of an old Indian encampment.

BIRCH CREEK, 84.8 *m.*, is at the southeastern corner of the Blackfeet Reservation.

At 86 *m.* is the junction with an improved dirt road *(see Side Tour from Tour 6, Sec. a)*.

DUPUYER, 94.7 *m.* (4,050 alt., 45 pop.), a supply point for stock ranches, came into existence as a stage stop on the bull freight route between Fort Benton and Fort Browning. Its name is from the French *depouille*, a word applied by trappers and explorers to the back fat of the buffalo, a delicacy esteemed by both Indian and white.

Right from Dupuyer on a graded road to the junction with another dirt road, 9 *m.;* R. here to SCOFFIN BUTTE, 14 *m.*, which is rich in fossilized dinosaur remains.

South of Dupuyer the road passes over broad cattle ranges. The region is a consistent producer of prize-winning stock. Local lore has it that riders sleeping in the open here sometimes wake to find a rattlesnake coiled cozily among the blankets, obviously in search of warmth. The early ranchmen, observing that the snakes most often attack horses on the nose or belly where the hair is short, concluded that they dislike horsehair, and adopted the practice of coiling a horsehair rope around their soogans (blankets) when sleeping on the ground. Early cartographers erroneously indicated a Lewis Range between this point and the Continental Divide.

At 107.6 *m.* is the junction with an improved road.

Left on this road is PENDROY, 1 *m.* (4,264 alt., 85 pop.), the terminal of a Great Northern branch from Great Falls, and a grain-shipping point.

BYNUM, 114.9 *m.* (3,970 alt., 94 pop.), is a shipping point in a region of large dry-land and irrigated wheat ranches.

CHOTEAU, 128.3 *m.* (3,800 alt., 997 pop.), seat of Teton County, was named for Pierre Chouteau, Jr., a member of a family of fur traders associated with Astor's American Fur Company. Montana also has a county named for Chouteau; to avoid confusion the town name is spelled without the first "u." Choteau was once headquarters for big cattle spreads (ranches) whose herds ranged over large areas of north-central Montana. There are still several large ranches near.

Right from Choteau on partly improved State 33, a part of a cut-off between this point and Helena. AUGUSTA, 33 *m.* (4,076 alt., 412 pop.), was named for the daughter of a pioneer rancher, D. J. Hogan. Sulphur deposits discovered near here in March 1885 caused much excitement, but proved unimportant commercially. A fairly prosperous farming area surrounds the town.

At Augusta are junctions with State 20 *(see below)* and an unnumbered dirt road; R. on the dirt road 17 *m.* to SUN RIVER MEDICINE SPRINGS, where warm water is piped to a small outdoor swimming pool.

State 33 approaches the rugged and abrupt main range of the Rockies, which is accessible by several foot and bridle trails. It crosses the Dearborn River, a tributary of the Missouri named by Lewis and Clark for Henry Dearborn, Secretary of War in 1806–07. The valley is largely sheep pasture.

WOLF CREEK, 76.1 *m.* (3,560 alt., 110 pop.), is something of a summer resort, with good fishing and beautiful mountain scenery. It is at the entrance to WOLF CREEK CANYON. The Indian name of the place was "the-creek-where-the-wolf-jumped-to."

At 76.6 *m.* is the junction with US 91 (see *Tour 6*).

Castellated PRIEST BUTTE (R), 130.3 *m.*, towers above the SITE OF ST. PETER'S MISSION, established in 1859 by Father Hoecken *(see HISTORY)*. This mission for the Blackfeet was not successful; after two years, Father Hoecken and his colleagues moved to Sun River.

At 142.2 *m.* the highway enters the GREENFIELD BENCH, the major unit of the SUN RIVER IRRIGATION PROJECT. It consists of 38,000 irrigated acres and 100,000 acres that can be irrigated; GREENFIELD LAKE (R) is the shallow reservoir of the system.

FAIRFIELD, 150 *m.* (3,999 alt., 227 pop.), a trimly built and well cared for village amid acres of grain, is the trading center of the Greenfield Bench. Before the development of irrigation, the grass here became scarce in dry summers, and stockmen were forced to move their herds. Consequently, the community was long known as "Freeze-out Bench."

On the broken country between the highway and the Rockies (R) a few remaining pronghorn antelopes graze, sometimes within sight of the road.

A panorama of the entire Greenfield region at 157.3 *m.*, shows SQUARE BUTTE and, in the distance, CROWN BUTTE (R), both south of Sun River. As the road descends to the Sun River Valley, the 506-foot smokestack of the Anaconda Reduction Works (L) at Great Falls is seen.

At 165.3 *m.* is the junction with State 20.

Right on State 20, which follows a route used by Capt. Meriwether Lewis and his party. A short section of State 20 is built on the Mullan Wagon Road, which came down through this region on its way between Fort Benton and the Prickly Pear, near Helena.

SUN RIVER, 0.8 *m.* (3,416 alt., 57 pop.), one of the oldest settlements in the State, is at the old Sun River crossing on the trail between Fort Benton and the gold camps. Before the railroads came, it was a lively place—a rendezvous for cowboys, bullwhackers, mule skinners, and trappers. Thousands of gold seekers and settlers passed through it.

FORT SHAW, 5.9 *m.* (3,502 alt., 85 pop.), the trade center of a beekeeping area, was settled in 1867 as a military post protecting travelers on the Mullan Road and settlers in the Sun Valley from Blackfeet raiders. It was named for Col. Robert G. Shaw, a veteran of the Civil War. One fort building, 125 feet long, was the scene of many dances, and was sometimes a theater. The movable benches had no backs and the floor was merely hard-trodden earth; when it was necessary to dim the footlights, members of the orchestra rose and turned down the wicks of the kerosene lamps that lined the stage apron. Despite the primitive living conditions, the place was the social center of a large area; the first professional stage performance in Montana was given on this stage.

From Fort Shaw Gen. John Gibbon in 1876 led the Seventh Infantry to join Generals Terry and Custer in the campaign against the Sioux and Cheyenne. It was while Terry and Gibbon were attempting an encircling movement that Custer was wiped out on the Little Horn.

General Gibbon was interested in more than military affairs. He planted trees and flowers and made lawns and gardens about Fort Shaw. In 1890, when the fort was abandoned, the Government turned it over for use as an Indian school. In 1910 the Indian school was closed and one for white children was opened.

SIMMS, 11.5 m. (3,563 alt., 464 pop.), is a farmers' town shaded by giant cottonwoods whose branches make vaulted corridors of the streets. Irrigation has reclaimed much formerly barren land about the town and made grain growing as important as cattle raising.

At 15.8 m. is the junction with a graded dirt road; R. here 1 m. to LOWRY (3,650 alt., 8 pop.), a river hamlet surrounded by hay ranches.

RIEBELING, 22.4 m. (3,755 alt., 14 pop.), is a ranch and post office.

At 33.1 m. is the junction with State 33. (see side tour above from Choteau).

VAUGHN, 173.4 m. (3,366 alt., 45 pop.), is at the junction with US 91 (see Tour 6). Between Vaughn and Great Falls, US 89 and US 91 are one route.

At 185 m. is the junction with State 29 (see Tour 14). US 89 crosses the Missouri River.

GREAT FALLS, 185.8 m. (3,300 alt., 28,822 pop.) (see GREAT FALLS).

Points of Interest: Russell Museum, State School for the Deaf and Blind, High School, Gibson Park, Black Eagle Falls, Giant Springs, and others.

Section b. GREAT FALLS to LIVINGSTON, 174.5 m., US 89.

Between Great Falls and Belt US 89 runs along the ancient bed of a glacial lake; near Belt it passes the line that marks the southern reach of the prehistoric continental ice sheet; it crosses the Little Belt Mountains, whose slopes are thickly covered with the pine, fir, and spruce of the Lewis and Clark National Forest; and continues southward between the Big Belt Mountains (R) and the Castle and Crazy Mountains (L). The Little Belts produce some coal, silver, lead, zinc, and gold.

In GREAT FALLS, 0 m., US 89 goes eastward on 2nd Ave. N., leaving the Missouri River and the giant smokestack of the reduction works behind.

Between the city and a junction near Armitage US 89 and US 87 (see Tour 3) are one route.

BELT BUTTE (L), 20.5 m., with its girdle of dark limestone, offers an explanation for the name of the Belt Mountains.

BELT, 22.2 m. (3,574 alt., 810 pop.), formerly called Castner, was founded by John Castner, whose coal mine, the first in Montana, supplied fuel to Fort Benton. In 1893 the Boston and Montana Mining Company began operation in the Belt coal field and was soon supplying all fuel for the smelter at Great Falls. Finns and Slavs settled the town. In 1930 the smelters at Anaconda and Great Falls began using natural gas piped in from the Cut Bank field (see Tour 2, Sec. b), decreasing the market for coal for the Belt mines, though they continue to produce for the region surrounding them.

ARMINGTON, 24.9 m. (3,558 alt., 150 pop.), is a coal miners' town.

At 26.6 m. is the junction (L) with US 87 (see Tour 3). US 89 swings R. through the deep gorge of Belt Creek.

It leaves the narrow canyon at 36.8 m. and climbs up the northern slope of the Little Belt Mountains in long curves. It runs across an eroded plateau, low and wide, with many spurs. The mountains are forest-clad, with yellow and lodgepole pine predominating.

MONARCH CANYON, 45.5 m., is a defile between steep limestone cliffs of various shades. A boundary of the LEWIS AND CLARK NATIONAL FOREST is crossed at 47.5 m. Several improved public campgrounds maintained by the U. S. Forest Service are near at hand.

Old silver mines are seen here and there in this region, some of them abandoned, some, after years of idleness, active again because of higher silver prices.

MONARCH, 48.8 m. (4,563 alt., 66 pop.), is an old, partly deserted mining town at the junction of two gulches whose creeks join the Belt. From this point prospectors, with some grub and an extra pair of socks in their packs, go into the hills to look for pay dirt. A mine that yields a profit, or at least gives a fair return in gold is known as "good ground." Placer gold is of four grades: nuggets, coarse gold, fine gold, and flour. Nuggets range from a dollar up in value. Coarse and fine gold can be caught in ordinary sluice boxes with little loss, but flour is so light that it washes out of the sluices with the water. When a considerable quantity of flour gold is found, miners use quicksilver in the riffles of their sluices and allow the mixture to settle in woolen blankets; they burn the blankets (if they are old) or wash them, to recover the amalgam, which is then heated to drive off the quicksilver. Several machines for recovering flour gold by combining gravitational separation with the amalgamation process, have been patented.

Left from Monarch on an improved dirt road to FINN CREEK, 8 m., whose waterfalls and sylvan charm amply repay a short walk up its narrow ravine.

HUGHESVILLE, 14 m. (4,960 alt., 66 pop.), is one of a group of mining camps settled in 1879. From this region rich silver and lead ores were hauled by bull team to Fort Benton, shipped down the Missouri and Mississippi to New Orleans, and transferred to ocean steamers for shipment to smelters at Swansea, Wales.

Since 1905 Hughesville has seen several mining revivals. The largest mine in the district is the BLOCK P, which has a mill of the most modern type, with a daily capacity of 1,000 tons of ore, and uses an improved flotation method (see Tour 18) of ore concentration.

Between Monarch and Neihart, US 89 again follows Belt Creek

through its deep, narrow upper canyon. Amethysts and marine fossils have been found here.

NEIHART, 62.2 *m.* (5,800 alt., 168 pop.), trading center of the Little Belt mining district, was named for J. L. Neihardt, uncle of the poet John G. Neihardt, and discoverer in 1881 of one of the richest deposits of silver-lead ore in the Little Belts; 40 mines have been operated in the vicinity. The igneous rock in which the ore is found is called pinto diorite because of its red-and-green spotted appearance. Great masses of it are near the town.

Some of the Neihart lodes yielded more than 500 ounces of silver to the ton. Among the largest producers were the Rochester, M and I, Florence, and Silver Dyke mines, the last having a large low-grade deposit. There was considerable new activity here between 1935 and 1937. Several properties yield zinc in addition to the silver-lead-gold combination. Even in inactive periods the people of the district have an air of expectancy, for they are certain that there are lodes, yet to be discovered, which will bring prosperity overnight.

South of Neihart the highway follows Sawmill Creek, and begins the climb to King's Hill, a pass through the Little Belts.

In the dark red and purple base rocks feldspar crystals are imbedded.

At 70.3 *m.* is the junction with the Chamberlain Creek road.

Left on this road to Chamberlain Creek, 1 *m.;* from the mouth of this creek a foot trail runs 2.6 *m.* to the SUMMIT OF NEIHART BALDY (9,000 alt.), from which, at night, the lights of Great Falls, 70 miles north, are visible. Two immense natural amphitheaters in the igneous rock of the southern slope show sharply projecting buttresses and talus slides. A lakelet, surrounded by talus heaps overgrown with stunted alpine growth, fills a hollow at the bottom of the longest slope.

The summit of KING'S HILL, 71.7 *m.* (7,300 alt.), has a ranger station and a public campground in groves of alpine fir. The highway, here known as King's Hill Road, winds down the southwest slopes of the Little Belt Mountains. At 90 *m.* it crosses the southern boundary of the LEWIS AND CLARK NATIONAL FOREST.

At 100.5 *m.* is a junction (L) with State 6 *(see Tour 11).* For 12 miles US 89 and State 6 are one route.

WHITE SULPHUR SPRINGS, 100.6 *m.* (5,200 alt., 575 pop.), seat of Meagher (pronounced mar) County, was so named because of mineral springs. The springs are now privately exploited. Indians came great distances to use the hot water here for medicinal purposes. White people who follow their example, report improvement in cases of rheumatism and some stomach disorders.

Meagher County was named for Gen. Thomas Francis Meagher, an Irish patriot and Civil War hero who came to Montana as a Federal official. Acting as Territorial Governor in the absence of Sidney Edgerton, General Meagher made a trip to Fort Benton, July 1, 1867, intending to go down the river to obtain arms for a campaign against the Indians. Late at night, on the eve of his expected departure from Fort Benton, he went to his stateroom on the steamer after a visit to a tavern, and was never seen again. For some time rumors were afloat that the general had been

US 89 NEAR NEIHART

pushed into the river while attempting to board the steamer, but this was denied by responsible citizens of Fort Benton who had escorted him to his room. He was a large, powerful man; it is improbable that he could have been forcibly taken from his stateroom and hurled into the water without a struggle that would have aroused the crew and passengers. What happened to him remains one of the mysteries of pioneer Montana.

Contemporaries say that Meagher was a quarrelsome person; that many of his decisions as Acting Governor had met bitter opposition and made enemies who might conceivably have seized the opportunity to do away with him. Some members of the Ancient Order of Hibernians took the stand that he was a martyr to the Irish cause and erected a statue of him on the capitol grounds at Helena, near the main entrance *(see HELENA)*.

White Sulphur Springs was the boyhood home of Taylor Gordon *(see THE ARTS)*, a Negro singer of spirituals.

The country around White Sulphur Springs offers excellent hunting and fishing, and is a popular summer-resort area. An annual Labor Day Rodeo in the town draws some of the best riders and ropers in the State.

The AUDITORIUM, built (1870) when plans were projected to make White Sulphur Springs a rival of the popular spa of the same name in West Virginia, boasts a false ceiling made of a "big top" purchased from the Ringling Brothers' circus.

Right from White Sulphur Springs on an oiled road to FORT LOGAN, 17 *m.* (3,972 alt.), a former military post established in 1869 to protect the mining camps and the Fort Benton freight route. First called Camp Baker, it was renamed in memory of a Captain Logan killed at the Big Hole Battle *(see HISTORY)*. The blockhouse still stands.

South of White Sulphur Springs the highway traverses the wide, open, sage-dotted Smith River Valley, in which are holdings of the Ringling family of circus fame.

At 112.5 *m.* is the junction (R) with State 6 *(see Tour 11)*.

RINGLING, 125.1 *m.* (5,304 alt., 152 pop.), was named for the circus Ringlings, whose ranch properties in this section formerly included more than 100,000 acres. The town is an important shipping point for Smith River Valley wheat, which has high protein content. It was the southern terminal of the old White Sulphur Springs and Yellowstone Park R. R., now a 23-mile spur of the Milwaukee; this short railroad for many years operated but one combination-train daily, yet paid regular dividends.

South of Ringling the highway crosses a low divide into the south central mountains. For a part of the way three ranges are in view—the Crazy (L), the Absaroka (straight ahead), and the Bridger (R).

WILSALL, 146.8 *m.* (5,048 alt., 413 pop.), at the northern end of a Northern Pacific Ry. spur, depends on the shipping and trade of homesteaders in the upper Shields River Valley, a region producing wheat, seed peas, hay, and livestock. The town's name is a combination of Will and Sal, nicknames of the children of an early settler.

Between Wilsall and Livingston the highway closely follows the course of the old Bridger trail *(see Tour 1, Sec. b)*.

CLYDEPARK, 154.6 *m.* (4,821 alt., 302 pop.), was named for a breed of horses popular here, and for the parklike appearance of the valley. Two cattle kings, Harvey and Tregloan, once had the run of the entire valley.

The highway swings into the Yellowstone Valley at 169 *m.*

At 174.1 *m.* is the junction with US 10 *(see Tour 1, Sec. b)*. Between this point and Livingston US 10 and US 89 are one route.

LIVINGSTON, 174.5 *m.* (4,490 alt., 6,391 pop.) *(see Tour 1, Sec. b)*, is at the junction with US 10 *(see Tour 1)*.

Section c. LIVINGSTON *to* WYOMING LINE, *60.2 m. US 89.*

This section of US 89 parallels the Yellowstone River between the Absaroka and Gallatin Ranges, and passes through a popular dude-ranch region. A dirt road on the west river bank follows the earliest trail used by white men in the area. The upper valley is rich in the lore of Yellowstone National Park; countless people were drawn through this approach to the park by tales of fabulous wonders, most of which were not wholly believed until the official Washburn-Langford expedition of 1870 confirmed them.

South of LIVINGSTON, 0 *m.*, for 5 miles US 89 follows the old trail on the right bank of the Yellowstone, then crosses to the left bank.

The snowcapped ABSAROKA RANGE is seen (L) at 20 *m.;* US 89

skirts EMIGRANT PEAK (10,900 alt.). The mountains (R) which cast their notched and somber shadows on the Absarokas are the Gallatins. At 25.2 *m.* is the junction with a dirt road.

Left on this road to CHICO HOT SPRINGS *(adm. 35¢; hotels, cabins; shower, tub, and vapor baths, mineral water, warm and hot plunges; horses available for saddle and pack trips into the Absarokas, and for fishing and hunting),* 1.4 *m.* (5,160 alt.). The resort is in sheltered EMIGRANT GULCH, where placer gold was discovered by Thomas Curry in 1862; the earliest trappers and prospectors bathed in crude vats built around the hot springs.

Jim Bridger is believed to have spent the winter of 1844–45 here, though legend and story set an even earlier date for his first visit.

When a train of immigrants arrived near the narrow entrance to the gulch in 1864, their attention was drawn to a lone pine with 18 to 20 elk horns around its base, so strongly imbedded that they could not be removed. In December of that year Jim Bridger and one of the settlers met at a primitive hotel near Bozeman. When, during the swapping of stories, the ring of elk horns was mentioned, Bridger asserted that he had placed them there 25 years before.

The ghost town of CHICO, 2.9 *m.* (5,020 alt.), is inhabited by a few families who work side-gulch placers.

In YELLOWSTONE CITY, 5.2 *m.* (5,250 alt.), only rotting log foundations of its early buildings remain, but some new cabins have been built by prospectors now plying pick and pan in the gulch.

Gold was found in upper Emigrant Gulch on August 30, 1864. The usual stampede followed, and Yellowstone City began as a tent camp. When cold weather froze the sluices, the miners moved down into the valley and lived in holes dug in the mountain sides. The first winter was severe and supplies ran short; a 96-pound sack of flour cost $28, tea sold for $2 a pound, and "chawing" tobacco for $5 a pound. Game, plentiful in the vicinity, provided most of the food.

Yellowstone City boomed briefly but the strike was not a rich one. Crow killed several whites, and in 1866, the place was abandoned.

In the cemetery nearby is the GRAVE OF DONALD L. BYNUM, judge of the miners' court that tried and convicted George Ives, the first of the Virginia City road agents to be brought to justice *(see HISTORY).*

The EMIGRANT FISH HATCHERY (R), 25.9 *m.,* rears blackspot, rainbow, eastern brook, and Loch Leven trout for stocking Montana streams.

Five-mile YANKEE JIM CANYON, 41 *m.,* was named for James George, a picturesque character of pioneer days. Almost single-handed he built the first road into Yellowstone National Park on what became the Northern Pacific right-of-way, paralleling the modern highway on the opposite bank. He had a tollgate at the narrowest point. When in 1883 construction began on the Yellowstone Park branch of the Northern Pacific Ry., he fought the company until it agreed to build another road for him in the hills above the right-of-way. The old man remained in the region for many years, trapping and serving as a guide. Rudyard Kipling visited him in 1890 and told of the experience in a volume on his American travels.

CORWIN HOT SPRINGS, 49.3 *m.* (5,133 alt.), has cabins, a dance hall, a restaurant, a golf course, and a plunge. It is owned (1938) by Walter Hill, son of James J. Hill, the railroad builder.

The DEVIL'S SLIDE, 51 *m.,* an exposed dike of bright-red iron-impregnated rock on Cinnabar Mountain, is (R) across the river. The mountain was named by early settlers who thought the red rock was cinnabar.

The legend of the Devil's Slide is told in a jingle:

> "Ages ago, one can easily see,
> Old Yellowstone Valley went on a spree;
> The mountains had risen, the valleys had sunk,
> And old Mother Nature got roaringly drunk.
> The Devil, as drunk as the Devil would be,
> Slid to the bottom of Cinnabaree."

GARDINER, 56 *m.* (5,287 alt., 350 pop.), is the northern entrance to Yellowstone National Park. Rude old log buildings stand in sharp contrast with newer structures of pink stucco, milled logs, and brick veneer, that are brilliantly lighted at night during the tourist season to attract patronage. In winter Gardiner is almost deserted.

The town was named for Johnston Gardiner, a trapper who worked along the upper Yellowstone and its tributaries in the 1830's. Early efforts at settlement were frustrated by the hostility of the Crow, who hunted in this area. In 1883 the building of the railroad provided the impetus to settlement, but disputes arose over the proposed townsite and the Northern Pacific established its terminal at Cinnabar, 4 miles north. Gardiner became known as "the town that waited twenty years for a railroad," because the line was not extended to it until 1902.

At 57.3 *m.* the road crosses the northern boundary of YELLOWSTONE NATIONAL PARK through the ROOSEVELT ARCH, the cornerstone of which was laid by Theodore Roosevelt in 1903.

At 60.2 *m.* US 89 crosses the Wyoming Line, 1.9 miles north of Mammoth Hot Springs, Wyo. *(see WYOMING GUIDE).*

◄◄◄◄◄◄◄◄◄◄◄◄◄◄◄◄◄◄◄☼►►►►►►►►►►►►►►►►►►►

Tour 5

Bozeman—Gallatin Gateway—Junction with State 1—West Yellowstone
—(St. Anthony, Idaho); US 191.
Bozeman to Idaho Line, 101.1 m.

Route paralleled by Chicago, Milwaukee, St. Paul & Pacific R.R. between Bozeman Hot Springs and Gallatin Gateway.
Hotels in Bozeman, Gallatin Gateway, and West Yellowstone.
Dude ranches, mountain resorts, tourist camps, and public campgrounds along route.
Oil-surfaced roadbed, open throughout year.

US 191, the Gallatin Way, winds up the rugged canyon of the Gallatin River between the Gallatin and Madison Mountains. One of the two most frequently used Montana approaches to the country's oldest national park, it offers an appropriate introduction, and effectively whets the appetite for the grandeur of Yellowstone. Numerous trails and roads along this short route strike into forested semiwilderness, where green hills and pure air offer rest and peace, mountain streams provide game fish, high ridges challenge exploration, and a great variety of bird and animal life tempts the naturalist and photographer. Much of the route traverses the Gallatin National Forest and for nearly 30 miles it skirts the western edge of Yellowstone National Park.

At intervals the canyon widens, and the summits of the mountains form a tremendous backdrop for the quieter landscape near at hand.

US 191 branches west from US 10 at BOZEMAN, 0 *m.* *(see Tour 1, Sec. b).*

At 0.4 *m.* (L) is MONTANA STATE COLLEGE *(see Tour 1, Sec. b).* Immediately adjacent are the college experimental farms.

The lower Gallatin Valley, across which the highway takes its course, bears abundant crops of hay, small grains, and garden truck. In summer the fields are blue and purple with flowering alfalfa and peas and along the roadside are brilliant wild flowers. According to an Indian legend, on the third day of a bloody battle here between Sioux and Nez Percé, the sun was blotted out, and from the terrifying darkness came a voice. It was the Great Spirit commanding the warriors to forget old wrongs and cease shedding blood, for they were in the Valley of Peace and Flowers. Then the sun shone again. Since then the Sioux and Nez Percé have been friends. Another legend declares that whoever drinks of the waters of the Gallatin will return to the valley before he dies.

When Lieutenant Clark camped here in July 1806, he noted in his journal: "I saw Elk, deer & Antelopes, and great deel of old signs of buffalow. Thie roads is in every direction—emence quantities of beaver on this Fork—and their dams very much impeed the navigation of it."

At 7.7 *m.* is the junction with a dirt road.

Right on this road is ANCENEY, 9 *m.,* headquarters of the Flying D Ranch. Charles L. Anceney was an early-day cattle baron, whose 2,500,000 acres were among the largest holdings in the State. The Flying D is still one of the State's largest ranches, though it is reduced to 399,350 acres and has to lease 1,500,000 acres of National Forest land for summer range. No dude ranch, it runs as many as 40,000 head of cattle in good years.

Modern ranch roundups differ somewhat from those of the open range, but the Flying D operations are as lively as any of the present day. The spring, or calf, roundup is held in May or early June. Riders, working from the various ranches, bring cows and calves in from river bottoms and other sheltered spots where they have wintered. Since the holdings are largely under fence, there are few if any strays, slickears, or mavericks; consequently no repping (checking of ownership) is necessary, as in the old days when neighboring spreads sent riders to see that their calves were branded with the proper irons. The calves are separated from the cows and steers and thrown into corrals; as in former days, smoke goes up from branding fires and mingles with the fumes of burning hair; but the calves are branded with a stamping iron while standing up in a chute, and so there is now no danger from the horns of the resentful mothers. Acid branding is increasingly used; it is quicker, safer, and more humane. The bull calves are castrated; some of the cows and steers are dehorned; all are checked for ticks, ringworm, blackleg, or other troubles.

The herds are wilder and more widely scattered in the fall when the beef roundup is held; it is simplified by the present-day freedom from cattle thieves and by the fact that railroad shipping pens are at most within a few days' drive, and overnight camps can always be made at ranch buildings.

When the range was wild, the roundup crew went out in the spring, equipped for several weeks in the field. It always had one chuck wagon, sometimes several; a wagon for bed-rolls and extra gear; and many horses. The riders scoured all the country between great natural boundaries, such as rivers or mountain ranges. What they gathered in a day they threw into a herd and held until they had covered a certain territory or had as many head as they could conveniently handle. Then, while some of the riders held the herd, others worked out the unbranded calves, cows, and steers, roped them, dragged them to a fire, and held them down by force while the iron was applied. The branded animals were kept apart from the unbranded until the whole herd had been worked; then the herd was sent back on grass, and the wagon went on to another part of the range. Riders slept on the ground, ate food cooked in a Dutch oven, and caught their horses in a flimsy rope corral, improvised daily by the wrangler. Each man had to stand guard during a part of the night, riding around the herd and singing to keep the cattle quiet. During storms, when the herd was likely to stampede, the riders were sometimes in the saddle 24 hours at a stretch. Double roundups were held in the fall, one in September, and another—for beef—in October. Then came the drive to the railroad, with stampedes, swollen rivers, soaked blankets, and cold supper or no supper, all in the day's work. The puncher's pay was $30 a month and grub.

BOZEMAN HOT SPRINGS, 8.5 *m.* (4,772 alt.), is a health and recreation resort. The springs provide mineral water at a temperature of 137.5° F. for the baths and plunge. Dances at the pavilion are summer attractions; but the big annual event is the night rodeo held under floodlights in August. Professional performers, many of whom have ridden and roped in Madison Square Garden, N.Y.C., demonstrate their skill on horses and steers who understand the act required of them.

GALLATIN GATEWAY INN, 13.3 *m.* (R), is a dude lodginghouse of Spanish-Romanesque architecture, operated during the park season *(June 20–Sept. 10)* by the C.M.St.P.& P.R.R. Its cream-colored stucco walls and red-tile roof stand out brilliantly against the green mountains.

GALLATIN GATEWAY, 13.7 *m.* (4,906 alt., 160 pop.), near the entrance to Gallatin Canyon is announced by an arch of logs over the highway. The town exists only through the tourist trade, and so its residents strive for rustic and picturesque effect in their buildings. Until the railroad company made it the terminus of a branch line to Yellowstone Park, it was known as Salesville, for Zach Sales who had a mill here in the late 1860's to saw logs driven down the Gallatin River.

The highway twice crosses the river, which winds through part of the Flying D range.

The entrance to narrow GALLATIN CANYON is at 19.6 *m.*

At 23 *m.* is a boundary of the GALLATIN NATIONAL FOREST, a 582,922-acre area that borders Yellowstone Park on the north and west. In season, hunters from all over the State come here to hunt the elk that drift over from Yellowstone Park when the snow is deep. Even without this immigration there are elk and a few moose in the area. Mule deer, whitetail deer, mountain sheep, and black and grizzly bear also range these forests. Marten, mink, beaver, badger, weasel, and skunk are the principal fur-bearing animals. Ruffed and blue grouse are plentiful. The streams are well stocked with eastern brook, Loch Leven, rainbow, and cutthroat trout.

The blue mountains that bulk on the sky line straight ahead are the Spanish Peaks of the Madison Range; BEEHIVE PEAK (10,500 alt.) and WILSON (10,194 alt.) are the most prominent. About 50,000 acres around them, accessible by trails, has been set aside by the U. S. Forest Service as the Spanish Peaks Primitive Area *(see RECREATION)*.

ROCK HAVEN (L), 23.6 *m.*, a group of log cabins, lies neat and snug along the riverbank. It is a summer camp maintained by the Presbyterian Church.

SQUAW CREEK RANGER STATION (L), 26.9 *m.*, is a typical Forest Service station, with neatly painted buildings, well-kept grounds, and an air of efficiency. Such posts are manned by well trained career men. The first forest ranger was perhaps a cowpuncher or homesteader before he took a Civil Service examination and went out to close-herd trees. His knowledge of botany, range conditions, silviculture, surveying, fire fighting, packing, road building, and a hundred other matters was picked up by haphazard practical experience. He had to mediate between angry ranchmen, all of whom regarded him as an intruder who ought to be shot; he had to placate a bewildering variety of short-tempered interests that did not at first like the new Forest Service; he had to prevent the slaughter of game by poachers. In handling such matters, he was thrust into the role of educator and apologist. He had to spend his evenings bruising two fingers on a typewriter, making out reports in duplicate, triplicate, infinity, and confusion. The early stations were stout log cabins that smelled of bacon and ham hung from the rafters, packsaddles and block salt, fire fighting tools oiled and stored, and, as the years went on, pack rats and skunks.

The modern ranger is college-trained and has a corps of trained helpers to handle details. He builds landing fields, and takes jealous care of his short-wave radio, barometers, and humidity charts. He is not much like his predecessor, the venturesome ex-cowpuncher who rode out, six-gun on hip, but he has made the forests much safer.

At the station is the junction with Hellroaring Trail.

Right on this to DEER CREEK LAKES, 15 *m.*, in the high-peak area.

An ASBESTOS MINE on the mountain side (R), 34.5 *m.*, is operated on a small scale by local people. It taps large deposits.

KARST'S RUSTIC KAMP (R), 35.3 *m.*, is a group of modern log cabins, where saddle horses and pack trains are outfitted for trips into the mountains. There is good fishing in the river.

At 37.7 *m.* is the junction with the Portal Creek Trail.

Left on this dirt road to HIDDEN LAKES, 4 *m.* Fishing is the main attraction here.

A saddle trail leads on 2 *m.* to the GOLDEN TROUT LAKES *(a plunge, cabins, saddle horses)*, named for the fish with which they are stocked.

SWAN CREEK FOREST SERVICE CAMPGROUND (L), 40.3 *m.*, lies along the river.

The highway crosses the West Fork of the Gallatin at 42.8 *m.* to the junction with a forest trail.

Right on this trail to OUZEL FALLS, 5.5 *m.*, a small, beautiful cataract, whose green water plunges in white foam over rocks. LONE MOUNTAIN (11,194 alt.) is R.

The highway, winding along close to the river, gains altitude steadily. At 45.8 *m.* is the junction with Beaver Creek Trail.

Right on this trail to BUCK CREEK RIDGE, 7 *m.*, the GALLATIN-MADISON DIVIDE, 9 *m.*, and YELLOW MULE RANGER STATION, 10 *m.*

Vivid rose-colored cliffs crowned with a heavy growth of dark green timber here rise 200 feet, the colors emphasized in the evening and the morning when sunshine floods the walls. The cliffs, broken and irregular, appear sometimes on one side, and sometimes on the other.

GALLATIN CAMP (R), 52.6 *m.*, a typical tourist camp, is a rest stop during the park season for Milwaukee Road busses, locally called "Gallagaters." Here tourists stretch themselves, and have pie and coffee, a can of beer, or a milk shake.

The CINNAMON CREEK RANGER STATION (R), 54.2 *m.*, is at the junction with the Cinnamon Creek Trail.

Right on this trail to BUCK CREEK BASIN, 6 *m.*, BUCK CREEK RIDGE, 10 *m.*, and the GALLATIN-MADISON DIVIDE, 13 *m.*

At 55.2 *m.* is the junction with the Buffalo Horn Road.

Left on this dirt road to BUFFALO HORN LAKE, 6 *m.*, RAMS HORN LAKE, 8 *m.*, and the EAST GALLATIN DIVIDE, 9 *m.* From the Divide a foot trail leads to the YELLOWSTONE RIVER, 20 *m.*

At 57.5 *m.* is the junction with Taylor's Fork Road.

Right on this dirt road to TAYLOR RANGER STATION, 6.5 *m.*, and WAPITI CREEK CAMP, 7.5 *m.*

Taylor's Peak (11,293 alt.) and the Wedge (10,508 alt.) bulk up R.

The highway leaves Gallatin Canyon at 57.8 *m.* to cross a high plateau.

SNOWFLAKE SPRINGS (R), 59 *m.*, is a small cascade foaming down a heavily timbered slope. It may have been named for a somewhat larger Snowflake Springs in Yellowstone Park, which is the source of the Gallatin River.

At 60.2 *m.* is a boundary of Yellowstone National Park, along which US 191 runs for about 20 miles.

BLACK BUTTE (L), 62.7 *m.*, is a peak so densely timbered that at a little distance its green appears heavily shaded with black.

SNOWSHOE CLIFF (R), 66.5 *m.*, is a very steep, heavily timbered ridge.

At 69.2 *m.* is the junction with a dirt road.

Right on this road to GALLATIN RANGER STATION, 0.5 *m.*

From the divide, 76.1 *m.*, between the Madison and Gallatin Valleys is a view embracing summits and ridges heavily furred with dark, bristling timber, and an occasional upthrust of gray crags. HORSESHOE CURVE, 76.3 *m.*, is sharp *(drive carefully).*

At 83.8 *m.* is the junction with State 1 *(see Tour 15).* South of this point the road becomes an aisle between impenetrable ranks of lodgepole pine, each shaft rising clean, straight, and lofty. So close do they stand that in late afternoon only an occasional gleam of sunshine reaches the road.

BAKER'S HOLE CAMPGROUNDS (R), 89.5 *m.,* is a Forest Service camp and picnic ground.

WEST YELLOWSTONE, 92.7 *m.* (6,665 alt., 300 pop.), the western entrance to the park, is a tourist town, full of eager competition and alert service. Here thousands arrive each summer—on the Union Pacific R.R., whose Yellowstone branch ends here, by automobile, and by plane from Great Falls or Salt Lake City. There are some visitors who have been here often but there is an ever-increasing horde of dudes. Every variation of western costume appears. In winter the town is abandoned, snow-bound, its many shops boarded up.

The Yellowstone area was known to the Indians as the Land of Evil Spirits. Most of them shunned it except when gathering obsidian for arrowheads.

Long ago the Sheepeaters, a peaceful people, lived in the lofty cliffs near the steaming hot springs, bubbling "paint pots," and spouting geysers that other tribes dared not approach. The men, skillful hunters of mountain sheep, their chief food, used bows made of rams' horns, bound with sinew. They fashioned their clothing of the skins of the dwarf whitetail deer that frequented the high forests and meadows. Their dwellings were frames made of poles covered with cedar bark and moss cemented with pitch.

These people chipped obsidian arrowheads of exquisite design that won them another name, the Arrow Makers. The history of these people is carved on the canyon walls near West Yellowstone, in what the Indians called the Country of the Painted Rocks. The picture writings, tribal emblems, and outlines of pygmy men and women are cut in irregular semicircles.

Some anthropologists believe the Sheepeaters were a remnant of a non-Indian race; others regard them as the descendants of outcast Bannack and Shoshone. Around their campfires, and in tribal ceremony and song the Sheepeaters told that their forebears had inhabited the geyser region "from the beginning," and that a large part of the tribe had once been destroyed by a terrible convulsion of the earth in the Upper Geyser Basin.

US 191 turns westward and cuts a broad avenue through forests of lodgepole pine; occasionally there are glimpses of the silver-white bark of young limber pine. As the road winds upward on the 400-foot rise to the Continental Divide, the sharp spires of alpine fir appear, together with bluish Engelmann spruce and Rocky Mountain red cedar.

TARGHEE PASS, 101.1 *m.* (7,078 alt.), named for a chief of the Bannack, was used by Chief Joseph on his way into Montana after his defeat of General Howard at the Battle of the Big Hole *(see HISTORY).* Just before Joseph entered the park area, he sent back a scouting party, which stole a hundred of Howard's pack mules and seriously hampered the pursuit.

At Targhee Pass US 191 crosses the Idaho Line, 68 miles north of St. Anthony, Idaho *(see Tour 1, IDAHO GUIDE)*.

◄◄◄◄◄◄◄◄◄◄◄◄◄◄◄◄◄◄◄◄ ☼ ►►►►►►►►►►►►►►►►►►►►►►

Tour 6

(Lethbridge, Alberta)—Sweetgrass—Shelby—Great Falls—Helena—Butte—Dillon—Monida—(Idaho Falls, Idaho); US 91.
Canadian Border to Idaho Line, 423.6 m.

Busses between Shelby and the Idaho Line; US 91 roughly paralleled by Great Northern Ry. between Sweetgrass and Butte, and by Oregon Short Line of the Union Pacific R.R. between Butte and the Idaho Line.
Varied hotel accommodations in cities and larger towns; tourist cabin camps here and there south of Great Falls.
Roadbed oil-surfaced throughout; open all seasons.

Section a. CANADIAN BORDER *to* GREAT FALLS, *127.4 m.,* US 91.

Between the Canadian Border and Great Falls, US 91 roughly parallels the Continental Divide 100 miles away which on clear days forms the western horizon. To the east only the unexpected upthrust of the Sweetgrass Hills breaks the monotony of the Great Plains. The road passes through oil fields and between great wheat and livestock ranches, and crosses several tributaries of the Missouri River.

US 91 crosses the Canadian Border, 0 *m.,* as a continuation of Alberta 4, 65 miles south of Lethbridge, Alberta.

SWEETGRASS, 0.1 *m.* (3,471 alt., 356 pop.), is a port of entry with U. S. customs and immigration offices. It was so named because of the abundance of sweet grass on the surrounding prairie. Only the invisible boundary line separates Sweetgrass from Coutts, the Canadian customs station, and they are often mentioned as a single place, Sweetgrass-Coutts. The Stars and Stripes and the Union Jack flutter above the twin villages.

In 1887 a narrow-gauge railroad called "the Turkey Track" was built across the border between Shelby and Lethbridge. Before that time the country was traversed only by range riders whose headquarters were south of the Marias River. Not until the coming of the dry-land farmer, about 1900, did Sweetgrass become much of a trading center.

The Sweetgrass Hills are visible (L) for nearly 15 miles. WEST BUTTE (7,000 alt.) is cone shaped; EAST BUTTE (5,000 to 6,000 alt.), consists of three peaks whose slopes bear lodgepole pine. MIDDLE BUTTE, locally called Gold Butte, is farther south, on a morainal ridge. Placer gold was found there by a Blackfoot in 1884. It was not a fabulous strike, as stampeders soon learned, but until the vein was worked out nearly every shovel of pay dirt yielded 25¢ in colors (gold left after waste has been washed away). Hence, the discovery canyon was named Two Bits Gulch.

Farthest south are the prominent Grassy and Haystack Buttes. A lobe of the great Keewatin ice sheet covered all this area to a depth of 2,000 feet and left behind a deposit of glacial drift from 15 to 100 feet deep. The glacial invasion smoothed the hills and filled the valleys between. Some of the high ridges were not entirely cut away, and new valleys were formed; the countryside was thus left with a billowy appearance.

The HUDSON BAY DIVIDE (4,000 average alt.) is visible (R) for about 27 miles.

The wide coulee in which Sweetgrass, Sunburst, Kevin, and Shelby are built is believed to have been the preglacial stream bed of the Milk River, only partly filled with glacial deposits. The present Milk River is like a bent bow lying across southern Alberta, with both ends in the United States.

US 91 closely follows the old Whoop-up Trail. In 1870 the U. S. Government outlawed the selling of whiskey to the Indians. Whiskey traders from Fort Benton thereupon established themselves in Canadian territory. According to the story, someone asked a Fort Benton trader how business was progressing at the new post. "Oh, they're damn well whoopin' it up," he declared. To stop the whiskey trade among the Indians, the Royal Northwest Mounted Police in 1874 built Fort McLeod on Old Man's River, 28 miles from Whoop-up. This caused most of the traders to return to Montana. The trail, however, was long used, all supplies for Fort McLeod being hauled by bull train from Fort Benton, the terminus of traffic on the Missouri.

At 8.9 *m.* is the junction with a dirt road.

Right on this road is SUNBURST, 0.3 *m.* (3,349 alt., 486 pop.), a gusher town, so named because the rising sun bursts over the Sweetgrass Hills.

The northern end of the KEVIN-SUNBURST OIL FIELD is (R) at 14.7 *m.* Between Sunburst and Shelby the prairie on both sides of the road is forested with derricks. This field and several others nearby are in the great Sweetgrass Arch (*see NATURAL SETTING*).

The producing sand of this oil field lies at the contact (plane between adjacent bodies of dissimilar rock) of the Ellis formation and the Madison limestone, at an average depth of 1,200 to 1,500 feet; its thickness ranges from a few inches to more than 20 feet. In nearly every well here is oil, gas, or sulphur water, in some wells all three. Three hundred feet above the Ellis-Madison contact is the Sunburst sand, the gas-producing horizon (deposit of a particular geologic time).

Dry holes as well as old stripper wells (those from which oil must be pumped) have been made to produce again by the acid treatment introduced in 1933. Gallons of a hydrochloric acid compound are dumped into the wells and when it reaches the Madison limestone a sulphur colored smoke rises. The acid makes the limestone porous and allows the oil or gas to gush through.

At 19.8 *m.* is the junction with an improved road.

Right on this road is KEVIN, 5 *m.* (3,331 alt., 324 pop.), near which the first gusher of the Sweetgrass Arch was drilled in 1922.

SHELBY, 36.3 *m.* (3,276 alt., 2,004 pop.) *(see Tour 2, Sec. b)*, is at the junction with US 2 *(see Tour 2)*.

From benchland the highway winds down between high and barren bluffs of glacial gravel into the valley of Marias River, a region of sage and parched grasses. This is the heart of the old Blackfeet country, where these Indians usually wintered. The cottonwoods and willows that fringed the river were among the advantages it offered.

US 91 crosses the Marias River at 43.7 *m.* The Marias is closely inter-woven with the early history of north-central Montana. In 1806 Capt. Meriwether Lewis, suspecting that it might be the main channel of the Missouri, and hoping that it might prove an important waterway to the north, left the main party and ascended it to a point near the site of Cut Bank *(see HISTORY)*. Later it was used by successive exploring and trading expeditions. In 10 days in 1831 James Kipp bought 2,400 beaver pelts from Indians who came to visit his new fort at its mouth.

At 52.5 *m.* is the junction with a dirt road.

Left on this road to a FOSSIL AREA, 8 *m.* The Dry Fork of the Marias, a peren-nial stream, has cut a deep channel through the Colorado shale and exposed many marine fossils of the Cretaceous period.

CONRAD, 64.1 *m.* (3,500 alt., 1,499 pop.), seat of Pondera County, is the distributing center of a prosperous grain-growing section. In the vicinity are oil wells that, like those in the Kevin-Sunburst field, produce from the Ellis-Madison contact.

1. Right from Conrad on Main St., which becomes a dirt road, to VALIER, 24 *m.* (3,802 alt., 575 pop.), on the shore of LAKE FRANCIS, the reservoir of an irrigation system capable of watering 100,000 acres. Formed by the damming of a coulee that cuts through a high bench, the lake has a 16-mile shore line. A spawning station is on the south shore, 5 miles from Valier. The lake is well stocked with fish, chiefly rainbow trout. Valier is served by the Montana Western Ry., 20.2 miles in length; its single daily freight-and-passenger train has run be-tween Conrad and Valier since 1909.

The country nearby was settled by Belgians imported in 1913 by the Great North-ern Ry. These people are now among the sturdiest and most prosperous citizens of the region. They maintain their national identity, speak their native language, and attend the Belgian Roman Catholic church.

2. Right from Conrad on an improved road to the VIRGELLE FORMATION, 9 *m.*, a sandstone group, eroded by wind and rain into all manner of grotesque figures, that lines both sides of the road for 5 miles.

3. Left from Conrad on Main St., which becomes a graveled road, to a DUTCH COLONY, 3 *m.*, established under the same conditions as was the Belgian colony near Valier *(see above)*. At 22 *m.* is a bridge crossing DEAD INDIAN COULEE. Right on foot along the coulee to a steep-walled 4-acre RATTLESNAKE PIT, which in August and September, before the time of hibernation, swarms with hiss-ing, writhing snakes. Altogether they possess enough venom to do away with an army—and they have plenty of relatives outside the pit. Hikers are comparatively safe but should exercise caution *(see GENERAL INFORMATION, and FAUNA)*.

BRADY, 75.6 *m.* (3,535 alt., 185 pop.), is a grain-marketing and distributing center for 5,000 acres of the Bynum Irrigation Project. Water
is conveyed to the Brady district through Muddy Creek from a reservoir
30 miles west.

The road crosses the Teton (Fr., *woman's breast*) River at 85.1 *m.*
The name was first applied to a mountain at the river's source.

DUTTON, 92.1 *m.* (3,535 alt., 350 pop.), is a small collection of
frame houses built around grain elevators and a flour mill. In normal
years it is one of the leading wheat-shipping points in the State; in 1934
it shipped 977 carloads. Dry-land farmers in its vicinity sometimes make
impressive income tax returns. A hard, heavy wheat, high in protein, is
produced.

A low range of hills at 93.8 *m.* (R), composed of loose piles of dirt,
rock, and debris, is a terminal moraine of the great Keewatin ice sheet.

At 101.9 *m.* is the junction with a graveled road.

Right on this road is POWER, 1 *m.* (3,681 alt., 120 pop.), a wheat-shipping
point on the Great Northern Ry. Its clustered grain elevators stand like lighthouses
in a sea of wheat.

At 108.4 *m.* is a wide view of the main range of the Rocky Mountains
(R) and the Great Plains (L). Here and there a brown butte, with spreading fingers of alluvium, rises above the prairie. The foliage is sparse,
bunch grass predominating. Cottonwoods and alders grow along the
stream courses, the only trees in this dry range country.

In a SALT MARSH, 109.8 *m.* (R), an alkaline crust covers considerable patches of ground *(see NATURAL SETTING).*

VAUGHN, 116 *m.* (3,366 alt., 56 pop.), is at the junction with US 89
(see Tour 4). Between this point and 6th St. W. in Great Falls, US 91
and US 89 are one route *(see Tour 4).*

GREAT FALLS, 127.4 *m.* (3,330 alt., 28,822 pop.) *(see GREAT
FALLS).*

Points of Interest: Charles M. Russell Memorial Museum, Giant Springs, State
School for the Deaf and Blind, Black Eagle Falls, Gibson Park, and others.

Great Falls is at the junctions with US 89 *(see Tour 4)* and State 29
(see Tour 14).

Section *b.* GREAT FALLS *to* BUTTE, *163.9 m.,* US 91.

South of Great Falls the highway winds through mountainous country.
The most glamorous pages of Montana's history were written here.

US 91 runs southwestward from GREAT FALLS, 0 *m.,* on 6th St. W.,
and crosses the railroad yards between double bends of the Missouri and
Sun Rivers.

US 91 crosses Sun River, 1.1 *m.,* near its confluence with the Missouri.
Blackfeet who hunted buffalo in this vicinity called the river the Medicine. On his return from the Pacific in 1806 Capt. Meriwether Lewis *(see
HISTORY)* crossed the Continental Divide from the Big Blackfoot Valley, followed the Sun River downstream, and camped at its mouth July 11,
1806. On the south bank (L) of Sun River is the MEADOW LARK

PAINTED ROCKS

COUNTRY CLUB. US 91 ascends from the river flat to a high bench affording a view of Great Falls. The Little Belt Mountains (L), then the Big Belts, form the horizon.

SQUARE BUTTE, 6.1 *m.* (R), large, flat-topped, and isolated, has an area of 650 acres on its top. Abandoned ranch buildings near a clear spring on the top are reached by a country road from Ulm.

Dry-land wheatfields stretch from the highway to the distant mountains. During times of drought the area is partly uncultivated. Russian thistles flourish by the roadside.

ULM, 11.6 *m.* (3,345 alt., 75 pop.), is a grain-shipping town. Three elevators, red storehouses for Missouri benchland wheat, rise above the small cluster of homes shaded and half hidden by clumps of gnarled cottonwoods.

At 25.9 *m.* is the junction with a graveled road.

Right on this road to the fire-swept ruins of ST. PETER'S MISSION, 17 *m.,* at the base of Bird Tail Divide on the old stage road to Helena. Across the road are the ruins of an early Jesuit school. The mission, which began work here in the stone buildings in 1886, had been established earlier just south of where Choteau now stands *(see Tour 4, sec. a)*; after two years among the hostile Blackfeet, who, unlike the Flathead, were content to do without the white man's religion, the priest and his assistants moved to Sun River, and then to Flood, 16 miles up the Missouri from Great Falls. Later the mission was transferred to Skull Butte near Cascade and then to this place.

Before its last move, St. Peter's had on its teaching staff Louis Riel, the man who had led the half-breed rebellion against the Canadian Government in 1869. By birth Riel was a quarter-breed, but his sympathies were those of a full-blood Indian. He became a citizen of the United States while at St. Peter's, but in 1885 he returned to Canada to lead another rebellion; it failed and he was captured and hanged.

CASCADE, 26.4 m. (3,378 alt., 520 pop.), like the county of which it is a part, was named for the falls of the Missouri, none of which are near the neat little town on the rolling bottom lands. Cascade was once the home of Charles M. Russell (see THE ARTS).

At 39.4 m. the valley narrows, and the highway crosses to the south side of the Missouri to run through BIG BELT CANYON, in which the walls are mottled with tints of red, moss green, and yellow which vary in brilliance with the amount of sunlight and shadow.

CRAIG, 50.6 m. (3,455 alt., 103 pop.), was named for an early settler in the valley.

At 52.8 m. is the junction with a dirt road.

Left on this road to HOLTER DAM (1912), 2 m., which backs up the Missouri River for 30 miles in a deep canyon, and forms Holter Lake. Broad at the dam, the lake narrows and twists and turns through Ox Bow Bend.

At 55.1 m. is the junction with State 33 (see Tour 4, Sec. a).

The road turns south through the precipitous canyon of Little Prickly Pear Creek. The roadway in many places is carved from vertical walls of stratified shale. At 68.1 m. it leaves the canyon, to ascend to a high, open, intermountain plateau. At 76.6 *m.* the Gates of the Mountains (L) become visible.

At 77.9 *m.* is the junction with a graveled road.

Left on this road, which turns sharply back toward the north, to the GATES OF THE MOUNTAINS, 3 *m.,* a deep gorge cut by the Missouri River in the Big Belt Mountains. Capt. Meriwether Lewis *(see HISTORY)* wrote of it in his journal:

"these cliffs rise from the waters edge on either side perpendicularly to the height of (about) 1200 feet. every object here wears a dark and gloomy aspect. the towering and projecting rocks in many places seem ready to tumble on us. the river appears to have forced it's way through this immense body of solid rock for the distance of 5¾ miles and where it makes it's exit below has thrown on either side vast collumns of rocks mountains high . . . it is deep from side to side nor is ther in the 1 st. 3 Miles of this distance a spot except one of a few yards in extent on which a man could rest the soal of his foot. several fine springs burst out of the waters edge from the interstices of the rocks. it happens fortunately that altho' the current is strong it is not so much so but what it may be overcome with oars for there is hear no possibility of using either the cord or Setting pole. it was late in the evening before I entered this place and was obliged to continue my rout untill sometime after dark before I found a place sufficiently large to encamp my small party; at length such an one occurred on the lar'd side where we found plenty of lightwood and pitch pine. this rock is black grannite below and appears to be of a much lighter colour above and from the fragments I take it to be flint of a yellowish brown and light creemcoloured yellow. from the singular appearance of this place I called it the gates of the rocky mountains."

At the end of the road is a boat landing. In summer motorboats make regular trips through the gorge. The cliffs are of limestone eroded into fantastic shapes, which have been given names suggestive of their forms: *Indian Head, Beartooth, Robber's Roost, Bride and Groom, Amphitheater.* On an island in the center of the gorge is the MERIWETHER CANYON PICNIC GROUND. Here the Lewis and Clark expedition camped July 19, 1805.

The highway descends to the PRICKLY PEAR VALLEY, 80 *m.,* usually called the Helena Valley, a scantily settled region of grain and dairy farms.

At 91.6 *m.* is the junction with a dirt road.

Right on this road to a GOLD DREDGE *(visited on application at office, Bank of Montana Bldg., Helena),* 0.2 *m.,* among conical heaps of dirt and debris, the tailings of its operations. The dredge operates along the lower reaches of Last Chance Creek and reaches to a maximum depth of 74 feet. The boulders and earth it scoops up are placed in a washing compartment, where the gold sifts to the bottom. As the dredge proceeds, it makes a small pond on which to float.

HELENA, 94.3 *m.* (4,124 alt., 11,802 pop.) *(see HELENA).*

Points of Interest: State Capitol, St. Helena Cathedral, Lewis and Clark County Courthouse, Public Library, Carroll College, Algeria Shrine Temple, Hill Park, Placer Diggings.

Helena is at the junction (R) with US 10 N *(see Tour 1A),* which unites with US 91 between Helena and a junction (L) at 96.2 *m.*

Across the Prickly Pear Valley (L) and above the low range of the Spokane Hills are the Big Belt Mountains. MOUNT ASCENSION (5,360 alt.) rises (R) above Helena.

The SITE OF MONTANA CITY, 104.9 *m.* (4,067 alt.), is marked by the weed-covered tailings of what were once extensive placer operations. Nothing else remains to indicate the site of a town that in its flourishing

days boasted a population of 3,000 and was mentioned as a possible capital of the State.

CLANCEY, 106.7 *m.* (4,213 alt., 125 pop.), a famous silver camp in
the late nineteenth century, is still a shipping point for ore from small
mines in the vicinity. The dumps of old mining operations are (L) near
the service station.

Right from Clancey on a dirt road is LUMP CITY, 2 *m.* (4,850 alt.), the scene
of extensive silver mining in the past. The Liverpool (R), most noteworthy of the
mines in and about Clancey, produced $1,500,000 in the late 1890's. Ore from the
Clancey district was so rich that it could be hauled by bull team to Fort Benton,
shipped by river and ocean to Swansea, Wales, and still net a profit. The only thing
left of the once lively mining town is a dilapidated, weather-worn schoolhouse inhabited by mountain rats.

ALHAMBRA HOT SPRINGS (L), 108.9 *m.* (4,265 alt.), is a quiet resort
*(cabins, saddle horses available; outdoor plunge, 25¢ and 50¢; vapor
baths, 50¢)*. The hot water, which has a high mineral content, flows underground from Lava Mountain (L), a high volcanic mound.

JEFFERSON CITY, 112.7 *m.* (4,708 alt., 68 pop.), began in 1864 as
a stage station on the line between Virginia City and Fort Benton. It has
been active at times as a mining town.

1. Right from Jefferson City on a dirt road to CORBIN, 2 *m.* (4,769 alt.), and
WICKES, 4 *m.* (5,165 alt.), mining and smelting camps in the boom days. Wickes
boasted of the first lead-silver smelter in Montana; the plant was dismantled in
the early 1890's. Near Wickes and Corbin are such gold and silver mines as the
Alta, with a reported production record of $32,000,000; the Gregory, with $9,000,-
000; the Ninah and the Bertha. Most of the important production came before
1892, but the district is still regarded as a potential source of silver, lead, zinc, and
gold. The Mount Washington Mine *(visited on application)* is 1 mile south of
Corbin.

2. Left from Jefferson City on a dirt road, barely passable for cars, to PRICKLY
PEAR DIVIDE, 12 *m.* *(Horses available at Jefferson City for trip.)* A good view of
the upper Prickly Pear Valley is obtained from the summit. Just over the divide are
three small lakes, the headwaters of Crow Creek.

3. Left from Jefferson City on a dirt road to the junction of Prickly Pear and
Golconda Creeks, 2 *m.;* R. across the Prickly Pear and along Golconda Creek to the
BUCKEYE MINE and the remains of an old Spanish ARRASTRA, 6 *m.*, a crude mill
for grinding gold ore, used by the first owners of the mine.

US 91 runs through a narrow winding canyon and ascends to the divide
between the Prickly Pear and Boulder Valleys. The descent that follows
is a series of loops and sharp turns.

BOULDER, 125.1 *m.* (5,158 alt., 760 pop.), seat of Jefferson County,
was named for the massive stones strewn about the valley. It was established in the early 1860's as a stage station on the Fort Benton-Virginia
City route, and later became the trade center of a mining and agricultural
area. The MONTANA SCHOOL FOR THE FEEBLE-MINDED *(open on application to superintendent)*, at the southern limits, cares for about 400 persons. Those capable of learning are trained in useful occupations; the
older boys do farm work and care for the dairy herd; the girls are taught
sewing, weaving, and housekeeping.

Left from Boulder on a dirt road to the junction with another dirt road, 2 *m.;*
L. 1 *m.* on the side road to BOULDER HOT SPRINGS (4,824 alt.). Here are vapor

baths *(adm. 50¢)* and a natural hot-water plunge *(adm. 25¢ and 50¢). (Equipment for saddle and pack trips and hunting and fishing available.)*

The dirt road winds southward along the mountain sides.

ELKHORN, 18 *m.* (5,430 alt.), is a former mining camp, established in 1872, that sent out $14,000,000 worth of gold and silver. In boom days this frontier town had 14 saloons; bullet holes in the buildings show how disputes were sometimes settled.

Left from Elkhorn 4 *m.* on a foot and bridle trail to ELKHORN PEAK (9,500 alt.); the last half mile must be climbed on foot. Near the peak the rock formation changes abruptly. Marble cliffs of dazzling white glisten in the sun on clear days.

WHITEHALL, 32 *m.* (4,371 alt., 553 pop.) *(see Tour 1, Sec. c)*, is at the junction with US 10 S *(see Tour 1).*

US 91 turns up the narrow canyon of Boulder River. There are gold and silver mines at the heads of many of the gulches that end in the valley.

At 132 *m.* is the junction with a dirt road.

Right on this road up High Ore Creek to the GRAY EAGLE AND COMET MINES, 4 *m.,* active silver and gold producers.

BASIN, 134.4 *m.* (5,306 alt., 250 pop.), a typical mining camp, booms or dozes as the price of metal determines. Most of the buildings are frame, with the second-story false fronts common in nineteenth century camps; some are squalid shacks. Across Boulder River (L) is the JIB MINE, a sensational gold producer in the 1920's.

The highway crosses Boulder River and follows the edge of a deep rocky gorge in whose walls red argillites predominate.

The SHAMROCK FOREST SERVICE CAMPGROUND, 141.6 *m.* (R), is in the DEER LODGE NATIONAL FOREST.

After the highway crosses Bison Creek it begins the ascent of a long hill, becoming a narrow shelf on the mountain side, with a stream rampaging over stubborn boulders far below.

ELK PARK CAMPGROUND (L), 144.9 *m.,* has outdoor stoves, tables, and other conveniences.

ELK PARK, 146.4 *m.* (6,237 alt.), a roadside service station, is on a flat plateau covered with dairy farms that supply milk to Butte. The farmers are of Swiss-Italian stock.

The CONTINENTAL DIVIDE, 158.9 *m.* (6,354 alt.), marks the boundary between Jefferson and Silver Bow Counties; the latter is Montana's smallest county in area, but the largest in population and wealth. The highway twists down through a bare and rocky canyon. At 160.1 *m.* BUTTE HILL (R), with its mine buildings, gallows frames, ore bins, and sprawling city, is in view across the valley.

MEADERVILLE, 161.8 *m.,* a suburb of Butte, has many important mines *(see BUTTE).* Its night clubs and Italian restaurants are numerous and popular.

BUTTE, 163.9 *m.* (5,755 alt., 39,532 pop.) *(see BUTTE).*

Points of Interest: Marcus Daly Statue, Smithers Historical Photographs Collection, Chinatown, Meaderville, Leonard Mine, State School of Mines, Columbia Gardens, and others.

Butte is at the junction (L) with US 10 S *(see Tour 1).*

Section c. BUTTE to IDAHO LINE, 132.3 m., US 91.

This section of US 91 crosses some of the finest grazing lands in the State, which are inside a great loop of the Continental Divide with eastward drainage through the Big Hole and Beaverhead Rivers. The valley bottoms, at an average elevation of 5,000 feet, are broad; the benches rise gently to low, rounded summits, treeless or only lightly forested.

This part of Montana was the first settled; it was easily reached from the Oregon Trail and the Mormon country to the south. The gold rush of 1862–63 attracted many fortune hunters who, after sampling the excitement of Alder Gulch and Grasshopper Creek, settled down in the verdant valleys and founded Montana's livestock industry.

Some mining is carried on in the mountains. Fishing and hunting are good.

Between BUTTE, 0 m., and a junction (R) at 5.7 m., US 91 and US 10 S (see Tour 1) are one route (see Tour 1, Sec. c).

South of the western junction with US 10 S, US 91 crosses the Milwaukee, the Union Pacific, and the Northern Pacific tracks; the Milwaukee Road is identified by the electric wires above the track. By an easy grade the road ascends to the CONTINENTAL DIVIDE, 14.8 m. (5,915 alt.), which here is scarcely recognizable as anything more than a high, sparse sheep range. South of the crest the waters drain into the Big Hole River, which flows into the Jefferson. "Hole," was the word used by early trappers to designate a mountain valley. Lewis and Clark, who followed the stream for a short distance in August 1805, named it Wisdom River.

DIVIDE, 25 m. (5,397 alt., 113 pop.), is a distributing and stock-shipping point for the upper Big Hole Valley.

Right from Divide on a graveled road along the Big Hole River to the RALSTON RANCH, 28 m., once a well-known stage station halfway between Divide and Wisdom, where the up stage and the down stage met, and where passengers and drivers enjoyed thick, tender steaks, crisp brown grayling from the river, and Mrs. Ralston's pies. Strings of freight wagons, each string drawn by 8 to 16 horses, rounded the curves in the road about dinnertime; fresh horses replaced the road-weary ones, which stayed here and were rubbed down, fed, and bedded for the night. Sometimes there was a dance at the station, in which cowboys, freighters, girls from surrounding ranches, and country schoolma'ams took part.

The Big Hole River is a natural habitat of grayling; rainbow trout have been planted in it. There is also excellent fishing in tributary streams. Cattle fattened on the nutritious wild grasses of the valley compete with the corn-fed stock of the Middle West. Men from many parts of the country come in for the late hay harvest, willing to work long and hard for the sake of a summer in this fastness of the old West, for top-notch haying hand's pay, and excellent food.

MELROSE, 35.2 m. (5,173 alt., 380 pop.), in large part consists of cabins that show the effects of time and storm. Nearby, along Big Hole River, are many inviting fishing holes; from Forty-five Bend, the best of them all, prize-winning rainbow trout have been taken with light tackle.

BROWNS, 41 m., is a roadside service station.

Right from Browns on a dirt road along Rock Creek to small BROWNS LAKE, 7 m., a favorite with Butte fishermen.

Big Hole River parallels the road for a few miles farther, then the stream turns sharply northeastward to join the Jefferson.

GLEN (Reichle P.O.), 46.2 *m.* (5,000 alt., 35 pop.), is a shipping point for surrounding hay ranches.

The road ascends the low divide between the Big Hole and Beaverhead Valleys. The rocky hillsides (R) are a retreat of rattlesnakes. Local people conduct occasional snake hunts during which they blast the rattlers from their dens.

As the highway enters the BEAVERHEAD VALLEY, fields of bunch grass, brome grass, sedge, and wild timothy flank the highway. In spring the bluebell, lupine, shooting star, buttercup, and daisy bloom profusely near the road. The sunflowerlike Wyethia, a comparatively rare plant in other sections of the State, is common here.

At 54.1 *m.* is the junction with a dirt road.

Left on this road to ZIEGLER'S HOT SPRINGS, 12 *m.*, on the Big Hole River. *(Cabins, campground; plunge and hot bath, adm. 50¢.)*

At 64.8 *m.* is the junction with State 41 *(see Tour 16).*

DILLON, 65.9 *m.* (5,057 alt., 2,422 pop.), seat of Beaverhead County, was named for Sidney Dillon, president of the Union Pacific R.R. It is a very important primary wool market, and the largest wool-shipping point in Montana. Dillon has the air of a much larger city, and an assurance and repose that it owes perhaps to its having known few economic setbacks. Many of the homes are typical of the early 1900's, while others are of modern design. A few of the first log cabins remain on the northern side of town. The broad, tree-shaded streets become country roads that lead to ranches much older than the city.

As the seat of the State Normal College, Dillon has a great variety of cultural activities, including those of literary and choral clubs, college and high school bands, and a college string orchestra. The college prepares teachers for the public schools of the State; the supervised practice work is done in the local schools, which serve as laboratories. This arrangement, in operation for many years, has provided unusual educational advantages for local children.

The position of the town, amid the low, lazy, rather arid hills, was determined by accident. Construction of the Utah and Northern R.R. was suddenly brought to a standstill in 1880, when a rancher on land here refused to give up land for the right-of-way. A few enterprising men engaged in business at or near the terminus banded together, bought the ranch, and gave the railroad company the right to go through. They continued their partnership by executing a trust deed, recorded on December 4, 1880, which marked the birth of Dillon. Lambert Eliel, trustee for the group, granted title to town lots, which were sold at public auction. The new town became the county seat when voters decided that Bannack was too far off the beaten track.

The WOOL WAREHOUSE, near the railroad station (R), is operated by a local company that markets wool for the growers at a charge of one cent for 10 pounds. The warehouse can hold 3 million pounds of wool, and has electric conveyors for loading and hauling the huge wool sacks.

MONTANA STATE NORMAL COLLEGE (L), near the southern city limits, has a main hall, a gymnasium, residence halls, and athletic fields on an attractive campus of 14 acres. There are about 350 students and 25 teachers. The small MUSEUM *(open when school is in session)* in MAIN HALL contains pioneer relics and Indian artifacts.

Right from Dillon on State 36, a graveled road, to the junction with an improved road, 8 *m.;* L. here 15 *m.* to BANNACK (5,510 alt., 180 pop.), Montana's oldest town, which was named for the Bannack Indians, who once roamed the region.

Here, on July 28, 1862, John White and a small party of prospectors from Colorado discovered a bonanza of placer gold along GRASSHOPPER CREEK. News of the strike spread, and in a few months a roaring, vigorous tent, shack, and log cabin city of about 1,000 people grew up. A horde of rough-and-ready adventurers from all parts of the West came in, among them scoundrels such as Henry Plummer, who had been run out of California and Nevada gold camps. For a year, until vigilantes caught up with him and his deputies, Plummer and his gang robbed and killed miners by the score *(see HISTORY).*

In September 1863 Sidney Edgerton, a brilliant lawyer of Akron, Ohio, who had been appointed chief justice of the newly created Idaho Territory, arrived here with his family. He was on his way to Lewiston, Idaho, but because of the lateness of the season and the difficulties of travel over the mountains, he decided to remain in the lively camp for the winter. In the spring he returned to Washington to advocate creation of a new territory. On May 26, 1864, Congress, heeding his pleas, created the Territory of Montana; President Lincoln named Edgerton its Governor and Bannack the temporary capital.

Governor Edgerton called the first Montana legislative assembly to order at Bannack on December 12, 1864. By that time the Grasshopper diggings had proved shallow and most of the miners had pulled stakes for the richer prospects in Alder Gulch; there Virginia City boasted a boom population of about 10,000, with as many more people in its vicinity. The first legislature therefore decided that the second session should convene at Virginia City.

Bannack remained a mining town, with small quartz mines and placer operations nearby. Its post office was closed in January 1938, but the weathered remains of the State's FIRST CAPITAL, FIRST JAIL, and FIRST HOTEL still face the single street in the narrow gulch.

At 32 *m.* on State 36 is the junction with a dirt road; R. here to ELKHORN HOT SPRINGS, 44 *m.* (4,830 alt.), in the BEAVERHEAD NATIONAL FOREST *(hotel, cabins, baths; an open plunge, adm. 50¢; guides, saddle horses, and pack outfits available for big-game hunting).* There is good fishing nearby. A general store and a Forest Service campground with free firewood make this an excellent base for visitors to the high mountains.

At the confluence of Beaverhead River and Rattlesnake Creek, 67.9 *m.,* in 1862 stood the only signpost in a vast wilderness. On one side of a rough-hewn board was daubed in axle grease:

> "Tu grass Hop Per digins
> 30 myle
> Kepe the trale nex the bluffe."

On the other side was:

> "To Jonni Grants
> one Hundred & twenti myle"

The "grass Hop Per digins" were at Bannack; "jonni Grant" was a rancher in the Deer Lodge Valley *(see Tour 1, sec. c).*

A monument (R) at 75.1 *m.* is on the westward route of Lewis and Clark through Beaverhead Canyon, and the later trail of prospectors coming up from Fort Hall on the Oregon Trail. Through this canyon the tracks of the first railroad in Montana were laid *(see TRANSPORTA-TION).* The canyon sides are dark with lodgepole pine, Engelmann spruce, and balsam fir.

ARMSTEAD, 89.3 *m.* (5,505 alt., 109 pop.), is at the junction of Prairie and Red Rock Creeks, which form the Beaverhead River. Capt. Meriwether Lewis, scouting ahead of his canoe party, turned west along an Indian trail by Prairie Creek, and found the camp of Cameahwait, Sacajawea's brother *(see HISTORY).* The meeting between Sacajawea and Cameahwait occurred a little way downstream.

Right from Armstead on a dirt road to ROCK PAINTINGS, 1 *m.,* believed to be the work of prehistoric Indians. Behind the first large red butte are lines of stones running from it across the valley like spokes radiating from a hub. At the foot of the butte are crude paintings in the center of a large ring of rock; it is supposed that the place was the scene of tribal rites.

RED ROCK, 93.1 *m.* (5,490 alt., 20 pop.), so named because of the predominant red of the rocks around it, is in Red Rock Valley, a fine broad sweep of irrigated hayland. Because of the elevation and the short growing season, sheep and cattle are the chief products of the ranches, whose prosperity is shown by their well-kept buildings.

DELL, 108.5 *m.* (6,050 alt., 45 pop.), is a trading center for valley ranchers.

LIMA, 116.9 *m.* (6,256 alt., 459 pop.), is a division point on the Oregon Short Line. Since the removal of the railroad repair shops it has lost much of its activity. Some of its stores are boarded up, and several houses have been deserted.

Left from Lima on a dirt road to LIMA RESERVOIR, 13 *m.,* which provides water for much of the grassland along Rock Creek. There is good fishing here.

MONIDA, 132 *m.* (6,798 alt., 75 pop.), on the Continental Divide, has a name composed of parts of the names of the States meeting here. It was a welcome stage stop on the old Salt Lake Trail, which in the 1860's brought people hungry for gold into Montana and took away those who were satisfied. The Centennial Mountains (L) and the Beaverhead Mountains (R) form the Continental Divide.

Left from Monida on an improved dirt road to LAKEVIEW, 29 *m.,* with hotel, auto camp, and general store overlooking the RED ROCK LAKES. Butte and Dillon sportsmen maintained a duck-hunting club here, until the area became part of a 50,000-acre migratory bird refuge. When drought struck the eastern part of the State there was a great concentration of ducks and geese on this preserve. White trumpeter swans, a species almost extinct in the United States, nest here. There is good fishing.

MONIDA PASS, 132.3 *m.* (6,823 alt.), is on the hardly perceptible CONTINENTAL DIVIDE, which here forms the Idaho Line, at a point 83 miles north of Idaho Falls, Idaho *(see Tour 2, IDAHO GUIDE).*

≪≪≪≪≪≪≪≪≪≪≪≪≪≪≪≪≪≪ ☿ ≫≫≫≫≫≫≫≫≫≫≫≫≫≫≫≫≫

Tour 7

(Cranbrook, B. C.)—Eureka—Kalispell—Missoula—Hamilton—(Salmon, Idaho); US 93.
Canadian Border to Idaho Line, 297 m.

Route served by bus lines; paralleled by Great Northern Ry. between Eureka and Kalispell, by Northern Pacific Ry. between Polson and Missoula, and also between Missoula and Darby, with logging and sugar beet trains in season.
Hotels and cabins in cities and larger towns; tourist camps at irregular intervals.
Oil-surfaced roadbed except between Canadian Border and Eureka and for 25 miles north of the Idaho Line. Open all seasons except south of Hamilton; winter travelers should ascertain conditions over Clark and Gibbons Pass.

Section a. CANADIAN BORDER *to* KALISPELL, 76.8 *m.*, US 93.

This section of US 93 in its general direction follows the Tobacco Plains Trail, through the country of the Salish and Kootenai Indians, an ancient pathway that became the route of fur traders and pack trains between Missoula and Vancouver, British Columbia. David Thompson, Alexander Ross, Finan McDonald, and Jacques Finlay, and other employees of the Hudson's Bay and the North West Companies, explored the region and established the trading posts that were the first white settlements in it.

After rich placer discoveries in the mountains drew prospectors who needed goods, long and heavily laden caravans of pack mules and horses toiled over this trail. Later the division of Indian lands brought settlers swarming to the fertile Kootenai and Flathead Valleys.

The highway passes through sections of the Kootenai National Forest, with tamarack and fir forming dense walls on both sides. Throughout this area, wood cutting is a major occupation. Great stacks of cordwood are piled along the highway awaiting transportation.

US 93, a continuation of an unnumbered British Columbia road, goes south from the Canadian Border, 0 *m.*, 0.1 mile south of Roosville, a Canadian customs station, and 86 miles southwest of Cranbrook, B. C. The U. S. customs and immigration station (R), a red-brick Colonial-type structure with white columns, is among low pine-covered hills. The two cottages back of it are the homes of officials.

The Whitefish Range (L), moderately timbered, is vividly green in the distance. MT. POORMAN (2,900 alt.) lifts its conical peak just south of the border. The Purcell Mountains (R) and the Cabinets (straight ahead), their summits often only vaguely discernible in a gray haze, form a dark horizon.

At 6.9 *m.* is the junction with State 37 *(see Tour 2, sec. c)*. Between this junction and Eureka US 93 and State 37 are united.

EUREKA, 8.9 *m.* (2,571 alt., 860 pop.), is slowly climbing up a hillside above its first buildings on the banks of Tobacco River. After its large sawmill burned in 1923, the town developed a Christmas market for evergreens; sixty-eight carloads of small firs were shipped to eastern markets in 1935. Huckleberries grow in abundance on the mountain sides.

US 93 follows the Tobacco River (R) through dairy and hay country. At 13.4 m. is the junction with a dirt road.

Left to GLEN LAKE *(cabins, boats)*, 3 m., a tarn in a dense forest.

Because of dense stands of larch and Douglas fir that border the highway, the slopes and summits beyond are only occasionally visible. At 20.6 m. is the junction with a dirt road.

Right on this road is FORTINE, 0.6 m. (2,955 alt., 100 pop.), one of those flag stops whose inhabitants gather on the station platform to watch the trains pass, then retire to the post office to gossip and await the distribution of letters and papers.

At 22.8 m. is the junction with a dirt road.

Right on this road to ANT FLATS RANGER STATION, 1 m., built of great rough-hewn logs.

MURPHY LAKE (L), 23.6 m., is long, narrow, and bordered with dense tamarack growth. A State game preserve surrounds it. There is an improved campground on its shore.

Between 25.4 m. and 27.4 m. the highway winds along the shore of the deep blue DICKEY LAKE (R), which has many small inlets. At 29.3 m. is the junction with a graded dirt road.

Left to FISH LAKE *(cabins and boats available)*, 3 m., which is annually re-stocked with trout.

WHITEFISH MOUNTAIN (7,445 alt.) towers (L) above lesser peaks. Immediately south of it is DIAMOND PEAK (7,285 alt.).

The highway makes an S-curve at 30.4 m. through a defile between jagged cliffs buttressed (L) by somber outcrops of rock.

SPRING CREEK CAMPGROUND (R) *(tables, outdoor stoves, good spring water)*, 35.4 m., is in a thinned grove of firs.

At 40.8 m. is the junction with a forest road.

Left on this through good hunting country to STRYKER RIDGE, 5 m. (7,000 avg. alt.), a rampart of the Whitefish Range.

The HEADQUARTERS OF THE STILLWATER STATE FOREST, 43.9 m. (R), is in six log buildings. The forest covers 90,000 acres. Within it are the headwaters of the Whitefish River, part of the Stillwater, and many small lakes.

STILLWATER LAKE (R), 44.9 m., formed by a dam on the Stillwater River, has a campground *(boats, cabins)* on its shore.

WHITEFISH, 61.3 m. (3,035 alt., 2,803 pop.), is a neat lake-shore town, with modern business buildings of brick, and dwellings of frame-and-stucco construction. Shaded streets border lawns ornamented with shrubs and trees.

The town is in the open upper Flathead Valley, with the Kootenai National Forest R., the Flathead L. It is a division point on the Great

Northern Ry., with railroad shops. Nearby sawmills give employment to many men.

WHITEFISH LAKE, 1 mile wide and 7 miles long, stretches northward with many summer homes and camps along its forested shores. Between the town and the lake is a public park and bathing beach. A regatta (July 4th) features outboard motorboat racing, aquaplaning, swimming, and diving.

At 63.3 *m.* is the junction with a dirt road *(see side tour from Tour 2, sec. c).*

KALISPELL, 76.8 *m.* (2,959 alt., 6,094 pop.) *(see Tour 2, sec. c)* is at the junction with US 2 *(see Tour 2).*

Section b. KALISPELL to MISSOULA, 123.2 m., US 93.

For more than 40 miles this section of US 93 winds along the western shore of Flathead Lake, the broad blue expanse of water now in view, now hidden beyond a higher part of the rough, wooded rim of the lake. Here and there an island, steep-sided and tree-covered, rises out of the water; the road makes innumerable loops and long curves around the large and small bays that indent the shore line. Almost all the way, the mighty Swan and Mission Mountains (L) are in view, awe inspiring in their austerity, always commanding. In contrast, the view R. is mostly of valley flats alternating with low, rounded hills.

US 93 follows Main St. in KALISPELL, 0 *m.*, around the courthouse and through a residential section to a level valley.

SOMERS (L), 9.5 *m.* (2,950 alt., 750 pop.), is a sawmill town by Flathead Lake. The buildings are of the frame type usual in mill towns; the water below is crowded with logs that have been shipped in by rail or driven down the Flathead and Stillwater Rivers and towed in by small steamers.

FLATHEAD LAKE, about 30 miles long and 10 miles wide, has an average depth of 220 feet. A product of glacial action, it is fed mostly by the icy waters of melting glaciers and snowbanks in the high mountains to the east and north. Its outlet during the glacial age was westward through the Big Draw at Elmo into Little Bitterroot River; as the ice receded, a new outlet, from Polson Bay into Flathead River, developed. Local lore has it that Paul Bunyan became interested in Polson *(see below),* and in an effort to boom that town dug the new channel that replaced the Big Draw.

Flathead Lake offers opportunities for boating, swimming, and fishing. *(Fishing best in June.)* It is stocked with salmon, trout, whitefish, and bass. Several charming islands lie near the west shore. Near Dayton, accessible only by boat, are the PAINTED ROCKS, signs and characters in vivid colors left by an unknown Indian artist or historian long before white men saw the region.

LAKESIDE, 14.9 *m.*, near the shore of the lake, exists to entertain tourists.

ANGEL POINT LOOKOUT, 19.5 *m.*, on clear days offers an unobstructed view across the lake to the Mission Range (L). The road sweeps down a hill and comes close to GOOSE BAY, 21 *m.* In a log house among the trees lived Frank B. Linderman, poet, novelist, and friend of the Indian *(see THE ARTS)*.

DAYTON, 30.5 *m.* (2,884 alt.), is the embarkation point for a 4,500-acre dude ranch on WILD HORSE ISLAND, 7 miles from shore.

Right from Dayton, on a dirt road to LAKE MARY RONAN *(cabins, boats)*, 7 *m.* It is stocked with silver salmon and Dolly Varden trout.

Between Dayton and Evaro, a distance of 70 miles, the route runs through the Flathead Indian Reservation.

BIG ARM, 40.2 *m.* (2,941 alt., 50 pop.), is a small Indian village on the lake shore. Indians here wear native dress and live somewhat as they did before the coming of the white man.

The road proceeds over a broad, rugged headland. There are several deceptively sharp curves.

POLSON, 53.1 *m.* (2,949 alt., 1,456 pop.), seat of Lake County, is in a natural amphitheater at the foot of the lake. The town, the trade center of one of the most fertile farming areas in Montana, has modern stores, and homes with delightful gardens. Within a block of the business district is a dock and breakwater. A 63-acre park on the lake shore affords facilities for golfing, playing tennis, and for boating and swimming. The Cherry Regatta on Polson Bay celebrates the cherry harvest *(1st week in August).* A 9-hole GOLF COURSE *(greens fee 50¢)* is L.

An increasing number of visitors outfit here for mountain trips *(saddle horses, $2.50 up; guides, $5 a day).*

Right from Polson on a dirt road to the GORGE OF THE FLATHEAD RIVER, 5 *m.* During May and June, flood season, water pours through this gorge at the rate of 500,000 gallons a second. The walls are perpendicular, and rise 200 to 500 feet above the white water.

Here is the $11,000,000 FLATHEAD DAM AND POWER PLANT, built on a site owned by the Confederated Tribes of the Flathead. This plant will be able to generate between 200,000 and 250,000 horsepower.

South of Polson the whole Mission Range is in view. The loftiest of these snow-capped peaks are at the southern end, with a very gradual diminution northward toward the mouth of Swan River, which cuts through the range. Among the higher peaks are glaciers, cataracts, and rocky precipices. The region was the ancient summer hunting ground of the Salish, and is rich in their lore.

At 54.8 *m.* is the junction with State 35 *(see side tour from Tour 2, sec. c).*

PABLO, 61.3 *m.* (3,100 alt., 150 pop.), a trading center for ranchers, was named for Michael Pablo, an Indian stockman, who reared a herd of bison in Flathead Valley. PABLO RESERVOIR (R) is a refuge for migratory waterfowl.

Between Pablo and St. Ignatius the route traverses the irrigated lands of the Flathead Indians. Between Pablo and Ronan, SHEEPSHEAD MOUNTAIN (L), named for its form, is in view.

RONAN, 66.8 *m.* (3,064 alt., 1,600 est. pop.), was named for Maj.

Peter Ronan, first Indian agent to the Flathead, who wrote a history of the valley tribes. It is a busy town with a flour mill; the population tripled between 1930 and 1937, partly because of a great influx of farmers into the lower Flathead Valley from the drought areas of North Dakota and eastern Montana. The area around Ronan, formerly part of the Flathead Reservation, was thrown open to white settlement in 1910, and 10,000 people soon established themselves on ranches and small irrigated farms. Many Indians and numerous horse-drawn vehicles are seen on the streets.

Above (L) is McDONALD GLACIER, on the north side of MOUNT McDONALD (9,800 alt.), the loftiest peak in the Mission Range. MOUNT HARDING, north of Mount McDonald, is only a little lower.

At 74.9 *m.* is the junction with a dirt road.

Left on this road to McDONALD LAKE (not to be confused with Lake McDonald in Glacier Park), 7 *m.*, fed by glacial waters from the Mission Range. *(Boats, campgrounds, good fishing.)*

ST. IGNATIUS, 81.2 *m.* (2,900 alt., 303 pop.), is a subagency almost at the center of the Flathead Reservation. The village is dominated by Indians. Like the ROMAN CATHOLIC MISSION, established here in 1854 by Fathers De Smet, Hoecken, and Menetrey, the town was named in honor of St. Ignatius of Loyola, the Spanish priest who founded the Society of Jesus.

The MISSION SCHOOL, CHURCH, and HOSPITAL are the results of nearly a century of patient, conscientious work among the natives. Early paintings used in teaching the Indians are on view.

Left from St. Ignatius on a dirt road to ST. MARY'S LAKE (not to be confused with the St. Mary Lakes in Glacier Park), 11 *m.*, which offers excellent trout fishing. The Salish called it "the waters of the forgiven"; their tradition is that a brave once expiated a murder on its shore. Another Salish legend tells that beautiful spirits inhabited the deep waters and lured careless warriors to destruction.

South of St. Ignatius US 93 makes a narrow winding turn (R) at the bottom of St. Ignatius Hill. Mostly R. is the FLATHEAD (formerly the Jocko) INDIAN RESERVATION, of 1,403,058 acres, created in 1855. The agency is 1 mile north of Dixon *(see Tour 12)*. The Indian population in 1936 numbered 3,400, with 3,051 enrolled in the Confederated Tribes of the Flathead (Salish, Kalispel, and Kootenai). Though enrollments are increasing, full-blood Indians (750 in 1936) decrease in numbers. The tribes have so intermarried that an accurate estimate of the number in each one is impossible. More than three-fourths have white blood. Many have French and Scottish names inherited from trappers and traders of the old North West Company, who married squaws *(see HISTORY)*. Allotted to individual Indians are 227,113 acres of reservation land; 255,000 acres are held by the tribal council as a grazing reserve for Indian herds. Much land is occupied by whites. Irrigation was begun in 1907.

Lewis and Clark, the first white men to visit the Salish (September 1805), called them the Ootlashoots. They were few in number (about 700), but loyal, honest, and respected by the Blackfeet for their fighting prowess. They believed in a Good Spirit, a Bad Spirit, and a summer

A FLATHEAD WOMAN

country where the good Indian, when he died, met his wife and children and found game plentiful. The bad Indian passed to a land of perpetual ice where, shivering, he saw fire, and, thirsty, he saw water—beyond his reach. Beavers, the Salish believed, were fallen Indians, condemned to their lowly state by the Great Spirit.

In early days Flathead Valley was inhabited by the Pend d'Oreille (Fr., *ear pendant*), or Kalispel; the Salish lived in the Bitterroot country. When the great council signed the reservation treaty in 1855, at Grass Valley, near Missoula, it was agreed that the Salish should remain in the Bitterroot Valley until the Government needed the land. Chief Victor probably did not fully understand what this meant. Two years after his death in 1870, his son Charlot refused to move to the Jocko Reservation. Thereupon, Alee (or Arlee), who was willing to move, was named chief of the Flathead. Charlot never recognized Alee as chief and it was not until 1891, after years of destitution, that he gave up his ancient home and led a band of about 200 remaining Salish to the reservation.

After the Indian Reorganization Act of 1934, the Confederated Tribes adopted a constitution under which a council is popularly elected; but hereditary chiefs head the tribal organization and are recognized by the U. S. Indian Service. Noted chiefs include Three Eagles, who ruled in the days of Lewis and Clark's visit; Bear Looking Up, who was chief when Father De Smet arrived; and Big Face, the first Salish Indian baptized a Roman Catholic.

Beadwork and the making of buckskin clothing are the principal traditional Flathead handicrafts. A few brass ornaments and pipes of stone and carved wood are made. Considerable beadwork in animal designs is used on horse trappings.

These Indians no longer use primitive methods of cookery but still preserve meat and roots by drying. The bitterroot is sun-dried on canvas until hard; camas, when not sun-dried, is pit-roasted. Strips of meat from the back of elk are dipped in grease and smoked.

Some of the Flathead depend on fishing and hunting for one-fourth of their food supply. In the fall many engage in a special hunt for meat and hides. The skins are soaked in water for 10 days, then treated with a mixture of brains and liver to waterproof them and rot the hair. After stretching and scraping, they are worked over carefully until soft enough to be used for moccasins and the like.

The annual bitterroot feast is held at Camas Prairie in the spring before the bitterroot blooms; the camas feast is in June. All full-bloods participate. Prayers are offered for good crops, and dried camas and bitterroot are eaten. Other ancient ceremonies still observed are the blue-jay dance (January), and war dances (*visitors admitted*) in July. These are also attended by the full-bloods. From 75 to 100 tepees are pitched in a circle around the war dance tent, which is a double lean-to of poles and hides.

To MOUNT E-TAM-A-NA, at the head of Crow Creek in the Mission Mountains, young braves used to come to fast and pray. If a petitioner dreamed about some animal or bird, it became his shumash (guide) through life, aiding him in battle and healing him in illness.

The NATIONAL BISON RANGE, 85 *m.*, is R. *(see Tour 12)*.

At 86.8 *m.* is the junction with State 3 *(see Tour 12)*.

RAVALLI, 87 *m.* (2,760 alt., 15 pop.), was named for Father Anthony Ravalli *(see HISTORY)*.

ARLEE, 96.9 *m.* (3,094 alt., 450 pop.), was named for Alee (Ind., *red night*), the Salish chief *(see above)*. The name is Arlee only in white usage, for the Salish language has no "r." Arlee is a small trading center for the Jocko Valley. Usually there are Indians on its streets; in summer they occasionally have powwows on the river flat at the edge of town.

Left from Arlee on a dirt road through the Mission Range to the CLEARWATER LAKES, 30 *m.* *(see Tour 8)*.

EVARO, 107.8 *m.* (3,972 alt., 25 pop.), a small cluster of houses at the top of a hill, is at the southern limits of the Flathead Reservation. The southern peaks (L) of the Mission Range are seen here rising 7,000 feet above the valley.

The highway descends through the narrow CORIACAN DEFILE, the gateway between the Flathead and Missoula Valleys. It is reputedly named for Koriaka, a Hawaiian, who was killed there during an attack by Black-feet upon a party of trappers and traders.

At 114.6 *m.* is the junction (R) with US 10 *(see Tour 1)*. Between this point and Missoula US 10 and US 93 are one route *(see Tour 1,. sec. d)*.

MISSOULA, 123.2 *m.* (3,233 alt., 14,657 pop.) *(see MISSOULA)*.

Points of Interest: Montana State University, Missoula County Courthouse, Catholic Group, Free Library, Bonner House, Greenough Park, Waterworks Hill, and others.

Missoula is at the junction with US 10 *(see Tour 1)*.

Section c. MISSOULA *to* IDAHO LINE, 97 *m.,* US 93.

US 93 traverses the entire length of the Bitterroot Valley, following in reverse order the route of Lewis and Clark from the Big Hole Basin to the Lolo Trail. Sheltered on the east and southeast by the rounded Sapphire Mountains and the southwestward loop of the Continental Divide, and on the west by the high, irregularly toothed Bitterroot Range, this valley is widely known as Montana's best—in some years, almost its only —fruit-growing area. Here, where the first crop in the State was planted in 1842 *(see HISTORY)*, rich fields, gardens, orchards, pastures, and meadows stretch from mountain range to mountain range.

South of MISSOULA, 0 *m.,* US 93 crosses Clark Fork of the Columbia, locally called the Missoula; then swings slightly R. and L. passing the WESTERN MONTANA FAIRGROUND and the MUNICIPAL AIRPORT (L), 1.9 *m.*

MOUNT LOLO (9,075 alt.), bearing permanent snow fields, is straight ahead; Squaw Peak *(see Tour 1)* is R.

At 2 *m.* is the junction with an improved road.

Right on this road to FORT MISSOULA, 0.5 *m.,* founded in 1877 when it was believed that efforts to remove the Salish from the Bitterroot Valley to the Jocko Reservation might cause an uprising. The only garrisoned post in Montana, it is manned by two battalions of the Fourth Infantry. The frame buildings at the western end of the reservation are headquarters of the CCC in Montana and northern Idaho.

The military reservation was formerly much larger, but squatters crowded in and were permitted to stay. Abandoned in 1898 the post was re-established in 1901; 5 years later the city of Missoula bought land and increased the reservation to about 3,000 acres. Fort Missoula became a regimental post, and permanent fireproof buildings were completed by 1910. It was abandoned again from 1912 to 1921, except as the site of a mechanics' school during the World War.

The officers' club, of logs, and the powder house, of stone, are all that remain of the early structures. They contrast oddly with the newer barracks and the tiled roof line of officers' residences.

The Missoula Valley was once the bottom of a lake that left the marks of successive water levels on Mounts Sentinel and Jumbo (L). In some places the soil is productive; in others the smooth water-washed stones lie near the surface, and the thin topsoil does not retain moisture long.

The road crosses the Bitterroot River, 4.2 *m.* The Bitterroot Valley was

ST. MARY'S MISSION, STEVENSVILLE

known to the Salish as Spetlemen *(place of the root),* for here, in June, they dug the brown bitterroot *(see FLORA)* and dried it for food.

LOLO (Ind., *muddy water*), 11.1 *m.* (3,198 alt., 102 pop.), is made up of a store, a beer hall, a service station, and a few houses and tourist cabins.

Right from Lolo on State 9, a graveled road through the LOLO NATIONAL FOREST, to the SITE OF FORT FIZZLE (R), 6 *m.* When Chief Joseph, on his retreat toward Canada in 1877 *(see HISTORY),* crossed the pass from Idaho, he found a barricade erected here to head him off. Joseph slipped past the barricade and continued down the Lolo Trail and up the Bitterroot Valley with all his tribe and a large herd of horses. The barricade became known as Fort Fizzle.

LOLO HOT SPRINGS (3,786 alt.) is at 30 *m.* *(hotel, cabins, campground; warm-water plunge, adm. 50¢).* The water is not mineralized.

The road ascends through heavy timber with only occasional far views to LOLO PASS, 37 *m.* (5,187 alt.), closely following the route of Lewis and Clark in 1805 *(see HISTORY).* At the pass State 9 crosses the Idaho Line, 10 miles north of Powell Ranger Station, Idaho *(see Tour 8, IDAHO GUIDE).*

FLORENCE, 20.1 *m.* (3,273 alt., 95 pop.), is a one-street trading center with a creamery and a cheese factory.

Left from Florence on a graveled road to a junction with a side road, 4 *m.;* L. here 6 *m.* to RED ROCK MINE *(open to visitors),* a gold property developed by shaft and crosscut.

The three pointed summits sharply outlined against the southern horizon (R) are the Como Peaks.

At 28.5 *m.* is the junction with a graveled road.

Left on this road to the SITE OF FORT OWEN, 0.5 *m.* (R), a trading post established in 1850 by Maj. John Owen. Nothing remains of the buildings but part of
one wall made of crude bricks. In the spring of 1841 Father De Smet and six companions *(see HISTORY)* had erected a small chapel here of whipsawed lumber held
together with wooden pins. They had built a sawmill and a gristmill, making the
saw from the iron band of a wagon wheel. The mill stones, shipped from Antwerp,
Belguim, had been brought ashore at Fort Vancouver on the Columbia and carried
overland. Oxen and wagons, carts and plows had also been brought to the mission
and in 1842 the Mission garden had produced some wheat and vegetables.

Major Owen differed from many of the early citizens of Montana in that he came
with definite intent to settle. He began by buying the buildings from the Catholic
authorities at St. Mary's Mission, and added others of his own. Refusing to be diverted by gold rushes and booms, he stayed at his fort and developed it into the
most important travel and trade center in the valley. A genial host, he made the post
popular with white and red visitors alike.

STEVENSVILLE, 1 *m.* (3,500 alt., 691 pop.), is a trade center for farmers in
this valley, which today produces grain, hay, sugar beets, seed and canning peas,
potatoes, apples, cherries, and strawberries. A cannery and a cooperative creamery
provide markets for local products. The creamery picnic held annually in August
is an event of much importance to the valley people.

ST. MARY'S MISSION (1867), near the southern edge of town, is a small log
church of conventional design. In the rear of the church is a small MUSEUM *(open)*
containing mementos of the early days of St. Mary's.

VICTOR, 35.8 *m.* (3,414 alt., 350 pop.), was named for Chief Victor
of the Flathead.

HAMILTON, 48 *m.* (3,600 alt., 1,839 pop.), seat of Ravalli County
and chief center of Bitterroot Valley business, in its modern business
buildings and attractive dwellings reflects the prosperity of the surrounding country. It owes much of its development to Marcus Daly, who established his Bitterroot Stock Farm east of town, and caused many fine
homes and stores to be built. He gave two lots to each of the town's religious congregations as sites for churches.

The U. S. PUBLIC HEALTH SERVICE LABORATORY *(open 2:30-4:30 by
appointment; guides),* 900 block on S. 4th St., is maintained for research
in the control of Rocky Mountain spotted fever *(see FAUNA).* It manufactures and distributes without charge phenolized virus prepared from
the tissues of infected ticks, which is used as a vaccine that lessens the
severity of this disease. Its use in the mountains and Pacific States has lowered the death rate from 85 to 26 percent or less. The laboratory produces
enough virus annually for 50 or 60 thousand vaccinations, which is less
than the demand.

1. Left from Hamilton on Adirondack St. to a comfortable FREE TOURIST PARK,
just out of town on a green meadow shaded by trees. It faces a tiny lake and has a
rustic lodge, and camp sites with outdoor stoves. Once part of the Marcus Daly
estate, it was used as a training ground for the Daly race horses.

2. Left from Hamilton on an improved road to the MARCUS DALY ESTATE
(private), 2 *m.,* a 22,000-acre ranch with a Colonial-type mansion at the end of a
shaded avenue. Deer graze on the front meadows.

At 50.9 *m.* is the junction with State 38.

Left on this partly improved dirt road, called the Skalkaho Trail, to BLACK BEAR
CAMP, 12.8 *m.* (R), a large Forest Service campground. Adjacent is the summer
camp, with log lodge, of Hamilton's Boy Scouts.

State 38 winds through a thick forest of lodgepole pine, to SKALKAHO (Ind., *many trails*) FALLS (L), 20.7 *m.*, a slender stream descending in long, graceful plunges from a heavily timbered mountain side, so near the road that light breezes blow spray across it. Large rocks border the falls on one side, on the other the mountain is steep and dark green. A smaller waterfall is beyond the first, hidden in the forest. The green and white water of the large falls passes under a bridge and descends again.

SKALKAHO PASS, 25.4 *m.* (7,258 alt.), is in the Sapphire Range, which forms the boundary between the Bitterroot and Deer Lodge National Forests.

Between Skalkaho Pass and Rock Creek lies a region that despite its network of trails, seems untouched wilderness. Color is everywhere. Distant timbered ridges are deep blue and purple beyond the dark green of nearer slopes. Light green aspen, cottonwood, and willow border the streams. Red-brown and blue-gray rocks and slaty to auburn logs are partly covered by the green, red, and yellow of flowering and berry-bearing undergrowth. Brown and yellow pine needles carpet the entire area.

ROCK CREEK, 36.7 *m.*, is an excellent trout stream. Sapphires are found along its course, often in old placer diggings.

At 52.3 *m.* is the junction with US 10 A *(see Tour 18)*.

At 62.8 *m.* is the junction with a dirt road.

Left on this road to SLEEPING CHILD HOT SPRINGS, 10 *m.*, in a wooded canyon below austere granite peaks. The name was "Weeping Child" in the Indian tongue. *(Hotel, cabins, campground; warm plunge, adm. 50¢.)*

DARBY, 64.9 *m.* (3,881 alt., 285 pop.), is the terminus of the railroad. Except for the handsome Forest Service dwellings among the trees (L), it consists chiefly of log houses and frame buildings with high false fronts. Prospectors dressed for the hills walk the streets, bargain for outfits in the stores, or "toss a poke" on a bar to pay in gold dust for a round of drinks.

DEND POND (R) is a rearing pool for trout.

Forested slopes at 70 *m.* form a foreground for the bare spire (R) of TRAPPER'S PEAK (10,175 alt.).

INDIAN MEDICINE TREE, 76.4 *m.* (L), is a large yellow pine. Above it, on the mountain side, the rock has profiles resembling human beings; one is fairly large and quite distinct. For many years it was the custom of the Salish to gather each summer at Medicine Tree for ceremonial dances. Offerings to the Great Spirit were hung upon the tree and the Indians prayed beneath it for special benefits and blessings.

According to legend, the Great Spirit once said to Coyote: "Go forth and discover all things that prey on human beings. You will always have a friend, the Fox, who will not be far behind you. You may be killed, but he will have power to bring you back to life."

Coyote was wise and cunning. He went forth as he was bidden. While traveling he one day stepped on a lark and broke its leg. He healed the injury, and the lark warned him of a wicked mountain ram that killed all who passed along the trail. When Coyote came to the ram's lair, he taunted him and urged him to show his strength. The ram accepted the challenge and buried his horn in the trunk of a pine tree. Before he could withdraw it, Coyote drew a great flint knife and cut off his head. He left the horn in the tree and threw the ram's head and body against the mountain side. Blood splashed upon the rocks and left the imprints resembling faces that now look toward the tree.

Old-timers in the Bitterroot Valley tell of seeing a horn imbedded in the tree. It was broken off in the course of time and bark grew over the hole it had made.

At 81.1 *m.* is the junction with a dirt road.

Right on this road to MEDICINE HOT SPRINGS, 1 *m.* *(cabins, hotel; warm plunge,* *adm. 50¢).* The Indians, who credited the waters with therapeutic qualities, called the spring "the dwelling place of the Great Spirit."

SULA, 84.2 *m.* (6,692 alt., 25 pop.), an attractive service station, built of logs, is at the bottom of the ascent to Gibbons Pass.

At 96.9 *m.* is the junction with State 36.

Left on this road to BIG HOLE BATTLEFIELD NATIONAL MONUMENT, 19 *m.* Here on August 9, 1877, troops under Gen. John Gibbon met Chief Joseph's band of Nez Percé *(see HISTORY).* The Nez Percé did not flee, as was the Indian custom under surprise attack, but bundled their women, children, and horses to safety, and put up a stiff fight. Joseph fired the Army's defense line; had the wind not changed, this maneuver would have routed the whites. In the evening Chief Joseph learned from a scout that General Howard was approaching, and withdrew toward the Yellowstone country *(see Tour 13 A).*
Bullet-riddled trees and rifle pits mark the site. A concrete shaft erected by the Government bears a bronze plate upon which are inscribed the names of those of Gibbon's command who fell in the battle.

GIBBONS PASS, 97 *m.* (6,982 alt.), on the Continental Divide, was named for Gen. John Gibbon.

Here US 93 crosses the Idaho Line, 50.2 miles north of Salmon, Idaho *(see Tour 5, Idaho Guide).*

◄◄◄◄◄◄◄◄◄◄◄◄◄◄◄◄◄◄◄◄◄❖►►►►►►►►►►►►►►►►►►►►►

Tour 8

Helena—Wilborn—Lincoln—Ovando—Bonner—Junction with US 10; unnumbered road, State 20, and State 31.
Helena to Junction US 10, 129.9 m.

Route paralleled between Ovando and Bonner by Blackfoot branch of C. M. ST. P. & P. R. R.
Hotels in Lincoln, Ovando, and Bonner; accommodations elsewhere limited.
Dirt roadbed between Helena and Clearwater, difficult except in good weather; graveled between Clearwater and Bonner. Open only in summer.

This combination of routes strikes across the lower end of one of the largest primitive areas in the United States—a vast expanse of forested mountains and valleys larger than some eastern States.
The unnumbered route between Helena and Lincoln passes along the shaded, yellow-brown foothills below the Continental Divide, and pene-

trates a region where mining, once impressively successful, is still pursued, but on a much smaller scale. The road winds over rocky ridges, through deep canyons, and past abandoned camps and workings. It crosses the Continental Divide through Stemple Pass, from which glittering peaks extend into blue distance. The descent into the Blackfoot Valley is through an extremely rugged, heavily timbered, and almost untraveled back country. Except for the absence of hostile Indians, travel on part of this route is as much an adventure as it was in the mid 19th century.

HELENA, 0 m. (4,124 alt., 11,803 pop.) (see HELENA).

Points of Interest: State Capitol, St. Helena Cathedral, Lewis and Clark County Courthouse, Public Library, Carroll College, Algeria Shrine Temple, Hill Park, placer diggings, and others.

North from US 10 N, 0 m. (see Tour 1A), on Benton Ave. in HELENA, crossing the tracks of the Great Northern and Northern Pacific Rys. to the unnumbered dirt road.

The NORTHERN PACIFIC DEMONSTRATION FARM (L), 1.9 m., for the breeding of registered cattle, has buildings that are Old English in style; stone walls enclose the yards.

From the sagebrush flats below Last Chance Gulch, the Big Belt Mountains (R) are seen. The umber tints of the rolling foothills, which are dotted with farms, change to deep blues and purples in the distance.

At 14.2 m. is the junction with a dirt road.

1. Right on this road to SILVER CITY, 0.5 m. (4,335 alt., 27 pop.), a station on the Great Northern Ry.

2. Left on this road along Silver Creek to MARYSVILLE, 6.5 m. (5,035 alt., 150 pop.), which in the 1880's and 1890's was the State's leading gold producer, with about 3,000 inhabitants. The remnants squat against high barren hills burrowed in innumerable places by prospectors. In the long years of decline, which began in the early part of the 20th century, the frame buildings decayed and sagged; the false fronts now lean at drunken angles. Broken boardwalks along the main street pass closed shops and saloons in which dust is deep on the window sills and bars and counters have been dulled by disuse. Goats graze over tumbled grass-grown mounds where cabins once stood. A rickety old backstop leans over a baseball field on which the miners played.

West and south of the camp is the DRUMLUMMON MINE. Thomas Cruse prospected along Silver Creek, which rises near Marysville, for nine years before 1876 when he struck the Drumlummon ledge. He named his strike for his native town in Ireland, and the town for Mrs. Mary Ralston, the first woman who came to the settlement. The Drumlummon was so rich in gold and silver that in 1882 English capitalists purchased it from Cruse for $1,500,000 cash and $1,000,000 in the stock of the corporation they formed to develop it. The corporation gave out no figures on production, but authorities have estimated that between 1885 and 1895 the output was worth $20,000,000. When the cyanide process for recovering gold and silver was perfected, a million tons of Drumlummon tailings were treated, and yielded an average of $8 a ton. Authorities estimate total production from the Drumlummon at $50,000,000.

Cruse went on to develop the Bald Mountain and West Belmont mines; these are said to have yielded metal worth $3,000,000. Others developed the Bell Boy, the Piegan, the Gloster, the Penobscot, the Empire, and the Shannon, which are said to have produced between $20,000,000 and $30,000,000 worth of gold. The English company eventually lost title to the Drumlummon on apex litigation (see HISTORY) started by owners of adjoining claims. New owners operated the mine until 1920; since then it has been worked by lessees.

Some geologists believe that rich ore bodies still exist in the old mines; and old-timers are sure that there will some day be another Drumlummon, Bald Butte, Bell Boy, or Shannon that will bring surging life again to Marysville.

CANYON CREEK, 19.8 *m.* (4,380 alt., 37 pop.), a tiny outpost for ranches of the Prickly Pear Valley, has a general store, post office, and filling station, all in one building.

The road swings sharply R. at 20.3 *m.* through the Little Prickly Pear Valley. No forests cover the brown, monotonous hills.

At 22.1 *m.* is the junction with a dirt road.

Left on this road to GRAVELLY RANGE LAKE, 3 *m.*, a small mountain pond surrounded by dense woods. Here and in nearby streams is good fishing.

The road swings out of Prickly Pear Valley at 23.8 *m.* and into the narrow canyon of CANYON CREEK. The yellow-brown foothills billow up against a distant blue and purple background.

WILBORN, 27.2 *m.* (5,125 alt., 40 pop.), is a supply point and post office for miners of the surrounding area. It is a mistake to speak of many such rough mountain settlements as towns; but Wilborn does have a school and a sawmill. Activity here is sporadic, depending on whether or not the mines are in operation.

Right from Wilborn on a dirt road to CAMP MASON, 0.3 *m.*, a cabin camp used by tourists, hunters, and fishermen. The dirt road proceeds by switchbacks through heavy timber to FLESHER PASS, 7.8 *m.* (6,200 alt.), an alternate crossing of the Continental Divide *(see below)*. Above the pass mountains rise in a series of old scarps; in the interstices of rocky outcrops, scrub timber lifts twisted greenery on the rims of somber cliffs.
The road follows Willow Creek to its junction with the Blackfoot River, and crosses the Blackfoot Valley to LINCOLN, 27.4 *m.* *(see below)*.

West of Wilborn the mountains are pockmarked with mine tunnels and shafts; some of the mines are being worked, others have been abandoned. Most of the active mines are in side gulches. There are deserted shacks and caved-in prospect holes near every creek. Typical of once wealthy workings that remain closed for long periods and are then reopened is the old GOULD MINE (L), 29 *m.*

The road follows Virginia Creek in its winding course through a canyon and at 31.5 *m.* crosses the eastern boundary of Helena National Forest.

The JAY GOULD MINE (L), 32.9 *m.*, and the NORTH GOULD MINE (R), 33.1 *m.*, are consistent producers equipped with modern mills that turn out gold bullion on the premises. The BACHELOR MINE (L), 35.9 *m.*, was formerly a large producer. Abandoned log cabins adjacent to it are all that remain of STEMPLE, a mining town.

STEMPLE PASS, 35.4 *m.* (6,600 alt.), leads over the Continental Divide. On the summit the rotting timbers of an abandoned mine shaft (R) evidence an ambitious effort to find gold on the roof of the continent.

West of Stemple Pass the road winds down a lane, shaded by lodgepole pine, that follows the course of Poorman Creek. Several of the pitches are steep, and the turns sharp. Forests are heavy on the western slope.

At 38 *m.* is the junction with Poorman Road.

Right on this road to GRANITE BUTTE LOOKOUT, 6 *m.*, one of the comparatively few Forest Service lookouts that can be visited by automobile. The ordinary lookout, such as this one, is a frame cabin about 15 feet square, anchored firmly to a peak and elaborately grounded against lightning. Large windows on all sides command the area the guard must constantly watch. In the single small room are his stove, bunk, emergency tools, and grub. Supplies are packed in at the beginning of the fire season, usually about the first of July. It is Forest Service policy to place two men at a lookout when possible; often a man and his wife occupy a cabin. Thus the peak is not deserted when one of the two leaves to snuff out a nearby smoke. If the guard is alone his solitude is nearly complete; he may see the packer and the ranger only once or twice in the 75 to 90 days he spends on guard. He soon grows bored with no other activity than chopping wood and carrying water, and exhausts his imagination in devising new things to cook. After he has memorized every contour in the area under surveillance, and the name of every lake, ridge, stream, and crag, he begins to talk to the ground squirrels. After he has read to shreds every magazine in his pack, he calls up his nearest neighbor for a chin-wagging. Three times a day he calls the ranger station to make his weather report. At night he may watch a lightning storm go around him, and count the flashes to himself. He busies himself with has alidade and mapboard, and tries vainly to guess where smokes will break. The smokes appear at last in half a dozen or more places; the wires hum with excited reports. Then the danger season sets in; smoke sometimes banks around until the guard cannot see more than the area close around his cabin. At night terrifying red flares glow behind distant ridges; a sheet of flame sweeps a nearby hillside, trailing a storm of sparks. By day planes go over the lookout, bearing men and tools. There is tension, weariness, and fierce drama. At the season's end perhaps a fog comes, cool and sweet after the stinging smoke; then rain or light snow begins, and finally the order is received for him to hit the downstream trail.

On more important peaks, the cabin has two stories—living quarters downstairs and workroom with mapboard, telescope, telephone, and possibly a short-wave set upstairs. Besides the lookout and his wife there may be one or several smoke chasers who go on foot to a fire as soon as the lookout detects it. Their job is to stop it while it is small, or hold it until crews can answer the lookout's call for help.

In every cabin are packages of emergency rations stamped with the slogans of the Forest Service: "Get 'em while they're small!"; "Don't leave 'em till they're out!"; and the like.

The guards, or lookouts, are usually young men, often students of forestry out to gain experience during their vacations. The smoke-chasers, or patrolmen, may be wire-bearded veterans who have tramped the forests all their lives.

RAMBLE INN CAMPGROUND (R), 43.8 *m.*, is in a grove of magnificent pine trees, where only the sound of running water breaks the stillness.

The road crosses the western boundary of the Helena National Forest at 45.4 *m.*, the BLACKFOOT RIVER at 50.5 *m.;* it follows the stream from this point to its confluence with the Clark Fork of the Columbia near Milltown *(see Tour 1, Sec. d)*. On his return from the Pacific in 1806, Captain Lewis worked his way up along the Blackfoot River to reach the Continental Divide.

LINCOLN, 49.6 *m.* (4,800 alt., 25 pop.), in a forest of Montana's largest pines, is buried under heavy snows in winter. In summer it is a place to which citizens of Helena come for rest and quiet. The stores and post office are in a clearing among the yellow pines, with summer homes in the woods around them. It was once important as a placer mining camp but only small operations are now carried on in the vicinity. Lincoln is a popular point of departure for fall hunting parties and summer fishermen.

At Lincoln is the junction with the Flesher Pass Road *(see above)* and with State 20. Left here on State 20.

At 51.5 *m.* is the junction with a dirt road.

Right on this road to LAKE SMITH *(good fishing)*, 1 *m.*, on whose shores are cabins.

An unimproved campground is L. at 63.8 *m.*

At 65.9 *m.* is the junction (L) with State 31, which is united with State 20 between this point and Clearwater.

Left on State 31 to the junction with a dirt road, 5 *m.;* L. here 1 *m.* to HELM-VILLE (4,255 alt., 202 pop.), a lonely village that is a gathering place for scattered farmers and ranchers in a large valley. Its annual Labor Day rodeo is widely known.

At 23 *m.* on State 31 is DRUMMOND *(see Tour 1, Sec. d)*, on US 10 *(see Tour 1)*.

BROWNS LAKE (R), 71.3 *m.*, is much frequented by duck hunters in season. The road makes a half circle through barren country along the south shore of the lake; the eastern sky line here is formed by irregular purple summits.

OVANDO, 82.2 *m.* (3,980 alt., 75 pop.), another backwoods place, was named for Ovando Hoyt, its first postmaster. It exists as a supply point for hay and sheep ranches and for the small logging camps in the heavy black forests that extend endlessly in all directions. Pack trains outfit here for trips into the South Fork of the Flathead Primitive Area *(see RECREATION and Tour 2, Sec. c)*.

At 87.2 *m.* is the junction with a dirt road.

Right on this road to WOODWORTH, 11 *m.* (3,750 alt.), headquarters of logging operations for the Bonner mill *(see below)*. A large crew of men is employed the year around cutting pine, fir, and tamarack. At the skidways about 30 flatcars a day are loaded with logs for the mill at Bonner. Caterpillar tractors have largely replaced horses and mules in logging; instead of the traditional "skinners" driving six- and eight-horse teams, the Woodworth operators have "cat skinners" and "gear jammers" to wrangle the big logs.

The camp has large, neat bunkhouses, a central mess hall, a commissary, a recreation hall, shower baths, a school for the loggers' children, and a branch of the Missoula County Library.

Many of the timber beasts (loggers) are of Scandinavian stock. Some students of folklore say that the Scandinavians created the legendary Paul Bunyan by bringing to America their tales of Thor, the Norse god of indomitable strength. They are prodigious chewers of *snus* (Dan. and Sw., snuff), and tellers of tales; and they are proud of their prowess in a difficult and hazardous occupation. They wear the traditional lumbermen's stag (or tin) pants, heavy woolen shirts, and logger boots. The pants, of tan, gray, or blue plaid, are pure wool, very thick and so closely woven as to be almost waterproof. They are "stagged," or cut off raggedly, so that the bottoms come just above the tops of eight-inch boots, a precaution against being snagged by low brush or broken limbs. The soles of the boots are heavily studded with sharp calks to guarantee sure footing, for a logger must move nimbly.

CLEARWATER, 97.3 *m.* (3,773 alt.), is a stock-loading point on the Blackfoot branch of the C. M. St. P. & P. R. R.

Right from Clearwater on State 31, a dirt road, to SALMON LAKE (L), 5.6 *m.*, the most southerly of the Clearwater Lakes chain, all of which have natural or improved campgrounds along their shores. They are connected by Clearwater River, a tributary of the Blackfoot. Summer cottages, many owned by Missoula people, dot the shore of Salmon Lake. The conspicuous house on the west side was the summer home of the son of W. A. Clark *(see HISTORY)*.

At the southern boundary of Lolo National Forest, 14.5 *m.*, is the junction with a dirt road; L. here 3 *m.* to PLACID LAKE, a popular place for fishing, swimming,

LUMBERJACKS

and boating. The Placid Lake road continues over the mountains to ARLEE, 25 *m.* (3,094 alt.) *(see Tour 7, Sec. b)*, which is on US 93 *(see Tour 7)*.

SEELEY LAKE (L), 14.6 *m.* on State 31, is the center of a recreational area second only to the Flathead Lake country in this part of Montana. The small, clear lake was named for J. B. Seeley, the first white man to make his home on its shore.

SEELEY LAKE POST OFFICE, 16.1 *m.,* serves the dwellers in the cabins and summer homes around the lake, and several dude ranches in the vicinity.

The SEELEY LAKE RANGER STATION (R), 17.5 *m.,* provides information concerning the trails and fishing and hunting opportunities of the Lolo National Forest.

At LAKE INEZ (L), 23.3 *m.,* the third of the Clearwater Lakes, the campground is on the heavily wooded west shore.

LAKE ALVA (L), 24.5 *m.,* and RAINY LAKE (L), 26.8 *m.,* are the smallest of the Clearwater Lakes. Rainy Lake is reached only by footpaths.

At 33.9 *m.* is the junction with a dirt road; L. here 4.7 *m.* to LINDBERGH LAKE, formerly Elbow Lake, whose name was changed in 1927 after Charles A. Lindbergh visited for a week in its neighborhood. Heavily timbered on three sides, it lies close against the base of the impressive, snow-crested Mission Mountains. On the eastern shore is a public campground and a rustic lodge kept (1939) by "Cap" Eli Laird, former captain of a packet on Coeur d'Alene Lake. His story telling is one of the attractions.

GORDON'S RANCH, 34.6 *m.,* is one of the largest dude ranches in the Clearwater Valley. Pack trains are outfitted here for trips into the Mission Mountains and into the South Fork of the Flathead Primitive Area.

At 34.8 *m.* is a junction with a dirt road; R. here 1.8 *m.* to HOLLAND LAKE. At 2.8 *m.* is HOLLAND LAKE LODGE, a cabin on the north shore of the lake. Except

HOLLAND LAKE

in a few places, dense stands of tamarack come down to the water's edge. At the northern end several waterfalls show against the dark forest mass. Sheer rock rises from the water on the east.

North of Holland Lake, State 31 runs through the heavy Flathead National Forest of the Swan Valley, a wild land with fish and game, rude trails, and lookout stations. The road is poor with an average of 20 curves to the mile. There are only occasional glimpses of the majestic Mission Mountains (L) and Swan Range (R). The forest silence is broken only by the calls of wild things, the splash and gurgle of tumbling streams, and the sound, like surf on a far shore, of wind flowing smoothly through the tops of tamaracks and firs. Nevertheless occasional cabins beside the road indicate that a few hardy human beings attempt to live here.

The emergency landing field at 43.1 *m.* is for planes bringing in fire fighters.

At 52.3 *m.* the road intersects an old Indian trail that crossed the mountains between the Flathead Valley and the Great Plains. Part of it is now a modern forest trail.

SWAN LAKE POST OFFICE, 106.4 *m.*, is at the upper end of SWAN LAKE, a long, narrow body of water whose clear surface reflects the rich emerald of the forest. On its shore, at 107.7 *m.*, are campgrounds, wharves, and a beach.

The road crosses the northern boundary of Flathead National Forest and continues along Swan Lake.

SWAN RIVER GORGE (R) is seen at 123.1 *m.*

BIGFORK, 123.3 *m.* (2,989 alt., 250 pop.) *(see side tour from Tour 2, Sec. c)*, is at the junction with State 35 *(see Tour 2).*

State 20 crosses the Blackfoot River, 100.1 *m.*, at its confluence with the Clearwater (R).

GREENOUGH, 105.2 *m.*, is a post office named for T. L. Greenough, an early settler who had extensive holdings in the valley.

POTOMAC, 113.5 *m.* (3,870 alt., 22 pop.), was named in 1883 by a settler who had formerly lived by the Potomac River. Ranchers, lumberjacks, miners, and prospectors make weekly trips to its general store and post office to get their mail and buy supplies. From 1925 to 1932 old-time dances held in the old log hall drew many people.

The highway crosses the Blackfoot River at McNamara's Landing, 122.2 *m.*, a loading point for sheep and cattle. From this place logs were formerly floated down river to Bonner.

BONNER, 129.4 *m.* (3,321 alt., 707 pop.), is a collection of neat company houses that vary only slightly in construction, but are painted according to individual taste; in them live the families of men who work in Montana's largest sawmill (R). The town lies mostly south of the mill buildings; the lumber yards, filled with great piles of newly sawed lumber, extend eastward. Around the mill the air is charged with the fresh, keen smell of the cut logs; near the sawdust dump it is sometimes dank and musty. Sawdust is fed to the great black burner beside the mill to provide heat for many buildings of the town.

The Margaret Hotel (R), on a fenced square near the center of town, was a show place when it was built in 1892. All the ornate detail of its period survives. Its entrance, in which gingerbread mingles with the dignified restraint seen in old southern hotels, faces the mill. Missoula clubs and social groups sometimes have their banquets in the building.

The Bonner Sawmill *(open; visitors' entrance at southeastern end),* on the bank of the Blackfoot River, was built in 1886, destroyed by fire in 1919, and rebuilt in 1920. It employs 400 men, but in off years there are several months during which the men work only part of each week.

The mill is a black frame shed, 300 feet long and 150 feet wide. Catwalks afford a safe view of the screeching, bellowing room; danger signs warn against going near the whirring machines. The logs, sawed into convenient lengths before they leave the woods, are hooked out of the pond in the rear of the plant by an endless belt, set with ugly sharp prongs, that carries them to the three saw carriages; band saws on pulleys rip through them. Sawdust is carried off to the engine room where it feeds the big furnaces that generate steam to operate the machines. Endless chains carry the boards to the planing department where they are smoothed or made into shingles and laths; or to other departments for special treatment. On the top floor of the shed is the filing room, where band saws are filed mechanically. All over the mill the men work fast; they wear clothing without loose ends. The noise seems almost unbearable to newcomers. Between 1898 and 1938 the mill turned out 3,990,-000,000 board feet of lumber. In an average eight-hour shift the saws cut 420,000 board feet of lumber and the planes finish 200,000 feet. The annual shipment of mine timbers, wedges, and other lumber to the Butte mines alone is 40,000,000 board feet.

At 129.9 *m.* is the junction with US 10 *(see Tour 1, Sec. c),* 7.3 miles east of Missoula.

Tour 9

(Charbonneau, N. D.)—Fairview—Glendive—Circle—Jordan—Grass Range; State 14, State 18.
North Dakota Line to Grass Range, 287.4 m.

Route served by Intermountain Transportation Co. busses between Glendive and Grass Range; paralleled by Northern Pacific Ry. between Sidney and Brockway, and by Chicago, Milwaukee, St. Paul & Pacific R. R. between Winnett and Grass Range. Hotels in towns; few tourist camps along route.
Roadbed oil-surfaced between Fairview and Circle; unimproved dirt between Circle and point 13.4 miles east of Jordan; improved between this point and the junction with US 87. Unimproved section poor in rainy weather.

State 14 follows the Yellowstone River through a rust-colored semi-badland, irrigated in part. Along the highway, traces of the old Fort Union Trail (L) are discernible. Here, in the late 1870's and early 1880's, stagecoaches, mail carriers, and freighters traveled between Fort Keogh and Fort Union. A few old rest camps, stables, and bunkhouses still stand beside the road. State 18 reaches across rolling, thinly settled plains, which, when carpeted with buffalo grass, were the pastures of millions of bison and, later, of cattle and sheep. Much of the grass cover has been removed by the plow or destroyed by overgrazing; monotonous stretches of eroded or weed-grown fields lie between the thinned pastures and patches of sage and cactus.

Montana 14 is a continuation of N. D. 23, which reaches the Montana Line 14 miles west of Charbonneau, N. D.

FAIRVIEW, 0 m. (1,902 alt., 576 pop.), on the State Line, with the Yellowstone River flowing by just east of it, has one street in North Dakota. The town was named for its panorama of fertile acres in the Yellowstone Valley. More arid lands, which in several areas take on the character of badlands, lie on the benches above the river bottoms. A lignite mine on the edge of town, employing about 20 men in winter, furnishes fuel for local consumption at moderate cost.

SIDNEY, 11 m. (1,928 alt., 2,010 pop.), seat of Richland County, is the trade town of farmers dependent on land producing under irrigation. Considerable wheat is grown under ditch (irrigation) in the vicinity, but 40,000 of the 60,000 irrigated acres are used to grow beets. Most of the work of thinning and topping sugar beets, formerly done by migratory Mexican and Filipino workers, has been taken over since 1930 by Montana and North Dakota farm families who have lost the battle with drought.

The RICHLAND COUNTY COURTHOUSE (R), one block from Main St., is the town's dominant building. In the sheriff's office is a collection of old firearms and of archeological finds of the county.

The SUGAR REFINERY *(open to visitors)*, near the northeastern city limits, is in operation in late fall and early winter. It produces 13 million pounds of sugar yearly.

Just north of Sidney, on a small flat behind Lovering Grove, are several low MOUNDS in zigzag formation. Each, 100 yards long, is larger at one end. Neither their purpose nor the date of their construction is known, but they appear much older than the ruins of Fort Union, the first white settlement in the region.

Right from Sidney on Main St., which becomes a dirt road, to a junction with another dirt road, 5 *m.;* L. here to THREE BUTTES, 10 *m.,* high sandstone domes that lie in an east-west line along the edge of the Missouri River badlands. West of the last butte is a large pit. The colors and formations are extravagantly varied. Numerous rattlesnakes make stout boots a necessity for visitors. *(See GENERAL INFORMATION.)* BLUE HILL, 6 miles south, is a flat-topped butte formerly used by Indians as a lookout.

Southwest of Sidney are miles of weirdly eroded buttes. Below the river breaks (R) lignite coal workings, large or small, are occasionally seen. Some, little more than holes in the hillsides, have been made by industrious farmers, who have dug their winter's supply of fuel out of veins 4 feet or less in thickness. Such mines do not justify the expense or trouble of installing equipment, and they are usually worked with the simplest tools. An auger and a tamping bar are used to place charges of blasting powder; in some places a single small home-made rail-car or wheelbarrow rolls out the coal. The miner must accustom himself to working in a cramped and, at first, uncomfortable position. He must also learn to recognize certain danger signs, for cave-ins are not unknown.

The larger mines are sometimes of the strip type. Several farmers bring horses or tractors, plows, and fresno scrapers, and remove the overburden. This may take days or weeks. They then blast the exposed coal into pieces small enough to be loaded on wagons and trucks, and haul it to some sheltered storage place, such as a cellar; coal of this type disintegrates rapidly when exposed to sunlight and air.

The river flats are natural hay meadows; many tons of speargrass (western needlegrass) have been cut in good years. Under irrigation the same land produces two or three crops of alfalfa a year. In 1936 Mormon crickets descended on forage crops here and forced livestock outfits to ship cattle elsewhere for winter feeding, or to import feed from western Montana. A discovery that sheep liked the insects for food was reported; large areas that showed signs of becoming breeding places were ranged over with good results.

At 17 *m.* is the junction with a dirt road.

Left on this road, across railroad tracks, to the O'BRIEN RANCH, 0.2 *m.* The older buildings *(open on application)* were a stage station on the Fort Union Trail. The oldest cabin, built in 1878 as a trading post by "French Joe" Seymour, is intact; the road ran directly in front of it. Opposite is a roomy log house, built by Jim O'Brien in 1882. It looks much as it did when dusty stage horses stopped at its door and sorely shaken travelers climbed out and gratefully sat down to a hearty meal of meat and beans. The dining room with raftered ceiling and blue-washed walls extends across the front. The whitewashed "bridal chamber" opens from the dining room; here the infrequent lady travelers were lodged for the night. Narrow stairs lead from the dining room to a large bunk room. The big kitchen, in which still sits the mammoth cast-iron army stove brought from Fort Buford upon the abandonment of the post in 1890, forms a T. The log store (L) was built a few years later than the house.

Badlands are (L) across the Yellowstone at 27.8 m.

SAVAGE, 31.6 m. (1,977 alt., 353 pop.), is a shipping point used by back-country grain farmers and river-bottom beet growers. The rock formations (R) resemble petrified trees.

The highway enters the breaks of the Yellowstone. Brilliantly tinted sandstone formations at this point give the valley a wild and rugged beauty.

INTAKE, 46.4 m. (2,031 alt., 45 pop.), came into existence when the irrigation dam (L) was built across the Yellowstone.

STIPEK, 55.4 m. (2,063 alt., 30 pop.), is a shipping and distribution point that comes alive briefly on Saturday, when ranchers and their families come in to shop and gossip.

At 63.5 m. is the junction with State 18 and US 10 (see Tour 1), just across the Yellowstone from GLENDIVE (see Tour 1, Sec. a). Between this point and a junction at 64.2 m., US 10 and State 18 are one route.

At 64.2 m. R. on State 18 across rolling range.

LINDSAY, 86.2 m. (2,203 alt., 50 pop.), a farmers' village, is only a dot on the prairie.

The highway descends from a hilltop at 95.8 m. to a deep dry cut; on both sides the buttes are much eroded.

Redwater Creek, 111.1 m., is a tributary of the Yellowstone. Abundant red shale lines its banks.

The highway turns sharply L. into CIRCLE, 112.2 m. (2,450 alt., 519 pop.), seat of McCone County. This is one of the towns that retain some of the flavor of the old cattle country; the cowpunchers on its streets are not ornaments hired to impress romantic visitors. "Circle" was the brand name of one of Montana's first cow outfits.

Right from Circle on a dirt road to the CIRCLE HOME RANCH, 1 m., with which nearly every old time range rider in Montana was familiar at one time or another. Punchers packed off to warmer climes in late fall nearly always returned to Circle in the spring; a man who could ride a horse and do his share of corral work was always sure of a job here. Many outfits used the nearby range for summer grazing, for water was always plentiful in creeks and prairie lakes, and the grass was unsurpassed for the fast finishing of steers.

BROCKWAY, 123.8 m. (2,593 alt., 130 pop.), the railhead for a vast inland stock and grain country, is identified by its white two-story frame boarding school. Long distances and inadequate roads make day schools impracticable in this area.

PARIS (R), 143.5 m., is an abandoned ranch that formerly held a post office. Around it the sunburnt range is dotted with red buttes and scarred with ravines.

Some of the infrequent ranch buildings along the road are of stone, a material far cheaper than lumber in this area. A few sod houses are still in use. Because drought has driven many families away, there are almost as many abandoned houses as inhabited ones.

WINDBREAK

The highway crosses LITTLE DRY CREEK at 161.7 *m*. Extensive fossil beds (R) have yielded skeletons and fragments of skeletons of pre-historic animals *(see NATURAL SETTING)*. The beds are reached only afoot or with horses.

VAN NORMAN (R), 162.6 *m.*, is a ranch post office in a sheep-grazing country. Dry Creek affords water holes, and gnarled cottonwoods give scanty shade on a sagebrush plain interrupted by buttes. Here and there the wagons and small "tarp" tents of herders dot the long reaches. In spring and fall large herds of sheep, cattle, and, sometimes, horses are trailed to Brockway.

At 180.6 *m.* is the junction with State 22 *(see Tour 10)*, which unites with State 18 between this point and a junction at 186.6 *m. (see Tour 10, Sec. b)*.

Before the country west of Jordan became a cattle-ranching and dry-land farming region, it was a range where Blackfeet, Gros Ventre, Assiniboine, and Crow hunted buffalo, especially in late summer. The Musselshell was known as the Dried Meat River because in its vicinity preparations for winter were made—meat was cured, and chokecherries were picked, dried, ground, and mixed with meat to make pemmican *(see BEFORE THE WHITE MAN)*.

Weather conditions in this region change rapidly. Rain frequently falls over very limited areas, and it is not unusual for one ranch to be well watered while another a few miles away is dry. Yarn spinners tell of a rancher who once attempted to outrun a storm with his team of fast horses. He heard the rain behind him but did not get wet; believing he had escaped, he turned to look back, and found, to his amazement, that the rear half of the wagon box was full of water.

SMOKY BUTTE *(see Tour 10)* rises above the prairie (R). Southwestward the countryside is gently rolling, carpeted here and there with grey-green sagebrush and low cactus. The plain is green under spring skies and dotted in the early hours with wild white morning-glories. With advancing summer the grass turns brown, and sage and cactus blur with dust.

An ABANDONED SHACK (R), 202.1 *m.*, made of sun-baked bricks, its interior smoothly plastered with mud, is representative of the houses often built by early settlers. They cost little to construct and were serviceable, warm in winter and cool in summer.

EDWARDS, 211 *m.* (2,206 alt.), is the site of one of the ranches of the old 79 outfit *(see Tour 11)*.

SAND SPRINGS, 219.2 *m.* (2,025 alt., 27 pop.), is a range-land post office.

Between 233.3 *m.* and 234.6 *m.* the road winds among rugged hills heavily covered with scrub pine, fir, and juniper on their western slopes. These hills are the divide between the Musselshell and Big Dry drainage areas.

MOSBY, 240.6 *m.* (2,280 alt., 6 pop.), is a post office and store on the east bank of the Musselshell.

Right from Mosby on a dirt road to the SITE OF FORT MUSSELSHELL, 35 *m.*, at the mouth of the Musselshell River. In the 1860's and 1870's this was an important post in the trade with the Gros Ventre. The traders, a few wolfers, and the woodchoppers who sold fuel to Missouri River steamboats, were the only white men in this part of the country. When the Indians were at peace, trade was profitable; the Gros Ventre gladly exchanged a buffalo robe for 10 cups of flour or 6 cups of sugar. The Assiniboine and Sioux, however, harassed the post incessantly, and at length forced its abandonment.

The highway crosses the Musselshell River. Somewhere in the breaks along this stream is a gold mine from which Indians brought dust and nuggets to Fort Musselshell. All but one of the Indian discoverers were killed in a skirmish with whites; the survivor said only that the mine was "two sleeps" from the post. Prospectors have repeatedly, but in vain, explored the country.

A tourist camp is on the riverbank at 241.3 *m.*

At 247.3 *m.* is the junction with a dirt road.

Right on this road to CAT CREEK OIL FIELD, 4 *m.*, whose 174 wells produce oil of high quality (50° A. P. I.). In 1936 each of 150 wells was pumping about 1,000 barrels a day. The field is a "stripper"—has wells that must be pumped—there are no gushers. Large pumping plants take out the crude oil, which is piped to Winnett, 20 miles away, for shipment.

When news of the Cat Creek discovery was flashed over the West, a mad stampede, resembling an old-time gold rush, occurred. Oil prospectors, however, reached their destination more swiftly and with less hardship than the pilgrims who came with pick and pan 50 years earlier. Every type of car was pressed into service; expensive limousines stirred the dust of old cattle trails beside wheezing models that wabbled along on warped wheels. One of the richest operators in Montana arrived in a flivver so dilapidated the cushion seat was gone; he had hurriedly left a less promising field and traveled to Glasgow by train, where he had had difficulty in obtaining a car. When a discouraged dry-land farmer happened to drive by, the oilman hailed him and inquired if he could spare his car for a few days. "Yep, I can spare her forever," said the farmer. "The old girl and me is about to part after some mighty tough experiences." The oilman peeled two ten-spots from a roll, and in another minute was on his way to Cat Creek in a cloud of exhaust smoke.

At 269.2 *m.* is the junction with a dirt road.

Left on this road is WINNETT, 0.7 *m.* (2,960 alt., 408 pop.), terminus of a C. M. St. P. & P. R.R. branch from Lewistown. A large refinery, and three storage tanks holding 100,000 gallons each, announce its chief reason for existence. Winnett is smudged with oil; the fumes of the product permeate the atmosphere. Some of the stores sell oil rigs, drills, and similar equipment.

Winnett is also the distributing center of a large area where wheat is grown. This country has suffered much from droughts but many farmers who stayed through the drought of 1917–1920 witnessed the miracle of seeing their parched lands yield "black gold" in fabulous amounts.

The Judith Mountains are straight ahead at 270.4 *m.*

YEGEN, 276.1 *m.* (2,087 alt.), is a railroad station named for the Yegen brothers, Swiss immigrants who began life in Montana as sheepherders, later operated a store here, and finally became prominent sheepmen and bankers of central Montana.

At 287.4 *m.* is the junction with US 87 *(see Tour 3),* 0.9 mile north of the center of Grass Range *(see Tour 3, Sec. a).*

<<<<<<<<<<<<<<<<<<<✿>>>>>>>>>>>>>>>>>>>>

Tour 10

(Moose Jaw, Sask.)—Opheim—Glasgow—Jordan—Miles City—Broadus —(Belle Fourche, S. D.) ; State 22.
Canadian Border to Wyoming Line, 385.1 m.

Frequent bus service between Glasgow, Wheeler, and Fort Peck.
Hotels and tourist camps in larger towns; few accommodations between them.
With exception of 15-mile oil-surfaced stretch between Glasgow and Wheeler, roadbed is unsurfaced or wholly unimproved between Canadian Border and Jordan; between Jordan and Broadus it is oil-surfaced; between Broadus and the Wyoming Line, graveled. Unsurfaced section dusty or muddy by turns.

Section a. CANADIAN BORDER *to* GLASGOW, *68 m.,* State 22.

State 22 crosses a section that is perhaps nearer to the frontier than any other part of Montana, for the people who began to farm it did not arrive until the early years of the World War; and it had no modern means of transportation until 1926. Cattlemen had long frequented the country because the wide grasslands dotted with small lakes were ideal for the rapid fattening of steers. For several years before the 1930's, with their depression and drought, this region produced almost fabulous crops. Farmers, striving to conquer the rich land, worked feverishly from dawn to dusk during the brief seasons of seeding and harvest. Sometimes they became wealthy from the profits of a single bumper year. But they used their profits to acquire more expensive equipment and larger areas for cultivation. Then suddenly they were paupers, and the land was dusty and barren under a sky dark with clouds but not with rain. It was one of the swiftest and most tragic economic transitions in the history of the State.

Many of the settlers stayed, counting on future seasons when rain would surely fall and grainfields again stretch deep green or pale gold to the horizon. Many others pulled stakes, to search bewilderedly for some new bonanza in a region where nature is less capricious. The once comfortable houses they abandoned stand gauntly on the dun prairie with glassless windows. Range cattle and horses have broken down the doors of some of them to find shade in summer and shelter from storms in winter.

State 22, a continuation of Sask. 2, crosses the Canadian Border, 0 *m.*, 1 mile west of West Poplar River, Sask., a Canadian customs station, and 115 miles southwest of Moose Jaw.

OPHEIM, 10.8 *m.* (3,263 alt., 510 pop.), a U. S. port of entry, is in one of the most fertile parts of the wheat-growing region that extends eastward through Daniels and Sheridan Counties and northward into Saskatchewan. The wheat marketed here, even in unfavorable seasons, almost invariably commands a high price because of its high protein content. Opheim had no railroad until 1926, when the Great Northern extended its Bainville-Scobey branch to the town. This was one of the last pieces of railroad building in Montana.

In the days of homesteading, Opheim was a hive of industry. Stores, banks, lumberyards, hotels, and bars did a very profitable business. Day and night the streets were crowded and noisy. In the surrounding country, the wild grasses grew stirrup-high, and prairie fires were annual events; but in a few short years most of the sod was turned under, the grass destroyed. With the profits from their first crops the farmers built large houses and barns; then modern schoolhouses were erected on land from which the hoofprints of buffalo had scarcely been effaced. When drought struck, some farmers sold out while the people at large still believed in their luck, and the land brought fair prices. Those who remained saw the countryside become almost an open range once more; but instead of the old, rich native grasses this range bore thick mats of the ugly, prolific Russian thistle.

These tough, gray-green weeds spring up profusely wherever the soil has been tilled, and in dry seasons absorb most of the scanty moisture stored up from the winter's snowfall. When mature, the plants break off and roll over the prairie, to lodge in great masses against fences, around buildings, and in windbreaks.

Many farmers have learned to use the thistles as emergency fodder, cutting and stacking them while they are heavy and green. The weeds cure in the stack, and if well salted, they have a taste that does not seem objectionable to most livestock. If unmixed and fed in large quantities, however, this fodder is dangerous, inducing a violent and exhausting colic, particularly in horses. The feed is never a satisfactory substitute for hay, but serves to keep stock alive during the long, lean winters when the range is buried under a heavy crust of snow and even the hardy bronc stands shivering with tail to the wind.

BAYLOR, 27 *m.* (3,251 alt., 15 pop.), a crossroads store and post office, was once a busy trading center for wheat farmers.

State 22 runs southward over great stretches of rolling benchland, and crosses deep coulees.

At 66 *m.* is the junction (L) with US 2 *(see Tour 2)*, with which State 22 runs into Glasgow.

GLASGOW, 68 *m.* (2,095 alt., 2,216 pop.) *(see Tour 2, Sec. a)*, is at the western junction with US 2 *(see Tour 2)*.

Section b. GLASGOW *to* MILES CITY, *175.4 m.,* State 22.

This section of State 22 traverses a rolling plain that, in part, is not quite so parched as the region north of the Milk River. Evening thundershowers are relatively frequent. Much of this country between the State's two largest streams remains cattle country.

In GLASGOW, 0 *m.,* State 22 follows Main St. which becomes an oil-surfaced road that crosses the Milk River, 3.2 *m.* There is continuous heavy traffic on this stretch, which was built to serve transportation needs during construction at Fort Peck Dam *(see Tour 10A)*.

WHEELER, 15.1 *m.* (2,125 alt., 4,000 est. pop.), a modern frontier town, is made up of shacks hurriedly built of tar paper, packing cases, shiplap, and canvas. Along the main street of the camp, neon signs announce the products of a more urbane world.

At Wheeler is the junction with an unnumbered oiled road *(see Tour 10A)*.

Between Wheeler and Jordan, a 75-mile stretch, there are few habitations or supply points. The dun color of the vast plains is varied only by intermittent growths of sage.

LISMAS FERRY, 20.4 *m.,* is the crossing of the Missouri River *($1 a car; service at any time; if ferry is on opposite side, blow horn to bring it across)*.

The highway traverses salt sage flats, then a region of hills and gullies, the Missouri River Badlands. Here the vegetation is more varied. Willows fringe many zigzag stream courses between the sparsely timbered hills.

HAXBY, 29.2 *m.* (2,018 alt., 5 pop.), a general store and post office, serves scattered ranches.

South of the hamlet the country is wild and rugged. Great boulders of amazing shapes and sizes are bright-colored under sunlight, shadowy and weird by twilight. The formations are largely brick-red scoria. There are large areas of gumbo and silty volcanic ash which, when wet, become very sticky. The barren Missouri breaks are a maze of eroded peaks, ridges, basins, and coulees. Wild animals are numerous. Coyotes and bobcats endanger the lives of calves and sheep, which range on the ridges dotted with scrub pine, spruce, and cedar. An occasional mountain lion stalks the deer along the river bottoms.

DAVIDSON, 58.4 *m.* (2,610 alt.), is a post office and general store.

PINEY BUTTES (3,000 to 3,500 alt.) parallel (R) the route between Davidson and Jordan. They are part of a broad land peninsula that juts into the Fort Peck Reservoir area, which includes the Missouri bottoms (R) and the flats along Big Dry Creek (L). "Big Dry" is from an Indian name that meant the creek was dry a "big" part of the time, and had no reference to its size as a stream.

All land along the Missouri, between Fort Peck and the mouth of the Musselshell, was condemned and bought by the Government after plans for the building of the dam and the creation of the reservoir were approved.

At 84.1 *m.* is a junction (L) with State 18 *(see Tour 9)*. Between this point and 90.1 *m.,* State 22 and State 18 are one route.

JORDAN, 89.7 *m.* (2,800 alt., 500 pop.), seat of Garfield County, is one of the State's real cow towns. In the winter of 1930 a New York radio station called it "the lonesomest town in the world," and certainly a New Yorker would find its isolation extreme. Until State 22 was carried through to Miles City and telephone service was established in 1935, its contacts with the world were few and sometimes broken for long periods. For several years the editor of the weekly Jordan *Tribune* had to depend on the world news he could pick up with his own short-wave radio. The material thus obtained appeared in a special column headed "A Hundred Miles from Miles." Miles City, 86 miles away, is the nearest railroad town.

In 1901, when it was founded by Arthur Jordan, the town was even more remote. For years long hair and beards were fashionable among the citizens simply because the settlement had no barber. The roads were merely paired ruts in the gumbo soil almost impassable in rainy weather. A story is often told of a Jordan farmer who started to market with a four-horse load of grain. Long delayed by rain and mud he arrived at Miles City with only two bushels of oats, and had to buy more at the elevator to feed his animals on the return trip.

In spring and fall this is a busy town. Sheep ranchers outfit their herders here for the summer's ranging and farmers come in long distances to buy six months' supply of food and clothing. The town now has a golf course, a swimming pool, movies on three nights a week, a commercial club, a hospital, and a high school.

At 90.1 *m.* is the junction (R) with State 18 *(see Tour 9)*.

South of this point is a grazing ground long used by antelopes. Their presence was a source of joy to the early cowboys, who, despite the law, did not hesitate occasionally to vary their monotonous diet of sowbelly and flapjacks with luscious roasts of antelope meat. Since game-law enforcement has become stricter, the animals are rarely killed. They are timid by nature and seldom let an automobile come near them, though they are sometimes seen grazing on distant hills.

SHEEP WAGON

SMOKY BUTTE (R), 91 *m.*, rises majestically from the open plain. A thick blue haze usually seems to hang about its gaunt basalt bulk.

COHAGEN, 114.5 *m.* (2,930 alt., 200 pop.), is a school and a general store surrounded by scattered homes. In 1919 it won brief local importance as Jordan's rival in a race for the county government.

Southeast of Cohagen the rolling prairie is carpeted with buffalo grass. Owls are seen meditating on fence posts along the road.

ROCK SPRINGS, 139.5 *m.* (2,870 alt., 6 pop.), by Rock Springs Creek, is a prairie post office, general store, and gas station.

Left from Rock Springs on an unimproved dirt road to a junction with another road, 10 *m.;* R. to CROW ROCK, 18 *m.*, a peculiarly shaped mound that has engaged the attention of geologists interested in oil. At its top are natural ramparts, behind which human bones have been uncovered. Legend tells of a band of 100 Crow who came here from their tribal lands south of the Yellowstone to hunt buffalo, and were attacked by a hunting party of Sioux, who forced them to retreat to the rock. Fighting without water, they were reduced to drinking the blood of their slain companions before the Sioux at length overpowered them, and scalped them to the last man.

ANGELA, 146.2 *m.* (2,490 alt., 5 pop.), is a crossroads post office, store, and gas station in gently rolling country harshly carpeted with cactus and low sagebrush.

State 22 crosses the Yellowstone River into MILES CITY, 175.4 *m.* (2,357 alt., 7,175 pop.) *(see Tour 1, Sec. a),* which is at the junction with US 10 *(see Tour 1).*

Section c. MILES CITY *to* WYOMING LINE, *141.7 m.,* State 22.

This section of State 22 passes through a land of grass and cattle, cowhands and Indians, a range from which the best Montana beef is shipped to eastern markets. Nutritious grasses, with an ample supply of water, make the entire district ideal for livestock raising. Farms—and hence fences—are few; it is the sort of region that cowboys dream about. Little grain is grown, and that little is used for winter feed. Only along the creeks, where irrigation is possible, has there been any continued effort to grow crops year after year.

Pioneers of this region tell of their concern when dry-land farming first began in Montana. They heard about other ranges that were being fenced in, and expected that their own would suffer the same fate. Some cowboys watched the newcomers "busting the sod" with their gang plows, and distastefully concluded that the only thing left for them was quitting the old life of the bunkhouse and the roundup to become farmers themselves. A popular bit of doggerel current here is: "I've hung up the saddle and turned out ol' Buck; I'm feelin' right solemn and blue. I'm a bowlegged puncher whose shore outa luck, and I reckon my punchin' is through. It don't matter which way I heads in the morn, I'm shore to fetch up at a fence; and I'm tired o' hearin' 'em talk about corn, and wheat that's gone up seven cents. Oh, I shore am atastin' of life's bitter dregs, and I'm gettin' right des'prate you'll see, for a country that's dealin' in butter and eggs, gets the goat of a hombre like me. So my mind is made up and my purpose is grim, and I blush at the thought of my shame, for it shore seems a pity that Montana Slim has to play such a card in the game. But my program is set and I can't back out now though I squirm in my grief and my sorrow, for I just bought a rake and a second-hand plow, and I starts in at farmin' tomorrow."

State 22 follows Main St. in MILES CITY, 0 *m.,* to Haynes Ave.; R. on Haynes Ave.; then southeast along the valleys of Tongue River and Pumpkin Creek. The red buttes in this country of coulees and canyons are composed of earthy hematite and scoria, a cindered lava much used in road construction.

BEEBE, 30.2 *m.* (2,349 alt., 7 pop.), is a ranch post office in a sparsely settled region.

VOLBORG, 46.8 *m.* (2,307 alt., 5 pop.), is a country store and post office.

COALWOOD, 56.5 *m.* (2,270 alt., 8 pop.), is on the flank of the large canyon of Home Creek, surrounded by towering red buttes. It is a combination store and post office; a gasoline pump has replaced the old feed store and smithy. The region around it was once a Cheyenne hunting ground. Tepee rings, arrowheads, and stone knives have been found on the sites of camps along the creek; an Indian skeleton, in almost perfect condition, was dug from a grave. Near it were weapons and shreds of a robe. The body had been buried in a sitting position.

South of Coalwood State 22 winds upward around pointed buttes and over ridges topped with scrub cedar, jack pine, and spruce, and at 70.7 *m.* crosses Mizpah Creek, a tributary of Powder River. The number of small ranches increases as the road runs southward; here and there are the sod-roofed log houses of farmers who wrest a scanty living from the rocky soil.

BROADUS, 80.2 *m.* (3,030 alt., 240 pop.), seat of Powder River County, is another of the "biggest little towns in the west"; its high school is the only one in a county of 3,275 square miles inhabited by 3,909 people. There is no railroad in the county, but good highways compensate for the lack.

Broadus is the trading center of a large part of southeastern Montana.

Right from Broadus on State 8, a partly improved dirt road, to CAMPS PASS, 22 *m.* (3,100 alt., 51 pop.), a settlement on a plateau between the Tongue and Powder Rivers.

State 8 enters the CUSTER NATIONAL FOREST through a canyon 50 feet wide and 500 feet high. HOME CREEK BUTTE, 30 *m.*, is a sandstone wedge with a sheer cliff overhanging the valley.

ASHLAND, 48 *m.* (3,200 alt., 82 pop.), on Tongue River, is the division head-quarters of the Custer National Forest, and the trade center for a group of cattle ranches that provide entertainment and recreation for vacationers.

LAME DEER, 69 *m.* (3,700 alt., 89 pop.) *(see side tour from Tour 1, Sec. a)*, is at the junction with State 45 *(see Tour 1)*. Between Lame Deer and a junction at 73 *m.* State 8 and State 45 are one route.

After the extermination of the buffalo (about 1885), the grasses of this region and its sheltered position in winter attracted cattlemen. An attempt of sheepmen to gain control of the section was defeated on January 3, 1901, when 11 masked men raided a sheep camp and killed 2,000 sheep in a single night.

CROW AGENCY, 123 *m.* (3,041 alt., 202 pop.) *(see Tour 3, Sec. b)*, is at the junction with US 87 *(see Tour 3)*.

At 80.9 *m.* State 22 crosses Powder River. Some historians believe the Verendryes *(see HISTORY)* reached this river in 1743, while seeking a route to the Pacific. In 1805 François Larocque journeyed almost the entire length of the stream as an agent of the North West Company. Trappers operated here briefly; Indians were the only inhabitants until stock growers came in 1880.

BOYES, 103.1 *m.*, is a general store and post office.

At 108.8 *m.* is the junction with an unnumbered dirt road *(see side tour from Tour 17)*.

HAMMOND, 109.7 *m.*, is a cluster of sod-roofed log cabins and a general store.

The highway at 138.1 *m.* crosses the Little Missouri River, a tributary of the Missouri.

ALZADA, 138.6 *m.* (3,622 alt., 50 pop.), is the most southeasterly settlement in Montana. Here saddle horses tied to hitching posts outnumber parked cars. Men in ten-gallon hats, faded shirts, and denim trousers, whose occupation is just plain cowpunching without any frills, loiter in front of the store.

Alzada was originally called Stonesville, for Lou Stone, who kept a saloon here in 1877–78, at the time Gen. Nelson A. Miles was building the telegraph line from Fort Keogh (Miles City) to Fort Mead, S. D. The Stonesville telegraph station was a rock-covered dugout at the top of a hill. The presence of older Stonesvilles in Montana led to confusion, so the town was renamed for Mrs. Alzada Sheldon, wife of a pioneer rancher.

At 141.7 *m.* is the Wyoming Line, 39 miles northwest of Belle Fourche, S. D. The route cuts diagonally for 24 miles across Wyoming, a stretch without a single town, and into South Dakota *(see Tours 3 and 13 in SOUTH DAKOTA GUIDE).*

<<<<<<<<<<<<<<<<<<<<<☼>>>>>>>>>>>>>>>>>>>>>

Tour 10A

Wheeler—Fort Peck; Fort Peck Rd. 4.2 m.

Frequent bus service.
Hotel and information bureau at Fort Peck.
Oil-surfaced roadbed; heavily congested.

This unnumbered oiled road branches east from State 22 *(see Tour 10)* at WHEELER, 0 *m.*

FORT PECK, 4.2 *m.* (2,100 alt., 6,000 est. pop., 1938), a planned city, seems strangely misplaced on the vast bare prairie. Built by the Government as a permanent town near Fort Peck Dam, today (1939) it has rows of barracks to house construction workers and a boulevard of stores and shops. South and west of the town is a maze of roads. The dam-building activities fill the valley.

At the main entrance to the city is an INFORMATION BUREAU, supplying maps and answering questions. East of the river, at an observation point overlooking the gigantic spillway and part of the dam site, is a small pavilion with maps and a large model of the completed spillway.

The construction of FORT PECK DAM, a PWA project, is under the supervision of U. S. Army Engineers. This great earth-fill barrier across the Missouri River is one of the largest structures of its kind in the world. Its maximum height is 242 feet, and its main length 9,000. A lower section on the west bank is 11,500 feet long. The dam stretches across the Missouri from bluff to bluff a distance of 3.68 miles. A highway 100 feet wide crosses its top. One hundred million cubic yards of earth, 4 million cubic yards of gravel, and 1,600,000 cubic yards of large rocks have been used in construction. At the beginning of 1938 it had cost $81,160,555, and it was believed that almost $11,000,000 more would be required for its completion by the end of 1939.

It takes several normal years for the Missouri River to bring here such a quantity of water (20 million acre-feet) as will be required to fill the space behind the giant wall. The length of the lake thus to be created is estimated at 175 miles, its shore line at 1,600 miles, its maximum depth at 240 feet.

On October 23, 1933, a small crew began clearing brush and cutting trees. By July 1934 more than 7,000 men were at work, and the town of Fort Peck was being built to house administrative personnel, engineers, concessionaires, and the many laborers. In addition to residences and barracks, schools, a hospital, a recreation hall, a laboratory, a town hall, a theater, and various shops have been constructed.

The huge filtration plant (L) was erected to provide the little city with pure water; three electric pumps force river water into the plant. A 288-mile power line from Great Falls, capable of carrying 154,000 volts, has been built to furnish electricity for construction purposes. At a boatyard 1 mile below the dam, pontoons, barges, and four great dredges have been constructed. The dredges have been biting deep into the bottom of the river for material to be pumped through pipe lines resting partly on pontoons to the earth fill.

The 2-mile wall of steel plating across the dam center was driven to a maximum depth of 163 feet to prevent excessive seepage below the dam. Each of four diversion tunnels, cut through the shale beds east of the river, has an inside diameter of 26 feet; their combined length is 25,294 feet. Each tunnel has a vertical shaft equipped with machinery to regulate the flow of water.

A large spillway from the reservoir provides an outlet for water that the diversion tunnels can not handle. It is 745 feet long and has 16 concrete and steel gates capable of discharging 250,000 cubic feet of water a second.

Great trestles span the site, carrying the railroad cars with material for the upstream and downstream gravel toes. The earth from the dredges is pumped in between these toes. The trestle on the downstream toe is part of a permanent road crossing to the east bank, where the tunnels are.

Construction of the dam will increase the navigability of the Missouri River, and aid development of irrigation, electric power, and flood control.

Navigation of the upper Missouri became important toward the close of the Civil War, when the gold camps in Alder, Last Chance, and Grasshopper Gulches were established *(see HISTORY)*. There were difficulties because of low water in late summer and fall, and trouble with Indians. In 1867 Comdr. E. H. Durfee and Col. Campbell K. Peck established the Indian agency and trading post of Fort Peck, a few miles from the present damsite, and undertook to pacify the Indians with food and gifts. Among the supplies they issued were 100-pound sacks of flour emblazoned on each side with great red circles composed of the words "Durfee and Peck." The Indians adopted the sacks for war dress, merely cutting holes for the arms and neck. The Hunkpapa, a Sioux tribe, especially valued the bright red circles as "good medicine."

Fort Peck enjoyed a monopoly of the fur trade with the Assiniboine and

Sioux, and became more important than Fort Union had been. Colonel Peck went to Washington in the first attempt to get Federal aid for the development of Missouri navigation. He died on his way back in 1869. His post was abandoned in 1879, and was later swept away by the river.

Underlying the glacial and stream deposits of the Fort Peck area are 20 to 40 feet of volcanic ash, in which fossils from the Age of Reptiles are found. There is a theory that the reptiles were exterminated when thousands of volcanoes erupted. A FOSSIL COLLECTION *(open during shows)* in the foyer of the Fort Peck theater contains more than 1,000 pieces gathered by project engineers. Remains of herbivorous and carnivorous dinosaurs, armored fishes, and swimming reptiles are among them. There is also a hindfoot of the Trachodon, a large duck-billed dinosaur, and a Triceratops horn core 2 feet long and 8 inches across, probably from a horn at least 4 feet long. Fossilized flora include a segment of palm leaf, wood of coniferous trees, and a dozen petrified figs, indicating the subtropical nature of this region at one period.

←←←←←←←←←←←←←←←←←←←←←☼→→→→→→→→→→→→→→→→→→→→→

Tour 11

Forsyth—Roundup—Harlowton—White Sulphur Springs—Townsend; State 6.
Forsyth to Townsend, 290.2 m.

Route served by Intermountain Transportation Co. busses; paralleled at intervals by the main line of the Chicago, Milwaukee, St. Paul & Pacific R. R.
Hotels and tourist camps in larger towns; many service stations.
Roadbed graded and drained between Forsyth and Melstone; rough and, in rainy weather, difficult between Melstone and Roundup; graded and, except for a 10-mile oil-surfaced stretch south of White Sulphur Springs, graveled between Roundup and Townsend.

State 6 traverses the central Montana range country, skirts the Bull and Big Snowy Mountains, slips between the Little Belt and Castle Ranges, and crosses the Big Belts into the upper Missouri Valley. The rolling plain and the foothills produce excellent hard wheat and afford pasturage for thousands of cattle and sheep. Mining for lead, silver, and gold is an important industry in the mountains. Antelopes graze north of the Mussel-shell River, coyotes slink over the hills and along the sides of coulees, and wolves are sometimes seen. A few wild horses still exist on the prairie. Several kinds of upland birds are hunted here in season.

Towns along the route are small and often far between.

State 6 branches northwest from US 10 *(see Tour 1)* at FORSYTH, 0 *m. (see Tour 1, Sec. a)*, crosses the Yellowstone River at 0.8 *m.*, and follows the railroad track and the river (L).

VANANDA, 23.1 *m.* (2,705 alt., 60 pop.), a village of general stores, a grain elevator, and a railroad station, serves the surrounding sheep and cattle outfits.

West of Vananda the highway passes over rolling country dotted with clumps of low sage and greasewood. Purple crocus, blue larkspur, and yellow mustard in turn lift their bright heads among the dry-land grasses, which are fresh and green in spring, dusty and dun in late summer. Large bands of sheep or herds of cattle crowd and push and bawl around occasional water holes.

The highway rises to the top of a ridge, 39 *m.*, that permits a view of a wide sweep of prairie.

INGOMAR, 49.9 *m.* (3,040 alt., 315 pop.), a trade center of the sheep-raising area, has one of the largest shearing plants in the State. It operates in May and June. *(For a description of shearing, see Tour 1, Sec. b.)*

GALBRAITH, 56.6 *m.* (3,111 alt.), is a railroad siding with stock-loading pens.

SUMATRA, 61.2 *m.* (3,186 alt., 300 pop.), is on an old trail that once connected Fort Musselshell, at the junction of the Missouri and Musselshell Rivers, with Fort Custer in the Big Horn country.

BASCOM, 72.1 *m.* (2,937 alt., 15 pop.), has four buildings—a general store and post office, a railway station, a one-room school, and the storekeeper's home.

State 6 crosses the Musselshell River, 75.1 *m.*, named by Lewis and Clark on May 20, 1805. Between farms and coal mines in this district are stock ranches. In autumn and winter, when ranch work is light, neighborhood hunting parties break the monotony of life for the inhabitants.

Indians believed the Musselshell Valley to be haunted by evil spirits, and seldom used it even as a passage to the buffalo grounds—a blessing to early settlers, who were thus spared the occasional Indian scares that afflicted other pioneer communities.

MELSTONE, 78.2 *m.* (2,897 alt., 217 pop.), was named for Melville E. Stone, general manager of the Associated Press (1893–1921), who once lived near here. It is a livestock-shipping point.

State 6 passes southwestward between towering rocky bluffs topped with scrub pine and cedar. Large cottonwoods border the river and give shade to livestock.

MUSSELSHELL, 92.7 *m.* (2,997 alt., 151 pop.), was named for the old stockmen's landmark known as Musselshell Crossing, where the herds of Texas longhorns driven north in the 1880's were bedded down for the last time before being "fanned out" in smaller herds to their ultimate Montana owners.

The crossing was established in 1877 on the north bank of the Musselshell River, opposite the present village. The trail between Fort Custer and Fort Maginnis passed through it. Three years later a store, which contained the post office, was opened here, and settlement of the valley began.

For 30 years the rule of the stockman was disputed only by rustlers, many of whom ended their lawless careers at the end of 20 feet of hemp. The cattle king's day ended here as it ended all over the State. In 1908 the railroad arrived and soon sodbusters were flocking in to break the great free range into relatively small cultivated tracts. Coal, the great mineral resource of the valley, was exploited. Villages sprang up amid the sage. The old West retreated before advancing barriers of barbwire, and grain farming superseded the livestock industry in importance.

Between Musselshell and Roundup, State 6 closely follows the Mussel-shell River, which winds intricately. When the C. M. St. P. & P. R. R. was built through the valley it was necessary to bridge the river 117 times in 115 miles.

State 6 enters the foothills of the BULL MOUNTAINS at 93.8 m. The rough higher ridges (L), which are old and eroded into fantastic pinnacles and deep gorges, contain many caves of various sizes. Rattlesnakes are numerous, but not particularly dangerous except in August, when they sometimes strike without warning (see FAUNA, and GENERAL INFORMATION).

DELPHIA, 100.1 m. (3,053 alt., 101 pop.), is the standard combination of general store and post office that is common on the plains.

GAGE, 109.2 m. (3,128 alt., 31 pop.), is one of the few remaining "cracker box communities" in Montana. Here, at the general store known as John Brown's, ranchers from the valley and homesteading bachelors from the hills buy groceries and "set awhile" to gossip and discuss politics. Old but comfortable chairs and upended apple boxes drawn about the stove in winter and the doorway in summer, testify that this is the community center.

ROUNDUP, 117.1 m. (3,184 alt., 2,577 pop.) (see Tour 3, Sec. a), is at the junction with US 87 (see Tour 3). Between Roundup and the junction at 118.7 m. State 6 is united with US 87.

At 140 m. on State 6 is the junction with a dirt road.

Left on this road is LAVINA, 1 m. (3,443 alt., 144 pop.), a prairie village that began as a trading post and a stage station on the route between Billings and Lewistown.

RYEGATE, 157 m. (3,641 alt., 292 pop.), is the seat of hopefully named Golden Valley County. A fine field of rye that attracted the attention of railway officials suggested the town's name. Since drought struck this rolling farm country, much of it is returning to range. The most fertile acres are to the south; dairying and turkey raising compete with livestock raising and grain growing.

Ryegate was built at the base of rimrocks 3 miles long that were once part of the shore of a large lake. Marine fossils are abundant here. Prehistoric inscriptions are still seen on the rocks; one crudely drawn picture, a mile west of town, shows six men and three antelopes. North of the rimrocks (R) the benchlands rise gently to the Big Snowy Mountains, 25 miles away.

Left from Ryegate on a graded dirt road is SEVENTYNINE, 16 *m.*, a community composed largely of people who speak both Russian and English. Most of the first settlers were from Odessa. They observe many of the customs of South Russia, and on feast days dance the *trepak* to the strains of the accordion and the balalaika.

The Russians and other farmers of this vicinity settled here in 1912 when the 79 Ranch, one of the largest old-time spreads in Montana was broken up. The ranch was named for 1879, the year John T. Murphy, president of the Montana Cattle Company, started it on Sweetgrass Creek. In 1881 the outfit moved to Big Coulee a few miles south of Seventynine. It built up its herds by trailing cattle from Texas and at its busiest ran 50,000 head of cattle and about 40,000 sheep. The home ranch was at Big Coulee, but there were three other large ranches, and the stock ranged from the Yellowstone to the mouth of the Musselshell. The greatest days of the 79 were, of course, those of the open range, but it did well enough later by purchasing railroad land and fencing it, fencing at the same time the Government land on alternate sections. To obey the letter of the law and still fatten their cows on Federal property, the men of the 79 ran fences right up to but not quite around the Government corners. The Government ended that practice in 1908, and in 1912 the company allowed its holding to be broken up.

BARBER, 163.5 *m.* (3,727 alt., 90 pop.), is a crossroads hamlet composed of a general store, a schoolhouse, and a railroad station.

DEADMAN'S BASIN (R), 170.7 *m.,* is a natural basin 2 miles square, with a storage capacity of 80,000 acre-feet of water, and an average depth of 58 feet. It is now filled for irrigation purposes by a 12-mile canal from the Musselshell River, which usually runs full only in April and May. A 1,000-foot tunnel at the northern end of the basin controls the supply of water for the irrigation of 21,000 acres of the lower benchlands along the Musselshell. Work on the project began in 1934 under the FERA, and has been continued by the WPA.

The name of the basin is of legendary origin. Indians are said to have found the bodies of two men here, one on each side of the basin.

SHAWMUT, 170.9 *m.* (3,857 alt., 100 pop.), is a country store and post office on a sparse sheep range covered largely with yucca, sage, and greasewood.

At 178 *m.* is the junction with a dirt road.

Left on this road, crossing railroad tracks and passing through the yard of the Winnecook Ranch to a FOSSIL AREA, 7 *m.,* locally known as Devil's Pocket. It was discovered in 1902. The specimens found here are similar to those found in the Crazy Mountains area *(see below)*, but less spectacular.

The CLIFF (R), 183.2 *m.,* is a piskun (buffalo leap) where many buffaloes were killed. Below it a highway cut exposes large numbers of buffalo bones.

HARLOWTON, 187.3 *m.* (4,167 alt., 1,473 pop.), seat of Wheatland County, is hidden by river bluffs until the road makes a turn and a descent about a mile from town. At the top of the hill is (L) the GRAVES HOTEL built in 1909 of stone quarried from the nearby rim rocks. The town's presence is first revealed by the concrete cylinders (R) of a flour mill. The road turns R. into the main street at the base of the hill. Local stone has been used in a number of buildings here. The town overlooks the Musselshell River and is protected to some extent from the almost continual northerly winds by the river bluffs. Many houses on the west side are perched on the very edge of the river-bank.

Harlowton was named for Richard Harlow, who built the "Jawbone Line" *(see TRANSPORTATION)*. It is a division point on the C. M. St. P. & P. R. R., whose electrified section begins here, and whose shops and yards provide much local employment. The flour mill, outstanding for this region, has 22 storage tanks with a capacity of 25,000 bushels each, and the daily output is 950 barrels of flour and large quantities of poultry and stock feeds. The town is the trading center for a steadily productive sheep and cattle region.

The RENÉ LA BRIE ARROWHEAD COLLECTION *(open on application; inquire at the Times Bldg., Main St.)* contains more than 1,000 arrowheads gathered over a period of 15 years. It is not completely catalogued, but includes most of the styles of points known to archeologists—the slender, fluted Folsom, the "Folsomlike," the Yuma, and many others. The range of size and types is as interesting as the variety of flints and other materials. Most of the points were found on Indian campgrounds, but many were obtained by laboriously screening tons of dirt from piskuns. Many of the Folsom and Yuma points were found buried near bones of mammoths, ground sloths, camels, and prehistoric horses. La Brie also has axes obtained by Indians from early fur traders, stones used for pounding pemmican, stones used in ceremonial games, war clubs, skinning knives, fleshers, pipe reamers, and medicine bowls.

The W. F. ALMQUIST FIREARMS COLLECTION *(open on application; inquire at the Times Bldg., Main St.)* is another valuable uncatalogued collection built up over a period of years. Some of the pieces, such as the Kentucky muzzle-loading rifles, have great beauty of workmanship. Others, such as the dragoon pistols and pepper-box revolvers, have more purely antiquarian interest. Most of the pieces have historical associations; many played a part in the making of Montana—the original derringer, the early Sharps, the Spencer, first repeating rifle, the first Colt revolver, and the Winchester. A number of the guns are in bad condition.

At 188 *m.* is the junction with State 19.

Left on State 19 to the boundary, 14 *m.*, of a FOSSIL AREA. For about 26 miles fossil beds extend along both sides of the highway, mostly L. The pockets are widely scattered. The Fort Union geological formation in this area contains some of the best examples of Cretaceous and Tertiary remains in North America. Bones of the earliest known primates were found here—animals ancestral to existing lemurs, monkeys, apes, and man. They were very small—about the size of squirrels—but are credited with the destruction of the dinosaurs, whose eggs they ate. More than 2,000 specimens of Paleocene mammals have been taken from the field; most of them are in the American Museum of Natural History in New York. Outstanding among the mammal finds was *Ptilodus montanus*, discovered in 1908 by Albert Silberling of Harlowton; it is one of the oldest known multituberculate mammalian skulls, being surpassed only by specimens found in Mongolia by Walter Granger and Roy Chapman Andrews. Other fossils found here include turtles, crocodiles, lizards, birds, plants, and several genera of dinosaurs, including the smallest one known—a birdlike creature only 14 inches long.

A little searching will unearth gizzard stones polished to a high gloss millions of years ago by the digestive processes of dinosaurs.

MELVILLE, 30 *m.* (5,000 alt., 25 pop.), a supply point for sheep camps in the Crazy Mountains, is also headquarters of the KREMER STOCK RANCH, which breeds the bucking horses and other stock used in rodeos of the West and also the annual

Madison Square Garden show in New York. Hundreds of horses are trained on the ranch each year.

State 19 follows a somewhat irregular route southward through grazing country, with impressive views of the mountains (R).

BIG TIMBER, 52 *m.* (4,072 alt., 1,224 pop.) *(see Tour 1, Sec. b)*, is at the junction with US 10 *(see Tour 1)*.

State 6 goes west up the Musselshell Valley. The Castle Mountains are straight ahead, almost indistinguishable from the Little Belts (R).

The sharp and rugged CRAZY MOUNTAINS (L), glittering in the clear air, are an isolated, geologically young range; they form an almost incredibly jagged upthrust of rock more than 11,000 feet high. Before white men ever saw them, Indians knew them as the Mad Mountains, and feared and avoided them. Their terrifying steepness, their awe-inspiring structure, and the demoniac winds that blow continually out of their strange canyons impressed white men as much as it had their coppery brethren, though with less superstitious awe. The epithet "Mad" became the more familiar "Crazy." The weird range is rarely visited.

DAISY NOTCH, slightly R., is a huge nick in the soft rock of a spur of Bluff Mountain in the Little Belts. At a distance it resembles a gunsight. The spur rises between Morrissey Coulee and Daisy Dean Canyon.

At 199.6 *m.* is the junction with a dirt road.

Left on this road is TWO DOT, 1 *m.* (4,434 alt., 179 pop.), named for an early cattle brand. It has won local fame as the scene of wild and violent dances that have more than once ended in free-for-all fights and grave injuries. A power sub-station here controls voltage for the electrified C. M. St. P. & P. R. R.

As the road goes south, R. is isolated COFFIN BUTTE, sometimes called Gordon Butte, in honor of a pioneer rancher. It rises steeply on the north side, but emerges into high grassland on the south and west. Now and then on summer nights, the sheepmen's lanterns glimmering on the slopes are reported as small forest fires by persons unfamiliar with the place.

The WALLIS HUIDEKOPER RANCH, 35,000 acres of hill and plain, is at 11 *m.* Strangers descending to it often mistake the collection of white-painted red-roofed buildings for a small village. The ranch at one time maintained a herd of buffalo from which came the largest buffalo head in the world, now in the Field Museum in Chicago. In the Huidekoper home are a number of oils by Charles Russell. One of them is *The Last of Five Thousand*, which brought Russell recognition *(see THE ARTS)*.

At 214.6 *m.* on State 6 is the junction with a dirt road.

Left on this road is MARTINSDALE, 2.4 *m.* (4,822 alt., 188 pop.), a sheepmen's town. West is the Smith ranch of 86,000 acres and east is the Bair ranch of 80,000 acres, two of the largest sheep outfits in the State. In 1910 Bair shipped east 44 carloads of wool, worth $500,000, the largest single shipment of wool that ever left Montana.

In the shearing season, blackjack and poker games often draw the itinerant workers from the shearing pens, and many shearers are as neatly "clipped" as the sheep.

Martinsdale is the home of Grace Stone Coates, novelist and poet *(see THE ARTS)*.

At 216 *m.* on State 6 is the junction with a dirt road.

Right on this road to FINDON, 10 *m.*, a country post office; L. from Findon on a dim and difficult trail to the Narrows of DAISY DEAN CANYON, 12 *m.* On the rock walls above the narrows are Indian picture writings partly obscured by the smoke of campers' fires.

At 219.9 *m.* State 6 turns northwest to run along the North Fork of the

Musselshell through a pass between the Little Belts (R) and the Castle Mountains (L). At intervals it follows an old Indian trail that ran between Judith Gap and White Sulphur Springs along the southern slopes of the Little Belts. The low Castle Mountains are timbered with lodgepole and yellow pine and, on the western slopes, with scrub cedar.

SUMPTER INN, 225.2 *m.*, is a tourist camp in a rugged, wooded canyon.

The deserted shacks and mine shafts of COPPEROPOLIS, 236.1 *m.*, a busy mining town in the 1890's, crown the divide between the valleys of the upper Musselshell and Smith Rivers. The Delpine Reservoir (R), a storage lake for irrigation waters, backs up through a long narrow valley.

The road here, surfaced with green, red, and yellow shales, swings south and descends through the Smith Valley.

At 244.7 *m.* is the junction (R) with US 89 *(see Tour 4)*. Between this point and the junction at 256.5 *m.* US 89 and State 6 are one route *(see Tour 4, Sec. b)*.

At 256.5 *m.* is the junction (L) with US 89 *(see Tour 4)*.

State 6 runs west through the foothills of the Big Belt Mountains and at 269.1 *m.* crosses the divide between the Smith and Missouri Valleys. It runs through narrow DEEP CREEK CANYON, where varicolored strata and curious rock formations tower 2,000 feet above the stream bed in some places. The descent toward the Missouri is long and winding.

DEEP CREEK RANGER STATION (L), 277.6 *m.*, is in the Helena National Forest, at the western end of Deep Creek Canyon.

At 279.2 *m.* the main range of the Rockies is seen straight ahead.

TOWNSEND, 290.2 *m.* (3,833 alt., 740 pop.) *(see Tour 1A)*, is at the junction with US 10 N *(see Tour 1A)*.

<<<<<<<<<<<<<<<<<<✿>>>>>>>>>>>>>>>>>>>

Tour 12

Ravalli—Plains—Thompson Falls—(Sandpoint, Idaho); State 3.
Ravalli to Idaho Line, 116.4 m.

Northern Pacific Ry. parallels entire route. Missoula-Hot Springs busses travel State 3 between Ravalli and Perma.
Better accommodations in towns; tourist camps along road.
Oil-surfaced roadbed; open throughout year.

State 3 is part of an alternate route to US 10 between Missoula and Spokane; though 40 miles longer than US 10, it is relatively free of traffic

NATIONAL BISON RANGE

and offers much more beautiful views. State 3 traverses the valleys of the Jocko River and the Clark Fork of the Columbia, with the deep green waters of the latter often in sight for nearly 100 miles. The road parallels the old Kootenai Trail, which was made by Salish Indians in prehistoric days. It was used by David Thompson, Finan McDonald, Jacques Finlay, and others of the North-West Company in the early 19th century and by prospectors and pack trains in the late 1860's, the boom days of the Coeur d'Alene and Kootenai mines. The Cabinet National Forest, adjacent to the highway at many points, has vast stands of white and yellow pine. The ravages of forest fires are frequently seen. Fishing is good in the Clark Fork and its numerous tributaries.

State 3 branches west from US 93 *(see Tour 7)* at RAVALLI, 0 *m.* (2,760 alt., 15 pop.) *(see Tour 7, Sec. b).*

The Jocko River (R) was named for Jacques Finlay, fur trader of the North-West Company and a member of David Thompson's exploring party *(see HISTORY).*

A heavy fence (R) marks the southern boundary of the NATIONAL BISON RANGE (18,000 acres) where the country's second largest herd of buffalo grazes. Among the 500 or so head is one of the only albino buffalo ever born in a supervised herd; it is estimated that only one of every seven million bison is an albino. The animals graze in scattered groups and often appear near the highway. Elk, deer, mountain goats, and other native animals share the range with them.

At 6.3 *m.* is the junction with a dirt road.

Right on this road to FLATHEAD INDIAN RESERVATION AGENCY, 1.2 *m.* *(see Tour 7, Sec. b)*; and MOIESE, 4.6 *m.*, headquarters of the National Bison Range *(conducted tours on Sat. afternoons and Sun.).* Moiese was named for a Salishan subchief.

DIXON, 7 *m.* (2,531 alt., 132 pop.), is a grain and cattle shipping center at the confluence of the Jocko and Flathead Rivers (R).

PERMA, 21 *m.* (2,512 alt., 30 pop.), is scarcely noticeable at a short distance. To the north and south stretches the open Camas Prairie of the Flathead Reservation. Salish and Kootenai come here annually in late spring to dig the bulbs of the camas, a member of the lily family that has an onionlike flavor. It was formerly one of the staples of their diet.

Right from Perma on an improved road to HOT SPRINGS, 22 *m.* (2,540 alt., 447 pop.). *(Riding, swimming, fishing, and hunting in summer.)* The springs are owned and maintained by the Government; the baths *(adm. 25¢ and 50¢)* are under the supervision of experienced attendants. The principal mineral ingredients in the hot water are silica, calcium, sodium, potassium, chlorine, carbonates, bicarbonates, and sulphates.

Between Perma and Paradise State 3 winds over a thickly wooded hill above a rocky gorge of the Flathead River. At 25 *m.* the Mission Mountains (R) are seen; a large glacier gleams on the face of McDONALD PEAK (9,800 alt.), the highest. The range was named for St. Ignatius Mission, established in 1854 by Jesuit missionaries *(see Tour 7, Sec. b).* McDonald Peak was named for Angus McDonald, the early North West trader operating in the Flathead and Clark Fork Valleys.

State 3 crosses the western boundary of the Flathead Indian Reservation at 30.6 *m.* *(see Tour 7, Sec. b).*

At 31.6 *m.* is the junction with the graveled St. Regis Cut-off.

Left on this road to QUINN'S HOT SPRINGS, 2 *m.*, where are hot mineral-water baths. *(Facilities for riding, swimming, hunting, and fishing.)*
ST. PATRICK'S NOB (6,866 alt.), directly across the Clark Fork from the hot springs, has a FOREST SERVICE LOOKOUT on its summit.

The Flathead River joins the Clark Fork, which the highway now closely parallels.

PARADISE (R), 34.2 *m.* (2,499 alt., 259 pop.), huddles on a grassy flat at the base of a bare mountain. Railroad yards are L.; Paradise is a division point on the Northern Pacific Ry., which here changes from mountain standard time to Pacific standard time. The town's name is a polite modification of Pair o' Dice, the name of a roadhouse on the trail.

From the mouth of the Flathead River the old Kootenai Trail followed the north bank of the Clark Fork to Idaho. Between 1810 and 1883, when the Northern Pacific was built, it was the main artery of travel through the lower Clark Fork Valley. Its identity was then lost, and most of the trail was obliterated.

Between Paradise and the Idaho Line are (R) the Cabinet Mountains

McDONALD PEAK, MISSION RANGE

and (L) the Coeur d'Alenes. Early French-Canadian trappers, noting box-like recesses in the gorge of the Clark Fork near the present State Line, applied to them the French word for cabinet or room, and this rock-walled gorge has since been known as the Cabinet Gorge. The name Coeur d'Alene seems to have had its origin in an epithet applied by Salish Indians to sharp-trading French Canadians, who translated it as "heart of an awl," and applied it to the Indians themselves. The shrewd practices referred to probably were not confined to the French. Another explanation is that early trappers said the Coeur d'Alene region was as hard to get into as "the heart of a shoemaker's awl."

PLAINS, 39.8 *m.* (2,582 alt., 522 pop.), straddles the highway, its business houses R., the railroad L. Beyond the stores are trim, neatly painted, frame dwellings, churches, and a school. Plains is the largest and oldest white community west of Missoula in the Clark Fork Valley, which at this point is about 15 miles wide. Because of the large herds of wild horses that once ranged the valley, the flats and town were originally called Wild Horse Plains. The Kootenai Trail ran near the site.

State 3 crosses the boundary of the CABINET NATIONAL FOREST at 46.2 *m.,* and Thompson River at 60.4 *m.* near the confluence with the Clark Fork. Large stands of western yellow pine border the stream.

The DAVID THOMPSON MONUMENT, 64.7 *m.,* erected by citizens of Thompson Falls to the memory of the explorer of the Columbia River watershed, stands close to the SITE OF SALISH HOUSE, built by Thompson in 1809. It is believed to have been the first roofed habitation of white men in the territory that later became Montana *(see HISTORY)*. David Thompson, a surveyor, was the first white man to follow the Columbia from its source to its mouth. Mapping this territory with sextant and compass, he traveled 50,000 miles on foot, on horseback, and by canoe. He built Salish House in a place from which he could readily see Indian war parties crossing Bad Rock *(Es-em-mowela,* or *Roche Mauvais)* on the Kootenai Trail.

Because of his seemingly magical instruments, Indians regarded him with superstitious awe, and called him Koo-koo-sint *(man who looks at the stars)*. They believed that his telescope enabled him to see all things, so that an Indian woman could not even mend a pair of moccasins without his knowledge.

Above the highway and the river is (R) Koo-koo-sint Ridge, overlooking the site of Salish House.

THOMPSON FALLS, 65.7 *m.* (2,463 alt., 464 pop.), seat of Sanders County, was named for David Thompson. At first glance this seems to be merely a one-street town, a short line of buildings containing a service station, a hotel, and a few stores. Closer inspection reveals homes and more stores in a forest of yellow pine and brush. The streets have an atmosphere of privacy and peace enhanced by the view of wooded summits to the south and by the calmness of the Clark Fork, which at this point is a lake.

With the completion of the Northern Pacific Ry. in 1883, Thompson Falls and Belknap, 7 miles west, became rivals. The railroad company favored Belknap, and refused to stop trains here. The citizens of Thompson Falls thereupon placed huge logs on the railroad tracks, and, while crews were removing the obstructions, boarded the trains and persuaded emigrants to settle here. In 1883, 10,000 people on their way to the Idaho gold fields wintered in the place. Twenty saloons were operated, in tents and wooden shacks, and vigilantes worked overtime to maintain order. They once mailed notices to 25 desperadoes, ordering them to leave town; 24 left at once but the twenty-fifth went away only after feeling a noose about his neck. A few log cabins near the riverbank, with bullet-riddled slab doors and window jambs, provide proof of the dangers of the period.

The town boasts of one of the natural marvels that are typical of so much of the northern mountain region. Crevices in the ground emit currents of air that range down to 33° F. This air has been piped and used for refrigeration since the first wells were dug 50 years ago.

The Clark Fork has been dammed at the natural falls (L) to produce 50,000 horsepower. The lake impounded for 2 miles behind the dam is the site of an annual regatta *(3rd week of July)*. Trout fishing is good in the lake, in the river below the falls, and in Prospect Creek, a tributary that enters L.

Left from Thompson Falls on unimproved State 4 (Prospect Creek Road) to OBSERVATION POINT, 1 *m.,* which affords a view of the Clark Fork, the dam, the falls, and the power-house. Driftwood high on the sides of the Clark Fork gorge indicates the fury with which water rushes through at the time of the spring rise, an event that attracts spectators from near and far. To the north extends the piled grandeur of the Cabinet Mountains.

The road runs southwest through the Cabinet National Forest and over the Coeur d'Alene Divide at Glidden Pass, 18 *m.* Approaching the summit, the road is narrow, with a few places where it is impossible for two vehicles to pass. This was the early trail from Thompson Falls to the placer gold discoveries at Murray, Idaho.

BELKNAP, 72.3 *m.* (2,460 alt., 113 pop.), has a post office and little else.

At 76.4 *m.* on State 3 is the junction with the Beaver Creek Road.

Left on this dirt road to the JACK WAITE MINE, 17 *m.*, a large lead, silver, and zinc producer on Beaver Creek.

WHITE PINE, 78.7 *m.* (2,380 alt., 175 pop.), is the shipping point for the Jack Waite Mine.

At 81.6 *m.* is the junction with an improved road.

Left on this road is TROUT CREEK, 0.1 *m.* (2,374 alt., 35 pop.), a coaling point for the Northern Pacific Ry.

State 3 passes through cool green stretches of cedar and tamarack, which flourish in the richer and moister soils near the river.

The road crosses SWAMP CREEK, 95.2 *m.*, and ROCK CREEK, 99.6 *m.* Trout fishing is good in both streams. A small section of the old Kootenai Trail is visible (R) near the junction of Rock Creek and the Clark Fork.

At 101.8 *m.* is the junction with a dirt road.

Left on this road, crossing the Clark Fork, to NOXON, 1 *m.* (2,187 alt., 151 pop.), which seems to be only a clearing in a densely forested area of indefinite extent. Around it, however, is one of the richest trapping areas in Montana, and a region of fabulous harvests of wild huckleberries. Agnes K. Getty, who once taught school there, described Noxon (Boxcar) in her novel *Blue Gold* (1934).

At 105.4 *m.* on State 3 is the junction with the Bull Lake Highway *(see Tour 2, Sec. c).*

At 113 *m.* is the junction with the Blue Creek Road.

Right on this improved dirt road to the SCOTCHMAN MINE, 4.5 *m.*, a producer of gold and silver. The road runs through a belt of cedar and white pine in the Cabinet National Forest.

At 116.4 *m.* State 3 crosses the Idaho Line and becomes State 3 in Idaho *(see Tour 11, IDAHO GUIDE)*, 34.4 miles east of Sandpoint, Idaho.

‹‹‹‹‹‹‹‹‹‹‹‹‹‹‹‹‹‹‹‹‹✿›››››››››››››››››››

Tour 13

Laurel—Rockvale—Warren—(Lovell, Wyo.); US 310.
Laurel to Wyoming Line, 55.9 m.

Route paralleled by Northern Pacific Ry. between Laurel and Bridger; by Chicago,
Burlington & Quincy R. R. between Bridger and the Wyoming Line.
Hotels and tourist camps in larger towns; cabin camps along route.
Oil-surfaced roadbed; open throughout year.

US 310 follows the old trail that ran between central Montana and
the fur traders' rendezvous on Green River, Wyoming. Explorers, prospectors, and trappers used this route continually, and Chief Joseph followed it in his retreat to Canada (see HISTORY). Most of the route ran
through the valley of Clark Fork of the Yellowstone, a region distinguished for wild beauty, with the impressive Beartooth Mountains to the
west and the Pryor Mountains on the east. From the prosperous farms that
cover the wide valley come livestock, sugar beets, grains, and hay.

US 310 branches south from US 10 (see Tour 1) at LAUREL, 0 m.
(3,311 alt., 2,558 pop.) (see Tour ·1, sec. b) and at 0.4 m. crosses the
Yellowstone River. RIVERSIDE PARK (L) is a picnic ground by the river.

SILESIA, 9.3 m. (3,404 alt., 40 pop.), a loading point for produce
from adjacent irrigated lands, was named, not for the German province,
but for nearby springs of siliceous water.

ROCKVALE, 12.1 m. (3,483 alt., 25 pop.), consists of a red gasoline
pump and a frame store and post office. A highway department port of
entry (see GENERAL INFORMATION) occupies a modernized log
cabin beside the road.

At Rockvale is the junction with State 32 (see Tour 13A).

At 16.4 m. on US 310 is the junction with a graveled road.

Left on this road is EDGAR, 0.3 m. (3,473 alt., 111 pop.), a village in the lower
valley of Clark Fork. It is named for Henry Edgar, one of the discoverers of Alder
Gulch (see Tour 16).

FROMBERG, 22.2 m. (3,538 alt., 550 pop.), shaded by cottonwoods,
resembles the agricultural villages of the Midwest. Its trim streets, faced
with white and gray stores, houses, and churches, have an air of peaceful
activity. Few of the buildings are new, but all are well kept.

Fromberg is the trade center of a section, productive when watered,
that is locally known as Poverty Flats because its settlers nearly starved
to death while waiting for a promised irrigation project. In summer the
air is full of the liquid song of red-winged blackbirds, which gather to
feed on the wildrice growing in roadside irrigation ditches.

The Pryor Mountains (L), named for Sergeant Pryor of the Lewis and

Clark expedition, are an outlying part of the Big Horn Range *(see Tour 3)*.

BRIDGER, 29.1 *m.* (3,664 alt., 567 pop.), is a sheep and cattle town set against rimrocks (R). Oil and gas from the nearby Dry Creek and Elk Basin fields have materially slowed down production in its once important coal mines. Bridger might well be the faded original of some frontier town described in fiction. The town was named for the greatest frontiersman in western history; the proof of his skill lies in the fact that though he was in the fur trade in 1810, he lived to be a very old man.

James Bridger (1795(?)–1881) began his frontier education at Fort Osage in 1810 and later worked with the Rocky Mountain Fur Company. He is sometimes called the discoverer of Great Salt Lake (1824), and was one of the first white men to explore the Yellowstone Park region extensively. Fort Bridger, the trading post he built in 1842 on the Black Fork of Green River, was of considerable importance on the Oregon-California Trail. He scouted many trails, including the one that bears his name *(see Tour 1, Sec. b)*. His advice as scout for the U. S. Army was law to prudent officers.

Bridger, alive, was a legend; dead, he inspired countless others. Ned Buntline (Edward Z. C. Judson), the popular pulp fictionist of Bridger's day, was responsible for the tradition that the scout was a great liar. In describing things that were new to the popular mind—in some instances new even to science—Bridger sometimes gave fantastic explanations. Like other frontiersmen he was not above exaggerating, particularly when talking to gullible tenderfeet. He stated, for example, that a certain river was hot on the bottom because it ran so fast over its rocky bed. His yarns of a glass mountain that magnified an elk feeding 30 miles away, and of a "peetrified bird sitting in a peetrified tree singing a peetrified song," were his means of expressing his scorn for the newcomers who annoyed him by their blundering.

In the 1840's Jim's stories of the Yellowstone Park region were national legend. Long before this a St. Louis editor set up his first and most sincere account in type, but he destroyed it when someone told him he would be laughed out of the country if he printed it.

In his later years Army officers vied with each other to obtain his services as a scout. Popular belief then held that he could map any part of the Rocky Mountains with charcoal on a piece of buffalo skin; Jim himself boasted that he could smell his way where he could not see it. His daily schedule was eccentric; he slept when he was tired, which was often in the middle of the afternoon, and ate when he was hungry, which was sometimes after midnight. Having eaten at some ungodly hour, he was likely to beat a tom-tom and sing Indian chants the rest of the night. To keep him awake till a decent hour and avoid these serenades, Capt. J. L. Humfreville started to read *Hiawatha* aloud to him. Jim was fascinated at first, but could not bear Longfellow's idealized Indians. Having heard of Shakespeare, Bridger sat for days by the Oregon Trail until he found an emigrant with a set of Shakespeare and then hired a boy at $40 a month to read to him. To the earlier plays he listened attentively, and memorized many scenes that he quoted later with his own emphasis; but when the boy reached *Richard the Third,* Jim threw the book in the fire. "No man," he shouted, "could be that mean."

Later in life Bridger retired to a farm near Kansas City, Mo. There he died, blind and poor.

The highway crosses the Clark Fork of the Yellowstone, 31.7 *m.* The river curves away R., the highway swings L. across an unfenced plateau, where short grasses provide excellent pasturage for sheep. Canvas-covered wagons stand here and there. Near each of them a herder and his dogs tend the sheep. Sometimes the dogs alone hold the sheep, while thin blue smoke drifts away from the wagon in testimony that the herder is preparing his beans and sauerkraut.

Herding is a weary task, not only because the herder sees few human beings during the summer, but also because of the stupidity of his charges, their monotonous bleating, the discomforts of bad weather, and the cheerlessness of his own prospects. Some herders occupy themselves with wood carving or basket weaving, or with gathering arrowheads or curious rocks. Others work stolidly, and, with almost infinite patience, save their small wages in the hope of some day buying herds of their own.

At 49.8 *m.* the Big Horn Mountains are straight ahead. Lt. William Clark named them in 1806, after killing two bighorn sheep in them.

WARREN, 51.3 *m.* (3,718 alt., 15 pop.), is a stock-loading point whose littleness and isolation are emphasized by the black ribbons of railroad track that stretch into the dim distance to east and west.

At 55.9 *m.* US 310 crosses the Wyoming Line, 27 miles northwest of Lovell, Wyo. *(see Tour 10 in WYOMING GUIDE).*

‹‹‹‹‹‹‹‹‹‹‹‹‹‹‹‹✹››››››››››››››››››››

Tour 13A

Rockvale—Red Lodge—Cooke—Silver Gate—(Yellowstone National Park); State 32.
Rockvale to Yellowstone National Park, 105.4 m.

Northern Pacific Ry. parallels route between Rockvale and Red Lodge.
Hotels in Red Lodge and Cooke. Dude ranches, mountain lodges, tourist cabins, and free public campgrounds along highway. Entrance fee to Yellowstone National Park, $3.00 for car.
Oil-surfaced roadbed; open only between late spring and early autumn. Climb to Beartooth Plateau is made over 5½ percent grade; turnouts provided for safe observation of canyons and peaks.
Temperatures drop nightly almost to freezing, making it imperative that campers carry adequate bedding.

MAE WEST CURVE ON STATE 32

State 32, one of five roads entering Yellowstone National Park, in part follows one of the oldest Indian trails in the State. It ascends and descends very steep grades, offering striking vistas of forests, and bare granite summits. It supplants old pack trails into a great recreational area, and provides an easy and rapid route for fire-fighting crews into a region of valuable timber. Near Red Lodge the highway ascends the gorge of Rock Creek Canyon until apparently insurmountable heights appear on all sides. The highest peaks in the State here rise abruptly from the Great Plains, many snow-capped throughout the year, others bearing glaciers in granite cirques (steep-walled mountain recesses eroded by glaciation). A vast region in these mountains has been set aside by the Federal Government as a permanent primitive area.

The Red Lodge-Cooke highway was cut through the Beartooth Mountains by the Federal Government at a cost of $2,500,000. The project was approved in January 1931. A construction camp moved in from Gardiner to the western end of the plotted route, taking its heavy machinery down an old "tote road." From Red Lodge another army of workers moved slowly up the mountain sides. High shelves were carved in canyon walls to carry the road. The two crews met on the summit of Beartooth Plateau.

State 32 branches west from US 310 at ROCKVALE, 0 *m.* (3,483 alt., 25 pop.) *(see Tour 13).*

The Beartooth Mountains are straight ahead at 0.1 *m.*

At 2.2 *m.* is the junction with a graded road.

Left on this road to MONT AQUA HOT SPRINGS *(warm plunge, adm. 35¢; tub baths, automobile campgrounds, modern tourist cabins, dining room),* 0.5 *m.,* on Rock Creek, a tributary of Clark Fork of the Yellowstone. From a 4,100-foot well water emerges at a temperature of 112° F. It contains 255 grains of minerals to the gallon and is nationally marketed.

JOLIET, 5.8 *m.* (3,728 alt., 359 pop.), is a shipping point for produce of the irrigated valley.

BOYD, 11.1 *m.* (3,898 alt., 33 pop.), lies on a gentle slope amid sweeping acres of grain irrigated by water from the melting snows of the Beartooths. Livestock, sugar beets, corn, wheat, hay, vegetables, and honey are the principal products. Most of the farmers are Finns; every home has a log-house steam bath, similar to those used in Finland. Steam is created by throwing water on heated rocks.

ROBERTS, 19.6 *m.* (4,585 alt., 200 pop.), a shipping point for Rock Creek Valley produce, clusters about its elevators and railway station in the fashion of villages everywhere in agricultural districts.

FOX, 26 *m.* (5,048 alt., 25 pop.), is a railroad siding used as a loading point for livestock.

RED LODGE, 32.4 *m.* (5,548 alt., 3,026 pop.), a progressive mining town, is the seat of Carbon County. Legend recounts that it was originally called Bad Lodge because of meat that spoiled, thereby ruining a Crow festival.

SILVER RUN PEAK (12,610 alt.), second highest mountain in Montana (R), seems, in the clear air, much nearer than it really is.

Red Lodge is headquarters for expeditions of the American Museum of Natural History and other scientific groups studying paleontology *(see NATURAL SETTING).* A human tooth found several years ago in coal of the Fort Union formation near Red Lodge, together with petrified bones of prehistoric mammals, gave some evidence that human life may have existed here earlier than was previously believed.

A collection of 3,000 Indian relics is on display at the BEARTOOTH CURIO SHOP *(open by appointment),* N. Broadway. Specimens of frozen grasshoppers from Grasshopper Glacier are exhibited in the office of the *Carbon County News.*

The RED LODGE MUNICIPAL TOURIST PARK, 33.2 *m.,* by the highway at the southern edge of town, a project of the CWA and FERA, was built entirely of local stone and timber with the labor of Finns, Swedes, and Norwegians. The architecture is Scandinavian. A rock wall of the ancient Roman style, built by Italians, completely encloses it. A stone fountain and pool containing native trout is in the center of a landscaped plaza. There is also a wading pool for children. Each of the 54 rustic cabins has one, two, or three rooms, a bath, and a private garage, and is equipped with electric light, gas, and hot and cold water. There is a recreation ground and laundry.

THE SEE 'EM ALIVE ZOO *(open May 15–Sept. 15, 9-sundown; adm. adults 10¢, children 5¢),* 33.5 *m.,* has 47 species of game animals, birds, and fish native to Montana, in surroundings simulating the natural. The zoo owner operates a silver-fox farm.

ROCK CREEK CANYON, 36.9 *m.*, has a narrow entrance, buttressed (R) by jagged outcroppings of granite known as POINT OF ROCKS, and is in the Limestone Palisades. Rock Creek (L) flows swift and clear over boulders.

The GREENOUGH RANCH (L), 38 *m.*, is the home of "Pack Saddle" Ben Greenough, who for years has conducted pack trains over treacherous mountain trails. His son and daughter form a rodeo team. In 1935 "Turk" was named king of bronc riders and in the same year Alice rode to victory in the world championship Boston rodeo. She has also won acclaim for distinguished riding in Spain, Italy, and Australia.

In the background is MOUNT MAURICE (L), with the Beartooth Geological Research Camp at its northern base.

The highway ascends steeply between sheer cliffs and unusual rock formations in the rugged foothills of the Beartooths, and at 38.1 *m.*, crosses the boundary of the CUSTER NATIONAL FOREST.

SHERIDAN CAMPGROUNDS, 38.2 *m.*, well equipped and modern, is maintained by the U. S. Forest Service. WAPITI MOUNTAIN is R.

CAMP RATIN (L), 41.1 *m.*, in a pine-belted clearing, is reached by a rustic bridge crossing Rock Creek. SHERIDAN PEAK rises L.; and R. is Silver Run Plateau (10,925 alt.).

At 43.5 *m.* on State 32 is the junction with a dirt road.

Right on this road 0.3 *m.* to RICHEL LODGE *(cabins and saddle horses rented)*.

At 45.3 *m.* on State 32 is the junction with an improved dirt road.

Right on this road to PARKSIDE CAMP *(tables, outdoor stoves, running water, sanitary conveniences)*, 0.5 *m.*, maintained by the U. S. Forest Service on the bank of Wyoming Creek.

At 47.5 *m.* on State 32 is the junction with a dirt road.

Left on this road to TIN CAN CAMP, 0.7 *m.*, another Forest Service campground.

PRIMAL SWITCHBACK, 48.2 *m.* (7,895 alt.), is the lowest of four great switchbacks that in 16 miles carry the highway to an altitude of 10,995 feet. The hairpin marks the spot where the herculean task of carving the highway from the rocky Beartooth Mountains really began. At BIG FILL TURN, 48.6 *m.*, a gigantic earth fill carries the road across the mouth of a steep gulch. In the steep ascent here, vegetation zones are well illustrated. At the lowest switchback, the road enters a belt of Engelmann spruce, above the Douglas fir and lodgepole pine belt of the valley. The spruce gives way to subalpine fir, which, as it nears the limits of its altitudinal range, is found in dense bushlike groups. The occasional mountain meadows are starred with bright blossoms.

At 50.5 *m.* is a turn-out from which is viewed the Wyoming Creek Valley and the vertical cliffs rising to snow-capped peaks above it.

DEADWOOD SWITCHBACK, 51.5 *m.* (8,625 alt.), has WYOMING ROCK TURN, 53.4 *m.*, as its chief curve.

At 54.5 *m.* the highway winds around sinuous MAE WEST CURVE (9,285 alt.). From KNOX POINT, 54.9 *m.* (9,465 alt.), is a good view of the curve immediately below, and of the far-flung reaches of green valley, timbered slopes, and parklike meadows. Sturdy CROME MOUNTAIN is R. with MOUNT REARGUARD (12,350 alt.) back of it, farther west. In the northwest SILVER RUN PEAK rises above HELLROARING PLATEAU.

The highway crosses timber line, 55 *m.*, leaving the alpine fir belt, and passes into the arctic-alpine meadows found in the northern Rockies at this altitude. Snow is still packed on the summit in July, and in shady places along the highway throughout the summer. The flowers spring up at the edge of the retreating snow. The alpine poppy, carpet pink, white dryad, phacelia, fireweed, Rocky Mountain laurel, heather, delicate alpine columbine, and various daisies and asters mingle with the rich cover of grass and sedge. Stems are short and the period of blooming is brief; in August goldenrod and late aster nod among the drying fruits of the brilliant early flora.

The wind that sweeps unendingly over the plateau is chilling even on the hottest days. Only below timber line on the southern edge of the high bench is there shelter from it.

The highway crosses the Wyoming Line, 55.2 *m.* (10,234 alt.), which is also the boundary between the Custer and Shoshone National Forests. Between this point and 93.2 *m.* the route dips into Wyoming.

TWIN LAKES, 55.9 *m.* (10,697 alt.), lie (R) far below the road in a craggy cirque, on whose walls snow remains the entire year. A turn-out on the highway permits a wide view from parked cars. The aloofness and ageless grandeur of this plateau made it one of the eternal things to the Indians, and their imaginations invested it with a soul.

BENNETT CREEK DIVIDE, 61.2 *m.* (10,931 alt.), is the watershed between flanking ranges of the Beartooths. RUBY PEAK is R., NIG PEAK, L.; GARDINER LAKE (10,500 alt.) is (L) at 62.5 *m.* and MIRROR LAKE (10,738 alt.) is (R) at 63.6 *m.*

Short switchbacks lead to the SUMMIT, 64.9 *m.* (10,995 alt.), of Beartooth Plateau (9,500 average alt.). The highway here is close to the trail followed by Chief Joseph and his Nez Percé followers after the burning of Cooke, on their retreat from Idaho to Canada (see HISTORY). Far in the northwest is GRANITE PEAK (12,850 alt.), Montana's highest, a stone pyramid thrusting into clouds. The panorama unfolded from the road's summit is vast and impressive. A sea of sunny plateaus, shadowy gulches, and mountains—some timbered, some snow-capped—stretch away as far as the eye can see. The great reaches of primitive lake-speckled wilderness below are accessible only on foot, and trails are few.

Hawks swoop toward dark canyons, sunlight glinting on their wings. Near the road at the summit whistling marmots sun themselves on the rock slides.

PILOT PEAK (11,740 alt.), first climbed in 1930, is visible (L) at 65.7 *m.* Near it INDEX PEAK (11,977 alt.) rises like a spire.

FROZEN MAN'S CURVE, 66.2 *m.* (10,450 alt.), a double S, looks down (R) 186 feet on tiny FROZEN LAKE, whose surface is often ice-covered even in summer. State 32 crosses a narrow neck of LONG LAKE (9,640 alt.) at 70 *m.*

At 70.1 *m.* is the junction with a dirt road.

Left on this road to LONG LAKE CAMP, 0.5 *m.*, a modern Forest Service picnic and camp site.

LITTLE BEAR LAKE, 71.1 *m.* (9,549 alt.), is R.

At 72 *m.* is the junction with a narrow dirt road.

Right on this road to ISLAND LAKE and ISLAND LAKE CAMPGROUND, 0.5 *m.*

BEAR CREEK links several mountain lakes; the road crosses it at 72.6 *m.*, near the outlet of Island Lake. Here, at timber line, the road drops down again from alpine meadows into the alpine fir belt and then into the more varied flora of lower mountain meadows.

BEARTOOTH LAKE (9,000 alt.), 75.1 *m.* the most popular lake in the Beartooth Mountains, provides excellent trout fishing. On its pine-clad shores are a store, a gas station, tourist cabins, and boating and camping facilities. Above the lake rises BEARTOOTH BUTTE, its front bright with ocher tints; a great variety of fossils has been found in its exposed rock. The BEAR'S TOOTH (10,420 alt.), a landmark known to the earliest Indians, projects from its face and gives the range its name.

BEARTOOTH FALLS (L), 75.6 *m.*, are visible. In June, when snows from the high mountain ranges are melting, the falls are a foamy trough in the dark green of the pine-rimmed gorge.

INSPIRATION POINT (8,745 alt.), 77 *m.*, has a parking area offering a magnificent view of the densely timbered Clark Fork Valley (L), and the high peaks of Yellowstone National Park; to the north lies a region spattered with lakes. The abundant flora all about has the high colors common on mountain benchlands in spring; death camas, wild onion, bitterroot, larkspur, lupine, buttercup, wild pansy, Indian paintbrush, and penstemon thrust up vivid heads among the less conspicuous grasses and their relatives, dappling the green background with yellow, red, and varying shades of blue and purple. Engelmann spruce gives way to the familiar Douglas fir and lodgepole pine; along the streambanks are quaking aspen, willow, alder, and the bright-colored flowers of moister, more sheltered habitats. Mingling with the fragrance of alpine flowers is the pungence of sun-warmed balsam and of pitch. Deer and elk browse in the meadows; a bear occasionally appears in a green space to busy himself with an ant-inhabited log.

State 32 crosses LAKE CREEK, 83 *m.*, between two cascades that drop 40 feet from the brink of the dark forest, to tumble over rocky ledges below.

Forest Service camp sites are (L) at 87.6 *m.* The highway crosses Clark Fork of the Yellowstone, 88.2 *m.*, and follows it for about 6 miles.

State 32 crosses the Wyoming Line at 93.2 *m.* and re-enters Montana. At 97 *m.* is the junction with a dirt road.

Left on this road 0.5 *m.* to SODA BUTTE CAMP *(tables, benches, outdoor stoves, running water).*

COOKE, 97.9 *m.* (7,535 alt., 102 pop.), busy with bright gas pumps and the needs of hungry tourists, began life as a prospect hole in the early 1870's. Behind the modern refreshment stands are weathered cabins with moss-covered roofs, twisted and sagging with age, and around the town are mountains pitted with old diggings and laced with prospectors' trails. Up quiet gulches men still "take a pan" and watch eagerly as the circular swish of the water washes away the lighter gravel, and the residue of black sand and gold forms a thin line around the edge of the pan.

Before railroads were built into the northern mountain region, Cooke was the receiving point for goods shipped by boat up the Missouri and Yellowstone Rivers and then forwarded by stage and pack train over the winding trail through Red Lodge. Here Buffalo Bill's Indian trade goods were transshipped for Cody, Wyo. The boisterous shouts of miners, and the deep rumble of "rock in the box," mingled with the rattle and creak of the slow ox and mule freight teams.

In 1877 Chief Joseph and his Nez Percé, on their retreat to Canada *(see HISTORY),* swept through Cooke and burned the gold mills. New mills were built and work was resumed for a time, but the crude methods and equipment of the day were unequal to handling the poorer ores; the "flour" (gold so fine that it does not settle in the sluice box) was lost. When the best of the pay dirt was gone, the miners who had stampeded here to dig the million dollars' worth of gold with which Cooke is unofficially credited, packed their picks, pans, and square-bladed shovels, and wandered away to richer fields.

BEARTOOTH FALLS

For 50 years before the opening of State 32, Cooke stood isolated, little more than a legend to the rest of the world. Saloons and mills decayed. Chipmunks played on the trestles and raced on the flumes. Cabins, taken over by pack rats, tumbled down and grass grew in the paths.

The decaying ALLEN HOTEL, erected in the 1880's of rough-hewn logs, is typical of the old buildings. It contains pieces of mahogany furniture brought here in a covered wagon, and hooked rugs more than 100 years old.

Several trails leading from the town into the mountains are suitable for hiking or riding, but strangers should be careful not to stray from the well-defined .ones, particularly where timber is heavy.

Right from Cooke on a mountain trail to GRASSHOPPER GLACIER, 14 *m.*, cradled between ICEBERG PEAK and MOUNT WILSE. All but the last half mile can be made on horseback.

The almost perpendicular face of the 80-foot cliff of ice is marked with black lines of frozen grasshoppers. The most widely accepted explanation is that swarms of the insects, carried by wind to great altitudes, were chilled in passing over the glacier, and fell. Snows covered them. Succeeding hordes met the same fate, and the glacier became striped with black bands of the frozen insects, some of them 60 feet deep from the present surface. The process is still going on. Warm summer thaws sometimes free great numbers whose decomposition creates an unforgettable stench.

This glacier loses height in summer, but invariably builds up again in winter, thus providing a field of practical study of glacial formation and disintegration.

To the northeast is GRANITE PEAK (12,850 alt.), scaled for the first time in 1923 by Fred Inabit and U. S. Forest Service officials.

SILVER GATE, 99.8 *m.* (7,470 alt.), is a summer hamlet of stores, amusement centers, tourist cabins, hotels, and gas stations, all catering to tourists. Soda Butte Creek (L) flows through pleasant, wooded land. SILVER MOUNTAIN (R) rises above the village.

At 101.9 *m.* State 32 crosses the northeastern boundary of YELLOWSTONE NATIONAL PARK.

SILVER GATE, 102.3 *m.* (7,350 alt.), is an official entrance to Yellowstone National Park.

At 105.4 *m.* State 32 crosses the Wyoming Line, 28.9 miles east of Tower Falls Junction *(see WYOMING GUIDE).*

Tour 14

(Manyberries, Alberta)—Havre—Fort Benton—Great Falls; State 29. Canadian Border to Great Falls, 157.3 m.

Route served by Intermountain Transportation Co. busses between Havre and Great Falls; same section paralleled by Great Northern Ry. branch.

Hotels in larger towns; tourist camps at long and irregular intervals.
Roadbed graveled or graded dirt between Canadian Border and Havre; oil-surfaced
between Havre and Great Falls; oil-surfaced section open all seasons.

This route forms a great inverted check mark across north-central Montana, with the short stroke extending across the grazing and dry-land farming country of the Milk River Valley, the longer one across the broad fields and buffalo-grass ranges between Havre and Great Falls. The rolling plain is divided into benches by the Missouri, Marias, and Teton Rivers and their tributaries. The isolated Bearpaw and Highwood Ranges raise bold barriers to a far eastward view; in the blue-banked westward distance foothills of the Rockies are seen.

Almost anywhere on the prairie route the eerie howl of coyotes is heard nightly. White-tailed jack rabbits leap like small kangaroos in the glare of automobile headlights. By day an occasional rattlesnake crawls in the dust of the prairie or among the rocks of the broken country. Canadian geese break migratory flights to rest on the streams and lakes in spring and autumn. Pheasant and grouse nest along country lanes, and feed in the farmers' fields. In the coulees and along the creeks. bullberries, huckleberries, chokecherries, serviceberries, and wild raspberries grow profusely.

State 29, a continuation of an unnumbered Canadian road, crosses the Canadian Border, 0 *m.*, 51 miles southeast of Manyberries, Alberta. North of Havre State 29 is known as the Wild Horse Trail. Over this trail, in the late 1880's, large herds of longhorn cattle were driven to the Canadian Cypress Hills for fattening, and back to the railhead in Montana for shipment.

SIMPSON, 2.1 *m.* (2,630 alt., 14 pop.), a post office and general store, is cut off from the world in winter. The trim buildings of an occasional large wheat farm contrast sharply with the many deserted houses and ruined barns along the road in this area. Russian thistles and yellow-flowered wild mustard grow rank in untilled fields. Great patches of ground are white with alkali where water has evaporated from ponds and stream beds.

The Bearpaw Mountains are straight ahead at 30.8 *m.*

The LIGNITE MINES, 38.6 *m.* (R and L), are in veins near the surface; the coal is removed entirely by undermining, without blasting.

HAVRE, 39.3 *m.* (2,486 alt., 6,372 pop.) *(see Tour 2, sec. a),* is at the junction with US 2 *(see Tour 2).*

NORTHERN MONTANA COLLEGE, 40.3 *m.* *(see Tour 2, sec. a),* is R.

State 29, here the Old Forts Trail, follows the first overland route between Fort Benton and Fort Assiniboine *(see below).*

At 40.4 *m.* is the junction with a graveled road.

Left on this road to BEAVER CREEK PARK (State Park No. 1), 19 *m.* *(free, improved camp sites),* which extends across 12 miles of thickly wooded country along Beaver Creek.

The BEARPAW MOUNTAINS (L) are now seen for 15 miles.

At 46.9 *m.* is the junction with a dirt road.

Left on this road to FORT ASSINIBOINE, 1 *m.*, established in 1879 to prevent the return of Sitting Bull and his Sioux warriors from Canada, and to overawe the restless Blackfeet. Many years later John J. Pershing served as a cavalry officer here. In the middle 1930's the fort was used as a transient relief camp. Several of the first buildings remain. Their sturdy construction was made possible by the fact that the sand and clay of Beaver Creek make excellent brick. Men who understood the manufacture of brick were specially enlisted for the building period.

LAREDO, 53.7 *m.* (2,423 alt., 225 pop.), is a grain-shipping point. South of it the road passes through a stock-growing region. At about midsummer large haying crews work at cutting and stacking alfalfa for winter feed. The work, so far as possible, is mechanized; great two- and four-horse sweeps pick up the bunched or windrowed hay and deposit it on the huge-toothed wooden forks of the stacker, which raise it to the top of the stack. There one man—sometimes two—works like a titan to tear apart the tangled bunches with his pitchfork and place the hay where it is needed to build a symmetrical stack.

BOX ELDER, 63.8 *m.* (2,682 alt., 127 pop.), is headquarters of a livestock firm whose buildings surround the village.

Left from Box Elder on a graded road to ROCKY BOY, 14 *m.* (3,100 alt., 40 pop.), agency of the ROCKY BOY INDIAN RESERVATION *(camp permits on application to superintendent)*. Nearly 100 years ago a large band of Chippewa (Ojibwa) from near Red Lake, Minn., moved west. The Sioux, who greatly outnumbered them, drove them into Canada, where they joined their kinsmen the Cree, and Kinnisto-no *(three of us)*. They hunted buffalo in what is now Montana, frequently warring with the Blackfeet, especially the Pikuni. In the spring of 1885, incited to revolt, they fought Canadian troops, and lost. Their leader, Louis Riel, a quarterbreed partly educated for the priesthood, was captured, convicted of murder, and hanged.

The rebellion crushed, many of the Chippewa, led by Stone Child whom white men dubbed Rocky Boy, escaped to Montana, and brought with them a band of Cree led by Little Bear, who asserted he had been born in Wisconsin of a Chippewa mother. Lacking country or friends, they became known as the Rocky Boy renegades. Until the buffalo disappeared they lived well enough. Then settlers began to complain of them. "They're Canadians. Send 'em home!" they cried.

Escorted across the border by soldiers, the Indians headed straight back, preceding their escorts home. Old-timers chuckled and let them alone. But now they had to scratch for a living.

From deer and elk skins they made moccasins, shirts, and beaded belts, to sell to white men, until stopped by game laws. Then they lived by gathering thousands of tons of buffalo bones scattered over the plains and stacking them in immense piles at the railroad stations. When the bones were gone they gathered the horns, and polished them for souvenirs. When the horns, the buffalo's last gift to them, were gone, they faced starvation. They built flimsy huts, and made stoves of iron washtubs taken from city dumps to save their scanty fuel. These stoves overheated, and made the air in the huts so foul that sickness followed. Harried by police and ruffians, the Indian women searched garbage cans, gathered offal from slaughterhouses, and even used the flesh of the occasional horse or cow found dead on the plains for food.

When the old Fort Assiniboine Military Reservation was abandoned, friends of the Indians persuaded the Indian Bureau to set aside 580,388 acres as a home for the wandering Chippewa and Cree. In 1916, 451 Indians were placed on this land, which became the Rocky Boy Reservation. Lying in the Bearpaw Mountains, 4,000 to 5,000 feet above the sea, it was level only in small patches. Here the hungry Indians cut logs, built a huddle of small cabins, and lived for 10 years on the scanty rations issued by the Bureau of Indian Affairs, whose sole concern was to keep them from bothering settlers.

Then a new policy was inaugurated. The Government gave the Indians work, and provided food, clothing, farming machinery, and seed to the value of $600 a man. When this sum had been repaid with work, further credit enabled the men to buy cattle and build homes. A farmer was hired to teach improved agricultural methods to the tribesmen. A flour mill and sawmill were built to handle the wheat they grew and the logs cut on the reservation. Roads were built by Indian labor; 25 percent of each worker's wages was applied on his private debt.

Drought made the first years difficult; not all the Indians took kindly to the new system. Improvement has been steady, however; there is scarcely a slacker on the reservation, and the per capita debt to the Government is less than $70.

Surplus flour from the Rocky Boy mill is sold to other reservations, and the proceeds applied against the tribal debt. At first the flour was sold to nearby merchants, but outside millers objected. Lumber from the tribal sawmill is, however, sold to white settlers as well as tribesmen. Children attend attractive schools equipped with kitchen, bath, laundry, and electric lighting. School gardens produce thousands of dollars' worth of vegetables; fresh milk is sent to the schools by the agency.

Of the 750 Indians on the reservation, 90 are farmers. In 1935 they shipped 220 steers to market. Even the old people work at $1 a day rather than accept issue rations. In 1935 beadwork worth more than $2,000 was sold by the Indians.

BIG SANDY, 74.7 m. (2,703 alt., 633 pop.), is one of the storied cowtowns of the old West. Charles M. Russell and other well known riders spent many active years on nearby ranches. The places they frequented—the blacksmith shop, Rusty Brown's saloon, the general store—are gone, replaced by modern plants that serve a changed community. But the region remains a meeting ground of fact and fiction, for Big Sandy is Dry Lake of the Flying U novels of B. M. Bower *(see THE ARTS)*, in which the town is described as it was at the turn of the century. Every ranch on the bench south of the Bearpaw Mountains has been pointed out as the "Flying U"; the honor has clung with particular tenacity to the old Eagle Creek outfit. A dozen "original Chips of the Flying U" have announced themselves. Mrs. Bower herself told of one of her characters who came to life.

"I . . . saw him perfectly, although he was like no one I know . . . Then I chanced to attend a dance in the Big Sandy schoolhouse . . . Perched on a corner of the rostrum, swinging one foot and chewing gum while he gazed around with his baby blue eyes, sat Cal Emmett, natural as life . . . I blurted to the woman alongside me, 'There's Cal Emmett!' and felt like a fool afterwards . . .'"

VERONA, 80.7 m. (2,721 alt., 41 pop.), is a busy hamlet in early fall when grain is brought to the elevators and livestock is trailed to town for shipment.

The Sweetgrass Hills and the HUDSON BAY DIVIDE are R. at 98.6 m.

LOMA, 102.6 m. (2,513 alt., 74 pop.), is just west of the confluence of the Marias and Missouri Rivers. The Indians called the Marias "the River that scolds all others" but Capt. Meriwether Lewis renamed it in honor of his cousin Maria Wood. The Lewis and Clark party camped at the mouth of the stream on June 3, 1805.

In 1831 Fort Piegan, a trading post, was established here by James Kipp for the American Fur Company. A year later the post was abandoned and hostile Indians burned it.

FORT BENTON, 111.7 m. (2,600 alt., 1,109 pop.), seat of Chouteau County, is one of the oldest communities in Montana *(see HISTORY)*.

FORT BENTON, 1869

Built at the head of navigation on the Missouri River, it was one of the most important of the early posts. Supplies for the gold camps of western Montana were transshipped here. Food, clothing, powder and ball, whiskey, and tobacco received at Fort Benton and sent on by ox team and pack train to camp traders in Montana, Idaho, and Canada, helped to found many great fortunes. The post was the point of debarkation for thousands of tenderfeet anxious to reach the gold fields. One of Fort Benton's older hotels has preserved the high ceilings, plush furniture, and glittering glass chandeliers that were the last word of fashion in the 1870's and 1880's.

Fronting the river on Main St. are the TOURIST PARK and OLD FORT PARK. A monument to Lt. John Mullan *(see HISTORY)* who surveyed and supervised construction of a military road between Fort Benton and Walla Walla, Wash. stands near the entrance to the Old Fort Park. A memorial seat of stone perpetuates the name of Milton Milnar, a picturesque character of range days.

The RUINS OF THE OLD TRADING POST AND BLOCKHOUSE are in a 5-acre tract two blocks west of the tourist park. One building and parts of two others remain. The fort, 250 feet square and built of adobe, had bastions at two corners. There was no stockade. An outer wall 32 feet thick formed the back of the buildings, which all faced the center of the grounds. A larger gate and a small one faced the river. In 1870 the American Fur Company closed its business and leased the fort to the Government. The Seventh Infantry occupied it for a short time.

The Highwood Mountains (L), seen at 121.6 *m.*, are thickly timbered with fir and lodgepole pine; they are in the Lewis and Clark National Forest, and are of volcanic origin.

At 154.2 *m.* is the junction with an oil-surfaced road.

Left on this road to BLACK EAGLE (Little Chicago), 0.5 *m.* (3,287 alt., 1,000 pop.), an industrial suburb of Great Falls in which employees of the copper and zinc refineries live. Many of these workers are of Balkan birth or descent, and retain the Balkan customs and habits and use Slavonic dialects. The town was named for Black Eagle Falls on the Missouri River *(see GREAT FALLS).*

The road follows Smelter Ave. eastward.

The COPPER AND ZINC REDUCTION WORKS *(open weekdays; tours 10 and 2; 2 to 3 hrs. required),* 1.2 *m.,* are (R) on a terraced hillside overlooking Great Falls, outside its limits but highly important to its development and prosperity. All buildings are of the modern type, of brick, steel, and cement, well lighted and ventilated; angularity of the groupings and the flat roofs is somewhat relieved by curving roadways and tramways. When lighted at night, as it is except during heavy bird migrations in spring and fall (birds blinded by light strike the stack and are injured), the 506-foot smokestack is visible 40 miles away.

No smelting has been done here since 1918; operations are confined to electrolytic refining of the copper and zinc smelted at Anaconda, and to the making of copper wire, cable, and rods. In the copper refinery the 600-pound anodes received from the smelter *(see Tour 18)* are placed in large tanks, decomposed by electric action, and recomposed as purified cathode copper.

There are 1,530 tanks in a room 535 feet long and nearly half as wide. Before the electrolyzed copper can be used in manufacturing it is melted and cast into bars by the furnace refinery nearby. A third plant receives undissolved anode scraps from the tankroom, and melts and recasts them for further tank treatment. The rolling mills, the first of their kind west of the Mississippi, contain rod-making and wire-drawing machinery, annealing furnaces, and stranding machines for making cable.

The zinc refinery has four divisions, one for each of the processes used in refining: roasting, leaching, electrolyzing, and casting. It was built in 1916, soon after research chemists discovered the electrolytic method of refining that transformed zinc from a nuisance to a valuable product *(see INDUSTRY AND COMMERCE).*

A brick factory near the west end of the grounds is capable of turning out 35,000 building bricks a day. It also makes fire brick and tile.

Electric power used in the reduction works is obtained from plants along the Missouri River; the maximum demand is 85,000 horsepower. An electric railway transports materials between departments.

As the road goes eastward from the reduction works, it descends 600 feet to follow the river between walls of reddish shale and sandstone. At about 2.3 *m.* the water toward the farther side is clear nd blue where the Giant Springs *(see GREAT FALLS)* pour their flood into the normally muddy Missouri.

RAINBOW FALLS (R), 4.5 *m.,* tamed by a dam, recover a little of their wild beauty only at high water in May and early June. The drop is 48 feet. "Here," wrote Robert Vaughn in *Then and Now,* "the entire river, 1,200 feet wide, hurls itself over an unbroken rocky rim . . . into a vast . . . amphitheater where, when the sun is shining, a rainbow spans the river from bank to bank." The Indian name for Rainbow Falls was Napa's Snarling.

At the base of the rocky terraces is the hydroelectric plant (50,000 horsepower). The grounds are handsomely landscaped.

CROOKED FALLS (R), 4.8 *m.,* are well named. At about the center of the drop, a notch like a great arrowhead points far back upstream. The road winds along the rim of the river gorge, which grows steadily deeper. At 8.8 *m.* is the junction with a side road; R. here 0.9 *m.* to the top of VOLTA DAM, which is 65 feet high.

The road bends (L) away from the river.

At 11.7 *m.* is the junction with a side road; R. here 1.4 *m.,* down a steep hill covered with green-spiked yucca, to the GREAT (or BIG) FALLS (R), largest of the falls on the Missouri, which are also deprived of their impressiveness except at unusually high water. The drop is 77.8 feet. Said Robert Vaughn: "The river . . . is . . . confined between rocky walls . . . 200 to 500 feet in height and is about 300 yards in width . . . Nearly half the stream descends vertically with such . . . force as to send . . . spray . . . 200 feet or more in the air. The other side . . . is precipitated over successive ledges . . . A vast basin of surging waters succeeds below, its deep green color . . . betraying prodigious volume and depth."

Great lines of steel towers stalk across the countryside from the 90,000 horsepower hydroelectric plant here. Below the falls a footbridge connects the bank with LEWIS AND CLARK PARK on a rocky island. The park has a kitchen with free use of electric plates and ranges. William Clark was the first to map the area above and below the falls.

At 13.7 *m.* on the main road is the junction with a side road; R. here 3 *m.* to. MORONY DAM, the latest (1930) of the dams near Great Falls. This plant generates 70,000 horsepower.

At 156.7 *m.* is the junction with US 89 *(see Tour 4)* 0.6 mile west of the center of GREAT FALLS *(see GREAT FALLS).*

<<<<<<<<<<<<<<<<<<<<✕>>>>>>>>>>>>>>>>>>>>

Tour 15

Junction with US 10 S—Ennis—Junction with US 191; State 1, 98.7 m.

Route paralleled by Northern Pacific Ry. branch between Junction US 10 S and Norris.
Accommodations limited.
Oil-surfaced roadbed; closed in winter south of Hutchins.

State 1 traverses almost the entire length of the Madison Valley, a generally wide, rolling park land between mountain walls. Beginning a dozen miles west of the point where the Madison and two other rivers pour their waters together to form the mighty Missouri it approaches the Madison at McAllister, crosses it near Ennis, and follows it closely between Ennis and Yellowstone National Park. On the west the Tobacco Root Mountains, deeply green on slope and summit, shelter the valley; to the east the Madison Range lifts its amethyst tops into the sky. The slate-colored Gravelly Range, near the southern end of the route, resembles vast banks of flowing sand.

The ascent into the upper valley is gradual. Sometimes the road crosses foothills carpeted with sagebrush; the land rolls away on both sides like a tumbling gray-green sea. Sometimes it runs smoothly over large flats on which sheep and cattle graze. The route as a whole traverses one of the best fishing areas in the Northwest.

State 1 branches south from US 10 S, 0 *m. (see Tour 1, Sec. c)*, 12.9 miles west of Three Forks. At 0.7 *m.* it crosses the Jefferson River, the most westerly of the three streams that unite to form the Missouri *(see Tour 1, Sec. b).* The river was named as a memorial to the man who, more than any other, was responsible for the acquisition of the West and who promoted the Lewis and Clark expedition.

HARRISON, 8.4 *m.* (4,903 alt., 154 pop.), is a ranch town with a single street and a small cluster of homes. Visible (R) north-to-south are Jefferson Mountain (10,640 alt.), Hollow Top (10,513 alt.), and Potosi Peak (10,096 alt.), summits of the Tobacco Root Range *(see Tour 16).*

Right from Harrison on a dirt road is PONY, 6.5 *m.* (5,443 alt., 200 pop.), trade center of an old mining district that returned to activity with the rise in metal values in the 1930's. The district has a number of placer and hard-rock claims.

The road southwestward through POTOSI CANYON in the Tobacco Root Mountains is a pine-scented lane, overhung and shaded by boughs. The summits of the mountains are often obscured by clouds. In a natural park, at the base of one, lies POTOSI HOT SPRINGS, 13.5 *m.*, with campground and swimming pool *(adm. 35¢).* Mule deer, bear, bighorn sheep, and elk often approach the springs. Within three miles are large tungsten deposits.

SURE SHOT LAKE, 15.6 *m.*, affords good trout fishing. In this lake lives the larval salamander known as axolotl.

NORRIS, 18.7 *m.* (4,848 alt., 75 pop.), sits snugly among cottonwoods in a dip between two hills. It is the center of a mining district with a history of large production from both placers and lodes. Corundum of gem quality is found in the placer diggings.

NORRIS PLUNGE, a community club project, is supplied with hot mineral water that flows out of the side of NORRIS HILL (L).

State 1 winds over Norris Hill. From the summit, 24.3 *m.* (5,300 alt.), is unfolded a panorama of the Madison Valley. Ennis Lake lies below (L).

McALLISTER, 28.7 *m.*, is a general store and post office. Ward Peak (10,267 alt.) is the most prominent summit (L) of the Madison Range in this vicinity.

Left from McAllister on a dirt road to ENNIS LAKE, 1 *m.*, the first of the hydroelectric projects on the Madison; it is merely an artificial widening of the stream, but that does not detract from the excellence of its rainbow trout fishing *(boats available).* Brief sudden squalls have taken several lives here. The road circles the lake, and gives access to many parts of the shore, and to cabins and dude ranches around it.

At 35.2 *m.* is a junction with State 34 *(see Tour 16).*

ENNIS, 35.3 *m.* (4,927 alt., 400 pop.), a typical western village of wide streets and one-story frame buildings, is shaded by the abrupt bulk of Fan Mountain (L) and in summer by its own willows, alders, and poplars. It was named for William Ennis, who came to Bannack (Grasshopper Gulch) in 1863, and later homesteaded on this site.

Right from Ennis on a dirt road to THOMPSON HOT SPRINGS, 1 *m.*, which has a warm plunge *(adm. 25¢).*

CAMERON, 46.4 *m.* (4,820 alt., 19 pop.), is a hamlet in the range district of the upper Madison. Rich grass grows on the untimbered lands around it. The Sphinx (10,860 alt.) is a peak (L) that vaguely resembles the Great Sphinx of Gizeh.

South of Cameron the country is an almost unfenced range. The wide upland valley has no towns and few ranch homes. Mounted men tend herds of cattle and flocks of sheep along the highway.

The MADISON PALISADES, 61.5 *m.*, rich sun-bright yellow and ruddy brown, tower above the plunging river.

HUTCHINS, 69.8 *m.* (4,637 alt., 8 pop.), is a ranch resort.

Right from Hutchins on a dirt road crossing the Madison River to a side road, 5 *m.;* R. on the side road to CLIFF and WADE LAKES, 7 *m. (cabins and boats).* From Cliff Lake 25-pound rainbow trout have been taken.

The main dirt road goes south through a forest of stunted pines broken by mountain meadows to RAYNOLDS PASS, 14 *m.* (about 6,050 alt.). In June 1860 Jim Bridger led a party of scientists under escort of Captain Raynolds, an army engineer, through this gap in the Continental Divide. Captain Raynolds reported: "This pass is so level that it is difficult to locate the exact point at which the waters divide. I named it Low Pass and deem it . . . one of the most remarkable . . . features of . . . the Rocky Mountains."

At Raynolds Pass the road joins a dirt road into the Henry's Lake region of Idaho *(see Tour 1, IDAHO GUIDE).*

At 77.8 *m.* the character of the country changes abruptly as the road swings sharply L. and enters MADISON CANYON. The highway winds through a shadowy evergreen forest where the river flows swiftly between buttressed banks; angular patches of sky show in the gaps between toothed and plumed summits.

BEAVER CREEK CAMPGROUND, 82.2 *m.*, is an improved site maintained by the Forest Service.

HEBGEN DAM *(fishing not permitted above footbridge)*, 85.3 *m.*, backs up the Madison to form a lake about 21 miles long and in places 5 miles wide. To some extent it controls the waters of the upper Missouri, and assures a steady flow for the hydroelectric plants downstream.

The highway follows the shore line of HEBGEN LAKE (R). The canyon widens to a broad plateau covered with parched gray sagebrush. Winds, dust-dry in summer, snow-laden in winter, lash this upland. The sky line of the Continental Divide (R) curves southward and eastward into Wyoming.

GRAYLING, 94.4 *m.* (6,675 alt., 5 pop.), is a lonely post office near one of the extremities of the lake.

At 98.7 *m.* is the junction with US 191 *(see Tour 5)*, at the boundary of Yellowstone National Park.

<<<<<<<<<<<<<<<<<<<✿>>>>>>>>>>>>>>>>>>>

Tour 16

Junction with US 10 S—Twin Bridges—Virginia City—Ennis; State 41 and State 34.
Junction US 10 S to Ennis, 69.8 m.

Route served by daily busses; paralleled at intervals between junction with US 10 S and Laurin by Northern Pacific Ry. branch.
Hotels in towns, tourist camps and campgrounds along route.
Oil-surfaced roadbed for 15.6 miles south of junction with US 10 S; graded dirt elsewhere.

Before this road was straightened and numbered, it was called the Vigilante Trail, one of the earliest routes of travel in Montana and part of a stage road between Last Chance Gulch (Helena) and Alder Gulch (Virginia City). South of Twin Bridges it was part of the route between Virginia City and Bannack (Grasshopper Gulch). As such it was closely associated with the activities of the road agents and of the men who, under the symbol "3-7-77," organized to clear them out of the territory.

White men first penetrated the region long before the time of the vigilantes. In 1805 Lewis and Clark camped in the Beaverhead valley and named the rivers. In 1810 Pierre Menard and Andrew Henry set traps along the waterways. In July 1840 Father De Smet crossed the Continental Divide near the headwaters of the Beaverhead, followed the Beaverhead to the Jefferson, and the Jefferson to the Missouri. In the presence of hundreds of Indians, he conducted the first Christian services in Montana.

Much of the region traversed by this route is semiarid, with hills, canyons, clumps of alder, greasewood, and sagebrush against a sky line of mountains—a land whose pitted hillsides, torn gravel bars, and diverted streams are like the scars of old wounds.

State 41 branches south from US 10 S, 0 *m.*, 6 miles west of Whitehall *(see Tour 1, Sec. c).*

SILVER STAR, 12.2 *m.* (4,538 alt., 35 pop.), a station on a branch of the Northern Pacific Ry., serves a small but fertile irrigated area in the Jefferson Valley. It is one of the oldest Montana villages. The Jefferson River (L) is here a winding stream of rapids with deep pools in which trout lie.

At BARKELL HOT SPRINGS (L), 12.9 *m.*, are a warm plunge *(adm. 35¢)* and campgrounds.

The road crosses the Jefferson River at 16.1 *m.* The prominent peak in the Tobacco Root Mountains (L) is Hollow Top (10,513 alt.). The name of the range is derived from a variety of the bitterroot that grows abundantly there. Shoshone Indians called it quee, and ate the roots; French voyageurs called it racine de tabac *(tobacco root)*, because, when cooked, it smelled like tobacco. The few white men who attempted to eat it became nauseated.

TWIN BRIDGES, 23.9 *m.* (4,868 alt., 671 pop.), is near the confluence of the tributaries of the Jefferson that Lewis and Clark in 1805 named Philosophy, Wisdom, and Philanthropy, for President Jefferson's "cardinal virtues." Philosophy became Willow Creek; Wisdom, the Big Hole River. Philanthropy was known for a time as the Passamari (Shoshone, *evil smelling)*, or the Stinking Water; then it became Ruby River. The earlier name referred, not to the crystalline waters of the river itself, but to sulphur springs near it.

The STATE ORPHANS' HOME *(open 2-4:30 weekdays when school is not in session; 10:30-11:30 and 2-4 Sun.)*, 3 blocks west of the center of town, was created by legislative act of 1893 to care for Montana's orphans, foundlings, and destitute children. The four modified Colonial-type brick cottages normally accommodate 200 children. A small brick hospital of modern functional design has a resident staff and is equipped to give medical and surgical care. A dairy herd and gardens are maintained. After the children have graduated from the home's elementary school, they attend Twin Bridges High School.

Right from Twin Bridges on State 41, a graded dirt road, to BEAVERHEAD ROCK (L), 13 *m.*, the great landmark, named by the Indians for its form, that helped Sacajawea *(see HISTORY)* identify this region as her home. It is 300 feet high and almost perpendicular; the Beaverhead River sweeps around its base. Seams in the rock contain crystals. Warm springs bubble up nearby.

Opposite the rock and beyond the river is BLAINE (4,987 alt.), a country post office.

At 27 *m.* on State 41 is the junction with US 91 *(see Tour 6, sec. c)*.

Left from State 41 at Twin Bridges on State 34, a graded dirt road.

The RUBY MOUNTAINS (R), 27.3 *m.*, a short range, were named for garnets found there, at first believed to be rubies.

SHERIDAN, 34.2 *m.* (5,079 alt., 525 pop.), named for Gen. Philip H. Sheridan, Civil War cavalry leader, is set in a sheltered bay of rich Ruby Valley farm land. It is headquarters for silver, lead, and gold mining operations in the Tobacco Root Mountains; mining gossip runs through the village like an electric current. There are four trout streams within walking distance of town.

ROBBERS' ROOST *(customary tip 25¢-50¢)*, 39.6 *m.*, is (L) in a fenced grove near a farmhouse. The rambling two-story log structure is approached through a turnstile; immediately within the gate is the old hitching rail where desperadoes' horses were tied. The ground-level porch, supported by logs, extends the length of the house and a similar veranda is accessible from the second story. In a large room (L) on the first floor is the bar at which many a dusty traveler of the 1860's quenched his thirst. The other furnishings were left by successive tenants. Pack rats inhabit the building; the doors swing on broken hinges, and the interior is stained with rain that has beaten in through open windows.

In 1863 Robbers' Roost was a stage station known as Pete Daly's Place. Most of the ground floor was a barroom, the undivided upper floor a dance hall. Here Sheriff Henry Plummer and his cutthroat associates, who called themselves "Innocents," planned their deeds of violence *(see HISTORY)*.

Nearing Laurin, the road crosses a region where fine herds of livestock graze.

LAURIN (pronounced Lawray), 43.1 *m.* (5,058 alt., 45 pop.), was originally the ranch of J. B. Laurin. The church (L) of local stone was his gift to the town.

1. Right from Laurin on an unimproved road that crosses the Ruby River to HANGMAN'S TREE, 0.3 *m.* Here Erastus (Red) Yager and G. W. Brown, messenger and secretary of Plummer's gang, were hanged on January 4, 1864 *(see HISTORY)*.

ROBBERS' ROOST

2. Right from Laurin on a dirt road is ALDER, 2.2 *m.* (5,128 alt., 158 pop.), sitting at the base of an unnamed mountain (L) and protected by a thick growth of cottonwood and alder along the river (R). The terminus of a Northern Pacific Ry. branch from Whitehall, it is a shipping point for livestock and farm produce of the Ruby Valley and for ore from Virginia City.

The highway skirts a series of conical mounds of gravel and boulders in the lower end of Alder Gulch. These mounds are the tailings left by a dredge that worked 11 miles of the gulch before and during the World War. The dredge, installed under the auspices of Harvard University, is locally declared to have enriched that institution by several million dollars.

RUBY, 47.6 *m.* (5,202 alt., 30 pop.), is now a cluster of miners' cabins, mud-chinked and sod-roofed, with a frame store and gas station. In the 1860's it was a crowded mining camp.

The Vigilante Trail turns R. up Alder Gulch. In the early 1860's the gulch was a continuous avenue of claims and miners' cabins. The ground was worked by sinking a shaft and drifting (tunneling) on bedrock; then the rich sand and gravel were hoisted to the surface and washed in a rocker or Long Tom. In the tailings that border the creek (R) are beams and bits of wood, the debris of pioneer operations.

NEVADA, 54.5 *m.* (5,267 alt.), a group of abandoned, crumbling buildings, was part of Virginia City in the first turbulent years of the Alder Gulch rush. Here is the site of the trial and hanging of George Ives, the first of Plummer's gang to meet punishment.

A GOLD DREDGE *(visited on application at office in Montana Power Bldg., Virginia City)* operates between Nevada and Virginia City.

VIRGINIA CITY, 55.7 *m.* (5,760 alt., 242 pop.), was the first in-corporated town in Montana (January 1864) and the second Territorial capital *(see Tour 6, Sec. c)*. Though it has kept a mere fraction of its boom-time population, it is one of the few gold camps that have long maintained existence. Prospectors still outfit in its stores, and dredge workers make it their home.

In May 1863 six miners led by young Bill Fairweather entered the hill country along the Madison River. The story of the next few days is told in the *Journal* of Henry Edgar, a member of the party:

"We crossed the Madison and came up . . . Wigwam Gulch. We camped beside a lake at the foot of Bald Mountain. We killed an elk there, and remained during the afternoon and overnight to dry and smoke the meat.

"The day after, we came down the lake and over the ridge. That was on May 26, 1863, about 4 o'clock in the afternoon . . . Fairweather and I were to make camp and stand guard. The other four proceeded up the gulch . . . prospecting. About sundown Bill went across the creek to picket the horses.

" 'There is a piece of bedrock projecting,' said Bill, 'and we had better go over and see if we cannot get enough money to buy a little tobacco.' So Bill took the pick and shovel and I took a pan and we crossed the creek. He dug the dirt up and shoveled it into the pan. I went down the creek to wash it. While I was washing the dirt, he scratched around in the bedrock with his butcher knife and . . . called: 'I've found a scad!'

"I had the pan about half washed down, and I replied: 'If you have one I have a thousand.' And so I had . . .

"We washed about three pans before dark and the three aggregated $12 and some cents . . . The other four returned tired and hostile because we hadn't taken care of the horses . . . I showed Sweeney what we had . . . 'Salted, by God,' exclaimed Sweeney.

" 'You know well enough if you pike me down and run me through a sluice you couldn't get a color,' I said . . ."

The first day after the discovery the six miners panned out about $180.

"We were tired and hungry and all out of provisions . . . Our supper consisted of antelope straight . . . We spent the next morning measuring the ground and staking it off . . .

" 'What shall we call the Gulch?' I asked. 'You name it,' Barney Hughes said. So I called it Alder Gulch on account of the heavy clump of alders along the . . . creek."

After a few days the party went to Bannack for supplies. They agreed to say nothing of their find, but the secret was written on their faces. Edgar wrote:

"Friends on every side. Bob Dempsey grabbed our horses and cared for them. Frank Buff got us to his cabin. Salt Lake eggs, ham, potatoes, everything! Such a supper!"

When the prospectors started back to their bonanza on June 2, the trail was crowded. At Beaverhead Rock a meeting was called, and a set of rules was drawn up to govern the claims. On June 6 the caravan reached

ROAD AGENTS' GRAVES, BOOTHILL CEMETERY, VIRGINIA CITY

Alder Gulch. "This is the creek," Edgar shouted, and the stampede began. Hustling, swarming life filled the gulch from Bald Mountain to the
valley of the Passamari.

Southern sympathizers among the gold seekers called the new town in
the gulch Varina, in honor of the wife of Jefferson Davis; but when Dr.
G. G. Bissel, a northerner and a miners' judge, was asked to head a legal
document with that name, he said "I'll see you damned first!" and wrote
it "Virginia." Because this name was as dear to the South as the other,
nobody objected. There was at first no safe way of shipping out the
millions in gold that the Alder Gulch placers yielded. The only stage route
was the one to Bannack. There was no post office in the Territory; letters
were carried from Salt Lake City across 475 miles of unsettled country,
first at $2.50 each, later at $1. Money was sent to the nearest express
office in private hands. The outlaws attracted by such conditions *(see
HISTORY)* were able to form, under Henry Plummer's leadership, an
amazing organization, complete with officers, secretary, and spies, that
for a time had everything its own way. Coaches were plundered and
scores of men were murdered. No relief by legal means was possible, for
no one within 400 miles had authority to administer an oath. Henry
Plummer, the bandit leader, was miners' sheriff. The robbery and murder
of the inoffensive Dutchman Nicholas Thiebalt for two hundred dollars

in gold dust brought matters to a crisis. George Ives, the killer, was apprehended, tried by a miners' court, and hanged *(see HISTORY)*. Other hangings followed in rapid succession; the vigilantes, first organized in Virginia City, spread to other mining camps, and remained active for several years. Their history was at first an honorable one, but the motives for some of their later deeds have been questioned. Several books have been written about them, both by men of their own day and by later investigators *(see THE ARTS)*.

CONTENT CORNER, Wallace and Jackson Sts., was the hub of activities at the height of the gold rush. The Territorial officers' building, on the southeast corner, is used as a grocery. The building opposite, once occupied by the *Montana Post*, the Territory's first newspaper, is now a hotel barroom.

The SITE OF THE VIGILANTE HANGINGS, Wallace and Van Buren Sts., is covered by a frame office building. Here the road agents George Lane, Boone Helm, Frank Parrish, Haze Lyons, and Jack Gallagher were strung up on January 14, 1864. Across the street is the SITE OF THE FIVE-STORY HOTEL, which was razed in 1935. This building was the subject of many jokes in the early days. Every stage driver on the way to Virginia City sang the glories and comforts of the five-story hotel. For its day, it was comfortable enough, but the five stories were in reality five successive levels on a steep hillside, each level one story high.

The THOMPSON MUSEUM *(open daily 9-5 in summer; 2-5 in winter)*, east end of Wallace St., contains many relics of the gold stampede days. Built of granite, in marked contrast with the whitewashed one-story cabins nearby, it was given to the town by William Boyce Thompson, a wealthy New Yorker who was born and reared in Virginia City. Its records and pioneer mementos are carefully cataloged. Picks and pans, packsaddles, muzzle-loading rifles, cap-and-ball pistols, Indian arrows and hunting equipment—all have a place here, carefully guarded but always available to the student. Among the irreplaceable items are bills of lading from shippers in St. Louis for goods sent up the Missouri River to Fort Benton and then by ox team overland to Virginia City. Proof of the hardships of pioneer life is contained in such things as bills for flour at $150 a sack. There are many old pictures.

The PLANT OF THE VIRGINIA CITY MADISONIAN *(open to visitors)*, Wallace St., has turned out a weekly grist of local history since the days of the vigilantes. Among the rafters in the rear room hang a number of yellowed knapsacks marked "U.S.," looking very much as they did when they were discarded one day in 1877 by a group of Virginia City men who had taken to the field to save their homes from a threatened attack by Chief Joseph *(see HISTORY)*. Hastily armed and equipped, they had rushed to the front only to find the Indians gone. Tired and disgruntled, they returned and tossed the knapsacks on the rafters, where they have been left undisturbed.

1. Left from Virginia City on Jackson St., which becomes a trail, to the SITE OF THE ALDER GULCH DISCOVERY, 0.3 *m.* A bronze monument has been placed here by Montana pioneers.

2. Right from Virginia City on Wallace St. to BUMMER DAN'S BAR, 0.8 *m.*, on the north side of Alder Gulch. It is not a place to drink. During the gold rush the camp was bothered by one Dan, who constantly begged and often filched food, but would not work. In a saloon one day Dan saw a patron order pie, a luxurious item in those days. When the pie was brought in, Dan snatched and quickly ate it. Instead of regarding the act as a joke, the patron called a camp meeting; it was the opinion of the camp that Dan should go to work. He was given a claim high on the side of the gulch, was loaned a pick and pan, and told to hop to it or get out. Dan went to work, and within a few weeks struck it rich. After panning thousands of dollars' worth of gold, he decided to go to the States, but was robbed on the way, and returned to Virginia City to bum once more.

3. Left from Virginia City on a dirt road to BOOTHILL, 0.4 *m.*, a low butte on which are the graves of road agents hanged in the town. Here, too, the GRAVE OF BILL FAIRWEATHER overlooks the site of the discovery that gave millions in gold to the world. Fairweather did not value his wealth; it was his pleasure to ride up the main street of Virginia City and scatter "dust" right and left to madly scrambling children and Chinese. After selling his claims in Alder Gulch, he prospected on the Peace River, and in Alaska from 1868 to 1872. In 1875, at the age of 39, he died at Robbers' Roost *(see above)*.

East of Virginia City State 34 winds over a barren mountain. From the summit, 58.1 *m.*, the Madison Range is seen ahead, a distant dark barrier. The road descends in a series of switchbacks through a country of brown and gray-green buttes scantily forested with scrub fir and jack pine.

ENNIS, 69.8 *m.* (4,927 alt., 278 pop.) *(see Tour 15)*, is at the junction with State 1 *(see Tour 15)*.

‹‹‹‹‹‹‹‹‹‹‹‹‹‹‹‹‹‹‹‹❀›››››››››››››››››››››

Tour 17

(Bowman, N. D.)—Baker—Miles City; US 12.
North Dakota Line to Miles City, 95.2 m.

Route paralleled by Chicago, Milwaukee, St. Paul & Pacific R. R. between North Dakota Line and Plevna.
Hotels in larger towns; tourist camps at Miles City.
Graveled roadbed between North Dakota Line and Plevna; oil-surfaced between Plevna and Miles City; open all seasons.

US 12 traverses a country that is often parched in summer, bleak and snow-bound in winter. Relentless sun and wind, driving hail, and swarming insect pests contribute to the desolation. The rolling semi-arid table-lands are briefly green in spring; then, except in rare rainy years, brown. Irregular masses of colored rock, predominantly brick red, crop out among the wind- and sun-cured grasses on the hills. Jack rabbits, gophers, coyotes, lizards, and rattlesnakes thrive on the scanty rations of the land; little mounds mark the villages of prairie dogs. Hawks and occasional eagles swoop and soar in search of prey.

Though great stretches here seem almost uninhabited, many dry-land farms challenge the stinginess of nature and defy the extremes of weather to which the region is subject.

Lying far from the important pioneer trails, this country saw little of the white man until the cattle kings appeared. Only traders and trappers from Fort Union to the north and from Yellowstone posts to the west visited the area, which until 1880 remained a buffalo range and an Indian campground. Then great herds of longhorn cattle from Texas spread out fanwise from the Powder River Trail. The winter of 1886–87 depopulated the ranges; it took years to build up the herds again. Only the more persistent cowmen stayed to become actual settlers.

Lignite coal, abundant throughout the region, is mined for local use.

US 12 crosses the North Dakota Line, 0 *m.*, 32 miles west of Bowman, N. D.

BAKER, 12.5 *m.* (2,929 alt., 1,212 pop.), seat of Fallon County, began as a camping place on the Custer Trail between Wibaux *(see Tour 1, sec. a)* and Camp Crook, S. D., because surface springs and grass were abundant here. The settlement that grew up was first known as Lorraine; it was renamed in 1908 to honor A. G. Baker, superintendent of construction on the Milwaukee Road. Wagon ruts of the old trail are still seen near town.

A typical market town in a grazing and farming region, Baker is exceptional only in being almost in the center of a great gas field *(see INDUSTRY AND COMMERCE)*, which extends southward 30 miles and northward almost to Glendive. A driller seeking water here in 1915 found gas; the well became ignited and remained a natural torch for six years. Three distinct gas sands have since been found in the Baker structure and now 200 wells are producing commercially.

BAKER LAKE, on the southeastern side of town, is an artificial body created in 1908 when a small creek was dammed to insure a water supply for locomotive boilers. The mile-long lake has become increasingly alkaline, and artesian wells have been bored to bring up good water; the lake now supplies recreational needs.

On the COURTHOUSE GROUNDS, near the southwestern edge of town, are PETRIFIED and AGATIZED TREES brought in from the surrounding country. Many of the varicolored specimens came from Cannonball Butte *(see below)* and from the region southwest of Baker. A specimen of giant sequoia in chalcedony is proof that this was once semitropical country.

The THOMAS CROW PLACE, two blocks west of the courthouse, has a cottage surrounded by terraced gardens *(open on application)* bordered with thousands of pieces of petrified and agatized wood of varied forms and colors, and with bits of lava, rose quartz, obsidian, petrified moss, marine fossils, and the tusks of prehistoric mammals.

1 Right from Baker on a graded dirt road to CANNONBALL BUTTE, 30 *m.*, on the southern extremity of a badlands area. Rounded, projecting sandstone formations extend from a butte that resembles the Rock of Gibraltar.

MEDICINE ROCKS

2. Left from Baker on State 7, an improved road, into the least developed part of Montana's plains. Badlands make up one-fourth of the region; side roads are twin tracks in the dust when the weather is dry, ribbons of greasy mud when it is wet. Many of the people living here dwell in makeshift shacks or in dugouts along shadeless streambanks; modern comforts are almost unknown. The available water has an unpleasant taste, and is so hard that it can be used for washing only with difficulty.

Most of the country is a rolling plain best suited to livestock production, but some crops are grown. Hills in the ordinary sense are rare, but rocky heights rise abruptly from the plain, affording a series of views of amazing sweep. The layers of sandstone, shale, clay, and various sedimentary materials enclose a wealth of fossils. It is a strange region, isolated and rude, but fascinating.

At 8.4 *m.* is the junction with a dirt road; L. here 10 *m.* to the 101 RANCH, established by the Standard Cattle Company of Texas in 1888 when new range was sought in the Northwest. Several herds of longhorn cattle, each containing 3,000 or 4,000 head, left Texas in the spring and arrived in the North in October. The 101 was the steer ranch; the stock or calf ranch was in Wyoming, where the herds wintered after the long summer on the trail. Each spring 30,000 two-year-olds were driven into Montana from the calf ranch; at autumn roundup time they were driven from the 101 Ranch to Wibaux *(see Tour 1, Sec. a)* for shipment to Chicago stock markets. The 101 brand is still used but the ranch is much reduced in size. Of the early improvements only the corrals remain.

On State 7 at the approach to a bridge, 28.1 *m.*, is the junction with a dirt road; R. here 3.4 *m.* to MEDICINE ROCKS, described by Theodore Roosevelt as "fantastically beautiful." Some of these strange sandstone buttes, which cover about one square mile, tower as sharp peaks or ridges 80 feet above low, sandy hills. Others have flat tops 25 to 200 feet wide. Eroded by wind and rain, they exhibit a confusion of spirals, columns, archways, caves, escarpments, and pyramids. In strong sunlight the rocky buttresses appear chalky white above the flowing sands; in moonlight they have the splendor of molten silver. The crannies in the rocks appear gray against the white, intensely black against the silver, and the whole has an effect of eerie unreality. The name of the rocks comes down from a time when Indian medicine men circled among them in weird ritual dances. Until white men came, several of the buttes bore Indian inscriptions. Among the names later carved on the sandstone is that of Theodore Roosevelt, whose stock ranch at Medora, N. D., was only a day's ride away.

At 36.7 *m.* on State 7 is a junction with State 30; L. here 23 *m.* to MILL IRON, a small streambank settlement that grew up on a ranch connected with the Hashknife spread, which ranged 65,000 cattle in Montana.

Between 36.7 *m.* and Ekalaka State 7 and State 30 run southwest together.

EKALAKA, 40.3 *m.* (3,031 alt., 475 pop.), dubbed Puptown because of the prairie dogs in its vicinity, began as a deadfall (saloon) for cowboys. Claude Carter, its founder, a buffalo hunter and bartender, was on his way to another building site, when his broncos balked at pulling his load of logs through a mudhole at this spot. Carter stopped the plunging animals. "Hell," he said, "any place in Montana is a good place to build a saloon." He began the erection of the Old Stand then and there. For more than 50 years its bar catered profitably to Carter County punchers.

Ekalaka was named for an Indian girl, Ijkalaka (Sioux, *swift one*) a niece of Sitting Bull. Women were the camp movers when the Sioux were on the trail, and Ijkalaka, the quickest breaker of camp, was honored with a name expressing her ability. In 1875 David Harrison Russell, the first white homesteader here, married Ijkalaka, and in 1881 he brought her to the little community that had grown up around the Old Stand. It was her home until her death in 1901.

After 50 years of cowtown existence, Ekalaka emerged as a fairly modern and ambitious village. As seat of Carter County, it has a high school with 120 students, some of whom travel 90 miles to reach it. Electricity for lighting is generated by a Diesel-powered plant installed in 1935. A city water system is maintained, though many homes still use wells. Two hotels, two garages, three stores, a theater, and a bank provide necessary community services. Commodities are trucked in from Baker.

The HIGH SCHOOL MUSEUM *(open)* exhibits a Triceratops skull 6 feet long, with excellently preserved supra-orbital horns and hood; a collection of plant and marine fossils; leg and toe bones of Tyrannosaurus rex; parts of Trachodon; teeth and tusks of a mastodon; primate vertebrae; fragments of prehistoric alligators and turtles; and the remains of an unidentified oreodont mammal. All were collected in Carter County.

At Ekalaka is the junction with State 30; R. here 2 *m.* to the junction with a dirt road; L. 25 *m.* to CHALK BUTTES, whose sheer white cliffs rise 20 to 30 feet above piny hilltops. On a butte known as STARVATION ROCK, according to legend, an Indian tribe once found refuge from its enemies, and guarded the single ascent until every member was dead of hunger and thirst.

PLEVNA, 26.7 *m.* (2,757 alt., 258 pop.), a neat village of white cottages and red elevators on Sandstone Creek, was settled largely by Russians after the building of the Milwaukee Road in 1907. It was named for a city in Bulgaria that was captured by Russian forces in 1877. The 200 families in the village and on small farms nearby retain many Russian peasant customs. Women wear the traditional small black head shawl; at meals the food is placed in a single large dish in the center of the table and all at the table eat from it. The Russian feast days are kept, and folk dances enliven community gatherings.

All about Plevna are fields of wheat, flax, oats, barley, rye, potatoes, and hay, less than 10 percent of which is grown on irrigated land. Every spring, farmers' tractors and teams move down the long fields, each tractor and team drawing a disk harrow, a drill, or some other of the implements of dry-land tillage. Each machine moves in a cloud of choking gray dust; the horses, in four- and eight-horse teams, snort at the dust and flies, and nod rhythmically as they throw the weight of lathered bodies against the harness. At other times horses and men toil at another task familiar on Montana farms—the clearing away of large and small boulders, which are loaded on wagons or stone boats and hauled out of the way, usually to a coulee, a gravelly knoll, or a fence corner. The largest ones are dragged out with heavy chains, often by the use of tractor power.

As summer advances into the critical days of June and early July, when the moisture reserves of winter have been exhausted by growing crops, the farmer is anxiously aware of every small cloud, every change in the direction of the lightest breeze. No other human creature is so whole-heartedly weather-conscious as the man who must force a living from land such as this. If it hasn't rained by the Fourth of July, the green fields and pastures turn brown, cattle begin to lose weight, and the long-suffering dry-lander tightens his belt once again.

If rain has come, harvest begins in August. Whirring machines—binders, headers, combines—cut wide swaths in the grain, and leave harsh, dust-gray stubble to catch next winter's snow. Threshing machines roar and cough; wind stackers moan and vomit straw. The indefinable yet unforgettable smells of chaff, steam, and warming metal parts mingle in the air with the stronger reek of oil and gasoline. Teams of draft horses plod to town, drawing wagons equipped with flareboarded grain tanks, and are passed on the way by modern trucks similarly equipped.

Before 1925 the threshing season normally began after all grain had been cut, and often continued into November. Mountainous yellow straw-stacks adorned every farmyard and field. When newfangled machines combined the operations of reaping and threshing, this season, once the heyday of the migratory worker, was cut to a few days in most communities. To take the place of the straw that had formerly been used for feed but was now left in the fields, where it was burned or plowed under, farmers bought hay shipped from the western valleys.

A service station (L) at 66.1 *m.* offers curios.

US 12 crosses Powder River, 66.3 *m.*, here fringed with cottonwood, ash, and various berrybushes. A popular description of the stream asserts that "she's 400 miles long, a mile wide, an inch deep, and runs uphill."

In this area the cowpuncher does his stuff with rope and rein, then goes to town to blow in his pay. If he is a "top hand," this may be as much as $50 a month and board; if he is an ordinary rider, it is $30 or $35. The saloon and the blackjack table usually get a generous share of it, though occasionally there is a puncher who saves his money, and invests in a herd of his own.

The road now enters rough country; high buttes marked with outcroppings of red shale support a scanty growth of jack pine. For many miles bare hills alternate with good grazing land; in places the soil is reddish.

At 93.7 *m.* is the junction with US 10 *(see Tour 1)*. Between this junction and Miles City US 10 and US 12 are one route.

MILES CITY, 95.2 *m.* (2,357 alt., 7,175 pop.) *(see Tour 1, sec. a)*, is at a junction with US 10 *(see Tour 1)* and State 22 *(see Tour 10)*.

◄◄◄◄◄◄◄◄◄◄◄◄◄◄◄◄◄◄◄◄◄◄◄◄☼➤➤➤➤➤➤➤➤➤➤➤➤➤➤➤➤➤➤➤➤➤

Tour 18

Junction with US 10 S—Anaconda—Philipsburg—Drummond; US 10 A.
Junction with US 10 S to Drummond, 66.8 m.

Route served by busses; roughly paralleled by Butte, Anaconda & Pacific R. R. between Butte and Anaconda, and by a Northern Pacific Ry. branch between Philipsburg and Drummond.
Accommodations limited except at Anaconda and Philipsburg.
Concrete roadbed between junction with US 10 S and Anaconda, oil-surfaced roadbed between Anaconda and Drummond; open all seasons.

Between the junction with US 10 S and Anaconda US 10 A is Montana's first paved road (1922). This section, with that between Anaconda and Georgetown Lake, is called the Lakes Trail. The entire route runs through a rugged region of mountains and barren hills. It rises slowly to Georgetown Lake, along a valley that is sometimes a canyon between pine-dark mountains; then it scales Flint Creek Hill and slides windingly down into Flint Creek Valley, a region rich in fishing streams and big game.

US 10 A branches west from US 10 S, 0 m. (see Tour 1, Sec. c), 14.8 miles west of Butte.

At 0.5 m. is the junction with a graveled road.

Left on this road to GREGSON HOT SPRINGS, 1.5 m. (see Tour 1, Sec. c).

At 7.1 m. on US 10 A is the junction with an oiled road.

Right on this road 2.1 m. to the 16-room EVANS HOUSE (open May–Nov.), built by Mrs. Gwenellen Evans in 1860 on the first plot of Montana land held by a woman. Both exterior and interior are well preserved. The original carpets, draperies, plush-covered furniture, square piano, 16-foot mirrors, and huge walnut doors and staircase remain. The rooms are filled with curios from many parts of the world.

The Washoe Smelter (L), with its huge smokestack, is seen at 8.2 m.
BURNT HILL (L), was once, according to legend, the scene of a battle between two Indian tribes. The losing tribe, to escape annihilation, fired the timber that covered the hill, and screened by the fire, found sanctuary beyond the mountain.

Slipping between desolate gray piles of slag, the road crosses Anaconda's bare front yard and follows Park Ave., which leads to Main St.

ANACONDA, 10.7 m. (5,331 alt., 12,494 pop.), set at the mouth of a narrow valley near the Continental Divide, is almost entirely dependent on the smelting of copper and zinc ores mined near Butte. When copper is in demand, the city has a smelter pay roll of about 3,500 men and is prosperous and, on the whole, content; when the market is sluggish and only skeleton crews work the town suffers.

For a smelter city a mile above sea level, Anaconda is not unattractive.

SMELTER, ANACONDA

It has many pleasant modern homes, with trees and lawns, to contrast with massive, pillared and turreted structures of the gingerbread period. Its streets are paved and well lighted. But the business section lacks liveliness except when copper is high. Certain districts are overcrowded and in the original settlement on the north side many old log buildings and flimsy frame houses of the mining-camp type are still in use.

Anaconda has an interest for sports that was encouraged by Marcus Daly, whose horses ran in important races both in America and England. The old race track, opposite Washoe Park, has been made into an athletic field. The city's recreational activities reach an annual climax in the Winter Sports Carnival *(see RECREATION),* which features ski jumping on Oimoen Hill, just south of the city.

Marcus Daly, the originator of Montana's copper industry, personally picked this place for the construction of a copper smelter because of its nearness to ample water and limestone. Daly's decisions were often abrupt and made by rule of thumb. While looking over the site, he saw a cow standing meditatively in the valley. "Main Street," he said to his engineers, "will run north and south straight through that cow."

The city, first called Copperopolis, was platted in 1883. When the postmaster, Clinton H. Moore, learned that a Copperopolis already existed in Meagher County, he looked about for a new name, and thought of the important Anaconda Mine in Butte. Mike Hickey, the discoverer of the

Anaconda, had named it after reading in an account of the closing campaign of the Civil War that "Grant encircled Lee like a giant anaconda." Moore chose Anaconda as the name for the new city. The aptness of this second name has been demonstrated by the entire social and economic history of Montana.

Anaconda expanded with the development of the copper industry, which about 1900 outgrew the smelter on the north side of town. A new one was erected farther south. Daly had high ambitions for the city he had founded, and was eager to see it grow. Old-timers say that when the Montana Hotel was being completed in 1888, the energetic Irishman stepped to a point of vantage across the street, took a good look at its two modest stories, then shook his head. "It doesn't look big enough," he said. "Put another story on it."

But Daly's plans for the city were not always successful. In 1889 he founded the Anaconda *Standard* to urge Anaconda's candidacy in the campaign for State capital. To impress the city's aliveness on the public mind, he gave the paper the make-up and features of a metropolitan daily. The candidate lost *(see HISTORY)*, but the campaign publication did better. In 1931, when the paper was reduced to tabloid size because of the growth of the *Montana Standard* of Butte, the news magazine *Time* devoted several columns to its history, stressing the fact that when the city had only 3,000 people the Anaconda *Standard* outbid the New York *Herald* for artists to prepare one of the first colored comic sections published in the Nation.

Among Anaconda's first inhabitants, people of Irish stock were predominant, but after 1900 there was a heavy influx of workers from the Balkan countries. Though, to a limited extent, the people of each national strain kept their own customs, beliefs, and distinctive organizations, all were soon bound together by their dependence on copper. Labor unions grew in strength, and eventually won such things for the workers as employment insurance, a system of "rights" depending on length of service, and wages based on the price of copper *(see HISTORY)*.

The MONTANA HOTEL, Main St. and Park Ave., is a three-story brick structure that is still proud of its bar, a reproduction of one in the old Hoffman House of New York. The woodwork is of Philippine mahogany, the floor of alternate strips of redwood and maple. Inlaid in the floor is a mosaic of Daly's race horse Tammany. A fresco of beer steins and ale glasses adorns the wall. It is said that late one night Daly arrived at the hotel, unannounced and unrecognized, and found the place filled. A printer just leaving for night duty on the *Standard* offered the stranger his room, "hoping he was a whisky drummer and might leave me a quart." Next morning the hotel manager informed the printer that from then on his rent was to be free.

The HEARST FREE LIBRARY *(open 10-9 weekdays)*, Main and 4th Sts., has more than 90,000 books and many newspapers and magazines, housed in a two-story brick building of simple design. The building was given to the city by Mrs. Phoebe Hearst, mother of William Randolph Hearst. The Hearsts were among Daly's original backers.

The CITY COMMON, a square bounded by Main, Hickory, 3rd, and

4th Sts., is given over to the children as a baseball field in summer and a skating rink in winter.

Left from Anaconda on 4th St., which becomes an improved road to the WASHOE SMELTER *(open 1 p.m. weekdays; guides)*, 1 *m.*, one of the largest copper smelters in the world. Its angular groups of brick and steel sheds cover the side of a hill surmounted by an enormous smokestack. Between the sheds and the stack extends a main flue half a mile long; from a distance it looks like a huge misshapen hot-water bottle flattened against the hill. The mountainsides for miles around are ugly and bare, or covered only with gaunt dead timber, destroyed, before the stack was built, by poisonous smelter fumes.

The stack, one of the landmarks of western Montana, rises 585 feet, has a diameter of 75 feet at the base and 60 feet at the top, and discharges 3 to 4 million cubic feet of gas a minute. Nearly 7,000,000 bricks were used in its construction.

Nearly all the zinc and copper ores mined in Montana are concentrated and smelted at this plant. Ore is hauled from Butte by the electrified Butte, Anaconda & Pacific R. R., delivered to high-line tracks in 50-ton cars, and dumped into bins by a rotary car dumper that can handle 1,000 tons an hour. It goes to a central crushing plant, and is then conveyed to the concentrating department, a close-set group of buildings left of the flue whose roofs give a terraced effect. Here the pulverized ore is passed through various screens, classifiers, and filters to great batteries of flotation machines.

In the flotation method of concentration the heavier minerals are made to float in water, while the lighter minerals sink. This phenomenon takes place when finely ground ore, with small quantities of oil and chemical substances added, is agitated and aerated. Some of the oil and chemicals cling to the heavy mineral particles; the mineral particles cling to air bubbles, which, because of the film of oil, expand without breaking and rise as froth to the surface. The method has been so perfected that certain minerals can be prevented from entering the froth if this is desired. In copper concentration, the iron-bearing minerals are to a large extent rejected. This is called selective flotation.

From the concentrators the ore goes to roasting furnaces where it is dried, and part of its sulphur is fumed off. It is then mixed with fluxing materials (limestone, silica, iron) and sent to reverberatory furnaces. There the slag is "tapped off," and the enriched copper product (matte) is drawn into 13-ton ladles and carried to buildings that contain rows of spectacular, pot-shaped, flame-belching converter furnaces, which produce "blister" copper, 98 percent pure. Further treated in refining furnaces, the metal is molded into slabs called anodes *(see Tour 14)*.

The LEACHING PLANT contains 12 great tanks in which tailings are treated with diluted sulphuric acid for recovery of copper that is present in the form of carbonates. The solution obtained is sent through scrap iron precipitating plants *(see BUTTE)*, where the metallic copper is recovered.

The ZINC PLANT is divided into concentrating, roasting, leaching, electrolyzing, and casting departments. The double lead-zinc concentrates *(see INDUSTRY AND COMMERCE)* are produced by selective flotation. In the electrolytic department are great tanks that hold the electrolyte solution from which the pure zinc is deposited on aluminum cathodes.

Lesser plants among the smelter group extract white arsenic from furnace fumes and flue dust, and manufacture wood preservatives, sulphuric acid, and phosphate fertilizer. A foundry and brick factory supply the smelter with the castings, fire brick, and building brick it requires.

US 10 A goes west from Anaconda on Park Ave.

The ANACONDA TOURIST PARK (R), 10.9 *m.*, is maintained by the city. *(Outdoor fireplaces, wood, water, and comfortable cabins.)*

At 11 *m.* is the junction with an improved road.

Right on this road to WASHOE PARK, 0.5 *m.*, a 15-acre playground *(picnic tables, benches, outdoor stoves, dance pavilion, tennis courts, swimming pool, artificial lake, fish hatchery)* with a zoo containing buffalo, bear, deer, antelope, and other large and small animals. Warm Springs Creek flows through the shady expanse of trees, shrubs, and lawn.

The wild, tumbled peaks of the Anaconda Range are on the L.

The highway crosses the boundary of the DEER LODGE NATIONAL FOREST at 19.8 m. Lodgepole pine predominates, with smaller stands of Douglas fir and Engelmann spruce in scattered areas. Near timber line are alpine fir and limber pine. Elk, deer, bighorn sheep, and mountain goats find pasture on the higher slopes; there are ducks on the rivers and lakes, and grouse in the smaller timber.

A FOUNTAIN (R), 21.2 m., was built of local stone by the State Highway Commission.

At 23.7 m. is a junction with a graveled road.

Right on this road to CABLE, 6 m., marked by the abandoned buildings of the ATLANTIC CABLE MINE, so named to commemorate the laying of the second transatlantic cable. Alexander Aiken, Jonas Stow, and John Pearson discovered the mine in June 1867 while tracking their horses, which had wandered into this neighborhood from their camp on Flint Creek. The ground was so rich that a cigar box full of samples of it was worth $1,000. Its estimated subsequent production of $6,500,-000 in gold included a nugget sold for $19,000 to W. A. Clark, who asserted that it was the largest ever found. Mill machinery was imported from Swansea, Wales, and freighted to the mine from Corinne, Utah, the nearest railhead. Mill whistles had been unknown in the Northwest up to that time; the old steamboat whistle installed by owners of the Cable Mine blew a blast audible twelve miles away on clear days.

Stow and Pearson sold their shares in the mine for $10,000 each. Aiken could not agree with his new partners, and became involved in lawsuits which wiped out his fortune. He left the country on foot, with his blankets on his back.

SILVER LAKE (L), 24.9 m., is a natural reservoir from which water is piped to the Anaconda smelter. Because of low water in this and adjoining lakes, work at the smelter was curtailed during the spring and summer of 1937 until lakes higher in the mountains could be tapped for an added supply.

The GOLD COIN MINE (R), 25.8 m., is an active gold producer that was once abandoned in the belief that its pockets were worked out.

GEORGETOWN LAKE (L), 26.5 m., an irregularly shaped artificial body, was created to supply hydroelectric power. Several fine summer homes are on its shores and it is noted for its large rainbow trout. During the winter of 1936–37 thousands of fish died in the lake because of a lack of oxygen caused by low water, long-continued ice cover, and a large amount of decaying organic matter.

The GEORGETOWN FISH HATCHERY (L), 27 m., is maintained by the State

GEORGETOWN, 27.3 m. (5,570 alt.), has cabins, a store, and boats that are rented to lake fishermen. Half a mile to the right are a few residences, the remains of an older Georgetown, built before US 10 A was routed along the lakeside.

Right from Georgetown on a forest road to SOUTHERN CROSS, 2 m., an almost deserted mining camp on the shoulder of Iron Mountain. Here a rich mine was abandoned because of flows of water that could not be pumped out. Vacant houses stand among the ore dumps, and rusty mining machinery lies scattered about. In all directions stretches a dark carpet of evergreens, unbroken except for a few bare

CONVERTERS

summits and an occasional patch of blue-gray water on the valley floor. Unemployed miners from Butte often prospect in the district.

ECHO LAKE *(boats available)*, 3.5 *m.*, is a favorite retreat for residents of Butte and Anaconda, whose summer homes line the shore.

At the summit of FLINT CREEK HILL, 29.2 *m.*, is a good view of the Continental Divide (L). The road descends Flint Creek Hill between walls of blue, orange-red, and brown rock.

At 34 *m.* is the junction with State 38 *(see Tour 7, Sec. c)*.

PORTER'S CORNERS, 34.4 *m.*, is a store and service station.

The road enters the broad Flint Creek Valley.

PHILIPSBURG, 40.1 *m.* (5,195 alt., 1,355 pop.), seat of Granite County, is a silver town whose mines also produce manganese *(see INDUSTRY AND COMMERCE)*. It clings precariously on the flank of a spur of the Rockies.

Luxurious automobiles move along its hilly streets, and stop before very simple houses. Bright sport outfits, smart street clothes, and white flannels mingle in democratic informality with calked boots, overalls, and mackinaws, at the talkies, on the streets, and in the homes.

Settled in 1866, Philipsburg was named for Philip Deidesheimer, superintendent of a silver-mining company. The county is named for a mountain of granite north of town, on which is the site of one of the region's first and richest mines *(see HISTORY)*.

HOPE MILL, one block south of Main St., is a ten-stamp silver mill built in 1867 to handle the free-milling ores from the Hope Mine, a mile north of town. It was the first silver mill in Montana. During Indian troubles it served as a fort.

The town is in a particularly good fishing region; at an Angler's Club fish-fry of 1928, 1,500 guests were fed with fish caught in one day in Rock Creek *(see Tour 7, Sec. c)*, 12 miles west of Philipsburg.

Right from Philipsburg on a dirt road to GRANITE, 1 *m.*, a bustling silver camp until 1893, when it was abandoned after the drop in the value of silver. The GRANITE BIMETALLIC AND HOPE MINES are nearby.

US 10 A goes north down the Flint Creek Valley, a grain and livestock region. At 52.1 *m.* is the junction with an improved road.

Left on this road is MAXVILLE, 0.2 *m.* (4,852 alt., 50 pop.), a distribution point once known as Flint. The name, changed to honor the first postmaster and merchant, R. R. Macleod, was intended to be Macville.

Between Maxville and Hall is (R) a stretch of man-made badlands, the result of hydraulic mining. Glacial deposits, immeasurably older, extend (L) along the valley floor.

HALL, 60.4 *m.* (4,215 alt., 151 pop.), is a livestock-shipping point. The Northern Pacific right-of-way in this vicinity was acquired from Henry Hall.

DRUMMOND, 66.8 *m.* (3,967 alt., 363 pop.) *(see Tour 1, Sec. d)*, is at the junction with US 10 *(see Tour 1)*.

Glacier National Park

(International Peace Park)

General Information

Season: Official season June 15 to Sept. 15; but entrances not closed to travel at earlier and later dates. Going-to-the-Sun Highway never clear of snow across the Continental Divide before June 15, but generally passable until sometime in October. Western entrance at Belton open all year; road beyond kept free of snow to Lake McDonald.

Administrative Offices: Park headquarters just inside W. entrance; address, Belton. Glacier Park Hotel Co. and Glacier Park Transport Co., Glacier Park Station; Glacier Park Saddle Horse Co., Kalispell, or, in summer, Glacier Park Station.

Admission: Free. Automobile permit $1, issued at any entrance during season.

Transportation: Park reached by Great Northern Ry. and US 2 *(Tour 2)* through Glacier Park Station (E) and Belton (W); by US 89 *(Tour 4)*, N. and SE.; by US 91 *(Tour 6)*, N. and SW.

Busses from Great Falls to Glacier Park Station in summer. Daily bus service within the park; Glacier Park Station to Two Medicine, St. Mary, Many Glacier, Waterton Lake, Going-to-the-Sun, Lake McDonald, and Belton; Belton to Lake McDonald, Logan Pass on the Continental Divide, Going-to-the-Sun, and St. Mary. Connections at St. Mary to Many Glacier, Waterton Lake, and Glacier Park Station. Glacier Park Transport Co. and Glacier Park Hotel Co. jointly offer all-expense tours by bus, ranging from $17 for 1 day to $42.50 for three days.

Saddle horses available at Glacier Park, Many Glacier, and Lake McDonald Hotels, Going-to-the-Sun Chalets, and Goathaunt Tent Camp. At Two Medicine Chalets, horses for local rides only. Trails total 900 *m.* Horseback trip expenses vary according to size of party and type of accommodation used. Average rate per person for 1-day trip in group with horses, guide, and box lunch, $5-$6. All-expense trips of several days, with stop each night at chalet or tent camp, about $10 a day per person. Private camping parties, with guide, cook, and other help, $11 to $27 a day per person. Experienced riders can use horses without guide at $1 an hr., $3 for 4 hr., $5 for 8 hr. *(see TRAIL TOURS)*.

Launch on Waterton Lake between Goathaunt Camp and Waterton Lake town site (Prince of Wales Hotel), Alta. (fare 75¢); on Josephine and Swiftcurrent Lakes from Many Glacier Hotel ($1); on Two Medicine Lake (75¢); Lake McDonald (75¢). Rowboats available at hotels and chalets on Two Medicine, St. Mary, Swiftcurrent, Josephine, Crossley, Red Eagle, and McDonald Lakes; 50¢ an hr., $2.50 a day. Outboard motors can also be rented.

Accommodations: Three hotels (Glacier Park, Many Glacier, Lake Mc-Donald); eight chalets (Two Medicine, Cut Bank, St. Mary, Many Glacier, Going-to-the-Sun, Granite Park, Sperry, Belton). Rates: Hotels, $6.50 to $14 a day American plan, $4.50 to $11 European plan; breakfast and lunch $1, dinner $1.50. Chalets, bed usually $2, breakfast and lunch 75¢, dinner $1. Going-to-the-Sun Chalet slightly higher for special accommodations. Ten percent discount for stay of week or more at one place.

Tent camps at Goathaunt on Waterton Lake, at Fifty Mountain on the Continental Divide in Kootenai Pass, and at Crossley Lake; used principally by saddle-horse parties, but open to hikers.

Privately owned cabins on Lake McDonald rented to tourists. Many tourist camps outside park along US 2 and 89, especially at Glacier Park Station and Belton. Rates lower than in park.

Free public automobile campgrounds, with pure water, firewood, cook stoves, and sanitary facilities, at Two Medicine, Cut Bank, Roes Creek, and Many Glacier on E. side; at Avalanche Creek, Sprague Creek (near Lake McDonald Hotel), Fish Creek (near Apgar), and Bowman Lake on W. side.

Climate, Clothing, Equipment: Riding breeches, golf pants, or slacks with puttees worn by both men and women. Shorts not good for hiking because trails are often closely fringed with bushes. Many hikers wear khaki, but wool is preferable to absorb sweat by day and to give warmth in evening. Stout shoes with thick soles essential for hiking on rocky trails; should be large enough to enable wearing of two pairs of socks, one pair thick wool. Warm sweater or jacket on trips; waterproof slicker is tied behind the cantle on every saddle horse.

All essential clothing and equipment can be purchased or rented at Glacier Park, Many Glacier, and Lake McDonald Hotels *(see STATE GENERAL INFORMATION).*

Medical Service: Trained nurses at hotels, resident physician at Glacier Park Hotel. In emergency a physician can be summoned by telephone from outside the park.

Post Offices: Mail forwarded to hotels and chalets. Mail to E. side should be addressed *via Glacier Park;* W. side, *via Belton.*

Communication and Express Service: Telephone, telegraph available at inns and ranger stations; express service to concentration points. Hand baggage (c.25 lb) free on busses; may be checked at entrances or re-checked to point of departure. No storage charges during trips.

Naturalist Service: Ranger naturalists at Many Glacier, Going-to-the-Sun, Two Medicine, Lake McDonald, Sprague Creek, Roes Creek Campground, and Avalanche Creek Campground deliver lectures, answer questions, conduct local field trips and campfire entertainments, and arrange flower exhibits.

Warnings and Regulations: Build fires only at designated places; be sure they are out before leaving them. Be careful with cigarettes, cigars, pipe ashes, and matches.

Speed limit of 35 m.p.h. must be reduced to 15 m. on sharp curves and in passing hotels and campgrounds. Keep cars in lower gears on grades. *Hunting or trapping prohibited.* Do not feed bears or leave foodstuffs where they can break into the containers; leave with camp tender, or hang in box out of reach. Do not pick flowers; get permit to collect specimens for scientific purposes. Do not destroy or injure natural features. Dead and fallen wood may be used for fires. *To camp* at other than designated campgrounds, obtain permit from ranger; leave campground clean; put refuse in containers provided, or bury it. (Get additional information in park.)

Best Fishing: (No license required, but get a copy of seasonal regulations as to limit, etc.) Two Medicine Lake—eastern brook and rainbow; Cut Bank Creek—eastern brook and cutthroat; St. Mary Lake—Mackinaw, cutthroat, rainbow; Red Eagle Lake and Creek—large cutthroat; Gunsight Lake—rainbow; Lake Sherburne—pike, whitefish, rainbow, cutthroat; Swiftcurrent, Josephine, Grinnell, and Ptarmigan Lakes—cutthroat, eastern brook, rainbow; Cracker Lake—small black-spot; Kennedy Creek—grayling, cutthroat; Belly River—large rainbow, cutthroat, grayling; Crossley Lakes—Mackinaw, cutthroat; Elizabeth Lake—rainbow, grayling; Waterton Lake—Mackinaw, cutthroat; Lake Francis—rainbow; Lake McDonald—cutthroat, Dolly Varden, western whitefish; Fish, Snyder, Avalanche, Lincoln, Trout, and Arrow Lakes—cutthroat; Lake Ellen Wilson—eastern brook; Harrison Lake—cutthroat; Logging, Quartz, Bowman, and Kintla Lakes—cutthroat, Dolly Varden. Excellent fishing in forks of Flathead River.

Centers of Interest: Outstanding scenery at Two Medicine, Red Eagle, Going-to-the-Sun, Many Glacier, Belly River Valley, Goathaunt, Granite Park, Logan Pass, Avalanche, Sperry, and North Fork. At Glacier Park Station, Blackfeet Indians camp, sing, dance, and tell stories. Water sports at Two Medicine, St. Mary (shingle beach), Going-to-the-Sun, Many Glacier, Goathaunt (launch from Waterton Lake village in Canada), Lake McDonald. Wild, primitive country in the North Fork, Two Medicine, Many Glacier, Goathaunt, and Granite Park regions; abundance of mountain flowers; animals such as mountain sheep and goats. Glaciers and first-rate climbing at Going-to-the-Sun (largest glacier in park), Many Glacier (best place to see mountain sheep), Logan Pass, and Sperry. Forest fire damage at Granite Park mars one of best views in park. On Logan Pass, brilliantly flowered meadows called Hanging Gardens are framed among high peaks. Abundance of huckleberries at Avalanche.

GLACIER NATIONAL PARK (1,534 sq. m.) straddles the Continental Divide between the Canadian boundary and Marias and Theodore Roosevelt Passes; it stretches from the Great Plains to the North Fork of the Flathead River. Its latitude and altitude make the climate temperate during short summers, cold and snow-blanketed through long winters. The heavy snows keep its streams full in summer, and feed gleaming emerald lakes and resplendent waterfalls.

The mountains of the park are young and spectacular—segments of the continental backbone, with a glacier, a lake, and a singing stream in every interstice. On the west the ascent to the summit is gradual—on the east the slope is so abrupt as to amount to an escarpment, a result of the Lewis overthrust fault, which uplifted and shoved the park area 15 to 25 miles out over the plains. On the eastern side there is an abrupt change from rolling shadeless plain to tremendously rugged timbered country. The sixty large and small glaciers that give the park its name are not strictly "rivers of ice," like those in Alaska and the Alps, but remnants of such rivers; they are bedded in glacial cirques and cling to high benches and northern slopes; every year they recede slightly. They have, however, all the glacial characteristics—movement, crevassed surface, and morainal deposits—but their day is spent. If there is no climatic change, they will be gone in a thousand years.

While the glaciers enhance the glory of the scene they are high in the mountains and accessible only by trail. The park is a wild mountainous area with an unusually wide range of appeal. To a rider the peak of appreciation may come as he dangles a leg over a thousand vertical feet of space; to a fisherman, when, knee deep in a rushing stream, he brings to net a fighting rainbow; to the hiker when he meets a bear or mountain goat on some high trail; to the picture hunter when he catches a bull moose wallowing along the edge of a marsh. Some will find the greatest lure in the loneliness of a summit.

The park is rimmed by roads, but there is only one highway across it. The most beautiful and dramatic spots are reached by foot and bridle trails that branch from the low roads and lead up valleys separated by the high, forested ridges of the generally impassable main range. Going-to-the-Sun Highway traverses a representative part of the park; nevertheless, valleys threaded only by trails have a charm impossible to places scarred with road cuts and tunnels. The area has infinite variety, and to know it well, visitors must come back for many seasons.

Adjoining, across the international line, is Canada's Waterton Lakes National Park, a limited area with topography and scenery like that of Glacier Park. Dedicated in 1932 as an international park, a symbol of the peaceful relationship between Canada and the United States, the joint area straddles the only long unfortified international boundary in the world. The two parks are under separate managements that cooperate closely.

The first white man in the Glacier Park area was probably Hugh Monroe, a Hudson's Bay Company trapper known to the Blackfeet as Rising Wolf, who arrived about 1815, and married a Piegan woman. The Blackfeet say that Father De Smet visited the region in 1846 and gave the name St. Mary to two mountain lakes shown to him by Monroe. The origin of the name is not otherwise explained.

The story of Marias Pass, which bounds the park on the south, is one of the most unusual in western annals. In 1806 Meriwether Lewis approached

LITTLE CHIEF MOUNTAIN

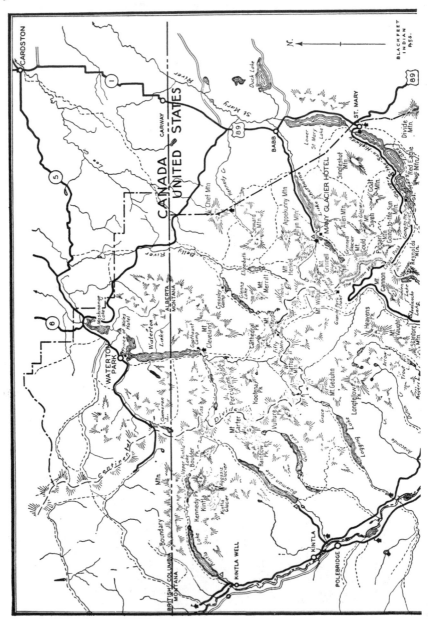

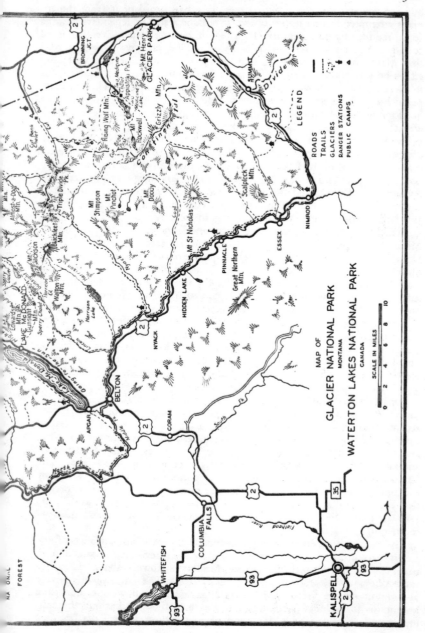

MAP OF
GLACIER NATIONAL PARK
MONTANA
and
WATERTON LAKES NATIONAL PARK
CANADA

SCALE IN MILES

LEGEND

ROADS
TRAILS
GLACIERS
RANGER STATIONS
PUBLIC CAMPS

but did not enter it. Later several men who had heard of it from the Indians attempted to find it, but failed. It became a sort of legendary passage for three-fourths of a century. In 1889, it became imperative that it be found as a route for a northern transcontinental railway. It is on record that Major Baldwin actually discovered it in October of that year; but either he was not given credit for it, or his report needed verification, for in December John Stevens set out from the East to find it. Though hampered by the lateness of the season and deserted by his superstitious Flathead guide, he set up his instruments on the plain near the present Meriwether station, took a bearing on the elusive gap, discernible from that point, and on December 11 walked into it. The Great Northern completed its road in 1892. In 1895 settlers cut a narrow trail through heavy timber from Belton to Lake McDonald. George Snyder shipped a steamboat to the lake and built a log hotel. Dr. Lyman B. Sperry penetrated to Avalanche Lake, reached the glacier that bears his name, saw the beautiful lake now called Ellen Wilson, and convinced the Great Northern's Jim Hill of the lucrative tourist business in store for his railway.

After 1900 mining excitement threatened an inrush of prospectors. Mining men persuaded Congress to obtain an area east of the Divide from the Blackfeet, but no ore of consequence was found. In 1898 rumors of oil had been disproved but because of them a 50-mile road had been cut from the foot of Lake McDonald to the foot of Kintla Lake—the first substantial step toward opening the region to travelers. Homestead booms populated the valleys; the Great Northern Railway began extensive advertising; and the Forest Service inaugurated a more careful patrol. Eventually on May 11, 1910, Glacier National Park was created by Act of Congress. Though the park is in the State of Montana, it is under the jurisdiction of the Federal Government, and violators of park regulations are tried before a United States commissioner at Belton. The policing is done by the chief ranger and 20 to 30 men.

Eons ago the land here rose, the sea drained off, and rock bodies upthrust by the wrinkling of the earth's crust became mountains. Snow accumulated and formed glaciers, and glacial erosion changed V-shaped valleys to U-shaped ones. The rocks were exfoliated by alternate thawing and freezing, and the glaciers plucked off the scales, forming cirques or amphitheaters, many of them now partly occupied by small lakes. The larger lakes are mostly the result of the damming of glacial valleys by moraines. Continued action of the ice cut into the steep walls that backed the cirques, so that where two glaciers lay on opposite sides of a wall, the crest dividing them was reduced in thickness, forming passes and sawtooth ranges.

The vast escarpment marking the end of the eastward advance of the Lewis overthrust is of old, hard limestone that resisted erosion, and in many places, most notably in Chief Mountain, towers above the softer sandstone and shale formations on which it rests. The fault, plainly visible at Summit on the Great Northern Ry. as a thin yellow line along the mountains to the north, is more clearly seen farther north along the eastern boundary of the park. It is conspicuous below Trick Falls on Two

Medicine Creek, and on both sides of the Narrows on St. Mary Lake. North of Swiftcurrent Valley it forms a barrier to every stream that crosses it, and on the forks of Kennedy Creek and Belly River, rises several hundred feet, giving the spurs and ridges between these streams almost unscalable fronts.

In general the weather during the official season is warm by day and cool at night. The winds that parch the Great Plains seldom reach these pine-scented valleys. In June, sometimes in July, cloud banks from the west slip over the saw-toothed crest, depositing their moisture as snow on the higher slopes and as rain in the valleys. Sudden thunderstorms with brief torrential downpours sometimes occur. Rainfall is about equal on the eastern and western slopes during the officially open season; earlier and later, it is much heavier on the western side of the Divide.

Nearly 1,000 species of plants bloom in the area, the most lavish display being in early July. The park is divided by exposure, precipitation, temperature, and other factors into three life zones—Canadian, Hudsonian, and Arctic-Alpine—with remarkable contrasts. Above timber line, the flowers follow retreating snowbanks; there are no successive flowering seasons, for all bloom nearly at once in a riot of color. High up, only the hardiest mosses and lichens, such as the thick-rooted stonecrops, cling among the constantly avalanching shales; only slightly lower grow rare sky-blue alpine columbine, forget-me-not, velvety dryad, globeflower, and carpet pink. A step lower, among stunted, gnarled alpine fir and white-barked pine, delicate glacier lilies push skyward through lingering snowbanks. Fringed parnassia, red and yellow mimulus, wild fragrant heliotrope, heather, and gentian add to the glow of color. Still lower, showy, creamy plumes of beargrass bloom in alternate years.

At the eastern base of the mountains are fields brilliant from earliest springtime with asters and flowering grasses that dazzle the eye until they fade and become tawny in the autumnal cold. Framing the highways in spring are passion flower, carpet pink, shooting star, buttercup; in late June, forget-me-not, blue Camassia, red and white geranium, scarlet paintbrush, bistort, and puccoon; in July, large flowering horsemint; in late summer, bronze agoseris, gaillardia, wild hollyhock, and in early autumn exuberant asters and yellow composites.

On the western, more humid slope the same flowers occur, but in smaller numbers and supplemented in places by trillium, fireweed, dwarf cornel, and calypso.

Forests composed almost wholly of coniferous trees lie far below the lofty peaks. In the valleys on the eastern side are stands of Engelmann spruce, alpine fir, lodgepole pine, and, rarely, Douglas fir and limber pine. Talus slides support a few rugged pines, and avalanche-ridden slopes bear mountain ash, maple, alder, and aspen.

The dense forests of the west slope, especially about Lake McDonald, have an almost twilight shade, even at noon. Composed chiefly of large trees, they are similar to forests of the Pacific coast. Western cedar and hemlock are interspersed with larch, grand fir, spruce, and pine. A few white pines in McDonald Valley below the Logan Pass road, and cedars around Avalanche Creek, stand nearly 200 feet high, with a basal diameter of 5 to 7 feet.

With abundant food, and protected by strict laws, nearly all species of big game of temperate North America thrive in the park. When tourists throng into the area they withdraw to undisturbed places, but the watchful traveler, especially on remote trails, can see white-tailed and mule deer, elk, moose, mountain goats and sheep, mountain lions, wolves, and grizzly and black bears. Moose frequent marshy ponds in the deepest forests; elk take to the open ridges; and mountain sheep and goats haunt the loftiest cliffs and meadows. The small valleys tributary to the North Fork of the Flathead are natural breeding grounds for moose, deer, and bear. On hot summer days, moose wade in shallow lakes or browse in the thick willows along streams. The great brown head and humped shoulders of a bull, with spade-like antlers set back against the hump, are often seen moving in the glacial waters of Trout Lake. In the water the moose is at a disadvantage; but it is unsafe to go very near to him, for he will fight as readily as a grizzly, and can crush a light craft with one stroke. Bears frequent campgrounds. The smaller animals—beaver, coyote, porcupine, otter, mink, weasel, wildcat, lynx, and marten—are found most readily by those who learn to tread softly and remain alert. Often, a man sitting quietly in the shade will see more wildlife in an hour than he would in a day of vigorous walking.

Fish are plentiful in all waters of the park. On the lakes the best fishing is usually near inlets or outlets, at about sundown. On the streams the time of day is not so important as cautious approach and quiet casting.

<<<<<<<<<<<<<<<<<<✿>>>>>>>>>>>>>>>>>>

Park Tour 1

St. Mary—Logan Pass—Lake McDonald—Belton; Going-to-the-Sun Highway. 51 m.

Oil-surfaced roadbed throughout.

Going-to-the-Sun Highway branches west from US 89 *(see Tour 4, sec. a)* at ST. MARY, 0 *m.* (4,478 alt., 103 pop.).

The auto checking station, 0.1 *m.*, registers incoming tourists.

Left from the checking station on an oiled road to the Swiss type ST. MARY CHALETS, 0.5 *m.*, just above the shingle beach of UPPER ST. MARY LAKE. The lakes were held in reverence by the Blackfeet as the home of the Wind Maker; the imaginative easily understand the origin of the belief, for Upper St. Mary's dark

GOING-TO-THE-SUN MOUNTAIN

blue waters are usually spangled with whitecaps. Rough water often makes fishing impracticable.

The highway skirts the northern shore of the upper lake. Across the water (L) the mountains, in succession, are Divide (8,647 alt.), Kootenai (8,300 alt.), Red Eagle (8,800 alt.), and Little Chief (9,542 alt.); R. are Singleshot (7,700 alt.), Whitefish (8,000 alt.), Goat (8,816 alt.), and Going-to-the-Sun (9,594 alt.).

The last-named peak, which grows more majestic as it is approached, is the locale of an Indian legend. Long ago great adversity visited the Blackfeet. Gone was their glory in war, gone their skill and strength; famine held them. Troubled by the distress of his favorite people, the Great Spirit sent among them a warrior of fine mien, a chief who knew all things, to instruct them in the way they should live. Again they became a great people, regaining their dominance over all tribes. As quickly as he had come, the chief departed up the lofty slopes of a mountain to the west, and as he went, amid lightning and thunder, clouds of snow eddied about him. After the storm the sun blazed forth, and the Blackfeet saw that the snow on the mountain formed the profile of the great chief as he was going to the sun.

At 6.4 *m.* is the junction with a secondary dirt road.

Right 0.5 *m.* on this road to ROES CREEK CAMPGROUND.

The NARROWS, 6.9 *m.*, mark the lake crossing of the Lewis overthrust fault. The yellow limestone, on both sides of the road is the lowest stratum of the rocks that were uplifted and pushed out over the plain. In most places in the park this hard lower limestone has not been broken through by the glaciers that scooped out the valleys, but forms a barrier over which waterfalls pour from the lakes behind it. The glacier that formed St. Mary Valley was one of the larger ones; the continuing line of the overthrust is plainly visible across the lake, bearing L. along the foot of Red Eagle Mountain, mounting high on Kootenai, and appearing near the top of Divide.

LOST LAKE (L), 9.7 *m.*, is a small circular body of water warm enough for comfortable swimming.

At 10 *m.* is the junction with a paved road.

Left on this road 0.3 *m.* to GOING-TO-THE-SUN CHALETS (4,500 alt.), usually called Sun Camp. The largest group of chalets in the park, they are, like most of the other chalets and hotels, of log construction in a local adaptation of the alpine style. Perched on the crest of a rocky eminence a little more than 100 feet above Upper St. Mary Lake, they afford a view of the lake and the encompassing heights. The azure water is rimmed with deep green forest; higher, the yellow, green, and red cliffs enfolding white snowbanks accentuate the verdant tones of the cirque meadows above the timber line. At this point the mountains visible (L. to R.) are Red Eagle, immediately across the lake; Little Chief; Citadel (9,024 alt.); Gunsight (9,250 alt.), farthest distant; Fusillade (8,747 alt.), a vast wedge; Reynolds (9,147 alt.), a higher triangle; Going-to-the-Sun, and Goat.

Trails branch from Going-to-the-Sun Chalets (*see Trail Tour 1*).

At 10.5 *m.* is the junction with a footpath.

Right on this path to SUNRIFT GORGE, 0.2 *m.*, a spectacular cleft in red argillite hardly more than 10 feet wide, with vertical walls 25 to 50 feet high, formed by a slip along a fault, and scoured into fantastic shapes by water. Windfalls, overgrown with moss and lichens, are continuously moistened by a curtain of mist from the rushing water below. Sunbeams slanting obliquely into the gorge touch the mist with rainbow colors.

The road mounts by an easy grade around Going-to-the-Sun Mountain (R), and at 13.5 *m.* swings L. across a tributary of Reynolds Creek to the side of Piegan Mountain (9,230 alt.). Across the narrow, forested valley (L) is Mount Reynolds. On a lower point of the latter is a lookout station commanding the St. Mary Valley.

A 408-foot TUNNEL, 17 *m.,* much of it on a shelf blasted out of solid rock, shows some of the difficulties and hazards encountered by the builders of this road. Several of the contractors and subcontractors failed financially during the 12 years of construction. Completed in 1933, the stretch between Going-to-the-Sun and Logan Pass was the final link. At the opening celebration in Logan Pass, west-side Indians met the Blackfeet and ceremoniously ended the age-old enmity between them.

LOGAN PASS, 18.3 *m.* (6,654 alt.), cuts the Continental Divide between the towering summits of Reynolds, Clements (8,764 alt.), and Oberlin (8,150 alt.) Mountains (L), and Piegan and Pollock (9,211 alt.) (R). The terraced meadows, more than a mile in diameter, in the open circle (L), are the HANGING GARDENS. Red and yellow mimulus, fragrant heliotrope, heather, glacier lily, fringed parnassia, gentian, and other species hardly less showy bloom at the edges of snowbanks and along hundreds of rills that net these uplands. From any elevated point in the Hanging Gardens can be seen the forested valley of St. Mary, with the lake far below filling a hollow between Going-to-the-Sun and Red Eagle.

At Logan Pass is the junction with a park trail.

Left on this trail is HIDDEN LAKE, 2 *m.* *(see Trail Tour 10).*

On the west slope the road for long stretches is on a man-made ledge on a steep wall, guarded on the outside edge. There are several turn-outs for parking. The deep Logan Creek Valley is precipitously below; Mounts Oberlin and Cannon (8,460 alt.) are L.; ahead across McDonald Valley the sweeping curve of a glacial wall leads to Heavens Peak (8,994 alt.). Above the road (R) the sharp outline of the Garden Wall is etched in saw-tooth scallops against the sky.

HAYSTACK BUTTE (R), 21 *m.,* around which the road winds, is a flying buttress of the Garden Wall. At one time it was between two arms of the glacier that carved out McDonald Valley.

CAMP NINE (L), 23.2 *m.,* is a road maintenance camp. Bears sometimes prowl about, just below the highway.

On the switch-back, 26 *m.,* where the road turns away from the Garden Wall, is a large parking space. The once beautiful view of McDonald Valley in both directions now illustrates the damage a major forest fire accomplishes in a few hours.

The place where the 1936 fire was started by lightning is plainly visible (L) on a low shoulder of Heavens Peak. The fire, quickly trenched about, smoldered for several days in crevices, defying efforts of men let down with ropes to put it out. A high wind scattered sparks over the valley, igniting spot fires that soon merged into a general conflagration.

The road enters a tunnel, 192 feet long, at 26.7 *m.;* two openings in the rock overlook McDonald Valley. From the tunnel the road drops rapidly into the heavy forest of the west side. Mountains towering against an unbelievably blue sky show through vistas of tall spruce, pine, and fir with thickset and cone-studded boughs.

At 28.1 *m.,* just before the road makes its last turn down to the valley floor, the north side of Mount Cannon and a small glacier near the summit are R., with a vivid green flank of Heavens Peak thrusting partly across the foreground. There is a similar view, with rushing water in the foreground, from the end of the horse bridge over McDonald Creek (R), 28.2 *m.,* just beyond the turn of the road. A footpath descends the bank. The creek affords good fishing in late summer, when the water is low.

The highway continues through a lane of evergreens with lush roadside flora.

AVALANCHE CREEK CAMPGROUND (L), 33.8 *m.,* is one of the best and largest campsites along the highway, with parking space for about 200 cars.

At the camp is the junction with a park trail.

Left on this trail to AVALANCHE LAKE, 3.5 *m. (see Trail Tour 8).*

LOGAN FALLS (R), 36.5 *m.,* large and noisy, are below but near the edge of the highway.

At 38.1 *m.* is the junction with a spur road.

Right on this road, which makes a turn around the head of Lake McDonald to McDONALD RANGER STATION, 1 *m.,* several summer homes, and a TOURIST CAMP, 2.5 *m.*

LAKE McDONALD (R), 38.5 *m.,* the largest lake in the park, is 10 miles long and more than a mile wide. Because of its depth (maximum, 437 feet), it is often ice free all winter, though the snow along its banks may be more than 4 feet deep. Fly fishing is good in deep water near the bank.

LAKE McDONALD HOTEL, 39.6 *m.* (3,167 alt.), is a log structure whose second and third story verandas overlook the lake. It is the center of west-side recreational activities and the hub of many trails. In the hotel lobby is a collection of mounted specimens of game native to the park. The view from the front lawn includes Stanton (7,744 alt.), Vaught (8,840 alt.), and Heavens Peak on the west, and the Garden Wall and Mount Cannon on the north. Mount Brown (8,541 alt.) towers a vertical mile above the hotel to the east.

1 Left from Lake McDonald Hotel on a park trail to SPERRY CHALET, 7 *m. (see Trail Tour 1, sec. d),* and MOUNT BROWN LOOKOUT STATION, 5 *m. (see Trail Tour 9).*

2. Right from Lake McDonald Hotel on a park trail to GRANITE PARK CHALETS, 18 *m. (see Trail Tour 1, sec. c).*

SPRAGUE CREEK CAMPGROUND (R), 40.4 *m.,* on the shore of Lake McDonald at the outlet of a rushing stream, has space for 75 cars. There is a sandy beach, but the lake water is cold even in August.

The road along the east shore passes many delightful picnic spots on gravelly points or wooded bays. The best view is to the rear.

LAKE McDONALD

APGAR, 48.6 *m.* (3,150 alt., 50 pop.), a community of tourist camps, stores, and places of recreation and refreshment, is at the lower end of Lake McDonald. The settlement dates from 1895 when Dimon Apgar and others cut a road from Belton through the heavy cedar forest to Lake Mc-Donald, and homesteaded there. In 1930 the Government purchased about half the privately owned land. A considerable acreage, still privately owned, is used for camp sites and summer homes.

At Apgar is the junction with the North Fork road *(see Park Tour 1A).* The west entrance checking station is at 50.7 *m.*

GLACIER NATIONAL PARK HEADQUARTERS, 50.8 *m.,* is a group of administrative offices, staff residences, and warehouses on the high banks of the Middle Fork of the Flathead.

The highway turns upstream (L) to a narrow crossing of the river, which in this area doubles back toward the south after a northward journey between the Flathead Range and the Continental Divide.

At BELTON, 51.6 *m.* (3,219 alt., 180 pop.) *(see Tour 2, sec. c),* is the junction with US 2 *(see Tour 2).*

◄◄◄◄◄◄◄◄◄◄◄◄◄◄◄◄◄◄☼►►►►►►►►►►►►►►►►►►►

Park Tour 1A

Apgar—Canadian Border; 59 m.

Narrow, graveled roadbed.

This highway follows the pioneer road built by prospectors in 1900 to reach a supposed oil field near Kintla Lake. Passing up and down steep timbered ridges along the valley of the North Fork of the Flathead, with only an occasional far view, it is used chiefly by those who wish to get into the back country for fishing and camping.

The road branches north from Going-to-the-Sun Highway *(see Park Tour 1)* at APGAR, 0 *m.* (3,150 alt., 50 pop.) *(see Park Tour 1).*

BULL HEAD LODGE (R), 0.6 *m.,* once the summer home of Charles M. Russell *(see THE ARTS),* is identified by the buffalo skull on the driveway arch.

At 1.5 *m.* is the FISH CREEK RANGER STATION (R). The North Fork road climbs to the crest of a hill, where a small public campground (R), in a stand of larch and lodgepole pine overlooks the lake.

The road mounts steadily between Howe Ridge (R) and the generally forested Apgar Mountains (L), the highest point of which is denuded Huckleberry Mountain (6,580 alt.) at the far end.

McGEE MEADOWS (L), 5 *m.*, is a marshy flat between the Fish and Camas Creek drainages.

At 5.5 *m.* is the junction with a dirt road.

Right on this road, barely passable even in dry weather, to muddy little HOWE LAKE, 1.5 *m.*, from which small, dark cutthroat trout are taken. A raft is provided for anglers.

CAMAS CREEK, 7 *m.*, drains Rogers, Trout, Arrow, and Evangeline Lakes.

At 7.5 *m.* is the junction with a park trail.

Right on this trail up Camas Valley to ROGERS LAKE, 3 *m.;* TROUT LAKE, 3.5 *m.;* and ARROW LAKE, 5 *m.*, at the foot of a CIRQUE WALL of which Rogers, Longfellow, and Heavens Peak, Mount Vaught, and Stanton Mountain are parts.

The road descends steeply to Dutch Creek, 10 *m.*, west of which it climbs again. Then it makes a long, steep, winding descent to Anaconda Creek, 13 *m.* Over the next ridge is LOGGING CREEK RANGER STATION (L), 18 *m.*

Right from Logging Creek Ranger Station on a park trail to LOGGING LAKE, 4 *m.* (3,800 alt.).

At 19.5 *m.* the road cuts in along the high, precipitous bank above the North Fork of the Flathead (L), with a view of the wooded Whitefish Range across the valley.

LAKE WINONA (L), 22 *m.*, is small and marshy. At 24 *m.* is LONE PINE PRAIRIE, an open space in the woods. The road again swings close to the North Fork at 25 *m.*, and angles down a long cutbank to the river level.

POLEBRIDGE RANGER STATION, 26.5 *m.*, is an entrance station at the park end of the bridge over the North Fork. Polebridge, a hamlet beyond the river, is on a Forest Service road that goes south to Columbia Falls and north to the Canadian Boundary.

At 26.9 *m.* is the junction with a dirt road.

Right on this narrow, winding road to BOWMAN LAKE, 6 *m.* (4,020 alt.), which is about 7 miles long, 0.5 mile wide, and 256 feet deep. The scene is somewhat similar to that at the foot of Lake McDonald, except that the valley is narrower. The forested Cerulean Ridge (R) culminates in Square Peak (9,800 alt.) and Rainbow Peak (9,860 alt.), whose bare escarpment rising from the lake shore is streaked with color. Indian Ridge (L) rises to an unnamed peak (8,300 alt.), beyond which, at the head of the lake, bulks Mount Peabody (7,282 alt.). The tops of many other mountains show behind the nearer fringe. The lodge and other buildings (L. of the public campground) were formerly occupied by a boys' camp.

Although the road closely parallels the North Fork, the river is usually out of sight. On BIG PRAIRIE, 30 *m.* to 33 *m.*, it passes two or three ranch houses. Few if any months are frost-free here.

At 38 *m.* is the junction with a dirt road.

Right on this road to LOWER KINTLA LAKE CAMPGROUNDS, 2 *m.* (4,000 alt.), a primitive site in a stand of tall spruce and fir. Kintla Lake, showing blue between forested slopes, extends eastward. It is about 6 miles long and 0.8 mile wide.
STARVATION RIDGE, north of the lake, leads to the Boundary Mountains, in which a series of peaks rises to about 8,000 feet. Parke Ridge (R) shuts off a clear view of Parke Peak (9,100 alt.). Kinnerly and Kintla Peaks (10,000 alt.) are

visible only from the upper lake, which is connected with the lower lake by Kintla Creek.

KISHENEHN RANGER STATION (R), is at 47 *m.*

The road crosses the Canadian Border at 59 *m.,* 1 mile south of Flathead, British Columbia.

◄◄◄◄◄◄◄◄◄◄◄◄◄◄◄◄◄◄☼►►►►►►►►►►►►►►►►►►►►

Park Tour 2

Junction with US 2—Two Medicine Chalets; 7.5 m.

This road angles sharply downhill, northwest from US 2 *(see Tour 2)* at TWO MEDICINE JUNCTION, 0 *m.,* to the level of LOWER TWO MEDICINE LAKE (L), 0.8 *m.* The dam at the lower end of the lake regulates the flow of water for minor irrigation along Two Medicine Creek on the Blackfeet Reservation. The valley is thinly wooded. Rugged mountains slant steeply above the treetops.

Two Medicine Valley was always a favorite camping ground of the Blackfeet, who met on the shores of the middle lake each year to make medicine and recount their exploits. Once when two factions developed, one camp was pitched on the upper lake and one on the lower. Some say this is the reason for the name "Two Medicine."

At 2.9 *m.* the road crosses the park boundary and at 3.8 *m.* is the entrance checking station.

At 5.5 *m.* is the junction with a footpath.

Right on this path to TRICK FALLS, 0.2 *m.,* amid spruces. Early in the season, when the volume of water is large, it looks like any other waterfall. But some of the water flows from a hole beneath its brink and, late in the season, water issues only from the hole. The ancient limestone edge of the falls marks a line of the Lewis overthrust fault across the valley. The glacier that scoured out the valley weakened this lowest limestone; the water of Two Medicine found an underground passage in the structure, thus making one waterfall above another. Many believe this phenomenon to be the origin of the name Two Medicine.

The road bridges Two Medicine Creek, and climbs (R) through dense evergreens to emerge at the foot of TWO MEDICINE LAKE (5,165 alt.) among the TWO MEDICINE CHALETS, 7.5 *m.,* which are large log cabins with sloping roofs designed to shed heavy winter snows.

Trails branch from Two Medicine Chalets *(see Trail Tours 3, 4).* From the shore of Two Medicine a slope (R) sweeps up out of lake and forest to the snowfields and purple-red summit of Rising Wolf Mountain

(9,505 alt.). Across the lake the crags of Sinopah (8,435 alt.) rise sheerly and hide the parent Mount Rockwell (9,250 alt.). Near the outlet (R) of the lake, and elsewhere along its shores, are beaver colonies.

<<<<<<<<<<<<<<<<<<<<<<<✿>>>>>>>>>>>>>>>>>>>>>

Park Tour 3

Junction with US 89—Rocky Mountain Trail Ranch; 6 m.

The road branches west from US 89 *(see Tour 4)* at CUT BANK BRIDGE, 0 *m.* *(see Tour 4, sec. a)*, following Cut Bank Creek through open and brushy country cut by many cattle trails.

CUT BANK RANGER STATION (R) is at 5 *m.*, and a small CAMPGROUND (R) at 5.5 *m.* in a grove of pines and fir.

Near the bank of the creek is the ROCKY MOUNTAIN TRAIL RANCH, 6 *m.*, with the former Cut Bank Chalets; it is now a dude ranch. At the head of this valley is TRIPLE DIVIDE PEAK (8,001 alt.), from which creeks, appropriately named Atlantic, Pacific, and Hudson Bay, flow to the three oceans touching North America.

<<<<<<<<<<<<<<<<<<<<<<<✿>>>>>>>>>>>>>>>>>>>>>

Park Tour 4

Babb—Many Glacier Hotel; 12.8 m.

The park road branches west from US 89 *(see Tour 4)* at BABB, 0 *m.* (4,461 alt., 25 pop.) *(see Tour 4, sec. a)*, crossing part of the BLACKFEET RESERVATION *(see Tour 2, sec. b)*.

Right, farthest out on the plain, is the yellow, truncated monolith, Chief Mountain (9,056 alt.); nearer is Sherburne Peak (8,500 alt.). The road winds around hills of drift deposited by the ancient glacier whose upper branches occupied Swiftcurrent and Boulder Valleys. These vast mounds, lying on each side of Swiftcurrent Creek (L), demonstrate impressively the amount of material a first-class glacier can transport. Thickets of small quaking aspens mottle their brown slopes.

A DAM (L), 5.7 *m.*, impounds the water of Swiftcurrent Creek, forming LAKE SHERBURNE. Excess water is diverted to St. Mary Lake and Milk River. BOULDER RIDGE, south of Sherburne Lake, was burned over in 1934, when a sheepherder neglected to extinguish his campfire.

The entrance station is at 8.6 *m.* As the road winds along the northern shore of Lake Sherburne, the mountains take on individual character and interest. Appekunny Mountain (9,053 alt.) rises R.; it bears the Indian name of James Willard Schultz *(see LITERATURE).* Near the head of the lake is rosy Altyn Peak (8,050 alt.), a lower summit of yellow Mount Henkel (8,700 alt.). At the foot of the cliffs around Appekunny and Altyn is the edge line of the Lewis overthrust, which superimposed ancient rocks upon more recent Cretaceous deposits. Altyn yellow limestone is lowest, then Appekunny green argillite, and Grinnell red argillite; Siyeh gray or yellow limestone forms the higher mountaintops. In some places the lower limestone is 1,500 feet thick; the green rocks occupy 2,000 to 3,000 feet; the red rocks about 2,000 feet. This banding, concealed in some places by the glacial debris that forms the slopes, is very apparent here.

Across Swiftcurrent Creek (L) is Point Mountain (8,300 alt.), with a ridge connecting it with Siyeh (10,004 alt.) farther back. Next is Allen (9,355 alt.) in the foreground; the gable end of Gould (9,541 alt.) interrupts the Garden Wall skyline. Grinnell (8,838 alt.) is straight ahead, coming to a reddish prominence in Stark Point, which rises sheerly above the small Swiftcurrent Lake, west of the head of Lake Sherburne. In the distance, R. of Grinnell, is yellowish Swiftcurrent (8,300 alt.), and farther R. is Wilbur (9,293 alt.).

The road swings L. across Swiftcurrent Creek, 12.6 *m.*, with a glimpse (L) of Swiftcurrent Falls. SWIFTCURRENT LAKE (R), formerly called McDermott, is in front of rambling, rustic MANY GLACIER HOTEL, 12.8 *m.* Evidence of the 1936 forest fire, which destroyed the former chalets, tourist camp, and store, is everywhere visible on the lower slopes here. *(See Trail Tour 1, secs. a and b, and 5 and 6.)*

The hotel, largest of the park buildings, is five stories high and accommodates 500 guests. It is built of logs and its design, adapted from those used for cottages in the Alps, is simple and charming. Balconies extend along the walls on each floor; at the ends are stairs leading to the ground. Within, great log columns extend from floor to roof around the rectangular lobby. There are two annexes.

‹‹‹‹‹‹‹‹‹‹‹‹‹‹‹‹‹‹‹‹‹☼›››››››››››››››››››

Trail Tour I

Going-to-the-Sun—Many Glacier—Swiftcurrent Pass—Granite Park—Lake McDonald—Sperry Glacier—Going-to-the-Sun. Piegan Pass Trail, Going-to-the-Sun Trail, and unnamed park trails; 66.2 m.

Hotels, chalets, or campgrounds near all major points of interest.
Trail requires caution in some places, but is nowhere unduly laborious.

Section a. GOING-TO-THE-SUN CHALETS *to* MANY GLACIER
HOTEL, *17.4 m.* Piegan Pass Trail.

Along the first part of this trail are meadows and also deep forests of alpine larch. From Piegan Pass is seen an endlessly fascinating sea of summits, crags, ridges, and valleys that continually vary in color and appearance according to the light and clouds.

Piegan Pass Trail branches west from GOING-TO-THE-SUN CHALETS, 0 *m.* (4,500 alt.) *(see Park Tour 1)*.

At 0.5 *m.* is a trail junction.

Right on this trail to BARING CREEK FALLS and SUNRIFT GORGE, 0.5 *m.* *(see Park Tour 1)*, SIYEH PASS, 5.7 *m.*, and PIEGAN PASS *(see below)*, 10.4 *m.*

At 2.5 *m.* is the junction with a spur trail.

Left on this trail 0.3 *m.* to ST. MARY FALLS.

At Reynolds Creek, 3.5 *m.*, is the junction with a park trail.

Right on this trail to SPERRY CHALETS, 12.5 *m.* *(see Trail Tour 1, sec. d)*.

The Piegan Pass Trail follows Reynolds Creek, passes REYNOLDS FALLS (L), and turns R. at a trail junction, 5 *m.* The real climb begins here, though this trail is not steep by mountain trail standards. The route underpasses Going-to-the-Sun Highway and proceeds up along a fork of Reynolds Creek through a forest, then through PRESTON MEADOWS, one of the few places in the park where alpine larch is found. Flowers, especially in July, border the banks of every little mossy rill, their crisp, delicate colors seemingly distilled from melted snow and mountain sunshine. Piegan Mountain (9,230 alt.) is L., Going-to-the-Sun (9,594 alt.), R. To the rear, the pyramidal peak in the middle distance is Reynolds (9,147 alt.), with Fusillade (8,747 alt.) just L. of it and Jackson (10,023 alt.) on the skyline beyond.

Right of Reynolds, in the distance, looking like the gable of a house with snow on the porch roof, is Edwards (9,055 alt.) and one edge of Sperry Glacier.

Near the summit of the pass the trail crosses two small creeks. The second, LUNCH CREEK, 8.2 *m.*, is the place where midday sandwiches are usually eaten.

PIEGAN PASS, 9.1 *m.* (7,800 alt.), is at the top of an open park that stretches around the flanks of Mount Siyeh (10,004 alt.) and Going-to-the-Sun Mountain (R). Left along the Continental Divide, part of the Garden Wall is in sight, with cliffs 2,000 to 4,000 feet high, interrupted just ahead by the dark bulk of Mount Gould (9,541 alt.). The dark band of rock so conspicuous along the Garden Wall at about the elevation of Piegan Pass, is diorite, a granular, crystallized material that intruded in the molten state between two layers of Siyeh limestone, bleached the rock along the lines of contact, and thus became fringed with white above and below. The limestone, extremely hard and resistant to erosion, accounts for the craggy summits along the Garden Wall.

At Piegan Pass is the junction with a park trail.

Right on this trail to SIYEH PASS, 4.7 *m. (see above)*, SUNRIFT GORGE, 9.9 *m. (see Park Tour 1)*, and GOING-TO-THE-SUN CHALETS, 10.9 *m. (see above; see Park Tour 1)*.

From Piegan Pass the trail descends steep, rocky switch-backs.

MORNING EAGLE FALLS (L), 11 *m.*, a thin, widespreading sheet of water, pours over cliffs of red argillite. The escarpments of Mount Gould and the Garden Wall seem to overhang the narrow valley.

FEATHERPLUME FALLS, 12 *m.*, is just R. of the summit of Mount Gould. The small volume of water starts a 2,000-foot drop but disappears in mist before it reaches the bottom.

The trail leaves the open parks and meadows along CATARACT CREEK (L), 13 *m.*, and enters a forest from which there are occasional far views. It descends an easy grade along the side of (R) ALLEN MOUNTAIN (9,355 alt.). Ahead is Lake Josephine; L., at the end of the Garden Wall skyline, are Mount Grinnell (8,838 alt.) and Grinnell Glacier.

At 16.1 *m.* is the junction with a park trail.

Left on this trail to GRINNELL GLACIER, 6.2 *m. (see Trail Tour 5)*.

MANY GLACIER HOTEL *(see Park Tour 4)*, 17.4 *m.*, is on Swiftcurrent Lake *(see Park Tour 4 and Trail Tours 5 and 6)*.

Sec. b. MANY GLACIER HOTEL *to* GRANITE PARK CHALETS, 7.8 *m.*

From MANY GLACIER HOTEL, 0 *m.*, the trail crosses Swiftcurrent Creek on a stone bridge at Many Glacier Hotel, and turns L. along the stream. Mount Henkel (8,700 alt.) is R., and across Swiftcurrent Lake (L) is Stark Point (7,800 alt.), a part of Mount Grinnell.

At 1.5 *m.* is the junction with a park trail.

Right on the trail to ICEBERG LAKE, 5.5 *m. (see Trail Tour 6)*.

The Swiftcurrent Pass trail crosses WILBUR CREEK, and continues up Swiftcurrent Creek (L) along the lower slopes of (R) MOUNT WILBUR (9,293 alt.).

At 4 *m.* is a trail junction.

Left on this trail 0.2 *m.* to REDROCK FALLS, whose waters pour over a 60-foot cliff of red argillite. Beyond the falls is (L) a marshy lake, pleasant to look at but harboring many mosquitoes.

At 5 *m.* the trail mounts the nose of a wall by switch-backs to gently rising meadows, passing several small waterfalls and lakes (L) and at 6 *m.* comes within sight of North Swiftcurrent Glacier (R) and the larger Swiftcurrent Glacier (L), whose front edge overhangs a 1,500-foot drop. The dark band of diorite that here forms the front edge of the cirque also outcrops in Swiftcurrent Pass and at Granite Park, and was mistakenly called granite by prospectors, who on this evidence hoped to find precious metals there.

SWIFTCURRENT PASS, 7 *m.* (7,176 alt.), provides an unusual view of the Continental Divide, which here unfolds its shining length in three directions. To the L. it meanders southward; to the R. the low summit of Flattop Mountain (6,500 alt.) carries it westward from the Lewis Range to the Livingston Range, whose snowy peaks then reach northward across Canada and become the front range of the Rockies all the way to Alaska.

Right from the pass 2 *m.* on a footpath to the yellow summit of SWIFTCUR-RENT PEAK (8,300 alt.); this easy trail can be climbed readily in about an hour, and the panorama the summit offers surpasses any other in the park—any other, at least, obtained with so slight an effort.

The GRANITE PARK CHALETS, 7.8 *m.* (6,600 alt.), are the only park hostelries that do not follow the conventional alpine type. The main lodge is a plain square structure of local stone, with a gabled roof and no ornamentation. Here is the junction with a trail to Logan Pass *(see Trail Tour 7).*

Section *c.* GRANITE PARK CHALETS *to* LAKE McDONALD HOTEL, *18 m.*

From GRANITE PARK CHALETS, 0 *m.*, the trail runs downhill through the center of the area burned in 1936, descending steeply through park-like meadows, and what was once a heavy stand of trees nearly 100 feet tall. Huckleberry bushes, formerly abundant, have sprung to life again only where the roots were not charred.

At 3 *m.* the trail circles close to the switch-back on the highway and goes below it to the valley floor near the junction of Mineral and McDonald Creeks. At about 5 *m.* it emerges from the fire-scarred area into a shady, fern-lined avenue of coniferous trees. Mount Cannon (8,460 alt.) is visible ahead over a shoulder of (R) Heavens Peak (8,994 alt.).

The trail crosses McDonald Creek, 6 *m.*, on a rustic bridge and closely follows the right bank for 10 miles. On the opposite side of the rushing stream is the highway. The trail is always in deep shade; there are changing views of the great peaks on both sides. Whitetail and mule deer frequent the forest and are sometimes seen along the path. Fishing in the creek is best in those pools that cannot be reached from the highway.

Sperry Glacier is visible (L) at 12 *m.* on a high shelf under Gunsight Mountain (9,250 alt.), at the head of Avalanche Basin between Mount Cannon and Mount Brown (8,541 alt.).

Between LOGAN FALLS, 15.5 *m.*, and McDONALD FALLS, 16 *m.*, the deep rocky channel of the creek is called PARADISE CANYON. At the end of the canyon the trail crosses the creek (L) on a rustic bridge, climbs the bank, overpasses the highway, and turns R., parallel to it.

JOHN'S LAKE, 16.5 *m.*, is a shallow pool, surrounded by sphagnum bog. Yellow waterlilies cover the surface.

At 16.5 *m.* is the junction with the Going-to-the-Sun Highway *(see Park Tour 1).*

Between this junction and Lake McDonald Hotel the trail and the high-way *(see Park Tour 1)* are one route. Bears often appear along the last mile of the trail.

LAKE McDONALD HOTEL *(see Park Tour 1)* is at 18 *m.* Trails branch from here *(see Trail Tour 1, Sec. d, and Tour 9).*

Section d. LAKE McDONALD HOTEL *to* SPERRY CHALETS, 7 *m.*

The trail branches L. from the LAKE McDONALD HOTEL MOUNTING STATION, 0 *m.*, crosses Going-to-the-Sun Highway *(see Park Tour 1)* at 0.2 *m.*, and proceeds along the left bank of Snyder Creek, through heavy forest in which cedar and western larch predominate, to CRYSTAL FORD, 1.5 *m.*, a trail junction.

Left here on a park trail to MOUNT BROWN LOOKOUT STATION (8,000 alt.) 3.5 *m. (see Trail Tour 9).*

The trail crosses Snyder Creek (R) on a footbridge, mounts a basal slope of Edwards Mountain (L), and enters the Sprague Creek drainage. Sprague Creek, in a densely wooded gorge below (R), is heard for 2 or 3 miles but not seen.

As the trail gains in elevation, Lake McDonald becomes visible in the rear, and R. appears a ridge with seven summits, the last of which is Lincoln Peak (7,400 alt.). The herbs, shrubs, and trees along the trail here represent all three life zones found in the park.

The stone Sperry Chalets, a thousand feet above, hardly distinguishable from the mountain background, show through the treetops at 4.5 *m.*

Above the trail are seen the bends and folds of the laminated red and gray argillite of the upper cliffs of EDWARDS MOUNTAIN (9,055 alt.). Their marine origin is shown by the ripple marks made on the face of the slabs when the material was soft beach mud, and in the patterns of sun cracks, which indicate that the mud was exposed to the air before the last deposits were added. At 5.5 *m.* the chalets are in full view (R) ; the trail swings R. across the creek and mounts the rise toward the open bench on which they stand. Edwards Mountain is L. and Gunsight R. of the high wall that hides Sperry Glacier from view.

The high stone SPERRY CHALETS, 7 *m.* (6,500 alt.), have more flavor of the Swiss Alps than anything else in the park. There are even goats around the place, not domestic, but mountain animals. Inasmuch as they have undisturbed possession of the sheltering porches for 9 months of the year, these ordinarily shy animals regard the chalets as their home, and continue to visit them all summer. Almost every night nannies and their kids clatter across one of the porches and bounce bleating into the bushes.

FAWN

On moonlit nights a dozen or more may frisk about close by. Marmots and conies are plentiful among the nearby rocks, and bears and mule deer are seen daily.

Left from Sperry Chalets, on a spectacular but safe ledge trail, to SPERRY GLACIER, 2.5 *m.,* named for Dr. Lyman B. Sperry of Oberlin College.

The trail swings in an arc up the wall beneath Gunsight Mountain (R), with a wide outlook over the ancient glacial basin to Lake McDonald, blue and shimmering in the sunlight. The closely encompassing mountains are extraordinarily bright colored, especially Edwards Mountain, with heavily folded rosy strata overlaid in places with alpine greenery. The trail mounts to the second bench and presently to the third bench of this compound cirque; on the floor of each is an alpine lake. The lower one is NANSEN; the upper, PEARY. All about are generous goat pastures.

The ascent of the last wall, about 100 feet, must be made on foot. A corridor with stairs has been blasted out of the rock, though the old iron ladder with 87 widely spaced rungs is still used by some visitors.

The glacier begins immediately beyond this wall. An excellent example of bench glacier, it is about 1.5 miles across the base, and extends upward approximately a mile. Its size has diminished rapidly since 1920, and it is ribbed with ledges. It is unsafe to cross it early in the season, for the ice is then covered with snow, and there are deep crevasses that only a party equipped with ropes should attempt to inspect.

In the late season Gunsight Mountain can be scaled from the glacier without great difficulty. Edwards (L) is possible for a careful climber.

Sec. e. SPERRY CHALETS *to* GOING-TO-THE-SUN CHALETS, *16 m.*

Going-to-the-Sun Trail swings south from SPERRY CHALETS, 0 *m.,* and ascends by a series of switch-backs to LINCOLN PASS, 1.5 *m.* (7,000 alt.), between Lincoln Peak (L) and a corbie-step gable of Gunsight Mountain.

Right on a footpath up a ridge 0.7 *m.* to the summit of LINCOLN PEAK. Almost 3,000 feet below is the blue pit of Lincoln Lake.

The main trail swings L. around LAKE ELLEN WILSON and, descending, turns the corner of one of Gunsight's fine buttresses. Right, far below the trail, the waters of Lake Ellen Wilson cataract almost straight down 1,700 feet into Lincoln Lake. The scrubby, gnarled, and twisted little alpine firs and pines along the trail are hung with shreds of white goats' hair. Gunsight Mountain (L) is one of the favorite pastures of park goats; in the late afternoon family groups often appear, picking precarious paths down from the higher ledges.

The trail crosses the tail-water of a foaming cataract, climbs a talus slope that bears some vegetation, and circles the east end of the lake.

GUNSIGHT PASS, 5 *m.* (6,900 alt.), looks down about 1,000 feet on serene Lake Ellen Wilson, lying in its high mountain cup almost surrounded by sheer, avalanching walls. Right are the crags and snowfields of Mount Jackson; back across the lake is Lincoln Peak, half hidden by a shoulder of Gunsight.

Below Gunsight Pass the trail crosses a heavy snowbank that pitches steeply down the mountain. In the early season, before the track has become imbedded in the bank, this hundred yards must be traversed cautiously because of the danger of slides. A small meadow beyond the snowbank is a pleasant place for lunch. Below is St. Mary Valley, closely hemmed on each side by colorful cliffs.

On a shelf of Mount Jackson, the trail continues around and above GUNSIGHT LAKE (L). The lake is cupped in a typical glacial cirque, but along the velvety looking sides of the bowl are deceptively tall alder bushes, through which a man can only flounder helplessly, once off the main trail.

Near the approach to a footbridge, 7.8 *m.,* which crosses the lake's outlet, is a trail junction.

Right from the footbridge on this dim trail, which bears R. around Mount Jackson and steadily gains altitude. At 2 *m.* the trail crosses a high lateral moraine, above which the shelving ledges of Mount Jackson climb to the lower elevation (*c.* 7,500 alt.) of BLACKFEET GLACIER, 2.5 *m.* This glacier, the largest in the park, covers about 10 square miles, with a fall of 3,000 feet from upper to lower ice. There are formations of all kinds, and the greatly crevassed surface is highly dangerous.

MOUNT JACKSON (10,023 alt.), the highest mountain directly on the Continental Divide in the park, can readily be climbed from this point by its series of smooth ledges. (*Climb should be attempted only in August, in clear weather, by well-seasoned and -equipped mountaineers.*) The rock surface is very slippery when wet. The great Blackfeet and Harrison Glaciers are seen from the summit, as are a half-dozen lakes and countless waterfalls. Innumerable lesser summits are seen in the distance.

The main trail crosses the Gunsight Lake outlet by ford and on a footbridge. The old, pack-ratty shelter cabin (R) has a couple of board bunks and a stove.

At 8 *m.* Gunsight Lake (5,276 alt.) glistens to the rear, between Jackson and Gunsight; Gunsight Pass forms a notch above its farther shore.

The trail loses altitude steadily around the flank of FUSILLADE

MOUNTAIN (8,747 alt.). This mountain (L) was named by George B. Grinnell, a conservationist who did much to bring the wilderness of Glacier Park to the world's attention. His party hunted goats on this mountain and fired a "perfect fusillade" without hitting one.

The trail follows Florence Creek to its confluence with St. Mary River. At 10 *m.* is a trail junction.

Left on a spur trail to FLORENCE FALLS, 0.4 *m.*, invisible from the main trail. Water from TWIN LAKES, in the cirque between Fusillade and Reynolds Mountains, drops 600 feet in a series of dizzy plunges.

The main trail follows the bank of St. Mary River through timber and occasional open glades where huckleberries are abundant.

Reynolds Creek, 12.5 *m.*, is crossed near its confluence with St. Mary River, by ford or on a footbridge. On the right bank is a snowshoe cabin equipped with telephone; in the winter it is used as overnight shelter by rangers on patrol, in summer it is a lookout station.

Between Reynolds Creek and GOING-TO-THE-SUN CHALETS, 16 *m.* *(see Park Tour 1)*, this route follows the Piegan Pass Trail *(see Trail Tour 1, sec. a)*.

≪≪≪≪≪≪≪≪≪≪≪≪≪≪≪≪≪✿≫≫≫≫≫≫≫≫≫≫≫≫≫≫≫≫≫≫

Trail Tour 2

Glacier Park Station to Scenic Point; Mount Henry Trail; 7.5 m.

The principal trail out of Glacier Park Station begins at GLACIER PARK HOTEL, 0 *m. (see Tour 2)*, which is on US 2 *(see Tour 2)*, and winds north through aspens that give way to limber pine, gnarled and twisted by heavy snows.

At 3 *m.* it mounts Bald Hill, and at 4 *m.* crosses Forty-one-Mile Creek, a favorite spot for a brief rest in the shade. BISON MOUNTAIN (7,835 alt.) is L.; it can be climbed advantageously from a high point at about 4.7 *m.*, midway between here and a second crossing of Forty-Mile Creek, 5.5 *m.* There is no trail, but the view from the top is worth the scramble up the steep ridge. Westward are noble peaks, green basins, snowfields, and waterfalls. Eastward the plains reach to dim distance beyond the Blackfeet Reservation.

From Forty-Mile Creek the trail winds steeply up to the crest, SCENIC POINT, 7.5 *m.* Ahead a maze of peaks and precipices looms, deceptively close across the clear void. Down 2,300 feet is Two Medicine Lake; a hundred smaller lakes are visible in the near and far distance. Rising Wolf Mountain (9,505 alt.) rears above the farther side of the lake, Pumpelly

Pillar at its head. Beyond are Mount Helen (8,540 alt.) and other peaks along the Continental Divide. Waterfalls of melted snow pitch over sheer cliffs.

Right from Scenic Point on a trail that descends the rocky ridges by switch-backs and then follows Appistoki 'Creek to APPISTOKI FALLS (L), 1.5 *m.*, and traverses heavily timbered country to TWO MEDICINE CHALETS, 3.5 *m.* (5,175 alt.) *(see Park Tour 2 and Trail Tours 3 and 4).*

<del>◄◄◄◄◄◄◄◄◄◄◄◄◄◄◄◄◄◄</del>✿<del>►►►►►►►►►►►►►►►►►►</del>

Trail Tour 3

Two Medicine Chalets to Upper Two Medicine Lake; 5.5 m.

From TWO MEDICINE CHALETS, 0 *m. (see Park Tour 2 and Trail Tours 2 and 4),* there are two trails leading around Two Medicine Lake, one along the south shore *(see Trail Tour 4),* another along the north.

The north trail turns R. at the footbridge over Two Medicine Creek, and L. along the shore.

The slope (R) sweeping up out of lake and forest to snowfields and a purple-red summit is Rising Wolf Mountain (9,505 alt.). The crags of Sinopah Mountain (8,435 alt.) at the head of the lake form the front peak of Mount Rockwell (9,250 alt.); L. of Rockwell in the distance is Grizzly (9,070 alt.). Ellsworth (8,595 alt.) and Appistoki (8,135 alt.) are across the water (L). There are beaver colonies along the shores of Two Medicine Lake.

At 3 *m.,* just beyond the end of the lake, is a trail junction.

1. Right on a mountain trail, which passes upward through timber for more than a mile and emerges into an upland of flowers, to a small unnamed lake (L), 1.5 *m.* Visible at the head of the lake is a small unnamed glacier. Goats are always in sight here. Behind the lake is Pumpelly Pillar, connected by a ridge with Mount Helen (8,540 alt.) on the Continental Divide. Right is Bighorn Basin, quarried by an ancient glacier, which with the help of another on the opposite side formed the pass ahead between (L) Helen and (R) Flinsch (9,225 alt.). At 3 *m.* is Dawson Pass (7,500 alt.). Westward some of the highest peaks of the park tower above the timbered green Nyack Valley; eastward is the familiar group around Two Medicine. The maze of cloud-wrapped mountaintops is so extensive that it is necessary carefully to study a topographic map in order to identify the peaks.

2. Left on the south-shore trail back to the Chalets *(see Trail Tour 4).*

PUMPELLY PILLAR, named for Prof. Ralph Pumpelly, who crossed the mountains from west to east by way of Dawson Pass in 1883, looms ahead. The trail runs up along Two Medicine Creek.

TWIN FALLS (L), 4 *m.,* is a cascade separated at the top and dashing thunderously together at the bottom. The shade here and the mist from the falls make this a pleasant spot to eat and rest. There are many small brook trout in the pool.

The trail continues upward through a forest of lodgepole pine and Englemann spruce, and emerges at UPPER TWO MEDICINE LAKE, 5.5 *m.*, a clear tarn with a beach of colored gravel. The lake occupies a glacial cirque with vertical walls on three sides. PUMPELLY PILLAR rises sheer (R), a splintered peak. Mount Lone Walker (8,580 alt.), named for a Blackfeet chieftain, dominates the head of the lake, and Mount Rockwell the left shore.

<<<<<<<<<<<<<<<<<<<<<<<<<☒>>>>>>>>>>>>>>>>>>>>>>>

Trail Tour 4

Two Medicine Chalets to Two Medicine Pass; 8 m.

West of TWO MEDICINE CHALETS, 0 *m.*, the trail follows the south shore of Two Medicine Lake through a lodgepole pine forest with occasional open parks, carpeted with flowers. At one of these the trail crosses Aster Creek.

PARADISE CREEK, 3 *m.*, the principal drainage from the south, carries a large volume of water. A footlog, upstream from the ford, provides a dry crossing.

At 4 *m.* is a trail junction.

Right on a park trail, 2.5 *m.*, to UPPER TWO MEDICINE LAKE (see Trail Tour 3).

Near the summit of a hill on the main trail is ROCKWELL FALLS (L), 4.3 *m.*

Left from Rockwell Falls on a dim trail that follows a branch of Paradise Creek down through HANGING GARDENS, 0.7 *m.*, seldom visited. Game is abundant.

The main trail makes a second crossing of Paradise Creek at 4.7 *m.*, then mounts steeply until it emerges from the forest at timber line. In the open upland there is a maze of game trails; the Two Medicine Pass trail crosses Paradise Creek to COBALT LAKE, 6 *m.*, which occupies a basin recently left by a glacier. Deer, elk, and bear are numerous; mountain sheep and goats frequent the ledges above the lake. Many kinds of flowers grow in this area. Above the lake the trail climbs steeply.

TWO MEDICINE PASS (7,675 alt.), 8 *m.*, lies between Mount Rockwell (R) and Mount Grizzly (L). Westward the timbered valley of Park Creek is visible; the thin wedge of Mount St. Nicholas (9,380 alt.) splits the sky. Right of St. Nicholas is Lake Isabel; farther R., Lake

GRINNELL LAKE AND GLACIER

Aurice. Left of Park Creek Valley is Mount Despair (8,585 alt.). East-ward are Ellsworth (8,595 alt.), Henry (8,870 alt.), and Appistoki (8,135 alt.), nearly in line. Scores of other peaks are in view.

<<<<<<<<<<<<<<<<<<<<<☼>>>>>>>>>>>>>>>>>>>>>>

Trail Tour 5

Many Glacier Hotel to Grinnell Glacier; 7 m.

Guides advised. Passage by launch ($1.00) from hotel to upper end of Lake Josephine shortens hike by more than 2 miles.

The trail leads west from MANY GLACIER HOTEL, 0 *m.* (*see Park Tour 4 and Trail Tours 1 and 6*), skirts the shore of SWIFTCURRENT LAKE for 0.8 *m.*, crosses a stone bridge over Swiftcurrent Creek, and turns L.

along the shore of LAKE JOSEPHINE. The beauty of the forest was destroyed by fire in the summer of 1936.

MOUNT GRINNELL (8,838 alt.) rises R. The trail winds steadily upward along its base.

At 1.3 m. is a trail junction *(see Trail Tour 1, sec. a)*.

GRINNELL LAKE (L), 4 m., a milky-blue circle about a mile in diameter, lies below the trail. The glacial scourings that pour into it give the water its curious color.

Across the lake a vast shoulder of Mount Gould (9,541 alt.) rises sharply; straight ahead is the ragged skyline of the Garden Wall, with Grinnell Glacier outspread beneath it. To the rear the many-topped Altyn Peak (9,335 alt.) lifts conspicuously beyond Swiftcurrent Lake. This scene combines all the pictorial elements for which the park is noted—glacier, waterfalls, brilliantly colored sheer cliffs, jagged sky line, cloud-flecked azure sky, blue lake, and pointed firs. It is the most reproduced of park views.

The trail mounts the debris at the foot of GRINNELL GLACIER, 7 m., which is about a mile wide and a mile long; the depth of the ice toward the wall is about 500 feet. It is not so heavily crevassed as some others, but the dangerous cracks make guide service necessary for exploration of its surface. There are ice caves at its foot.

<<<<<<<<<<<<<<<<<<<<<<✿>>>>>>>>>>>>>>>>>>>>>>>

Trail Tour 6

Many Glacier Hotel to Iceberg Lake; 6 m.

Between MANY GLACIER HOTEL, 0 m. *(see Park Tour 4 and Trail Tours 1 and 5)*, and 1.5 m. this trail and the Swiftcurrent Pass trail are one route *(see Trail Tour 1, sec. b)*.

From the junction this trail (R) follows Wilbur Creek (L). Mount Wilbur (9,293 alt.) is L. and yellow-topped Mount Henkel (8,700 alt.) R.; a high ridge, part of the Ptarmigan Wall, is ahead.

At 3 m., near the falls of Wilbur Creek, is a trail junction.

Right here to PTARMIGAN LAKE, 2.5 m. The climb is steep, passing from forest to open meadow, with many small waterfalls and cascades along the creek. The intensely blue lake, hardly more than a mile across, is surrounded by ruddy shales.

The trail mounts in short zigzags to a low sag in the skyline behind the lake, goes through a tunnel for 183 feet, and emerges on the precipitous north face of PTARMIGAN WALL (7,500 alt.), 3 m. Below is the wild Belly River country. Serene Lake Elizabeth is imbedded in a rich green setting, two miles away at the nearest point and 2,300 feet below. The South Fork of the Belly River, a great green trough, extends away over hazy distances to the plains. The chain of mountains, L. of Lake Elizabeth, with snow or ice in every depression, is regarded as one mountain mass, called Mount Merritt (9,924 alt.).

Right of the valley is Gable Mountain (9,200 alt.), whose high shoulder partly blocks the view toward the plains. Nearer is the bright-colored shaly slope of Mount Seward (8,879 alt.), called the Rainbow Slide. The trail goes down the valley, passes LAKE ELIZABETH, 4 *m.*, and DAWN MIST FALLS of the Belly River, 4.3 *m.*, and swings L. around Mount Merritt to CROSSLEY LAKE and a tent camp, 12 *m.*

The view of the tremendous CATHEDRAL WALL culminating in Mount Wilbur becomes more impressive as the trail approaches Iceberg Lake. The parklike meadow below the lake is bright with flowers; a small stream cascades across the green slopes in foamy leaps.

ICEBERG LAKE AND GLACIER, 6 *m.*, are small. The edge of the glacier that touches the water occasionally breaks off, and the miniature bergs float here all summer. The summer temperature of the water is 39° F. There are no fish in the lake, though wags say it is the home of "fur-bearing trout." The easiest approach to the glacier is across the shallow outlet creek and around the right shore of the lake. Mountain sheep and goats frequent the ledges of the 3,000-foot wall at the rear of the cirque.

<<<<<<<<<<<<<<<<<<<<<<<<<✿>>>>>>>>>>>>>>>>>>>>>>>>>

Trail Tour 7

Granite Park Chalets to Logan Pass; 8 m.

The most traveled section of the Garden Wall trail maintains an even elevation above timber line, making pleasant hiking. There is a brief climb over a low ridge that connects Haystack Butte with the Garden Wall.

The main trail branches south from GRANITE PARK CHALETS *(see Trail Tour 1, Sec. b)*.

At 0.8 *m.* is a trail junction.

Left on a footpath that slants up the shale to a low saddle of the GARDEN WALL, 0.5 *m.* It is a stiff climb of about 1,500 feet with one bit of ledge to cross. Horses can manage the first part of the climb, but the upper part must be traveled on foot. The top of GRINNELL GLACIER is almost even with the saddle on the eastern slope; a yawning gap between mountain and ice is partly filled with rubble. This bergschrund (mountain crevice) is an interesting illustration of how the precipitous back walls of cirques are created by glaciers. As the space between mountain and glacier fills each winter with snow and ice, and melts each summer, the expansion and contraction disintegrate some of the rear wall, which falls and is slowly carried away on the bed of the glacier. Where glaciers are present on two faces of a ridge, as was true along the Garden Wall, the crest becomes very thin and in some places is worn completely through to form saddles like this one, or, if both glaciers persist long enough, low passes.

The view east of the saddle embraces Mount Gould, Grinnell and Josephine Lakes, lying between Mounts Grinnell (L) and Allen (R), and sweeps on down Swiftcurrent Valley to the plains. West, the Livingston Range stretches northward in a great arc from Lake McDonald, visible betwen Mount Cannon (L) and Heavens Peak (R), to the cloud-streaked Canadian Rockies.

A dim continuation of the path goes to a second saddle, 1 *m.*, which affords a closer view of the awesome upper cliffs of Mount Gould.

At 1 *m.* on the main trail is a trail junction.

Right here on a spur trail to GOING-TO-THE-SUN HIGHWAY, 3 *m.* *(see Park Tour 1).*

The main trail winds around projecting buttresses just under the high cliffs of the GARDEN WALL (L). Many little streams formed by melting ice and snow trickle across it. There are occasional short stretches of difficult ledge trail above a precipice. Along these places the outside edge is guarded by a low retaining wall, and the inside face has been blasted out to make travel safe.

Alpine flowers of many colors border the path; in alternate years the creamy plumes of beargrass feather the slopes. This area is the home pasture of a small band of mountain sheep separated from the large herd that winters about Many Glacier; they are sometimes seen both above and below the trail.

HAYSTACK BUTTE (7,405 alt.) is a low, bare summit directly ahead. At 4 *m.* the trail mounts the ridge that ties it to the Garden Wall. Pollock Mountain (9,211 alt.) is the high point of the wall ahead (L).

Heavens Peak (8,994 alt.), nearest (R) across McDonald Valley, thrusts a gleaming snowy summit above the heavy forest of its lower slopes *(see Park Tour 1).* Mount Oberlin (8,100 alt.), not high but spectacular, is R. of Logan Pass ahead. Just before the pass is reached, the trail is rather difficult for a considerable distance.

LOGAN PASS, 8 *m.* (6,654 alt.) *(see Park Tour 1),* is crossed by Going-to-the-Sun Highway.

<<<<<<<<<<<<<<<<<<<<<☼>>>>>>>>>>>>>>>>>>>>>

Trail Tour 8

Avalanche Creek Campground to Avalanche Lake; 3 m.

There are only three short climbs on this easy trail.

East of AVALANCHE CREEK CAMPGROUND, 0 *m.* *(see Park Tour 1)* the trail follows AVALANCHE CREEK, a foaming torrent, full of whirlpools, that has cut a deep, winding gorge through red argillite, and scoured out many potholes in its bed. The banks of the gorge, continually bathed with mist, are covered with thick, emerald-green moss; the overhanging hemlocks and cedars are festooned with goatsbeard lichen. The gorge is the home of the water ouzel, which flies about in the spray and dives under water for food.

The trail passes through a mixed forest that contains some of the largest trees in the park. Rugged MOUNT CANNON (L) was called Goat Mountain by pioneers. In 1901, when Mr. and Mrs. Walter Cannon of Boston visited the park, Charles Howe, an old settler, told them that Goat Mountain had never been climbed, and promised that it would be named for Mrs. Cannon if she climbed it. The Cannons accepted the challenge, set out with a guide and pack outfit, reached the top (8,460 alt.), and erected a cairn there. Later they met a U. S. Geological Survey party, and reported their exploit. Thus Mount Cannon was named for the first woman to climb a major peak in the park—and incidentally for her husband.

Mounts Brown (8,541 alt.) and Edwards (9,055 alt.) are R. A sharp low peak between them is called the Little Matterhorn.

AVALANCHE LAKE, 3.5 *m.*, has milky water heavily impregnated with glacial scourings; it should be drunk only sparingly. The view from the foot of the lake includes a perfect glacial cirque, with four cascades from Sperry Glacier plunging over its 1,500-foot wall. Vegetation in the basin is dense, and in late July huckleberries are abundant a little way from the trail.

◄◄◄◄◄◄◄◄◄◄◄◄◄◄◄◄◄◄◄✯►►►►►►►►►►►►►►►►►►►

Trail Tour 9

Lake McDonald Hotel to Mount Brown; 6.5 m.

Between LAKE McDONALD, 0 *m.*, and CRYSTAL FORD, 1.5 *m.* *(see Park Tour 1)*, this tour and Trail Tour 1 are united *(see Trail Tour 1, Sec. d)*.

Above Crystal Ford the Mount Brown trail goes L. through thin forest, predominantly larch, with heavy undergrowth of beargrass and huckleberry bushes.

At 2 *m.* is a trail junction.

Right on a park trail to LOWER SNYDER LAKE, 3 *m.* SNYDER BASIN is a compound cirque, and the wall above the lower lake is only 400 to 500 feet high. There is no trail to the upper lake, but it is not a very difficult scramble up the talus slope to the second level. UPPER SNYDER LAKE is larger and entirely in the open.

The main trail turns R. up the mountain at 2.1 *m.* The ascent is a long, steady grind with little variation in the gradient of the trail, which mounts the south ridge by many switch-backs. As the trail winds over the ridge,

Lake McDonald below is occasionally seen. Snyder Basin and a score of peaks are R. The three most prominent are Edwards Mountain (9,055 alt.), Gunsight (9,250 alt.), and Jackson (10,023 alt.).

The trail continues across open, flowery parks and swings L. up the last ridge.

The LOOKOUT STATION, 5 m., is on the lower summit of MOUNT BROWN (8,541 alt.). Nine-tenths of the park peaks are visible from here; as one climber wrote in the register the view includes "more scenery than there seems to be any use for." The attendant will explain the use of instruments for spotting and locating smoke.

The UPPER SUMMIT, 6.5 m., about 500 feet higher, can be scaled only by skilled and well-equipped climbers.

‹‹‹‹‹‹‹‹‹‹‹‹‹‹‹‹‹‹‹‹‹✕›››››››››››››››››››››

Trail Tour 10

Logan Pass to Hidden Lake; 2 m.

This easy trail branches south from Going-to-the-Sun Highway, 0 m. (see Park Tour 1), at LOGAN PASS (see Park Tour 1) and winds across terraces of the HANGING GARDENS, which early in the season are rather wet in some places. At 1 m. the trail climbs the lateral moraine of a glacier invisible from the trail.

Right, climbing at any convenient point, to CLEMENTS GLACIER, 0.1 m. This tiny remnant, hardly more than a hundred acres in extent, is sometimes called Museum Glacier, because it exhibits the principal features of larger ice fields in its crevasses, caves, and moraines.

The Hidden Lake trail runs through a low, grassy pass between an unnamed elevation (L) and Clements Mountain (R). It ends at the edge of precipitous cliffs, 2 m.

HIDDEN LAKE, 500 feet below, occupies a cirque only recently evacuated by ice. Its blue is reminiscent of that in the paintings of Maxfield Parrish.

The only way to get down to it is to circle far R. along the steep slope of Clements Mountain and follow one of the small watercourses that go down to enter the lake near its outlet.

Trout planted in the lake a few years ago have accustomed themselves to subsisting on its minute water life, and usually refuse the offerings of the most ingenious fisherman. Rarely is one caught. The usual weight is 5 or 6 pounds.

The mountain beyond the lake, named by old timers, is SHEPHERDS PEAK (8,740 alt.). Goats clamber along its ledges.

PART IV

Appendices

Montana Glossary

Badlands—Barren lands, with fantastically eroded horizontal strata.

Bedding ground—Sheltered place where stock beds down at night, usually in a ravine or a clump of brush.

Bench—Plain rising above lowland. Where bench succeeds bench over vast areas, they are numbered: first bench, second bench, etc. Some are named: Plentywood Bench, for example.

Between hay and grass—In difficult times, as in early spring, when hay is gone and grass has not come up.

Biddy—Aged and toothless ewe.

Biddy bridle—Old-fashioned bridle with "blinders."

Bonanza—A rich vein of ore, or any easy source of wealth.

Boothill—Cemetery where pioneers who died "with their boots on" were buried.

Box canyon—A canyon closed at one end by high cliffs.

Brains, the—Engineers; white-collar workers.

Brand blotting—Making a brand indistinct and alterable by applying heat through a wet sack or blanket.

Bronc—Unbroken horse; broken, but wild, horse.

Bronc buster—Rider who specializes in breaking wild horses.

Broomtail—Range or scrub horse of doubtful value.

Bucking rolls—Leather pads on the pommel that enable a rider to clamp his knees to the saddle.

Buffalo chips—Dried buffalo or livestock manure used for fuel.

Buffalo wallow—Depression where buffalo rolled in the dust.

Bulldog—To throw a steer by leaping from the saddle, grasping his horns, and twisting his neck.

Bull-mooser—Drill used in sinking shafts and winzes.

Bullwhacker—Driver of oxen.

Bum lamb—Lamb which has lost its mother and wanders about trying to get food from other ewes.

Butte—A conspicuous hill or mountain, usually a hard core left standing in an area reduced by erosion.

Buzzard head—Mean-tempered range horse.

Buzzies—Stoping-machine drills.

Cavvy—Herd of horses (from Spanish *caballada*).

Cayuse—Horse of doubtful lineage, usually an Indian pony.

Cedar breaks—Broken land overgrown with scrub cedar.

Chaps—Leather or goatskin riding pants worn for protection from cold or whipping brush growth. Originally *chaparajos*.

Chinook—A warm southwest wind that removes snow in winter.

Circle—Area a roundup rider must inspect in a day. Several men riding separate circles cover the range thoroughly.

Close herdin'—Cheek-to-cheek dancing.

Corral—Livestock pen of poles or boards.

Coulee—A small valley in prairie country.

Cowpuncher—Ranch hand. In Montana the term is preferred to "cowboy," which is regarded as slightly less virile.

Crazy as a sheepherder—(Cattlemen's expression.)

Crow hop—Straight jump made by a bucking horse, especially in leaving the chute (at a rodeo).

Cutting horse—Quick horse, good at cutting out.

Cut out—To separate (an animal) from the herd.

Ditch rider—Irrigation patrolman who turns water into laterals and watches for breaks in ditch banks.

Dogies—Cattle; sometimes motherless calves.

Drift fence—Fence set up to stop straying livestock.

Drop band—Band of ewes being lambed in the spring.

Dry, the—Room where miners change clothing after work.

Dry band—Band of sheep without lambs or gravid ewes.

Dust, the—Silicosis, caused by breathing dust in mines.

Duster—Dry oil well.

Fan the hammer—To fire rapidly with a single-action revolver on which the trigger catch has been filed down. The gun was held in the right hand, the hammer drawn back and released with the heel of the left.

Father up the herd—To get the herd bedded down at night.

Feel one's oats—To get cocky.

Filly—Unmarried woman.

Fool—Person of more than ordinary aptitude; as "a ridin' fool" for an uncommonly good rider.

Fool brand—Brand too complicated to be described by a brief name.

Fork a horse—To mount.

Go into the hills—To start on a prospecting expedition.

Go on top—To come out of a mine.

Hardrocker—Quartz miner; miner who digs ore out of rock.

Hell-for-leather—In great haste. "Ridin' hell-for-leather" suggests very hard use of leather (i.e., whip).

Hill rat—Prospector.

Hog leg—Six-shooter in a holster (from its form).

Hombre—Man (Spanish); pronounced "umber" in Montana.

"It's deep enough for me"—Miner's notice to employer. Miners superstitiously avoid making such statements as "I'm quitting," or "This is my last shift."

Kack—Saddle.

Lamb licker—Sheepman (derisive), from a ewe's habit of licking a newborn lamb.

Lariat—Light, strong rope with a running noose, used for catching and tying livestock.

Larrup—To strike, thrash.

Larrupin' truck—"Great stuff."

Lasso—Lariat; also (v.) to catch with a lariat.

Line fence—Dividing fence between range outfits.

Lobo—Wolf that hunts alone. Hence, a solitary person.

Loco—Poisonous weed that destroys muscular control; also (adj.) crazy, and (v.) to craze.

Lone ranger—Unmarried man.

Long, the (or long steel)—In mining, a drill used to finish holes to a depth of 5 to 7 ft.

Long yearling—Colt or calf between one and two years old.

Loose herdin'—Dancing with decorous space between partners.

Nester—Homesteader.

Nipper—Supplier of powder and sharp steel in mines.

On the prod—Out of sorts; as, a cow ready to use her horns.

Peel broncs—To ride, drive, or break horses, especially with free use of the whip.

Pile—To throw. "That horse piled me."

Plugger—Machine for drilling boulders, for blasting.

Pool camp—Roundup camp of several ranches, each one's interests being in the hands of a "rep" (which see).

Pop—In mining, a drilled hole less than 2 ft. deep.

Pull freight—To go away; move on.

Pull leather—To hold on to the saddle in riding a bucking horse. In rodeos it disqualifies the rider. Hence, to reach for support (in argument and the like).

Put a loop on—To lasso.

Rattle one's hocks—To get going; to move along.

Rep—Representative; roundup hand who looks after the stock of a particular ranch in pool camp.

Ride the owlhoot trail—To ride at night (as an outlaw).

Ridin' herd on (*a woman*)—Courting.

Ridge runner—Wild horse which keeps to a ridge or high point to watch for danger and warn the herd.

Road agent—Old-time robber of stage route travelers.

Roll your bed!—"You're fired."

Rope—To lasso. The favorite Montana term.

Roundup—Periodic gathering of range cattle for branding and the like.

Running iron—Straight iron without a brand design, with which any brand can be applied.

Rustle—To make one's way. To obtain; as food, wood, water. To steal (livestock). To ask for a job.

Sack out—To break a shying horse by tying him up and throwing sacks at him until he no longer shies.

Salivate—To "liquidate"; to shoot full of holes.

Savvy—To understand (Spanish, *sabe*); also (n.) knowledge, grasp. "He's got lots of savvy."

Shifter—Boss of a shift in a mine.

Show daylight—In bronc busting, to let light show between man and saddle; a usual preliminary to being "piled."

Slick ear—Animal without earmark.

Slicker—Unbranded animal.

Slow elk—Beef butchered without the owner's knowledge.

Sodbuster—Homesteader.

Soogan—Quilt, blanket.

Sourdough—Bread leavened with sponge from a previous baking.

Stampede—Properly, the disorderly running away of a herd of animals. Loosely, any confused activity.

Steel—Mine drills generally.

Stray—Animal off its home range; hence, a stranger.

String—Saddle horses kept for the use of a single rider.

Sunfish—To buck with a sidewise, writhing motion or by rapidly lowering and lifting the shoulders.

Swing team—Any pair between leaders and wheelers in a multiple team.

Tally—Time to go off shift (miner's slang).

"Tap 'er light"—Parting admonition among miners.

Throw a wide loop—To be careless as to whose stock one ropes; to take more than one's share of anything.

Tin pants—Heavy, stiff, waterproof garment worn by woodsmen. "Stand your tin pants in the corner."

Tommy-knocker—Ghost of a man killed in a mine. Miners say he returns to work the shift on which he was killed. They thus explain the creaking of timbers and similar sounds.

Top a horse—To ride an unbroken horse, partly taming him.

Top hand—First-rate cowpuncher.

Top railer—Person who sits on the top rail of a corral and advises the men who do the work and take the chances. The back-seat driver of range land.

Vented brand—Brand blotted out before witnesses, when the legal ownership of an animal is changed.

War bag—Bag containing a cowpuncher's personal effects.

Woolies—Sheep.

Wrangler—Herder in charge of saddle stock.

Chronology

1743   The Verendryes, presumably traversing southeastern Montana, sight what they call the "shining mountains."

1749   The elder Verendrye dies; sons are deprived of their grants; French and Indian War puts an end to all expeditions of discovery.

1763   New France passes into British hands; Louisiana (reaching to the Rockies), into control of Spain.

1804   March 9. Montana east of the Rockies becomes part of the United States through transfer from France of Upper Louisiana, carrying out terms of the Louisiana Purchase of 1803.
May 14. Captain Meriwether Lewis and William Clark set out from St. Louis to explore the region.

1805   Sacajawea, Indian wife of the French-Canadian trapper Charbonneau, joins Lewis and Clark at the Mandan villages as interpreter. April 26. Lewis and Clark reach the mouth of the Yellowstone; June 14, Great Falls; July 19, Gates of the Mountains; July 25, Three Forks; August 12, Lemhi Pass, where Captain Lewis passes over the Continental Divide and they meet the Shoshone; and September 11, Lolo Pass on the future State Line.
François Larocque, first white man on lower Yellowstone.

1806   June 29. Lewis and Clark, returning from the Pacific, reach Travelers' Rest near mouth of Lolo Creek; then next day divide the expedition to explore vast areas before their reunion at the mouth of the Yellowstone, August 12.
September 23. Lewis and Clark arrive at St. Louis.

1807   Manuel Lisa establishes first trading post in Montana at junction of Big Horn and Yellowstone Rivers.
John Colter, a veteran of the Lewis and Clark Expedition working for Lisa, crosses Yellowstone Park, a region known for years thereafter as Colter's Hell.

1809   David Thompson, for the North-West Company, builds Salish House near present site of Thompson Falls; makes expedition into Flathead Region.

1810   Killing of twenty men by Indians leads to abandonment of the new post at Three Forks established by Menard and Henry.

1811   Manuel Lisa's post abandoned because of Indian troubles.

1822   Andrew Henry builds a trading post on the Yellowstone for Gen. William H. Ashley of St. Louis.

1823   In spring, while traveling up the Missouri, Henry is attacked by Blackfeet near Great Falls, and forced to turn back.

1824   Alexander Ross and party travel through Hell Gate Canyon near site of Missoula.

1828   Kenneth McKenzie builds for the American Fur Company a trading post, Fort Floyd, at the mouth of the Yellowstone near the site of Fort Henry. Fort Floyd later became Fort Union.

1831   Flathead delegation visits St. Louis, asking for missionaries to teach them Christianity.

1832   Fort Piegan established near mouth of Marias River.
Fort McKenzie built on Marias River following abandonment and burning of Fort Piegan.
First steamboat, the *Yellowstone,* reaches Fort Union; among the passengers is George Catlin, famous painter.
Alexander Culbertson arrives at Fort Union.

1833   Prince Maximilian of Wied-Neuwied arrives at Fort Union on the *Assiniboine,* American Fur Company steamer.

1835   Flatheads again ask for missionaries.
Fort Van Buren, second American Fur Company post, established on the Yellowstone near the mouth of the Tongue.

1839   Third Flathead request for missionaries.

1840   Father de Smet, after celebrating mass with Flatheads in Wyoming, travels north with them into Gallatin Valley.

1841   September 24. Father de Smet founds St. Mary's Mission near present site of Stevensville in the Bitterroot Valley.

1842   In spring Father de Smet plants first Montana crops—wheat, oats and potatoes—at St. Mary's Mission.

1843   John James Audubon, famous naturalist, visits Fort Union.
Fort McKenzie burns. Fort Chardon, at the mouth of the Judith, and Fort Sarpy, 25 miles below the mouth of the Tongue, built by American Fur Company.

1845   Father Ravalli sets up first Montana gristmill at St. Mary's Mission.

1846   American Fur Company builds Fort Lewis (*see below*) near mouth of Marias River.
Northwest Montana becomes United States territory by treaty with England fixing international boundary at forty-ninth parallel.

1850   Major John Owen establishes Fort Owen in the Bitterroot Valley at the site of St. Mary's Mission.
Fort Lewis rebuilt and rechristened Fort Benton by Major Alexander Culbertson.
Steamboat *El Paso* reaches mouth of Milk River.

1852   François Finlay, known as Benetsee, finds gold on what is now Gold Creek, between Garrison and Drummond.

1853   Gov. Isaac I. Stevens explores a route across Montana for a railroad from St. Paul to the Pacific.
John Grant brings in the first considerable herd of cattle, most of it picked up along the Oregon Trail.

1854   Father Hoecken founds St. Ignatius Mission in Mission Valley.
        Sir St. George Gore, Irish sportsman, and large party arrive in
        Montana.

1855   Governor Stevens signs treaties with the Salish Indians at Council
        Grove, near the mouth of the Bitterroot River, and with the Black-
        feet, at the mouth of the Judith River.
        St. George Gore and party, with Jim Bridger as guide, explore and
        hunt in the Powder River region.

1858   Mullan Wagon Road from Fort Benton to Walla Walla, Wash-
        ington, begun.
        The Stuart party finds gold on Gold Creek, near site of Finlay's
        earlier discovery.

1859   July 2. Stern-wheeler *Chippewa* is first steamboat at Fort Benton;
        Key West arrives a few hours later.

1862   Gold rush to Bannack, when John White and William Eads find
        placer deposits.
        Mullan Wagon Road is completed.
        September 26. Capt. John Fisk's expedition of 100 men and 30
        women and children from Minnesota, arrives at Gold Creek.

1863   May 28. Gold discovered in Alder Gulch, near present site of
        Virginia City, by Edgar-Fairweather party.
        Idaho Territory organized, including Montana.

1863–64 December 20–February 5. Hanging, by Bannack and Virginia City
        vigilantes, of twenty-four outlaws, including the sheriff, Henry
        Plummer, and two deputies; eight others banished. Prisoners admit
        murdering 102 persons in Montana.
        First schools started at Bannack and Virginia City.

1864   May 26. Montana Territory created; Bannack, first capital.
        G. O. Humphreys and William Allison stake out first claims on
        Butte Hill.
        July 14. Gold discovered in Last Chance Gulch, present site of
        Helena.
        Montana *Post*, first important newspaper in the Territory, is started
        at Virginia City.
        December 12. First Territorial legislature meets at Bannack.
        Placer discovery in Confederate Gulch.
        John M. Bozeman leads first wagon train over Bozeman Trail, a
        cut-off to Montana gold camps from Fort Laramie on the Oregon
        Trail.

1865   February 2. Montana Historical Society incorporated.
        February 5. Original nine counties of Montana established.
        February 7. Virginia City becomes Territorial capital.
        Placer gold mining at its height; sensational recoveries in Confed-
        erate Gulch.

1866   Acting Gov. Thomas Francis Meagher drowned at Fort Benton.
        Indian troubles bring about establishment of Fort C. F. Smith to
        protect Bozeman Trail.

Nelson Story trails in first herd of cattle from Texas.

First constitutional convention at Helena.

First National Bank of Helena is first bank in Montana.

1867 Fort Shaw established on Sun River to protect Mullan Road; Fort Ellis, near present site of Bozeman.

John M. Bozeman killed by Piegans near Livingston.

August 2. Helena *Herald* first issued.

1868 Fort C. F. Smith and Bozeman Trail abandoned to placate Indians.

1869 Camp Baker (later Fort Logan) established in Big Belt Mountains, east of Helena.

Fort Benton taken over by United States Government.

1870 Piegan War; Baker massacre of non-combatant Indians.

Population (U. S. Census), 20,595.

1871 February 10. David D. Carpenter receives patent on first homestead entry filed at Helena Land Office (August 1, 1868).

1872 Congress creates Yellowstone National Park.

1874 First shipment of Montana cattle to the East made from Ogden, Utah, by James Forbes; the stock had been driven south from the range of Conrad Kohrs on Sun River.

1875 Seat of government moved from Virginia City to Helena.

Rich silver strike made at Butte by William Farlin. W. A. Clark begins development of Travonia mine, and Marcus Daly arrives from Salt Lake City.

June. General Forsythe, under orders from General Sheridan, explores Yellowstone region.

1876 June 17. Battle of the Rosebud; the Sioux, under Crazy Horse, defeat General Crook.

June 25. Battle of the Little Big Horn; General Custer and five troops of the 7th U. S. Cavalry cut off and killed by Sioux. (Historians differ as to number killed, estimates varying from 208 to 277.)

Gen. Nelson A. Miles establishes Fort Keogh, the beginning of Miles City, at the mouth of the Tongue River.

1877 Miles campaigns successfully against Sioux and Cheyenne.

Nez Percé War. August 9, Chief Joseph defeats General Gibbon at the Battle of the Big Hole.

October 8. Surrender of Chief Joseph in the Bear Paw Mountains.

Fort Missoula, west of the Rockies, and Fort Custer, near the mouth of the Big Horn, are established.

1879 Fort Assiniboine Military Reservation south of Havre established.

1880 Utah & Northern completed to Dillon.

Fort Maginnis in Judith Basin.

Silver surpasses gold. Montana mines have produced more than $200,000,000.

Population, 39,159.

1881 Northern Pacific Railway enters Montana from the east.

Marcus Daly begins copper mining at Butte.

Helena incorporated as a city.

1882 Fort Benton abandoned as a military post, marking decline of fear of Indians.

Paris Gibson files on site of Great Falls. Billings, Livingston, Lewistown, and other town sites laid out.

Utah and Northern completed to Garrison.

1883 Henry Villard, president of the Northern Pacific Ry., drives last spike in ceremony at Gold Creek.

1884 Last of the buffalo. Extension of the cattle industry. Stockmen fight organized cattle thieves.

January 14–February 9. Second constitutional convention at Helena; November 4, constitution ratified, and Congress asked to admit Montana as a State.

July 28. Montana Stockgrowers Association organized at Miles City, with Theodore Roosevelt as a charter member.

1885 Billings and Missoula incorporated as cities.

1887 Hard winter starts decline of cattle industry; worst storm, January 28-30.

Legislature provides for observance of Arbor Day.

James J. Hill's construction crews lay tracks of St. Paul, Minneapolis & Manitoba R.R. at record speed.

1888 Coal mining begins in Cascade County.

Great Falls incorporated as a city.

1889 Montana Central Railroad completed to Butte.

July 4. Third constitutional convention at Helena.

October 1. New constitution ratified.

November 8. President Harrison's proclamation announces admission of Montana into Union as a State.

November 23. First State legislature convenes at Helena.

1890 Great Northern builds west from Havre through Marias Pass. End of steamboat traffic on the Missouri in Montana.

Hydroelectric plant and smelter established at Great Falls.

Population, 142,924.

1892 Great Northern Railway completed through State.

Fort Shaw abandoned as a military post.

1893 Legislature establishes State University at Missoula, State College at Bozeman, Montana School of Mines at Butte, and State Normal College at Dillon.

September 15. Montana State College opens at Bozeman.

Five new counties created.

1894 Helena wins capital election in competition with Anaconda.

Chicago, Burlington & Quincy R.R. completed to Billings.

1895 University of Montana opens at Missoula.

The bitterroot selected as the State flower.

Montana Trades and Labor Council organized at Butte.

Blackfeet sell their mountain lands to the Government.

1896   Blackfeet and Fort Belknap reservations open to settlement.
Silver mining declines; copper mining increases.

1897   State Normal College opens at Dillon.

1898   July 18. First Montana Infantry leaves for Philippines.

1899   July 4. Cornerstone of capitol at Helena laid.
State Board of Agriculture created.
W. A. Clark's senatorial campaign.

1900   Montana School of Mines opens in Butte.
Great expansion in sheep industry.
November 12. Marcus Daly dies in New York.
Population, 243,329.

1902   Homestead entries for dry-land farms increase.
Fort Custer abandoned.

1906   Chicago, Milwaukee, St. Paul and Pacific R.R. enters Montana.

1907   Coal mining begins in Musselshell field at Roundup.

1908   C. M. St. P. and P. R.R. is completed across Montana.
Great Northern builds from Great Falls to Billings.
Billings Polytechnic Institute is founded.

1909   Mount St. Charles (later Carroll) College established at Helena.

1910   Glacier National Park created.
Population, 376,053.

1911   Fort Assiniboine abandoned as a military post.

1913   Highway Commission created.
Natural gas discovered near Glendive.

1914   July–December. Decline of labor unions and establishment of open
shop in Butte mines.

1915   Price of farm land increases because of European War.
Bumper wheat crop harvested.
Oil discovered in Elkhorn Basin.
Workmen's Compensation Act passed by legislature.

1916   Another record wheat crop harvested.
Copper mining has its greatest year.
Second Montana Infantry serves on Mexican border.
Jeannette Rankin, first Congresswoman, elected.

1917   Second Montana Infantry goes overseas.
Drought begins, causing collapse of homestead boom.

1919   Horse raising profitable due to war demand.

1920   Cat Creek oil field discovered.
Falling land prices in fourth year of drought ruin many farmers.
Population, 548,889.

1921   Newly created State Highway Commission plans better roads. First
gasoline tax enacted.
Good crop year.

1923   Open pit mining with power machinery at Colstrip, Rosebud County, produces 50 tons of coal per man daily.
Kevin-Sunburst oil field discovered.
Legislature enacts Old Age Pension Law.

1924   Fort Keogh abandoned as a military post.
Good crop year.

1926   Heirs of W. A. Clark sell Butte properties to Anaconda Copper Mining Company.

1927   Gasoline tax increased.
Bumper grain crop.

1928   Bumper grain crop.

1929   Beginning of another series of drought years.

1930   Population, 537,606.

1931   General drought brings desolation to eastern Montana.
Cut Bank gas and oil field discovered.

1933   Named Attorney General in Roosevelt Cabinet, Senator Thomas J. Walsh, first Montanan appointed to a Cabinet post, dies before taking office.
Montana ratifies repeal of prohibition; Liquor Control Board set up for sale of liquor by State.

1934   Construction work begins at Fort Peck Dam.
Great activity in road building. Tourist traffic increases.
State Planning Board created.
May–September. Miners on strike at Butte; closed shop restored.

1935   Helena damaged by a series of earthquakes.
Montana Highway Patrol organized.

1936   Revival in business, but drought continues.
Great activity in metal mining districts, especially at Butte, Helena, and Philipsburg.

1937   Copper mines at Butte and reduction plants at Anaconda and Great Falls operate at capacity.
Legislature enacts law permitting sale of liquor by licensed retailers.
Shortage of hydroelectric power due to low water in Montana rivers.

1938   Custer Creek crash, night of June 18-19. Cloudburst floods creek, and carries away bridge. Milwaukee R.R. express, the *Olympian*, plunges into creek. More than 40 killed, and 80 injured.

Bibliography

Abbott, N. C. *Montana Government*. Billings, Gazette Print. Co., 1937. 239 p. front., illus.

Aikman, Duncan. *Calamity Jane and the Lady Wildcats*. New York, Blue Ribbon Books, 1937. 347 p. front., plates, ports.

Alter, J. Cecil. *James Bridger, Trapper, Frontiersman, Scout and Guide;* A Historical Narrative. Salt Lake City, Shepard Book Co., 1925. 546 p. front., plates, ports., map.

Bailey, Vernon, and Florence Merriam. *Wild Animals of Glacier National Park*. Washington, Govt. Print. Off., 1918. 210 p. illus., plates, map.

Bancroft, Hubert Howe. "History of Montana." (In his *History of the Pacific States of North America. Washington, Idaho, and Montana, 1845–1889*. San Francisco, The History Co., 1890. v. 26, p. 589-808.)

Brady, Cyrus Townsend. *Indian Fights and Fighters*. Garden City, N. Y., Doubleday, Page & Co., 1916. 423 p. illus.

Brissenden, Paul. *The I. W. W.; A Study of American Syndicalism*. New York, Columbia University Press, 1920. 438 p. fold. chart.

Byrne, Patrick E. *Soldiers of the Plains*. New York, Minton, Balch & Co., 1926. 260 p. Describes the Indian wars, 1866–77.

Chittenden, Hiram M. *The American Fur Trade of the Far West;* A History of the Pioneer Trading Posts and Early Fur Companies of the Missouri Valley and the Rocky Mountains. New York, F. P. Harper, 1902. 3 v. illus., maps.

———. *History of Early Steamboat Navigation on the Missouri River;* Life and Adventures of Joseph La Barge. New York, F. P. Harper, 1903. 2 v. front., ports., plates, map.

Commons, John R. *History of Labor in the United States*. New York, Macmillan, 1918–35. 4 v. diagrs.

Dimsdale, Thomas J. *The Vigilantes of Montana;* or, Popular Justice in the Rocky Mountains. Narrative of the chase, capture, trial, and execution of Henry Plummer's road agent band . . . interspersed with sketches of life in the mining camps. 3rd printing. Butte, W. F. Bartlett, 1915. 276 p. (1st ed. Virginia City, Mont., 1866.)

Dingman, Oscar A. *Placer Mining Possibilities in Montana*. Butte, Montana School of Mines, 1931. 83 p. (Montana. Bureau of Mines and Geology. Memoir 5.)

Elrod, Morton J. *Elrod's Guide and Book of Information of Glacier National Park*. Approved by the National Park Service. 2nd ed., rev. and enl. Missoula, M. J. Elrod, 1930. 208 p. illus., maps.

———. "The Montana National Bison Range." *Journal of Mammalogy*, Feb. 1926, v. 7:45-48. plates.

Fisher, Arthur. "Montana, Land of the Copper Collar." (In Gruening, Ernest, ed. *These United States.* 2nd series. New York, Boni & Liveright, 1924. p. 34-47.)

Fuller, George W. *A History of the Pacific Northwest.* New York, Knopf, 1931. 383 p. front., plates, ports., maps, bibliographical notes. Standard authority.

Glasscock, C. B. *The War of the Copper Kings;* Builders of Butte and Wolves of Wall Street. Indianapolis and New York, Bobbs-Merrill, 1935. 314 p. front., plates, ports., facsims.

Greenfield, Thomas L. *Montana in Rotogravure.* San Francisco, Pacific Rotogravure Co., 1930. 72 p. illus.

Grimsby, Oscar Melvin P. *The Contribution of Scandinavian and Germanic People to the Development of Montana.* Missoula, University of Montana, 1926. 144 p. (M. A. thesis)

Hamilton, William T. *My Sixty Years on the Plains Trapping, Trading and Indian Fighting.* Ed. by E. T. Sieber; with 8 full-page illus. by Charles M. Russell. New York, Forest & Stream Pub. Co., 1905. 244 p. front. (port.).

Haywood, William D. *Bill Haywood's Book.* New York, International Publishers, 1929. 368 p. incl. front. (port.).

Hennen, Jennings. *The History and Development of Gold Dredging in Montana.* Washington, Govt. Print. Off., 1916. 63 p. (U. S. Bureau of Mines. Bulletin 121.)

Henry, Alexander, and David Thompson. *New Light on the Early History of the Greater Northwest.* Manuscript journals of Alexander Henry, furtrader of the Northwest Company, and of David Thompson, official geographer and explorer of the same company, 1799–1814. Ed. by Elliott Coues. 3 v. New York, F. P. Harper, 1897. front. maps.

Hosmer, J. Allen. "A Trip to the States in 1865." *Frontier,* Jan. 1932, v. 12: 149-172. A reprint of the diary of the 16-year-old son of• Montana's first Territorial chief justice, Judge Hezekiah L. Hosmer. Ed. with foreword by Edith M. Duncan.

Housman, Robert L. *The Beginnings of Journalism in Frontier Montana.* Missoula, 1935. 10 p. (Sources of Northwest History, no. 22. Montana State University. Repr. from *Frontier and Midland.*)

Howard, Oliver Otis. *Nez Perce Joseph;* An Account of His Ancestors, His Lands, His Confederates, His Enemies, His Murders, His War, His Pursuit and Capture. By O. O. Howard, Brig. Gen. U. S. A. Boston, Lee & Shepard, 1881. 274 p. front., port., maps.

Irving, Washington. *The Fur Traders of the Columbia River and the Rocky Mountains,* as described by Washington Irving in his account of "Astoria" and the record of "The Adventures of Captain Bonneville," with some additions by the editor. Ed. by Frank Lincoln Olmsted. New York and London, Putnam, 1903. 222 p. front., plates. (The Knickerbocker Literature Series.)

James, Will. *Lone Cowboy;* My Life-Story. Illus. by the author. New York, Scribner, 1930. 431 p. front. (port.), plates.

Jones, Marcus E. *Montana Botany Notes.* Missoula, 1910. 75 p. illus., plates. (Univ. of Montana. Biological Series 15. Bulletin 61.)

King, Captain Charles. *Campaigning with Crook and Stories of Army Life.*

New York, Harper & Bros., 1890. 295 p. front. (port.), plates. Describes frontier warfare in the late 1870's.

Langford, Nathaniel Pitt. *Vigilante Days and Ways.* New York and St. Paul, D. D. Merrill, 1893. 485 p. front., ports. Accepted authority on Montana's early mining days.

Laut, Agnes C. *Pathfinders of the West.* The Story of Radisson, La Verendrye, Lewis and Clark. New York and London, Macmillan, 1904. 380 p. front., illus., plates, maps.

Lewis, Meriwether, and William Clark. *Original Journals of the Lewis and Clark Expedition, 1804–1806.* Ed. by Reuben Gold Thwaites. New York, Dodd, Mead & Co., 1904–5. 8 v. fronts., illus., maps, facsims.

Linderman, Frank Bird. *American;* The Life Story of a Great Indian, Plenty Coups, Chief of the Crow. New York, John Day, 1930. 313 p. front., illus.

———. *Indian Old-man Stories;* More Sparks from War Eagle's Lodge-fire. Illus. by Charles M. Russell. New York, Scribner, 1920. 169 p. col. front. and plates.

McBain, J. Ford. *Geography of Montana.* Boston, New York, etc., Ginn & Co., 1931. 39 p. illus. maps.

Maximilian, Prince of Wied. *Travels in the Interior of North America, 1832–1834.* Cleveland, Arthur H. Clark Co., 1906. 4 v. illus., plates, facsim., map. (Vols. 22-25 of *Early Western Travels, 1748–1846,* ed. by Reuben Gold Thwaites.)

Montana. Dept. of Agriculture, Labor and Industry. *Montana Resources and Opportunities* (1933 ed.). Helena, Naegele Print. Co., 1933. 127 p. illus.

Osgood, E. S. *Day of the Cattleman.* Minneapolis, Univ. of Minnesota Press, 1929. 283 p. front., illus., maps, plates. Study of the northern range, 1845–90.

Palladino, Lawrence B., S. J. *Indian and White in the Northwest;* A History of Catholicity in Montana, 1831–1891. Lancaster, Pa., Wickersham Pub. Co., 1922. 512 p. front., illus., ports., plates.

Phillips, Paul C. "The Archives of the State of Montana." (In American Historical Association. *Annual Report,* 1912. Washington, 1914. p. 295-303.)

Renne, Ronald R. *Organization and Costs of Montana Schools.* Bozeman, 1936. 104 p. (Montana. Agricultural Experiment Station. Bulletin 325.)

Richardson, Jessie E. *The Quality of Living in Montana Farm Homes.* Bozeman, 1932. 45 p. (Montana. Agricultural Experiment Station. Bulletin 260.)

Roberts, Edwards. "Two Montana Cities." *Harper's Magazine,* Sept. 1888, v. 77:585-596. Article on Helena and Butte.

Ronan, Peter. *History of the Flathead Indians, Their Wars and Hunts, 1813–1890.* Helena, Journal Pub. Co., 1890. 80 p. front., engravings.

Roosevelt, Theodore. *Hunting Trips of a Ranchman. Outdoor Pastimes of an American Hunter. A Book-lover's Holidays in the Open. Autobiography* (chapter 4). New York, Scribner, 1926. (Vols. 1, 2, 3, and 30 in *The Works of Theodore Roosevelt.*) In numerous editions.

Rowe, Jesse Perry. *Montana Coal and Lignite Deposits.* Missoula, 1906. 82 p.

illus., plates, maps. (Univ. of Montana. Geological Series 2. Bulletin 37.)

Russell, Charles M. *Good Medicine;* Memories of the Real West. With an introduction by Will Rogers and a biographical note by Nancy C. Russell. Garden City, N. Y., Garden City Pub. Co., 1936. 162 p. col. front. Letters of Russell illus. by himself.

Schultz, James Willard. *My Life as an Indian.* Ed. by George Bird Grinnell. New York, Doubleday, Page & Co., 1907. 426 p. front., plates.

Shields, George O. *The Battle of the Big Hole.* A History of General Gibbon's Engagement with Nez Percé Indians in the Big Hole valley, Montana, August 9, 1877. Chicago and New York, Rand, McNally & Co., 1889. 120 p. front., plates, port.

Smalley, Eugene V. *History of the Northern Pacific Railroad.* New York, Putnam, 1883. 437 p. steel engravings, maps.

Smet, Pierre Jean de. *Life, Letters and Travels of Father Pierre Jean de Smet, S. J., 1801–1873;* Missionary Labors and Adventures among the Wild Tribes of the North American Indians. Ed. by Hiram Martin Chittenden and Alfred Talbot Richardson. New York, F. P. Harper, 1905. 4. v. fronts., plates, ports., map. Invaluable records bearing on the early history of Montana.

Standley, Paul C. *Flora of Glacier National Park, Montana.* Washington, Govt. Print. Off., 1921. 203 p. plates. (Smithsonian Institution. U. S. National Museum. Contributions from U. S. National Herbarium, v. 22, pt. 5.)

Stuart, Granville. *Forty Years on the Frontier as Seen in the Journals and Reminiscences of Granville Stuart.* Ed. by Paul C. Phillips. Cleveland, Arthur H. Clark Co., 1925. 2 v. ports., plates.

Teit, James A. "The Salishan Tribes of the Western Plateaus." Ed. by Franz Boas. (In U. S. Bureau of American Ethnology. *Forty-fifth Annual Report, 1927–28.* Washington, 1930. p. 23-396. illus., plates.)

Thompson, Mrs. Margaret. *High Trails of Glacier National Park.* Caldwell, Idaho, Caxton Printers, 1936. 167 p. illus.

U. S. Bureau of Mines: *Technical Paper 260, Miners' Consumption in the Mines of Butte, Montana.* Preliminary report of an investigation made in the years 1916-19 by Daniel Harrington and A. J. Langa. Washington, Govt. Print. Off., 1921, 19 p.

U. S. Bureau of Mines. *Bulletin 257. Review of Safety and Health Conditions in the Mines at Butte.* By G. S. Rice and R. R. Sayers. Washington, Govt. Print. Off., 1925. 27 p. illus., plates.

Weed, Walter Harvey. *Geology and Ore Deposits of the Butte District, Montana.* Washington, Govt. Print. Off., 1912. 256 p. (U. S. Geological Survey. Professional Paper 74.)

Whitney, C. N., R. N. Cunningham, and S. V. Fullaway. *Montana Forest and Timber Handbook.* Missoula, Missoulian Pub. Co., 1936. 162 p. illus., charts, tables.

Willard, Daniel E. *Montana, the Geological Story.* Lancaster, Pa., Science Press Print. Co., 1935. 373 p. front., illus., tables, charts, maps, bibliography. Written for the tourist.

Wissler, Clark. *The Sun Dance of the Blackfoot Indians.* New York, The

Trustees, 1918. (In Anthropological Papers of the Am. Museum of Natural History. v. 16, pt. 3. p. 223-270.)

(For novelists and poets who have written about Montana, see essay THE ARTS.)

Index